INTERNATIONAL HANDBOOK OF THREAT ASSESSMENT

INTERNATIONAL HANDBOOK OF THREAT ASSESSMENT

EDITED BY

J. REID MELOY

JENS HOFFMANN

OXFORD
UNIVERSITY PRESS

Oxford University Press is a department of the University of Oxford.
It furthers the University's objective of excellence in research, scholarship,
and education by publishing worldwide.

Oxford   New York
Auckland   Cape Town   Dar es Salaam   Hong Kong   Karachi
Kuala Lumpur   Madrid   Melbourne   Mexico City   Nairobi
New Delhi   Shanghai   Taipei   Toronto

With offices in
Argentina   Austria   Brazil   Chile   Czech Republic   France   Greece
Guatemala   Hungary   Italy   Japan   Poland   Portugal   Singapore
South Korea   Switzerland   Thailand   Turkey   Ukraine   Vietnam

Oxford is a registered trademark of Oxford University Press
in the UK and certain other
countries.

Published in the United States of America by
Oxford University Press
198 Madison Avenue, New York, NY 10016

Library of Congress Cataloging–in–Publication Data
International handbook of threat assessment / edited by J. Reid Meloy, Jens Hoffmann.
pages cm
ISBN 978-0-19-992455-4
1. Violence—Forecasting.   2. Threat (Psychology)   3. Risk.   4. Violent crimes—Prevention.
I. Meloy, J. Reid.   II. Hoffmann, Jens, 1968–
RC569.5.V55I57 2014
363.32—dc23
2013028677

Cover art by Gustav Klimt, *Death and Life*, 1910. Oil on canvas.
Courtesy of the Leopold Museum, Vienna, Austria.

3   5   7   9   8   6   4   2
Printed in the United States of America
on acid-free paper

Stars, hide your fires!

Let not light see

My black and deep desires.

Macbeth, Act 1, Scene 4

CONTENTS

FOREWORD

Over the last several decades, law enforcement in the United States has seen a shift in mission and focus. Once charged with capturing offenders and gathering evidence, police organizations and professionals increasingly have been asked to *prevent* certain kinds of violent attacks.

In the 1980s and 1990s there were well-publicized workplace attacks, stalking that resulted in murder, intimate partner attacks, and school shootings. Attention to these events pressed law enforcement officers, security professionals, psychologists, psychiatrists, and others to learn how to gather information and to intervene *before* an attack was mounted. This movement toward threat assessment and management was highlighted after the attacks of September 11, 2001. The FBI was given, as a primary mission, the job of *preventing* terror attacks in the United States. Attacks at university campuses, shopping centers, movie theaters, places of worship, and most recently an elementary school in Newtown, Connecticut, provided further impetus to the emerging discipline of threat assessment.

We came to our interests in threat assessment and the prevention of targeted violence from different backgrounds. Robert Fein was trained as a clinical and forensic psychologist and spent nine years assessing and treating mentally disordered, violent men in a security hospital. He was asked to be a consultant to the Intelligence Division of the US Secret Service in the early 1980s and helped review "protective intelligence" cases. Bryan Vossekuil became a law enforcement professional and a special agent of the US Secret Service, with investigative and protective responsibilities concerning the safety of the President and other persons protected by the Secret Service. He conducted criminal and protective intelligence investigations, served on the President's security detail, and became a supervisor in the Intelligence Division.

In the late 1980s, four cases came to attention that caused concern within the Secret Service. In these cases, individuals took weapons to places where they thought a protectee might be, with the intention of shooting. None of these persons fit the then conventional wisdom about presidential assassins: No subject had made a threat to kill the President. Two appeared mentally ill, and two did not appear to be mentally ill. None had a history of violence. And importantly, the Secret Service did not learn about either of these men until *after* they had made efforts to approach a protectee with a weapon.

Concern about these cases led the director of the Secret Service to ask us to conduct a study that would strengthen Secret Service efforts to prevent assassination attempts. We first reviewed all English-language literature we could find about assassins and assassination. We then decided to conduct an operational study. This study included the preattack behaviors of all persons in the United States from about 1950 on who were known to have selected a target by virtue of that target's prominent public status—and to have attacked or approached the target with a weapon with the apparent intention of attack. Our goal was to collect and analyze information that might help agents to prevent attacks on Secret Service protectees.

This study, the Secret Service Exceptional Case Study Project, led us to consider and contribute to the developing field of threat assessment. To differentiate assassination from general violence, we coined the term *targeted violence*. We thought of targeted violence in the context of certain types of workplace violence, stalking, and, later, school shootings.

Our findings included the following: (1) assassination is the end result of an understandable and often discernible process of thinking and behavior; (2) there is no accurate descriptive, demographic, or psychological "profile" of an assassin or school shooter; and (3) persons who *pose* threats often do not *make* threats. Our hope was that our research and thinking about assassination and school shootings would foster further information gathering, analysis, conceptualization—and improvement of practice—in threat assessment and management.

Over the last 15 years, many researchers and practitioners around the world have contributed to the field of threat assessment. Often spurred by tragedy, psychologists, law enforcement professionals, psychiatrists, investigators, protectors, attorneys, and others have worked to understand and prevent targeted violence. They have studied—and worked to thwart—violence related to stalking behaviors, workplaces, schools, universities, intimate relationships, and public figures and officials.

To their great credit, Drs. Reid Meloy and Jens Hoffmann have assembled an impressive collection of data-based studies, description, and discussion about threat assessment and management. This book, the *International Handbook of Threat Assessment*, is graced by work conducted by many of the best thinkers and practitioners—on both sides of the Atlantic and in Australia—who work on the prevention of targeted violence.

Drs. Meloy and Hoffmann—in their scholarship, teaching, and practice over the years—have set high standards. Dr. Meloy has been one of the world's powerful forces for the advancement of research on threat assessment and management. He has published over 200 articles on these and other related topics, written or edited 10 books, collaborated on research with colleagues around the world, taught thousands of practitioners, consulted on many high-status and lower-status cases, and worked with diligence and intensity to bring a scientific focus to threat assessment. Dr. Hoffmann is an increasingly well-known scholar, teacher, presenter, and practitioner. He has published widely and coedited seven books on topics relating to stalking, intimate partner violence, school shootings, and domestic violence. He has worked with police services in Germany and Austria.

The *International Handbook of Threat Assessment* provides a comprehensive overview of the discipline of threat assessment and management today. Chapters in this rich volume present current and useful theory that illuminates practice. They lay out what is known about a range of targeted violence attacks and describe innovative threat assessment and management services in the United States, Canada, the United Kingdom, Europe, and Australia. Other chapters, sometimes directly, sometimes by implication, point to the limitations of current knowledge of threat assessment and management. A thoughtful reader will find much to chew on and many paths forward.

Anyone who has sat with, worked with, or studied perpetrators of targeted violence comes to recognize that much targeted violence is preventable. In many situations today, with the right information, prevention professionals are thinking clearly and comprehensively about how to evaluate a given situation and how, if appropriate, to intervene. If threat assessors had more useful and accurate information about persons and situations of concern, more attacks could be stopped.

The *International Handbook of Threat Assessment* will provide a great public service if, as we expect, it stimulates better and further research and practice to help prevent targeted violence, save lives, and avoid needless pain and suffering. Those who read these papers will benefit. And importantly, many who do not read this book but are served by those who do read it will also benefit greatly.

Robert A. Fein, PhD
Bryan M. Vossekuil
The Metis Group, Inc.
March 2013

ABOUT THE EDITORS

Dr. Reid Meloy is a diplomate in forensic psychology of the American Board of Professional Psychology and consults on criminal and civil cases throughout the United States and Europe. He is a clinical professor of psychiatry at the University of California, San Diego, School of Medicine and a faculty member of the San Diego Psychoanalytic Institute. He is a fellow of the American Academy of Forensic Sciences and the Society for Personality Assessment, and is past President of the American Academy of Forensic Psychology. He is an elected affiliate member of the International Criminal Investigative Analysis Fellowship. He has received a number of awards from various professional organizations and is chairman of Forensis, Inc., a nonprofit public benefit corporation devoted to forensic psychiatric and psychological research (forensis.org). He is also a founding board member of Forensis Europa. Dr. Meloy has authored or coauthored several hundred papers published in peer-reviewed psychiatric and psychological journals and has authored, coauthored or edited a number of books. His first book, *The Psychopathic Mind* (Aronson, 1988), was an integration of the biological and psychodynamic understanding of psychopathy. His recent edited book with Drs. Jens Hoffmann and Lorraine Sheridan, *Stalking, Threatening and Attacking Public Figures: A Psychological and Behavioral Analysis* (Oxford University Press, 2008), led to a commissioned study, published in 2011, for the National Academy of Sciences on threats to public figures (www.nap.edu). Dr. Stephen White and he created the WAVR-21 (Specialized Training Services, 2007), a scientifically based structured professional judgment instrument for the risk assessment of workplace targeted violence. Dr. Meloy is also a consultant to the counterintelligence division of the FBI and intermittently teaches at the Behavioral Analysis Units in Quantico, Virginia. He is a member of the Fixated Research Group for the United Kingdom's Home Office concerning threats to the British Royal Family and other political figures and is also a consultant for Team Psychology & Security in Germany. He is a senior action editor of the new APA *Journal of Threat Assessment and Management,* and is periodically quoted in the *New York Times* concerning stalking, threats toward public figures and serial and mass murder cases. He has been a technical consultant to the television program CSI since its inception in 2001.

Dr. Jens Hoffmann is a forensic psychologist and the head of the Institute of Psychology and Threat Management, a private research and training organization based in Darmstadt near Frankfurt, Germany. Currently the institute is involved in two interdisciplinary research projects funded by the German Federal Ministry of Education and Research and the European Union. In one project, an online training course is being developed for threat assessment teams that are to be installed in schools; the other project is analyzing different forms of mass murder for better prevention of these crimes. Dr. Hoffmann has published more than fifty papers and book chapters on the topics of stalking, workplace violence, targeted violence in schools and universities, spousal homicide, and attacks on public figures. On behalf of the German Bureau of Criminal Investigation, he has written a textbook on offender profiling. He is chairman of Forensis Europa, a nonprofit public benefit corporation devoted to forensic psychiatric and psychological research. In his role as an expert, Dr. Hoffmann assisted the German Bundestag in rendering the act of stalking a criminal offence in

Germany. He has given lectures and workshops in 10 European countries and the United States. Together with Dr. Meloy he has taught for the Dutch National Police. Dr. Hoffmann is a board member and the former President of the Association of European Threat Assessment Professionals (AETAP). Together with two former police psychologists, Dr. Hoffmann also heads the firm Team Psychology & Security. One of their main tasks is conducting threat management for national and international groups and public figures. They have handled more than two thousand cases of threatening behavior and unwanted pursuits. Dr. Hoffmann and his team were involved in creating and implementing the first threat assessment programs in universities, companies, hospitals and courts, in German-speaking countries. In a two-year project in the Swiss canton of Solothurn, he was the main consultant in developing a regional interdisciplinary threat management program covering the whole spectrum of targeted violence. Dr. Hoffmann also designed System Safe School, a concept for threat management teams. System Safe School was implemented in several hundred schools and was chosen by the German state of Saarland and the Swiss canton of Solothurn as their primary prevention program for school shootings. He is also the main architect of the family of online risk assessment tools known as DYRIAS (dynamic risk assessment system), which assesses the risk of spousal homicide, school shootings, and other forms of targeted violence.

CONTRIBUTORS

Henrik Belfrage, PhD, Professor of Criminology, Mid Sweden University, Sundsvall, Sweden

Eric Bell, MA, Scientist, Pacific Northwest National Laboratory, Richland, WA, USA

James Biesterfeld, Special Agent (retired), US Army Intelligence, USA

Alana N. Cook, MA, Simon Fraser University, Burnaby, British Columbia, Canada

Eugene R. D. Deisinger, PhD, Deputy Chief of Police and Director, Threat Management, Virginia Tech, Blacksburg, VA, USA

Margaret L. Diekhuis, MSc, Investigative Psychologist, Ministry of Interior and Kingdom Relations, The Hague, The Netherlands

Keith Dormond, MSW, Constable, Vancouver Police Department, Vancouver, British Columbia, Canada

Jeffrey Dunn, Officer-in-Charge, Threat Management Unit, Los Angeles Police Department, Los Angeles, CA, USA

Linda Ekman, MSc, Analyst at Stockholm County Police, Sweden

Frank R. Farnham, BSc, FRCPsych, Consultant Forensic Psychiatrist, Clinical Director, National Stalking Clinic, London, UK

Robert A. Fein, PhD, The Metis Group, Inc.

Justine Glaz-Ocik, MA, Institute of Psychology and Threat Management, Darmstadt, Germany

Stephen Hart, PhD, Simon Fraser University, Burnaby, British Columbia, Canada

Jens Hoffmann, PhD, Institute Psychology and Threat Management, Darmstadt, Germany

Angela Guldimann, MA, Forensic Psychiatric Service, University of Bern, Bern, Switzerland

David V. James, MA, FRCPsych, Consultant Forensic Psychiatrist, Strategic Director, Fixated Threat Assessment Centre, London, UK

P. Randall Kropp, PhD, British Columbia Forensic Psychiatric Services Commission, Vancouver, British Columbia, Canada

Rachel D. MacKenzie, DPsych(Clin), The Victorian Institute of Forensic Mental Health, Melbourne, Victoria, Australia

Jennifer McCarthy, DPsych(Clin), MAPS, The Victorian Institute of Forensic Mental Health, Melbourne, Victoria, Australia

Troy E. McEwan, DPsych(Clin), MAPS, Centre for Forensic Behavioural Science, Monash University and the Victorian Institute of Forensic Mental Health, Melbourne, Victoria, Australia

Liam McGrath, MA, Scientist, Pacific Northwest National Laboratory, Richland, WA, USA

J. Reid Meloy, PhD, ABPP, Clinical Professor of Psychiatry, Univ. of California, San Diego, CA, USA

Kris Mohandie, PhD, ABPP, Operational Consulting International, Pasadena, CA, USA

Paul E. Mullen, MB, BS, DSc, FRCPsych, FRANZCP, Centre for Forensic Behavioural Science, Monash University and the Victorian Institute of Forensic Mental Health, Melbourne, Victoria, Australia

Jeffrey J. Nolan, JD, Dinse, Knapp, & McAndrew, P.C., Burlington, VT, USA

Mary Ellen O'Toole, PhD, FBI Behavioral Analysis Unit (retired), Quantico, VA, USA

Marisa Reddy Randazzo, PhD, Managing Partner, Sigma Threat Management Associates, Alexandria, VA, USA

Karoline Roshdi, MA, Institute of Psychology and Threat Management, Darmstadt, Germany

Gregory Saathoff, MD, School of Medicine, University of Virginia, Charlottesville, VA, USA

Antonio Sanfilippo, PhD, Chief Scientist, Pacific Northwest National Laboratory, Richland, WA, USA

Mario J. Scalora, PhD, University of Nebraska-Lincoln, Lincoln, NE, USA

Ronald Schouten, MD, JD, Harvard Medical School, Boston, MA, USA

André Simons, MA, Unit Chief, Behavioral Analysis Unit, FBI, Quantico, VA, USA

Lorraine Sheridan, PhD, Curtin University, Perth, Western Australia

Sharon S. Smith, PhD, CEO, Forensic Psycholinguistics, LLC, Fredericksburg, VA, USA

Rachel B. Solov, JD, Deputy District Attorney, San Diego County District Attorney's Office, San Diego, CA, USA

Ronald Tunkel, MCJ, Senior Special Agent, ATF Representative to the Behavioral Analysis Unit, FBI, Quantico, VA, USA

Bram B. Van der Meer, MSc, Director, Van der Meer Investigative Psychologists, The Hague, The Netherlands

Dorian Van Horn, Special Agent, Naval Criminal Investigative Service (NCIS), Retired

Lisa J. Warren, MPsych(Clin), PhD, MAPS, Centre for Forensic Behavioural Science, Monash University, Melbourne, Victoria, Australia

Bryan Vossekuil, The Metis Group, Inc.

Stephen G. White, PhD, President, Work Trauma Services, Inc., San Francisco, CA, USA

Simon P. Wilson, MA, FRCPsych, Consultant and Honorary Senior Lecturer in Forensic Psychiatry, Institute of Psychiatry, London, UK

Robert B. Woyach, PhD, Social Science Automation, Inc., Columbus, OH, USA

Katherine Timmel Zamboni, MSc, Swiss Federal Institute of Technology Zurich (ETH Zurich), Switzerland

PART I

Foundations

1

Threat Assessment and Threat Management

J. REID MELOY, STEPHEN D. HART, AND JENS HOFFMANN

Threat assessment and *threat management* are terms used interchangeably in many different fields of study—including military matters, engineering, finance, computing science, public policy, and others—to refer to the general process of identifying, evaluating, and mitigating the risk of harm to relevant assets. This handbook is concerned with a particular kind of threat: the risk that acts of violence or other forms of harassing or aggressive behavior will be perpetrated.

The goal of our chapter is to define the nature of threat assessment and threat management. It is divided into three major parts. The first deals with basic concepts. The second delineates the similarities between threat assessment and violence risk assessment and the ways in which they differ in both practice and theory. The third gives a brief overview of the research findings, theoretical avenues, and examples of measurements specific to the discipline of threat assessment and management.

PART 1: BASIC CONCEPTS

Definitions

What is meant by "threat"? Threat has two distinct meanings in English. One refers to the perceived possibility of harm (i.e., potential danger). The other refers to a statement conveying an intention to cause harm (i.e., a menacing utterance). Threat assessment and threat management rely on the first meaning— that is, threat as hazard or risk.

The key feature of a threat, risk, or hazard is that it is uncertain. We are unsure of exactly what will happen

(its nature), how bad the consequences will be (severity), when it will happen (imminence), how often it will happen (frequency), how long it will last (duration), or the probability that it will happen (likelihood). This is in part because a threat arises and exists in specific circumstances. As we do not know exactly what the future will look like, we cannot anticipate threats with certainty. A threat is inherently dynamic, changing over time, and contextual, changing in response to the environment (Borum et al., 1999).

By violence we mean any actual, attempted, or planned injury of other people, as well as any communication or behavior that causes other people to reasonably fear for their health or safety; it is intentional, nonconsenting, and without lawful authority. It makes intuitive sense to add the latter proviso because that is how we distinguish violence from legitimate activities such as sport, medical treatment, or sanctioned use of force (e.g., by health care, police, or military). But why do we say that violence must be intentional? We are emphasizing that violence is goal-directed behavior: The actor forms a goal, then forms an intent to work toward it, and then forms behavioral plans consistent with the goal and intent. The basic sequence, then, is goal → intent → behavior. Although all violence requires cognitive activity, it doesn't necessarily require much thought. Decisions to act can be made rapidly, shifting from goal to intent to behavior in mere moments. Also, actors may not be aware (i.e., self-aware or self-conscious) of their own goals and intentions prior to behaving. When the thought process that precedes violence is more slow and self-conscious, the violence is typically character- ized as "deliberate" or "premeditated"; when it is more rapid and less self-conscious, it is typically character- ized as "reckless" or "impulsive." Threat assessment and threat management clearly assume that violence is goal-directed; this may be particularly useful when violence is more deliberate and premeditated. It makes little sense to spend much time or energy eval- uating and intervening with individuals if violence is just accidental, instinctual, or reflexive.

What is meant by "assessment"? Assessment is, most generally, the process of gathering information for use in making decisions. In light of the preced- ing discussion, it should be clear that the informa- tion that needs to be gathered concerns if, why, and how a person has formed violent goals, inten- tions, and behavioral plans; the extent to which these goals, intentions, and behavioral plans are stable and coherent; and how best to interrupt the goal-intent-behavior sequence in light of the person's likely future life circumstances.

An obvious way to gather information about a per- son's past and present goals, intentions, and behavioral plans with respect to violence is to talk to that person directly. But, as discussed previously, goals, intentions, and plans can change, so talking to someone at a sin- gle point in time may be of limited use. Even if such people are stable over time, they may be confused, dis- organized, or ambivalent. Even if they are stable and coherent, they may not have good insight. And finally, even if such people have good self-awareness of their goals, intentions, and plans with respect to violence, they may be unwilling or unable to talk about them in an honest, sensible manner.

For this reason, threat assessment relies as much or more on information gathered from other sources as it does on interviews with those who are the focus of the assessment. That information may include interviews with collateral informants such as fam- ily members, friends, coworkers, neighbors, health care and social service providers—in fact, just about anyone who may be acquainted with the person of interest. Other sources of information may be docu- mentary, including such things as health care, police, corrections, education, employment, military or social service records. A final and important source of information is behavioral observation, including virtual behavior that is communicated through the Internet, cyberspace, or other social media devices.

Threat assessment does not require the evalua- tor to gather extensive, full, or complete information.

Indeed, the nature, extent, and quality of information available vary dramatically according to the circum- stances in which the threat assessment is conducted. The available information in some cases comprises a few brief communications from an unknown person; in other cases, it may include dozens of hours of inter- views with the person of interest and collaterals, along with literally thousands of pages of records, spanning decades. But the dependability and accuracy of a threat assessment is clearly limited by the nature and quality of the information on which it is based.

What is meant by "management"? Management is the process of acting to gain or maintain control of a situation. In the current context, then, threat manage- ment refers to violence prevention—the actions that can be, should be, or have been taken to prevent vio- lence. Effective management requires planning that is strategic (i.e., that identifies, sets, and prioritizes goals and objectives), tactical (i.e., determines what operations are needed to achieve goals and objec- tives), and logistical (i.e., ensures the availability and coordination of resources needed to execute and support operations).

There is a clear and direct link between assess- ment and management: assessment precedes and guides management, and management may alter subsequent assessment. First, we understand the threat of violence that exists; next, we take steps to minimize the threat. It is impossible to take sensible steps to minimize the threat without a good assess- ment; but unless it assists management, assessment is pointless.

Synthesis. Based on the foregoing discussion, we can define threat assessment as the process of gather- ing information to understand the threat of violence posed by a person, and threat management as the process of developing and executing plans to mitigate the threat of violence posed by a person. This defini- tion is broadly consistent with definitions offered by various authorities in the past, although some people refer to both processes by a single name (Calhoun & Weston, 2003; Meloy, 2000; Mohandie, 2000; Turner & Gelles, 2003).

Threat assessment in contemporary literature was advanced by the work of Dietz and Martell (1989) when they outlined the "warning signals" that likely preceded an attack on a public figure. Their archival research suggested that imitating assassins, develop- ing a "hit list," writing in a diary words that implied the stalking of a public figure, and attempting to procure a weapon were behaviors of concern. The *concepts* of threat assessment and targeted violence and their theoretical premises and rationale were further advanced by the descriptive research within the US Secret Service two decades ago (Borum, Fein, Vossekuil & Berglund, 1999; Fein & Vossekuil, 1998a,b, 1999; Fein, Vossekuil & Holden, 1995) and were specifically tailored to address the problem of extremely low base-rate[1] violence toward their protectees, including the President of the United States.

The assessment of risk for other acts of violence, moreover, was enhanced by the US Secret Service's threat assessment model and included problematic approaches, communicated threats, and attacks on other public figures, workplace homicides, adolescent and adult mass murder, high school shooters, campus and university shooters, stalking of private citizens, and acts of both foreign and domestic terrorism. The concept of threat assessment was a paradigmatic shift in thinking (Kuhn, 1970), since traditional methods of violence risk assessment— such as utilizing base rates for violence in a particular group as an anchoring point for predicting violence in an individual—did not work because of the rarity of such incidents. What was desired was a new theoretical paradigm, threat assessment, which then had to be articulated.

Threat assessment was defined as a "set of investigative and operational techniques that can be used by law enforcement professionals to identify, assess, and manage the risks of targeted violence and its potential perpetrators" (Fein, Vossekuil, & Holden, 1995, p. 5). Three principles of threat assessment bear repeating:

> First, targeted violence is the result of an understandable and often discernible process of thinking and behavior; second, violence stems from an interaction among the potential attacker, past stressful events, a current situation, and the target; and third, the key to investigation and resolution of threat assessment cases is identification of the subject's "attack related" behaviors. (Borum et al., 1999, p. 329)

PART 2 THREAT ASSESSMENT AND VIOLENCE RISK ASSESSMENT

The Nature of Violence

Research over more than half a century, beginning with the work of Hess and Brugger (1943), who studied "affective defense" in cats (the genesis of the term *affective violence*), and Wasman and Flynn (1962), who studied "quiet biting attack" in cats (the genesis of *predatory violence*), has continued to support the theory that there are two quite distinctive biological modes of aggression in mamms, including humans (Siegel & Victoroff, 2009). Affective violence—sometimes referred to as reactive, impulsive, or emotional violence—is preceded by autonomic arousal, caused by a reaction to a perceived threat, and accompanied by intense feelings of anger and/or fear. It is a defensive violence, and its evolutionary basis is self-protection to live another day (Meloy, 1988, 1997, 2006, 2012). Predatory violence, sometimes referred to as instrumental or premeditated violence, is characterized by the absence of autonomic arousal and emotion, the absence of an imminent threat, and planning and preparation beforehand. It is offensive violence, and its evolutionary basis is hunting for food to live another day. None of us would be here if our ancestors had not excelled at both affective and predatory violence; hence the theory that we have the biological capacity for both modes of violence and the accumulating empirical evidence that this is correct (Gregg & Siegel, 2001; McEllistrem, 2004; Raine et al., 1998; Viding & Frith, 2006). Although the concept is overly simplistic, affective violence originates in the limbic areas of the brain, while predatory violence is initiated in the higher cortical areas of the brain (Blair, 2010).

Threat assessment presupposes predatory (instrumental) violence. This is apparent in the work of the US Secret Service (Fein & Vossekuil, 1999), later theoretical formulations (Borum et al., 1999; Borum, Fein, Vossekuil, Gelles, & Shumate, 2004; Calhoun & Weston, 2003), and the cumulative research on attacks and assassinations of public figures (Meloy, Sheridan & Hoffmann, 2008; Meloy, 2011), wherein a "pathway" is assumed. Similar although not identical concepts to predatory violence in the threat assessment literature are targeted violence, defined as "incidents where an identified (or identifiable) target is selected by the perpetrator before the attack" (Vossekuil et al., 2002, p. 79), or intended violence, which is based on the three elements of intent, lack of profit in the motive, and plans to damage, injure, or kill (Calhoun & Weston, 2003).

In fact, the entire enterprise of threat assessment stands or falls on the ability to factually discern through intelligence gathering the warning behaviors that will precede the targeted violence by hours, days, weeks, or months, thus allowing for a considered determination of risk. If there are no warning behaviors before an attack, threat assessment is virtually impossible (Unsgaard & Meloy, 2011).

Similarities

Threat assessment and violence risk assessment differ in a number of ways, but they also have striking similarities. First, both are practiced by people with diverse professional backgrounds. The education, training, and skills required to conduct them do not fall within the domain of a single profession; many professions have something to contribute to their practice. Second, the ultimate goal of both is the prevention of violence, although threat assessment is usually initiated to protect a potential victim and violence risk assessment is initiated to manage a potential perpetrator. Third, both focus on assisting the decisions or actions of a range of people working within various legal frameworks. Fourth, both view the evaluations as a process, something that occurs and changes over time, rather than an event that occurs at a fixed time. Fifth, the process is something that is and should be structured or guided as much as possible by relevant theory and research. Sixth and finally, both view violence as the result of a decision process that is affected by individual and situational factors that may change over time. The differences between threat assessment/threat management and violence risk assessment/violence risk management, then, are primarily a matter of degree rather than kind. This is important, as it suggests that the theory and research relevant to one can inform the other.

Differences

There are also notable differences between threat assessment and violence risk assessment.

An Operational Context

Threat assessment typically occurs in an *operational* context and can be conducted by law enforcement, mental health, national security, private or corporate security, and human resources professionals; violence risk assessment, on the other hand, is usually done in a *judicial* context and conducted by mental health, corrections, and social service professionals. For example, a threat assessor for a public university consults with his or her threat assessment team to determine the risk posed by a graduate student who was heard to tell another that he would kill his dissertation chairman if he did not pass his oral defense and receive his doctoral degree. The threat assessor

meets with the team over the course of weeks, helps to steer the investigation of the student and, at one point, sits down and interviews the student as to his motivation and actual intent. An example of a traditional violence risk assessment involves a forensic psychiatrist being retained by a court to render an opinion as to whether a forensic patient could be safely released to the community if he remained in a supervised outpatient treatment program. The evaluator reviews all evidence in the case, including the patient's history of psychiatric disorder, the police investigation of his committing offense, and his behavior and treatment in the hospital. She then writes a formal report for the court, which is submitted as evidence prior to the hearing for release. The doctor then testifies about her opinions concerning the patient's *general* risk of violence.

A Dynamic Emphasis

Threat assessment typically emphasizes *dynamic* (often behavioral, clinical, or situational) variables when determining level of risk, whereas violence risk assessment has traditionally relied on *static* (often historical or dispositional) or "status" variables in determining level of risk. Research has suggested that static variables are more robust predictors of general violence risk over time, and they have been emphasized in actuarial instruments such as the Violence Risk Appraisal Guide (VRAG) (Quinsey, Harris, Rice, & Cormier, 2006). Other research, however, has found that dynamic factors are most salient in the assessment of short-term risk of violence, such as the Short-Term Assessment of Risk and Treatability (START) (Webster, Nicholls, Martin, Desmarais, & Brink, 2006), and a distinction is now made between more stable (slow-changing) dynamic factors and more acute (fast-changing) dynamic factors (Skeem & Monahan, 2011). However, structured professional judgment instruments, such as the HCR-20 Version 2 (Webster et al., 1997) and Version 3 (Douglas et al., 2013), have substantial dynamic content. In the Workplace Assessment of Violence Risk (WAVR-21) (White & Meloy, 2010), a structured professional judgment instrument for workplace-targeted violence risk, one of the five "critical items" (weapons skill and access) combines both historical data (weapons skill) with situational data (weapons access). There is no bright line between static and dynamic factors in contrasting violence risk and threat assessment but rather a difference in emphasis. For example, threat assessments tend to deemphasize psychiatric diagnosis while accentuating current psychiatric symptoms and their relation to violence risk. This approach is supported by research, which has found that analysis at the level of manifest symptom is more helpful than precision in diagnosis in determining the relation of psychosis to violence (Douglas, Guy, & Hart, 2009). Research and newer empirical studies support the clinical experience that the content of delusions may play a central role in the motivation for attacks (Hoffmann et al., 2011; Lammel et al., 2011). The trigger for an attack may be based on a delusional misinterpretation of the world—such as the assumption that others have a hostile intention to hurt or kill people. Violence by the delusional individual then is often motivated by self-defense. This is why delusional disorders and schizophrenia with paranoid perceptions pose a risk of offending, since the paranoid individual often feels that he or she is in danger. A workplace violence case may illustrate such a dynamic: A female paranoid schizophrenic employee believed that a coworker planned to kill her. She thought that the woman had fallen in love with the same male colleague as she fancied and therefore became jealous. The female worker felt so frightened that she could no longer sleep. Her job performance dramatically decreased, and she was dismissed by her employer. She threatened the female coworker and eventually stabbed her, believing that it was a matter of life and death and that only one of them would survive.

An Idiographic (Case-Driven) Approach

Threat assessment is an idiographic, or case-driven approach, whereas violence risk assessment is a nomothetic or group-data approach. Threat assessment is a highly individualized approach to determining risk that focuses on the current behaviors and circumstances of a subject who has come to the attention of the threat assessor. It is primarily an inductive or, more precisely, an abductive approach,[2] meaning that one moves from particular facts about a case—a subject of concern has told his friend he will murder his wife—to a general principle—"all subjects who leak such intent are dangerous.[3]" On the other hand, there is the deductive approach of violence risk assessment, which moves from an empirical research finding—psychopaths are at greater risk for instrumental violence than nonpsychopathic criminals—to a probable conclusion regarding an individual who fits into that large group—"this psychopath will likely be instrumentally violent." Violence risk assessment has historically depended on the study of large groups of violent individuals in comparison to other nonviolent groups to determine variables that predict violence, which are then applied to the individual case. Two essentially equivalent (Yang, Wong, & Coid, 2010) deductive approaches moderately predict general violence risk: the actuarial measures, which render a quantifiable probability estimate of risk (Hart, Michie & Cooke, 2007), and the structured professional judgment instruments, which help to organize data but leave the final combining of factors and generation of opinion of risk to the evaluator (Hart, 2001, 2003; Monahan, 2007, 2008; Skeem & Monahan, 2011). In recent years, however, violence risk assessment has emphasized the importance of "individualizing" judgments regarding risk based on unique characteristics of the subject of concern (Otto & Douglas, 2009), whereas threat assessment is attempting to develop a better empirical foundation of characteristics and behaviors for those who commit targeted violence. As a deductive effort (Hoffmann et al., 2011), this convergence is both predictable and welcome.

Low Base Rates for Targeted Violence

Base rates (the frequency of a behavior in a particular group while controlling for time) have been historically fundamental to the anchoring of probability estimates for violence in violence risk assessments (Monahan, 1981). For example, how often does violence occur over the course of a year within a group that is most similar to the individual being assessed? Base rates allow for actuarial predictions of risk but must be sufficiently high to minimize the risk of false positives—predicting violence in an individual when in fact he will not be violent—and false negatives—predicting no violence in an individual when in fact he will be violent. The rarity of events such as attacks and assassinations of public figures—the research focus of the Exceptional Case Study Project (Fein & Vossekuil, 1998a,b, 1999) and the genesis of contemporary threat assessment—underscored the uselessness of base rates and became a central impetus for the case-driven, fact-based behavioral focus of threat assessment.

Risk Management Instead of Prediction

Prediction in the form of probability estimates of violence risk has arguably become an achieved goal—with moderate success—in violence risk assessment (Yang et al., 2010). Prediction, however, has not been the goal of threat assessment; it is, instead, to risk-mitigate a subject of concern so that she or he does not become violent. Risk management is the end product of threat assessment, but the irony is that if done effectively—often risk management is modified as the dynamics of the threat assessment change—the threat assessor will never know whether the subject would have become violent or not without intervention. Furthermore, given the low base rates of targeted violence, it would take quite a long time to determine whether a threat assessment program actually reduced incidents of targeted violence. Such data are much more readily available, and over briefer periods of time, in violence risk assessment. For example, a sample of subjects with a 25% to 30% annual base rate for violence, such as males discharged from an acute psychiatric inpatient unit (Monahan et al., 2001), could be subjected to an outpatient treatment program, with a comparative no-treatment group, and followed for a year to see whether their violence rate were less. As a counterpoint, imagine attempting to draw conclusions as to whether the US Secret Service had been effective in protecting the president by comparing the number of presidential assassinations in the 120 years prior to the founding of their agency in 1902[4] ($n = 3$ [Lincoln, Garfield, McKinley]) and those that occurred during the 110 years after they began their protective duties ($n = 1$ [Kennedy]). Statistical inference is impossible owing to the low sample size despite the passage of 230 years, even if one could control for all other confounding variables, such as a substantial increase in public figure attacks and assassinations over the past several decades (Hoffmann et al., 2011; Schlesinger & Mesa, 2008).

The Potential Victim and Offender

Violence risk assessment has traditionally focused upon a probability estimate of general violence, whether the method is actuarial, such as the VRAG (Quinsey et al., 2006), or structured professional judgment, such as the HCR-20 (Webster et al., 1997; Douglas et al., 2013). Actuarials will usually express the risk of general violence as a quantitative estimate, whereas structured professional judgments will communicate the risk through the use of an adjective, such as *low, moderate,* or *high. Targeted violence,* a term coined by Fein and Vossekuil (1998a, 1999) and the provenance of threat assessment, balanced the locus of interest between the subject and the potential victim, which necessarily involved the relationship between the two, whether actual or fantasy-based, and broadened risk management to potentially include alterations in the subject's behavior, environmental or

situational factors, and the potential victim's vulnerability. One of the bridges to this changed formulation was the elucidation of "potential victim pools" in the early research concerning violence risk assessment (Meloy, 1987; Monahan, 1981).

Likely Urgency

A threat assessment is typically done much faster than a violence risk assessment. In this sense, it is a "hot" assessment vs. a "cold" assessment, since time is of the essence despite the fact that information is initially quite limited and often in flux. After the identification of a threat, a preliminary investigation will be conducted to determine whether a formal investigation is warranted and a case management plan formulated (Fein & Vossekuil, 1998b). All this is done in real time, as the threat may be increasing, decreasing, or stable while the threat assessors work. The formal investigation will typically encompass a broad range of topics, including the subject's motivations and current behaviors, level of organization, warning behaviors, and social/environmental factors that will likely affect his risk of violence. The methods of such data gathering typically involve multiple independent sources to heighten veracity (Borum et al., 1999). Kropp, Hart, and Lyon (2008) put it well:

> The context of the evaluation places important limits on the information that is gathered. For example, some risk assessments are conducted as a prelude to, or as part of, an ongoing investigation. These "operational" risk assessments, sometimes referred to as threat assessments, are often conducted by law enforcement, security, or human resources professionals....When the purpose of the risk assessment is to make operational decisions, though, evaluators may have no choice but to rely on a limited information base... . Evaluators should recognize that the quantity and quality of information they review set fundamental limits on the consistency (reliability) and accuracy (validity) of their judgments. (pp. 12-13)

Predatory (Instrumental) Violence

In the brief history of violence risk assessment, the mode of violence has typically not been a point of analysis; there has been the wrongful assumption that all violence is homogeneous and not biologically distinctive. In threat assessment, the assumption, often

TABLE 1.1. SIMILARITIES AND DIFFERENCES BETWEEN THREAT ASSESSMENT/
MANAGEMENT AND VIOLENCE RISK ASSESSMENT/MANAGEMENT

	Threat Assessment	Violence Risk Assessment	Consensus: TA and VRA Agree
Evaluator	Law enforcement and (public or corporate) security professionals	Health, corrections, and social service professionals	Professionals with diverse expertise (education, training, experience)
Context	Guiding front-line action (i.e., operational)	Assisting legal decision-making (i.e., consultive)	Serving a range of goals within various legal frameworks
Process	"Hot"/Rapid/A process (i.e., with no scheduled start or end dates)	Cold/Slow/An event (i.e., with scheduled start and end dates)	Reflective of the fact that judgments about violence risk are limited by (a) the accuracy and completeness of the information base, and (b) the dynamic nature of risk
Goal	Protection of victim(s)	Management (especially detention) of perpetrator(s)	Implementation of a broad range of strategies
Structure	Flexible/discretionary/-idiographic/individual-focused/inductive (abductive)	Fixed/nondiscretionary/nomothetic/group-focused/deductive	Structured and systematic, to the extent possible or practical
Time horizon	Short-term, so greater focus on Situational/motivational/dynamic factors	Long-term, so greater focus on Personological/-dispositional/historic factors	Evidence-based (i.e., informed by relevant theory and research) and ecological (i.e., reflective of the relevant social, psychological, and biological context)

unstated but behaviorally implied, is that the violence will be predatory or instrumental in nature: the *idea* of violence—thought as experimental action (Freud, 1911)—is incubated in the mind of the perpetrator. Threat assessment is limited, moreover, to predatory or instrumental violence, given the nature of the task: an implied pathway (Calhoun & Weston, 2003; Fein & Vossekuil, 1998a,b) and discernible warning behaviors (Meloy et al., 2012) that can be assessed in advance. In this sense, violence risk assessment encompasses a broader range of violent acts (both affective and predatory) by relying on static as well as dynamic risk factors.

Table 1.1 represents an attempt to synthesize the similarities and differences between threat assessment/management and violence risk assessment/management according to the evaluator, goal, context, process, structure, and time horizon.

PART 3 RESEARCH, THEORY, AND MEASUREMENT[5]

Research Findings

Notwithstanding the important early work of Régis (1890), Laschi and Lombroso (1886), and MacDonald (1911) on threatening and attacking public figures; Esquirol's discovery of erotomania (1965/1845) and clinical explanation of a dangerous erotomanic subject's pursuit of "a beautiful actress"; Krafft-Ebing's (1912) description of celebrity obsession; Hoffman (1943) and Sebastiani and Foy's (1966) study of psychotic visitors to government offices and the White House; Freedman's (1971) study of the psychopathology of assassination; and J. MacDonald's (1968) groundbreaking research on homicidal threats—among other studies concerned with the yet unnamed phenomenon of targeted violence—the contemporary science further advanced with the work of Dietz and Martell (1989) and their exploratory archival studies of those who problematically approached Hollywood celebrities and US congressmen, and Dietz's (1986) earlier study on mass, serial, and sensational homicides. Their work coincided in time with the research and subsequent publications of Fein and Vossekuil (1998a,b, 1999; Fein, Vossekuil & Holden, 1995), who conducted the first operational study of attackers and assassins of public figures in the United States, involving interviews with approximately one fourth of their subjects. Fein and Vossekuil originated the terms "targeted violence" and "posing a threat," and elaborated upon their meaning within the context of threat assessment in subsequent papers (Borum et al., 1999). At the same time, Calhoun (1998) published his archival study of those who problematically communicated with, threatened, and attacked federal judicial officials. These first contemporary efforts were characterized by a zest for empirical data, a focus on public figures, and an emphasis on either problematic approachers or attackers, two relatively disparate subject pools (Meloy, 2011). In the context of threats, and threat assessment, de Becker also made very important contributions to an understanding of threats, victimology, and public figure attacks (de Becker, 1997; de Becker, Taylor, & Marquart, 2008).

The 1990s also saw a veritable explosion of research on stalking, a behavioral prelude to violence in many cases, which was first criminalized in the United States in California in 1990—although Denmark was the first country to have a codified stalking law in 1933. Other states and countries followed suit. This rather complex pattern of threatening behavior held within it the notion of a single target and began to inform the literature on targeted violence. One current example is the finding that nonintimate stalkers of private citizens are quite similar to public figure stalkers (James et al., 2010a). Forensic research programs on stalking unfolded in the United States (Harmon & Owens, 1995; Meloy, 1989, 1998; Meloy & Gothard, 1995; Zona, Sharma, & Lane, 1993), Canada (Kropp, Hart, Webster, & Eaves, 1994), Europe (Hoffmann, 2005; Boon & Sheridan, 2002), and Australia (Mullen, Pathé, & Purcell, 2000), the last having arguably been the best-funded enterprise focusing on the understanding and treatment of stalkers and their victims (Mullen et al., 2009). Problematic approach, threatening, and attack research also continued throughout the decade, with seminal contributions from the US Capitol Police (Scalora et al., 2002a,b, 2003), the FBI (O'Toole, 2000), the Home Office of the United Kingdom (James et al., 2007, 2008, 2009, 2010, 2011) concerning threats to the British Royal Family and attacks on western European political figures, and expansive efforts by the US Secret Service, particularly in the areas of threats to education and school shootings (Fein et al., 2002; Randazzo et al., 2006; Reddy et al., 2001; Vossekuil et al., 2002; Drysdale et al., 2010) and the courts (Vossekuil et al., 2001). Studies of adult mass murder charted a different, more clinical course but informed the "pathway" theory and a fuller understanding of psychosis and instrumental violence (Hempel et al., 1999, 2000; Katsavdakis, Meloy, & White, 2011; Knoll, 2010a,b; Meloy, 1997; Meloy et al., 2004). Violence and aggression research generally continued to challenge the belief that violence was

homogeneous, and studies emerged that clarified the nature of both predatory (instrumental) and affective (emotional, reactive) violence (McEllistrem, 2004; Siegel & Victoroff, 2009), the former describing the biological substrate for the operational term, targeted violence. All these efforts have largely continued, led by a second generation of targeted violence researchers (Guldimann, Ekman, MacKenzie, Warren, McEwan, Kropp, Deisinger, Randazzo, Hoffmann, Schoeneman, Simons, Roshdi, Van der Meer, Bootsma, Cook, Glaz-Ocik, McCarthy), many of whom have contributed to this book.

Theoretical Models

Theory without data is just speculation. Data without theory is just counting. The march of science, however, is defined by their dynamic interplay. The research on attack-related behaviors—as well as the clinical and case experience in dealing with threatening behavior—has led to the construction of theoretical models describing a process that may end in a violent attack. For example, the idea of a pathway to violence became a central assumption in the theoretical foundation of threat assessment. Pathways to violence can focus on behavioral, cognitive, or emotional evidence or on a mixture of several of those elements (Meloy, Sheridan, & Hoffmann, 2008). One of the first models in the field stressed the internal factor of cognition while describing a process ending in workplace violence. Several stages were postulated, starting with a traumatic experience, followed by perceptions that problems were unsolvable, a projection of all responsibility onto the situation, and an increasingly egocentric frame of reference leading to the final assumption that a violent act was the only way out (Kinney, 1995). Another early model, underpinned by psychodynamic theory, was proposed by Meloy (1998), who described a specific escalation process in stalking. Following the experience of being rejected, a stalker passes through a sequence of internal states of shame and rage that may lead to aggressive behavior, at times even lethal, the motivation and consequence being to devalue the actual object of pursuit and restore once again an idealized fantasy relationship with the victim. The words of O. J. Simpson are an example of the restoration of this "linking fantasy"—often characterized by loving feelings and grandiosity—spoken several years after he was tried for killing Nicole Brown, his former wife, and Ron Goldman, her friend: "She comes to me from time to time in my dreams, and it's always a positive dream.

Occasionally I dream that I single-handedly solve the case" (*Newsweek*, June 23, 1997).

A behavioral pathway model inspired by empirical research was introduced following two US Secret Service studies of public figures and school shootings (Fein & Vossekuil, 1998a, 1999; Vossekuil et al., 2002). The researchers described a route from idea to action (Freud, 1911) wherein phases of ideation, planning, preparation and implementation were present. Calhoun and Weston (2003) further advanced this work by specifying in detail six markers along a general pathway to violence: grievance, ideation, research and planning, preparation, breach, and attack. This model became very popular in the threat assessment community, although for years no further scientific studies were conducted to test its value. Recent research on several sample cases of targeted violence has begun to empirically validate the pathway concept (Hoffmann et al., 2011; Meloy et al., this volume, Chapter 3). However, when a large random sample of problematic approachers to the British Royal Family was examined, one study questioned whether a pathway existed at all (James et al., 2010b); admittedly, none of these subjects appeared to have a motivation to attack a subject, leaving the question of a pathway in the context of attack-related behavior empirically unresolved.

The map is never the territory, and it is likely that pathways exist in both multiple and complex forms and sometimes not at all. For example, targeted violence can range from mass murders in public places to intended spousal homicides, both sharing general characteristics on the one hand and specific differences on the other (Calhoun & Weston, 2012). White and Meloy (2010) proposed five critical items suggesting a high or imminent risk of workplace violence: motives for violence; homicidal ideas, fantasies, or preoccupation; violent intentions and expressed threats; weapons skill and access; and preattack planning and preparation. MacKenzie et al. (2009) proposed five "red-flag risk factors" for stalking violence: suicidal ideation, homicidal ideation, last-resort thinking, high-risk psychotic phenomena, and psychopathy.

After extensive research on international cases of school shootings, Hoffmann and Roshdi (2013) developed a four-stage pathway model of severe targeted violence in schools. This process is accompanied by an ongoing crisis and an emerging pattern of warning behavior. The model describes the inner world of the perpetrator as well as an outside perspective showing how he acts. Each stage is marked by a typical pattern of behavior and an evolving internal state of mind (See Figure 1.1).

These are but three more examples of the emerging complexity of pathway models, few of which have been empirically validated. They posit a mixture of inferred internal states, traits, explicit behaviors, and social context. All of these indicators stand on the shoulders of others' work on violence risk, most importantly Monahan et al. (1981, 2001, 2007, 2008).

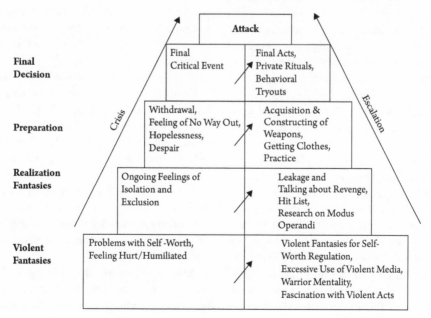

FIGURE 1.1 Pathway model of severe targeted violence in schools.

On the one hand, the pathway-to-violence models provide a descriptive and theoretical framework for threat assessment. They have also been adopted as instruments for the assessment of actual cases. The rationale is that the pathway models describe a number of stages that an offender must go through before he attacks, and that this sequential structure can be used as a type of inferred ordinal scale. A threatening individual's pattern of behavior is compared with the prototypical pathway model. Then the individual's location on the pathway, speed of movement, and direction can be theoretically ascertained. The closer he or she is to the final stage of attack, the higher the risk. Such an approach begs the question of validity: How useful is this model and others as an assessment tool of risk for targeted violence? In a recent contribution, the concept of pathway has been relegated to one of eight warning behaviors (Meloy et al., 2012) for targeted violence; the presence of a pathway may be necessary but not sufficient as patterns of threat emerge and risk management strategies are planned. This model, however, is also in need of empirical validation (see Meloy et al., Chapter 3).

Instruments

The theory and research within threat assessment have given rise to practical instruments for professional users. The major difference between traditional violence risk assessment instruments, such as the VRAG and the HCR-20, and threat assessment instruments is that *the latter will include the gathering of data on a specific victim or group of victims*, also keeping in mind situational, environmental, and contextual variables. This is one of the basic theoretical formulations in the development of the theory of threat assessment (Borum et al., 1999).

In the 1980s and 1990s a number of assessment tools were published by experienced threat management practitioners. These tools were designed to improve systematic assessment for violence risk in an operational setting. Most of these tools were based solely on case experience as no empirical testing of these tools appeared in the peer-reviewed scientific literature. De Becker (1997) theorized with his JACA instrument that the decision to attack is dependent on how a person perceives the justification, alternatives, consequences, and ability to use violence. De Becker also developed his MOSAIC systems for assessing violence risk in various settings. Likewise O'Toole (2000) described, in her assessment model for risk of school shootings,

three levels of risk, analyzing how specific, direct, detailed, and plausible a formulated threat appears. Based on her work, Cornell (2006) later made the distinction between transient and substantive threats as a foundation for his school threat assessment model. In the next decade, however, testing of these instruments accelerated. Roehl et al. (2005), for example, did a large and comprehensive study of several domestic violence instruments, including the DV MOSAIC (de Becker, 2000).

Another early prototype of a scientifically based threat assessment tool was provided by Dietz and Martell (1989) in their research report on approach behavior to public figures. It included calculation tables that allowed the reader to estimate the probability that a letter writer would try to physically approach a politician or celebrity. Almost two decades passed as more structured risk assessment instruments (Hart & Logan, 2011) were designed for threat assessment purposes.

In 2007 the first edition of the Workplace Assessment of Violence Risk (WAVR-21) was published, a structured professional judgment instrument assessing the risk of targeted workplace violence (White & Meloy, 2010; White, this volume, Chapter 6). The WAVR-21 is designed to consider target and contextual factors and also change over time in the risk behavior of a person of concern. Research was conducted assessing the interrater reliability of the instrument (Meloy, Hart & White, in press), which was found to be excellent for summary judgments of risk as calculated by psychologists and good for other non-mental health threat assessors. Item interrater reliability ranged from poor to excellent.

A year later a structured risk assessment instrument for stalking was introduced (Kropp, Hart & Lyon, 2008; Kropp & Cook, this volume, Chapter 11). The Guidelines for Stalking Assessment and Management (SAM) considers risk factors in three domains: the nature of the stalking, the victim, and the perpetrator. A dynamic component is part of the instrument owing to a creative "risk scenario" design. Successful research studies on the reliabilty and validity of the SAM have been conducted in different countries (Kropp, Hart, Lyon, & Storey, 2011).

Shortly thereafter, the Stalking Risk Profile (SRP), another instrument for risk assessment in stalking cases, was released by an Australian-British group (James, Farnham, & Wilson; McEwan,

MacKenzie & McCarthy; all this volume, Chapters 20 and 25; MacKenzie et al., 2009). A unique feature of this instrument is that it offers, in addition to violence risk, assessments of persistence, recurrence, and psychosocial damage to the stalker. The SRP group (www.stalkingriskprofile.com) is conducting validity and reliability research on the Internet.

That same year the first instrument of the Dynamic Risk Assessment (DYRIAS) family was released (Hoffmann & Roshdi, 2013). DYRIAS is a research-based online tool combining a clinical approach to gathering information with an actuarial calculation process. Different behavioral pathway models form the scheme of the DYRIAS system, and its dynamic structure allows it to reassess the case whenever a change of risk may have occurred. Currently two separate DYRIAS instruments have been designed to assess the risk of severe targeted violence in schools and the risk of spousal homicide. For both instruments validity studies were conducted, in each case analyzing samples of attackers as well as threateners who did not act (Hoffmann & Glaz-Ocik, 2012; Hoffmann, Roshdi & Allwinn, in press).

CONCLUSION

Threat assessment and management can be regarded as an embryonic scientific field and an advanced topic of interdisciplinary professional practice. We have attempted to define basic terms, address the similarities and differences between violence risk and threat assessment, introduce the research and theory grounding the latter, and give some examples of instrumentation to help the threat assessor. Professional associations of threat assessors currently operate on four continents, and a newly inaugurated APA scientific publication, the *Journal of Threat Assessment and Management*, will likely stimulate even more efforts to advance this promising scientific and applied field. As Freud wrote many years ago, "the voice of the intellect is a soft one, but it does not rest till it has gained a hearing" (Freud, 1927, p. 53).

NOTES

1. A base rate is the occurrence of a particular behavior in a particular group over a particular period of time. Low base rates preclude prediction because attempts to do so generate unacceptably high levels of false positives—that is, individuals who are predicted to be violent, and subsequently are not. The goal of threat assessment is not to predict violence but to mitigate the risk of violence in an individual of concern. Whether or not a particular

individual would have been violent if intervention had not occurred cannot be known.

2. Abductive reasoning is an inference to the best explanation, with an emphasis upon economy and sufficiency.

3. Inductive approaches are more vulnerable to cognitive bias than deductive approaches, particularly availability bias, confirmatory bias, and the predictable world bias (Kahneman, 2011).

4. Two operatives were assigned to protect President Theodore Roosevelt following a congressional request subsequent to the assassination of President William McKinley. Formal legislation for such protection was passed in 1912.

5. In light of the breadth and complexity of threat assessment and management over the past 30 years—and the other chapters in this book—this section is meant to convey a brief and selective review and in no way should be considered a comprehensive history of threat assessment.

KEY POINTS

- Threat assessment is the process of gathering information to clarify the threat of violence posed by a person or persons.
- Threat management is the process of developing and executing plans to mitigate the threat of violence posed by a person or persons.
- Threat assessment and violence risk assessment are both similar and different across evaluators, goals, context, process, structure, and time horizon.
- There are two psychobiologically distinctive modes of violence, affective (reactive, defensive) and predatory (instrumental, offensive). Threat assessment is primarily focused on the latter, wherein a specific person is targeted and the violence is intended.
- The past several decades have seen the beginnings of research, the elaboration of theory, and the development of measurement instruments in the field of threat assessment and management.

REFERENCES

Blair R. (2010). Neuroimaging of psychopathy and antisocial behavior: A targeted review. *Current Psychiatry Reports, 12,* 76–82.

Boon, J., & Sheridan, L. (2002). *Stalking and psychosexual obsession: Psychological perspectives for prevention, policing and treatment.* Chichester; Wiley.

Borum, R., Fein, R., Vossekuil, B., & Berglund, J. (1999). Threat assessment: Defining an approach to evaluating risk of targeted violence. *Behavioral Sciences and the Law, 17,* 323–337.

Borum, R., Fein, R., Vossekuil, B., Gelles, M., & Shumate, S. (2004). The role of operational research in counterterrorism. *International J Intelligence and Counterintelligence, 17*, 420–434.

Calhoun, F. (1998). *Hunters and howlers: Threats and violence against federal judicial officials in the United States, 1789–1993*. Arlington, VA: U.S. Marshals Service.

Calhoun, F., & Weston, S. (2003). *Contemporary threat management*. San Diego, CA: Specialized Training Services.

Calhoun, F., & Weston, S. (2012). *Concepts and case studies in threat management*. Boca Raton: CRC Press.

Cornell, D. G. (2006). Student threat assessment. In E. Gerler (Ed.), *Handbook of school violence* (pp. 115–136). London: Routledge.

de Becker, G. (1997). *The gift of fear*. New York: Random House.

de Becker, G. and associates (2000). Domestic Violence Method (DV MOSAIC). www.mosaicsystem.com/dv.htm

de Becker, G., Taylor T., & Marquart, J. (2008). *Just 2 seconds*. Studio City, CA: The Gavin de Becker Center for the Study and Reduction of Violence.

Dietz, P. (1986). Mass, serial and sensational homicides. *Bulletin of the NY Academy of Medicine, 62*, 477–491.

Dietz, P., & Martell, D. (1989). *Mentally disordered offenders in pursuit of celebrities and politicians*. Washington, DC: National Institute of Justice.

Douglas, K., Guy, L., & Hart, S. (2009). Psychosis as a risk factor for violence to others: A meta-analysis. *Psychological Bulletin, 135*, 679–706.

Douglas, K., Hart, S., Webster, C., & Belfrage, H. (2013). *HCR-20 Version 3: Assessing risk for violence--User guide*. Burnaby, Canada: Mental Health, Law, and Policy Institute, Simon Fraser University.

Drysdale, D., Modzeleski, W., & Simons, A. (2010). *Campus attacks: targeted violence affecting institutions of higher education*. U.S. Secret Service, U.S. Dept. of Homeland Security, Office of Safe and Drug-Free Schools, U.S. Dept. of Education, and Federal Bureau of Investigation, U.S. Dept of Justice. Washington, DC: authors.

Esquirol, J. E. (1965). *Mental maladies: A treatise on insanity*. (translated by R. de Saussure). New York: Hafner. (Original work published in 1845.)

Fein, R., & Vossekuil, B. (1998a). Preventing attacks on public officials and public figures: A Secret Service perspective. In J.R. Meloy (Ed.), *The psychology of stalking: Clinical and forensic perspectives* (pp. 176–194). San Diego: Academic Press.

Fein, R. & Vossekuil, B. (1998b). *Protective intelligence and threat assessment investigations: A guide for state and local law enforcement officials*. Washington, DC: National Institute of Justice.

Fein, R., & Vossekuil, B. (1999). Assassination in the United States: An operational study of recent assassins, attackers, and near-lethal approachers. *J Forensic Sciences, 44*, 321–333.

Fein, R., Vossekuil, B., & Holden, G. (1995). *Threat assessment: An approach to prevent targeted violence* (Publication NCJ 155000). Washington, DC: U.S. Department of Justice, Office of Justice Programs, National Institute of Justice.

Fein, R., Vossekuil, B., Pollack, W., Borum, R., Modzeleski, W., & Reddy, M. (2002). *Threat assessment in schools: A guide to managing threatening situations and to creating safe school climates*. Washington, DC: U.S. Department of Education and U.S. Secret Service.

Freedman, L. Z. (1971). Psychopathology of assassination. In W. J. Crotty (Ed.) *Assassination and the political order* (pp. 143–160). New York: Harper & Row.

Freud, S. (1958). Formulations regarding the two principles in mental functioning. *Standard edition. Vol. XII* (pp. 215–226) (translated and edited by James Strachey). London: Hogarth. (Original work published in 1911.)

Freud, S. (1961). The future of an illusion. *Standard edition, Vol. XXI* (translated and edited by James Strachey). London: Hogarth. (Original work published in 1927.)

Gregg T, Siegel A. (2001). Brain structures and neurotransmitters regulating aggression in cats: Implications for human aggression. *Progress in Neuropsychopharmacology and Biological Psychiatry, 25*, 91–140.

Harmon, R., & Owens, H. (1995). Obsessional harassment and erotomania in a criminal court population. *Journal of Forensic Sciences, 40*, 188–196.

Hart, S. (2001). Assessing and managing violence risk. In K. Douglas, C. Webster, S. Hart, D. Eaves, & J. Ogloff (Eds.), *HCR-20 violence risk management companion guide* (pp. 13–25). Burnaby, BC: Mental Health, Law, and Policy Institute, Simon Fraser University.

Hart, S. (2003). Violence risk assessment: An anchored narrative approach. In M. Vanderhallen, G. Vervaeke, P. J. Van Koppen, & J. Goethals (Eds.), *Much ado about crime: Chapters on psychology and law* (pp. 209–230). Brussels: Uitgeverij Politeia NV.

Hart, S., Michie, C., & Cooke, D. (2007). Precision of actuarial risk assessment instruments. *British Journal of Psychiatry, 190*, s60–s65.

Hart S., & Logan, C. (2011). Formulation of violence risk using evidence-based assessments: The structured professional judgment approach. In: P. Sturmey & M. McMurran (Eds.), *Forensic case formulation* (pp. 83–107). London: Wiley.

Hempel, A., Levine, R., Meloy, J. R., & Westermeyer, J. (2000). A cross-cultural review of sudden mass assault by a single individual in the Oriental and Occidental cultures. *Journal Forensic Sciences, 45*, 582–588.

Hempel, A., Meloy, J. R., & Richards, T. (1999). Offender and offense characteristics of a nonrandom sample of mass murderers. *Journal of the American Academy of Psychiatry and the Law,27*, 213–225.

Hess W. R., & Brugger M. (1943). Das subkortikale Zentrum der affektiven Abwehrreaktion. *Helvetica Physiologica et Pharmacologica Acta, 1*, 33–52.

Hoffman, J. (1943). Psychotic visitors to government offices in the national capital. *American Journal of Psychiatry, 899,* 571–575.

Hoffmann, J. (2005). *Stalking.* Heidelberg: Springer.

Hoffmann, J., & Glaz-Ocik, J. (2012). DyRiAS—Intimpartner: Konstruktion eines online gestützten Analyse-Instruments zur Risikoeinschätzung von tödlicher Gewalt gegen aktuelle oder frühere Intimpartnerinnen. *Polizei & Wissenschaft, 2,* 46–57.

Hoffmann, J., Meloy, J. R., Guldimann, A., & Ermer, A. (2011). Attacks on German public figures, 1968–2004: Warning behaviors, potentially lethal and nonlethal acts, psychiatric status, and motivations. *Behavioral Sciences and the Law, 29,* 155–179.

Hoffmann, J., & Roshdi, K. (2013). School shootings in Germany: Research, prevention through risk assessment and threat management. In: Böckler, N., Seeger, T., Sitzer, P., & Heitmeyer, W. (Eds.), *School shootings: International research, case studies, and concepts for prevention.* New York: Springer, 363–378.

Hoffmann, J., Roshdi, K., & Allwinn, M. (in press). DyRiAS—Schule: Entwicklung und Validierung eines online gestützten Analyse-Instruments zur Risikoeinschätzung von schwerer zielgerichteter Gewalt an Schulen. *Polizei & Wissenschaft.*

James, D., Mullen, P., Meloy, J. R., Pathé, M., Farnham, F., Preston, L. & Darnley, B. (2007). The role of mental disorder in attacks on European politicians 1990-2004. *Acta Psychiatrica Scandinavica, 116,* 334–344.

James, D. V., Mullen, P. E., Pathé, M., Meloy, J.R., Preston, L., Darnley, B., et al. (2009). Stalkers and harassers of royalty: The role of mental illness and motivation. *Psychological Medicine, 39,* 1479–1490.

James, D., McEwan, T., MacKenzie, R., Meloy, J.R., Mullen, P., Pathé, M., Farnham, F., Preston, L., & Darnley, B. (2010-a). Persistence in stalking: A comparison of associations in general forensic and public figure samples. *Journal of Forensic Psychiatry and Psychology, 21,* 283–305.

James, D., Mullen, P., Meloy, J. R., Pathé, M., Preston, L., Darnley, B. Farnham, F. & Scalora, M. (2011). Stalkers and harassers of British royalty: An exploration of proxy behaviours for violence. *Behavioral Sciences and the Law, 29,* 64–80.

Kahneman, D. (2011). *Thinking, fast and slow.* New York: Farrar, Straus & Giroux.

Katsavdakis, K., Meloy, J. R., & White, S. (2011). A female mass murderer. *Journal of Forensic Sciences, 56,* 813–818.

Kinney (1995). *Violence at work.* Englewood Cliffs, NJ: Prentice Hall.

Knoll, J. (2010a). The "pseudocommando" mass murderer: Part I, the psychology of revenge and obliteration. *Journal of the American Academy of Psychiatry and the Law, 38,* 87–94.

Knoll, J. (2010b). The "pseudocommando" mass murderer: Part II, the language of revenge. *Journal of the American Academy of Psychiatry and the Law, 38,* 262–272.

Krafft-Ebing, R. von (1912). *Psychopathia sexualis.* Stuttgart: Verlag von Ferdinand Enke.

Kropp, R., Hart, S., & Lyon, D. (2008). *Guidelines for stalking assessment and management (SAM).* Vancouver, BC: ProActive ReSolutions.

Kropp, R., Hart, S., Lyon, D., & Storey, J. (2011).The development and validation of the guidelines for stalking assessment and management. *Behavioral Sciences and the Law, 29,* 302–316.

Kropp, R., Hart, S., Webster, C., & Eaves, D. (1994). *Manual for the spousal assault risk assessment guide.* Vancouver, BC: British Columbia Institute on Family Violence.

Kuhn, T. (1970). *The structure of scientific revolutions* (2nd ed., enlarged). Chicago: University of Chicago Press.

Laschi, M., & Lombroso, C. (1886). Le délit politique. In *Actes du Premier Congrès International d'Anthropologie Criminelle, Rome 1885* (pp. 379–389). Turin, Florence, & Rome: Bocca Frères.

Lammel, M., Sutarski, S., Lau, S., & Bauer, M. (Eds.). (2011). *Wahn und Schizophrenie.* Berlin: MWV.

MacDonald, A. (1911). Assassins of rulers. *Journal of the American Institute of Criminal Law and Criminology, 2,* 505–520.

MacDonald, J. (1968). *Homicidal threats.* Springfield, IL: Charles C. Thomas.

MacKenzie, R. D., McEwan, T. E., Pathé, M., James, D. V., Ogloff, J. R. P., & Mullen, P. E. (2009). *Stalking Risk Profile: guidelines for the assessment and management of stalkers.* Melbourne, Australia: Centre for Forensic Behavioral Science.

McEllistrem J. (2004). Affective and predatory violence: A bimodal classification system of human aggression and violence. *Aggression and Violent Behavior, 10,* 1–30.

Meloy, J. R. (1987). The prediction of violence in outpatient psychotherapy. *American Journal of Psychotherapy, 41,* 38–45.

Meloy, J. R. (1988). *The psychopathic mind: Origins, dynamics, and treatment.* Northvale, NJ: Jason Aronson.

Meloy, J. R. (1989). Unrequited love and the wish to kill. *Bulletin of the Menninger Clinic,53,* 477–492.

Meloy, J. R. (1997). Predatory violence during mass murder. *Journal Forensic Sciences, 42,* 326–329.

Meloy, J. R. (Ed.). (1998). *The psychology of stalking: Clinical and forensic perspectives.* San Diego: Academic Press.

Meloy, J. R. (2000). *Violence risk and threat assessment.* San Diego, CA: Specialized Training Services.

Meloy, J. R. (2006). The empirical basis and forensic application of affective and predatory violence. *Australian and New Zealand J Psychiatry, 40,* 539–547.

Meloy, J.R. (2011). Approaching and attacking public figures: A contemporary analysis of communications and behavior. In C. Chauvin (Ed.), *Threatening communications and behavior: Perspectives on the pursuit of public figures* (pp. 75–101). Washington, DC: National Research Council, National Academies Press.

Meloy, J. R. (2012). Predatory violence and psychopathy. In Hakkanen-Nyholm, H. & Nyholm, J. (Eds.), *Psychopathy and law* (pp. 159–175). London: Wiley.

Meloy, J. R., & Gothard, S. (1995). A demographic and clinical comparison of obsessional followers and offenders with mental disorders. *American Journal of Psychiatry, 152,* 258–263.

Meloy, J. R., Hart, S., & White, S. G. (in press). Workplace assessment of targeted violence risk: the development and reliability of the WAVR-21. *Journal of Forensic Sciences.*

Meloy, J. R., Hempel, A., Gray, T., Mohandie, K., Shiva, A., & Richards, T. (2004). A comparative analysis of North American adolescent and adult mass murderers. *Behavioral Sciences and the Law, 22,* 291–309.

Meloy, J. R., Hoffmann, J., Guldimann, A., & James, D. (2012). The role of warning behaviors in threat assessment: An exploration and suggested typology. *Behavioral Sciences and the Law, 30,* 256–279.

Meloy, J. R., Sheridan, L. & Hoffmann, J. (eds) (2008). *Stalking, threatening, and attacking public figures: A psychological and behavioral analysis.* New York: Oxford University Press.

Mohandie, K. (2000). *School violence threat management.* San Diego, CA: Specialized Training Services.

Monahan, J. (2007). Clinical and actuarial predictions of violence. In D. Faigman, D. Kaye, M. Saks, J. Sanders, & E. Cheng (Eds.), *Modern scientific evidence: The law and science of expert testimony* (pp. 122–147). St. Paul, MN: West Publishing.

Monahan, J. (1981). *The clinical prediction of violence.* Washington, DC: U.S. Government Printing Office.

Monahan, J. (2008). Structured risk assessment of violence. In: R. Simon, K. Tardiff, eds. *Textbook of violence assessment and management* (pp. 17–33). Washington, DC: American Psychiatric Publishing.

Monahan, J., Steadman, H., Silver, E., Appelbaum, P., Robbins, P., Mulvey, E., ... & Banks, S. (2001). *Rethinking risk assessment.* New York: Oxford University Press.

Mullen, P., Pathé, M., & Purcell, R. (2000). *Stalkers and their victims.* London: Cambridge University Press.

Mullen, P., Pathé, M., & Purcell, R. (2009). *Stalkers and their victims* (2nd ed.). London: Cambridge University Press.

O'Toole, M. E. (2000). *The school shooter: A threat assessment perspective.* Quantico, VA: Critical Incident Response Group, FBI Academy, National Center for the Analysis of Violent Crime.

Otto, R., & Douglas, K. (2009). *Handbook of violence risk assessment.* New York: Taylor & Francis.

Quinsey, V., Harris, G., Rice, M., & Cormier, C. (2006). *Violent offenders: Appraising and managing risk* (2nd ed.). Washington, DC: American Psychological Association.

Raine A, Meloy J. R, Bihrle S., Stoddard J., LaCasse L., & Buchsbaum, M. (1998). Reduced prefrontal and increased subcortical brain functioning assessed using positron emission tomography in predatory and affective murderers. *Behavioral Sciences and the Law, 16,* 319–332.

Randazzo, M. R., Borum, R., Vossekuil, B., Fein, R., Modzeleski, W., & Pollack, W. (2006). Threat assessment in schools: Empirical support and comparison with other approaches. In S.R. Jimerson & M. J. Furlong (Eds.), *The handbook of school violence and school safety: From research to practice.* Mahwah, NJ: Lawrence Erlbaum.

Reddy, M., Borum, R., Vossekuil, B., Fein, R., Berglund, J., & Modzeleski, W. (2001). Evaluating risk for targeted violence in schools: Comparing risk assessment, threat assessment, and other approaches. *Psychology in the Schools, 38,* 157–172.

Régis, E. (1890). *Les Régicides dans l'Histoire et dans le Présent.* Paris: Maloine

Roehl, J., O'Sullivan, C., Webster, D., Campbell, J. (2005). *Intimate Partner Violence Risk Assessment Validation Study, Final Report.* Washington, DC: U.S. Dept. of Justice. Accessed at: www.ncjrs.gov/pdffiles1/nij/grants/209731.pdf

Scalora, M. J., Baumgartner, J. V., Callaway, D., Zimmerman, W., Hatch-Maillette, M. A., Covell C. N., ...Washington, D. O. (2002a). An epidemiological assessment of problematic contacts to members of Congress. *Journal of Forensic Sciences, 47,* 1360–1364.

Scalora, M. J., Baumgartner, J., & Plank, G. (2003). The relationship of mental illness to targeted contact behavior toward state government agencies and officials. *Behavioral Sciences and the Law, 21,* 239–249.

Scalora, M. J., Baumgartner, J. V., Zimmerman, W., Callaway, D., Hatch-Maillette, M.A., Covell, C.N., ...Washington, D. O. (2002b). Risk factors for approach behavior toward the U.S. Congress. *J Threat Assessment 2,* 35–55.

Schlesinger, L., & Mesa, B. (2008). Homicidal celebrity stalkers: Dangerous obsessions with nonpolitical public figures. In J. R. Meloy, L. Sheridan, & J. Hoffmann (Eds.), *Stalking, threatening, and attacking public figures: A psychological and behavioral analysis* (pp. 83–104). New York: Oxford University Press.

Sebastiani, J., & Foy, J. (1966). Psychotic visitors to the White House. *American Journal of Psychiatry, 122,* 679–686.

Siegel, A., & Victoroff, J. (2009). Understanding human aggression: New insights from neuroscience. *International Journal of Law and Psychiatry, 32,* 209–215.

Skeem, J., & Monahan, J. (2011). Current directions in violence risk assessment. *Current Directions in Psychological Science, 20,* 38–42.

Turner, J., & Gelles, M. (2003). *Threat assessment: A risk management approach.* New York: Haworth Press.

Unsgaard, E., & Meloy, J. R. (2011). The assassination of the Swedish minister for foreign affairs. *Journal of Forensic Sciences, 56,* 555–559.

Viding E, & Frith U. (2006). Genes for susceptibility to violence lurk in the brain. *Proceedings of the National Academy of Sciences, 103,* 6085–6086.

Vossekuil, B., Borum, R., Fein, R., & Reddy, M. (2001). Preventing targeted violence against judicial officials and courts. *Annals of the American Academy of Political and Social Science, 576,* 78–90.

Vossekuil, B., Fein, R., Reddy, M., Borum, R., & Modzeleski, W. (2002). *The final report and findings of the Safe School Initiative: Implications for the prevention of school attacks in the United States.* Washington, DC: U.S. Department of Education and U.S. Secret Service.

Wasman M, & Flynn J. (1962). Directed attack elicited from hypothalamus. *Archives of Neurology, 27,* 635–644.

Webster, C., Douglas, K., Eaves, D., & Hart, S. (1997). *HCR-20 assessing risk for violence, version 2.* Burnaby, CA: Mental Health, Law, and Policy Institute, Simon Fraser University.

Webster, C., Nicholls, T., Martin, M., Desmarais, S. & Brink, J. (2006). Short-term assessment of risk and treatability (START): The case for a new structured professional judgment scheme. *Behavioral Sciences and the Law, 24,* 747–766.

White, S., & Meloy, J. R. (2010). *The WAVR-21: A structured professional guide for the workplace assessment of violence risk, second edition.* San Diego, CA: Specialized Training Services.

Yang, M., Wong, S., & Coid, J. (2010). The efficacy of violence prediction: A meta-analytic comparison of nine risk assessment tools. *Psychological Bulletin, 136,* 740–767.

Zona, M., Sharma, K., & Lane, J. (1993). A comparative study of erotomanic and obsessional subjects in a forensic sample. *Journal of Forensic Sciences, 38,* 894–903.

2

Explicit Threats of Violence

LISA J. WARREN, PAUL E. MULLEN, AND TROY E. MCEWAN

In real life most threats are mundane if occasionally unpleasant utterances that create no real apprehension and have no implications for future events. Many of us have used a threat as a throwaway statement to express exasperation or possibly even humor. Very few of us have intended to cause actual distress, let alone fear, by our words except possibly on the sports field. Threats intended to induce fear are relatively infrequent, but when they occur the question arises of whether they will be carried out or enacted.

Meloy (1996) has argued that threat research is hampered by the lack of a widely accepted definition of a threat. The *Oxford English Dictionary* (Oxford University Press, 2012) notes *threat* as being derived from the old English word for painful pressure, which acquired the meaning of "a declaration of hostile determination or of loss, pain, punishment, or damage to be inflicted in retribution for, or conditionally upon some course." (www.lib.monash.edu.au/oed.com). To threaten is defined in terms of pressing, urging, or inducing. These definitions assume that threats are either menaces intended to induce compliance with the wishes of the threatener or promises of revenge for experienced harm that, in themselves, can cause painful pressure or torment. These definitions leave no room for any threats that in practice are no more than expressions of emotion, thoughtless reactions, or even jokes. The threat that is not a threat does not make the person a source of risk. Thus a distinction can be made between making a threat and being or posing a threat—a distinction

properly made between the content and the implications of a threat, rather than a distinction between threats and other forms of menacing behavior.

Social psychologists have explored the interpersonal elements of threatening, suggesting that they are intended to communicate such matters as (1) anger, (2) a desire for attention, (3) the threatener's current state of mind, and (4) hostile intentions (deBecker, 1997; Felson & Tedeschi, 1993; Hough, 1990; Milburn & Watman, 1981; Tedeschi, Malkis, Gaes, & Quigley-Fernandez, 1980).

Threats can be spoken, written, gestured, or symbolic (such as sending a bullet engraved with the target's name). While the content of threats ranges between threats of physical, psychological, and reputational harm, the focus of this chapter is on expressing the intention to injure or kill. Threats can be uttered directly to the target or *leaked* to third parties such as friends, family, teachers or health professionals (O'Toole, 2000; *Tarasoff v. Regents of University of California*, 1976). Here we will focus on the threats uttered to an individual or group of potential targets.

Among animals threatening behaviors are usually modulators of aggression designed to establish dominance or shield against antagonists or predators (Darwin, 1872/1998). Thus the threat in the animal kingdom is a way of potentially avoiding the use of force. This remains true in practice even if it sometimes turns out to be the prelude to open aggression when the challenge implicit in the threat is accepted. The purpose of threats and threatening for humans is less obvious.

The broadest and most basic definition of threat is *an utterance whose content implies an intention to do harm.* Utterances include spoken and written communications as well as actions intended to convey a message. This definition does not distinguish between the most common types of threat, which do not reflect any commitment by the threatener to future action, and those threats where there is, at least at the time, some degree of commitment to carry out the expressed intention. This distinction between intention and commitment may be of value in considering the transition to action (Calhoun & Weston, 2003). For example, we may express the wish to become rich and famous. If we do not have any real commitment to the effort and sacrifices that might make this possible, the expressed intent is without weight and lacks even a predisposition to action. The commitment to the intention to harm expressed by the threat can vary from zero to total. The risk of the threat leading to enactment depends therefore less on the expressed intent and more on the commitment to action. Central to assessing the risk in a threatener is evaluating the progress of the degree and nature of the commitment to act on the threat.

Threats can arise either in response to a provocation, as part of a plan to put pressure on someone, or as a less than specific expression of an angry or fearful preexisting state of mind. Threats are uttered in social and interpersonal contexts. Although the willingness to resort to threatening depends on the threatener's personal characteristics, the context usually determines the motivation. Figure 2.1 illustrates a simple model of the connection of threat to enactment of the threat.

There are a number of ways to classify threats. There is much to be said for simply dividing threats according to the context in which they occur. For example, those who threaten to harm partners or other family members, public figures, those they are stalking, or broad groups of the general population, would constitute various categories. There is, in our view, value in progressing beyond this to consider the types of threats that can occur in the different contexts.

Clinically we have developed a broad typology of threats based on their motivation and function, which relates to the likely degree of commitment to act on the threat. As with all typologies the types may overlap, and once knowledge advances this approach will probably be replaced by a more firmly grounded classification. With apologies for the struggle after alliteration, we suggest five types of threatener:

1. *Screamers:* whose threats are responses to provocations in the form of expressions of emotion that are cathartic. The threats take the form of an expletive, usually in response to an exciting situation. These are the commonest type of threat uttered in the community. Members of this group rarely find themselves in court or in a consulting room on account of their threats. Screamers usually make threats in a context and manner where they and their target(s) understand that no harm is intended or contemplated. The context and nature of the threats usually make clear they are expressions of emotion

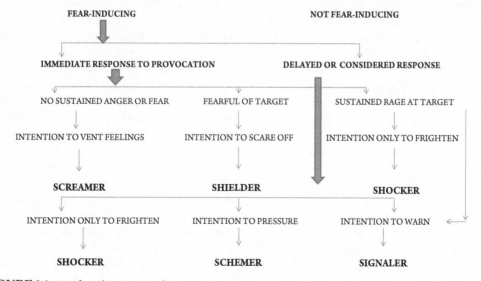

FIGURE 2.1 A guide to threatener typology.

rather than commitments to act ("I'll kill that bloody ref," "If you keep pushing yourself between me and the ball I'll murder you," "I'll murder that husband of mine" uttered upon finding the car's fuel gauge low again, etc.). They rarely produce fear or distress in those who overhear or to whom the threat is addressed. Uttering the threat makes the threatener feel better at the cost of mildly irritating or amusing the recipients. In short, when uttered, such threats are rarely accompanied by any commitment to action. Those rare instances where there may be some commitment involve angry and resentful individuals who typically threaten repeatedly in response to a wide range of provocations and direct their threats to more than one victim. In the small subgroup of screamers who go on to enact the threats, the target of the violence may be one of the people they have threatened or someone else entirely. This is because both the threats and the violence are driven by an underlying, relatively nonspecific rage at the world.

2. *Shockers:* whose threats are calculated to induce fear and produce an immediate impact in terms of increased anxiety in the target. Typically this is primarily a way of striking out and harming the targets or of establishing dominance over them. Occasionally such threats are intended to bring attention to the threatener. They take the form of stating an intention to engage in behavior that will have terrible consequences. The commitment is to producing an immediate reaction in the target rather than to any subsequent action. Only if pushed to prove it are they likely to progress to enactment.

3. *Shielders:* whose threats are self-protective in that they are intended to ward off potential aggression or incursions by others. Threats from shielders take the form "I am more dangerous than you think, so do not interfere with me." The commitment is to self-protection.

4. *Schemers:* whose threats are instrumental and motivated by the desire to influence or coerce others into complying with their wishes. These threats are usually premeditated and take the form of promising to engage in behavior harmful to the person or persons targeted unless they comply with the threatener's stated demands. The commitment is to further the shielder's interests, which, when the threat is insufficient and the commitment sufficiently strong, may be followed by enactment.

5. *Signalers:* whose threats are warnings that promise future harm to the target. Such threats take the form of stating an intention to engage in

retaliation against the target for actual or perceived harm caused to the threatener. There is a commitment to enactment inherent in such threats. Whether the commitment will lead to action depends on both the target's responses and the threatener's personality, defined by such variables as prudence, social conformity, and impulsivity.

All types of threat can induce fear in a target and may be harbingers of violence, but the frequency with which this occurs varies widely. The commonest types of threats in everyday life are the expletive screams. Such threats rarely create apprehension and usually carry no commitment to action. They can, however, occasionally evoke a response in the target, which leads to escalating confrontation from which violence can emerge. They may also reflect a preexisting angry or fearful state of mind and presage further aggression, though not necessarily against the person threatened. Those whose intention is to protect themselves behind a shield of threats are if anything committed to avoiding violence. If violence does emerge, it is likely to be from a failure to deter the target. To some extent such individuals need to create apprehension to avoid an escalation to violence. Those who threaten in order to shock are using the threat itself as a weapon to dominate or distress; unless provoked in some way to prove their seriousness, they have no reason to go further. Those who threaten to signal intent usually produce apprehension in the target. Those who scheme to coerce through menacing behavior probably should, but often do not, evoke fear. The chances of producing fear and of enactment vary widely between the different types of threat. If threats are all lumped together, there is a risk that the danger signaled by some threats is lost among the noise of threatening utterances of no consequence.

Those determined to attack disadvantage themselves by giving warning via a threat. Threats may on occasion be an attempt to remove the need for an attack. In the case of a suicide threat, we have no trouble recognizing the "cry for help" aimed at producing responses that will prevent the threatener's self-harm. In the threat to harm others, there may also be an attempt to avoid enactment by evoking responses that will limit the threatener's potential to harm others. Those adept at violence who have already decided to act do not intentionally warn their victims. Growing up in a rough neighborhood usually teaches people to threaten when they want to avoid a fight, but to strike first and without warning when they have decided that physical conflict is inevitable. Thus, in the threat, there may lie the threatener's hope to avoid enactment. Conversely, threats may perform the role of building up the threatener's commitment to attack and/or be part of his or her self-justification.

Threats can be implied or veiled, as in "I know where you live" or "This is my last resort, and if it fails I cannot be held responsible for the consequences." Such veiled threats require a degree of deliberation and a calculation of their likely impact. They are not suited to expletive screams. In part they may represent an attempt to maintain potential deniability should the threatener be challenged. On occasion the need for the target to interpret the overt statement as a threat may increase the degree of apprehension evoked. The very fact that the threats are so deliberate is also likely to heighten their impact. There is a degree of unpleasantness in the slyness of a veiled threat, but does this imply a greater likelihood of enactment compared with direct threats? No systematic studies, to our knowledge, address this question, in part because studies tend to conflate direct and veiled threats. Some experts express the view, based on clinical experience, that certain types of indirect threats should be regarded as indicating substantial risk.

This chapter will now focus on the relatively small minority of uttered threats that have evoked fear and/or concern. For brevity's sake, we will not add a qualification of being fear-inducing, as that should be assumed.

THREAT CRIMES

Threat crimes offer one source of data to investigate not only whether threats are followed by violent enactment but also the personalities, social situations, and motivations of threateners. In most jurisdictions various statutes can be used to prosecute those who utter threats. The choice of legislation is generally based on the content of the threat, the method of delivery, the manner in which the threat is to be carried out, and the identity of the target (Alldridge, 1994). Inherent in all statutes, however, is a requirement that the threatener was reckless in his or her statements or intended to cause distress by creating a reasonable belief that the threat would be carried out. The law usually attempts to protect people's right to express themselves freely, while also precisely defining those utterances with consequences that are unacceptable and consequently criminal.

As an informative population, threateners who are arrested, charged, and convicted of threat crimes

have advantages and disadvantages. The road from uttering a threat to appearing in court involves a process of several levels of selection.

In the general community

Surveys examining rates of victimization in the general community often examine threats to harm. The question used in surveys typically seeks information about whether the respondents had been threatened with damage or hurt in a way that actually frightened them (Hough, 1990). Victim surveys in the United States suggest that each year 1.6% of the population experience such threats (Bureau of Justice Statistics, 2006). The International Crime Victims Survey has been administered to over 300,000 people in 78 countries over the past 20 years (van Dijk, Mayhew, van Kesteren, Aebi, & Linde, 2010). Threat crimes were identified as among the most common person-based crimes. It was estimated that each year some 5% of the population is threatened in a manner inducing fear and/or distress. Roughly 30% of those threatened in this manner will report the offense to the police, which is lower than reporting rates for assault (45%) but similar to those for sexual assault (28%) (Hough, 1990; van Kesteren, Mayhew, & Nieuwbeerta, 2000).

Police responses to reports of being threatened are likely to be variable. The only data available suggest that the frequency of individuals being charged with a threat crime has escalated rapidly over the last 20 years. This probably reflects largely an increased willingness of victims to report and the police to act on complaints rather than a true increase in threatening behaviors (van Kesteren et al., 2000). To qualify as an offense, a threat must induce fear (or be likely to do so in a reasonable person). The police presumably act more often if they can understand why the threat in the particular circumstances would be fear-inducing. For a conviction, the court must come to the same conclusion. A final complication in using threat crime statistics is the tendency for police to use this as a "loading charge." In robberies, assaults (both sexual and nonsexual), and when arrest was resisted, threats are frequently uttered. The police and prosecution have considerable discretion in whether to specify this as a separate offense. When they do, the offense is centered on a crime other than threatening—that is, a mere by-product.

Those convicted of threat crimes who are referred for mental health evaluations are reputed to have high levels of psychopathology, in particular personality disorders and problems of substance abuse (Barnes, Gordon, & Hudson, 2001; Häkkänen, 2006). In a study of 613 individuals convicted of making threats to kill, over 40% had had prior contact with mental health services; in some 60% there was a history of substance abuse; and schizophrenia (3%) was significantly more common among such offenders than in the general community (0.7%) (Wallace et al., 1998; Warren, Mullen, Thomas, Ogloff, & Burgess, 2008).

Warren et al. (2008) followed up 613 convicted threateners for 10 years. Over 40% were subsequently convicted of a violent offense, including 19 (3%) homicides and 8 (1.3%) attempted murders. In those whose index offenses included threatening to kill as the only or the most serious crime ($n = 207$), violent reoffending occurred in one third, and 5 (2.4%) committed a homicide. This high level of subsequent violence was surprising and at odds with prior studies of threats to public figures, which had often failed to establish links between threats and subsequent aggression. In part the high level of subsequent violence probably relates to the frequency of threats to kill directed at an intimate (approximately 40%), which is reported to be associated with a higher risk of subsequent violence (Meloy, 1998). In part the selection process—which required the victim to be frightened and had to convince police, prosecutors, and a court that the fear was justified—guaranteed a sample of threateners whose utterances carried considerable weight. Humans, like all animals, are good at recognizing what poses a threat and separating this from those uttered threats that are mostly harmless. Were they not, their survival chances would be reduced. The visceral response produced by some threats should not be ignored, as it is relevant information, and, we believe, relates to risk.

Warren and colleagues (2008) studied threats that did not arise in the commission of another crime; they were predominantly verbal (87%) and usually uttered in domestic or work-related situations. In these circumstances threats uttered in a manner that produces fear need to be taken seriously.

If threats that evoke fear and result in the threatener's prosecution and conviction are associated with greatly increased rates of violence at a later date, then violence should be associated with prior convictions for threatening. A study of 555 consecutive homicide convictions revealed that 82 (15%) of these individuals had been charged with threatening to kill, almost all in the weeks and months prior to the killing. By chance only one or two would have been expected to have faced such charges (Warren, Mullen, Davis, & Ogloff,

2013). Interestingly, although 24 went on to kill the person they were charged with threatening, no less than 57 killed someone else. This study points to lost opportunities: 15% of those who were to kill were not only known by the police to be uttering threats to kill but had created sufficient concern in the law enforcement agencies to have been charged with making a threat to kill. The lost opportunity highlights the need for forensic sciences to further explore and publicize the risks presented by persons who make such threats.

The frequency with which those killed were not those who reported the threat raises a problem. The model of threat and enactment proposed earlier placed emphasis on the motivation and relationship to the target. That threatening behavior may not always reflect a victim-specific form of animosity but a more generalized predisposition to violence should be taken into account in considering assessment and management (Soothill, Francis, Ackerley, & Fligelstone, 2002; Warren et al., 2008).

Threats in the Clinical Setting

There are three aspects to threats in the clinical setting: the first is when threats are directed at clinical staff, the second is when an intention to harm third parties is confided to a health professional, and the third is when a threatener is referred for assessment.

Staff working in health services are not infrequently the target of threats from both patients and the relatives of patients. The highest-risk area is probably the emergency room, but mental health is a clinical specialty where threats to staff also often occur (Bernstein, 1981; Brown, Dubin, Lion, & Garry, 1996; Coverdale, Gale, Weeks, & Turbott, 2001; Faulkner, Grimm, McFarland, & Bloom, 1990; Guy, Brown, & Poelstra, 1990).

A wide range of studies have examined threats in terms of to whom, by whom, when, and where as well as their impacts on clinical staff (Coverdale & Roberts, 2005; Crabbe, Alexander, Klein, Walker, & Sinclair, 2002; Guy et al., 1990). The literature on threats to others confided to mental health staff is even richer. This is because of the medicolegal issues around duty to warn and subsequent liability should the patient act on the communicated threat (Carstensen, 1994; McMahon, 1992; Mendelson & Mendelson, 1991; Mossman, 2007). Liability and the existence of a legal assumption of a duty to warn vary widely between and within nations' laws. In some jurisdictions, such as the majority of the states in the United States, which encourage or mandate reporting, clinicians assume that they have a legal duty to warn the person whom they know to be threatened. Other nations, however, use professional codes of conduct (rather than legal mechanisms) to support the reporting of those who threaten to harm. The debate around the world on this point is a spirited one, seeking to clarify the obligations of clinicians by resolving these legal, ethical, and moral dilemmas.

It is another question whether warning those threatened may help to protect patients from proceeding to acts of violence, which will bring unnecessary harm to them as well as to their victims. Attacks on other people rarely have positive outcomes. In contrast to the substantial literature on the context and impact of threats in clinical practice and the medicolegal and ethical dilemmas they raise, there is a remarkable paucity of studies on whether such threats are followed by other forms of aggression.

Studies on whether those referred to mental health services for making threats to kill were likely to act on such threats had an early and auspicious start. MacDonald (1968) followed up, for five years, over 90 patients seen in a Colorado emergency room after they had made threats to kill. Of these, 3 (3.9%) committed a homicide and 4 (5.2%) killed themselves. This is an extraordinary mortality rate. This study was not replicated over the next 50 years, had no influence on the later development of risk assessment techniques, and fell into undeserved obscurity. The mortality in this study mirrors more recent follow-up studies on those convicted of threat crimes as discussed previously. A recent study from Australia followed up 144 patients referred to a forensic community mental health service because they had made threats to kill (Warren, Mullen, & Ogloff, 2011). The 12-month follow up indicated that 33 (23%) had subsequently been charged with a violent offense, including one homicide (Warren et al., 2011). Whatever the criteria for referring threateners in California in the 1960s, and in Australia more recently, they identified a group with a high risk of future violence. For clinicians seeing such patients the message is clear: these patients should be prioritized for a finely tuned assessment where their risks and needs are identified; then they should be treated by those who have the matching expertise.

Threats to Commit Mass Homicide

Mass killings—when a gunman goes into a public space and begins shooting people apparently at random—have become part of the landscape of twenty-first-century western societies (Cantor,

Mullen, & Alpers, 2000; Meloy et al., 2004; Mullen, 2004). Direct threats do not often precede these massacres except when adolescents are involved (Meloy et al., 2004; Meloy, Hempel, Mohandie, Shiva, & Gray, 2001). Indirect or veiled threats occur, but their significance is rarely recognized at the time. Communications with family, friends, or like-minded groups may suggest that such murderous behavior is being contemplated, and these statements may leak into more public forums, providing a potential warning (Twemlow, Fonagy, Sacco, & Vernberg, 2008; Warren et al., 2008).

In contrast, some individuals make explicit threats to commit a massacre to authority figures such as teachers, police, and health professionals. They may also place such threats on websites clearly identifying themselves as the senders. These threats tend to come thick and fast in the days following the publicity attending an actual massacre. Such threats may precipitate a referral to a mental health professional with a request to assess the risk.

CASE EXAMPLE

A 23-year-old university student handed in an essay that seemed to imply an intention to kill himself after slaughtering as many fellow students as possible. When questioned he made no attempt to evade the issue but stated that this was indeed his plan. The essay had been written a day or so after the massacre at Virginia Tech in 2007. The university he attended had suffered a campus shooting five years previously.

In the circumstances, the response was measured and appropriate. Immediate contact was made with the student counseling service and he was seen the same day. The psychologist, perhaps because of the university's unfortunate history, was well versed in the literature on massacres. She did not panic but was sufficiently concerned to make an urgent appointment with our forensic service, which the student agreed voluntarily to attend.

He arrived for his appointment wearing army camouflage gear and lace-up military boots and immediately launched into an account of his plans for mass murder/suicide. He gave a history of self-harm involving cutting and overdoses in his teens. He said he was chronically depressed, but what he described were brief, intense periods of despondency lasting a day or so and usually in response to the reversals and stresses of daily life. He had had a number of sexual relationships, the longest for two years, which had recently ended. He was a regular user of cannabis. He expressed vague leftish political views. He had never owned or used a gun. He expressed himself to be antimilitary and antiauthoritarian. The thought of killing fellow students had first occurred recently. He had made no detailed plans, had not acquired a weapon, and had not indulged in fantasies about such an action. He had no obsessional traits—in fact, quite the reverse. He feared that he was on the way to failing the year and was uncertain about pursuing his university studies. Uttering the threats, he had assumed, would make the decision to leave university for him. He had made sure that his ex-girlfriend would hear of what was to happen and believed that this would make her take him more seriously.

Those adults (over 18 years of age) who commit mass killings have usually planned the killings in great detail. They are often not just gun owners but gun collectors and/or gun-obsessed. They are loners who often have a rich fantasy life around themselves as soldiers or warriors. They lack functional intimate relationships, can live isolated lives, tend to hold right-wing and elitist political views. They are often rigid or obsessional and manifest a higher than expected rate of psychotic disorders. Those who openly threaten mass killings often present as having less evolved homicidal plans and a lesser interest in guns and weaponry, especially in countries such as the United Kingdom and Australia, where rates of gun ownership are far lower than in the United States, making those who possess arsenals actual anomalies. The stand-out feature of their presentation is a need to make flamboyant threats in an attempt to convey their intense distress. The threat is the plea for help to relieve this distress.

They have chaotic, disorganized lives but usually manage some semblance of intimate relationships. They are not lone fantasizers but gregarious boasters. They do not admire authority or the military and are unhappy, unstable, and looking for help rather than determined to commit suicide. They are also contemptuous of everyone, particularly those offering help. This type of threatener aims to shock and by doing so acquire some secondary gain.

In our own clinical series of threateners there were eight who had threatened a massacre. The threats were aimed at shocking and bringing attention to the threateners' current plight. All were managed in the community, and although three committed some minor offenses in the follow-up period, none killed or injured others or themselves (Warren et al., 2011).

Repeated Threats to Kill Members of the Public

Repeated threats are typically uttered by those who experience the reinforcing consequences of threatening, such as the domestically violent who control their partners' lives by choosing judicious moments to threaten them (Felson & Messer, 2000). Repeated threatening is a phenomenon that has been reported in the literature in two ways: (1) repeatedly using this form of communication in all manner of interactions and (2) selecting a situation where the repeated use of threats brings a desired outcome, albeit intermittently.

Threats as a communication style were well explored by social psychology researchers throughout the 1970s and 1980s. More than describing the message sent, these studies highlight the techniques involved in sending, receiving and decoding threats (deBecker, 1997; Felson & Tedeschi, 1993; Hornstein, 1965; Milburn & Watman, 1981). Sending includes the threatener's intent, which is encoded into a particular message influenced by past experience and the current environment (Milburn & Watman, 1981). The content can be conditional, but this is not mandatory. Receiving is the response of the threat's audience, and decoding is the process of modifying—by way of values, arousal level, and memory—the meaning of the threat (Milburn & Watman, 1981). This research explored the relationship between the parties and the environmental milieu that impacted the communication process.

Repeated threatening in selected situations has been explored as part of the research on those situations. An excellent example is the stalking literature, where threatening is either the only repeated, unwanted intrusion or one of many intrusions into the stalking victim's life. Many stalking victims are threatened (Harmon, Rosner, & Owens, 1998; Mullen, Pathé, Purcell, & Stuart, 1999; Pathé & Mullen, 1997), and those threatened have been found to be three times more likely to be assaulted (McEwan, Mullen, MacKenzie, & Ogloff, 2009). This highlights the need to take such threats seriously and explore their significance when repeated. For some the significance is that the threat fails to achieve the sought response, which becomes the catalyst for escalation. This has been seen time and again among those who supposedly *snap* when a pathway to violence, including direct or leaked threats, had arisen but failed to be identified. For others, the significance of repeated threats is that they reliably produce the desired outcome. One man we assessed had used threats to kill in each of the six armed robberies he had committed. His explanation was that people "behaved themselves" when threatened, meaning that he got his loot and made his escape (in the short term at least).

Among recidivist threateners we have discovered an unusual group of female threateners who repeatedly target emergency services. They utter many threats to commit serious acts of violence, often bombings, against the general public or prominent people. They usually communicate threats to police via the phone but occasionally use the press or terrorist hotlines. They often identify themselves or make their apprehension straightforward. Being questioned by police was often a desired consequence, especially when the attending officers were male, uniformed, and easy on the eye.

CASE EXAMPLE

A woman in her early twenties was referred for the management of recidivist threatening. Her threats were delivered by post or telephone and peaked at a frequency of more than 10 per day. She favored death threats and bomb threats, often directed to local news presenters or authorities. She had been charged and convicted of the relevant offenses many times but this had done little to deter her behavior. Several police officers reported a belief that contact with them was more of an attraction than a deterrent. Her referral to forensic mental health was as much of a cry for help from the frustrated criminal justice system as a means to offer her a therapeutic intervention.

Assessment revealed a chaotic childhood but no major mental illness or substance abuse. She had been previously considered to be psychotic by medical officers in police cells because she had laughed at and talked with specific spots on cell walls or ceilings. As her arrests often occurred in the minutes after telephoning a threat, it was later ascertained that her hilarity was the result of the use of atypical inhalants (such as Texta pens [felt-tipped markers] and correction fluid).

Axis II psychopathology was more complex. Assessment of intellectual capacity revealed low functioning but no disability. Traits of Borderline Personality Disorder were evident but subclinical. The welfare staff supporting her reported adaptive functioning in several life domains, particularly an evenness in her rapport with them.

Treatment was primarily psychological counseling focusing on criminogenic needs and social skills

training. Cognitive distortions about emergency service workers were challenged and social cognition theory underpinned the rehabilitation model (Gilbert & Daffern, 2010).

Threateners of this type are often of low intelligence and/or have disorganized personalities together with chaotic social and developmental histories. When seen, they will usually admit that they enjoy the drama their threats engender. Some give histories of having been treated with kindness and concern by police and other agencies when they first made a threat. Most admit that with every repetition their reception becomes less friendly. In some there is an overt sexual element connected to being caught, held, and humiliated. Typically the threats are made impulsively in response to a distressing event. They are akin to shockers who attempt to distress and disrupt with the additional element of attention seeking. In addition to threats, this group often make false reports of accidents, fires, and crimes. Self-harm, in particular cutting, often occurs as an accompaniment.

They are a sad and needy group but one that can create serious disruption to the emergency services. If they persist, the final stop is usually prison. Managing them requires psychological and social support over lengthy periods. On the positive side, they usually grow out of the behavior. On the negative, the treating clinic can easily become a target of their false reports.

Threats to Public Figures

If we confine ourselves to explicit threats to kill directed at a public figure, the picture is reasonably clear. Early studies found no relationship or even an inverse one between direct threats and either attacks or unwanted approaches (used as a proxy for attacks) (Dietz et al., 1991; Freedman 1971). Scalora et al. (2002), using a large database, also failed to demonstrate a connection between direct threats and subsequent unwanted approaches to politicians, but they noted that "Threats cannot be ignored because...42% of violent approaches involved prior threatening behavior" (p. 3).

The Exceptional Case Study Project (ECSP), focusing on assassination and attempted assassination of 83 public figures in the United States, also failed to find an association between explicit threats to the individual and subsequent attacks (Fein & Vossekuil, 1999; Fein, Vossekuil, & Holden, 1995). It did, however, note that over 60% of attacks were preceded by a history of indirect or conditional threats about or against the target (Fein and Vossekuil, 1999). The Fixated Research Group based in London investigated serious attacks on European politicians, noting that nearly half were preceded by warning behavior, though none by directly communicated threats (James et al., 2007). This finding was confirmed by a German study (Hoffmann, Meloy, Guldimann, & Ermer, 2011). A further study on attacks on British royalty found similar associations (James et al., 2008). A larger study of those who made inappropriate communications including explicit threats were less likely to try to approach a member of the Royal Family. Such threateners were, however, overrepresented in the more violent attempts to breach cordons and reach royalty (James et al., 2009). A study of disturbing communications and approaches to the Dutch Royal Family also confirmed the inverse relationship between direct threats and approach behavior (Van der Meer, Bootsma, & Meloy, 2012).

The apparent differences between the original US studies, which placed little or no value on threats as predictors of escalation or violence, and the more recent studies can be resolved. Explicit threats to public figures have only a modest association to future aggressive attempts to approach. Warning behaviors other than direct threats have a more substantial association to escalation and violence. Meloy et al. (2011) reexamined the earlier data sets and found that despite the implications drawn from them at the time, they also supported a substantial relationship between warning behaviors and later aggression. Although explicit threats are a poor and unreliable risk factor, combining information about the motivation and psychiatric status with a range of the threatener's warning behaviors (Meloy et al., 2012; chapter 3, this volume) provides a more robust predictor of escalation and violence.

Threats in the Workplace

The uttering of threats at work is a significant problem for employers and those responsible for creating and maintaining safe workplaces. Threats tend to arise in one of four contexts: (1) an employee expressing thoughts of harming colleagues and/or superiors; (2) a customer of the product or service provided by the company making threats to employees; (3) a personal conflict, often with an intimate partner, spilling into the workplace; and (4) a person or persons targeting the company in the belief the company has committed acts of environmental or humanitarian abuse. In each context threats can culminate in distressed workers, damaged reputations, and acts of targeted violence.

One scenario that has been explored ad infinitum is the disgruntled employee or ex-employee arriving at work armed and ready to kill. The history was often that harm had been threatened, usually leaked to third parties rather than uttered directly to targets, often as a way of vainly trying to address a grievance the employee perceived as unresolved. Such acts, colloquially referred to as *going postal* after several highly publicized shootings by US Postal Service employees in the 1980s, are fodder for media agencies trolling for sensational stories; they are also perpetuating the myth that this is the fate of companies with disgruntled employees (Denenberg & Schneider-Denenberg, 2012). The danger of such myths is that they trump and therefore mask the breadth and complexity of threatening and violent behaviors that occur in workplaces. Workplace violence is now the business of threat assessment and management (TAM), a set of practices widely adopted as a gold-standard intervention in cases of targeted violence (e.g., Turner & Gelles, 2003).

The place of uttered threats is prominent within TAM, partly owing to their frequency (Maes, Icenogle, Shearer, & Fowler, 2000) and partly because of the acknowledgment by researchers that the comments people make about violence, and its place in the constellation of human interactions, can be a risk factor for the perpetration of physical violence (McCann, 2002; McEwan, Mullen, & Purcell, 2007; Scalora et al., 2002; Warren et al., 2008).

TAM practices have seen the creation of several instruments designed to guide the professional judgments of those who have responsibility for responding to threats, physical violence, and acts of psychological torment. The Workplace Assessment of Violence Risk (WAVR-21, second edition) is such a tool (White & Meloy, 2010). It guides users to evaluate 21 factors that research has found have a demonstrated relationship to violent behavior occurring in the workplace. Item 3 (Expressed Violent Intentions and Threats) examines uttered statements about the use of violence at the workplace (leaked or direct), and several consider statements made by the individual indicating that he or she thinks about acts of violence, believes that violence is a viable choice, and/or has a history of perpetrating violence (see chapter 5 of the WAVR-21 manual, White & Meloy, 2010).

Threats in Domestic Violence and Discord

Threat is inherent in domestic violence. An environment of intimidation is created by words and actions that warn of a potential attack. Explicit threats to kill and injure can occur in addition to the less specific but no less oppressive warning behaviors.

Campbell and colleagues (2003) reported that over 70% of men who killed their partners had previously made explicit threats to kill them. Studies in those with excessive and morbid jealousy who make explicit threats to kill their partners show a high rate of subsequent attacks (Kingham & Gordon, 2004; Mullen, 1990; Roberts, 2005). Threats to kill the partner suspected of infidelity should always be taken very seriously, particularly in cases where there is a history of violence between the couple.

Threats Within Stalking

Threats occur frequently in stalking situations. Epidemiological studies report prevalence rates between 40% and 50% (Baum, Catalano, Rand, & Rose, 2009; Purcell, Pathé & Mullen, 2002); in forensic samples, rates tend to be higher, ranging from 50% to 70% depending on the context in which the sample was collected (Brewster, 2000; McEwan et al., 2009; Mohandie et al., 2006; Sheridan & Roberts, 2011). Although threats are common and psychologically damaging to many victims, their import for violence risk differs depending on who utters them and the function of the wider stalking behavior. The vast majority of threats in stalking situations are made by two types of stalkers—disgruntled former sexual partners and vengeful stalkers who are targeting a stranger or acquaintance that they perceive has done them harm (McEwan et al., 2009). In a smaller number of cases, intimacy-seeking stalkers will make threats, although these usually occur in the context of anger toward someone they perceive to be interfering in the longed for relationship or when they realize that such a relationship will not eventuate.

For some years the role of threats in predicting stalking violence was unclear, with some writers concluding that threats were in fact weakly related to stalking violence unless the target was a prior sexual intimate (Meloy, 1998). Reanalysis of composite data in 2007 showed that stalking victims who had been threatened were 3.6 times more likely to be assaulted (McEwan et al., 2007). This led to a reevaluation of the significance of threats and the conclusion that threats were in fact a pertinent risk factor for targeted violence in the stalking situation. Subsequent research has clarified the role of threats further, showing that the prior relationship between stalker and victim moderates the relationship between threats and stalking violence. McEwan and colleagues (2009) separately analyzed the relationship between threats and violence among ex-intimate partner stalkers and stalkers with stranger or acquaintance relationships to the victim, finding that threats were strongly associated with violence by former intimate partners but only weakly associated with violence by other types of stalkers. This relationship was suggested in earlier data (Meloy & Gothard, 1995) and theorized by Calhoun & Weston (2003) in their formulation of the "intimacy effect."

There is some evidence, however, that the moderating role of relationship is not as relevant in assessing for risk of *serious* stalking violence (violence causing serious injury or death). Sheridan and Roberts (2011) analyzed the responses of over 1,500 stalking victims and concluded that threats were a risk factor for life-threatening violence regardless of the prior relationship between victim and stalker. This is consistent with the finding of James and Farnham (2003) that threats were a significant predictor of serious stalking violence in a nondifferentiated sample of stalkers who engaged in serious violence.

While threats are an important risk factor for stalking violence, the relationship between the two is not straightforward, and threats should be only one variable considered in a comprehensive risk assessment of any stalking situation. Moreover, while threats are related to the risk of stalking, they do not appear to be relevant to other types of risk present in stalking, such as the risk of the stalking episode continuing or recurring in the future.

Personality, Psychopathology, and Background of Threateners

The psychology and psychopathology of those who make threats to harm others, explicit or otherwise, has not, to date, attracted much research interest. An exception was a study on the personality profiles of 45 men incarcerated for threatening the life of the US president; it found high levels of social deviance and a variety of pervasive personality problems as measured by the Minnesota Multiphasic Personality Inventory (Hathaway & McKinley, 1951; Megargee, 1986). Another study of 128 male threateners referred for a mental health assessment found them to be unusually suspicious and prone to excessive anger, with little insight into their own or others' emotional states. Testing suggested them to be evasive, overly sensitive to criticism, and high on measures of hostility (Warren, Ogloff, & Mullen, 2012). This group had IQ scores ranging from 63 to 125 (mean 90) with, in many, a significant discrepancy between verbal and performance scores in favor of performance (mean difference 13.8). These findings make intuitive sense given that if one is hostile, overly suspicious, and takes offence easily but lacks the verbal skills to express feelings in an appropriate and effective manner, threats can become the default response. Care must be taken in overgeneralizing these results as the group studied was heterogeneous in terms of why, where, and to whom the threat was made.

The interpersonal style of threateners tends to be one of discomfort with self and others. They struggle with their emotions and see the people they interact with as typically hostile. Only one in five report secure adult attachments. The majority (62%) shun intimacy and 17% become overly preoccupied by their relationships (Warren et al., 2012). The ability to empathize is more complicated than might be assumed, since threateners were found to experience sympathy as readily as most but to have great difficulty in taking another's point of view.

Threateners can be angry people. Our study suggested that many felt threatening to be preferable to other anger management strategies they had used, such as door slamming, property damage, and acts of physical violence. One threatener in the study indignantly declared that discussing threats was unhelpful since he thought that he was no longer violent, having now chosen to threaten rather than hit his partner (Warren et al., 2011). In cases such as these, anger management programs developed for violent offenders may be useful (see Howells, 1998).

There are more studies of major psychopathology in threateners. Those convicted of threat crimes are reported to have significantly elevated rates of depressive disorders, schizophrenias, and personality disorders, with over 60% in one series having either prior treatment for substance abuse or convictions for drug- or alcohol-related offenses (Wallace et al., 1998). Those who threaten public figures appear to have very high rates of psychotic disorders, and threateners referred for mental health management have similarly elevated rates of serious psychiatric disorder (Barnes et al., 2001; Häkkänen, 2006; Warren et al., 2011).

Suicide Among Threateners

In MacDonald's (1968) follow up of threateners referred for psychiatric evaluation, 4 (5.2%) killed themselves in the five years after the index threat to kill. In Warren et al.'s (2011) follow up of 144 subjects referred because of threats, 2 killed themselves within 12 months. In the same author's follow up of 613 individuals convicted of threats to kill, 16 (2.6%) committed suicide in the 10-year follow-up period, which did not differ significantly from the rate of homicide (n = 19, 3%) (Warren et al., 2008). Taken together, these studies suggest that uttering threats to kill others is a risk factor for suicide. The rates of attempted suicide or self-harm were not reported in these studies, but it would be surprising if it were not far greater than for completed suicide.

Assessing and Managing Risk in Those Who Make Threats to Kill

The management of threateners is directly related to the risk assessment that forms the basis for developing a plan of clinical management. In our view as clinicians, risk assessment should always be primarily about developing a management plan to reduce the *risk to patients* of damaging themselves and others (Mullen and Ogloff, 2005). Our own group takes a problem behaviors approach to managing threateners. This approach, as its name suggests, focuses on the behavior itself, in this case the issuing of threats to kill.

Learning from the Assessment and Management of Suicide Threats

Homicide threats, like suicide threats, can be both signposts to the distress of threateners and indications of how they are thinking of behaving. They always point to a need for an examination of the individual and the situation from which the threat emanated.

Threats to commit any physically harmful act create dilemmas for everyone involved. Clinicians who witness such statements are compelled to make a choice. Do they assume the threatened act probable and act accordingly, or do they focus on the psychological processes that led the person to make such dramatic utterances? Threateners, when their threats are taken seriously, also thrust themselves into a dilemma by saying something that instantly narrows their options on what to do next. Do they carry through and make good or backpedal and make excuses such as "I was angry," "I was joking," "It's just what I say when I'm upset."

Schacter (1988) opined, "Since most who threaten suicide do not suicide and most who do suicide have threatened, we have a real dilemma. How do we tell which of our patients are the ones in danger?" (p. 146). One answer that will not serve is to assume that because only a tiny percentage who threaten go on to act on those threats, then this amounts to no more than harmless howling. This was the approach once taken by many clinicians to suicide threats. They assumed, because fatal outcomes were rare and even self-harm uncommon, that those who threaten suicide may occasionally self-harm but not in a lethal manner. This is now recognized as an error, and an error that we were in danger of repeating with threats to kill.

The assessment of suicide risk is a well-established practice. The response to suicide threats is now always to take the threat seriously. The genesis of the threat is explored. Is the threat an impulsive utterance in response to a brief albeit severe lowering of mood, or is it the expression of the utter hopelessness of a sustained depression? Is suicide threatened in the hope of changing the attitudes of others or even to punish those who care but are judged to have failed to support and aid? Is the suicide threat an expression of the fear of a progressing and potentially fatal disease or of exhaustion and the wish to escape from the pain and disability of a chronic illness? The commitment to self-destruction accompanying the suicide threat is assessed by such factors as the existence of a plausible plan, the amount of preparation for self-destruction, and the degree to which threateners have persuaded themselves it is the best course of action for themselves and those they care about. Prior attempts and their nature add relevant information, though it is not wise to assume that past attempts of low potential lethality are necessarily predictive of a low risk of completed suicide. Age, gender, substance abuse, social isolation, the nature and extent of mental disorder, completed suicide in family members or close friends—these and other factors have well-established influences on risk. Often, perhaps too often, the presence of a significant degree of sustained depression is regarded as one of the most important prognostic factors. The assessment of suicide risk is linked to management strategies to reduce risk. There are still gaps in our knowledge about suicide relevant to assessment and management, but this is a far more developed area of clinical practice than the assessment and management of threats to kill others. Common sense dictates that we learn from, where relevant, the approaches we make to suicide threats and apply them to threats to

kill. Making a threat to kill is a risk factor for killing oneself. Part of a thorough assessment of anyone who has made a threat to kill is assessing his or her risk of suicide or self-harm.

Is Risk Assessment in Threats to Kill Much the Same as in Violence in General?

The temptation is to answer yes and no. A safer response is, however, no. This is because although there are common risk factors, such as substance abuse, there are enough differences to support a separate and distinct approach to risk assessment. One obvious difference is that a past history of assault or other criminal behaviors does not reliably predict whether a threat will be enacted. There is even a suggestion in the literature that when those without such histories make a threat in a manner that induces fear, they may be more likely to act upon it than would more obviously antisocial individuals (Warren et al., 2008).

The assessment of the risks of the threat being enacted is in part determined by the context. Threats in the context of stalking have been the subject of extensive research that allows their assessment and management to be incorporated into the developing clinical practice of the stalking field. Threats to kill in the context of domestic disputes may well be best regarded as part of the assessment and management of domestic violence, although the literature and practice here regarding threats is less well established. Threats to public figures are similarly best dealt with as part of the wider threat assessment and management literature and practice in this specific area.

If a threat has been taken sufficiently seriously to justify a referral to police or a mental health professional, then it is wise to approach the assessment on the assumption that risk must be excluded rather than demonstrated.

The Target

The nature of the person threatened has such an important influence on the level of likely risk that this is the place to start. Threats to partners probably carry the greatest risk of some sort of enactment. Threats by a stalker to his or her victim have a similar level of risk. When it is an ex-partner being stalked, this produces a particularly troubling combination in terms of enactment. At the other end of the scale are explicit threats to public figures with whom the threatener has no actual relationship and to whom he or she has no easy access. Here attempts to carry through the threat are uncommon, and success in harming the target is fortunately rare. The primacy of the relationship of threatener to target leads to a management strategy aimed at separating the threatener from the target and the context in which the threat emerged. This is easier said than done. In the domestic situation, partners often fail to take the threat with sufficient seriousness to accept advice for even temporary separation. In the workplace, separation is not always practical without injustice to either the threatener or the threatened. As a result, attempts to alter the context are sometimes perceived as encouraging threatening behavior.

How the Threat Is Delivered

Threats confided to third parties are particularly problematic. As noted, this may indicate that the threatener is asking for help to control his or her wish to harm someone. The function of the threat may be largely related to the relationship with the person to whom the threat is delivered, being intended to raise concern about the threatener or be a boast to establish a more powerful threatening identity.

It is tempting to assume that death threats delivered to the potential target face to face are more likely to be acted upon than those sent via phone, letter, email, or text. The assumption is that if you can get close enough to threaten in person, you are likely to be able to get the access you need to perpetrate physical violence. This assumption has been tested in studies comparing the access threateners have to those they know well vs. targets they would have to struggle to access, such as celebrities. Such studies found that an *intimacy effect* does exist where the better acquainted the threatener is with their target, the higher the risk that he or she will do harm (Calhoun & Weston, 2003; Meloy & Gothard, 1995; Mullen, Pathé, & Purcell, 2009). A partner, for example, with whom the threatener is in day-to-day contact, is usually threatened face to face, while public figures are almost always threatened by other means.

There is, however, to our knowledge no evidence that threats delivered face to face are more likely to be enacted once the influence of the relationship, or *intimacy*, is controlled for. Until there is evidence to the contrary, it is wise to assume that threats carry a similar level of risk however they are delivered.

What the Threat represents

Was it primarily a spontaneous reaction to a provocation or disturbing situation? ("I was so upset it just slipped out"). If so, the threatener will usually be able to describe the provocation, will deny having premeditated the threat, and will not attribute the threat largely to any previously existing angry or fearful state of mind. Alternatively, the threatener may attribute uttering the threat, at least in part, to how he or she was feeling ("If I hadn't been in such a bad mood I would never have..."). The threatener may also acknowledge that the threat emerged in an effort to coerce compliance ("I had no choice, he wouldn't listen or take me seriously, so..."). In practice some threateners lack the verbal skills and/or insight into their own behavior to make clear distinctions. The nature of the target, method of delivery, and context will usually help to distinguish between spontaneous reactions, threats intended to advance an agenda, or expressions of a preexisting emotional state. The reactive threats, which keep recurring in various contexts, suggest that underlying anger or heightened fear are important drivers.

Management in those who repeatedly make threats because of high levels of poorly controlled anger or from ongoing fear for their own safety has to include addressing what is driving the rage or fear. In some, persecutory beliefs, delusional or preoccupying, will reflect a major mental disorder that requires treatment. High levels of ongoing anger usually arise from long-standing grievances compounded by current psychosocial stressors. Again, these elements needs to be clarified and managed. This may involve anger management therapies or forms of focused psychotherapy (Howells, 1998; Howells & Day, 2003; Novaco, 1997).

Psychopathology

Threats may reflect experiences influenced by or rooted in abnormal states of mind. Most prominent are delusional states where the anger, fear, or fixation on a quest derive from the patient's psychotic state. There is suggestive evidence of increased risk from the high rates of subsequent violence found among convicted threateners with schizophrenic illnesses and from the prevalence of querulants among those who progress from threats to attempted enactment against public figures (James et al., 2009, 2010; Mullen, 2009; Mullen & Lester, 2006).

Morbid jealousy is preoccupying, intense, and often associated with erroneous, absurd, or delusional beliefs about infidelity. The risks of serious violence in this group are very high (Mullen, 1990). Threats are warning behaviors in this context and indicators to separate the partners. Separation, if not permanent, should at least continue until the jealousy has been managed in a manner that has reduced the level of intensity and preoccupation to reasonable levels. Jealousy does not appear on actuarial risk assessment instruments used in general clinical practice. This is because extreme jealousy does not occur, or more likely is not noted, with sufficient frequency in the populations used to establish the associations to violence. However, jealousy is one of the most common triggers for men to assault and kill their partners (Adinkrah, 2008; Easteal, 1994). Never fail to explore jealousy issues in couples whose relationship is marred by threats or the occurrence of violence. Never ignore threats to kill or harm in the context of jealousy. Death threats by the morbidly jealous are an indication for immediate admission, involuntary if necessary (Kingham & Gordon, 2004; Mullen, 1990).

Suicidal individuals often make threats to kill others as well as themselves. Profoundly depressed people see themselves as having nothing left to lose, which removes a potent inhibitor of violent and antisocial behaviors. On the plus side, depression is usually, but not always, associated with a loss of drive, energy, and initiative. This increases the safety of those threatened unless they are family members or in close contact with the depressed threatener. Even though convincing data are yet to be published, increased caution with this group is recommended. Threats by mothers or fathers to harm their children should always evoke grave concern and an active response.

Disorders that impair impulse control range from brain damage and frontal dementias to personality disorders or intoxications. Such conditions are associated with increased rates of threatening and probably with the enactment of threats. Substance abuse is now a well-established risk factor for the enactment of threats (Warren et al., 2008, 2011). Again, management needs to be targeted at the disordered states that drive and sustain the threatening behaviors. We have found this to extend beyond the effects of intoxication and well into the chaos of the lives of most chronic abusers.

Type of Threatener
Screamers

Most reactive threats that occur spontaneously are expletives uttered by the threatener type we have called a *screamer*. Screamers are likely to be referred for assessment only when the threats have become both a habitual response to a range of provocations and are creating fear and distress in the target or targets. It is among this group of screamers who repeatedly threaten because of an underlying anger at the world that a predisposition to violence can be found. Such threateners present an ongoing risk of escalation to violence against a range of potential targets. In another group of recidivist threateners, uttering threats as expletives has become a kind of tic of no great significance. The difference is usually obvious given the suppressed rage of one and the simple bewilderment that they have been taken seriously by the other. Several of our patients have expressed surprise that their threats were taken as anything other than expressions providing emphasis. One added that in the world of prisons and gangs, where he had lived for most of his life, threats were just part of everyday conversations. Threats of this type are the equivalent of the expression of interest and sympathy that pepper the conversations of the polite and articulate and are equally devoid of any commitment to action.

CASE HISTORY

A man in his late forties was referred for assessment following an interim revocation of parole with regard to the risk he posed if he were returned once more to the community. He had been convicted 20 years previously of a homicide, which occurred during a barroom brawl. He was an enormous man, made even more ferocious in appearance by facial tattoos. In his years on parole he had complied with all conditions, held down a job, not returned to substance abuse, and established a stable relationship. The revocation followed a complaint by a next-door neighbor of having been threatened in a manner that terrified him. Our man had recently moved to the neighborhood. Disagreement had occurred over the placement of refuse bins for collection. The neighbor had pushed over the subject's bin on one occasion because he believed it intruded on the area in front of his house. When this occurred a second time, our man became incensed and made a number of threats to harm the neighbor. These were expressions of anger in response to a provocation with no apparent commitment to action. In short, they were screams expressing righteous indignation. Although we believed that no actual threat of enactment existed, the man was seen on a number of occasions after his return to the community to help him understand that someone who looked like him and had a history like his simply could not make threats to anyone in any circumstances without evoking fear. The only long-term consequence was increased civility and tolerance on the part of the neighbor.

Shockers

Members of this group usually have a plan involving the use of a threat to distress the target. If the threat produces the desired result, they have no need to escalate their behavior. Problems arise when the threat is ignored or dismissed as just words. This is a challenge to a threatener to prove that he or she is serious. Such challenges are usually ignored, but there is a risk that the threatener will respond by escalating her or his behavior to prove that their threats are worthy of respect.

CASE HISTORY

A young woman was referred after she had threatened a psychiatrist she had been seeing privately for some time. The psychiatrist had terminated the treatment following long-standing problems over late payments and unscheduled visits. The patient had broken into his office, poured red paint over a phrenology head sitting on his desk, and left a knife and a note promising that his head would be next. On assessment it was clear that she enjoyed the fear and fuss she had produced. She was quite satisfied that she had "got her own back" and had no continuing interest in her one-time therapist. Last heard of she was training to be a therapist.

Schemers

Management in this group is aimed at both helping them to understand the self-defeating nature of their strategy and equipping them with more functional, or at least socially acceptable, strategies for expressing their feelings. Members of this group are pursuing a plan to coerce their targets into complying with their wishes. For some inarticulate individuals, this becomes one of their only methods of trying to get their way. Such people are not likely to escalate to violence but are in need of improving their communication skills. Those whose manipulative threats arise from deeply held convictions, which they are committed to realizing, are more difficult to assess. In those like the querulants obsessed with obtaining what they regard as their rights, there may be a commitment to action, including violent action if threats fail to attain their

goal (NSW Ombudsman, 2012). The central questions in threateners who are schemers are how committed they are and how far they will go to attain their ends.

The best management of querulants remains an unresolved issue. The easiest to manage are those with an underlying major mental disorder, but they are in the minority. In those lacking verbal skills, management is directed at improving their capacity to use words other than threats to obtain their ends. This is often less difficult than it sounds given the wide discrepancy between verbal and performance IQ in many within this group. They often have a reasonable grasp of interpersonal conflict but lack the confidence and experience to try to resolve their issues verbally.

CASE HISTORY

A man in his early sixties was referred for a presentence report following convictions for making death threats to politicians and perpetrating a bomb hoax. The man had been disabled in an accident at work that left him with severely impaired vision. His claims for Workers Compensation had been poorly handled. Initially, the insurers attempted to avoid liability, then they tried to limit liability by claiming that the man had failed to abide by safety regulations. Eventually he received compensation and a pension, but even then there were reasonable grounds for suspecting a degree of underpayment. He had pursued his claims through the court over many years, appearing as an unrepresented litigant. Finally he had been declared vexatious. He then began, with his wife's assistance, petitioning and writing to a range of political and public figures. He progressed to picketing and putting up posters outside politicians' homes and offices. His wife produced the posters to his specifications. Threats to kill followed, and finally a threat was made to blow up the parliament if his demands were not met. He distributed copies of the threats to the media in advance.

When seen, he brought with him reams of documentation that he believed supported his claims. Like many querulants he spoke at great length of his grievances, which he framed not just as a battle for his rights but as a quest for justice that would transform the basis for Workers Compensation and litigation throughout the world (Mullen & Lester, 2006). He had no history of violence, no knowledge of guns or explosives, and had taken no steps to prepare an attack on anyone. He expressed satisfaction at the media coverage his threats had been given, believing that this would advance his cause. He made clear that he would continue his quest but that he would never resort to violence (as it would make him as bad as "them"). His wife was loyally supportive but sensibly skeptical. She expressed the view that the poor man couldn't do much else, and at least this kept him occupied and for most of the time hopeful and cheerful.

The report assisted the court to follow its preferred option of a noncustodial sentence (a $50 fine). Our querulant showed his gratitude by putting a giant poster outside our clinic condemning our collusion with the courts in denying him justice. The provision of ongoing contact with a mental health professional in these cases often helps to ameliorate the behavior. Central to such management is confronting the patients with the price that they and their families are paying for pursuing their quest. This, combined with encouragement to view the campaign as having been successfully pursued as far as is reasonable, often over time (a long time) helps to reduce or stop the behavior.

Shielders

This type of threatener often has a preexisting fear of either particular people or situations or of the world in general. This fear can be reality-based or due to either oversensitivity and suspiciousness or persecutory beliefs. Such individuals overreact to situations that they perceive as threatening by uttering threats to warn off those who have frightened them. Whether they escalate to greater aggression depends on the nature of their fears and the effectiveness of the threat as a deterrent. Generally, as they are trying to avoid confrontation, they present a low risk.

CASE HISTORY

A middle-aged man was referred after an incident on a late-night train when he had been caught on video threatening three young men while brandishing a machete. He lived a solitary life, spending most of his time in his apartment reading and writing articles on arcane subjects that were occasionally published. His only recreation was attending orchestral concerts, thus his presence on the late train. He had no history of any offending and had always regarded himself as a peaceful person. He was shy, oversensitive, and self-referential.

He had frequently been frightened, while traveling at night, by gangs of youths who behaved in an aggressive and disorganized manner. A year previously a gang had pushed him around, made fun of him, and threatened him with a knife. He had been

badly shaken. He reported this to the transport police, who apparently said something to the effect that this was always happening and they did their best, but what can you expect. Subsequently, whenever he was on a train with anyone he thought might be a threat to him, he would loudly tell them to keep away or he wouldn't be responsible for what might happen. He admitted to embellishing the threat with obscenities and by reaching into his bag as if for a weapon. This seemed to work well for several months, although he said that the usual response was something along the lines of "What's wrong with you?"

A few weeks before the incident, a young man laughed at him and said, "Go on, show me what's in the bag." It was after this that he obtained and began carrying the machete. When questioned, he admitted that if threats failed and anyone tried to attack him or even harass him, he would be prepared to use the weapon. He assured us that he had purchased a replacement for the one taken by the police and to prove his point took a large machete from his bag.

This person responded well to a management approach that involved ameliorating his anxieties, encouraging more appropriate responses to fear of others, finding less troubling ways of traveling at night, and encouraging his involvement with like-minded groups of music enthusiasts with whom he often traveled to concerts. His second machete was confiscated, with his reluctant consent, at the assessment interview.

Signalers

This type of threatener already has a predisposition to act violently and is giving, with the threat, a warning of his intentions. This predisposition may flow either from anger at the target or a less focused enmity directed at all those he believes have harmed him or been complicit in harming him. We have found that in signaling a warning by making a threat, many are announcing/signaling as a means to avoid progressing to violence. Signalers usually deliver threats in a manner that would alarm even the most insensitive or stoical. This group are often described as threatening in a cold, deliberate manner. Unlike those of schemers, their threats are not a form of "if you do not" but instead are statements of intent. How great the commitment is to act on the stated intention may not be clear; at best it is likely to have a degree of ambivalence. Whereas sound threat assessment practice is to take the threat seriously, it is also helpful in these cases to explore any secondary gains and any indications of ambivalence on the part of the threatener. In these conversations the skilled threat assessor can help the threatener find ways to acknowledge his or her disgruntlement and choose more prosocial responses.

Lessons Learned from Research on Threats to Commit Suicide

Plausibility, preparation, motivation, rationalization, prior history of acting on threats or of violence in general, and substance abuse can all be assumed to translate from the field of suicide risk assessment to threatener risk assessment. In suicide, the older and more socially isolated are at higher risk. In threat enactment, the younger and socially dysfunctional, rather than the isolated, are probably of greater risk. The increased risk for males is even more marked.

SPECIAL ISSUES IN MANAGING THE THREATENER

General

Mental health services, and forensic services in particular, must have policies and procedures in place to deal with threats to all types of staff. The policies should be based on the principles of:

1. Taking all threats seriously while not overreacting or promoting groundless fears
2. Ensuring staff safety
3. Prioritizing the care and treatment of patients whenever possible
4. Supporting, not blaming, the staff member who has been threatened

Procedures should involve:

1. Recording the nature, context, and impact of the threat
2. An assessment of the risk of enactment and/or repetition
3. The development of a management approach to the threatener
4. The assistance to be provided to the victim
5. A consideration of whether current practices may be aggravating situations likely to predispose to threats and aggression

Staff must not be left uncertain as to how to react and what to do if threatened. Policies and procedures with regard to threats should, however, be templates, not rigid mandated rules, which leave room for clinicians to exercise judgment while providing a framework within which such autonomy can safely be practiced.

Direct Threats to the Clinician

Never ignore a direct or implied threat made to you by a patient. If your patient goes to the trouble of threatening you, politeness requires that you respond. Not to respond is to treat the threatener and his or her threat as of no interest or consequence. The failure to respond may be motivated by the desire to avoid either escalation or reinforcing the behavior. It is, however, likely to be experienced as an insult and potential provocation that invites at best resentment and at worst an escalation toward enactment.

Label the threat. "That was a threat." Ideally express that the threat affected you ("I found your threat distressing and/or frightening") even if you did not. This tells the patient that you are listening and that you take the threat and the patient seriously.

The response to labeling the threat may be denial or minimization, "It wasn't a threat," "I did not mean to…," or an apology, "Sorry, I was carried away." Although neither a denial nor an apology should simply be accepted, such responses open up the opportunity for a dialogue on the meaning and intention of the threat. If labeling the threat is followed by a reiteration or a challenge, "So what are you going to do about it?" the interview should usually be ended. When the clinician knows the patient well and continues to feel safe in the situation, there may be a case for continuing, but termination of the session remains the default position. In our view the stopping of the interview should be explained except when the clinician senses imminent danger. Words to the effect of, "I am sorry but I am too distressed to continue, we will have to discuss other arrangements for you to be seen again in the waiting room." This assumes that you are not unwise enough to see threateners in solo unsupported practice and you have a public area with other staff and patients to which to return. We believe it is important for your safety and the patient's ongoing management to make clear to the threatener that he or she is not going to be entirely rejected because of the threat. Any attempt to escalate the threatening or stop the clinician from exiting the consulting room is an indication, in almost all cases, to push the emergency button to call for aid or otherwise seek immediate help.

The future management of someone who has made a threat that caused a degree of fear or distress to a staff member needs to be discussed with fellow clinicians and the discussion carefully recorded in the patient notes. A number of outcomes are possible.

Continue as before if the clinician and the subsequent risk assessment indicate this to be safe and acceptable. Transfer to a new therapist if and only if the original therapist prefers not to continue or believes the threat to arise from some personal quality (e.g., gender, approach, prior conflicts and misunderstandings). Remember that we all have patients with whom there is a clash that is difficult or impossible to ameliorate. Continue future sessions in a safer environment, such as together with another therapist or in an office open to observation where there are in fact observers. One clinician we know of who had had a troubling record of threats and overt violence from individuals referred for court assessment began seeing cases considered at risk of such behavior in an office in a nearby police station. Although an effective strategy, this was not without its clinical, ethical, and practical problems.

In practice most threats can be managed safely, and on occasion they create therapeutic opportunities. There is no room in managing threateners for macho attitudes ("You don't frighten me") or of therapeutic omnipotence ("No need to worry, I can manage these types of people with no trouble"). Confidence—based on careful initial assessment and ongoing assessments of risk combined with clear therapeutic goals—is the appropriate response.

Fortunately the use of judgmental psychobabble about failing to manage the transference is less and less a problem among today's clinicians. Unfortunately knowledge of the well-based observations on how attitudes and moods in both the clinician and the patient can be induced and mirrored in the therapeutic situation, and an appropriate understanding of transference and countertransference, are also being lost. A therapist can experience fear because a patient is frightened, and an insecure clinician can destabilize a patient. Fear, anger, distrust, and hopelessness experienced by clinicians in interaction with patients may well be created by a mirroring and the inducing effect of a patient's state of mind, which in turn can be substantially influenced by the patient's psychological history. Such experiences should not be ignored. Threats can emerge when a patient begins to experience fear of the clinician. Clinicians who are frightened of the patients they see in practice need to change themselves or their area of specialization (Meloy & Reavis, 2007).

CONCLUSION

Threats to harm others, particularly when they evoke apprehension in the target or recipient, always need to be taken seriously. Although the vast majority of threatening utterances are not associated with any commitment to acting on the threat, some are warnings of intent.

Any threat to kill is a problem behavior (Warren, MacKenzie, Mullen, & Ogloff, 2005). These utterances are damaging regardless of whether they culminate in physical violence. Threatening to kill or harm is never an advisable way to communicate. Assessing and managing them is part of the core business of mental health professionals.

KEY POINTS

- All threats by all threateners can escalate to violence and need to be acknowledged as an unacceptable form of communication; any indication of violence risk requires assessment.
- Many threats will never be enacted, but many who commit acts of violence threaten first (often leaked to a third party rather than uttered directly to the target).
- Threatening can occur for a myriad of reasons where the motivation to threaten differs, as does the relationship between the threatener and target. The typology presented in this chapter categorizes these differences and helps tailor threat assessments.
- The management of threateners requires that the safety and well-being of all relevant parties be prioritized while addressing the threatener's skills deficits and enhancing his or her abilities to resolve matters prosocially.

REFERENCES

Adinkrah, M. (2008). Husbands who kill their wives. *International Journal of Offender Therapy and Comparative Criminology, 52*(3), 296–310.

Alldridge, P. (1994). Threat offences: A case for reform. *Criminal Law Review, 8,* 176–186.

Barnes, M. T., Gordon, W. C., & Hudson, S. M. (2001). The crime of threatening to kill. *Journal of Interpersonal Violence, 16*(4), 312–319.

Bernstein, H. A. (1981). Survey of threats and assaults directed towards psychotherapists. *American Journal of Psychotherapy, 35,* 542–549.

Brown, G. P., Dubin, W. R., Lion, J. R., & Garry, L. J. (1996). Threats against clinicians: A preliminary descriptive analysis. *Bulletin of the American Academy of Psychiatry and the Law, 24,* 367–376.

Bureau of Justice Statistics. (2006). *Criminal victimization in the United States: National crime victimization survey.* (U.S. Department of Justice Publication No. NCJ 223436). Retrieved from http://www.bjs.gov/content/pub/pdf/cvus06.pdf.

Calhoun, F. S., & Weston, S. W. (2003). *Contempoary threat management.* San Diego, CA: Specialized Training Services.

Campbell, J. C., Webster, D., Koziol-McLain, J., Block, C., Campbell, D., Curry, M. A.,...Laughon, K. (2003). Risk factors for femicide in abusive relationships: Results from a multisite case control study. *American Journal of Public Health, 93*(7), 1089–1097.

Cantor, C. H., Mullen, P. E., & Alpers, P. A. (2000). Mass homicide: The civil massacre. *Journal of the American Academy of Psychiatry and the Law, 28*(1), 55–63.

Carstensen, P. C. (1994). The evolving duty of mental health professionals to third parties: A doctrinal and institutional examination. *International Journal of Law Psychiatry, 17*(1), 1–42.

Coverdale, J., Gale, C., Weeks, S., & Turbott, S. (2001). A survey of threats and violent acts by patients against training physicians. *Medical Education, 35*(2), 154–159.

Coverdale, J. H., & Roberts, L. W. (2005). Protecting the safety of medical students and residents. *Academic Psychiatry, 29*(4), 329–331.

Crabbe, J., Alexander, D. A., Klein, S., Walker, S., & Sinclair, J. (2002). Dealing with violent and aggressive patients: At what cost to nurses? *Irish Journal of Psychological Medicine, 19*(4), 121–124.

Darwin, C. (1872/1998). *The expression of emotion in man and animals* (3rd ed.). Oxford: Oxford University Press.

deBecker, G. (1997). *The gift of fear: Survival signals that protect us from violence.* Boston: Little Brown.

Denenberg, R. V., & Schneider-Denenberg, T. (2012). Workplace violence and the media: The myth of the disgruntled employee. *Work, 42*(1), 5–7.

Easteal, P. (1994). Homicide-suicide between adult sexual intimates: An Australian study. *Suicide and Life Threatening Behaviour, 24*(2), 140–151.

Faulkner, L. R., Grimm, N. R., McFarland, B. H., & Bloom, J. D. (1990). Threats and assaults against psychiatrists. *Bulletin of the American Academy of Psychiatry and the Law, 18*(1), 37–46.

Fein, R. A., & Vossekuil, B. (1999). Assassination in the United States: An operational study of recent assassins, attackers, and near-lethal approachers. *Journal of Forensic Sciences, 44*, 321–333.

Fein, R. A., Vossekuil, B., & Holden, G. A. (1995). *Threat assessment: An approach to prevent targeted violence:* National Institute of Justice: US Department of Justice.

Felson, R. B., & Messer, S. F. (2000). The control motive in partner violence. *Social Psychology Quarterly, 63*(1), 86–94.

Felson, R. B., & Tedeschi, J. T. (1993). A social interactionist approach to violence: Cross-cultural applications. *Violence and Victims, 8*, 295–310.

Gilbert, F., & Daffern, M. (2010). Integrating contemporary aggression theory with violent offender treatment: How thoroughly do interventions target violent behaviour. *Aggression and Violent Behavior, 15*(3), 167–180.

Guy, J. D., Brown, C. K., & Poelstra, P. L. (1990). Who gets attacked? A national survey of patient violence directed at psychologists in clinical practice. *Professional Psychology: Research and Practice, 21*(6), 493–495.

Häkkänen, H. (2006). Finnish bomb threats: Offence and offender characteristics. *International Journal of Police Science and Management, 8*(1), 1–8.

Harmon, R. B., Rosner, R., & Owens, H. (1998). Sex and violence in a forensic population of obsessional harassers. *Psychology, Public Policy, and Law, 4*(1-2), 236–249.

Hathaway, S. R., & McKinley, J. C. (1951). *Minnesota Multiphasic Personality Inventory manual.* New York: Psychological Corporation.

Hoffmann, J., Meloy, J. R., Guldimann, A., & Ermer, A. (2011). Attacks on German public figures, 1968-2004: Warning behaviors, potentially lethal and non-lethal acts, psychiatric status, and motivations. *Behavioral Sciences and the Law, 29*(2), 155–179.

Hough, M. (1990). Threats: Findings from the British Crime Survey. *International Review of Victimology, 1*, 169–180.

Howells, K. (1998). Cognitive behavioural interventions for anger, aggression and violence. In N. Tarrier, A. Wells & F. Haddock (Eds.), *Treating complex cases: The cognitive behavioural therapy approach* (pp. 295–318). New York: Wiley.

Howells, K., & Day, A. (2003). Readiness for anger management: Clinical and theoretical issues. *Clinical Psychology Review, 23*, 319–337.

James, D. V., Meloy, J. R., Mullen, P. E., Pathé, M., Farnham, F. R., Preston, L. F., & Darnley, B. J. (2010). Abnormal attentions toward the British royal family: Factors associated with approach and escalation *Journal of the American Academy of Psychiatry and the Law, 38*(3), 329–340.

James, D. V., Mullen, P. E., Meloy, J. R., Pathé, M. T., Farnham, F. R., Preston, L., & Darnley, B. (2007). The role of mental disorder in attacks on European politicians 1990-2004. *Acta Psychiatrica Scandinavica, 116*(5), 334–344.

James, D. V., Mullen, P. E., Pathé, M. T., Meloy, J. R., Farnham, F. R., Preston, L., & Darnley, B. (2008). Attacks on the British royal family: The role of psychotic illness. *Journal of the American Academy of Psychiatry and the Law, 36*, 59–67.

James, D. V., Mullen, P. E., Pathé, M., Meloy, J. R., Preston, L., Darnley, B., & Farnham, F. R. (2009). Stalkers and harassers of royalty: The role of mental illness and motivation. *Psychological Medicine, 39*(9), 1479–1490.

Kingham, T., & Gordon, H. (2004). Aspects of morbid jealousy. *Advances in Psychiatric Treatment, 10,* 207–215.

MacDonald, J. M. (1968). *Homicidal threats.* Springfield, IL: Charles C. Thomas.

Maes, J. D., Icenogle, M. L., Shearer, R. A., & Fowler, C. M. (2000). Handling the threat of organisational violence: An OD approach in a government agency. *Equality, Diverstiy and Inclusion: An International Journal, 19*(5), 14–22.

McCann, J. T. (2002). *Threats in schools: A practical guide for managing violence.* New York: Haworth Press.

McEwan, T., Mullen, P. E., MacKenzie, R. D., & Ogloff, J. R. P. (2009). Violence in stalking situations. *Psychological Medicine, 39,* 1469–1478.

McEwan, T., Mullen, P. E., & Purcell, R. (2007). Identifying risk factors in stalking: A review of current research. *International Journal of Law and Psychiatry, 30,* 1–9.

McMahon, M. (1992). Dangerousness, confidentiality and the duty to protect. *Australian Psychologist, 27*(1), 12–16.

Megargee, E. (1986). A psychometric study of incarcerated presidential threateners. *Criminal Justice and Behavior, 13*(3), 243–260.

Meloy, J. R. (1996). Stalking (obsessional following): A review of some preliminary studies. *Aggression and Violent Behavior, 1,* 147–162.

Meloy, J. R., & Gothard, S. (1995). Demographic and clinical comparisons of obsessional followers and offenders with mental disorders. *American Journal of Psychiatry, 152*(2), 258–266.

Meloy, J. R., Hempel, A. G., Gray, B. T., Mohandie, K., Shiva, A., & Richards, T. C. (2004). A comparative analysis of North American adolescent and adult mass murderers. *Behavioral Sciences and the Law, 22,* 291–309.

Meloy, J. R., Hempel, A. G., Mohandie, K., Shiva, A. A., & Gray, B. T. (2001). Offender and offence characteristics of a non random sample of adolescent mass murderers. *Journal of the American Academy of Child and Adolescent Psychiatry, 40*(6), 719–728.

Meloy, J. R., Hoffman, J. L., Guldimann, A., & James, D. V. (2012). The role of warning behaviors in threat assessment: An exploration and suggested typology. *Behavioral Sciences and the Law, 30*(3), 256–279.

Meloy, J. R. & Reavis, J. (2007). The dangerous cases: when treatment is not an option. In van Luyn B, Aktar S, Livesley, J. (Eds.), *Severe personality disorders: Major issues in everyday practice.* London: Cambridge University Press, pp. 180–194.

Mendelson, D., & Mendelson, G. (1991). Tarasoff down under: the psychiatrist's duty to warn in Australia. *The Journal of Psychiatry and Law, 19*(1-2), 33–61.

Milburn, T. W., & Watman, K. H. (1981). *On the nature of threat: A social psychological analysis.* New York: Praeger Publishers.

Mossman, D. (2007). Critique of pure risk assessment, or Kant meets Tarasoff. *Cincinnati Law Review, 75,* 523–610.

Mullen, P. E. (1990). Morbid jealousy and the delusion of infidelity. In R. Bluglass & P. Bowden (Eds.), *Principles and practice of forensic psychiatry* (pp. 823–834). London: Churchill Livingstone.

Mullen, P. E. (2004). The autogenic (self-generated) massacre. *Behavioral Sciences and the Law, 22*(3), 311–323.

Mullen, P. E. (2009). Querulous behaviour: Vexatious litigation, abnormally persistent complaining and petitioning. In M. G. Gelder, N. C. Anderson, J. J. Lopez-Ibor Jr., & J. R. Geddes (Eds.), *New Oxford Textbook of Psychiatry,* 2nd ed. (Vols.1-2, pp. 1977–1980). Oxford: Oxford University Press

Mullen, P. E., & Lester, G. (2006). Vexatious litigants and unusually persistent complainants and petitioners: From querulous paranoia to querulous behaviour. *Behavioral Sciences and the Law, 24,* 333–349.

Mullen, P. E., Pathé, M., & Purcell, R. (2009). *Stalkers and their victims,* 2nd ed. Cambridge: Cambridge University Press.

Mullen, P. E., Pathé, M., Purcell, R., & Stuart, G. (1999). Study of stalkers. *American Journal of Psychiatry, 156*(8), 1244–1249.

Novaco, R. W. (1997). Remediating anger and aggression with violent offenders. *Legal and Criminological Psychology, 2,* 77–88.

NSW Ombudsman Office. (2012). *Managing unreasonable complainant conduct: A manual for frontline staff, supervisors and senior managers* 2nd ed.). Retrieved from http://www.ombo.nsw.gov.au/__data/assets/pdf_file/0004/3568/GL_Unreasonable-Complainant-Conduct-Manual-2012_LR.pdf

O'Toole, M. E. (2000). *The school shooter: A threat assessment perspective* (pp. 1–46). Quantico, VA: Critical Incident Response Group, National Center for the Analysis of Violent Crime.

Oxford University Press. (2012). *The Oxford English Dictionary,* from http://www.oed.com

Pathé, M., & Mullen, P. E. (1997). The impact of stalkers on their victims. *British Journal of Psychiatry, 170,* 12–17.

Roberts, K. A. (2005). Women's experience of violence during stalking by former romantic partners factors predictive of stalking violence. *Violence Against Women, 11*(1), 89–114.

Scalora, M. J., Baumgartner, J. V., Zimmerman, W., Callaway, D., Maillette, M., Covell, C., … Washington, D. O. (2002). Risk factors for approach behavior toward the US Congress. *Journal of Threat Assessment, 2,* 35–55.

Soothill, K., Francis, B., Ackerley, E., & Fligelstone, R. (2002). *Murder and serious sexual assault: What criminal histories can reveal about future serious offending.* London: British Home Office.

Tarasoff v. Regents of University of California, 17 Cal. 3d 425, 551 P.2d 334, 131 Cal. Rptr. 14 C.F.R. (1976).

Tedeschi, J. T., Malkis, F. S., Gaes, G. G., & Quigley-Fernandez, B. (1980). First impressions, norms, and reactions to threats. *Human Relations, 33*(9), 647–657.

Turner, J., & Gelles, M. (2003). *Threat assessment: A risk management approach.* New York: Hayworth Press.

Twemlow, S. W., Fonagy, P., Sacco, F. C., & Vernberg, E. (2008). Assessing adolescents who threaten homicide in schools. *Clinical Social Work Journal, 36,* 131–142.

van Dijk, J., Mayhew, P., van Kesteren, J., Aebi, M., & Linde, A. (2010). *Final report on the study on crime victimisation* (T. r. w. c. b. Eurostat, Trans.). Tilburg, Netherlands: International Victimology Institute.

van Kesteren, J. N., Mayhew, P., & Nieuwbeerta, P. (2000). *Criminal victimisation in seventeen industrialised countries: Key findings from the 2000 International Crime Victims Survey.* The Hague, Netherlands: Netherlands Ministry of Justice.

Wallace, C., Mullen, P. E., Burgess, P., Palmer, S., Ruschena, D., & Browne, C. (1998). Serious criminal offending and mental disorder. *British Journal of Psychiatry, 172,* 477–484.

Warren, L. J., MacKenzie, R., Mullen, P. E., & Ogloff, J. R. P. (2005). The problem behavior model: The development of a stalkers clinic and a threateners clinic. *Behavioral Sciences and the Law, 23,* 387–397.

Warren, L. J., Mullen, P. E., Davis, M. R., & Ogloff, J. R. P. (2013). *Threats to kill by homicide offenders.* Manuscript in preparation.

Warren, L. J., Mullen, P. E., & Ogloff, J. R. P. (2011). A clinical study of those who utter threats to kill. *Behavioral Sciences and the Law, 29,* 141–154.

Warren, L. J., Mullen, P. E., Thomas, S., Ogloff, J., & Burgess, P. M. (2008). Threats to kill: A follow-up study. *Psychological Medicine, 38*(4), 599–605.

Warren, L. J., Ogloff, J. R., & Mullen, P. E. (2013). The psychological basis of threatening behaviour. *Psychiatry, Psychology and Law, 20*(3), 329–343. doi: 10.1080/1 3218719.2012.674716

White, S. G., & Meloy, J. R. (2010). *A structured professional guide for the workplace assessment of violence risk.* San Diego, CA: Specialized Training Services.

3

Warning Behaviors and Their Configurations Across Various Domains of Targeted Violence

J. REID MELOY, JENS HOFFMANN, KAROLINE ROSHDI, JUSTINE GLAZ-OCIK, AND ANGELA GULDIMANN

A new typology of warning behaviors was introduced into the violence risk and threat assessment literature as a "useful means of conceptualizing behavioral patterns indicating increasing threat" (Meloy, Hoffmann, Guldimann & James, 2012, p. 260). It was mentioned in an abbreviated and preliminary form in Meloy and O'Toole (2011) and Meloy (2011). The concept of "warning behaviors" was advanced in the studies of the Fixated Research Group concerning abnormal communications and approaches to the British Royal Family during the previous decade (James et al., 2007, 2008, 2009, 2010, 2011) and has been termed by others as "signaling the attack" (Vossekuil, Reddy, Fein, Borum, & Modzeleski, 2000), "tell-tale behaviors" or "high risk indicators" (Calhoun & Weston, 2003), "stalking-type behavior" (Mullen et al., 2009), "pre-attack signals" (Dietz & Martell, 2010), and "red flag indicators" (White & Meloy, 2007).

The typology is not another model of risk factors but instead captures supraordinate behavioral *patterns* that constitute change and may evidence accelerating risk. Warning behaviors contain within them dynamic rather than static variables, the former typically offering more substantial contributions to the assessment of short-term violence risk (Gray, Snowden, & MacCulloch, 2004; Nicholls, Brink, Desmarais, Webster & Martin, 2006; Skeem & Mulvey, 2001). The typology was generated to carefully define and systematize such patterns—a problem that, when unaddressed, typically hampers social science research—which heretofore had not been done in the threat assessment literature. The original study reviewed in detail the

previous research attempting to identify these acute and dynamic variables in various domains of targeted violence: attackers and assassins of celebrities, politicians, and other public figures; psychiatric patients; adolescent mass murderers and school shooters; adult mass murderers; spousal homicide perpetrators; workplace violence attackers; and federal judicial threateners and attackers (Meloy et al., 2012). The factors identified in the typology were gleaned from the research on targeted or intended violence, discussions with colleagues, and the casework experience of the original authors. It is a rationally derived typology:

1. *Pathway warning behavior*—any behavior that is part of research, planning, preparation, or implementation of an attack (Calhoun & Weston, 2003; Fein & Vossekuil, 1998a, b, 1999).

2. *Fixation warning behavior*—any behavior that indicates an increasingly pathological preoccupation with a person or a cause (Mullen et al., 2009). It is measured by (a) increasing perseveration on the person or cause, (b) increasingly strident opinion, (c) increasingly negative characterization of the object of fixation, (d) impact on the family or other associates of the object of fixation if present and aware, (e) angry emotional undertone. It is typically accompanied by social or occupational deterioration.

3. *Identification warning behavior*—any behavior that indicates a psychological desire to be a

"pseudo-commando" (Dietz, 1986; Knoll, 2010), have a "warrior mentality" (Hempel, Meloy, & Richards, 1999), closely associate with weapons or other military or law enforcement paraphernalia, identify with previous attackers or assassins, or identify oneself as an agent to advance a particular cause or belief system.

4. *Novel aggression warning behavior*—an act of violence that appears unrelated to any targeted violence pathway warning behavior and is committed for the first time. Such behaviors may be utilized to test the ability (de Becker, 1997) of the subject to actually do the violent act and may be a measure of response tendency, the motivation to act on the environment (Hull, 1952), or a behavioral tryout (MacCulloch, Snowden, Wood, & Mills, 1983). When homicide occurs within this warning behavior, it may be "proof of kill" (G. Deisinger, personal communication, February 2011).

5. *Energy burst warning behavior*—an increase in the frequency or variety of any noted activities related to the target, even if the activities themselves are relatively innocuous, usually in the days or weeks before the attack (Odgers et al., 2009).

6. *Leakage warning behavior*—the communication to a third party of an intent to do harm to a target through an attack (Meloy & O'Toole, 2011).

7. *Last resort warning behavior*—evidence of a "violent action imperative" and "time imperative" (Mohandie & Duffy, 1999); increasing desperation or distress through declaration in word or deed, forcing the individual into a position of last resort. There is no alternative other than violence, and the consequences are justified (de Becker, 1997). The subject feels trapped (S. White, personal communication, October 2010).

8. *Directly communicated threat warning behavior*—the communication of a direct threat to the target or law enforcement beforehand. A threat is a written or oral communication that implicitly or explicitly states a wish or intent to damage, injure, or kill the target or individuals symbolically or actually associated with the target.

The typology has face validity and appears to embrace within it most of the universe of warning behaviors in intended and targeted violence. However, further empirical research is necessary. One of the first questions we attempt to answer is whether the typology has external or ecological validity. In other words, does it serve a useful purpose in the real world by classifying warning behaviors that have preceded acts of targeted violence? We therefore applied the typology to five small samples of individuals: (1) assassins and attackers of US presidents and national political figures, (2) public figure attackers in Germany during the latter half of the twentieth century (Hoffmann et al., 2011), (3) school shooters in Germany, (4) school threateners in Germany, and (5) spousal homicide attackers in Germany.

ASSASSINS AND ATTACKERS OF US PRESIDENTS AND NATIONAL POLITICAL FIGURES

This small sample ($N = 18$) was derived from the work of Clarke (1982, 1990, 2007) and consisted of those individuals who attacked or assassinated a US president or a recognized national political figure. The subjects in the study are listed in Table 3.1.

TABLE 3.1. ATTACKERS AND ASSASSINS OF US PRESIDENTS OR NATIONAL POLITICAL FIGURES

Name	Date of Attack	Target
Richard Lawrence	Jan. 30, 1835	Andrew Jackson
John Wilkes Booth	April 14, 1865	Abraham Lincoln
Charles Guiteau	July 2, 1881	James Garfield
Leon Czolgosz	Sept. 6, 1901	William McKinley
John Schrank	Oct. 14, 1912	Theodore Roosevelt
Giuseppe Zangara	Feb. 15, 1933	Franklin Roosevelt
Carl Weiss	Sept. 8, 1935	Huey Long
Oscar Collazo	Nov. 1, 1950	Harry Truman
Griselio Torresola	Nov. 1, 1950	Harry Truman
Lee Harvey Oswald	Nov. 22, 1963	John Kennedy
James Earl Ray	April 4, 1968	Martin Luther King
Sirhan Sirhan	June 5, 1968	Robert Kennedy
Arthur Bremer	May 15, 1972	George Wallace
Samuel Byck	Feb. 22, 1974	Richard Nixon
Lynette Fromme	Sept. 5, 1975	Gerald Ford
Sara Jane Moore	Sept. 22, 1975	Gerald Ford
John Hinckley, Jr.	March 30, 1981	Ronald Reagan
Francisco Duran	Oct. 29, 1994	Bill Clinton

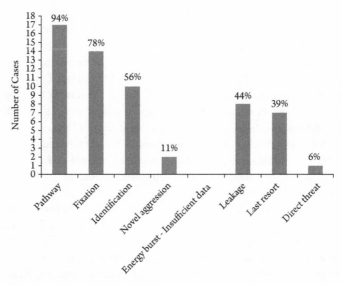

FIGURE 3.1 US presidential and political attackers and assassins ($N = 18$).

Fixation: 6 cause, 7 person, 1 person + cause; in two additional cases there was a fixation on a person but not the target. *Note*: The percentage for the known *N* is reported.

Other sources were utilized to supplement the work of Clarke if there were insufficient or ambiguous data concerning warning behaviors. The warning behaviors for this sample are presented in Figure 3.1.

In this sample, pathway warning behavior occurred in virtually every case, with a fixation on either a cause or a person in the vast majority of the cases. There was identification warning behavior in slightly more than half the cases and leakage in almost half the cases. A sense of desperation or distress, last resort warning behavior, was evident in one third of the cases. Direct threats were almost nonexistent ($n = 1$). There were insufficient data to code for energy burst warning behavior. This sample is a subsample of the Exceptional Case Study Project (ECSP) (Fein & Vossekuil, 1998a, b, 1999) analyzed from a somewhat different perspective—the emphasis being on patterns of accelerating behavior that would warrant concern by the threat assessor. However, as in the ECSP study, there is no comparison or control group, so this is not evidence that warning behaviors predict or even correlate with an attack. It is indicative of the degree to which the warning behaviors can be usefully applied to a real world sample of subjects who engaged in targeted violence toward a US president or national political figure. The fatality rate in these cases was 39% ($n = 7$), underscoring the high mortality risk of an attack even though one rarely occurs.

DESCRIPTION OF THE GERMAN SAMPLES

Primary data were used as the basis of analysis for all of the German samples. The primary data consisted of court records, investigative files, and official reports. In addition to the primary data, more information from the public domain was gathered whenever this was reasonable—for example, autobiographies or interviews with the attackers or interviews with other individuals involved in the case. In two of the German samples (public figure attackers and school shooters) the universe of cases was included.

Attackers of German Public Figures

This study covered all nine lethal or potentially lethal nonterroristic attacks against public figures in Germany after World War II. In every case deadly weapons such as guns, knives, or bombs were used by the attackers. Five nonlethal attacks against German public figures were also studied. The public figures in these cases were assaulted, for example, by a slap in the face, thrown eggs, or paint bombs.

Of these offenders, 9 were male (64%) and 5 were female (36%). There were only two incidents in which the public figure targets had a nonpolitical background (14%): one was an athletic star and the other a television presenter. In all of the other attacks the public figures were politicians. In 9 of the attacks the public figure was injured (64%), in 3 of these cases (30%) in a life-threatening manner. None of the victims died during or directly after the attack.

The oldest offender was 83 years old and the youngest 22; the average age was 40 years. Almost half of the offenders (42%) had a severe mental disorder and psychiatric history before the attacks. All of these individuals except one warranted a psychiatric diagnosis or had identifiable psychiatric features (ICD-10/DSM-IV-TR): 5 (36%) were psychotic at the time of the attack and 3 were diagnosed with paranoid schizophrenia (21%). More details of the study can be found in Hoffmann et al. (2011).

German School Shooters

The second highest number of school shootings worldwide have taken place in Germany, only superceded by the United States. Between 1999 and 2010, nine German cases were identified in which the offender carried out an attack with a lethal weapon. All of the attackers were male; their ages ranged between 15 and 23 years, with an average of 18 years. The majority were former students who returned to their schools for the rampage ($n = 5$; 56%); the others were students at the time of the attacks.

As for the victims, 37 died; 19 were teachers, 11 were students, and one was a secretary. Six victims were from outside the school: one police officer, two former supervisors in a company, and three random victims who were shot while the offender was on the run. Five of the offenders committed suicide (56%); two others tried to kill themselves immediately after the attack but survived (22%).

In 78% of the attacks firearms were used; in 44% explosives and smoke grenades were the weapons of choice, and 22% of the attackers used knives. The highest international number of casualties per event in the last two decades were found in Germany: the rampage school attack in Erfurt (2002) killed 16 people, and 16 people were shot in Winnenden (2009).

German Threateners of School Shootings

In the school threateners' sample ($n = 17$), cases were included only if there was no serious intention to commit a school shooting. In a first step, a sample of cases was identified by researching news reports on the Internet. Then the courts that handled those cases were contacted and asked to provide court records and investigative files for a research project. In a review of the files, any case was excluded where

interventions could have played a role in keeping a threatener from becoming an attacker. This resulted in the final nonrandom sample of 17 cases.

The age of the youngest threatener was 12 years and that of the oldest 22 years; the average age was 16 years. In contrast to the group of school shooters, who were all males, three of the threateners were female students (18%). In the vast majority of the cases (89%) the threatener was a current student of the school, unlike the school shooters, who were usually former students.

German Intimate Partner Homicide Perpetrators

The 70 offenders in this sample were drawn from an original published study of male intimate partner homicide perpetrators (Glaz-Ocik & Hoffmann, 2011). Cases were included if lethal intention was highly likely although death did not result; this was decided by the utilization of a deadly weapon or the force used by the male attacker was judged to be potentially lethal. In 51 of the offenses (73%) the women died. At the time of the attack, 70% of the female victims were estranged from their partners. The sample was gathered by first reviewing news reports of such attacks and then requesting primary data directly from the courts.

The average age of the attackers was 39 years; that of the female victims was 33 years. The 27% of female victims who survived were able to flee the scene despite their severe injuries or received immediate medical help, which saved their lives. Next to the female primary victim, a third party was attacked in 16 cases (21%); 10 of these secondary victims were killed. In most of these cases, the assumed or real new partner was the target of the offender, followed by children and individuals who tried to help the victim. A minority of 15 offenders (21%) tried to commit suicide after the attack; 4 succeeded.

RESULTS OF WARNING BEHAVIORS WITHIN THE GERMAN SAMPLES

The results of warning behaviors within the German samples are illustrated in Figures 3.2 through 3.5.

DISCUSSION

It is clear that not one single and universal pattern of warning behaviors exists in comparing the various domains of targeted or intended violence. But different domains of targeted violence appear to show typical

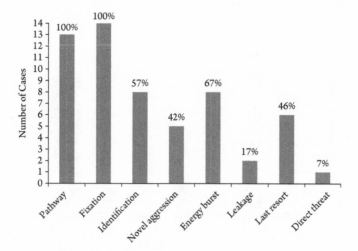

FIGURE 3.2 German public figures attackers (*N* = 14).

Fixation: 9 cause, 5 person. *Note*: The percentage for the known *N* is reported.

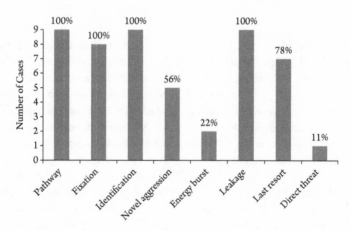

FIGURE 3.3 School shooters (*N* = 9).

Note: The percentage for the known *N* is reported.

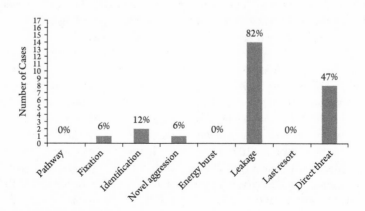

FIGURE 3.4 School threateners (*N* = 17).

Note: The percentage for the known *N* is reported.

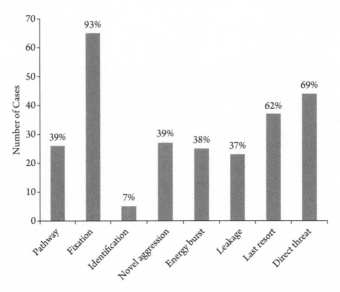

FIGURE 3.5 Intimate partner homicide perpetrators ($N = 70$).

Note: The percentage for the known N is reported.

profiles of warning behaviors (table 3.2). This is especially evident in the two public figure attack groups, the only domain of targeted violence in this study where two independent samples could be analyzed. Although different cultural backgrounds and historical time frames are apparent, the similarities between these two groups of public figure attackers within the same domain are striking (Figures 3.1 and 3.2).

Public Figure Attacks

In all of the US sample and most of the German sample, the targets of the attacks were politicians. Some warning behaviors with less precise definitions were analyzed in one study of attacks on European politicians (James et al., 2007); in an earlier research project on assassinations and attacks in the United States conducted by the US Secret Service, the majority of victims were also politicians (Fein & Vossekuil, 1998, 1999).

The majority of the European attackers (79%) and virtually all of the US assassins (97%) planned their offenses in advance—a marker for pathway warning behavior. This clearly fits with the high frequency of pathway warning behavior present in both of these samples of our study (94% and 100%).[1]

In the European attack study (James et al., 2007), however, the rate of fixation warning behavior (54%) was at first glance significantly lower than in our US (78%) and German (100%) samples. A closer look at the German sample reveals that in the original

study a distinction was made between a mild and a heavy fixation (Hoffmann et al., 2011). If one considers only the cases of heavy fixation, the frequency drops to 69%, closer to the percentage in the group of attackers of European politicians.

A history of interest in assassination, such as reading books or watching movies on this topic, or even emulating other assassins, was seen in 44% of the attackers from the US Secret Service sample. Such activities fulfill one criterion of identification warning behaviors (Meloy et al., 2012). Our German (57%) and US (56%) samples showed a slightly higher rate of identification warning behavior, but other markers such as a warrior mentality and a close association with weapons and military paraphernalia were included in this category, which may account for the higher percentages.

In the US Secret Service study, 44% of the attackers displayed signs of serious depression or despair and 41% uttered suicide threats. This is a typical mindset of offenders seeing themselves in a position of last resort and is also almost identical to the frequency of last resort warning behavior in our German (46%) and US (39%) samples.

In the US Secret Service study, two thirds of the assassins and near-assassins were known to have spoken or written in a manner that suggested that they were considering mounting an attack against a target—a loosely defined leakage warning behavior. This rate is much higher than the percentage of leakage in our German (17%) sample and some-what higher in the US (44%) sample; however, our more restrictive definition of leakage as noted above likely accounts for this difference (Meloy & O'Toole, 2011). For example, acts of writing in a diary about an intent to attack that were not or could not be known by authorities were not included in our definition.

Not a single successful assassin in the US Secret Service sample or any of the attackers of western European politicians communicated a direct threat to their victims or law enforcement before the attack. In our two samples, composed of both attackers and assassins, the communication of a direct threat was rare: 6% in our US sample and 7% in our German sample.[2]

A comparison of these two independent samples within the domain of public figure (mostly political) attackers and assassins yields some preliminary findings. Attackers and assassins engage in patterns of behavior that can be logically grouped according to the warning behavior typology. However, there may be other warning behaviors which are unknown at this time. Such warning behaviors in these two independent samples provide similar profiles as outlined in Figures 3.1 and 3.2. The most frequent warning behaviors are pathway and fixation, with identification warning behavior appearing in half of both samples at an almost identical rate. Fixation on a *cause* is slightly more frequent than fixation on a person among these attackers and assassins.

Both novel aggression and energy burst warning behaviors were more frequent in the German sample than the US sample, but this may be an artifact of observation bias—insufficient data available from the US sample owing to the nonexistence of this typology at the time of data gathering. Energy burst, in particular, is difficult to measure without establishing a baseline of activity over time for the subject of concern.

Leakage—the communication to a third party of intent to attack a target—occurred in nearly half of the US sample but less than one in five subjects in the German sample. The US data are quite consistent with previous research on the importance of leakage among adolescent and adult mass murderers (Meloy et al., 2004), and a strong disparity between more leakage and less direct threats in intentional and targeted violence is, once again, confirmed by both of these new public figure data sets, albeit small in size. Last resort warning behavior, first noted by Mohandie and Duffy (1999) in their concepts of

violence and time imperatives, is apparent in about 40% of these two samples.

School Shooters and School Threateners

A number of US studies have taken a closer look at warning behaviors in school shootings (Meloy et al., 2001, 2004; Newman, 2004; O'Toole, 2000); the most detailed and comprehensive research project was the Safe School Initiative, which analyzed 37 incidents of targeted school violence involving 41 attackers (Vossekuil et al., 2002). Important similarities in four domains are found in comparing data from the Safe School study with the profile of the warning behaviors in our smaller German sample.

Almost all US attackers (93%) planned and prepared their school shootings, a finding very consistent with the German attackers, who all followed a pathway warning behavior, including the last steps of research, planning, preparation and implementation (see Figure 3.3).

The very high frequency of US school shooters who exhibited a history of suicide attempts or thoughts (78%) was identical to the frequency of last resort thinking in the German sample of school shooters. This warning behavior is described as an increasing desperation or distress through declaration in word or deed, forcing the individual into a position of last resort. Suicidal ideation appears to be a strong behavioral marker for last resort warning behavior.

Leakage was present in all the German cases and also in 81% of the US school shootings; at least one person had information that the attacker was thinking about or planning the school assault. The rate of directly communicated threats was predictably very low in both samples: 17% in the US sample and 11% in the German sample.

We then compared the warning behaviors of German school shooters with the warning behaviors of German school threateners with no intention to attack (Figure 3.4).

To our knowledge, this is the first time that threateners and attackers within any targeted violence domain have been studied to test the null hypothesis that there would be no differences between the two groups. Given the small sample sizes and a total N of only 26, we first inspected the frequency of warning behaviors in each group and then inferentially compared only five warning behaviors across the two groups that appeared to be different and would increase risk. *Pathway* warning behavior was present in every school shooting and completely absent in the threatener sample ($P = .000$; phi = 1.0). Statistically significant differences between the two groups also occurred in *fixation* warning behavior ($P = .000$; phi = .915), *identification* warning behavior ($P = .000$; phi = .850), *novel aggression* warning behavior ($P = .010$; phi = .561), and *last resort* warning behavior ($P = .000$; phi = .834). Owing to cell frequencies less than 5, the Fisher Exact Test is reported instead of chi-square. Phi coefficients were calculated and interpreted as a measure of effect size according to Cohen (1988; 0.10 = small, 0.30 = medium, 0.50 = large). The effect sizes were all large in our small sample.

The school shooters' and school threateners' warning behaviors yield important findings. School shooters in the United States and Germany produce similar warning behavior profiles despite differences in geography, language, culture, and history: frequent pathway, leakage, and last resort warning behaviors and infrequent directly communicated threats. Pathway, fixation, and identification profiles are prominent and quite similar in comparing the German school shooters and the German and US public figure attackers.

Whereas both school shooters and school threateners frequently leak their intent to others, *the warning behaviors of pathway, fixation, identification, novel aggression, and last resort significantly discriminate the shooters from the threateners* and are suggestive patterns for high-risk cases, especially in the combination of several of these warning behaviors. Directly communicated threats appear to be a negative correlate for an attack to be carried out; however, 53% of the threateners did not communicate a direct threat and 11% of the attackers did communicate a direct threat. The interactive structure of the warning behavior typology may be useful for single case assessment.

Intimate Partner Homicide Offenders

Figure 3.5 profiles the warning behaviors in a sample of 70 intimate partner homicides. Such killings are often assumed to be affective—impulsive, reactive, and emotional—without any preparation or planning; however, recent studies have found that spousal homicides are planned in a minority of cases, thus qualifying as intended and targeted acts of violence. In a Canadian sample of spousal homicides there was evidence for planning in 13% of the cases (Dutton

& Kerry, 1999). In a Danish study the homicide was planned before the crime 22% of the time (Leth, 2009). In our German sample, there was evidence of pathway warning behavior in 39% of the cases, or higher than expected.

Virtually all the cases involved fixation on the person as a warning behavior prior to the killing. Such a finding highlights the importance of a pathological preoccupation with the victim and is also consistent with other findings that implicate stalking as a risk factor for spousal homicide (Campbell et al., 2003).

In our sample last resort behavior was also present in the majority of the cases (62%). Almost two decades ago another study of male spousal homicide attackers in Germany analyzed in a very detailed way conflicts and crisis that are typical of last resort situations (Burgheim, 1993). It was found that in 67% of those cases the spouse had a new partner, a breakup occurred in 69%, a final meeting in which the future of the relationship should be decided was scheduled in 43% of the cases, and in 54% the offender uttered threats of suicide connected with his relationship problems before the killing.

The most extensive internationally researched warning behavior in spousal homicide is direct threats. In a US study 74% of the offenders threatened to kill the woman before the attack (Campbell et al., 2003). In a Swiss sample 50% of the subjects threatened before killing (Zoder, 2008), and in a German group 66% threatened before killing (Burgheim, 1993). In our German case files direct threats were present in 69% of the cases, very similar to the US and the German study. In a different research approach, victims of attempted homicide were interviewed (Adams, 2007); of these, 90% reported that they were threatened by the offender before the attack. This high number may not reflect the true amount of threats before killings, since the dead can no longer speak. Such findings, especially when contrasted with the infrequent use of direct threats in the other domains we studied, underscore the "intimacy effect" (Calhoun & Weston, 2003): the more intimate the relationship has been, the more important are directly communicated threats in assessing risk of targeted violence.

Identification warning behaviors were very infrequent, unlike all the other targeted violence domains, yet novel aggression, energy burst, and leakage were consistently found in about one third of the cases, signifying their importance in the analysis of a subject of concern.

CASE STUDY: THE WARNING BEHAVIORS OF ANDERS BEHRING BREIVIK

At 1647 on July 22, 2011, a ferryman was asked to transport a police officer to the island of Utøya, located in a lake about 35 kilometers (20 miles) northwest of Oslo, the capital of Norway. The captain of the ferry helped the police officer carry a case onto the island. The police officer announced that he wanted to inform the members of the Labour Party youth camp on Utøya about a massive bomb explosion in the City of Oslo at 1525 that—as would later turn out—had killed eight people. But shortly after the boat reached the shore, the man revealed his true intentions and started to shoot the defenseless and trapped people on the island.

It was only about an hour later that actual police officers arrived on the island and apprehended Anders Behring Breivik. By then he had killed 69 people, mostly adolescents, with a Ruger Mini 14 and a Glock 34 pistol—the weapons he had secretly carried in the case onto the island (BBC, May 3, 2012).

The mass murder shocked a worldwide audience and was judged to be one of the most tragic events in recent history. The trial that followed in 2012 was accompanied by a heated debate surrounding the mental health of the accused. Two court-ordered forensic evaluations came to opposite diagnostic and criminal responsibility conclusions: the first found him to have paranoid schizophrenia and to be without criminal liability, whereas the second opined that he was a disordered man with a narcissistic and antisocial personality who was completely culpable (*The Guardian*, June 18, 2012).

While Breivik's mental state is a highly relevant question, we instead focus on the warning behaviors that Breivik exhibited before he carried out his attack on July 22. Warning behaviors are not linked to a particular psychiatric diagnosis but instead focus on accelerating patterns of concern for risk of targeted violence (Meloy et al., 2012). They can be observed whether the attacker is mentally ill or not, but are likely influenced by mental state and psychodiagnostic realities.

The information regarding the eight warning behaviors come from various public sources, including the 1,500 pages of Breivik's manifesto, which he called *2083—An European Declaration of Independence* (hereafter called Manifesto) and posted on the web the day of the attack. Other sources of data include the first original forensic evaluation, trial transcripts, and documents reported in the international media as well as other secondary news reports about Breivik. Such reporting includes statements by him and by other people such as his friends, family members, and other persons who made significant observations regarding his behavior leading up to the attack. The information on the warning behaviors is by far not complete but does unveil some of the major steps Breivik took in the run up to the attack. However, all reported subject material, especially from secondary sources (newspapers, media), should be viewed with great caution. We have attempted to confirm the veracity of such data that was utilized in this case study.

Pathway Warning Behavior

Breivik spent a tremendous amount of time to plan/research, prepare and carry out the attack. According to Breivik, he started to earn and save money between 2002 and 2006:

> I am required to build a capital base in order to fund the creation of the compendium. I don't know if I will ever proceed with a martyrdom operation at this point as it simply seems too radical (p. 1416, Manifesto).

He planned on saving 3 million Euros, but as of 2005 he had reportedly accumulated only 500,000 Euros. He boasted of several financially successful companies, but the Norwegian police later questioned these so-called businesses and they were debunked at trial. He did move back in with his mother in 2006 because it helped him to save money. That same year he started writing the Manifesto. He also conducted basic research on body armor, weapons, and explosives/chemicals (p. 1416, Manifesto).

Breivik joined a pistol club in 2005 just in case he should one day need to buy a gun legally (p. 1430, Manifesto). In order to have a credible coverup to buy explosives or components to explosives (i.e., fertilizer), he created the company Geofarm in the autumn of 2009 (p. 1417, Manifesto).

That same month he opened two Facebook accounts to collect the email addresses of nationalists and other like-minded people, asking them to accept his Facebook invitation. According to Breivik, he ended up with a total of 5,700 Facebook contacts and 8,000 high-quality email addresses in March 2010, representing all spheres of culturally conservative thought (p. 1420, Manifesto). It is around this time that he began worrying about appearing on a

Norwegian government counterterrorism watch list (p. 1420, Manifesto).

In 2010, he received the medical certificate he needed to obtain a new driver's license (psychiatric forensic report, 2011). Since traveling by car was vital to his attack plans, this was an important step toward preparing for the attack (Calhoun & Weston, 2003).

In July 2010, a year before the deadly attacks, he buried his body armor in the Norwegian forest in order to hide it from the authorities (p. 1421, Manifesto). Later that summer, he traveled to Prague, where he tried to purchase weapons but failed, since he could not adequately approach "shady figures" (p. 1423, Manifesto). Back home, he applied for a rifle permit and stated that he wanted to hunt deer. The proposal was accepted and the permit issued in October 2010 (p. 1424, Manifesto).

In preparation for the attack, Breivik conducted 15 sessions of pistol training between November 2010 and January 2011. Pistol training was initiated in order to fulfill the government requirement for purchase. He sent the application in January 2011. He joined the pistol club as early as 2005 in a planned move to increase his chances for legally obtaining a semiautomatic Glock pistol. In the same time frame he conducted three rifle training sessions in order to acquire experience with the Ruger Mini 14 (p. 1430, Manifesto).

Toward the end of 2010, Breivik started to buy chemicals (p. 1426, Manifesto). This triggered his fear of detection and he started to motivate himself with steroids and caffeine, the computer game "World of Warcraft," and his favorite music (e.g., music groups SAGA and Helene Bøksle—one of the voices of the title song of the computer game "Age of Conan") (Wikipedia, 2012).

Breivik bought a digital camera for photo sessions in early 2011 (p.1431, Manifesto). In order to promote his manifesto and get his message across, he created a video ("marketing movie trailer") between February 15 and 26, 2011 (p. 1432, Manifesto), five months before the attacks.

In early 2011, he converted the public listing of his company Geofarm from regular to agricultural. This move allowed him to rent and register a farm with accompanying fields. The fields, registered through Geofarm, came with a specific "farming ID number," which is a requirement for ordering large amounts of fertilizer from the national supplier (p. 1438, Manifesto). Breivik moved further along his pathway to violence when he left his mother's place and moved into the farmhouse in early May

2011. He also rented a Fiat Doblo and removed all the "AVIS" insignias (p. 1454, Manifesto).

On April 27, 2011, Breivik ordered 300 kilograms of fertilizer and started to build the bomb on the farm between May and July 2011 (p. 1455, Manifesto), describing in detail each step in the process of making the bomb in his writing. The bomb ingredients were virtually the same as those utilized by Timothy McVeigh in the United States in 1995. Breivik tested the bomb device on June 13, 2011, at a very isolated site (p. 1460, Manifesto). During his time on the farm, Breivik's neighbor observed that the windows of the farm were darkened. Breivik tried to avoid anyone who attempted to visit him (Der Spiegel, August 1, 2011).

Breivik used to exercise physically for years but not necessarily on a regular basis. In order to be physically and mentally fit for his attack, he trained and used steroids in three cycles beginning in early 2010, wanting to build up strength and speed and become a "one-man army" (psychiatric forensic report, 2011).

In July 2011, Breivik prepared the last steps before the attacks. He familiarized himself with the routes to the attack sites and programmed his GPS (p. 1464, Manifesto). He dug out the body armor that he had buried in the Norwegian forest a year earlier and bought upgraded ammunition (p. 1465, Manifesto). He rented a second car, a Passat, on July 16 and again removed all stickers (p. 1469, Manifesto).

He put the bomb in his rented Passat (p. 1470, Manifesto) and wrote a time schedule for the attack, but he would fail to adhere to his plans.

Breivik seems to have spent his last night at his mother's place. He slept till 0800 and started to install a high-speed modem for the distribution of his writing. This task took longer than planned. He drove his Fiat to Hammersbourg Square and took a taxi back to his mother's home, where he uploaded his "marketing video" on YouTube and made this entry in the Manifesto: "I believe this will be my last entry. It is now Fri July 22nd, 12.51. Sincere regards, Andrew Berwick, Justiciar Knight Commander, Knights Templar Europe, Knights Templar Norway." Breivik tried to send his manifesto to the 8,000 cultural conservatives whose email addresses he had collected earlier (psychiatric forensic report, 2011).

Breivik then walked to his Passat, which he had parked with the bomb in the trunk. He had the foresight to bring along a sign stating "sewer cleaning in progress" to avoid drawing attention to the smell of sulfur from the homemade explosives in the back of his vehicle (ABC News, April 27, 2012). In his vehicle, he changed into military clothes and attached blue lights to the roof so that he could approach his target, the *Regierungsviertel*, undetected. He parked the Passat with the bomb in front of the building and put on a helmet with a visor and a protection vest. He lit the fuse and moved away with the Glock in his hand, a scene that was caught on a surveillance camera and later published. After driving two blocks in his other car, the Fiat, he heard the explosion behind him (psychiatric forensic report, 2011).

After setting off the bomb, he drove to the ferry and deceived people with his police uniform and fake police identification papers in order to finish the second part of his plan: the slaughter of the children of the liberal politicians in power, whom he detested—those who were loved the most by his enemies (BBC, May 3, 2012).

Fixation Warning Behavior

Over the years, Breivik became more and more obsessively preoccupied with his cause—namely, a violent response to the Islamization of Europe through the multiculturalism of liberal politicians and their social dominance in government. He invested a great amount of his energy, time, and money in carrying out his plans. His project took nine years and cost about 300,000 Euros (230,000 USD, p.12, Manifesto), resulting, among other things in a 1,500-page compendium. Toward the end, he isolated himself from his social circle to work undisturbed by reporting to others, "I have a book deal" (p. 1435, Manifesto). Breivik also claimed that because of his project, long romantic relationships would not have been possible. His mother reportedly told the forensic experts that she observed his behavior becoming more erratic: "He lectured me about politics all the time." His friends also observed erratic behavior. They told the court that he spoke more often about politics in the months before the attack than in the past on the rare occasions when they met. To some he appeared depressed and had seemingly lost his "spark." It was only shortly before the attack that his friends thought he was doing a little bit better. Little did they know that the imminent implementation of his secret attack plans gave him back his spark (*The Guardian*, August 24, 2012)—what the sociologist Randall Collins calls "clandestine excitement."

Identification Warning Behavior

Breivik exhibited the aspect of identification called a "warrior mentality" (Hempel, Meloy & Richards, 1999). He wore a wet suit and posed with an automatic weapon in pictures in his compendium. In another picture he wore a uniform with medals. He seemed to have an admiration for the Israel Defense Forces and wore one of their protective vests during the attack (Manifesto, pp. 1510-1513). He idealized the Knights Templar of the eleventhth to thirteenth centuries and even claimed that he took part in a Knights Templar meeting in London in 2002, a likely fantasy (Manifesto, 1415). He also identified himself as "Commander Breivik who just performed an operation on behalf of Knights Templar" while speaking with the police on the phone during the attack (*UK Telegraph*, November 24, 2011). He also played "World of Warcraft," a military strategy game, and in the first pychiatric forensic report in 2011 called it his martyrdom gift.

Another aspect of identification is the study of previous assassins and warriors so as to become like them. Breivik copied and pasted passages in his compendium from the so-called Unabomber, sometimes only replacing words such as "leftist" with "cultural Marxist." Breivik plagiarized his inspirational source, Theodore Kaczynski, who was arrested in 1996 after his US serial bombings killed three people and injured 23 between 1978 and 1995. Timothy McVeigh, who was responsible for the 1995 Oklahoma City bombing which left 168 dead, also appeared in Breivik's writing (*The Telegraph*, July 24, 2011):

> I am really beginning to understand why Mr. McVeigh limited his manufacturing to 600 kg. He probably encountered much of the issues I did and he probably had to learn everything the hard way just as I have done (p. 1467, Manifesto).

Notice the degree to which Breivik becomes *like* McVeigh in his own mind, a core element of the psychology of identification. Breivik also mentioned that he liked the movie about the German Red Army faction leaders "Baader-Meinhof" and tried a special bomb making technique once used by Baader–Meinhof (*The Guardian*, August 24, 2012; Manifesto, pp. 1425, 1458).

Breivik thought of himself as an agent to advance a particular cause or belief system, the third facet of identification. He chose to become a resistance fighter against multiculturalism, Marxism, and the Islamization of Europe.

Novel Aggression Warning Behavior

Novel aggression warning behavior, describing acts of violence unrelated to attack behavior that are committed for the first time, could not be found in the Breivik case based on the information we gathered. However, if there is such a thing as "*virtual* novel aggression," which we did not think about in our original formulation but may be quite relevant as a warning behavior, Breivik's activity with "World of Warcraft," wherein he engages in virtual behavioral tryouts, would fit. (http://www.guardian.co.uk/world/2012/apr/19/anders-behring-breivik-trial-live)

Breivik said he "trained" for the attacks using the computer game "Call of Duty: Modern Warfare." The 33-year-old said he practiced his shooting using a "holographic aiming device" he had bought for the war simulation game, which he said is used by armies around the world for training. "You develop target acquisition," he said. He used a similar device during the shooting attacks on Utøya. He also said the computer game helped him to rehearse various scenarios, including fighting his way out of the government quarter after the car bombing in the event he was spotted while planting the bomb (*The Guardian*, April 19, 2012).

Energy Burst Warning Behavior
Breivik became increasingly active in the last two years (2009-2011) before the attack, and the warning behaviors increased after he rented the farm where he prepared and tested the bomb. He isolated himself more and more to focus on his "project" and to avoid discovery, but he purposely maintained a few social relations so that no one would become suspicious (Manifesto, p. 1416ff).

Leakage Warning Behavior
On July 17, 2011, the following tweet appeared online: "One person with a belief is equal to the force of 100,000 who have only interest." This quotation from British philosopher John Stuart Mill was later attributed to Breivik (*Der Spiegel*, July 23, 2011). Although it is not specific leakage as we have defined it, it points to Breivik's determined mind frame in the final days before the attack. The leakage in the Breivik case occurred when he posted his manifesto online, wherein he described his bomb-making step by step; he also posted a 12-minute long manifesto marketing video on his Facebook site just a few hours before he drove to the central goverment district to begin his killings.

Last Resort Warning Behavior
Breivik showed last resort warning behavior. It seemed clear to him that the Progress Party was too "moderate" and that it would never be in a position to

change Norway. He had lost confidence in the democratic processes (p. 1401, Manifesto). Since multiculturalismn was spreading rapidly, a "time imperative" (Mohandie & Duffy, 1999) for his actions is evident in his writing. He believed that alternative options to violence had been tried but he deemed them unsuccessful, a "violence imperative" (Mohandie & Duffy, 1999). According to him, the media carried most of the responsibility for his acts because they did not publish his opinions before the attack (psychiatric forensic report, 2011). He wrote that "the time for dialogue is over" in his manifesto (p. 1377), and it was obvious that he felt violence was justified ("He who saves the country, violates no law," quote from Napoleon, p. 684, Manifesto). During the trial on April, 17, 2012, he underscored his last resort attitude for the killings when he said, "I did this out of goodness, not evil. I acted in self-defense on behalf of my people, my city, my country. I would have done it again" (*New York Times*, April 18, 2012, p. A9).

Direct Threat
None of the information indicated that Breivik communicated a direct threat to anyone before the attack. If anything, he strove to maintain a very low profile, recognizing that as he moved down the pathway, his behaviors would become more detectable and more clearly illegal.

Breivik was positive for seven out of eight of the warning behaviors.

CONCLUSION
A typology of warning behaviors in threat assessment appears to have some usefulness in identifying accelerating patterns of risk. Our findings across five groups and three domains of targeted violence—public figure attacks, spousal homicide, and school shooters—suggest distinctive profiles, especially when spousal homicide perpetrators, prior sexual intimates of the victim, are contrasted with targets having no actual relationship with their perpetrators. Perhaps most important is the statistical significance between a sample of German school shooters and school threateners and the large effect size between certain warning behaviors in each group. These empirical findings support the theory that this typology has face validity, embraces within its categories most of the universe of warning behaviors in intended and targeted violence, and may provide a useful beginning structure for further operational thinking and research.

TABLE 3.2. SUMMARY OF WARNING BEHAVIORS ACROSS DIFFERENT SAMPLES

	German Public Figure Attackers (N = 14)	US Presidential & Political Attackers (N = 18)	School Shooters (N = 9)	School Threateners (N = 17)	Intimate Partner Homicide Perpetrators (N = 70)
Pathway	100% (13/13)	94% (17/18)	100% (9/9)	0% (0/17)	39% (26/66)
Fixation	100% (14/14)	78% (14/18)	100% (8/8)	6% (1/17)	93% (65/70)
Identification	57% (8/14)	56% (10/18)	100% (9/9)	12% (2/17)	7% (5/70)
Novel aggression	42% (5/12)	11% (2/18)	56% (5/9)	6% (1/17)	39% (27/70)
Energy burst	67% (8/12)	Insufficient data	22% (2/9)	0% (0/17)	38% (25/66)
Leakage	17% (2/12)	44% (8/18)	100% (9/9)	82% (14/17)	37% (23/62)
Last resort	46% (6/13)	39% (7/18)	78% (7/9)	0% (0/17)	62% (37/60)
Direct threat	7% (1/14)	6% (1/18)	11% (1/9)	47% (8/17)	69% (44/64)

Note: The percentage for the known *N* is reported.

These data, however, are not without limitations. The samples are small with the exception of the spousal homicide perpetrators, and no other inferential comparisons were undertaken owing to the many other variables that differentiated the groups, most notably geography, culture, and time of data gathering. In some cases the samples represent the virtual universe of cases (German public figure attackers and US attackers and assassins); in other domains the cases were nonrandom samples of convenience (school threateners). We also make no assertions that these warning behaviors predict targeted violence, although the consistency with which the warning behaviors are represented in the various domains supports the argument that these may be correlates of targeted violence in general and have real-world validity.

Once again, we acknowledge the cognitive bias of overconfidence: that we have identified all warning behaviors and there are no others of which we are unaware. In other words, we know what we know and what we don't know. Unfortunately the history of science is littered with the unknown unknowns, in this case warning behaviors that we don't know we don't know.

NOTES

1. Note, however, that our US sample is a subsample of the US Secret Service study, otherwise known as the Exceptional Case Study Project (Fein & Vossekuil, 1999).

2. There was also overlap between the European attacks study (James et al., 2007) and the German attacks study (Hoffmann et al., 2011), with the latter capturing virtually all of the cases on record while the James et al. (2007) study did not.

KEY POINTS

- There are eight warning behavior patterns: pathway, fixation, identification, energy burst, novel aggression, leakage, last resort, and direct threat.
- There appear to be distinctive configurations of warning behaviors across various domains of targeted violence.
- The warning behaviors of pathway, fixation, identification, novel aggression, and last resort were significantly more frequent when a small sample of German school shooters were compared with German school threateners.
- There is no evidence yet that warning behaviors predict targeted violence.
- Anders Breivik demonstrated most of the eight warning behaviors in his preattack history.
- Further research needs to be done.

REFERENCES

Adams, D. (2007). *Why do they kill? Men who murder their intimate partners.* Nashville, TN: Vanderbilt University Press.

Burgheim, J. (1993). *Psychologische Bedingungen bei Entstehung und Verlauf von Tötungsdelikten in der Situation der Partnertrennung.*Konstanz: Hartung-Gorre.

Calhoun, T., & Weston, S. (2003). *Contemporary threat management.* San Diego, CA: Specialized Training Services.

Campbell, J. C., Webster, D., Koziol-McLain, J. et al. (2003). Risk factors for femicide in abusive relationships: Results from a multisite case control study. *American Journal of Public Health, 93,* 1089–1097.

Clarke, J. W. (1982). *American assassins: The darker side of politics.* Princeton, NJ: Princeton University Press.

Clarke, J. W. (1990). *On being mad or merely angry.* Princeton, NJ: Princeton University Press.

Clarke, J. W. (2007). *Defining danger.* New Brunswick, NJ: Transaction Publishers.

Cohen, J. (1988). *Statistical power analysis for the behavioral sciences.* Mahwah, NJ: Lawrence Erlbaum Associates.

De Becker, G. (1997). *Gift of fear.* Boston: Little Brown.

Der Terrorist und die Brandstifter (August 1, 2011). *Der Spiegel.* Retrieved from http://www.spiegel.de/spiegel/print/d-79723321.html

Dietz, P. E. (1986). Mass, serial, and sensational homicides. *Bulletin of the New York Academy of Medicine, 62,* 477–491.

Dietz, P., & Martell, D. (1989). *Mentally disordered offenders in pursuit of celebrities and politicians.* Washington, DC: National Institute of Justice.

Dutton, D. G., & Kerry, G. (1999). Modus operandi and personality disorder in incarcerated spousal killers. *International Journal of Law and Psychiatry, 22,* 287–299.

Fein, R., & Vossekuil, B. (1998a). Preventing attacks on public officials and public figures: A Secret Service perspective. In J.R. Meloy (Ed.), *The psychology of stalking: Clinical and forensic perspectives* (pp. 176–194). San Diego, CA: Academic Press.

Fein, R., & Vossekuil, B. (1998b). *Protective intelligence and threat assessment investigations: A guide for state and local law enforcement officials.* Washington, DC: National Institute of Justice.

Fein, R., & Vossekuil, B. (1999). Assassination in the United States: An operational study of recent assassins, attackers, and near-lethal approachers. *Journal of Forensic Sciences, 44,* 321–333.

Glaz-Ocik, J., & Hoffmann, J. (2011). Gewaltdynamiken bei Tötungsdelikten an der Intimpartnerin. In C. Lorei (Ed.), *Polizei & Psychologie 2009* (pp. 263–286). Frankfurt am Main: Verlag für Polizeiwissenschaft.

Gray, N., Snowden, R., & MacCulloch, S. (2004). Relative efficacy of criminological, clinical, and personality measures of future risk of offending in mentally disordered offenders: A comparative study of HCR-20, PCL:SV, and OGRS. *Journal of Consulting and Clinical Psychology, 72,* 523–530

Hempel A., Meloy, J. R. & Richards, T. (1999). Offender and offense characteristics of a nonrandom sample of mass murderers. *Journal of the American Academy of Psychiatry and the Law, 27,* 213–225.

Hoffmann, J., Meloy, J. R., Guldimann, A., & Ermer, A. (2011). Attacks on German public figures, 1968-2004: Warning behaviors, potentially lethal and nonlethal acts, psychiatric status, and motivations. *Behavioral Sciences and the Law, 29,* 155–179.

Hull, C. (1952). *A behavioral system.* New Haven, CT: Yale University Press.

James, D. V., Meloy, J. R., Mullen, P., Pathé, M., Farnham, F., Preston, L., & Darnley, B. (2010). Abnormal attentions towards the British Royal Family: Factors associated with approach and escalation. *Journal of the American Academy of Psychiatry and the Law, 38,* 329–340.

James, D. V., Mullen, P., Meloy, J. R., Pathé, M., Farnham, F., Preston, L., & Darnley, B. (2007). The role of mental disorder in attacks on European politicians, 1990-2004. *Acta Psychiatrica Scandinavica, 116,* 334–344.

James, D. V., Mullen, P., Meloy, J. R., Pathé, M., Preston, L., Darnley, B., … Scalora, M. (2011). Stalkers and harassers of British royalty: An exploration of proxy behaviours for violence. *Behavioral Sciences and the Law, 29,* 64–80.

James, D. V., Mullen, P., Pathé, M., Meloy, J. R., Farnham, F., Preston, L., & Darnley, B. (2008). Attacks on the British Royal Family: The role of psychotic illness. *Journal of the American Academy of Psychiatry and the Law, 36,* 59–67.

James, D. V., Mullen, P., Pathé, M., Meloy, J. R., Preston, L., Darnley, B., & Farnham, F. (2009). Stalkers and harassers of royalty: The role of mental illness and motivation. *Psychological Medicine, 39,* 1–12.

Knoll, J. (2010). The "pseudocommando" mass murderer: Part I, the psychology of revenge and obliteration. *Journal of the American Academy of Psychiatry and the Law, 38,* 87–94.

Leth, P.M. (2009). Intimate partner homicide. *Forensic Science, Medicine, and Pathology, 5,* 199–203.

MacCulloch, M., Snowden, P., Wood, P., & Mills, H. (1983).Sadistic fantasy, sadistic behavior and offending. *British Journal of Psychiatry, 143,* 20–29.

Manifesto of Anders Behring Breivik (2011). *2083—A European Declaration of Independence.* Retrieved from web July 23, 2011; no longer posted.

Meloy, J. R. (2011). Approaching and attacking public figures: A contemporary analysis of communications and behavior. In C. Chauvin (Ed.), *Threatening communications and behavior: Perspectives on the pursuit of public figures* (pp. 75–101). Washington, DC: National Research Council, National Academies Press.

Meloy, J. R., Hempel, A., Gray, T., Mohandie, K., Shiva, A., & Richards, T. (2004). A comparative analysis of North American adolescent and adult mass murderers. *Behavioral Sciences and the Law, 22,* 291–309.

Meloy, J. R., Hempel, A. G., Mohandie, K., Shiva A., & Gray B. T. (2001) Offender and offense characteristics of a nonrandom sample of adolescent mass murderers. *Journal of the American Academy of Child and Adolescent Psychiatry 40*(6), 719–728.

Meloy, J. R., Hoffmann, J., Guldimann, A., & James, D. (2012). The role of warning behaviors in threat assessment: An exploration and suggested typology. *Behavioral Sciences and the Law, 30*, 256–279.

Meloy, J. R., & O'Toole, M. E. (2011). The concept of leakage in threat assessment. *Behavioral Sciences and the Law, 29*, 513–527.

Mohandie, K., & Duffy, J. (1999). First responder and negotiation guidelines with the paranoid schizophrenic subject. *FBI Law Enforcement Bulletin*, December, pp 8–16.

Mullen, P., James, D., Meloy, J. R., Pathé, M., Farnham, F., Preston, L., ... Berman, J. (2009). The fixated and the pursuit of public figures. *Journal of Forensic Psychiatry and Psychology, 20*, 33–47.

Newman, K. S. (2004). *Rampage. The social roots of school shootings*. New York: Perseus.

Nicholls, T., Brink, J., Desmarais, S., Webster, C., & Martin, M. (2006). The Short-Term Assessment of Risk and Treatability (START): A prospective validation study in a forensic psychiatric sample. *Assessment,13*, 313–327.

Odgers, C. L., Edward P. Mulvey, E. P., Skeem, J. L., Gardner, W., Lidz, C.W., & Schubert, C. (2009). Capturing the ebb and flow of psychiatric symptoms with dynamical systems models. *American Journal of Psychiatry, 166*, 575–582.

O'Toole, M. E. (2000). *The school shooter: A threat assessment perspective*. Washington, DC: Federal Bureau of Investigation, U.S. Department of Justice.

Psychiatric forensic report on Anders Breivik translated into English by Christian Skaug (2011). Retrieved from http://www.document.no/2012/02/forensic-psychiatric-statement-anders-behring-breivik-iii/

Skeem, J., & Mulvey, E. (2001). Psychopathy and community violence among civil psychiatric patients: Results from the MacArthur Violence Risk Assessment Study. *Journal of Consulting and Clinical Psychology, 69*, 358–374.

Vossekuil, B., Fein, R., Reddy, M., Borum, R., & Modzeleski, W. (2002). *The final report and findings of the safe school initiative*. Washington, DC: U.S. Secret Service and Department of Education.

Vossekuil, B., Reddy, M., Fein, R., Borum, R., & Modzeleski, M. (2000). *USSS safe school initiative: An interim report on the prevention of targeted violence in schools*. Washington, DC: U.S. Secret Service, National Threat Assessment Center.

White, S., & Meloy, J. R. (2007). *Manual for the workplace assessment of violence risk (WAVR-21)*. San Diego, CA: Specialized Training Services.

Wikipedia (2012). Helene Boksle. Retrieved from http://de.wikipedia.org/wiki/Age_of_Conan

Zoder, I. (2008). *Tötungsdelikte in der Partnerschaft*. Neuchatel, Germany: Bundesamt für Statistik.

The following internet citations were utilized in the writing of the case of Breivik. Interested readers are referred to the web addresses for the specific articles that were used:

Anders Behring Breivik trial live (April 19, 2012). *The Guardian*. Retrieved from http://www.guardian.co.uk/world/2012/apr/19/anders-behring-breivik-trial-live

Anders Breivik: Unraveling Violent Crimes and Mental Illness (April 27, 2012). *ABC News*.Retrieved from http://abcnews.go.com/blogs/health/2012/04/27/anders-breivik-unraveling-violent-crimes-and-mental-illness/

Anders Breivik believes court will rule this week that he is sane (June 18, 2012). *The Guardian*. Retrieved from http://www.guardian.co.uk/world/2012/jun/18/anders-behring-breivik-rule-sane

Anders Behring Breivik spent years training and plotting for massacre (August 24, 2012). *The Guardian*. Retrieved from http://www.guardian.co.uk/world/2012/aug/24/anders-behring-breivik-profile-oslo

Blond, blauäugig, skrupellos (July 23, 2011). *Der Spiegel*. Retrieved from http://www.spiegel.de/politik/ausland/mutmasslicher-attentaeter-blond-blauaeugig-skrupellos-a-776076.html

Norway shooting: Anders Behring Breivik plagiarised "'Unabomber'" (July 24, 2011). *The Telegraph*. Retrieved from http://www.telegraph. co.uk/news/worldnews/europe/norway/8658269/Norway-shooting-Anders-Behring-Breivik-plagiarised-Unabomber.html

Tape of Anders Behring Breivik's phone call to police after mass murder on Utoya released, November 24, 2011). *Telegraph*. Retrieved from http://www.telegraph. co.uk/news/worldnews/europe/norway/8913536/Tape-of-Anders-Behring-Breiviks-phone-call-to-police-after- mass-murder-on-Utoya -released.html

Utoeya witnesses tell court of Breivik's fake police ID (May 3, 2012). *BBC News Europe*. Retrieved from http://www.bbc.co.uk/news/world-europe-17938773

4

Collecting and Assessing Information for Threat Assessment

BRAM B. VAN DER MEER AND MARGARET L. DIEKHUIS

False facts are highly injurious to the progress of science, for they often endure long. But false views, if supported by some evidence, do little harm, for everyone takes a salutary pleasure in proving their falseness.

CHARLES DARWIN, 1871, *The Descent of Man*

Whether a threat assessment expert is asked to provide a case consultation or a formal threat assessment, one of the major responsibilities for the assessor is to ensure the quality and the completeness of the information on which the assessment and threat management strategies will be based. The expert needs to be aware of limitations or mistakes that could have occurred prior to, during, and after the information gathering process. Such mistakes obviously have negative effects on the quality of the information and can compromise the overall integrity of the threat assessment process.

The threat assessment professional must be able to isolate, from diverse sources of information, specific factors that increase or decrease the violence risk for a specific individual or situation. The identification of relevant factors must be followed by appropriate strategies to stabilize the situation, reduce the risk, and protect the individual or target from harm. Achieving this goal is impossible when information that the professional has to work with is incomplete, inaccurate, or out of date. It can result in a low-quality assessment, potentially leading to incorrect or inadequate management strategies with the potential for devastating, even life-threatening consequences.

Experience indicates that threat assessment professionals are not always focused (or not focused enough) on the necessity of critically examining the value of the information they are working with. Experts sometimes seem to accept too easily that the information they receive in a case file is a true reflection of what has happened and that those who provide information are reliable sources. Instead of such acceptance, the professional must ask such questions as: What or who is the source of the information? How was this collected or maintained prior to being included in the case file? Are there alternative scenarios or explanations for the current situation? Did the reporter of the information observe, interpret, register, and reproduce the information correctly? These are a few examples of questions that the professional should ask and answer before regarding the information fit or reliable for use in a threat assessment.

QUALITIES OF THE THREAT ASSESSMENT PROFESSIONAL

It is considered self-evident that the person conducting the assessment must be a professional in the field in which the assessment is requested. No matter how reliable or sufficient the information gathered, the resultant threat assessment will be flawed, incomplete, or inaccurate if the assessor does not have the requisite education, experience, or subject matter expertise. The professional acts as a human instrument of data collection.

Four elements can be identified as important to guarantee a good-quality threat assessment: (1) education, experience and subject matter expertise; (2) access to sufficient information to perform the assessment; (3) a level of certainty that the received information is indeed reliable; and (4) a professional objective assessment of the available material.

These elements are crucial because the work that threat assessment professionals do has far-reaching consequences for the individuals and families involved. The impact of the process of threat assessment itself and the burden of the ongoing implementation of threat management strategies on the personal lives of victims (targets) is often underestimated. Feelings of fear, depression, desperation, and anger can be expected; in some cases a psychiatric diagnosis is involved, such as posttraumatic stress disorder. For instance, targets for whom personal protection measures are necessary may be uncertain whether the guard will be effective in the event that a violent incident occurs. They wonder what to tell their families about the level of risk faced and are worried about the impact on their personal lives and safety once the protection ends.

I was not that concerned about my personal safety. My elderly mother was more afraid that something would happen than I was. She did not believe that the protection would be sufficient. I felt very well protected by the officers, and they did everything to make it as comfortable as possible for me. Nevertheless, we were forced to adjust our whole family life; it had a negative influence on my relationship and led to several emotional situations in our house. They (the guards) were there all the time; it had a tremendous impact on my and my family's life. Going for a Sunday morning walk, they were there walking behind us, going to the movies, they were sitting close. When I forgot to buy milk at the grocery store and needed to go and fetch it quickly, I first had to make a phone call to arrange for them to walk with me. My two teenage children were afraid that something would happen to them because they did not receive protection. It was very difficult for me to decide what I should and should not tell them.

This is the impact as reported by a public figure who received personal protection over several months. It is clear that the threat management in this particular situation had a significant influence on many facets of life, not only for the protected individual but for family members as well. In this case information was received from a criminal informant that members of a well-known violent organization were planning on killing him. The public figure received personal protection shortly after being made aware of the threat.

On the basis of the content of the information, most professionals would agree that the assessment was accurate. Unfortunately in this case, the information was not of good quality. The assessors involved failed to thoroughly investigate the source of the information. The information was accepted as valid and legitimate and therefore acted upon, creating the stressful situation described by the public figure.

In an effort to prevent errors like this, a threat assessment professional in the above case must ask, at an early stage of his or her work: From where did the informant get the information? Would it be possible for him or her to get such sensitive information from the criminal organization? If yes, why would the informant be privy to such information? Why would the informant risk his or her own safety by providing this information to authorities?

After a more thorough assessment, the answers to these questions led to the conclusion that the informant was not reliable. It was deemed unlikely that he would ever be in a position within the criminal organization to access such information. As a result of further investigation, it was determined that he was in a financial crisis because of his drug abuse and in need of money (which he hoped to get by providing the authorities with information and being rewarded for it). Furthermore, there was no indication from other collateral sources that an attack against this official was planned. The personal protection of the public figure was no longer necessary. A more complete assessment and critical analysis of the original information might have spared this public figure such a lengthy and invasive case management strategy.

This case shows how important it is that assessments and management advice be substantiated by facts or evidence and multiple sources of information if possible. It is also critical that the assessor have the ability to analyze not only the evidence itself but also any underlying motivations of the complainant. Of course there are times when immediate protection is necessary, so that there is no time to wait for a comprehensive examination of the information. In such situations it has to be communicated very clearly to the "victim" or target that the protection is a precaution that is necessary so as to allow investigators to gather additional information.

Everything should be done to reduce the risk of error in judgment. Besides the importance of working with good information, this example also illustrates the importance of professional objectivity. The assessor must not be influenced by personal judgments or moral opinions. In the case above, although the informant appeared to be truthful, could tell a convincing story, and create a scenario that even the authorities found credible, the assessment team needed to rely on an objective analysis and not be influenced by the subjective appearance of credibility.

Such a neutral and "fact based" approach is one of the core competencies of the threat assessment professional. Often the cases assessors deal with are highly emotionally charged, which increases the risk that judgments will be influenced by these subjective experiences. For instance, the "victim" has a strong emotional reaction to the threat, is very upset, and reacts with fear. The assessor interviewing her is influenced by this behavior and could have difficulty exploring the possibility of false victimization. For instance, scientific research shows that emotional reactions that people show in speaking about a memory do not mean that the memory is accurate (Wolters & Odinot, 2010). Professionals should be aware that what they sometimes experience as reality is in fact not objective judgment but subjectively determined and therefore dangerous. Different people assign different meanings or labels to the same experience, in which social learning plays an important role (Bensaou & Earl, 1998). Professionals who need to judge information are therefore advised to discuss their evaluations and assessments with independent colleagues. Such reflections help rule out subjective perceptions. What will also reduce the risk of error is to trust a multidisciplinary threat assessment team working on the same case.

THREAT ASSESSMENT AS AN ONGOING AND DYNAMIC PROCESS

A threat assessment looks at facts and circumstances at a fixed moment in time, using information that is available at that specific moment, but this is problematic. Imagine looking at the photo of a balloon. One cannot know if it is rising or falling. For as long as the unwanted situation (threat) is continuing, the assessment process must continue and be constantly updated with new developments and additional information as soon as it becomes available. One small piece of new information can completely change the level of risk and the direction of further information gathering in the case. What may

be considered a high-risk situation today, based on information that a violent incident will occur, can be reduced to a low risk status tomorrow should this single source information no longer be deemed reliable through the collection of information from other independent sources. New information, or an interpretation of old information in the context of new developments, can move the assessment in a completely different direction. Any generalization must be considered a "working hypothesis," not a conclusion.

The following case example shows the importance of recognizing information in the right context. If the circumstances and the exact roles of the people involved are understood incorrectly, information might be complete but at the same time be misinterpreted.

The manager of a small construction firm contacts a threat assessment professional for assistance with the following situation: A team of 12 construction workers are working on a project that is of such a large scale that it will take at least 14 months to complete. An existing farmhouse is being renovated. The homeowners are Geoff and Susan White. Susan works as a translator and has her office at home; Geoff is the CEO of a large electronics firm and travels a lot. One of the construction workers assigned to the project is Lee Richards. Three days ago Susan wrote an email to the manager of the construction firm with the following content:

"The construction work has been going on for 3 months now and I know all of the workers. They are nice guys and every now and then, during their breaks I join them for tea. I bake cookies and we chat. Lee was a nice guy at first, but his behavior has changed lately. He has started making sexual comments—that he likes my tight shirt and that my hair makes me look very sexy. He has offered to take my dog out for a walk during the evenings, which I thought was a good idea at first. On Saturday he asked me to join him for a walk. I agreed, but then I cancelled because I did not feel comfortable with him anymore. He seemed very disappointed and ignored me for two days in a row. Since then he has called me several times on my mobile phone, asking me to have a talk about what is wrong in our relationship. I have the feeling that he is watching me. I am very scared.

I looked up his name on the Internet and found an old news article from 16 years ago saying that a man named Lee Richards was sentenced to 12 years in prison for killing his ex-wife after years of stalking her".

Given this information, it could very well be that Susan is at risk. At first analysis, factors indicating the risk for future violence are evident. There is the potential history of previous violence committed by Lee, he appears to be making attempts to establish a relationship with Susan, and he may be suffering from her rejection. There are indications of stalking behavior, one of which is the news article that Susan is referring to. This case requires immediate attention and further assessment. The first steps in the assessment are to weigh the information that is already available and then to collect additional information. Although Lee's behavior may be consistent with that described in the news article, it would be naïve not to first find the news article to which Susan is referring. This original source of information can be used to confirm whether the Lee Richards who is working on Susan's property is actually the same person referred to in the news article. If this is determined to be the case, the risk for future violence toward Susan increases dramatically. The case would then need to be carefully analyzed and closely monitored. Protective surveillance or other security measures might even be considered. This intrusive level of monitoring may be important from a safety perspective while allowing for simultaneous information collection by an independent agent. This information is valuable and necessary for the ongoing threat assessment process.

MAKING A TIME LINE

New and developing information needs to be monitored constantly and evaluated on a regular basis for as long as the case remains active. It is recommended that any new information be added to an existing document or time line. This time line is a document created as a separate running log of events kept within the case file. When a new incident or event occurs or other relevant information is received, the assessor makes an entry on the time line document. The date of the event is recorded, the event is summarized briefly, and, in a separate section or column, the assessment professional writes an opinion about the consequences this has for both risk and management strategies.

As an example, information is obtained that Lee Richards has been seen following young women in his car. For the purpose of the threat assessment case file, the date, time, and location of these incidents are recorded, as well as other relevant contextual factors including a description of his behavior. This time line is valuable in establishing a baseline for behavior and any escalation or de-escalation over time. It can also help to illustrate inconsistencies and contradictions within the information already obtained. It helps in ruling out or confirming previous findings and conclusions. By using this simple tool, information is recorded in a structured way, allowing the professional to quickly get a good overview of the case. Information recorded in this manner helps the professional in the ongoing assessment and management of the case. The time line reinforces the fact that threat assessment is an ongoing and dynamic process. When threat management strategies are implemented, the process of gathering information, assessing information, and readjusting the management strategies continues.

Threat assessment and management as well as information collection run parallel: (1) collecting information (e.g., the stalker is trying to purchase a firearm); (2) examining information (e.g., examining whether the person who reports that the stalker is trying to purchase a firearm is providing reliable information, examining any alternative motives that the reporter might have to report this, etc.); (3) drawing new conclusions about the case (e.g., purchasing a firearm could mean that the stalker plans to use it on the victim, which means that threat is increasing); and (4) determining and implementing new strategies in order to manage the threat (e.g., placement of the victim in a women's shelter).

INFORMATION MANAGEMENT

One of the problems threat assessment professionals encounter is that large amounts of information, which may or may not be relevant, are gathered over time. Finding an effective way to identify relevant information from all this falls to the assessor to discern.

An equally problematic issue for assessors is ensuring that complainants or clients are aware of the importance of providing information. Ensuring that this information comes to the attention of a qualified assessor can be challenging. Individual clients may unwittingly screen information prior to notifying the threat assessment professional. This vetting process may be an honest attempt to reduce the bulk of information provided, or it could be intentionally vetted to hide potentially embarrassing information from coming forward. In either case, the client must be educated about the necessity of presenting any and all new information to the assessor. The client is too closely involved in the matter to have insight into her or his own risk or potential for escalation. He or she needs to understand that small changes that may seem insignificant could in fact signal a marked escalation to a threat assessment professional. Professional threat assessment has no value if information is not freely shared. An effective system guarantees that the latest relevant information is provided to the assessor in a timely fashion.

One of the most important lessons learned about ineffective information sharing is what has been defined as the "silo effect" (Calhoun & Weston, 2012; Meloy et al., 2012). This effect implies that large agencies each hold information within their own closed systems. It is accessible, but only within the agency and to a selected group. Other important pieces of the information puzzle are gathered and stored in other organizations. If all relevant pieces of information could be collected across agencies, a higher level of understanding of the totality of the circumstances would result. When agencies protecting the information are not communicating, crucial information relating to the case is not shared and the potential for unidentified risk escalates. This is further complicated when threat information involves national security and there are classified documents that cannot be exchanged. Even among those who have the requisite security clearances, the operative principle may be "need to know" rather than "need to share," thus further exacerbating the silo effect (Soufan, 2011).

In Lee Richards's case, for example, the police may know that he has been convicted of several violent crimes against women, including domestic violence. Mental health agencies may know that Lee has issues with anger, frustration, and violent fantasies. Lee's colleagues might know about his violent fantasies. Now a threat assessment professional is asked to assess the case of Lee Richards, who is reportedly stalking a woman. As long as these different institutions or professionals have no established protocol for confidential information sharing, important information will be missed, assessments will be incomplete, and dangerous situations may come into being or escalate without anyone knowing.

Information management problems of this kind have resulted in disastrous situations and continue to pose challenges. Initiatives in which organizations (police, intelligence, mental health, etc.) work together and carefully share information on specific cases should be supported in every way possible. Concerns about interagency information should be explored at the agency level. There is frequently a misperception that information cannot or should not be shared. The reality in many instances is that there is an existing information-sharing protocol, especially where safety issues can be articulated. This issue must be explored in considering the possibility of physical harm to a target; the statement "safety trumps privacy" should inform any information-sharing considerations.

GATHERING INFORMATION

In the case of Lee Richards and Susan White, it is necessary to collect more information before the assumed threat can be assessed thoroughly. The assessor needs to gather more information about Lee Richards. Information is needed about his criminal background, including the specifics of his offense behavior and precursors to the offense. Information about his day-to-day activities and general behavior is also needed.

A potential strategy is to approach the subject and discuss concerns directly with him. This must be considered carefully once a great deal of information has been gathered and considered. By approaching the subject, the assessor educates the subject as to the nature of the enquiry, thereby potentially escalating risk to a target. As risk is dynamic, it is contrary to the practice of threat assessment to actually be responsible for further escalating a situation. Another concern about speaking directly to the subject is the value of any self-reported information gleaned, which is counterbalanced by the risk of unintentional information sharing by the interviewer. After careful consideration, it may be more prudent to interview collaterals, such as the manager of the company where the subject is working or a parole officer responsible for offender management in order to gather this type of collateral information.

In addition to the need for relevant information about the subject, a better understanding of the victim (or target) and the context of the case is necessary for a thorough assessment. An interview with the victim (target) is important. This interview has to be well prepared, understanding that potentially sensitive issues will be discussed. An understanding of the dynamics between the subject and the target needs to be established. The subject may have misunderstood or misread the behavior of the target and interpreted it as a desire for further communication. Examples to be included in an interview with Susan might be: How was contact with Lee Richards initiated and how did it develop to where it is now? When did he start to make sexual comments and under what circumstances? How do the other workers react to Susan? Why did she decide to join them during the tea breaks? How did the workers react to that? How does Susan in general approach these men and what is her behavior like during the personal contacts? How did it happen that Susan agreed that Lee could take her dog out, and why did she say yes to his invitation to go out for a walk? Why was he still around on a Saturday? Is Susan's husband aware of the situation and what is the status of their relationship? What was the behavior that caused Susan to conclude, "He seemed very disappointed when I canceled and sort of ignored me"? How many times has Lee called, what does he talk about, and how does Susan respond to him during these phone calls?

Observing Susan's nonverbal behavior toward the interviewer while answering questions, especially if he is a male in this case, may provide further data on ways in which she unwittingly contributed to the current threat.

INFORMATION ASSESSMENT

Threat assessment is all about understanding human behavior, identifying behaviors that cause concern, and contemplating whether or not these concerning behaviors will escalate to violence. It is essential that threat assessment professionals be focused on whether or not they interpret (understand) the behaviors that they identify correctly. The threat assessment professional must collect information that either supports or refutes hypotheses about an individual's behavior and intentions. Lee Richards's behavior, for instance, may have an alternate explanation. There is information that Susan has the tendency to approach Lee in a flirtatious manner, she dresses in a way that could be interpreted as provocative, and she initiates the personal contact between them. This information about Susan would help the assessor understand why Lee told her that he wanted to have a talk about what was "wrong in their *relationship*." It now seems more "understandable" that Lee experienced his contact with Susan as the start of a romantic relationship.

In the process of collecting data, the professional must objectively assess the subject of the assessment and the information he or she is providing. In interviewing Susan, the observer needs to understand whether Susan can be considered a stable, trustworthy, reliable, and truthful source. Is there any other source that can confirm or corroborate the information that she is giving? It would be a naïve assumption and a dangerous approach in threat assessment to assume that the information provided by the witness or complainant is always truthful. It is better to maintain a position of healthy skepticism, always weighing the motivation for the interviewee's statements, whether fully conscious or not.

An informant can have several reasons for providing information that is wholly or partly untrue. A victim of stalking can be afraid of the perpetrator and might exaggerate what really happened in order to motivate the police to arrest the stalker. A worker in a company might lie about receiving threatening and harassing communications from his boss because he does not like her and merely wants to cause trouble in her life. Sometimes there is a personal reason for the informant to give specific false information. The motivation can be anger, fear, financial benefit, status, or personal attention. On occasion the informant could be delusional. Information from those who tend to take an overly active role in providing information and repeatedly come forward with new information must be handled with great care. When there are indications of personality disorder, one has to be highly critical or suspicious of the procured information. In the case of those with borderline personality disorder, manipulation and the emotional need for personal attention or to be the center of attention is frequently present. It should be noted that false victimization is not a rare phenomenon in threat assessment practice (Pathé et al., 1999). However, providing misleading or untruthful information is not always intentional or motivated by personal interest. There are several reasons why incorrect or flawed information may be unintentionally provided. One very fundamental reason could be the cognitive processing of information. Some information is registered and processed in our brains and other information is filtered out (Swaab, 2010). When human beings recall past experiences, there is always a question regarding the accuracy of the recall and whether the memory is a true representation of what actually transpired. It is well known that memory is unstable; it can be influenced by all kinds of factors over time. Emotional experiences lead to a better memory of details that draw the most attention, such as a victim's memory of the weapon that the offender used to threaten him or her. Less central experiences are known to be less well remembered, such as the clothes that the threatening individual was wearing (Christianson, 1992). Very strong emotions, as during the experience of a traumatic event, can lead to posttraumatic stress disorder, which is characterized by poor storage of memories of such events. On the other hand, experiences with such a large emotional impact can lead to very strong memories of emotions that were experienced during the event and of fragments of the event itself (flashbacks). The problem is that although emotional events increase the subjective experience of the memory, they do not enhance the objective correctness of the memory (Phelps & Sharot, 2008).

When assessors have received information from those suffering from mental retardation or psychiatric illness, the information provided should be handled with even more care. Psychotic individuals have episodes where they experience difficulty in critically distinguishing between fantasy and reality. If the threat assessment professional has no behavioral expertise or background, it is advised that he or she consult with a psychologist or psychiatrist. Threat assessment professionals frequently encounter persons with disorders such as schizophrenia and delusional disorders. A recent study on communications and approaches to the Dutch Royal Family (Van der Meer, Bootsma & Meloy, 2012) showed that the most prevalent psychiatric disorders for those who approached inappropriately were in the psychotic spectrum. 75% of a total of 107 subjects had psychotic symptoms and/or were diagnosed with schizophrenia.

INTERVIEWING AS A TOOL FOR GATHERING INFORMATION

There are different methods of collecting information from human subjects. The goal is to collect information as purely as possible from the source, with minimal disturbance of the natural context in which the information is disclosed. Some government organizations involved with threat assessment work have the ability and legal justification to use special techniques of information gathering—for instance wiretapping and methods such as infiltration and undercover operations. In most threat assessment cases, such methods and techniques are

not available and one has to search for other opportunities. The interview is one of the most frequently used methods.

It can be relevant to interview the victim or target in the case, other witnesses, or sometimes the individual who is making or posing the threat. The last is not always possible owing to judicial, practical, or investigative reasons; in some instances it may even be counterproductive. For instance in the case of Lee Richards, as discussed earlier, it is likely better to collect information from other collateral or indirect sources.

Part of the skill set of a threat assessment professional is the competence to collect useful and reliable information while interviewing. Interviewing is not about asking questions and ticking off a checklist of required information. Such a clinical "question-answer" interview style seldom proves to be effective. The interview style and the way in which the interviewee is approached are important determinants of the success of the interview. The interviewer needs to establish a trustworthy and professional "working relationship" with the interviewee in order to increase the likelihood of obtaining sensitive information that the interviewee might be otherwise reluctant to share.

It should be underlined that what the authors define as the "threat assessment interview" is different from a police interrogation in which the interviewee is the suspect of a crime. It can, of course, be that the person interviewed in the context of a threat assessment is also a suspect in an ongoing investigation, but that is not the status in the threat assessment interview. The threat assessment interview takes place separate and apart from any criminal investigation. The main difference is that the threat assessment interview is focused on the identification of risk factors in order to help prevent future violence. The interrogation, on the contrary, is aimed at finding evidence of whether or not a certain crime has been committed and that can be used for prosecution.

Reasons for Interviewing

Four reasons for using an interview in the context of threat assessment can be identified. The first and foremost is to collect reliable information on risk factors—finding additional risk and protective factors or information that can help substantiate or contradict previously identified risk factors. Second, the interview can be a useful method to find collateral information or evidence on data that have been received from other sources. When the description that Susan White gives us of Lee Richards's behavior corresponds with how his boss describes his experiences with Lee, a more solid basis for our findings is created. Third, the interview can be considered one of the very few methods to reach a good understanding of the interviewee. It can be used as a tool to access information that would otherwise not have been discovered. If the professional interviewing Susan White is skillful and chooses the right approach, he or she might be able to get Susan to speak more openly about the short sexual relationship she had with Lee. Information of this nature is sensitive but crucial for a successful assessment. Finally, the interview creates an opportunity to inform the threatening individual what he should and should not do in order to avoid getting into trouble or being arrested by the police. Boundaries can be set, agreements can be made, and through the interview the assessor can gather information on how the individual can be helped in order to decrease the risk of violence. This will provide useful information for the threat management process (Calhoun & Weston, 2003, 2009).

Although we have no statistics, it is also our experience, having done many interviews in the context of threat assessment, that most people who threaten or stalk are willing to be interviewed and to speak about their personal experience of the situation, to discuss the reasons why they react or behave in a certain way, and to explore what should happen in order to solve the problem. An explanation of this willingness could be a general need to be heard, a need to have an opportunity to release their frustrations, and in some instances a need to identify possible opportunities to communicate with the victim.

Understanding the Interviewee
Creating proper conditions and setting a proper interview climate when speaking with the subject may increase the likelihood of the interviewee being more willing to share personal insight and useful information. Keywords for the approach in the "threat assessment interview" are an objective and neutral, but nevertheless friendly, understanding, and a non-judgmental and subtly supportive approach. In order to find a deeper level of understanding of the person and to be able to "see the world through her eyes," the interviewer will have to be sufficiently attentive. Only then can a situation be reached where there is more access to sensitive matters and to understanding not only the surface meanings but also the

meanings that lie somewhat beneath the surface. The professional strives for empathic neutrality (Patton, 2002; Rogers, 1980).

Whenever possible and safe, it is recommended to speak to the person in the environment where he or she lives. Thus the interviewee may feel more relaxed and comfortable. The living circumstances and the home environment of the interviewee can also provide interesting and valuable contextual information. It is also important, when a home visit is considered, that the violence risks for the interviewer be carefully assessed prior to the interview.

> A man named John Watson is living in a rental apartment. He writes a short letter to the owner of the apartment building. He states in his communication that there is "confidential information about an upcoming attack from the Middle East" and that they should take "serious security and protection measures." He threatens to kill the "terrorists" who are making phone calls from the phone booth on the other side of the street. Neighbors of this individual have informed the owner of the building that he has converted his apartment into what looks like a military shelter. His windows are painted green, he has dug trenches in his small garden, and entrances to several rooms in the house are being camouflaged and blocked. The man is warning his neighbors of upcoming terrorist attacks, and invites them to see his apartment in order to show them what they should do to protect themselves.

A threat assessment professional is asked to assess the risk for violence against anyone making phone calls from the phone booth and against anyone in the close vicinity of this individual. The expert decides to interview John Watson. The above information provides very important cues for the way the interviewee should be approached and the topics that need to be addressed.

It is our experience that persons with paranoid personality traits or with paranoid delusions are in general reluctant to participate in interviews. The interviewer may not be believed or trusted, or the intentions of the interviewer may be misinterpreted, owing in large part to the nature of the disorder. In such cases it is important to create an interview climate that will help the interviewee feel more comfortable. A calm and friendly approach is recommended, and it is important to be as transparent as possible. The interviewers must introduce themselves properly and explain the reasons for the interview and its importance. Such individuals usually have a higher sensitivity to recording devices; therefore it is recommended to gain consent prior to producing any technical equipment.

Preparing for the Interview

Thorough preparation and detailed knowledge about the facts in the case are crucial to a successful interview. Up-to-date knowledge about the details of the case will make the interviewer more confident and the process more efficient. The interviewer will be more aware of what information is lacking for the threat assessment and will be able to detect inconsistencies with information compared with that obtained from other sources. If necessary, such findings can be directly discussed with the interviewee.

It is recommended that two professionals conduct interviews of this nature. From a personal safety perspective, it should be noted that enquiring about personal frustrations, stressors, or other sensitive matters with vulnerable persons can lead to aggressive reactions. A second reason for recommending two interviewers is that the second interviewer is available to take notes and ensure that everything relevant is recorded; this reduces the risk of missing important information. A third reason for having two interviewers is that the second person can assist by asking supplementary questions or introducing topics that may have been overlooked.

Although it is strongly recommended, it is not always possible to make a voice recording of the interview. Also, interviewers sometimes seem reluctant to record their interviews. It is our experience that in the context of threat assessment, few interviewees are resistant to recording. It can be explained to the interviewee that the recording will prevent any future confusion about what was actually discussed in the interview. This can be seen as a protective measure for the interviewee. Offering the interviewee a copy of the recording directly after the interview is recommended. When interviewers make up reports after completing interviews, it is important for them to realize the importance of writing as literally as possible what has been asked and answered. Making a summary of an interview can be dangerous because of the risk of introducing a subjective interpretation.

Interviewers prepare for the interview by considering the potential psychological traits or behavioral dynamics of the interviewee. They need to consider what the most effective approach will be, given the psychological characteristics of the interviewee. In the case of John Watson, the tenant in the apartment building—and where there are indications of delusional beliefs—the approach will be different than in a case in which an interviewee is known to have antisocial personality traits. In an interview of this nature, the antisocial individual will be much more manipulative and provocative. When the interviewers have no psychiatric or psychological expertise, it is advised that they consult with a behavioral expert or conduct the interview with a behavioral expert.

The preparation for the interviewers should include a discussion about the goal of the interview: What do they want to obtain from the interviewee? Once this is clear, they will be able to identify the discussion topics that must be introduced in order to achieve the goal. Under every identified topic chosen to be included in the interview, specific questions should be formulated and listed. For example, in preparing for an interview with John Watson, an important topic should be his *mental health*. Examples of questions listed under this topic are previous hospital admissions, use of medication, acceptance of psychiatric problems, and content of delusions. Another recommended topic is *previous deviant/criminal behavior*, with questions to determine the type of crimes committed in the past, the role of violence, and the frequency and intensity of deviant behavior. Topics should be discussed in a logical order. Sensitive or painful topics must be introduced with care and appropriateness. Experienced interviewers will be able to move subtly toward sensitive issues in a way that feels natural to the interviewee and will not do so abruptly. Even in areas where deception is likely, the interviewee's responses can be compared with the known historical data; thus his or her propensity to deceive can be assessed.

Stages of the Threat Assessment Interview

Four stages of the interview can be identified (Gudjonsson, 2003), as described below.

Introduction

In this first stage it is important to explain to the interviewee the reasons for the interview, what the goal of the interview is, and what will be done with the collected information. The interviewers introduce themselves as professionals and discuss their roles and the judicial status of the interviewee. Creating a safe and comfortable interview atmosphere is important at this stage. We explain at the start of the interview that all questions asked during the interview are relevant for the assessment and that some topics will be personal and may be frustrating or difficult to speak about. This introduction will help to reduce the chance that the interviewee will argue later on about the necessity of discussing certain topics. It is our experience that such a transparent approach reduces the stress experienced by the interviewee.

Sometimes interviewers make the mistake of spending too little time addressing the above issues and quickly go through the formalities. Thus the interviewee might feel disrespected or not taken seriously. In speaking with delusional individuals, this can lead to increased suspicion and a reluctance to cooperate.

Free Recall

The interviewer introduces the first topic and allows the person to speak freely about the matter, without interruption. When the interviewee is too brief in his narrative, the interviewers can add open-ended questions so as to motivate the interviewee to be more comprehensive. When the interviewee is allowed to use his or her own words and determine his or her own order of event telling, possible contamination of the statement is reduced.

Questioning

In this phase the interviewers ask their prepared questions and questions that were noted during the free recall or pure version phase. The questioning is thorough and detailed, with an answer to a specific question leading to a new set of questions. This enables the interviewer to dig "under the surface," creating opportunities to find new information.

In the following situation the interviewer wants to obtain more information about how John experiences his diagnosed psychiatric disorder:

Interviewer: So, John, you just told us that you have to use medication for your psychological problems. Can you tell us more about that?
John: They say it will make me feel less anxious and upset.
Interviewer: Who tells you that?
John: The psychiatrist I have to visit every two weeks.
Interviewer: Tell us a bit more about how you feel about these visits.

John: I don't think it is necessary to go, so I don't. There is nothing wrong with me.
Interviewer: How can it be that the doctor says you have this problem, and you say there is nothing wrong with you?
John: They are making up stories like this, to make me look crazy when I warn everyone about terrorists taking over our country and killing us. I would not be surprised if the psychiatrists are supporting the terrorist organization.
Interviewer: So, do I understand correctly John, you don't go to see the psychiatrist because they intentionally want to make you look crazy because they form a team with the terrorists?
John: Yes, exactly. I am sure it is one big conspiracy. I have seen the doctor making strange phone calls when I was there once. It was getting dangerous, so I had to get away.
Interviewer: How does that make you feel?
John: Angry, scared, like I have to protect myself.
Interviewer: How do you protect yourself?
John: Making sure my house is safe, observing the phone booth. I don't have any weapons to protect myself so this is all I can do.
Interviewer: So how about the medication?
John: It is poison.
Interviewer: It is poisonous?
John: Yes, so I can't use it. I told you the doctors are conspiring with the terrorists; they want to kill me for making the truth come out.

When the interviewer has extensively questioned the interviewee about a topic and feels that enough information has been collected, he or she will naturally move to the next topic. In this interview not only information about John's mental disorder and how he experiences it is gathered but, while speaking about this, the interviewer finds opportunities to collect other useful information too—about weapons availability and medication use. Later on in the interview, if necessary, the interviewer can come back to these points to ask additional questions. Also note that the interviewer is asking open-ended questions, being very careful with leading the interviewee to a specific answer. The question "So how about the medication?" will probably provide more and more reliable information than if the question had been, "Are you using your prescribed medication?"

In general it is important to be aware of the risks of using closed, leading, and suggestive questions. If the interviewee is considered mentally unstable, the risk of getting wrong information is increased (Gudjonsson, 2003). In most cases such a questioning style will increase the likelihood of gathering unreliable information.

Ending the Interview

When all the topics have been fully explored, the interview is concluded.

Checklists

It is strongly recommended that existing empirically based threat assessment tools be utilized in determining which information is necessary in order to complete a comprehensive threat assessment. Structured professional judgment tools, such as the WAVR-21 (White & Meloy, 2007) for workplace violence situations, the B-SAFER (Kropp et al., 2010) for domestic violence casework, the SARA (Belfrage et al., 2011) for the assessment of spousal assault risk, or the Stalking Risk Profile (MacKenzie et al., 2009) when the assessment focuses on stalking can be used when identifying topics and specific questions for the interview. Tools like these are obviously used for the actual threat assessment. They can also play a role in giving direction and topics for the interview.

Those whose professional duties require that they engage in short contacts or very brief interviews with potential offenders—like security guards, bodyguards, or protection officers—can also benefit from scientifically or empirically based checklists. For example, in 2010 the Netherlands Police Academy developed a questionnaire (Calis, 2011) for police guards protecting the Royal Palace. These officers are often confronted with individuals who seek contact, threaten, or for other reasons attract attention. The guards' accurate reports of such incidents and the information collected are crucial for anyone conducting a formal threat assessment later in the process. In the established questionnaire, 10 topics are identified, with specific, detailed questions under each topic. Examples of topics are "the motivation of the person to be there," "earlier attempts to approach public buildings or public figures" and whether or not the person is dealing with "psychological problems or psychiatric care."

An addendum to the questionnaire is a short checklist that the officer can fill out after the incident. In this section the officer is guided to give a detailed description of (1) the physical appearance of the individual, (2) his or her behavior, and (3) the context in which the incident took place.

STATIC, DYNAMIC, AND CONTEXTUAL INFORMATION

One must distinguish between information that is factual, static, and dynamic. Static information is that which will not change over time. It includes information about the offender (the name of a person, his age, whether or not he has a military background, etc.). Dynamic information describes information that can change over time (addiction to drugs or alcohol, attitudes, future intentions, etc.).

In the following example a protection or security guard has contact with an individual walking repeatedly back and forth in front of an identified politician's office. Information gathered by the guard is important input for the analysis and evaluation by threat assessment professionals. In his statement he writes: "The man approached me, he looked like a tramp, or maybe a drug addict. He was confused and I had the impression that he wanted to enter the building. He threatened me when I did not allow him to pass the gates." These three sentences in his report do provide relevant information, but if the guard had been more specific and factual in reporting this incident, it would have been much more useful for the person who later had to conduct a threat assessment. A more useful report of the situation would have been as follows:

> I saw a man approaching me. It was 10.19 pm, Tuesday January 19, 2012. He looked me straight in the eyes while walking up to me. The man was dressed in a stained shirt and worn out jeans. It was cold outside (4 degrees Celsius). He started talking to me but his speech was very chaotic and I could make no sense at all what he was saying. I did have the impression that he wanted to enter because he was constantly looking to the front door of the house, and he tried to push me aside once. He did not do this in an aggressive way. I told him "no, you are not allowed to go inside, you need to leave." Then the man said that I would be killed.

For the guard in this case the main objective was to collect information and reproduce it in as much detail as possible. In this first example of information gathering his task should not be an interpretation of the situation as he experienced it, and he should certainly not give his personal recollection of the incident and the behavior of the observed.

However, sometimes the interpretation of such an observer can be helpful to the assessment once the more concrete facts are recorded. Even his emotional perceptions (e.g., that he was scared by the intimidating physical appearance and the loud screaming of the person observed) can be useful for the assessment as long as this interpretation can be justified through the facts of the circumstance.

Especially helpful and therefore strongly recommended to those who have to report on situations and behavior of individuals (e.g., bodyguards, protection officers, security officers) is providing contextual information. The fact that the reporter in the above case mentioned that it was 10.19 pm is relevant for the assessment because the perpetrator wants to enter the office of the politician after working hours. Also the report that it was cold outside and the person was dressed only in jeans and a t-shirt could be useful information from a psychiatric perspective. Psychotic individuals have the tendency to experience stimuli such as pain or temperature differently (Kaplan & Sadock, 2003). This can be because of the illness itself or a result of antipsychotic medication, which can lead to differences in the perception of pain. Contextual information gives a better understanding of the behavior and helps the assessor to form an opinion on whether or not the behavior was appropriate or normal for that specific situation.

In the following example it is shown how contextual information can change the interpretation of an entire situation and have the potential to alter the direction of an assessment. The guard at the Royal Palace writes: "I saw a man running towards the gates of the Royal Palace, he was laughing and shouted at the other protection guard that he wanted to personally meet with the queen. He then attempted to climb over the fence. The man was alone." By comparison:

I saw a man running toward the gates of the Royal Palace; he was laughing and shouted at the other protection guard that he wanted to personally meet with the queen. He then attempted to climb over the fence. Three other males accompanied the man. There was a lot of public activity, people hanging around, and many drunken people singing and celebrating Queen's Day. It all happened last Tuesday night, 9.15 p.m.

KEY POINTS

- The threat assessment professional needs to be aware that all kinds of limitations and mistakes could have occurred in the information gathering process. He has to critically examine the value of the information with which he is working.
- Informants and complainants are not always reliable sources. The assessor has to thoroughly investigate the source and his underlying motivations and see whether or not the information provided by the source can be accepted as valid and legitimate and acted upon.
- Threat assessments and management strategies have to be substantiated by facts and evidence as well as multiple sources of information.
- Professionals should be aware that what they sometimes experience as reality is in fact not objectively true, but subjectively determined and therefore dangerous to the assessment.
- In addition to the need for relevant information about the subject, a better understanding of the victim (or target) as well as the context of the case is necessary for a good assessment.
- Part of the skill set of a threat assessment professional is the competence to collect useful and reliable information via interviewing. Such skills should allow him to be sufficiently attentive to sensitive matters and to understand not only the surface meanings but also the meanings that lie beneath.
- Using closed, leading, and suggestive questions, especially when the interviewee is considered mentally unstable, has a strong negative influence on the reliability and overall validity of the information gathered.
- Empirically based threat assessment tools should be used in order to complete a comprehensive threat assessment. Such tools can also provide direction for interviews and help identify topics for further information gathering.

REFERENCES

Belfrage H., Strand, S., Storey, J. E. Gibas, A. L., Kropp, P. R., & Hart, S. D. (2012). Assessment and management of risk for intimate partner violence by police officers: Using the Spousal Assault Risk Assessment Guide (SARA). *Law and Human Behavior, 36*(1), 60–67.

Bensaou, M., & Earl, M. (1998). The right mind-set for managing information technology. *Harvard Business Review*, September-October, 119–128.

Calhoun, F., & Weston, S. (2012). *Concepts and case studies in threat management*. Boca Raton, FL: CRC Press.

Calhoun, F. S., & Weston, S. W. (2003). *Contemporary threat management*. San Diego, CA: Specialized Training Services.

Calhoun, F. S., & Weston, S.W. (2009). *Threat assessment and management strategies*. Boca Raton: CRC Press.

Calis, A.L. (2011). *Wat doet u hier? Een vragenlijst voor beveiligers en politieambtenaren in het eerste contact met "approachers."* Master thesis, Netherlands Police Academy. http://forensiseuropa.wordpress.com/published-research/

Christianson, S. (1992). Emotional stress and eyewitness memory: A critical review. *Psychological Bulletin, 112*, 284–309.

Darwin C. (1871). *The descent of man, and selection in relation to sex*. London: Murray, 1871.

Gudjonsson, G. H. (2003). *The psychology of interrogations and confessions: A Handbook*. Chichester: Wiley.

Kaplan, H. I., & Sadock, B. J. (Eds.). (2003). *Synopsis of psychiatry. Behavioral sciences/clinical psychiatry*, 9th ed. Philadelphia: Lippincott Williams & Wilkins.

Kropp, P. R., Hart, S. D., & Belfrage, H. (2010). *Brief Spousal Assault Form for the Evaluation of Risk (B-SAFER), Version 2: User manual*. Vancouver: Proactive Resolutions Inc.

MacKenzie, R. D., McEwan, T. E., Pathé, M. T., James, D. V., Ogloff, J.R.P., & Mullen, P. E. (2009). *The stalking risk profile. Guidelines for assessing and managing stalkers*. Melbourne: Centre for Forensic Behavioural Science.

Meloy, J. R., Hoffmann, J., Guldimann, A., & James, D. (2012). The role of warning behaviors in threat assessment: An exploration and suggested typology. *Behavioral Sciences and the Law, 30*, 256–279.

Pathé, M., Mullen, P. E., & Purcell, R. (1999). Stalking: False claims of victimization. *The British Journal of Psychiatry, 174*, 170–172.

Patton, M. Q. (2002). *Qualitative research & evaluation methods*, 3rd ed. Thousand Oaks, CA: Sage.

Phelps, E. A., & Sharot, T. (2008). How (and why) emotion enhances the subjective sense of recollection. *Current Directions in Psychological Science, 17*, 147–152.

Rogers, C. (1980). *A way of being*. Boston: Houghton Mifflin.

Soufan, A. (2011). *The black banners*. New York: Norton.

Swaab, D. (2010). *Wij zijn ons brein*. Amsterdam: Contact.

Van der Meer, B. B., Bootsma, L., & Meloy, J. R. (2012). Disturbing communications and problematic approaches to the Dutch Royal Family. *Journal of Forensic Psychiatry and Psychology, 23*, 571–589.

White, S. G., & Meloy, J. R. (2007). *A structured professional guide for the workplace assessment of violence risk*. San Diego, CA: Specialized Training Services.

Wolters, G. & Odinot, G. (2010). Zijn zekere getuigen betrouwbare getuigen? In P.J. van Koppen, H. Merckelbach, M. Jelicic & J.W. de Keijser (Eds.), *Reizen met mijn rechter* (pp. 529–538). Deventer, The Netherlands: Kluwer.

5

Legal Issues in Threat Management

KRIS MOHANDIE AND JENS HOFFMANN

Threat management options and practice are necessarily informed by and operate within a legal context. Legal regulation for threat assessment practice originates in a variety of arenas, including (1) penal code statutes that identify criteria and thresholds for violations, arrest, incarceration, and release of offenders; (2) civil rights-related laws pertaining to protected speech, regulations on interviews and interrogations, limitations on searches and seizures, use of surveillance and nonconsensual monitoring, and the regulation and possession of firearms or other weapons; (3) employment law and regulations specific to various settings such as schools; (4) laws that task organizations and employers with providing a safe and harassment-free workplace or school; (5) the legal basis for involuntarily hospitalizing an individual for mental health, substance abuse, or likelihood of reoffending; (6) special rights that juvenile subjects may possess; and (7) developing case law relevant to threat management practice. This chapter will provide an overview of the legal basis for threat management in the United States, Germany, and other European countries, present the results of an international survey of threat management laws, and discuss future trends and needs in this area.

UNITED STATES

Penal Code Statutes

Penal code statutes are valuable tools for threat assessment and threat management. It is important for the professional to be aware of the elements of various crimes that surface during threat assessment

investigations so that the criminal justice system may be used to bring control to a subject's behavior. These statutes can be quite varied given the endless range of fact patterns present in cases: antistalking and criminal harassment, conspiracy to commit murder, attempted murder, terrorism, illegal weapons possession and modification, criminal threats, assault, vandalism, burglary, trespassing, theft, domestic violence, explosives possession and manufacturing, child and elder abuse or endangerment, public intoxication, filing a false police report, and illegal immigration. In one hospital setting workplace violence threat case, it was discovered that the offender had "accidentally" injured a coworker with whom he had a dispute using a defibrillator. Further investigation addressing the technology of the device determined that the power adjustment had been modified to many times the safe setting and that the subject had violated the terms of his American work visa. Ultimately he was convicted of attempted murder (rather than the lesser crime initially charged of assault), sentenced to prison, and deported from the United States following his release from prison. Knowledge and use of the penal code statutes afforded greater protection through the extension of confinement and removal of the offender from target access both while in prison and upon release.

Stalking, as another example, is a crime that, in the United States, is covered by both local and federal law. Generally stalking statutes have several elements, including a pattern of pursuit that is unwanted and unwelcome to the victim, a credible threat, and the creation of fear, or intent to induce fear in the victim. A case that might initially appear to involve lower-level criminal infractions such as trespassing, annoying phone calls, burglary, and vandalism may actually represent a course of conduct chargeable as stalking. This may allow accurate identification by the criminal justice system of the salient behavioral issues and enable appropriate controls and sanctions to be brought to bear on the subject's behavior.

Child and Elder Abuse Laws

State child abuse reporting laws mandate reporting incidents of suspected child abuse—including physical and emotional abuse, sexual abuse, and child neglect—to appropriate authorities. Child abuse and neglect issues may come up from time to time during threat assessments. Neglect in particular may be part of what is leading a child or teen to acquire access to firearms. These laws may sometimes be invoked to remove an at-risk individual from such an environment or to provide external social agency monitoring of risk-relevant issues. Similar laws apply to elder and dependent abuse, which may be relevant where subjects may be abusing an elderly person or dependent.

Search and Seizure Exceptions

New Jersey v. T.L.O., 469 U.S. 325 (1985), is a decision by the US Supreme Court that stemmed from a question of the constitutionality of a search of a public high school student for contraband after she was caught smoking. The subsequent search of her purse revealed drug paraphernalia. The student posed a Fourth Amendment challenge to the search, and the Court agreed, finding that public school officials act under the umbrella of government authority and are thus subject to the constraints of the Fourth Amendment. However, based on the circumstances unique to a school setting, school officials need not have probable cause but the search must be reasonable under the circumstances. In this case, the Court found the school had "reasonable suspicion" to conduct the search and the search was upheld.

When campus-based law enforcement officers are involved, there is a split in authority regarding whether the standard to be applied is probable cause or reasonable under the circumstances. The lower reasonableness standard may apply when campus-based law enforcement act as agents of the school, as in *State of Florida v. N.G.B.*, 806 So.2d 567 (Fla.2d DCA 2002); however, the higher probable cause standard may apply if the school conducts the search at the request of the campus-based law enforcement officer, as in *State of New Hampshire v. Heirtzler*, 147 N.H. 344 (2001). Outcomes will likely be fact-driven.

Civil and Individual Rights

US civil rights laws protect the individual from unwarranted interference and abuse of power by the government. Many of these civil rights are guaranteed in amendments to the US Constitution and represent the basic rights of all Americans on US soil. The First Amendment protects an individual's right to freedom of speech (Cohen, 2009). The Second Amendment ensures the right to bear arms and is the basis for legal firearm possession by US citizens. The Fourth Amendment safeguards against unlawful search and seizure by the government; absent an exception such as exigent circumstances, law enforcement officers are subject to the "probable cause" standard and, prior to searching a person or place without consent, must obtain a search warrant. The Fifth Amendment protects people from being held for a crime unless they are properly indicted, affords the individual the right not to have to testify (and make statements) against herself or himself, and provides other due process guarantees. A person also has a right, as reflected by the *Miranda* case law, "to remain silent, to have an attorney appointed..." (*Miranda v. Arizona, 1966*). In many jurisdictions, juveniles have the same rights and can ask to have a parent or guardian present during questioning. These rights serve as limitations on how invasive threat assessments may be without consent of the subject, and may in fact determine whether the subject's behavior is considered a threat at all. A subject may make statements others perceive as threatening, yet the statements or behavior may be protected speech. Subjects may acquire and possess firearms as long as they do so legally. They may have a wealth of incriminating and relevant information on their person or property (including computer, cyberspace, and cell phone), but without their consent or a search warrant, this information may not be legally available to the threat investigation. They may also refuse to cooperate with attempts to interview them, and juveniles often have greater protections for such refusals than adults. Thus it behooves those investigating and assessing threats to have competent and informed legal professionals advising them for the more difficult scenarios.

US Patriot Act

The controversial Patriot Act, enacted in the wake of the 911 terrorist attacks on the United States, granted wide exceptions to a variety of US civil rights. This federal law expanded the right of the government to conduct searches and surveillance without court order and now applies to certain domestic terrorism situations, which may include "lone wolves" who are not affiliated with any particular group but are bent on mass destruction. It also broadened the discretion of law enforcement and immigration authorities to detain and deport immigrants suspected of involvement in terrorist activities.

Case Law Relevant to Individual Rights

The rights afforded by these various civil rights are not infinite. American courts, through a variety of cases, have helped to define the boundaries of some of these civil rights, and local statutes have further codified interpretations.

"Free speech" is an individual freedom; it is not without boundaries and limitations that have direct implications for threat assessment. Justice Oliver Wendell Holmes, in one of his most famous opinions, wrote: "The most stringent protection of free speech would not protect a man in falsely shouting fire in a theater and causing a panic.... The question in every case is whether the words used...create a clear and present danger" (*Schenck v. United States*, 1919).

In its current formulation of this principle, the Supreme Court held that "advocacy of the use of force or of law violation" is protected unless "such advocacy is directed to inciting or producing imminent lawless action and is likely to incite or produce such action" (*Brandenburg v. Ohio*, 1969).

Similarly, the Court held that a statute prohibiting threats against the life of the president of the United States could be applied only against speech that constitutes a "true threat" and not against mere "political hyperbole" (*Watts v. United States*, 1969). In *Rankin v. McPherson*, 483 U.S. 378, 380 (1987), the Court upheld the right of an employee to remark, after hearing of an attempt on President Reagan's life, "If they go for him again, I hope they get him." The Court considered the fact that the statement dealt with a matter of public concern, did not amount to a threat to kill the president, did not interfere with the functioning of the workplace, and was made in a private conversation with another employee and therefore did not discredit the office. Furthermore, as the employee's duties were purely clerical and encompassed "no confidential, policymaking, or public contact role," her remark did not indicate that she was "unworthy of employment."

In *Virginia v. Black*, 538 U.S. 343, 360-363 (2003), the Court noted that "Intimidation in the constitutionally proscribable sense of the word is a type of true threat, where a speaker directs a threat to a person or group of persons with the intent of placing the victim in fear of bodily harm or death.... The First Amendment permits Virginia to outlaw cross burning done with the intent to intimidate because burning a cross is a particularly virulent form of intimidation. Instead of prohibiting all intimidating messages, Virginia may choose to regulate this subset of intimidating messages." A plurality held, however, that a statute may not presume, from the fact that a defendant burned a cross, that he had an intent to intimidate. The burden of proof is on the state to establish this intent.

Free Speech Exceptions

The landmark decision *Tinker v. Des Moines Independent Community School District*, 393 U.S. 503 (1969), established the test about what is considered free speech on school campuses. This case stemmed from protests to the Vietnam War when a group of high school students decided to demonstrate their opposition to the war by wearing black armbands to school. In reaction to this plan, the school district adopted a policy prohibiting the wearing of armbands to school. The Supreme Court supported the rights of the students, opining that the district's preemptive ban was an unconstitutional interference with their rights: "First Amendment rights, applied in light of the special characteristics of the school environment, are available to teachers and students." They rejected the district's argument that the ban on the armbands was reasonable because it was based on a fear that they would lead to a disturbance on campus, noting: "in our system, undifferentiated fear or apprehension of disturbance is not enough to overcome the right to freedom of expression." The Court then offered what is now a test of whether a student's private expression of opinion at school is protected speech: Conduct by the student, in class or out of it, which for any reason—whether it stems from time, place, or type of behavior—materially disrupts classwork or involves substantial disorder or invasion of the rights of others is, of course, not immunized by the constitutional guarantee of freedom of speech. Students do have a constitutional right to freedom of speech and expression while at school as long as the speech does not *materially disrupt* the educational environment or *substantially disorder or invade the rights of others* (Lam, 2002, p. 2).

Two other key Supreme Court cases—*Bethel School District No. 403 v. Fraser*, 478 U.S. 675, 682 (1986), and *Hazelwood School District v. Kuhlmeier*, 484 U.S. 260 (1988)—stand in contrast to *Tinker*, as both rein in students' speech at school. In *Fraser*, the Court held that a student's lewd speech at a school assembly was not constitutionally protected, reaffirming the principal cited in *New Jersey v. T.L.O.* 496 U.S. 325, 340-342 (1985), that "the constitutional rights of students in public schools are not automatically coextensive with the rights of adults in other settings." In *Hazelwood*, the Court found the First Amendment is not violated by educators exercising reasonable editorial powers over a school newspaper (Lam, 2002, p. 3).

In *Arnett v. Kennedy*, 416 U.S. 134 (1974), the Supreme Court balanced governmental interests and employee rights and this time sustained the constitutionality of a federal statute that authorized removal or suspension without pay of an employee "for such cause as will promote the efficiency of the service," where the "cause" cited was an employee's speech. The employee's speech in this case, however, consisted in falsely and publicly accusing the director of his agency of bribery. The Court interpreted the statute to proscribe only that public speech which improperly damages and impairs the reputation and efficiency of the employing agency, and it thus imposes no greater controls on the behavior of federal employees as are necessary for the protection of the government as employer. The decision is not directed exclusively at speech but at employee behavior including speech that negatively affects the efficiency of the employing agency.

In *Garcetti v. Ceballos*, 547 U.S. at 418 (1988), the Court wrote that, if an employee did not speak as a citizen on a matter of public concern, then "the employee has no First Amendment cause of action based on his or her employer's reaction to the speech."

These cases demonstrate that the First Amendment has limitations: the Court will consider time, place, manner of expression, and organizational and individual impact in determining whether the speech is protected or not; that is, it will consider context. Thus threat assessment professionals should consider, assess, and document contextual issues in conducting their assessments.

Relevant Restrictions and Exceptions to Constitutional Law

There are other exceptions to civil rights that can assist with threat management. The Second Amendment, the right to bear arms, has limitations that have been carved out by various state and federal statutes, something which continues to evolve. High-profile events—such as the December 2012 mass shooting at the Sandy Hook Elementary School in Newtown, Connecticut—often result in a public outcry to restrict access to firearms, debate between opposing interests such as the National Rifle Association and victims' groups, and adjustments to these rights. At the time of this writing, this process was in full swing in the United States.

If an individual has been subject to certain kinds of restraining orders, has been arrested for domestic violence or threats, is on probation or parole, or has been convicted of a felony, he or she is usually banned from possessing firearms and other weaponry. To legally purchase a firearm, an individual must now go through a background check for these kinds of issues and will also be asked about any mental health history. In California, if an individual has been involuntarily hospitalized for mental health reasons, particularly if he or she has been kept longer than 72 hours, the institution is supposed to notify the Department of Justice, thus subjecting the individual to a firearms prohibition. Such a prohibition cannot be reversed without a court proceeding. Although individuals may certainly acquire illegal or black market firearms, these kinds of legal restrictions make it more difficult for anyone to procure them legally. In threat cases where these issues may apply, it is often the case that the local authorities have not adequately addressed these prohibitions.

School-Specific Threat Management Statutes and Case Law

Several laws in the United States are directly relevant to school and campus threat management situations (Lam, 2002). The Federal Gun Free Schools Act (GFSA) of 1994 mandates that every state receiving funds under the Elementary and Secondary Education Act (ESEA) must have a law that mandates a minimum one-year expulsion for any student caught carrying a firearm to school. It also mandates reporting to local law enforcement for appropriate action. The expulsion requirement may be modified on a case-by-case basis by the local chief administering officer. School districts do not violate the GFSA if they provide educational services in an alternative setting to a student who has been expelled from her or his regular school. All local educational agencies receiving ESEA funds must refer any student who brings a firearm to school to the criminal or juvenile justice system. The GFSA specifically requires that it must be implemented in a manner consistent with the Individuals with Disabilities Education Act (IDEA) (Mohandie, 2000).

Under the IDEA, school personnel may deal with a student with a disability who carries a weapon to school or to a school function by removing him or her to an interim placement for up to 45 days. This interim placement can be extended for an additional 45-day period if a hearing officer determines that it would be dangerous to return the student to his or her normal placement. Appropriate educational services must be provided to the student at the alternative site. IDEA does not permit discipline that changes a student's placement, such as an expulsion, if the student's behavior was a manifestation of his or her disability. IDEA does make clear that school personnel can report crimes committed by students with disabilities to appropriate authorities. If a student with a disability brings a firearm to school, a school district can comply with both the GFSA and the IDEA by using the provision of the GFSA that permits modification of the expulsion requirement on a case-by-case basis (Mohandie, 2000).

Privacy in school settings is another issue: federal laws bar the disclosure of medical information except under defined circumstances, and laws such as the Family Educational Rights and Privacy Act (FERPA) mandate the privacy of student records and prohibit disclosure of academic and disciplinary issues to anyone other than those who have a legitimate need to know. Institutions should define those involved with threat assessment on campus as having a legitimate need to know this information (Deisinger, Randazzo, O'Neill, & Savage, 2008). FERPA provisions also include exceptions that allow information sharing in the case of emergency situations and/or situations where public safety is a concern. Of note, according to the US Department of Education (2008), when a student turns 18 years old or enters a postsecondary institution at any age, all rights afforded to parents under FERPA transfer to the student. However, FERPA also provides ways in which schools may share information with parents without the student's consent. Schools may disclose education records to parents if the student is a dependent for income tax purposes, if a health or safety emergency involves a son or daughter; and if the student who is under age 21 has violated any law or its policy concerning the use or possession of alcohol or a controlled substance. Communicating

with parents or guardians under such legally defined exceptional circumstances may further buttress threat assessment and intervention efforts.

Guidance issued by the US Department of Education since the massacre at Virginia Tech clarified that it is up to the individual institution to decide whether there is an emergency or public safety concern (Deisinger et al., 2008). Further, it does not extend to communications, observations, and other forms of information that members of the threat assessment team may need to share, such as materials that are not written down. FERPA also does not apply to the records of law enforcement units; thus some schools may wish to have the threat assessment team under the umbrella of their police department, designated law enforcement entity, or unsworn security operation (Deisinger et al. 2008).

Many states have enacted laws that mandate programs to address school safety and documentation of violence that occurs during the school year. For example, California has the California Comprehensive School Safety Plan (Mohandie, 2000).

With regard to oral threats in school, a Ninth Circuit case, *Lovell by and through Lovell v. Poway Unified School District*, 90 F.3d 367 (1996), illustrates both leakage and the court's reaction to it. Sarah Lovell, a 15-year-old tenth grader at Mt. Carmel High School in Poway, California, visited her guidance counselor to request a schedule change. After several hours of confusion relating to the rearrangement of Lovell's classes, the counselor told her that another administrator had placed her in overloaded classes. At that point, Lovell told the counselor, "If you don't give me this schedule change, I'm going to shoot you!" The counselor reported Lovell's conduct to an assistant principal and "told [him] that she felt threatened by the statement and was concerned about some future reprisal by Lovell." The Ninth Circuit Court of Appeals held that Lovell's conduct was not protected by the First Amendment or by any other federal or state law. The court noted that it was not required to consult the US Supreme Court cases governing students' on campus free speech rights because "threats such as Lovell's are not entitled to First Amendment protection in any forum." The fact that the threat was made by a student in the school context did not matter. In analyzing that issue, the Ninth Circuit returned to the doctrine formulated by the US Supreme Court in *Watts v. United States, supra,* to address threats in the First Amendment context where the Court distinguished between a "true threat" and mere political hyperbole. Although political hyperbole and other "uninhibited, robust, and wide-open" debates on public issues are protected by the First Amendment, true threats are not. The issue, the Court explained, is how to distinguish a threat from constitutionally protected speech.

In *United States v. Orozco-Santillan*, 903 F.2d 1262 (1990), the court, taking note of the *Watts* true threat doctrine, referred to past cases that defined a threat as "an expression of an intention to inflict evil, injury, or damage on another." *Orozco-Santillan* also offers an "objective standard" for evaluating whether a statement constitutes a true threat and is thus unprotected by the First Amendment: "whether a reasonable person would foresee that the statement would be interpreted by those to whom the maker communicates the statement as a serious expression of intent to harm or assault." The court added that "Alleged threats should be considered in light of their entire factual context, including the surrounding events and [the] reaction of the listeners" (*United States v. Orozco-Santillan, 1990; Lam, 2002, p. 4*).

Cases involving students' written speech—in the form of threatening or potentially violent poems, notes, or Internet websites—are further testing the boundaries of the First Amendment. *LaVine v. Blaine School District*, 257 F.3d 981 (2001), involved a California eleventh grader whose poem, "Last Words," led to his temporary emergency expulsion. After a 17-day absence, following a psychiatric evaluation and counseling at the district's expense, LaVine was allowed to return to school. Nonetheless, because of a dispute between the LaVine family and the school district regarding how their son's expulsion was characterized in his school file, the family sued, alleging violation of James LaVine's First Amendment rights. After determining that LaVine's poem fell under the purview of *Tinker, supra*, the Ninth Circuit employed a "totality of the relevant facts" analysis and ultimately ruled that the school district did not violate LaVine's First Amendment rights. The court explained that "Taken together and given the backdrop of actual school shootings, we hold that these circumstances were sufficient to have led school authorities reasonably to forecast substantial disruption of or material interference with school activities—specifically, that James was intending to inflict injury upon himself or others." (Lam, 2002, pp. 4-5).

D. G. v. Independent Sch. Dist. No. 11, 2000 U.S. Dist. LEXIS 12197 (N.D. Okla. Aug. 21, 2000), also involved a student who was disciplined for a writing with themes of violence—a poem written by an eleventh-grade student entitled "Killing Mrs.

[Teacher]." The Court looked to both *Watts* and *Tinker* for guidance. After assessing the student's intent and the school district's response to the poem, it decided that, according to the *Tinker* test of "material disruption" or "substantial interference," the district had violated D. G.'s First Amendment rights. The court therefore granted D. G.'s motion for a preliminary injunction prohibiting the district from suspending her. The court also weighed in on zero-tolerance policies, using both the *Watts* "true threat" doctrine and the *Tinker* standard as benchmarks for punishing student speech (Lam, 2002, p. 5). They ruled on the impossibility of having a "no tolerance" policy against "threats" if the threats involve speech.

> A student cannot be penalized for what they are thinking. If those thoughts are then expressed in speech, the ability of the school to censor or punish the speech will be determined by whether it was (1) a "true" or "genuine" threat, or (2) disruptive of the normal operation of the school. Neither of those circumstances exist in the case before the [c]ourt. In sum, the court finds that any commotion caused by the poem did not rise to the level of a substantial disruption required to justify a suspension of [student].

The Internet is a developing area in terms of the law as it relates to students' First Amendment rights against the needs of educators to keep their schools safe. Only a few cases illuminate the current state of the law with regard to student speech in this (usually) off-campus forum. In *J. S. v. Bethlehem Area School District*, 569 Pa. 638 (Pa. 2002), J. S., an eighth grader, posted a website entitled "Teacher Sux" from his home computer, which made offensive comments about his algebra teacher and principal and used vulgar and profane language to describe them and their alleged activities. It included a section titled "Why Should [the teacher] Die?" that featured a drawing of his teacher with her head cut off and blood dripping from her neck as well as a solicitation for $20 per viewer so that J. S. could fund a hit man to kill her. An anonymous email about the website was sent to a teacher at the school, who in turn alerted the principal about the online posting. The principal contacted local law enforcement and the FBI. After both agencies identified J. S. as the creator of the website, the district suspended him for 3 days, which was modified after a hearing to a 10-day suspension. The district also initiated expulsion hearings. J. S. and his parents challenged the decision in state courts. The Court used *Tinker, Fraser,* and *Lovell* as well as other cases dealing with the issue of whether students may be disciplined for conduct occurring off school premises. Concluding that "it is evident that the courts have allowed school officials to discipline students for conduct occurring off of school premises where it is established that the conduct materially and substantially interferes with the educational process," the court affirmed a lower court's decision that the school district did not violate J. S.'s rights by expelling him in response to his website (Lam, 2002, p. 6).

The *Boman* and *D. G.* courts, using nearly identical language, ruled that following a threat, school districts are justified in taking some time to determine whether it poses a potential hazard to school safety. Thus short-term suspensions may be warranted. But once the school district has "gathered the facts...and the context of the [threat becomes] clear," if there is no danger—and if the speech is not covered by *Kuhlmeier, Fraser,* or *Tinker*—then it is protected by the First Amendment and further discipline of the student is unwarranted (Lam, 2002, p. 9).

Threat Assessment Team Documentation

Another important issue in school-based threat assessment cases is protecting the confidentiality of information generated by the threat assessment team, given that documentation is critical for a variety of reasons (Mohandie, this volume, Chapter 8). This file should be treated as a confidential file and secured in a manner that limits accessibility as much as possible to those who "need to know." One goal is to limit the subject's potential access in order to protect information sources and methods, while another is to avoid giving the subject something new to obsess about or perceive grievance over. It has been suggested by some (Deisinger, Randazzo, O'Neil, & Savage, 2008) that housing the threat assessment team records within the campus law enforcement or security operation may provide such extra protection for those records as well as allowing 24/7 access, particularly in settings that have 24-hour operations. They opine, citing the US Department of Education, that law enforcement unit records "created and maintained by these law enforcement units are not considered education records subject to FERPA" (Deisinger et al., 2008, p. 78). According to the US Department of Education, it appears that it is important to ensure that no personally identifiable information from the student's educational record be blended with the law enforcement unit records. Otherwise the usual protections afforded FERPA materials might apply, including, potentially, subject access to such files.

Duty to Warn

Individuals who are subject to threat investigations have often had contact with mental health professionals, with such treatment and evaluation usually protected by the legal concept of privilege (federal and state) and the ethical issue of confidentiality (American Psychological Association, 2010). However, there are recognized allowable exceptions and mandates to breach such protections, codified at the state and federal levels, known as *Duty to Warn* and *Duty to Protect* obligations that usually involve notifying the intended victim and police when a threat is made by a patient in the presence of a mental health professional. These laws usually apply to mental health professionals but might also be relevant to other professionals who have a "special relationship" with a subject or potential victims. The genesis of these exceptions and mandates was the landmark California case *Tarasoff v. UC Board of Regents,* 17 Ca.3d 425 (1976), and its further refinement in the *Ewing v. Goldstein,* 120 Cal.App.4th 807 (2004) decision. These cases and laws often have bearing on threat assessment matters when that warning call is made to a potential victim, making the company or other potential target aware, often for the first time, that there is a potential danger. Knowledge of these legal issues may give threat assessment professionals a tool to persuade treating mental health professionals to provide critical feedback during high-risk scenarios when the subject is in treatment.

The *Tarasoff* case stemmed from a 1969 university-based stalking and homicide case and mandates a duty to warn the intended victim and the police in the event of a serious threat of physical harm being made against a reasonably identifiable victim or victims. It has been codified and clarified in the California Civil Code. An interesting development, however, is the amplification of this in *Ewing v. Goldstein* as stated by the court:

> The intent of the statute is clear. A therapist has a duty to warn if, and only if, the threat which the therapist has learned—whether from the patient or *a family member*—actually leads him or her to believe the patient poses a risk of grave bodily injury to another person.

The expanded duty from now on applies to credible threats received from the patient, or the patient's family; however, the court made clear that its decision did not go beyond "family members."

When it is discovered that an offender is in current or was in recent mental health treatment, further amplification of these legal notification issues is a distinct possibility as wrongful death and other personal injury related litigation unfold. The treatment provider is often at the center of these adversarial matters. Whatever the outcome in such events, each case stands as a potential example of the critical identification role that—by virtue of the legal duties to warn and/or protect—treating mental health professionals play in prospective threat assessment. Generally speaking, privacy and privilege end where public peril begins.

Involuntary Hospitalization and Other Civil Commitment Issues

There are a variety of state laws that allow involuntary mental health-related hospitalization and other civil commitment procedures. In most states (Florida under the Baker Act and California under Welfare and Institutions Code 5150, for example), individuals may be involuntarily hospitalized for defined lengths of time in a locked mental health facility based upon having a mental health disorder and having been assessed as a danger to self, danger to others, or gravely disabled to the extent that they are unable to care for themselves. The typical procedure involves initial suspicion and documentation to support holding the person against his or her will for further evaluation and assessment, often up to 72 hours. At this point or sometimes earlier, the person may be released or kept after a hearing for additional time, which may involve days, weeks, or longer, depending upon the issues. The individual is afforded various due process protections that include regular hearings, during which evidence is presented to support and refute the need for additional commitment time. In tandem with many of these state-level commitment procedures may also be firearms removal and prohibitions, whereby the commitment facility must notify the US Department of Justice (the entity that conducts background checks for firearm purchase applications) of the involuntary hospitalization.

Other commitment procedures include conservatorship proceedings to remove the person's right to make decisions for himself or herself and may also include mandated lengthier periods of institutionalization (often up to a year), as is the case in California. These laws are often used to remove dangerous people from access to potential victims during high-risk windows of vulnerability, confine them for treatment, establish external behavioral control, and create structure after release. However, because individuals do get released and can obtain weapons illegally, it is important for threat assessment professionals to monitor their presence in these systems.

Restraining and Other Protective Orders

Restraining orders are sometimes sought as a tool in threat assessment investigations. Such orders, which may be issued by a civil or criminal court, preclude the subject from harassing or approaching the victim. Many other conditions and boundaries may be sought and obtained in threat situations, including firearms bans, the surrender of computer equipment, and restrictions upon where the offender may travel. Restraining orders were noted to improve control of the subject 60% of the time but were violated 40% of the time, with escalation noted in 21% of the latter cases (Spitzberg, 2002). Thus restraining orders are a potential legal tool that may be helpful in many cases but need close monitoring to assess their true efficacy in individual cases.

Bail, probation, and parole conditions are parameters established by the courts and criminal justice systems for arrestees and offenders being considered for release. These legal strategies have the added advantage of immediate arrest or return to confinement based upon violations and can be very effective for managing threat subjects. The threat of going back to jail or prison is sometimes sufficient to maintain the compliance of many subjects; certainly there is utility in the confinement of those who are not compliant.

THE EUROPEAN SITUATION

Europe is a continent with 46 different states and a corresponding number of discrete jurisdictions. There are notable differences between diverse legal traditions of European countries regarding the government role in protecting citizens from threatening, harassing, and violent behavior. This backdrop has a direct impact on the legislative process and determines whether laws are introduced that support a threat management oriented approach as well as available legal procedures to intervene when a citizen is a target of harassment or aggression. As a general trend over the past three decades within the western world, interpersonal violence is considered more and more unacceptable. Historically, for example, a man assaulting his wife or children was seen as doing no more than engaging in unpleasant behavior. Officially, such actions resided in the realm of private life and were far away from being legally relevant. This began to change in the final quarter of the last century, when the women's movement gradually gained more social influence. Domestic violence was criminalized. Years later, following the United States, a number of European countries identified and codified stalking as illegitimate and illegal behavior.

Antistalking Laws in Europe and Their Influence on Threat Management

The discipline of threat assessment focuses not only on isolated acts of aggression but also tries to identify and assess patterns of problematic behaviors that may lead to violence—that is, violent pathways that are unfolding. In Europe, the juridical discussion on stalking opened the door for an initial examination of threat assessment in such a way. In 1997, the United Kingdom was the first European member state that passed antistalking legislation. As of 2009, nine European states had introduced special laws against stalking (De Fazio, 2009). An awakening awareness of risk issues by public authorities went hand in hand with antistalking legislation. The European legislative focus thus shifted from distinct acts of violence to patterns of problematic behavior, which advanced the threat assessment perspective.

These changes were reflected in police interventions following the introduction of antistalking laws. Police officers started to take a much more proactive approach—for example, engaging in the "knock and talk" strategy for confronting the stalker face to face to stop the harassing behavior. Research has shown that such an offensive strategy by the police is often helpful (Williams, Lane, & Zona, 1996). Police officers, particularly those dealing regularly with stalking, have evolved in their appreciation and approach to dangerousness assessment. They no longer restrict their emphasis to seemingly isolated acts of behavior as the only risk marker, and have begun to take on a broader approach to problem identification and threat assessment. Having the stalking statute in mind, officers started to look for patterns of actions.

Such a perspective of course fits better with the philosophy of threat assessment.

This assumption is supported by a study comparing police efficacy between countries with and without antistalking laws (Hoffmann, Özsöz & Voß, 2004). Stalking victims were asked about the effectiveness of police intervention in Germany prior to the introduction of an antistalking law and concurrently in England, where antistalking legislation had already been in effect for several years. The results revealed significant differences: in England, stalking victims asked much earlier for police support, the intervention of the officers was perceived as much more successful than in Germany, and in both countries an aggressive police intervention including confronting the stalker was rated as the most effective strategy. The study demonstrated that having a stalking legal statute directly influenced the effectiveness of police work in such cases as well as the willingness of stalking victims to report concerning behavior to police or other agencies, thus enabling prospective threat assessment to occur.

Involuntary Hospitalization in Europe

Like the United States, most European countries adopt a high threshold for involuntary hospitalization and compelled psychiatric treatment. There are a few European jurisdictions—such as England and Wales—where compulsory detention is not exclusively based on dangerousness criteria but can be undertaken in the interests of the individual's health (James, Farnham, & Wilson, this volume, Chapter 20). These legal boundaries are important factors in threat assessment work. A case example is illustrative. In Germany, a delusional young man fixated for several years on a female public figure and then followed and harassed her in a severely disturbing manner. The stalker suffered from erotomania and therefore was convinced that he had a romantic relationship with this celebrity. His approach to this public figure was intended to reestablish the romantic bond. His delusional state was very apparent in his numerous communications. Although mental health services and police were actively involved in the case, they had no legal ground to bring the young man into treatment against his will, so his harassment continued. The stalker then pursued another female public figure in another European country. In this country there was a lower legal threshold for involuntary mental health treatment, so the young man was hospitalized for several months and treated with medication. His mental condition improved and he returned to Germany. To date, he occasionally writes odd letters to the German celebrity but no approach attempts or more serious stalking behavior toward her or any other public figure have been reported since the intervention.

In most European countries, a requirement for involuntary hospitalization is an acute danger of harm against others or suicidal tendencies. When a threatening subject is brought to a mental institution it is typical that the psychiatrist must quickly decide whether or not the person poses a real risk and is responsible to present supporting evidence to a judge. If a threat assessment expert is already involved in the case and aware of the legal situation, she or he can actively support the psychiatric system. The coauthor of this chapter has often served in this role and proactively provided input to mental health professionals conducting these assessments. Procedurally, it is clarified up front that the intent is to provide written or verbal documentation of the subject's threatening or other concerning behavior and not to influence the psychiatrist in an unethical or partisan manner. The preparation of a fact-based report with traceable information sources may assist the evaluating mental health expert to convince the judge, as appropriate, that there is risk of violence and the necessity of a higher level of care (involuntary or continued involuntary hospitalization) to mitigate violence risk. Supporting the psychiatrist with critical information can often help place potentially dangerous individuals in treatment, thus lowering the probability of a later assault and imminent dangerousness during the period of institutionalization.

Privacy Protection and Data Security in a European Context

Regulations concerning privacy not only vary across European countries but sometimes even within different regions of the same country, as in Switzerland. In establishing interdisciplinary threat assessment networks and teams, it proves helpful to consider privacy protection and data security from the very beginning forward. One example of an interdisciplinary group is the Fixated Threat Assessment Centre (FTAC), based in London, whose mission is to protect the British Royal Family and politicians from assaults and other forms of threatening and disturbing acts. The FTAC consists of police experts and health care professionals within interdisciplinary teams. Owing to privacy

protection, each group has access only to databases of their own profession (James, Farnham, & Wilson, this volume, Chapter 20). Another example is the newly formed threat management group in the Swiss canton of Solothurn: there, police officers, psychologists, psychiatrists, and representatives of public authorities work together on cases. The data protection official of Solothurn was part of the project from the very beginning, which led to an amendment in local data protection laws supporting the threat management team's efforts within a better operational foundation.

Forming threat assessment teams inside of organizations like companies, universities, or schools is usually not as difficult from a privacy protection perspective. It is often sufficient to define that team as an official professional group inside the organization with mandatory rules of confidentiality and data protection.

INTERNATIONAL SURVEY OF THE LEGAL FRAMEWORK FOR THREAT ASSESSMENT PROFESSIONALS

While preparing this chapter the authors developed an online questionnaire that was distributed to international threat assessment experts with whom they were professionally associated. The study aimed to determine the legal basis supporting practical threat assessment casework in their respective jurisdictions, their experiences with a number of different types of laws, and areas for improvement. It was hoped that this preliminary, nonrandom inquiry could inform legal commonalities and nuances between international jurisdictions. We would like to thank our colleagues for their participation in this study.

Sample Description

The questionnaire was completed by 56 threat assessment experts (65% male, 35% female) from nine different countries: Australia (7%), Canada (7%), Germany (13%), Great Britain (9%), Luxembourg (2%), Netherlands (5%), Sweden (3%), Switzerland (29%) and the United States (25%). The experts had different professional backgrounds, the largest group being psychologists (34%), followed by police officers (21%), corporate threat assessment professionals (13%) and other private security experts (7%), psychiatrists (11%), members of domestic violence support organizations (5%), legal experts (5%), and university threat assessment professionals (4%).

In their casework, these threat assessment experts address a number of issues, with most handling cases involving different forms of violence and threatening behavior. Eighty-four percent had been involved in stalking cases, 60% domestic violence, 58% workplace violence, 47% threatening behavior against public figures, 44% targeted violence in schools, 36% targeted violence in universities, and 18% terrorism.

Antistalking Laws
71% of the experts worked in a country where antistalking laws were in effect. Of those professionals, 73% applied such laws in casework, with 38% reporting positive, 3% negative, and 59% mixed experiences. A number of professionals criticized the inconsistent application of antistalking laws by police and prosecution. Others reported that the law was sometimes difficult to apply if no violence was present in the stalking case or the risk was assumed to be low. In some jurisdictions, the legal requirement of victim fear was seen as a problem, especially in public figure protection. As a positive aspect of antistalking laws, it was reported that such laws often facilitated mental health assessment and treatment of the stalker and provided a legal basis for police intervention.

Restraining Orders
Eighty-nine percent of the responding experts reported laws pertaining to restraining orders in their country. Of the threat assessment professionals who had experience with restraining orders in their casework (74%), 42% reported positive, 8% negative, and 50% mixed experiences. A frequent criticism was that restraining orders did not work well in serious cases or would sometimes destabilize or trigger the person of concern, leading to escalation of the case. The experts consistently warned that restraining orders should not automatically be the first option. Nevertheless, a number of professionals reported that restraining orders worked well in less serious cases.

Laws Against Making Threats
Antithreat laws were present in every country. Eighty-two percent of the threat assessment experts applied such a law, with 60% reporting positive, 7% negative, and 33% mixed experiences. It was reported that having such a law enabled police to act more expeditiously. It seemed to be more successful in lower-risk cases and had the potential to influence the threatener, especially when the subject had no previous experience with law enforcement or the criminal justice system.

Duty-to-Warn Law
Less than half of the experts (47%) reported a legal duty-to-warn obligation in their country. When such a law was present, 63% applied it, with 75% reporting positive, 6% negative, and 19% mixed experiences. It was seen as very helpful to be able to warn potential victims. The experts proposed broad-based training of all psychologists and psychiatrists in risk and threat assessment so that they would be better able to determine whether a patient poses a risk.

Laws That Allow Involuntary Psychiatric Hospitalization
Such laws are present in every country of practice among the polled experts. It was applied by 84% of the experts, with 41% reporting positive, 2% negative, and 57% mixed experiences. A repeated criticism was that such psychiatric interventions are often of short duration, resulting in the threatening person being prematurely released. It was also noted that information sharing and management (e.g., between the psychiatric and judicial systems) can be a problem. On the positive side, it was noted that such laws offer the possibility for immediate intervention and buy time to organize resources and establish greater control.

General Criminal Statutes Frequently Utilized to Manage Those Deemed to Be a Potential Risk (e.g., Illegal Weapon Possession, Trespassing)
As expected, such laws were present in every respondent country and were used by 62% of the experts for threat assessment work. Fifty-two percent reported positive, 12% negative, and 36% mixed experiences. In most cases, laws addressing weapons possession were applied, often resulting in the confiscation of guns from threatening individuals.

Data Privacy Laws
Data privacy laws were also present in every respondent's country. They were applied by 55% of the experts, with 18% reporting positive, 32% negative, and 50% mixed experiences. It was repeatedly noted by multiple respondents that data privacy laws make it difficult to share information with

other professionals as well as to obtain information from others. The overall impression was that threat assessment experts often operate in privacy law gray areas. One positive feature noted by respondents was that it was often helpful to protect victim data and information from being released to the offender.

Discussion

As a major result of the survey, it becomes evident that for all countries varying laws are applied on a regular basis by threat assessment experts, ranging from 55% to 84%, depending on statute. Legal foundations directly influence threat assessment and management. The experts from three continents seemed to have remarkably similar experiences with the diverse types of law. For all statutes except the data privacy law, the positive experiences outweigh the negative aspects in casework. Training and knowledge of the legal basis are important for every profession being involved in threat assessment. The importance of having legal experts on every threat assessment team or network should be emphasized.

CONCLUSION

We have attempted to provide a nonexhaustive yet representative overview of the legal contexts that threat assessment professionals may find themselves operating within and to familiarize the reader with various laws that might be relevant to threat management practice. That being said, neither of us is an attorney and this chapter should not be taken as a substitute for legal counsel. Access to legal counsel is a key component of threat assessment methodology.

ACKNOWLEDGMENTS

The authors would like to thank LA Unified School District Attorney Belinda Stith and San Diego District Attorney Rachel Solov for their tireless review and input into this chapter.

KEY POINTS

- Threat assessment and management occur within a legal context. It is imperative for threat assessment professionals to be aware of the laws that restrict threat management activities.

- In most democratic countries there is an important balancing act—regulated by conflicting laws—that compels the threat assessment professional to consider safety concurrently with the rights of the individual. Safety is generally the first consideration, with individual rights in close second.
- Legal issues include personal rights to privacy, weapon and firearm possession, freedom from unreasonable search and seizure, and freedom of expression. However, these rights, which are common to free societies, are not without limitation. It is these limitations that enable threat assessment professionals to respond and limit problematic behaviors.
- Criminal statutes are quite varied for dealing with threat cases and may include antistalking and criminal harassment, conspiracy to commit murder, attempted murder, terrorism, illegal weapons possession, criminal threats, assault, vandalism, trespassing, theft, domestic violence, explosives possession and manufacturing, child and elder abuse, public intoxication, and illegal immigration.
- Some legal techniques involve setting other limits on the subject's behavior, such as bail, probation, and parole conditions; civil and criminal restraining orders; involuntary hospitalization, civil commitments, and conservatorships; and other statutes that allow a person to be declared a dangerous or mentally disordered offender.

REFERENCES

American Psychological Association. (2010). *Ethical principles of psychologists and code of conduct with the 2010 Amendments.* Washington DC: author..

Arnett v. Kennedy (1974) 416 U.S. 134.

Bethel School District No. 403 v. Fraser (1986) 478 U.S. 675, 682.

Boman v. Bluestem Unified School District No. 205, 2000 U.S. Dist. LEXIS 5389, at 1,2.

Brandenburg v. Ohio (1969) 395 U.S. 444, 447.

Cohen, H. (October 16, 2009). *Freedom of speech and press: Exceptions to the First Amendment. CRS report for Congress.* Prepared for members and committees of Congress. Congressional Research Service. www.crs.gov

D. G. v. Independent Sch. Dist. No. 11 (2000) U.S. Dist. LEXIS 12197. (N.D. Okla. 2000)

De Fazio, L. (2009). The legal situation on stalking among the European member states. *European Journal on Criminology and Research,* 15 (3), 229–242.

Deisinger, G., Randazzo, M., O'Neill, D., & Savage, J. (2008). *The handbook for campus threat assessment and management teams.* Boston: Applied Risk Management.

Ewing v. Goldstein (2004) 120 Cal.App.4th 807.

Garcetti v. Ceballos (1988) 547 U.S. at 418.

Hazelwood School District v. Kuhlmeier (1988) 484 U.S. 260.

Hoffmann, J., Özsöz, F., & Voß, H.-G. (2004). Erfahrungen von Stalking-Opfern mit der deutschen Polizei. *Polizei & Wissenschaft, 4,* 41–53.

J. S. v. Bethlehem Area School District (Pa. 2002) 569 Pa. 638.

Lam, A. D. (2002). Student threats and the First Amendment. *School Law Bulletin,* XXXIII, 1–11.

LaVine v. Blaine School District (2001) 257 F.3d 981.

Lovell by and through Lovell v. Poway Unified School District (1996) 90 F.3d 367.

Miranda v. Arizona (1966) 384 U.S. 436.

Mohandie, K. (2000). *School violence threat management.* San Diego, CA: Specialized Training Services.

New Jersey v. T.L.O. (1985) 469 U.S. 325.

Rankin v. McPherson (1987) 483 U.S. 378, 380.

Schenck v. United States (1919) 249 U.S. 47, 52.

Spitzberg, B. (2002). The tactical typology of stalking victimization and management. *Trauma, Violence, and Abuse, 3,* 261-288.

State of Florida v. N.G.B. (Fla.2d *DCA 2002*) 806 So.2d 567.

State of New Hampshire v. Heirtzler (2001) 147 N.H. 344.

Tarasoff v. UC Board of Regents (1976) 17 Ca.3d 425.

Tinker v. Des Moines Independent Community School District (1969) 393 U.S. 503.

United States v. Orozco-Santillan (1990) 903 F.2d 1262.

United States v. Orozco-Santillan (9th Cir. Cal. 1990) 903 F.2d 1262, 1265.

Virginia v. Black (2003) 538 U.S. 343, 360-363.

Watts v. United States (1969) 394 U.S. 705, 708.

Williams, W. L., Lane, J., & Zona, M. A. (1996). Stalking: Successful intervention strategies. *The Police Chief, 2,* 24–26.

PART II

Fields of Practice

6

Workplace Targeted Violence

Threat Assessment Incorporating a Structured Professional Judgment Guide

STEPHEN G. WHITE

"Work is about a search for daily meaning as well as daily bread, for recognition as well as cash, for astonishment rather than torpor; in short, for a sort of life rather than a Monday through Friday sort of dying."

——STUDS TERKEL, *Working*

As a noted author of stories about common people, Studs Terkel (1972) suggests that work fulfills many needs and inevitably is part of our identity. Work may be uplifting, satisfying at the least, or present some of life's most painful setbacks. Frustration, conflict, and disappointment in varying degrees are unavoidable, posing personal challenges that must be navigated. In our work we are interdependent and only in partial control of our circumstances. Real or perceived injustice, losses, rejection, or wounded pride will lead some to varying degrees of emotional wounds, reacted to with aggression. A few will react violently, and a very small number will respond with homicidal violence.

The subject of this chapter is the assessment of workplace targeted or intended violence: the conscious decision to kill or physically harm identified or symbolic targets in a workplace or work context. Intended violence is consistent with predatory violence—planned, emotionless, and offensive—in contrast to affective violence, which is reactive, emotional, and defensive (Calhoun & Weston, 2003; Meloy, 1988, 2000, 2006). Contrary to repeated misstatements in the media, it is a myth that workplace perpetrators of such violence merely "snap": the attacks are not impulsive but are consciously planned (Hempel, Meloy, & Richards, 1999; Meloy, Hempel, Gray, Mohandie, Shiva, & Richards, 2004; White & Meloy, 2007).

Incidents of workplace targeted homicide account for approximately 25% to 30% of the annual number of workplace homicides, statistics that appear to be fairly stable (US Department of Justice: Office of Justice Programs, 2011; US Department of Labor: OSHA Administration, 2011). Workplace targeted violence is not an "epidemic," in spite of subjective or media led impressions. In 2010 there were approximately 177 victims in this category, or 34% of the total number of workplace homicides that year. The largest category of homicide in the workplace is accounted for by robberies and similarly motivated acts and is not the subject of this chapter. More frequent than homicide but commonly underreported (Chappell & DiMartino, 2006) are acts of nonfatal violence in the workplace: rape, sexual assault, robbery, and aggravated and simple assault. These crimes may involve different motives and vary as to how personal or impersonal the perpetrator's relationship is with the targeted individual or group. In 2009 there were at least 572,000 nonfatal violent crimes directed at individuals while at work or on duty. Those most at risk for nonfatal violence include law enforcement officers, security guards, mental health workers, bartenders, and sales employees (US Department of Justice: Office of Justice Programs, 2011; US Department of Labor: OSHA Administration, 2011). Workplace assaults are usually affective acts of violence but can be predatory, as in some cases of rape or sexual assault.

Numerous case studies and retrospective accounts (e.g., Calhoun & Weston, 2003; Kelleher,

1997; Meloy, 1997; Perline & Goldschmidt, 2004) reveal that homicidal targeted workplace violence begins with a deeply felt personal grievance, often the loss of a job or a significant career setback, at times with parallel personal losses, especially financial stress. An accumulation of difficulties and frustrations and resultant real or felt insults may contribute to the momentum toward violence. Amid a life often spiraling downward, the perpetrator escalates within a varying time frame along a "pathway to violence" to achieve his or her definition of justice (Borum, Fein, Vossekuil, & Bergland, 1999; Calhoun & Weston, 2003; Meloy, Hoffmann, Guldimann, & James, 2012; White & Meloy, 2007). These individuals usually perceive themselves as victims and believe that nonviolent alternatives to resolve differences are unattainable, frustrating and unsatisfactory, or untrustworthy. They possess a rigid "black or white" cognitive style, an often striking sense of entitlement, and a limited capacity for positive self-directed change. Their interpersonal histories are frequently replete with conflict and many ups and downs. Chronic anger, expressed or not, is common. The primary causal factors for some and a contribution to risk for others are troubling mental states—delusions, paranoia, and extreme moods, especially depression—that lead the individual to fixate on victims in the workplace. The scenario may be a highly personal one—for instance, rejection by an intimate partner resulting in violence at her workplace by her aggrieved husband or lover.

The violence may be clinically understood as rooted in an extreme sensitivity to *narcissistic injury,* a felt insult to one's sense of self or identity (Gilligan, 2003; Kohut, 1972); the wound is beyond the bounds of angry feelings experienced by more resilient employees following a job or career setback (Feldmann & Johnson, 1996). Angry remarks such as, "This job is my whole life," or, "I've given you everything!" often betray this deeply felt emotional state.

So unbearable is such a state of mind that the violent perpetrator is, in most instances, willing to sacrifice his or her own physical life, with a concluding act of suicide or by provoking a fatal response by law enforcement—a "suicide by cop" – in order to restore some final twisted sense of pride and self-importance (Feldmann & Johnson, 1996; Mohandie & Meloy, 2000; Perline & Goldschmidt, 2004). By destroying hated or envied others, he denies them what has been lost to him: life and its possibilities. In his eyes, by demonstrating ultimate power over his dismissive rejecters, he forces them to respect him (Gilligan, 2003). Rage fuels the decision but is unlikely to be felt immediately preceding or during the attack. For the workplace avenger, violent action is often an acceptable and final *solution* to his or her own assessment of the current circumstances, if not a dark reflection on a life unrealized.

Targeted violence is not only about individual risk factors, since it always occurs within an interpersonal context. The assessment of workplace violence includes situational and organizational risk factors. Those around an individual who is considering violence may be highly influential by ignoring, permitting, encouraging, or provoking a subject's violence (Borum et al., 1999; Denenberg & Braverman, 1999; Innes, Barling, & Turner, 2005; Monahan, 1986; White & Meloy, 2007).

Although classic literature reveals tales of "workplace murder," there are virtually no references to this category of crime in any systematic or statistical format prior to 1980 (Kelleher, 1997). In the following decade a number of high-profile workplace mass murders widely reported in the media created public awareness and concern about a relatively new perpetrator of violence: the disgruntled homicidal-suicidal employee. The field of workplace threat assessment and violence prevention has since emerged and is now widely practiced. An informed method to assess the risk of targeted violence in the contemporary western workplace, however, remained to be developed. A seminal monograph by Monahan (1981) concluded that clinicians did no better than chance in predicting violence. This led to new research efforts in violence risk assessment since that time, resulting in a robust body of continuing empirical and theoretical work (Otto & Douglas, 2010). Although numerous case studies have resulted in the recognition of widely accepted warning signs as well as an intuitive understanding of risk factors and their interaction, (e.g., Turner & Gelles, 2003), more systematic research on the predictors and conditions of workplace targeted violence is lacking (Schouten, 2008; Meloy et al., 2012). Schouten (2008) delineates various reasons why this is so. Among them are the shortage of perpetrators to study owing either to their death in the incident or their unwillingness to participate in research; the varying quality of information available from incidents, much of it coming from sensationalized or premature media counts; and court documents that reflect biased adversarial views of the perpetrator from opposing counsels. The reluctance of organizations to allow access to incident or contextual details in the inevitable legal aftermath of violent events is an additional factor.

Empirical evidence for the effectiveness of workplace-specific interventions to prevent targeted violence is also lacking. As Schouten (2008) points out, prospective controlled studies of employee and organizational risk characteristics for homicide with random assignment to intervention strategies are not possible for ethical and legal reasons. Risk management operational decisions rely largely on the application of "clinical judgment" (Binder, 2006), regardless of an intervener's specific professional discipline. Beck (2008, pp. 237-238) succinctly describes the circumstances and challenge for the assessment professional:

> *There is no substitute for clinical judgment* in assessing the risk of violence and in making the many decisions involved in treatment. Actuarial methods are helpful..., but only as background. For example, it helps to know that young people are more often violent than older people, that men are more often violent than women, that people brought up in violent circumstances are more likely to be violent than those brought up in safety, and so on. However, knowing all the actuarial data will not in the end serve to reduce the necessity for making a clinical assessment of risk. The person in the clinical encounter is unique; the circumstances of his or her life are unique and may be changing, rapidly or slowly, in ways that affect risk. It is the clinician's responsibility, difficult as this may be, to learn about this person and the circumstances of his or her life, and on this basis to make the best estimate of risk. This is true in all clinical settings.

THE WAVR-21[1]

The Workplace Assessment of Violence Risk, or WAVR-21, is an evidenced-based structured professional judgment (SPJ) guide for assessing workplace-related targeted violence risk in a systematic and organized manner (White & Meloy, 2007). Like other SPJ guides described in this text, the WAVR consists of empirically supported static and dynamic risk and protective factors. Selection of risk and protective-factor items was based on a review of research findings, existing case studies, the

professional literature, and the developers' extensive case experience. The WAVR-21, consistent with other SPJ guides, recognizes the essential role of clinical judgment in reaching decisions about risk, and its nature, severity, frequency, and imminence in individual cases. Structured guides should ideally assist assessment professionals in formulating a comprehensible "anchored narrative" of practical use by the professional's clientele who need to know how the subject, in light of past and present circumstances, is likely to respond to possible future events and scenarios (Hart, 2011a). SPJ guides also bolster the defense of risk management strategies in any litigation subsequent to a case. According to Monahan (2008), courts uniformly find risk assessments based on the use of structured instruments to be admissible scientific evidence.

The WAVR-21 includes 19 risk factors, one protective factor, and an organizational impact factor, the last being not a risk factor per se but almost always important in assessing and managing workplace threat cases. The first five items are considered "red flag" indicators, as they assess violent motives, ideation, intent, weapons skill, and preattack planning: late-stage behaviors along the pathway to violence. Additional items assess the contribution of mental disorder, negative personality factors, and organizational and situational factors. The full WAVR-21 "grid" (see Table 6.1) may be used by qualified clinicians sufficiently trained in risk assessment and familiar enough with workplace contexts, human resource and employment law principles, and organizational dynamics. The items are coded either "absent," "present," or "prominent," and definitions of these three levels are provided for each item. Raters may also indicate dynamic change for any item. An accompanying manual describes the items in detail, including inquiry questions and supportive research literature (White and Meloy, 2007).

The WAVR-21 is not a psychological test and there are no norms. A reliability study of the instrument included 11 raters who each rated 12 randomly assigned cases from actual files of workplace threat scenarios (Meloy, White, & Hart, in press). Summary interrater reliability correlation coefficients (ICCs) for overall presence of risk factors, risk of violence, and seriousness of the violent act were in the fair to good range, similar to those of other SPJ instruments. A rating group of only psychologists produced an ICC of 0.76 for summary rating of violence risk, which is in the excellent range. Some of

TABLE 6.1. WAVR-21 CODING GRID

1. Motives for Violence	12. Anger Problems
2. Homicidal Ideas, Violent Fantasies or Preoccupation	13. Depression and Suicidality
3. Violent Intentions and Expressed Threats	14. Paranoia and Other Psychotic Symptoms
4. Weapons Skill and Access	15. Substance Abuse
5. Pre-Attack Planning and Preparation	16. Isolation
6. Stalking or Menacing Behavior	17. History of Violence, Criminality, and Conflict
7. Current Job Problems	18. Domestic/Intimate Partner Violence
8. Extreme Job Attachment	19. Situational and Organizational Contributors to Violence
9. Loss, Personal Stressors and Negative Coping	20. Stabilizers and Buffers Against Violence
10. Entitlement and Other Negative Traits	21. Organizational Impact of Real or Perceived Threats
11. Lack of Conscience and Irresponsibility	

the individual items had poor reliability, likely due to both clinical and statistical reasons. Predictive validity studies—the true test of an instrument's ability to correctly identify violent individuals before the fact—are the next step in the development of the WAVR-21. Such studies are sophisticated and expensive; they require large sample sizes owing to the issue of base rates: Among those individuals who make threats or create concern, only a very few ever commit a workplace homicide (Hart & Logan, 2011).

Contributing significantly to the content, language, and queries of the WAVR-21 is the threat assessment approach developed largely by Fein et al. (1995), Fein & Vossekuil (1998, 1999), and Borum et al. (1999); their research concerned targeted violence toward public figures—specifically the protectees of the US Secret Service but also some celebrities and CEOs of major corporations. This fact-based approach focuses on ideas, motives, emotions, and behaviors that may lead to violent action. Similar notions parallel this line of thinking: for example, De Becker's (1997) JACA formulation that the subject feels *justified* in using violence, believes that *alternatives* to violence will not achieve the desired outcome, and considers the *consequences* of violence to be acceptable; in addition, the subject possesses the *ability* to act violently. Hart and Logan (2011) refer to decision theory in proposing that violence is a choice and is preceded by a four-step thought process of varying time frames on the part of the subject: the thought of acting violently is entertained, the act would pay off in some manner, any negative consequences are considered acceptable, and finally a method is chosen on how to gain access to and attack the target or targets.

These pathway-to-violence factors—cognitive, emotional, and behavioral—are incorporated into the WAVR-21. The tool can be applied to workplace crises or evolving situations as well as to those cases developing more slowly where concern about risk exists but without the urgency of a crisis. Although the threat assessment approach in the workplace de-emphasizes the role of major mental disorders, it does not dismiss them. The focus is more on acute symptoms and their contribution to pathway behaviors than on diagnostic categories per se. Knowing the diagnosis of a subject's mental disorder that is contributing to risk is often very relevant to risk management decisions.

Following is a description of the WAVR-21 items—the 19 risk factors, a stabilizing factor, and the organizational impact factor as currently defined in the WAVR-21 second edition manual (White & Meloy, 2010). The risk factors are identified as either static or dynamic: whether or not they are changeable through intervention.

1. *Motives for Violence*: Evidence of a felt motive to act violently as a legitimate means to address a grievance or achieve an objective; e.g., to seek revenge or "justice," end pain, gain notoriety, or bring attention to or solve a problem. This is generally a dynamic factor.

2. *Homicidal Ideas, Violent Fantasies or Preoccupation*: Homicidal ideation or thoughts especially toward anyone in the workforce; preoccupation with violent themes, fantasies, weapons, or violent groups; approval of violence, especially workplace violence; and identification with perpetrators of violence. This is generally a dynamic factor.

3. *Violent Intentions and Expressed Threats*: Any threats, specific plans, or

expressed intentions to harm any members of the workforce (e.g., spoken, written, electronic, or symbolic); a time imperative may indicate a more imminent intention to act. This is generally a dynamic factor.

4. *Weapons Access and Skill*: Firearms or weapons possession and skill; evidence of bringing weapons to the workplace. This is generally a static factor (i.e., once attained, skill does not usually decrease). However, the factor is dynamic in that access can be interrupted and prevented.

5. *Preattack Planning and Preparation*: Preparations for violence: planning and/ or practice; increased weapons acquisition; access to potential targets; research to increase knowledge of targets' whereabouts; or actions to increase access to targets. This is a dynamic factor.

6. *Stalking and Menacing Behavior*: Stalking; current case-related pattern of fear-inducing harassment; covert or deceptive contact with a target-victim; probing of targeted victims' physical boundaries; defiance of workplace rules or authority; security breaches or attempts. This is a dynamic factor as it is not meant to refer to past history but to current, case-related behavior.

7. *Current Job Problems*: Recent or likely termination; significant performance, conduct, or job status issues; pattern of under- or unemployment over a period of months or years. This can be either a static or dynamic factor depending on the case.

8. *Extreme Job Attachment*: Strong personal and emotional attachment to job; significant discrepancy between the employee's and the employer's view of his or her work contribution. This can be either a static or dynamic factor depending on the case.

9. *Loss, Personal Stressors, and Negative Coping*: Observable stress, desperation, despair, or humiliation in reaction to a significant loss, death, rejection, or setback (e.g., death of a family member, breakup of a marriage or relationship, loss of status, financial resources, property, or good health; failed civil actions); generally very poor coping ability when stressed. Loss per se is usually a static factor, whereas stressors

can be either static or dynamic. Negative coping is a dynamic factor.

10. *Entitlement and Other Negative Traits*: Strong sense of entitlement and self-centeredness; very defensive, blaming of others, intolerant; "black or white" thinking; preoccupation with felt insults; holds grudges; vindictive. This is most likely a static factor, since it is related to personality traits, including narcissism.

11. *Lack of Conscience and Irresponsibility*: Callous disregard for or exploitation of others; lack of remorse for wrongdoing; habitual lying; habitual pattern of violating work policies or laws. This is a static factor as it is related to personality traits, specifically psychopathy.

12. *Anger Problems*: Angry outbursts; "ready to explode" appearance; impulsive reactions to frustration; physical displays of anger (e.g., throwing objects, property destruction, vandalism; pattern of bullying, belligerence, intimidation; expression of anger leads to noteworthy fear in others; escalation in expressions of anger over days or weeks, or sudden absence of chronic anger). This can be either a static (trait anger), dynamic factor (anger related to a particular context or issue), or both.

13. *Depression and Suicidality*: Notably depressed mood, strong feelings of hopelessness or "nothing to lose"; suicidal ideas or actions, including history of attempts; anger associated with depressed mood or suicidal feelings; noncompliance with recommended mental health treatment. Depression is usually a dynamic factor but it can also be static. Suicidality is a dynamic factor.

14. *Paranoia and Other Psychotic Symptoms*: Persecutory or delusional beliefs or hallucinations, especially if linked to an intention to attack perceived enemies; highly elevated, grandiose mood; impulsive behavior; agitation; anger or acts of violence associated with any of the above; noncompliance with mental health treatment for any of the above. This can be either a static or dynamic factor.

15. *Substance Abuse*: Alcohol abuse or dependence; amphetamine/cocaine

abuse or dependence; other drug abuse or dependence; anger expression and/or violence associated with alcohol or drug abuse or dependence; recent history of treatment noncompliance for drug or alcohol problems. This is a dynamic factor.

16. *Isolation*: Active avoidance of social and intimate bonds; increasing preference for isolation. This is usually a static factor as it generally refers to a personality trait. But when it is dynamic (i.e., the individual is becoming more withdrawn), it warrants greater concern.

17. *History of Violence, Criminality, and Conflict*: History of violence, especially recent, frequent, or severe; denial or minimization of known violence history; history of being restrained by protective orders or violating protective orders; history of nonviolent criminality, interpersonal conflict, filing grievances or litigiousness; childhood exposure to violence. This is a static factor.

18. *Domestic/Intimate Partner Violence*: History of partner assault, escalation, harassment, surveillance, or stalking; history of assaulting previous partners; jealousy, especially toward work relationships; recent separation and/or partner in new relationship, especially with a coworker; threatening contacts with partner in the workplace; workplace romantic triangle involving subject and two other coworkers. This is both a static (historical) factor as well as a dynamic factor relating to current behavior.

19. *Situational and Organizational Contributors to Violence*: Presence of negative situational influences such as subject's family, peer group, or community support for violence; supervisor or coworker provocation; a notably demanding workload; poor physical work environment; negative management practices or adversarial management-workforce relationship; lack of management violence prevention knowledge and protocol; others' denial of subject's violence potential. This is usually a dynamic factor.

20. *Stabilizers and Buffers Against Violence*: General characteristics of resilience; positive and supportive family or intimate attachments; other prosocial attachments and involvement; genuine remorse for fear-inducing conduct or policy violations; genuine respect for authority; positive or appropriate response to defusing, limit-setting, or negotiating; appropriate help-seeking for problems (legal advice, mental health treatment, career guidance, spiritual support); motivation to avoid legal consequences for threatening or criminal behavior. This is both a static (positive traits) and dynamic (effective behaviors) factor and is coded in an *opposite* direction from the previous risk factors.

21. *Organizational Impact of Real or Perceived Threats*: Removal of targeted employees from workplace; employees' fear of violence; work group's decline in performance, attendance or morale; employees' demands for management response to threat situations. This item is not a risk or protective factor but is useful to interveners and others who must restore order and reduce fear following threat scenarios.

Gender and age are not identified as WAVR-21 risk factor items but should be noted and considered in evaluating workplace violence risk. Males are typically more violent than females and the vast majority of workplace homicidal perpetrators are male (Kelleher, 1997). Younger males are more violent than older males (Beck, 2008; Swanson, Holzer, Ganju, & Jono, 1990; Tardiff, 2008), but this does not necessarily hold true for workplace violence. The relevance of both age and gender will vary with the context of a workplace case.

In practice the evaluator examines the evidence for each of the risk factors in relation to the evidence for the other factors, relying on his or her clinical judgment to reach an opinion as to the nature, severity, and time line of violence risk. For instance, does a jealous subject fixated on his wife at her workplace (captured by item number 18: Domestic/Intimate Partner Violence) also have access to firearms, or is he also paranoid, captured by other items on the WAVR? As with other SPJ guides, the evaluator must *integrate and weigh* the evidence present for all of the WAVR-21 factors in formulating his or her current opinion of risk (Meloy, White, & Hart, in press; Tardiff, 2008).

PERTINENT LEGAL
ISSUES[2]

Employers must respond to potential threats to the workforce in a manner that is both legal and ethical. A full discussion of the legal issues pertinent to workplace violence is beyond the scope of this chapter and the author's expertise; however, a few remarks of importance to evaluators are in order.

During the incident management process, the employer must navigate and balance significant legal issues, responding so as to maintain a safe workplace while respecting the various rights of the employee of concern. According to the General Duty Clause of the federal Occupational Safety and Health Act of 1970 (OSHA), employers must maintain a workplace "free from recognizable hazards that are causing or likely to cause death or serious harm to employees" (Occupational Safety and Health Act 1970). State laws impose similar requirements. Employers who do not properly manage and respond to workplace violence risk expose themselves to a variety of possible legal claims, particularly those involving negligence, whether it is negligence in hiring, retention, or supervision. Employers have been held liable for failing to safely remove a potentially violent employee and, in certain circumstances, from failing to screen out a job applicant with a violent history or apparent violent proclivities (Lies & Powers, 2008; Speer, 2003). Additional legal theories focus on the employer's mismanagement of the investigative or risk management process, where shortfalls in these practices can generate claims that include discrimination, wrongful termination, invasion of privacy, defamation, and violation of rights under applicable collective bargaining agreements.

The Americans with Disabilities Act (ADA) and corresponding state laws add further complexity to the legal issues an employer must consider during the threat management process. The ADA protects employees and job applicants from discrimination based on a known or perceived mental disability. Mental disorders covered by the ADA include, among others, depression, schizophrenia, bipolar disorder, posttraumatic stress disorder, and borderline personality disorder. Many state laws provide similar protections. As the WAVR-21 items clearly indicate, a risk assessment at times will require an evaluation of whether an employee's known or suspected mental disorder may have contributed to the problematic behavior that gave rise to the need for an assessment, and whether the disorder might contribute to a risk

of potential future violence. In general, the ADA and corresponding state laws should not prevent an employer from conducting a risk assessment or from taking steps to protect the workplace from violence. As a general matter, the ADA and corresponding state laws do not require an organization to employ someone who poses a "direct threat" to the workplace, as legally defined, or who cannot meet standards of workplace behavior even with reasonable accommodations. Nonetheless, the existence or perception of a known or suspected mental disorder generates for the employer a need to carefully examine potentially complex legal requirements under the ADA and corresponding state laws, and it places a premium on proper communication between the evaluator and the organization's employment law counsel and/or human resources staff.

In particular, an appropriate strategy must be implemented for properly handling information about a known or suspected mental disorder during a threat assessment and subsequent discussions by the evaluator with the employer.

The evaluator, in remaining mindful of these various legal exposures faced by the employer, may encounter a workplace context where varying degrees of disclosure or speculation about an individual's real or presumed mental disorder otherwise exist. For instance, a delusional employee may have openly shared with coworkers that, "The Gods are telling me I am the one to rid the earth once and for all of evildoers!" As a further example, employees may report "a 'paranoid' coworker who thinks we are hacking his computer and poisoning his coffee." Other individuals who raise concern may, when interviewed by a team member, voluntarily respond with comments such as, "It's because I'm bipolar." A further possibility is the professional arriving at the opinion, through his or her own assessment, that a mental disorder (e.g., a major depression) is an important contributor to an employee's angry outbursts that raised concern about violence risk.

In all of these scenarios the evaluator and the organization's legal counsel should carefully confer about what is communicated *by the evaluator* in his or her feedback and reports, verbal or written, *and to whom*, thinking through as well what information should be kept privileged. In general the employer's designated representatives need to know, in straightforward language, the subject's probable motives and explanations for his or her conduct of concern; the nature, severity, and time frame of possible risk; the likely targets; and what would escalate or ameliorate any risk. The evaluator's assessment narratives and subsequent discussions do not need to include diagnostic information to address the employer's risk management issues. At times it is indeed pertinent to reveal the relative treatability of a contributing mental disorder, whether or not it is specifically named by any party, in the interest of risk management decision making. Risk assessment professionals should understand that ultimately with ADA cases the employer needs to (1) weigh the legal requirements related to ADA and corresponding state laws, (2) decide what and how much the evaluator will communicate to the employer about a known or suspected mental disorder relevant to any risk issues, and (3) be especially careful in handling information confidentially during the threat management process.

THE WORKPLACE
PRACTICE CONTEXT

It is now standard practice for large organizations to establish and train in-house threat management teams, although there are no statistics on the extent of these proactive programs. Teams are made up primarily of security, human resource, legal, and mental health professionals. A truly collaborative spirit among the members enhances success and minimizes problematic missteps such as the silo effect: information from one resource not being shared with another when it should be in the interest of effective case management. In smaller organizations these duties will likely fall upon a human resources or administrative manager. The WAVR "tool kit" provides two short forms for use by nonclinicians in these multidisciplinary roles: a 12-item risk screening form, "Violence Risk," and a seven-item protective factor form, "Protect." These tools, clinically but not statistically related to the full WAVR-21 grid, avoid the use of clinical language and focus more on observable behaviors associated with risk.

Compared with other contexts such as prisons or the courts, the workplace defines important behavioral frequencies and organizational issues that dictate how threat assessment must be practiced. First, the base rate for workplace targeted homicidal violence is very low, since this is a population of individuals presumably stabilized by the protective factor of employment. Second, employers must respond appropriately to a wide range of aggressive and often fear-inducing conduct that comes to their attention. This requires assessors to recognize and interpret for their clientele

the meaning and implications of these less serious but disruptive behaviors, such as bullying, intimidation, some forms of sexual harassment, stalking, angry outbursts, and bizarre behavior or communications. Various WAVR-21 items capture these entities, which may be included in some definitions of "workplace violence" (Rugala, 2004; Schouten, 2008). Third, workplace threat assessment and case management is very much a dynamic and ongoing process, at times conducted in a crisis atmosphere. Initial incident reports or requests for assistance provide only partial information. Responders must make fairly rapid judgments as to how serious a situation may be, balancing the need for more information with the need for speed in responding.

In this sense workplace risk assessment reflects current thinking: it is not "prediction based," but is rather a process of "risk management" (Borum et al., 1999; Hart, Kropp, Laws, Heilbrun, 1997; Klaver, Logan, & Watt, 2003; Meloy et al., 2012; Turner & Gelles, 2003). The goal is to assess both static (e.g., history of violence) and dynamic—changing and therefore changeable—risk factors (e.g., level of anger, degree of psychosis, or possession of weapons). Dynamic risk factors become the focus of interventions intended to reduce risk. In practice, workplace threat assessment and threat management are usually very much *intertwined*. Assessment is ongoing, and an individual's response to various interventions (e.g., escalation, de-escalation, or no apparent change) becomes part of the evolving and/or changing opinion of risk level. This back-and-forth dynamic is apparent to threat management practitioners as they work their cases. For example, they will note how subjects respond to being placed on administrative leave and informed that their allegedly threatening remarks will be investigated. Do they escalate or instead accept the imposed structure and implications? This response informs the interveners' decisions as to what they do *next*.

Case management interventions vary along a continuum from nonconfrontational to confrontational, from dismissing a subject after a screening interview to physically protecting targets and criminal prosecution for threat-related crimes (Calhoun and Weston, 2003; White & Cawood, 1998). Intervention measures include defusing and limit-setting interviews with a subject, protective and restraining orders, voluntary and involuntary treatments, target hardening or removal, security protection including armed professionals at a work site, surveillance, law enforcement liaison, arrest, detention, and prosecution. None of these can or should be applied in a "menu" fashion. Most have certain downsides and selecting any of them should be based on the best current assessment information as well as the stakes involved if no action is taken. Professionals and teams need to be aware of *the intervention dilemma*: any intervention intended to prevent violence can have three possible outcomes—it may decrease risk, increase risk, or have no effect on whether a given individual chooses to act violently (De Becker, 1994; White & Cawood, 1998).

Given the operational aspect to workplace threat assessment practice, it is more appropriate to discuss opinions of risk in terms of "level of concern" versus level of risk (Meloy et al., 2012; Scalora et al., 2002). Information is inherently incomplete even as cases progress, and higher levels of "concern" should lead to interventions that reduce any possibility of harm. Thus the actual risk is never realized if interveners act appropriately and are successful. Definitions

of levels of concern for workplace practices are offered in Table 6.2 and have important operational implications.

The central task of a workplace threat assessment protocol is to (1) sort out the large majority of cases that present a very low level of concern for violence and do not need intensive case management; (2) identify the few cases that credibly suggest a high or imminent level of concern about serious violence and therefore justify the necessary, costly, and potentially disruptive measures to protect safety; and (3) for the midlevel cases, find appropriate and reasonable strategies for ongoing assessment and monitoring until the pathway toward or away from violence is clear.

Knowledge of workplace violence risk factors does not translate into a static profile of the "potentially violent employee" (Turner & Gelles, 2003; Day & Catano, 2006; Schouten, 2008). Communicated threats and disturbing behavior have widely differing meanings and may stem from

---

TABLE 6.2. OPERATIONAL DEFINITIONS OF RESPONSE TO LEVELS OF CONCERN AND/OR RISK

Low Level of Concern–Likely Low Risk

Operational Definition: The existing information suggests that a risk of violence is nonexistent or very low. Additional data gathering may be desirable. It is safe and appropriate to otherwise proceed with standard employee relations and management responses to the particular situation. Monitoring for any changes in risk factors or warning signs may be appropriate. Full involvement of the organization's incident management team or representatives is usually not indicated, but conferring between at least two team members or representatives is prudent for concurrence of opinion.

Moderate Level of Concern–Likely Moderate Risk

Operational Definition: The existing information suggests that violence could possibly occur, although the situation is not urgent. Risk cannot be ruled out. Monitoring and additional actions are necessary or desirable to further evaluate and respond to the situation to a point of resolution. If not yet conducted, formal professional risk assessments are usually indicated where strategically possible and wise. Not responding appropriately could lead to violence, workplace disruption, or other exposures. Involvement of the organization's incident management representatives is necessary.

High Level of Concern–Likely High Risk

Operational Definition: The existing information suggests that violence is entirely possible and within the near future or following any triggering events. Immediate and continuing attention is required of incident management resources to assure a safe resolution and/or to manage workplace fear and disruption. Timely formal risk assessments are likely desirable where strategically possible and wise. Risk reducing interventions and security actions and/or law enforcement liaison need to be carefully considered and decided upon by the organization and its threat management representatives or team.

Assumption of Imminent Risk

Operational Definition: The existing information suggests that a 911 emergency exists. Contacting law enforcement and taking other immediate actions to protect the safety of exposed individuals is the necessary action. Notifying incident management team members, following immediate safety steps, is a necessity for further follow-up actions.

different motives or causes (Meloy, 2000; Meloy & O'Toole, 2011; Warren, Mullen, Thomas, Ogloff, & Burgess, 2007; Warren et al., chapter 2, this volume; White & Meloy, 2007). Along with those individuals with no violent intent are others who are ambivalent about such a decision and can be dissuaded from such a destructive pathway.

Certain scenarios and individuals of concern will frequently be presented to threat management teams and assessors. These generally include, with room for individual variation, the functioning accusatory paranoid; the disgruntled contemplator of revenge; the decompensating psychotic; the economically distressed, midlife male; the angry "short fuse" employee; the vexatious litigant; stalkers with differing motives and targets; workplace romantic triangles; bullies and their dysfunctional work groups; and an employee's jealous ex-intimate. Many individuals of concern have histories of being "difficult employees" with poor emotional regulation, interpersonal skills, or problem solving abilities. They are noteworthy for overestimating their work performance or potential, their unrealistic expectations, lack of empathy and abrasive styles, and inability to persist with longer-range goals. Underlying insecurities may be masked with bravado, intimidation, and emotional outbursts that make these individuals appear threatening. Serious personal losses, setbacks, and family deaths, including the effects of an increasing economic squeeze on the middle and working classes (Pew Research Center, 2012), may add to the mix.

ROLE OF THE THREAT ASSESSMENT PROFESSIONAL IN AN ORGANIZATIONAL CONTEXT

The threat assessment professional has a distinct role in the management of workplace threat cases. Ideally he or she is a specialist, knowledgeable about violence risk factors and possessing the analytic ability and clinical judgment to "connect the dots" from the available data in a meaningful way (Prince & Phelps, 2010). Within this dynamic process the professional offers viable and safe intervention alternatives. This skill is often combined with the contributions of the other members of the employer's multidisciplinary team who are more knowledgeable about the organization's culture, dynamics, and practices. In-house clinicians may also serve or assist in an assessment role. Security and human resource professionals,

especially in large organizations with a high volume of cases, may demonstrate and contribute their considerable experience and confidence in screening and assessing risk situations. Past case experiences fundamentally increase the likelihood of future case successes, and all participants should be aware of their limitations. The outside risk assessment professional needs to appreciate this multidisciplinary collaborative model and, when it is properly conducted, its benefits to his or her effectiveness.

There is no current professional certification or standard for conducting risk assessments, however, and no clear delineation between experts and nonexperts (Hart, 2011b). Risk assessment mental health clinicians are the most qualified to assess the role of major mental and personality disorders and symptoms in individual violence risk cases. Violence risk assessment is comprehensible but complex, in that many factors, distal and proximal, conscious and unconscious, contribute to these final deadly acts. There are many idiosyncrasies in individual cases and many nuances in their management. The threat assessment professional must be comfortable in an environment where the stakes may be high and yet decisions must often be made with insufficient information. Peer and cross-disciplinary consultation should be an option for even the most experienced practitioners. The false-positive bias—overestimating risk leading to overreacting in practice—is most evident in risk assessors with little experience. Risk opinions should neither be minimized nor inflated (Beck, 2008; MacKenzie, McEwan, Pathé, James, Ogloff, & Mullen, 2009), as subsequent tactical decisions can have a significant influence on the course and outcome of a particular situation, including effects on the civil liberties of the subject. This is not to dismiss the possibility that the employer, given the liability for any level of risk, may decide, even when the risk is judged to be low, to take extra security measures "out of an abundance of caution." In these scenarios the threat assessment professional—much like the airline pilot who is the reference point for passengers on the difference between turbulence (a low-risk frequent event) and an emergency (a high-risk very infrequent event)—possesses a great deal of influence on how a case will be perceived and how it may be addressed and resolved.

The professional may conduct a *direct* assessment, which includes a face-to-face clinical evaluation of the employee-subject and relies as well on additional information such as incident reports, collateral interviews, and input from the organization's team. Given the nature of the workplace context, professionals will also be asked for their opinion when a direct assessment is not possible or not desirable. This may arise, for instance, in the case of a former employee or the current or former intimate partner of an employee—outsiders whose current conduct has raised concern. In the case of such *indirect* assessments, the professional will base his or her opinion "on the information available to me so far," and denote the inherent limitations of an opinion in these instances. Indirect workplace threat assessments are common and necessary and are understood as having limitations by the user organization. They are consistent with the American Psychological Association's Code of Ethics, which states that when an individual examination is "not practical" or "not warranted or necessary," consulting psychologists "clarify the probable impact of their limited information on the reliability and validity of their opinions and appropriately limit the nature and extent of their conclusions and recommendations" (American Psychological Association, 2010, p. 12).

CASE EXAMPLE

The following case illustrates the stages and dynamic nature of workplace targeted violence risk assessment. Common issues and decision points are presented. Operational measures such as security, law enforcement, and legal actions are alluded to but not discussed in detail, as the emphasis here is to illustrate the assessment process. Two variations on the case are offered to illustrate different risk scenarios and more serious levels of concern.

The Initial Incident Report, Engagement of the Professional, and Intake

An incident or information of concern is initially reported from various possible sources to an appropriate organizational resource, usually a manager, security personnel, or human resources. The facts—who, what, where, and perhaps why—are collected in varying degrees of completeness by the threat management designee or team representative. This information may then be communicated to the assessment professional.

The provocative incident. The subject, Gabe, is a 29-year-old technical contributor in a minor role, hired eight months earlier by a high-tech firm. Recently he sent some threatening emails to Andy, his supervisor, who is about the same age as Gabe and who has been attempting to manage his unacceptable performance. Andy reported to the team,

> From the beginning Gabe had an agenda to advance into another specialty area for which he was not hired and is not qualified. He can't multitask, lacks professionalism in many forms, and is arrogant. His work is inconsistent, yet he seeks unwarranted praise and deflects any negative feedback. He is disrespectful of other team members, especially the women.

Gabe reacted to Andy's closer supervision and limit setting with increasingly angry, defensive, accusatory emails. Gabe sent the following email to Andy, copied to the other eight team members:

> When are you going to get off my back? Like I told Claire [another team member], I can't let things go. What you call "out of line" I call sticking up for myself. The training you have given me is crap and does not help me in my career path. You don't understand whom you are messing with.

Management's initial response. In a meeting with him, Andy and Shelly, the human resources manager, confronted Gabe about the inappropriateness and threatening nature of his email. Defensive and claiming that he "wasn't threatening and didn't break any laws," Gabe was given a written warning informing him firmly that any further examples of such misconduct would lead to further disciplinary action "up to and including termination."

Subsequent events and responses. Two days later Gabe sent an email to the team, claiming his worth and adding, "Andy is out to get me and I'm not going to sacrifice my pride by walking away." This concerned the team, who were aware of Gabe's prickly nature, lack of competence, and big ego. When Shelly called Gabe in and asked him what he meant in the email, he answered, "Knowing you, you are probably thinking the worst." He refused to explain himself any further and would repeat his response: "You are trying to get me to testify against myself when you should be doing something about Andy." Shelly placed Gabe on a paid administrative leave while the company conducted a further investigation and considered its options. When Andy informed his team that, "Gabe will not be at work for the time being" and "I am not at liberty to say anything more," everyone pretty much figured out what was going on and wondered if the situation could pose a risk of harm. When members of a workforce experience concern or fear, one or more individuals will often come forward and volunteer additional information. In this case it was team member Claire who approached Andy and told him, "Gabe talked about guns and how much he liked them. He was angry at you, said he knew a lot more than you did and tried to get me to agree with him which I would not." When queried, Claire indicated that Gabe said nothing more about weapons and did not make threats to physically harm anyone.

Engagement of the assessment professional and further data gathering. In a long team discussion that included Andy's boss, the group reviewed the WAVR-21 Short Forms, noted several risk factors to be present, and decided to confer with the company's outside threat assessment professional. The clear sentiment was to terminate Gabe, but the group realized, as is the *common dilemma*, that terminating him could trigger a violent retaliation on Gabe's part.

The team presented their case information to the professional, who in addition learned the following: Gabe also claimed that he had discussed "a great idea" of his with a manager in the IT security department and had made "a significant contribution" to their ongoing project to strengthen the company's firewall. He subsequently insisted that he was not getting due credit for it and "his good name" was being damaged. When Shelly asked Amir, the manager, about this allegation, he stated,

> We only talked about it over lunch one day when Gabe approached me. He sent me several emails about his ideas, in fact a rather obsessive number of them, which were technically considerably subpar. I rather politely dismissed him. He was a bit pushy and I assure you his comments were nothing contributory to our work.

Gabe is single and moved from another state to accept his current job. His resume states that he has a bachelor of science degree. So far little is known about his family, personal life, or outside activities except that he is rumored to frequent bars on weekends and has implied that he enjoys "tying one on."

Initial Questions and First Impression

Using the WAVR-21 risk domains to guide his inquiry with the in-house representatives, the threat assessment professional learns important information about Gabe, even though many areas of interest remain unanswered. In consultation with the team members, the professional attempts to answer the following *initial questions*, leading to a first impression and plan for proceeding.

1. What is the subject doing or saying that raises concern about violence?
2. What is an apparent explanation for the subject's behavior (his "grievance," motive, goal, problematic or bizarre thinking or perceptions, etc.)?
3. To what extent does the subject see violence as a means to resolve his situation?
4. Does he have the weapons or means and capacity to act violently?
5. What might trigger him to be violent?
6. What actions might reduce the likelihood of violence?
7. What information should be pursued, how and by whom?

Is Gabe contemplating violence, especially if he were terminated? Could termination be a trigger for violence, and does he have the means to be violent? The assessor's first impression, referring to the WAVR-21 items, is that Gabe could pose a risk, given his sense of injustice. At the least, risk cannot be ruled out at this point. Gabe's grievance, stemming from his own internal dynamics and not reality-based, is that he is being mistreated and thwarted in his career. Evidence exists for veiled threats, current job problems, fixation ("I can't let things go"), entitlement, grandiosity and other negative traits, and anger at his supervisor and perhaps others. He may have paranoid tendencies as well and allegedly has implied that he may own or have access to firearms. The assessor would like to know whether he feels some degree of extreme job attachment or whether his demeaning attitude toward his position could allow him to let go of it with prideful disdain. Gabe's very poor judgment in the face of adversity, as well as his failure to conduct himself reasonably and civilly, forces the employer to address his employment status and thus Gabe's possible reactions. The assessor may begin to note whether WAVR items are present or prominent, make distinctions between the absence of an item and insufficient information, and note the direction of any change in a dynamic item.

It is also possible that Gabe poses very little or no risk and that he is just posturing. He does engage in some bullying. He is also demonstrating very poor judgment, perhaps stemming from his apparent narcissistic tendencies. These are very common scenarios and present a low risk. It will cost him his job and be a hard lesson, but it is not about a life-defining and intolerable humiliation and he will not retaliate with a homicidal act. Perhaps he will take some other vindictive action, such as vandalism or a righteous email campaign to demean others and defend himself. Perhaps legal action against the company will be his response. All this remains to be seen and comprises the assessor's *working hypotheses*. Risk assessment is not risk prediction. Which lines Gabe crosses and abides by—his communications and especially his behavior—are the most relevant continuing assessment data.

To paraphrase Borum et al. (1999), targeted violence is dynamic—it can change; continuous—it can vary in its seriousness; and contextual—it involves others and their reactions, and in this instance the outcome may hinge on the organization's response. The threat assessment approach—a "protective investigation"—is about safety and is distinct from misconduct or criminal investigations, even if the last two efforts are also being conducted (Calhoun and Weston, 2003).

Collateral Interviews and Data

Collateral data are essential in conducting risk assessments, preferably from multiple sources and using differing methods (Hart, 2011a; Meloy, 2000; Monahan, 1993; Monahan et al., 2001; Schouten, 2008; Turner & Gelles, 2003). Self-report by a violence risk subject is rife with potential errors (Tardiff, 2008). Workplace perpetrators may "leak" intentions to do harm to third parties, commonly in the absence of directly communicated threats to their targets (Meloy et al., 2012; Meloy & O'Toole, 2011; O'Toole, 2000). In the workplace context, the evaluator, in consultation with team members, must weigh several factors in considering whom to interview: the value of what might be learned; the discretion, credibility, and reluctance of potential witnesses; and the impact on the workplace

when employees are involved in a sensitive investigation. Assessors will commonly encounter "he said-she said" controversies and the natural tendencies of some to minimize or to exaggerate risk-relevant information; it will therefore be necessary to consider informants' personal motivations. The professional must weigh how much he or she should rely only on the collateral interview data provided by the team representatives. The more serious the case, the more he or she should conduct his or her own interviews, preferably in person if at all convenient. Collateral information usually reaches a certain point of consistency and redundancy regarding the subject, as well as the subject's motives and behavior.

An additional source of collateral data is a background check of a subject's criminal and civil public records. The details of this aspect of a protective investigation are beyond the scope of this chapter; the reader is therefore referred to other sources (e.g., Cohen, Duffy, Eisenberg, Heffernan, & Moll, 2008; Turner & Gelles, 2003; White & Cawood, 1998). Background checks are particularly valuable when there is evidence or suspicion of a subject's past criminal or violent conduct, when protective orders had previously been served against him or her, or when the current case appears to pose a serious risk. Most background checks of workplace subjects of concern reveal no records of convictions or civil actions. That should not lead to false reassurance if the current presence of risk factors suggests otherwise. Background checks should be conducted with the guidance and under the auspices of the organization's legal counsel.

On the following day the assessor conducts collateral interviews with Andy, the supervisor, Claire, the coworker, and Shelly, the human resources manager.

The coworker. The assessor learns from Claire that Gabe bragged about how much he knew, how much he was going to achieve, and how his job kept him "boxed in." He thought Andy was "an idiot." He would alternately speak with high praise about certain "geniuses" in the industry and previous "great mentors" he had had, but stated that his last job was also "a dead end." He said "If it weren't for the dumb asses in my way I would have gotten a lot farther by now." Claire noted that Gabe was mediocre at best, made excuses about what he didn't know, and was generally emotionally draining as a coworker. She eventually avoided him as much as possible, but then he would complain, "You're not doing your share of the work." In fact he was trying to get her to cover for his poor performance. Claire had no further information about Gabe's gun talk, but he did talk about an incident at a previous job where he allegedly "duked it out" with a coworker. She believed this to have happened when he was much younger, working in some kind of warehouse. The assessor does not otherwise find any evidence of "leakage" of threats by Gabe to Claire, to whom he otherwise frequently confided his thoughts and disgruntlement.

The supervisor. Andy is weary from his efforts to manage Gabe and frustrated that he "just doesn't get it." Now he is also mildly fearful that he could be targeted. The assessor does not learn significant new information about Gabe but does gain a deeper understanding of how quick he is to anger and how defensive he is. At a young age Andy possessed something Gabe does not and likely unconsciously envies: competence and promise. Andy offers examples of how Gabe has to navigate at work to cover his limitations and bolster his grandiosity.

The human resources manager. Shelly confirms that Andy is a good supervisor and that no one else complains about him. Gabe's personnel file reveals that his parents are his emergency contact, hopefully suggesting a positive attachment to them. The assessor also discerns that Shelly is a capable professional, perceptive and fair in her judgments of employee issues and firm in the face of intimidating individuals such as Gabe. This is relevant, since the assessor is determining the capabilities of those he is assisting in this collaborative model—their judgment, objectivity, personal resilience, and receptivity to input. Item 19 on the WAVR—Situational and Organizational Contributors to Violence—addresses this factor, which so far is viewed as absent in this case.

Based on what he knows at this point, the professional is prepared to recommend a face-to-face risk assessment of Gabe; his reasoning is that he feels he could not assure the company that the risk of violence is very low or nonexistent; secondly, an assessment would contribute significantly to the database, including a proposed exit strategy if Gabe were separated from the company. However, Gabe himself changes the stakes of the situation.

Escalation and Increasing Level of Concern

Dynamic threat assessment involves following the subject—who may or may not escalate—through time, observing his behavior, and seeing how he reacts to the interventions of the organization or other authorities.

On what is now Day 5 since the original incident, Gabe posts on YouTube a video of himself practicing at a firing range. In the video he is rapidly firing and reloading a semiautomatic handgun. In the next segment he holds up his target profile, on which he has drawn a human upper body. He shows the well-placed holes and says to the camera, smiling, "Pretty good, huh?! I never miss!" He then sends an email with a link to the video to his team members, which states, "Thought you guys would like to see this. I do think of you when I'm not there."

In addition, Gabe sends an email to Amir, the IT manager with whom he had met and to whom he then subsequently had sent a number of emails. It states, "Amir, you know I gave you great input on the firewall project. Not recognizing this is just another way you and the company are trying to take credit for my contributions. You have stolen my ideas. There are various ways for me to make this right. But I can only think of one."

This leads the company to change its plans. They decide to report Gabe to the police, perceiving him as now making credible threats to harm his coworkers. The security manager contacts the watch commander in the neighboring community where Gabe lives, a person with whom the manager fortunately has an established relationship. All of the company's information pertinent to the situation is provided to the police, who take the report and decide to meet with Gabe at his apartment. Meanwhile a background check on Gabe is conducted by the security manager, revealing that Gabe has a clean record.

The police report back to the security manager that Gabe acted appropriately when the police conducted their "knock and talk." Although guarded, he acknowledged the video posting but claimed he was only "spouting off" and had no intention to harm anyone at the company. He said, "If they fire me I will see them in court. I was set up by my supervisor." Gabe admitted to owning firearms and showed the police the closet where they were kept. He acknowledged that he enjoyed target shooting. With the information they had, the police did not consider Gabe an imminent threat, nor did they take any further action. They counseled him that further threats could get him into serious trouble. They also recommended to the company that it obtain a restraining order. If Gabe violated it, the police could take possession of his firearms.

The sentiment to terminate Gabe is now strong, but so is the concern that he would react violently.

The in-house team members debate that Gabe's reaction to the police was reassuring—he backed down and is not a serious threat—vs. "he told them what they wanted to hear" and he is still contemplating violence. The professional recommends that a risk assessment remains advantageous: key questions would be better answered with more information and there is little downside to requiring Gabe to undergo an evaluation. If he refuses, the employer must make its decisions based on the information it has.

The Risk Assessment Interview

The directive to appear for a violence risk evaluation is a very significant event for the employee of concern. His job is usually at stake, if not his reputation. The context is a humiliating one. Apprehension is appropriate, as he is not sure what to expect, even if it is explained to him beforehand, as it should be. The interviewee is in a Catch-22: if he tells the truth about forbidden thoughts or agrees with damning incident reports, he may lose his job. If he is perceived as lying about or minimizing the seriousness of his alleged misconduct, he is still subject to judgment. It is also possible that he may not care. Some subjects may be the victims of others' exaggerations, and a few the legitimate scapegoats in a dysfunctional work group. In most instances the employee is relatively eager to present and defend his point of view, and this desire of his serves the purpose of the interview.

The setting can be at the workplace, the professional's office, or some other location or conference room, depending on the practices of the employer, the assessment professional, and the circumstances and level of concern posed by the case. Discrete security may be arranged and the details of this plan must be thoroughly discussed with the security professionals.

Relatively little has been written about the workplace threat assessment interview. There is no specific format for how the interview should be conducted, but there are fairly identifiable stages and specific goals (Turner & Gelles, 2003). The interviewer identifies herself and her professional status and conducts the informed consent process, first verbally and then followed by a written consent that the subject reads and signs if he or she agrees to proceed. The interviewer explains that she has been asked to conduct a risk assessment of the employee based on recent and/or alleged communications or behavior that have raised concern that the employee could pose a risk of harm to others in the workplace and/ or to himself. The interview is not confidential and

the professional, although she has discretion, will be providing the employer's designated managers or representatives with her findings, opinions, and recommendations. With certain exceptions, there is no release to third parties. The subject may agree to release his health providers and the assessor to discuss his condition, risk issues, and treatment. The assessor, should she believe that a credible threat exists, has the duty to warn any possible targets of the subject as well as to inform law enforcement. How these releases and communications are conducted and managed, or variations on this general procedure, may be discussed with management as well as with the subject.

The interviewer should be attentive to the subject's demeanor and degree of anxiety, anger, or felt insult at the requirement to be evaluated, and should promptly work to establish rapport. It is important that the interviewer convey in the beginning her interest in hearing the subject's version of events and his perspective on his situation. Stating, "I am here to understand better what is going on as well as to conduct an assessment," may help reassure the subject and set a respectful tone. The interviewer may gather basic demographic and work activities information as a way to warm up in a less threatening manner. The more the employee perceives the interviewer as being objective, fair, and patient, the more he is likely to provide information in a relatively unguarded manner. In all of this, even if he is defensive and protective, the subject is revealing himself to the interviewer—his personality structure, cognitive style, emotional control, perceptions of others, and what he perceives is at stake for him. The interviewer can validate pain and frustration without endorsing fear-inducing or unacceptable behavior. Nor can the interviewer allow herself to be intimidated by the subject. It is advisable with some subjects to get promptly and directly to the point; no niceties are required when the individual is ready to deal with the specifics of why he is there. This preference may reflect a need to have some control over his circumstances. Flexibility is the key to successful interviews. Interviews, in the workplace assessment context, are about understanding, not interrogating or psychologically stripping the subject bare. Even though she is attempting to uncover the true motives and intentions of the subject, the interviewer should remain cognizant of the need to maintain the subject's dignity and to not increase his sense of shame or his anger.

The WAVR-21 manual provides inquiry questions for each of the 21 items that the interviewer can use to guide or inform her assessment meeting.

Familiarity with these allows the professional to ask and phrase the questions in a more seamless and sensitive rather than a rote manner.

Shea (1999) has described interview techniques in assessing suicide risk that, with some modifications, can be adapted to assessing violence risk, especially given the prominence of suicide as the final act in some targeted violence scenarios. Basically the techniques involve asking questions, adapted here for a workplace violence risk assessment, in a manner that enhances the elicitation of ideation and intent. These include *shame attenuation* ("Do you find your boss is unfairly getting on your case?"); *normalization* ("I know organizations aren't perfect. Many of the people I interview tell me how angry they are. What's it like for you?"); *denial of the specific*—that is, eliciting answers to a series of questions about a topic versus a general question (instead of "What drugs have you used?" ask, "Have you ever tried cocaine?...acid?...meth?...marijuana?..."); and *symptom amplification*, which counteracts tendencies to downplay the frequency or degree of concerning behaviors ("How many times have you gotten into a fight in your whole life—5?, 10?, 20?").

Questions can be asked in a relatively neutral manner to maintain the level of the subject's ongoing disclosures. For example, when he pauses, respond with, "Is there more?" Direct questioning about violent thoughts and feelings must be asked at some point, however adroitly the interviewer has otherwise attempted to get at these inner processes. For instance, "Do you have any thoughts or feelings about hurting anyone here?...Can you imagine any circumstance where violence would be justified?...What about your supervisor?"

The essential task of the interviewer is to assess the balance between the subject's contemplation of violence (or other aggressive, disruptive behavior) as a response to his situation, versus his more rational, prosocial resourcefulness and vision of a worthwhile future beyond his immediate problems or predicament. Does he feel hopeless, or trapped between his goals or aspirations and reality? Could notoriety appeal to him in a "nothing to lose" mind set? What are his problem solving abilities and his personal, family, and economic resources? An important objective is to understand the subject's felt grievance from his point of view, his real or perceived losses and their impact on him, and what he wants. An additional area of inquiry is to compare the subject's view of his conduct, performance, and value to the organization, with that of the employer's view. This is a potential measure of his grandiosity and denial, assuming the employer's view is reality-based and reasonable. The degree of his attachment to his job must be ascertained. Ultimately, the subject must be asked about his reaction if he were to no longer work for the organization. Questions along these lines are, "What if this doesn't work out here?...Suppose they decide not to retain you?...What if you ultimately lost your job for some reason?...How would you feel about that?...How would you react?" It is generally inadvisable to suggest remedies to the subject, for example, "You can always sue them." However, if a subject volunteers that pursuing a lawsuit, for example, is what he contemplates, it is appropriate to respond with, "That is certainly your right."

A case must be evaluated on its own merits; the interviewer must not be falsely reassured by the statistical improbability of workplace violence. The interviewer is seeking to discern violent *intent*—the most crucial risk factor—from violent thoughts, past statements, or aggressive conduct. Intent is ultimately *inferred* from the assessor's total current picture of the subject. From all that he knows, the professional develops some informed hypotheses as to what the subject's course may be. Will it be to act violently, toward whom, and when, by what means, and how seriously? If so, the focus becomes to risk manage the subject. Or does he appear to be traversing another path, away from violence, and likely to choose other solutions to his situation? Perhaps the opinion will be, as is common, that violence is a highly unlikely choice for the subject in spite of the evidence for some risk factors.

The assessment interview also offers an important opportunity, usually toward the end of the session, to leverage protective factors and begin to *search for and construct a dignified and acceptable resolution to the situation* for the benefit of all parties. Calhoun and Weston (2003) refer to this as the "hybrid mix" in interviews—assessment and case management are going on at the same time. It is usually appropriate for the evaluator, even though he is retained by the employer, to express his interest in the welfare of the interviewee (Beck, 2008). If perceived as genuine by the subject this can create some alliance between him and the interviewer, however short-term, to possibly reduce risk, and at the least, the subject's agitation and isolation. Comments such as, "I'm concerned that your actions would destroy you, not just others," or, "What about *you* and your life?" delivered at an appropriate moment, convey this attitude on the part of the professional.

The interviewer should not be a negotiator on behalf of the employer or his neutrality will be compromised. But he can open the door with queries such as, "Sometimes companies work out settlements with employees in these situations, some kind of agreement, helping you with a transition. Would you be open to that?" The subject will likely be curious about the details. The interviewer may state he will convey this to the organization. Implicitly the employer must indicate beforehand that the interviewer has this option. In many cases a "benevolent severance" is workable and desirable, where legal parameters and the employer's policies are flexible enough. The employee is separated, even allowed to resign. He is offered a modest severance, usually one to three months' pay and an extension of benefits intended to bridge him to the next job. Benefits extension is especially advisable when a mental disorder is a significant risk factor, the employee is undergoing treatment, and he or she is motivated to continue. Any such considerations require review from the organization's legal and management stakeholders. The overall goal is safety first, less agitation for the subject, and thus reduced situational tensions for the involved parties. Overly generous financial packages, however, are transparent in revealing the employer's fear of an attack, will feed some subjects' grandiosity, and will embolden them to ask for more or attempt further manipulations. When the outcome is that the subject is judged not to pose a risk, the employer may then exercise various options: termination for misconduct (i.e., the employee does not *pose* a threat but he still *made* a threat) or returning her or him to the workplace, perhaps with counseling, final warnings, or referral for professional services. Various reparative interventions or directives with the work group and supervisors may be in order.

Gabe is called and told to report for the interview, to which he agrees. The location is away from his immediate workplace, in an interview room near the entrance to the building lobby. Two armed security professionals are in the adjoining room, out of an abundance of caution and unbeknownst to Gabe.

Following the introductory remarks, informed consent process, and signing of the document, Gabe is quite talkative. He claims that concerns about him being violent are "a bunch of shit." He frames his YouTube video as follows:

Well, they messed with me, so I messed with them. Yea, maybe I was trying to shake them

up and it felt good doing it. I got a laugh. But they should get over it. What they are doing to me is worse—just screwing me and picking at little things when I haven't been given the right training. Plus Amir stole my ideas.

The interviewer listens attentively and is privy to Gabe's cognitive distortions, poor tolerance for normal work expectations and the accompanying stress, and especially his minimization of his serious behavior. He senses how Gabe cannot maturely integrate negative feedback; it feels humiliating and categorizes it as an attack. Gabe escapes these painful intolerable affects by counterattacking with projected blame. The YouTube video was an impulsive act to alleviate a distressing mood, the assessor silently concludes.

The interviewer navigates through the WAVR-21 items, at times eliciting information in conversation, at times doing so by direct questioning. He asks Gabe what he meant by the emails: "I can't let things go," "I'm not going to sacrifice my pride by walking away," and "I can only think of one way to make this right." In his own words Gabe describes his prideful side and a history of being sensitive to "insults, especially from idiots." The interviewer senses that Gabe gets a certain sadistic satisfaction from intimidating others. "Red flag" indicators reveal violent ideation, threats, and weapons skill and access but not a convincing violent motive: violence is not a truly acceptable alternative for Gabe. He is not in a "nothing to lose" tailspin. He goes to the range fairly regularly and this is likely an emotional, ego-boosting outlet for him. The interviewer carefully inquires about Gabe's rituals when he is there and looks for such signs as rehearsal of "overkill" shooting or personal photo target selection during other target practice situations. Because these rituals may be common among some gun enthusiasts, any such behaviors must be evaluated in the context of Gabe's work or life problems, as represented by other WAVR items. Gabe describes his three firearms in technical detail. They are proud possessions. But there is no apparent evidence of preattack planning. Gabe denies any intent to harm anyone at work, especially Andy. Current job problems are certainly present, but fortunately Gabe is not strongly attached to his job. He answers the crucial, "What if you lost your job over this?" with, "If they fire me I will sue them and go and get another job." (A more concerning response would be a pause, perhaps followed by a remark such as, "They should not push me too far" or "We may assure each other of our mutual destruction.")

Gabe's definition of the company as beneath him actually serves as an ingredient for a peaceful resolution, even though it is clear that he holds grudges. He has engaged in menacing behavior and is subject to impulsive actions short of physical harm. There is no evidence of significant recent personal losses. Narcissistic entitlement and other negative traits are present but he does not display psychopathic traits. Clearly he has anger problems, and these fuel undesirable behaviors on his part. He does not appear depressed and denies any suicidal history, ideation, or intent. The interviewer listens for paranoia, an important risk factor as well as a common determinant of challenging behavior. Gabe distorts events but is not clinically paranoid. He is alcohol dependent but not addicted and admits to occasional recreational drug use in the past. He denies the use of amphetamines or other stimulants, but it is based only on his self-report. Corroborative evidence does not suggest a direct contribution of stimulant drugs. He says he has friends and does not appear overly isolated. He says he is in relatively frequent contact with his parents. He speaks as though he wished to rise above the economic and social level of his family of origin. The interviewer perceives hints of a demanding but unsupportive father, but Gabe underestimates this influence on his own unrealistic self-expectations. Gabe admits to the incident of a fight with a previous coworker about five years ago and "two or three bar fights when I was a young hothead. But a broken nose cured me of that." He currently is not dating, has had several girlfriends in the past, and denies any intimate partner violence. "I am an arguer for sure. My ex-girlfriends will tell you that. When they check out, who cares?" Denigrating his rejecters seems to work for Gabe, at least at this point in his life.

Ultimately the interviewer opines that Gabe has no homicidal intent toward anyone at work. Knowing that the chances that Gabe will retain his job are slim and that the employer is not inclined to provide any severance unless strongly recommended, the interviewer brings the meeting to a close, thanking Gabe for his time and wishing him well, whatever the outcome. Gabe says, "Thanks. They should make up their mind," and leaves without incident.

The interviewer presents his findings to the employer's team in a verbal narrative, helping them to understand Gabe and the various bases for his behavior more clearly. He considers Gabe a low risk to harm anyone if he is terminated, but certain temporary security precautions are in order, as the risk is too high and Gabe can be impulsive. He would clearly remain a problem employee, given his nature and defenses; he has seriously violated personal conduct policies; and the relationships are now largely beyond repair. Pursuing a restraining order is discussed and the evaluator offers his opinion, reviewing the pros and cons in this case. The decision is ultimately the employer's.

Gabe is terminated the next day by Andy's boss, Matt, who is chosen for this task to shield both Andy and Shelly from any further involvement with Gabe. Matt has been apprised of all events along the way and has been involved in all the case management decisions, but he has remained "above the fray" and his higher position may add a tone of both seriousness and calm to the proceedings. Gabe is terminated by telephone as there is no necessity to do this at the work site, given standard safety precautions and the occasion for emotions to spike. (This is not usually the preference, as in general the more respectful way is to terminate someone in person.) Gabe is instructed to have no further contact with anyone except Matt or a designated male representative in the human resources department. This defines a clear structural boundary which, if not heeded by Gabe, should be considered an indication of renewed concern. He asks, "Will any of this be disclosed to a future employer?" This is a good sign that he is orienting toward the future. He is informed there will be no such disclosures. Security is maintained at the site for one week as a precaution. The assessor is given the details of the termination conversation, since this is an important data point.

The professional should document all findings, opinions, and recommendations in the course of the case and ultimately in some form of report or detailed notes. Written reports are privileged and belong to the employer, to be released only with the organization's authorization or by court order. The degree of formality of written reporting will vary according to the case and the employer's preferences, but the professional is always responsible for his or her documentation and the justification for all opinions and recommendations. The WAVR-21 provides for note taking regarding individual items, critical risk factor items, and additional case-relevant risk factors. The WAVR-21 grid may be completed at some logical juncture in the case, noting that it is always subject to updated circumstances and changes in the constellation of factors.

From an investigative and legal standpoint, both the employer and the assessor should consider whether the protective investigation was based on a reasonable belief, was generated by adequate information, and was gathered in an effective and unbiased fashion (R. Speer, personal communication, January, 2012). Employers are also required—by federal and state safety statutes, common law duty, and ethical considerations—to warn identifiable targets of credible threats (Speer, 2003). In practice it is often necessary to consider very carefully the wording of such communications so as to balance the duty to warn with the need to protect the subject employee's privacy, and otherwise minimize the risk of defamation claims.

VARIATIONS ON THE CASE

The above scenario is very typical of many workplace threat assessment cases. Warning signs and risk factors are present and the situation requires careful assessment and management. But the outcome is common: The risk is none to low and very manageable. Continuing to use the case of Gabe as a foundation, here are other possible scenarios that pose more risk:

The Paranoid Employee

In this version the subject is described as posing a moderate risk for violence and requiring more intense and ongoing case management.

Gabe reacts even more strongly to Andy's tightening supervision, revealing a highly suspicious nature. He is silent, with a vigilant look at team meetings, and soon expresses paranoid ideas of reference: "People are talking about me in that conference room." Frank delusional content shortly appears, as he claims that his team members are playing "dirty tricks" on him and "implanting bugs on my computer." Angrily and with a red face, he accuses others of these misdeeds. These affective outbursts quickly create fear of an impulsive assault or a predatory attack. He insists on taping the meeting with Shelly, who refuses to allow this. This leads to Gabe demanding that her boss "investigate the entire situation, including Shelly, who should be fired." He is increasingly adamant with his complaints of a "hostile workplace," but when queried his explanations and offers of evidence are increasingly rambling and incoherent. He makes frequent references to legal action and says that he cannot wait to see the wrongdoers "criminally prosecuted before a jury."

In such a scenario attempting a risk assessment must be weighed against the likelihood that it will be too inflammatory for the subject, who will claim that the company is "demonizing me by bringing in a psychologist when it's all about my rights being violated." The professional may recommend that he only conduct an *indirect assessment*, using the data available without a face-to-face evaluation. This is particularly true with highly litigious and calculating paranoids who go on to become vexatious litigants (Mullen & Lester, 2006). Whether such a subject is interviewed or not, there are two areas to assess for risk with paranoid individuals, represented primarily by Item 14 on the WAVR: Paranoia and Other Psychotic Symptoms. First, they may attempt to preemptively eliminate a perceived imminent threat to their safety. They will attack before being attacked, usually in the form of an assault. Second, accumulated rejections, criticisms, or defeats may lead to intolerable resentment and the decision to retaliate in a planned and predatory manner against perceived current foes or symbolic targets (Meloy et al., 2004). Such an accumulation of slights may take weeks, months, or years to build up.

Establishing rapport and trust with a paranoid interviewee is inherently challenging. Evaluators should remember that the subject is basically afraid, realize that workplace demands and especially competition are likely very threatening to him, and acknowledge that his beliefs are sincere in spite of evidence to the contrary. The assessment should seek to answer two questions: (1) Whether the subject feels a need to launch a self-protective attack to prevent being harmed, and (2) how he might otherwise respond if he encountered those who had "wronged" or "harassed" him.

In spite of efforts to be as fair and sincere as possible with him, an inevitable self-fulfilling prophecy often occurs—the individual's insistent or disruptive behavior forces the employer to take limit-setting actions. This further increases the paranoid employee's fears that the employer or others are conspiring against him. It is particularly important to seek a face-saving way out for the subject. Some paranoid subjects will resign their position as a way to manage their anxiety (White, 2011). Such a self-initiated departure should not be prevented if other remedies are unworkable, which is often the case. An assessment of the subject's tolerance for anxiety and frustration informs the urgency of the situation and strategic decisions. Paranoia appears in many psychiatric diagnoses, but treatability can vary considerably (Gabbard, 2007).

Workplace Stalking

This scenario describes Gabe as the subject of an ongoing case of workplace stalking:

Gabe's early signs of fixation on his work issues become focused on Andy and Amir. After being terminated he continues with an intense campaign of derogatory emails and phone messages. He then begins to show up at the work site parking lot. He purposely blares his car radio so loudly that employees are distracted and frightened. He leaves each time before the police arrive. He also appears at the homes of Andy and Amir. Personal and corporate restraining orders are served him. He is indignant with police and insists he is not in the wrong as he is "on public property." He eventually is arrested but released. He becomes well known to the law enforcement agencies in the jurisdictions of the company and the residences of Andy and Amir. He hacks the Facebook page of Amir's teenage daughter and uses this information to make intrusive and disparaging sexual remarks about her in emails to Amir's colleagues.

There is no nuance or persuasive strategy in dealing with Gabe. He must be managed and his targets actively protected as necessary. Assessment should include attending to what transgressions Gabe does *not* engage in, suggesting what price he appears unwilling to pay, in spite of his maliciousness and irrationality. His writing and voice messages are reviewed for changes suggesting an attack—ultimatums, a desperate tone, and frank psychotic content with violent delusions. Law enforcement and the local district attorney's office are enlisted to prosecute Gabe to the fullest extent possible. This requires considerable liaison efforts on the part of the company and its legal representatives.

The WAVR-21 includes a Stalking and Menacing Behavior item (Item 6), and the assessor should note the degree of contribution from other WAVR items in a workplace stalking case. In the above case, Item 12: Anger Problems, and Item 10: Entitlement and Other Negative Traits (especially pathological narcissism) would figure prominently in a direct or indirect assessment, both contributing to the motivation for stalking and perhaps physical violence. A WAVR-based assessment may be augmented with other stalking-specific SPJs, such as the *Stalking Risk Profile* (MacKenzie et al., 2009) or the SAM, *Guidelines for Stalking Assessment & Management* (Kropp, Hart, & Lyon, 2008). According to the RECON typology (Mohandie, Meloy, McGowan, & Williams, 2006), Gabe would be categorized as an acquaintance stalker. The general, nonhomicidal violence rate for this group is 27%.

Domestic or Intimate Partner Violence and the Workplace

The WAVR-21 is designed to include the assessment of threats posed by the rejected or controlling partners of employees. These are usually outsiders, but the concern could be created by a coworker with whom the targeted individual has had an intimate relationship. The perpetrators are predominantly male and they most often have communicated some manner of threat to harm the target and/or others at her workplace. Outsiders would not usually be evaluated by a mental health professional assisting the organization, but security professionals or law enforcement may undertake this task when the circumstances warrant it.

The targeted employee is typically under a great deal of stress, balancing her fear of being harmed and the consequences to her career for being perceived or judged for "bringing her personal problems" into the workplace. She is a very helpful source of information about the subject and his risk potential. In-house team members do not always appreciate the value and feasibility of conducting a thorough collateral interview with her or may be reluctant given their training to respect employees' privacy. Domestic violence cases are complicated and the employer may be privy only to "tip of the iceberg" information about an employee's abusive or threatening personal situation (Paziotopoulos & Runge, 2008). In principle, anyone with relevant information should be expected to cooperate with a protective investigation if a credible threat is posed to the workplace. Targeted intimate partner interviews can be conducted respectfully and sensitively. They give the professional, who legitimately may ask probing personal questions related to abuse and escalation, the opportunity to assess the target's intentions as well as the risk to her and possible others in the workplace. In general, the more committed she is to ending the relationship and the more final the message she has given the subject, the higher the risk (Walker & Meloy, 1998). The target may also underestimate the current risk posed by her partner and not be able to recognize a true escalation from a baseline of taunting and threats, which were previously only intended by the subject to control her. Questions from Campbell's (2004) *Danger Assessment* may supplement WAVR-related queries from Item number 18: Domestic/Intimate Partner Violence, as well as the other WAVR items.

Workplace romantic triangles involve a targeted employee, a coworker with whom there is a new relationship or interest, and a rejected partner who is most often an outsider but on occasion is a coworker. This is a potentially high-risk scenario. Whether true or not, the rejected partner's perception of such a relationship and the degree of associated pathological jealousy are highly relevant to assessing risk. The targeted woman may offer useful insights on how she thinks the subject would react to various actions on the part of the employer or authorities, such as protective orders and cease and desist letters, or law enforcement welfare checks to engage the subject for assessment and limit-setting purposes.

CULTURE AND WORKPLACE VIOLENCE

A word is in order about the role of culture in workplace violence, given that this is an international text, and in light of the United States and other western nations becoming increasingly multiethnic and polycultural. There is very little systematic knowledge or research on the role of personal cultural variables in targeted violence, including workplace violence. Most of the literature addresses the issue from a western perspective, and statistics and history clearly indicate that workplace targeted homicide is predominantly an "American" problem. Bullying, mobbing (bullying instigated by a group of coworkers against an individual target), and assaults are more often the "workplace violence" issues in Europe (Chappell & Di Martino, 2006).

Culture refers to the unique behavior and lifestyle shared by a group of people, and includes customs, habits, beliefs, and values that shape emotions, behavior, and life patterns (Tseng, 2003). Any risk factor is subject to being influenced by culture, to either increase risk or to decrease it, as a subject's cultural background and related beliefs may also serve to inhibit violent tendencies (Lim & Bell, 2008). Acculturation, culture clash, and immigration stress may contribute to and exacerbate risk (Meloy, 1992; Tseng, 2003).

When professionals are evaluating a subject outside their own cultural realm of experience, the following considerations may serve as guidelines (White & Christiansen, 2012):

1. Obtain cultural background information relevant to a particular case so as to distinguish common collective behavior from deviant behavior. For instance, consult with someone of the same cultural background as the subject, attempting to illuminate relevant attitudes and practices regarding courtship, marital practices, and gender dynamics; methods and rituals for coping with stress and loss; and definitions of sanctioned violence.

2. Consider enlisting an interviewer from the same culture as the subject if possible.

3. Be aware of problems with language and translation, such as culture-specific idioms, nonmatching vocabulary words, or differences in the meaning of particular words.

4. Consider differences and nuances of etiquette in interviewing that may enhance rapport and minimize the risk of "microinsults." Subjects from nonwestern countries in particular may react with deep shame, which may be either expressed or hidden, to being evaluated by a mental health professional.

5. With caution and realizing that any subject may be dishonest and attempt to present himself or herself in the best light, ask the individual to assist in understanding people of his or her cultural background. This is accomplished with such questions as "How do they think, behave, and react in situations such as yours?" and "What would be their interpretation of your behavior?"

6. Assess the subject's degree of acculturation and understanding of "local" laws, judicial processes, behavioral expectations, and right vs. wrong.

7. In assessing imminent or high-risk scenarios, refer to *known universal risk factors*: motives to harm, intent, fixation, entitlement, psychosis/violent delusions; mood disturbance, especially anger and rage as motivators; substance abuse; firearms/weapons access and capacity; and perturbation (an unbearable sense of pain, dread, hopelessness, and shame). Although influenced by cultural beliefs and attitudes, the issue and indicators are primarily the same—an individual harbors a strongly felt reason or motive for harming an identified or symbolic target and some means to commit the act.

8. When a risk scenario is primarily culturally driven—as with the rising problem of "honor-based" family violence (see Belfrage & Ekman, Chapter 17)—rely on the relevant body of knowledge addressing the assessment and management of that phenomenon as well as the counsel of properly qualified experts.

NOTES

1. Full disclosure: The author and first editor have a commercial interest in the WAVR-21.

2. The author would like to acknowledge Rebecca Speer, Esq., for her assistance with the discussion of legal issues.

KEY POINTS

• The assessment of workplace targeted violence risk first emerged in the 1980s in response to the social and occupational issue of workplace shootings and mass murders. Its principles and practice are consistent with the threat assessment model most clearly articulated in the 1990s by the behavioral scientists of the US Secret Service.

• Risk is complex, involves inherent uncertainties, and is dependent on many factors. Structured professional judgment guides such as the WAVR-21 assist professionals with organizing and coding empirically based risk data.

• Clinical judgment and the experience it reflects will remain the essential tool for the workplace threat assessment professional.

• The practitioner of workplace targeted violence risk assessment must be able to function in dynamic organizational contexts and collaborate with in-house stakeholders, whose experience and resilience may vary widely. The professional may serve a critical role in helping his or her clientele understand the meaning of behaviors of concern, which can be wide-ranging in their nature as well as the risk they may pose.

• Paraphrasing Hart (2011a) and applying his comments to the workplace, risk assessment is inductive, speculative, and idiographic. The endeavor, although it should be based on empirical knowledge of violence risk, is less about probability statements than about language, narratives, and providing action plans for future contingencies.

REFERENCES

American Psychological Association (2010). *Ethical principles of psychologists and code of conduct.* Washington, DC: Author.

Americans with Disabilities Act (1970). 42 U.S.C. § 12113(b).

Beck, J. (2008). Outpatient settings. In Simon, R. I., & Tardiff, K. (Eds.), *Violence assessment and management* (pp. 237–257). Washington: American Psychiatric Publishing.

Binder, R. L. (2006). Commentary: The importance of professional judgment in evaluation of stalking and threatening situations. *Journal of the American Academy of Psychiatry and the Law, 34,* 451–454.

Borum, R., Fein, R., Vossekuil, B., & Bergland, J. (1999). Threat assessment: Defining an approach for evaluating risk of targeted violence. *Behavioral Sciences and the Law, 17,* 327–337.

Calhoun, F. S., & Weston, S. W. (2003). *Contemporary threat management: A practical guide for identifying, assessing, and managing individuals of violent intent.* San Diego, CA: Specialized Training Services.

Campbell, J. (2004). *Danger assessment.* Baltimore, MD: Johns Hopkins University School of Nursing. www.dangerassessment.org.

Chappell, D., & Di Martino, V. (2006). *Violence at work,* 3rd ed. Geneva, Switzerland: International Labour Office.

Cohen, G. S., Duffy, B., Eisenberg, A. L., Heffernan, W. R., & Moll, J. (2008). Strategies for preventing workplace violence. In M. A. Lies II (Ed.), *Preventing and managing workplace violence: Legal and strategic guidelines* (pp. 166–204). Chicago: American Bar Association.

Day, A. L., & Catano, V. M. (2006). Screening out violent employees. In E. K. Kelloway, J. Barling, & J. J. Hurrell (Eds.), *Handbook of workplace violence* (pp. 549–577). Thousand Oaks, CA: Sage.

De Becker, G. (June 1994). *A white paper report: Intervention decisions: The value of flexibility.* Paper presented at the annual meeting of the Association of Threat Assessment Professionals, Anaheim, CA.

De Becker, G. (1997). *The gift of fear: Survival signals that protect us from violence.* Boston: Little Brown.

Denenberg, R. V., & Braverman, M. (1999). *The violence-prone workplace: A new approach to dealing with hostile, threatening and uncivil behavior.* Ithaca, NY: Cornell University Press.

Fein, R., Vossekuil, B. & Holden, G. (1995). *Threat assessment: an approach to prevent targeted violence (Publication NCJ 155000).* Washington, DC: U.S. Dept of Justice, Office of Justice Programs, National Institute of Justice

Fein, R., & Vossekuil, B. (1998). Preventing attacks on public officials and public figures: A Secret Service perspective. In J. R. Meloy (Ed.), *The psychology of stalking: Clinical and forensic perspectives* (pp. 175–191). San Diego, CA: Academic Press.

Fein, R., & Vossekuil, B. (1999). Assassination in the United States: An operational study of recent assassins, attackers, and near-lethal approachers. *Journal of Forensic Sciences, 44,* 321–333.

Feldmann, T. B., & Johnson, P. W., (1996). Workplace violence: A new form of lethal aggression. In H. Hall (Ed.), *Lethal violence 2000.* Kammela, HA: Pacific Institute for the Study of Conflict and Aggression.

Gabbard, G. (Ed.). (2007). *Treatments of psychiatric disorders,* 4th ed. Washington, DC: American Psychiatric Association.

Gilligan, J. (2003). Shame, guilt, and violence. *Social Research, 70,* 4, 1149–1180.

Hart S. D. (2011a). Complexity, uncertainty, and the reconceptualization of violence risk assessment. In Abrunhosa, R. (Ed), *Victims and offenders: Chapters on psychology and law* (pp. 57–69). Brussels: Politeia. (Original work published in 2004.)

Hart, S. D. (April, 2011b). *Professionalizing threat assessment: Should we, have we, can we?* Paper presented at the annual meeting of the Association of European Threat Assessment Professionals, Tallinn, Estonia.

Hart, S. D., Kropp, P. R., Laws, D. R., Klaver, J., Logan, C., & Watt, K. A. (2003). *The Risk for Sexual Violence Protocol (RSVP).* Burnaby, BC, Canada: Simon Fraser University, Mental Health, Law, and Policy Institute.

Hart, S. D., & Logan, C. (2011). Formulation of violence risk using evidence-based assessments: The structured professional judgment approach. In Sturmey P., & McMurran M., (Eds.), *Forensic case formulation.* Chichester: Wiley-Blackwell.

Heilbrun, K. S. (1997). Prediction versus management models relevant to risk assessment: The importance of legal decision-making context. *Law and Human Behavior, 21,* 347–359.

Hempel, A., Meloy, J. R., & Richards, T. (1999). Offender and offense characteristics of a nonrandom sample of mass murderers. *Journal of the American Academy of Psychiatry and the Law, 27,* 213–225.

Innes, M., Barling, J., & Turner, N. (2005). Understanding supervisor-targeted aggression: A within-person between-jobs design. *Journal of Applied Psychology, 90,* 4, 731–739.

Kelleher, M. D. (1997). *Profiling the lethal employee: Cases studies of violence in the workplace.* Westport, CT: Praeger.

Kohut, H. (1972). Thoughts on narcissism and narcissistic rage. *The Psychoanalytic Study of the Child, 27,* 360–400.

Kropp, P. R., Hart, S. D., & Lyon, D. R. (2008). *Guidelines for stalking assessment and management (SAM).* Sydney, NSW, Australia: ProActive ReSolutions.

Lies, M. A., & Powers, J. J. (2008). Employer liability and workplace violence. In M. A. Lies II (Ed.), *Preventing and managing workplace violence: Legal and strategic guidelines* (pp. 258–289). Chicago: American Bar Association.

Lim, R. F., & Bell, C. C. (2008). Cultural competence in violence risk assessment. In Simon, R. I., & Tardiff, K. (Eds.), *Violence assessment and management* (pp. 35–57). Washington, DC: American Psychiatric Publishing.

MacKenzie, R. D., McEwan, T. E., Pathé, M. T., James, D. V., Ogloff, J. R. P., & Mullen, P. E. (2009). *Stalking risk profile: Guidelines for the assessment and management of stalkers.* Elwood, Victoria, Australia: StalkingInc. Pty Ltd & the Centre for Forensic Behavioral Science, Monash University.

Meloy, J. R. (1992). *Violent attachments.* Northvale, NJ: Jason Aronson.

Meloy, J. R., Hempel, A. G., Gray, B. T., Mohandie, K., Shiva, A., & Richards, T. C. (2004). A comparative analysis of North American adolescent and adult mass murderers. *Behavioral Sciences and the Law, 22,* 291–309.

Meloy, J. R., Hoffmann, J., Guldimann, A., & James, D. (2012). The role of warning behaviors in threat assessment: An exploration and suggested typology. *Behavioral Sciences and the Law, 30,* 256–279.

Meloy, J. R., & O'Toole, M. E. (2011). The concept of leakage in threat assessment. *Behavioral Sciences and the Law, 29,* 4, 513–527.

Meloy, J. R., White, S. G., & Hart, S. D. (in press). Workplace assessment of targeted violence risk: the development and reliability of the WAVR-21. *Journal of Forensic Sciences.*

Meloy, R. (1988). *The psychopathic mind: Origins, dynamics, and treatment.* Northvale, NJ: Jason Aronson.

Meloy, R. (1997). Predatory violence during mass murder. *Journal of Forensic Sciences, 42,* 326–329.

Meloy, R. (2000). *Violence risk and threat assessment: A practical guide for mental health and criminal justice professionals.* San Diego, CA: Specialized Training Services.

Meloy, R. (2006). The empirical basis and forensic application of affective and predatory violence. *Australian and New Zealand Journal of Psychiatry, 40,* 539–547.

Mohandie, K., & Meloy, J. R. (2000). Clinical and forensic indicators of "suicide by cop." *Journal of Forensic Sciences, 45,* 2, 384–389.

Mohandie, K., Meloy, J. R., McGowan, M., & Williams, J. (2006). The RECON typology of stalking: Reliability and validity based upon a large sample of North American stalkers. *Journal of Forensic Sciences, 51,* 147–155.

Monahan, J. (1981). *Predicting violent behavior: An assessment of clinical techniques.* Beverly Hills, CA: Sage Publications.

Monahan, J. (1986). Dangerous and violent behavior. In O. B. Dickerson & A. J. Kaminer (Eds.), *Occupational medicine state of the art reviews: The troubled employee* (559–568). Philadelphia: Hanley & Belfus.

Monahan, J. (1993). Limiting therapist exposure to Tarasoff liability: Guidelines for risk assessment. *American Psychologist, 48,* 242–250.

Monahan, J. (2008). Structured risk assessment of violence. In Simon, R. I., & Tardiff, K. (Eds.), *Violence assessment and management* (pp. 17–33). Washington: American Psychiatric Publishing.

Monahan, J., Steadman, H. J., Silver, E., Appelbaum, P. S., Robbins, P. C., Mulvey, ... Banks, S. (2001). *Rethinking risk assessment: The MacArthur study of mental disorder and violence.* New York: Oxford University Press.

Mullen, P., & Lester, G. (2006). Vexatious litigants and unusually persistent complainants And petitioners: From querulous paranoia to querulous behavior. *Behavioral Sciences and the Law, 24,* 333–349.

Occupational Safety and Health Act (1970). 29 USC § 654.

O'Toole, M. (2000). *The school shooter: A threat assessment perspective.* Quantico, VA: Critical Incident Response Group, FBI Academy, National Center for the Analysis of Violent Crime.

Otto, R. K., & Douglas, K. S. (Eds.). (2010). *Handbook of violence risk assessment tools.* Milton Park, UK: Routledge.

Paziotopoulos, P., & Runge, R. (2008). What employers can do to minimize the impact of domestic violence and stalking in the workplace. In M. A. Lies II (Ed.), *Preventing and managing workplace violence: Legal and strategic guidelines* (pp. 258–289). Chicago: American Bar Association.

Perline, I. H., & Goldschmidt, J. (2004). *The psychology and law of workplace violence: A handbook for mental health professionals and employers.* Springfield, IL: Charles C. Thomas.

Pew Research Center. (2012). Fewer, poorer, gloomier: The lost decade of the middle class. Available at: http://www.pewsocialtrends.org/files/2012/08/pew-social-trends-lost-decade-of-the-middle-class.pdf

Prince, P., & Phelps, A. (2010, August). *Partnering for Client Safety.* Paper presented at the annual meeting of the Association of Threat Assessment Professionals, Anaheim, CA.

Rugala, E. A. (Ed.). (2004). *Workplace violence: Issues in response.* Quantico, VA: Critical Incident Response Group, FBI Academy, National Center for the Analysis of Violent Crime.

Scalora, M. J., Baumgartner, J. V., Callaway, D., Zimmerman, W., Hatch-Maillette, M. A., Covell C. N., ... Washington, D. O. (2002). An epidemiological assessment of problematic contacts to members of Congress. *Journal of Forensic Sciences, 47,* 1–5.

Schouten, R. (2008). Workplace violence and the clinician. In Simon, R. I., & Tardiff, K. (Eds.), *Violence assessment and management* (pp. 501–520). Washington, DC: American Psychiatric Publishing.

Shea, S. C. (1999). *The practical art of suicide assessment: A guide for mental health professionals and substance abuse counselors.* New York: John Wiley & Sons.

Speer, R. A. (2003). Workplace violence: A legal perspective. *Clinics in Occupational and Environmental Medicine, 3,* 733–749.

Swanson, J., Holzer, C., Ganju, V., & Jono, R. (1990). Violence and psychiatric disorder in the community: Evidence from the epidemiological catchment area surveys. *Hospital and Community Psychiatry, 41,* 761–770.

Tardiff, K. (2008). Clinical risk assessment of violence. In Simon, R. I., & Tardiff, K. (Eds.), *Violence assessment and management* (pp. 3–16). Washington: American Psychiatric Publishing.

Terkel, S. (1972). *Working: People talk about what they do all day and how they feel about what they do.* New York: The New Press.

Tseng, W. (2003). *Clinician's guide to cultural psychiatry.* London: Academic Press.

Turner, J. T., & Gelles, M. G. (2003). *Threat assessment: A risk management approach.* New York: Haworth Press.

US Department of Justice: Office of Justice Programs. (2011).

US Department of Labor: OSHA Administration. (2011).

Walker, L. E., & Meloy, J. R. (1998). Stalking and domestic violence. In J. R. Meloy (Ed.), *The psychology of stalking* (pp. 140–161). New York: Academic Press.

Warren, L., Mullen, P., Thomas, S., Ogloff, J., & Burgess, P. (2007). Threats to kill: A follow-up study. *Psychological Medicine, 38, 4,* 599–605.

White, S., (April 2011). *The paranoid employee.* Paper presented at the annual meeting of the European Association of Threat Assessment Professionals, Tallinn, Estonia.

White, S. G., & Cawood, J. C. (1998). Threat management of stalking cases. In J. R. Meloy (Ed.), *The psychology of stalking* (pp. 295–315). New York: Academic Press.

White, S. G., & Christiansen, R. (August, 2012). *The role of culture in stalking and violence risk: A case study and assessment format.* Paper presented at the annual meeting of the Association of Threat Assessment Professionals, Anaheim, CA.

White, S., & Meloy, J. R. (2007). *The WAVR-21: A structured professional guide for the workplace assessment of violence risk.* San Diego, CA: Specialized Training Services.

White, S. G., & Meloy, J. R. (2010). *The WAVR-21: A structured professional guide for the workplace assessment of violence risk, Second edition.* San Diego, CA: Specialized Training Services.

7

Threat Assessment and Management in Higher Education

Enhancing the Standard of Care in the Academy

EUGENE R. D. DEISINGER, MARISA R. RANDAZZO,
AND JEFFREY J. NOLAN

Following the April 2007 tragedy at Virginia Tech, numerous US and international educational, governmental, and professional organizations conducted reviews on an array of issues related to campus safety and violence prevention (e.g., Leavitt, Spellings, & Gonzalez, 2007; Virginia Tech Review Panel, 2007). Those reviews recognized that having a threat assessment and management (TAM) process was critical for enhancing early identification and intervention with situations that posed a risk of violence or significant disruption to the campus environment (e.g., ASME Innovative Technologies Institute, 2010; International Association of Campus Law Enforcement Administrators, 2008; National Association of Attorneys General, 2007). In the ensuing years, many institutions of higher education have created multidisciplinary teams or enhanced the operations of existing teams.

Within the United States at least, there is an emerging standard of care with respect to implementing and operating a threat assessment team on campus (see ASME Innovative Technologies Institute, 2010; Nolan, Randazzo, & Deisinger, 2011). To enhance the safety and well-being of college campuses, institutions must do more than simply form a team. Such a team can only operate effectively when it facilitates a systematic process that (1) enables centralized awareness of developing concerns through an active outreach program, (2) conducts a thorough and contextual assessment of the situation, (3) implements proactive and integrated case management plans, (4) monitors and reassesses the

situation on a longitudinal basis, (5) staffs the process with an effective and relevant multidisciplinary team, and (6) conducts all of these practices in accordance with relevant laws, policies, and standards.

Some institutions have focused on the implementation of a multidisciplinary team without the foundation of a clear purpose or an effective and systematic process (Nolan et al., 2011; Randazzo & Plummer, 2009). Forming and operating a threat assessment and management team (TAM team) without a clear mission or systematic process is an approach that is fraught with limitation, error, and liability. In such cases, *form* attempts to drive *function* and campuses end up with multidisciplinary teams (and campus communities) that are unsure of their mission, purpose, operation, and utility. This chapter will address key components in working toward an effective threat assessment and management process, including recommendations for the staffing and operation of a multidisciplinary team to facilitate the process. This will allow form to follow function rather than the reverse.

UNDERSTANDING TARGETED VIOLENCE IN HIGHER EDUCATION

To support understanding and response to cases involving threatening and disruptive behavior, practitioners should have a working understanding of issues related to targeted violence in colleges and universities. In 2010, the US Department of Education, US Secret Service, and Federal

Bureau of Investigation released a joint reported entitled *Campus Attacks: Targeted Violence Affecting Institutions of Higher Education* (Drysdale, Modzeleski & Simons, 2010). The report's authors reviewed incidents of targeted violence that had affected colleges and universities during the twentieth century. They found 272 cases that met the inclusion criteria for targeted violence. Approximately 80% of those incidents of violence occurred on campuses: Residential settings (i.e., campus dormitories or apartments), public grounds, and administrative or classroom buildings were the most common locations in which victims were attacked. The study also looked at incidents that occurred off campus (but that were related to the subject's or victim's affiliation with a campus) and found that nearly 20% of overall incidents occurred at off-campus locations. Again, residential settings and public areas represented the most common areas for an incident to occur.

Precipitating events were identifiable in over 80% of cases; however, the subjects engaged in pre-incident threats or aggression to targets in only 29% of cases. In 31% of cases, concerning behaviors (of the subject) were identified prior to the incident of targeted violence.

Consistent with research from other venues, there was no single demographic profile of perpetrators. Although males represented 80% of perpetrators, there was a marked range in age from the youngest at 16 to the oldest at 62 years of age. Students accounted for approximately 60% of perpetrators, with two thirds of those being currently enrolled. The remaining perpetrators were former students, raising the question as to whether separation by itself was an effective deterrent to escalation toward violence. Similarly, faculty and staff accounted for about 11% of perpetrators with about half of those being currently employed and the remainder being former employees. Intimate partner violence was a significant factor in overall incidents. Beyond those incidents in which perpetrators were directly affiliated with the campus (students, faculty, or staff), another 20% of perpetrators were only indirectly affiliated with the campus, primarily through their involvement in an intimate relationship with a member of the campus community. Finally, the study reported a disturbing finding in that 9% of the perpetrators had no affiliation with the campus on which the incident occurred.

Reports such as the campus attacks study provide an overview of the range, nature, and process of violence that affects campuses. Such an overview informs safety professionals on the range of indicators of concern that may be related to a case in question. Additionally, as perpetrators of targeted violence often show some identification with prior perpetrators and study the tactics and methods of those predecessors, safety professionals are well advised to develop a similar familiarity with incident and perpetrators with whom a subject may identify.

STEPS IN THE CAMPUS THREAT ASSESSMENT AND MANAGEMENT PROCESS

There are several steps to the campus threat assessment and management process, from encouraging the campus community to report concerns or consult with the threat assessment team, to the point where the TAM team first learns about a threat or other disturbing behavior, to a team's screening of initial reports, conducting full inquiries and assessments, engaging in case management planning and implementation where necessary, to the closure of the case (Deisinger et al., 2008; Nolan et al., 2011; Randazzo & Plummer, 2009). Details about the core steps in the best practices for campus threat assessment and management are summarized below.

ENHANCING CENTRALIZED AWARENESS OF CONCERNS

Our tendency as humans is to not want to report concerns or threats unless they are truly alarming—and even then we tend to be bad at reporting. But the easier we can make it for people to report concerns, the more likely they will be to report. Beyond facilitating community members' willingness to report information, which is more of a passive and unidirectional process, effective teams strive to build a culture of consultation which is a much more interactive, collaborative, and engaged process.

The campus community should be able to report possible threats, or other concerning behaviors, to the threat assessment team 24 hours a day, 7 days a week. The more ways that students, faculty, staff, and parents can report concerns to the team, the greater the likelihood that the team will receive reports as early as possible. Many colleges and universities provide their community with a means of anonymous reporting, such as a single telephone number, or dedicated webpage, that can be used to provide information about a person in question without revealing information about the caller. While it may be helpful (and in some jurisdictions may be mandated) to have a means of anonymous reporting, it is important that the anonymous reporting mechanism not be the community's primary or only means of communicating concerns about suspicious or troubling behavior. The team should utilize multiple mechanisms to facilitate reporting to, and consulting with, the team. These mechanisms may include such low-tech options as periodic liaison discussions with each department to remind them that a student or colleague might come to them with some concerning information and that they can, in turn, report that information to the team. It also means having mechanisms (where the reports come in) that facilitate the information gathering process, including searchable records of previous contacts with the threat assessment team, cross-referencing with other police or security contacts, and that the review process involves personnel trained in how to act on reports quickly and effectively.

To enhance reports and consultations with the team, community members need to know it is their role and responsibility to consult with the TAM team about concerns they have. The team should provide examples of the nature and types of behaviors about which community members may seek consultation, as well as where and with whom community members can consult. To facilitate early identification and intervention with developing concerns, the team should clearly convey that such consultation is wanted, even if the initial report turns out not to be a problematic or dangerous situation. The often compartmentalized nature of situations means that individual community members will rarely have awareness of the entirety of a situation, and thus they will seldom be able to rule in or rule out a situation (as a threat) by themselves. It is also critical that the community is aware that, once concerns are identified, reasonable and thoughtful action(s) will be taken to assess, understand, and (where necessary) mitigate concerns. Because higher education populations experience significant turn-over on an on-going basis, there is need for an active outreach program through which the team provides regular and repeated reminders of the consultative process as a resource.

Figure 7.1 shows examples of various sources—on and off campus—that may report concerns to the

FIGURE 7.1 Examples of sources that may report concerns to the threat assessment team.

threat assessment team. Note that the model reflects communication to the team, as well as communication from the team back to the reporting party, to foster ongoing awareness of situations. The figure also reflects examples of where a threat assessment team may actively reach out to see if concerns have developed, to get updates on existing situations, to provide guidance about case management, and to support community members in those roles.

The TAM team serves as a centralized location where an individual can report alarming behavior or troubled suspicions. Based upon an initial report, the team can gather more information from others who know the person in question, piecing together scattered fragments to create a more comprehensive picture of the individual and the threat that he or she may pose. Once the TAM team has this information, the team can develop a strategy to monitor the situation or intervene with the person, if necessary, to reduce the threat. By facilitating communication, collaboration, and coordination across departments, offices, and entities on campus and off, a TAM team can markedly improve an institution's response to developing concerns (Jaeger et al., 1993).

CONDUCTING A THOROUGH AND CONTEXTUAL ASSESSMENT OF IDENTIFIED CONCERNS

Screening Initial Reports and the Role of Triage

Upon receipt of a report of a concerning situation, the team should first determine whether that situation poses a serious and imminent danger or an emergency (Deisinger et al., 2008). This determination is based both on the nature of the initial report (e.g., "John just threatened to kill his supervisor and is walking into the building with a rifle!"), as well as any other information that the team (or the recipient of the initial report) may already have about the context of the situation being reported. When initial reports indicate the presence of an emergent situation, law enforcement and security resources should be immediately notified and dispatched to address and resolve the acute threat. Following the crisis response, it is important for the team to review and assess the situation to determine if there is an on-going threat posed, and if so, to develop a case management strategy to continue to mitigate that threat to the extent possible.

Where the initial report does not suggest an emergent situation (and thankfully, most initial reports do not), the team should triage the initial concern to evaluate whether the reported situation falls within the mission, scope, and authority of the team. From the experience of the authors, the threat assessment process is best used to supplement and enhance existing mechanisms for managing situations, and should not usurp or unnecessarily replace existing mechanisms. This collaborative approach (with other campus and community resources) supports community investment in the process, minimizes abdication of responsibility by those having a legitimate role in addressing concerns, and enhances oversight and transparency of the process for the assessment and management of cases.

Conducting the Threat Assessment Inquiry/Investigation

Upon receipt of information about a situation that meets the criteria for review and management, the threat assessment team must conduct a fair, objective, reasonable, and timely inquiry or investigation both to gain a contextual understanding of the situation and from which to base a meaningful case management strategy (Deisinger et al., 2008; Randazzo & Plummer, 2009). To conduct a full threat assessment inquiry or investigation, the TAM team should review any existing sources of information for the persons and settings involved. This would include the identified subject of concern, as well as any identified targets of grievances or violence, reporting parties, and information about the settings where the subject's behavior is drawing attention. Teams should "ping" their systems, that is, check records/sources that already exist for information relevant to the situation. These sources may include a centralized TAM database, conduct or disciplinary records, criminal history, contact with police/security services that did not result

in charges, performance evaluations, transcripts, etc. The team should also consider seeking information from relevant persons (e.g., roommates, family members, colleagues, etc.) and other sources that may have information about the person/situation of concern. The team should consider a range of persons that may serve as sources of information and monitoring about the subject of concern. These may include persons who regularly interact with the subject of concern, as well as those who may occasionally be in a position to observe the person even if they do not frequently interact with the subject. Consideration should be given to gathering information both from people inside the institution (e.g., faculty, resident advisors, supervisors, etc.) as well as from off-campus sources where appropriate (e.g., previous employer, previous school(s), public internet activity (such as social media sites), and family members.

The team should carefully weigh the risks and benefits from each of these potential contacts in considering not only who to interview, but also when and in what setting, as well as selecting the best person or role to gather the information or conduct the interview (Pollard et al., 2012). However, this information-seeking mandate, to enhance understanding of context, is an important role that distinguishes TAM teams from traditional student assistance or behavioral intervention processes, which typically respond to the incident in question (and the information provided about the incident) but do not seek out additional information from multiple sources that allows for richer understanding and confirmation (or disconfirmation) of reports (Nolan et al., 2011).

Several authors (Calhoun & Weston, 2003; Cawood & Corcoran, 2003; Delworth, 1989; Fein & Vossekuil, 1998; Meloy, 2000; Mohandie, 2000; Vossekuil et al., 2002) have elaborated on potential indicators of concern and advocated a systematized approach to assessing those indicators, which we have summarized into four domains referred to as STEP (Deisinger et al., 2008):

S—Behaviors, traits, characteristics and history of the *subject* of concern

T—Vulnerability of the identified (or identifiable) *target*

E—An *environment* (or system) that facilitates, permits, or does not discourage violence

P—*Precipitating events* that may trigger escalations in concerning behavior

Team members utilize their respective positions and sources to gather relevant information in each of these domains, using several investigative questions (see e.g., Deisinger et al., 2008; Fein & Vossekuil, 1998) to determine whether the person of concern poses a threat to others or the community; that is, whether the subject has developed a plan to do harm and is taking steps to implement that plan.

Forming the Evaluation of the Nature and Level of Threat Posed

As it gathers information through the threat assessment investigative process, the team forms their assessment based on the totality of the circumstances as they are known or reasonably knowable. The team then determines whether the reported situation poses a threat that meets the criterion for continuing intervention by the team, identifies the nature and process of that threat, and uses that conceptualization to guide development of an integrated case management strategy.

In cases in which the team determines that the situation poses a threat, they will develop, implement, monitor, and (on an on-going basis) review a case management plan to intervene and mitigate the threat posed, to the extent reasonably possible. In cases where the team determines that the situation does not pose a threat (and no further reasonably foreseeable precipitating events are identified), the team would close the case. In situations where the threat appears to ebb and flow but is currently at a low level (that does not require active efforts to manage) the team would monitor the person/situation for a period of time and regularly re-evaluate the case to determine whether a threat then exists or may be evolving (Pollard et al., 2012).

DEVELOPING AN INTEGRATED CASE MANAGEMENT PLAN

When the team has determined that the situation poses a threat of violence or significant disruption (meeting the criterion for team involvement) they would then develop, implement, monitor, review, and document an integrated case management plan to intervene and mitigate the identified threat(s). Each case management plan is based on an individualized and contextual understanding of the case, rather than on any proscriptive rubric or formulae. In developing the case management plan, the team must consider not only the needs or potential areas of intervention in a given case, but also the resources and mechanisms available to address

those concerns. The case management plan is designed not only to address identified and acute concerns, but also to help move the subject of concern away from a path of violence and disruption to others.

Similar to the contextual assessment process, integrated case management incorporates coordinated interventions in each of the relevant domains of assessment and intervention outlined by Deisinger et al (2008). An integrated case management plan involves relevant strategies to :

S—De-escalate, contain, or control the *subject* who may take violent action

T—Decrease vulnerabilities of the *target*

E—Modify physical and cultural *environment* to discourage violence or escalation

P—Prepare for and/or mitigate *precipitating events* that may trigger adverse reactions

Subject-Based Strategies

Strategies that are intended to de-escalate, deter, contain, or control the subject of concern would strive to utilize the least intrusive measures that are likely to help achieve movement toward the case management goals (Calhoun & Weston, 2003). Examples of such strategies may include:

- Maintaining communication and engagement with subject
- Involving an ally or trusted person to monitor (and where appropriate) to intervene with the subject of concern. This may be a family member, or peer that has an established relationship with the subject, or may be a team member who develops such a relationship
- Assisting the subject in problem-solving and access to services for assistance/support
- Referring for mental health evaluation and/or treatment
- Mandating psychological evaluation (where lawful and appropriate)
- Involuntary hospitalization for acute mental health assessment
- Confronting the subject and establishing expectations regarding behavior
- Control-based approaches:
  - Discipline
  - Student conduct
  - Criminal prosecution
  - Mandated assessment

- Involuntary hospitalization
- Suspension
- Expulsion
- Termination

It is important to note that such control-based strategies tend to be short-term interventions and do not address ongoing goals of:

- Moving the subject away from thoughts and plans of (and capacity for) violence and disruption
- Connecting the subject with on-going support resources (where needed)
- Monitoring the subject when he or she is no longer connected to the campus community

Teams should use these control-based approaches with the understanding that separation does not equal safety; they should proceed with intentionality and awareness of the limitations and potential consequences of such interventions, including escalation of volatility by the subject (Deisinger et al., 2008; Randazzo & Plummer, 2009). This is not an admonishment against control-based strategies. In fact, failure to hold a subject accountable for inappropriate behavior can contribute to an environment that is conducive to further inappropriate behavior and violence. Rather, it is a caution that such approaches, when used in isolation, rarely resolve significant, ongoing, concerns and are therefore best used as part of an integrated approach that addresses both acute safety concern and ongoing needs of the situation. Where possible in addressing cases involving subjects of concern within the campus community, teams should strive to sustain key relationships (with subject, target, and witnesses) as channels of communication for information gathering and assessment, intervention, support, and monitoring of the situation.

Target-Based Strategies
Many targets/potential victims have little experience in monitoring or addressing their personal safety. Team members can provide coaching regarding personal safety and encourage targets to engage in a variety of interventions, including:

- Setting clear and reasonable limits with the subject(s) of concern
- Making clear statements to the subject when contact and communication are unwanted

- Avoiding/minimizing further contact with (or response to) subject's attempts to communicate
- Documenting of subject behaviors that cause concern and the impact of those behaviors
- Maintaining awareness of surroundings
- Limiting public availability of personal information
- Varying routines
- Traveling in company of colleagues and friends
- Using protective services and surveillance
- Developing contingency plans for escape, shelter, and support should the subject attempt to confront the target
- Developing skills in personal defense
- Making referrals for support and assistance to deal with the stresses and impact of victimization

In his book, *The Gift of Fear*, Gavin De Becker (1997) articulates the core needs that all victims have when they are dealing with safety concerns. De Becker notes that victims want to know that safety professionals (and, by extension, TAM team members) care about them as people and not solely as "cases." De Becker further comments that victims want certainty for their safety, which no one can provide. A TAM team can, however, provide certainty about its processes (i.e., what the team can and cannot provide to support the victim in enhancing his or her safety). De Becker notes that victims need a sense of consistency and that this is supported and upheld by regular, timely, and meaningful communication between the safety professional and the target/victim. When subjects engage in threatening behavior, it is much too easy to become focused on what the team should do *to* the subject of concern rather than what it should do *for* the victim and the community. This balance must be continually struck for the team to maintain effectiveness and credibility.

Environmental Management Strategies
Often in the course of the case it becomes apparent that, beyond the actions of the subject, there are environmental, systemic, or cultural factors that affect a case. Environmental management strategies may include the following:

- Address systemic, policy, or procedural problems that may serve as precipitating events

- Implement prevention/intervention programs to address bullying, harassment, sexual assault, relationship violence, etc.
- Enhance campus climate by working toward a caring community and building a culture of care and consultation
- Intervene with associates that support or encourage violent or disruptive behavior
- Support and expect timely accountability for inappropriate behavior
- Encourage early identification and intervention approaches
- Maintain a culture of setting reasonable and timely expectations
- Enhance conflict management skills
- Enhance supervisory skills
- Implement active crime prevention programs

Monitoring and Mitigating Potential Precipitants

In practice, many precipitating events may not be preventable, and some are not reasonably foreseeable. The task for the TAM team is to better anticipate and plan for the impact of such precipitants, so that a negative impact (on the subject) can be mitigated where possible, and to make plans to monitor and respond to subjects as the case moves forward.

MONITOR AND REASSESS

Cases handled by a TAM team generally remain open until the person of concern no longer appears to pose a threat. This may be well beyond the point when criminal cases are closed or mental health services are completed (Deisinger et al., 2008). Whether the case remains open or is closed, the TAM team should document how they handled the case and include the report that first came to the team's attention, the information the team gathered, the evaluation it made, the case management plan it developed and implemented, and any evaluations or monitoring that the team conducted after the initial evaluation and case management efforts.

A person can continue to pose a threat even after he or she is no longer a member of the campus community. The team's focus should be on whether the person continues to pose a threat regardless of whether he or she is still part of the campus community. If the TAM team believes the person does still pose a threat, the team should continue to monitor the plan and modify it as needed for as long as the person/situation may still reasonably pose a threat. It may be necessary for the TAM team to continue to refer the person of concern to necessary resources outside of the campus community and/or take other follow-up steps as the situation and level of concern dictate, such as notifying local law enforcement where the person of concern now lives.

Finally, as the TAM team considers what may affect the person's behavior in the short, mid- and long term, the team should anticipate the impact of future precipitating events (i.e., important dates or events such as anniversaries, failing a course, termination of benefits, the ending of a relationship, or the occurrence of mass attacks elsewhere) that could prompt the person to become a greater threat. The team should develop contingency plans and take necessary steps to reduce or mitigate the anticipated threats. This on-going, longitudinal view of cases is another aspect that differentiates threat management processes from traditional incident or crisis based interventions that respond at a point in time, rather than across the life span of a case.

UTILIZING MULTIDISCIPLINARY TEAMS

There are certain hallmarks or characteristics of what makes an effective TAM team (Deisinger et al., 2008; Nolan et al., 2011). One such hallmark is that effective TAM teams continually seek to improve communication to *and* from the team in lawful and appropriate ways. Multidisciplinary teams can facilitate and enhance communication as they include persons that can serve as information sources owing to their connections across campus. Team members facilitate the process of information getting to the team through a broad range of channels. Similarly, team members can facilitate the dissemination of information to relevant constituencies across campus. Team members work continuously to identify gaps in communication and to enhance timely and effective flow of information. In short, they agree to share their concerns and their resources.

Another hallmark is that effective TAM teams view issues related to safety and violence as community problems, requiring community collaboration, investment, and partnerships. Team members agree to work together toward shared goals for enhancing the safety and well-being of the campus community.

Through increased communication and a spirit of collaboration, team members can be better able to coordinate activities and interventions. This minimizes risks of individual departments taking actions that interfere with team goals or the actions of other departments. It better allows for interventions and follow-up to be done consistently and more effectively.

Teams make the best possible use of the resources and skills that are available to them. The good news is, especially in times of diminished resources, that many campuses have a range of staff, skills, and resources that are already in place and have an existing role in addressing concerns regarding the safety and well-being of the campus community. The team approach helps maximize the effectiveness and efficiency of those resources. In short, the emphasis is to begin with what you have and make it better as you go.

There are several people and roles that can contribute to threat assessment teams. Common representatives include those from offices such as the following:

- Academic Affairs/Provost/Graduate College
- Employee Assistance
- Human Resource Services
- Police/Security
- Residence Life
- Student Affairs/Dean of Students
- Student Health/Counseling Service
- University Counsel/Attorney

The size and membership of the TAM team will be determined, in large part, by the team's workload and the resources and structure of the institution. Core team membership should be driven by the communication and working relationships that are necessary to achieve the mission of the team. The institution can decide on the team's initial membership and then expand or contract as conditions dictate. A general guide is to have as few core members as are necessary to provide for a timely and objective review of cases. Having too many core members may make for difficult scheduling of regular meetings.

TAM teams handle day-to-day reports submitted to the team, conduct full inquiries, and implement/monitor case management activities. But to be more fully effective, a TAM team needs support from key resources and activities on campus and in the community.

A full discussion of these resources and their usefulness for enhancing TAM team operations and effectiveness is beyond the scope of this

chapter. However, more information can be found at Deisinger et al. (2008). Some examples include:

- Support/backing from the university's leadership
- Administrative support
- Access to mental health services
- Involvement of law enforcement and security services
- Active outreach and training to the community
- Engagement with gatekeepers of all types, at all levels
- Clear policy and procedures for TAM team authority and operations

Threat assessment and management teams must have the authority for managing cases and making decisions, or (in the absence of such authority) have direct and timely access to those with decision-making authority on their campus.

A threat assessment team should be part of a comprehensive and proactive safety and crisis management plan that addresses prevention and mitigation of violence, preparedness, response to active threats and crises, and recovery from critical events (Jaeger et al., 1993).

Having a threat assessment team can be particularly effective at an institution that already has a proactive approach to campus safety. We see threat assessment as an integral part of campuswide efforts to prevent violence, identify persons at risk, intervene with developing concerns, respond to violent events, and recover from any violent events. We recommend that campuses consider conducting an overall vulnerability assessment, consistent with the International Association of Campus Law Enforcement Administrators *Blueprint for Safe Campuses* (2008) and the Massachusetts Higher Education report (O'Neill et al., 2008), to identify areas where enhancement may be needed.

LAW AND THE STANDARD OF CARE

Legal Duties

Maintaining a safe and secure campus is foundational to providing an effective environment for learning and for challenging the development and application of knowledge. While violence occurs in all types of settings, most campuses are relatively safe environments, with low rates of violent crime (in relation to the communities in which the campuses exist). Institutions of higher education often provide a range of services and programs to sustain the safety of the campus environment. Over the past few years, increasing numbers of campuses have implemented threat assessment and management processes as part of larger efforts to enhance campus safety. Enhancing the safety and well-being of the campus is the primary goal of the TAM process (Dunkle et al., 2008). In the course of developing, implementing and operating these teams, myriad legal issues and liability concerns can arise. While liability concerns are always secondary to safety considerations, legal issues are relevant and important considerations in the threat management process. Campus administrators and TAM team members can best support and implement effective threat assessment and management strategies when they understand the legal issues that can be involved.

The following discussion summarizes legal issues that have implications for the TAM process under the legal system of the United States. Practitioners in other parts of the world should consult with their local legal advisors to determine the extent to which analogous legal issues apply in their country. This discussion will summarize general legal principles and issues for consideration, with the understanding that there are variations across jurisdictions in the manner in which some of these principles are applied. TAM team members are encouraged to seek out relevant legal expertise with knowledge of both the domains of law relevant to the case at hand, and the application of law in that particular jurisdiction.

Institutions of higher education are generally accepted to have duties to exercise due care to provide a campus and workplace environment that is *reasonably* safe from foreseeable acts of violence or harm to others. Common law is the most universal source of such duties. Common law stems from the legal principles developed over time by judges in the form of case law, rather than by legislators through statutes. Details of common law vary from state to state, and an analysis of every jurisdiction's laws is beyond the scope of this chapter. However, a legal resource known as the Restatement of Torts (American Law Institute, 2011) does provide a foundation for understanding the legal principles likely to be applied in many states.

If a college or university causes harm to a student or visitor through the acts or omissions of a campus employee, then the institution is likely to be liable for negligence if the employee failed to exercise reasonable care and thereby created a risk of physical harm (American Law Institute, 2011). The legal duty can be thought of then as a duty to avoid doing harm.

When considering issues related to campus violence and threat assessment, communities tend to think in terms of violence perpetrated by students, and do not consider acts perpetrated by employees. This discussion will focus on duties owed to students and visitors, but not on employees, because workers' compensation statutes typically provide the exclusive remedy for employees injured or killed within the scope of their employment. Some sections of the Restatement (e.g., Restatement (Third) of Torts, § 40(b)(4)(a) and § 40, cmt. k; American Law Institute, 2011) and some jurisdictions do consider institutional liability to employees, but such issues are state-specific and beyond the scope of this chapter. In any case, institutions will strive to take reasonable steps to keep employees safe from physical attacks on campus, even in the absence of a general legal duty to do so. The duties of most importance to the campus TAM context are those described in Sections 40–43 of the Third Restatement. We will discuss each in turn.

Duties Based on a Special Relationship with the Injured Person

Section 40 of the Restatement (American Law Institute, 2011) states that "an actor in a special relationship with another owes the other a duty of reasonable care with regard to risks that arise within the scope of the relationship," and provides that one of the "special relationships" that creates a duty is the relationship of "a school with its students (American Law Institute, 2011; Restatement (Third) of Torts, § 40(a), § 40(b)(5))." A statement within section 40 makes clear that by "school" the Restatement intended the section to apply to institutions of higher education. Section 40 of the Restatement also recognizes that "because of the wide range of students to which it is applicable, what constitutes reasonable care is contextual—the extent and type of supervision required of young elementary school pupils is substantially different from reasonable care for college students." The section further states that "[c]ourts are split on whether a college owes a duty to its students," and that courts that do find a duty reach that conclusion based on a broad variety of sometimes questionable rationales. The Restatement appears to recognize that the law is far from settled on this point. Nonetheless, institutions of higher education are encouraged to plan and operate as if courts will recognize *some* level of duty to protect students from other students or third parties. Practitioners and attorneys who are interested in the specific cases cited and annotated in the Restatement should refer to Nolan et al. (2011). Section 40 of the Third Restatement (American Law Institute, 2011: Restatement (Third) of Torts, § 40(b)(3)) also states that organizations that hold their premises open to the public have a "special relationship" with, and a duty to reasonably protect, those who are lawfully on their grounds. Institutions of higher education that maintain open campuses would typically be assumed to fit within this definition. The Restatement also states (and courts have regularly recognized) that landlords have a duty to exercise reasonable care to protect their tenants from foreseeable criminal activity (American Law Institute, 2011: Restatement (Third) of Torts, § 40(b)(6)). Courts that may be hesitant to find a "special relationship" based on the student-university relationship alone, may fit hazing and criminal assault cases into a "business invitee" or "landlord-tenant" framework in which a duty may attach; team members should recognize that these legal interpretations continue to provide avenues for those claiming that colleges and universities have a duty to exercise reasonable care to prevent foreseeable incidents of violence that occur on campus.

Duties Based on a Special Relationship with the Subject Posing the Risk

Section 41 of the Restatement focuses on situations in which an institution may have a "special relationship" with the subject who is posing a risk for violence, and a duty to exercise reasonable care to prevent the person from harming others. Employers are generally liable for the acts of employees if those acts are within the scope of employment, i.e., the acts are motivated at least in part by a desire to serve the employer (see Restatement (Third) of Agency, § 2.04 (American Law Institute, 2011). Acts of violence are, thankfully, outside the scope of employment for most jobs. However, Section 41 of the Restatement states that employers can still be held liable for acts outside the scope of an employee's employment "when the employment facilitates the employee's causing harm to third parties" (American Law Institute, 2011: Restatement (Third) of Torts, § 41(b)(3)). To

"facilitate" could be as simple as providing access to physical locations (e.g., dormitories or classrooms) by virtue of a person's employment. Institutions of higher education should assume that they "have a duty to exercise reasonable care in the hiring, training, supervision, and retention of employees" (Nolan & Moncure, 2012). Therefore, institutions (and TAM team members) should understand that they will likely be found to have a duty to use reasonable care in utilizing their threat assessment team when an employee's actions or comments raise concerns as to whether the employee may pose a threat to others.

Section 41 of the Restatement identifies another "special relationship" as that which a mental health professional has with patients (American Law Institute, 2011; Restatement (Third) of Torts, § 41(b)(4)). The duty relating to that special relationship comes from state laws and court decisions that implement the principles outlined in the California Supreme Court's decision in *Tarasoff v. Regents of the University of California* (551 P.2d 334 Cal. 1976). Generally speaking, legal principles based on the *Tarasoff* guidelines either require or permit mental health professionals to release information (that would otherwise be protected under therapist-patient privilege) where the mental health professional reasonably believes that the patient may pose an imminent risk of harm to an identified individual or individuals. Section 41 of the Restatement recommends that mental health professionals use "reasonable care" to warn identified targets and/or take other reasonable steps to prevent specific, imminent harm. Note that there is significant variation from state-to-state as to whether and how such duties (to warn and/or protect) are specified in statute or outlined by court findings. Mental health professionals on TAM teams should have a working knowledge of the mental health professional-patient rules in their state, and should also take steps to ensure that other mental health professionals on campus have a clear understanding of those rules (Jed Foundation, 2008). Of course, mental health professionals, such as counseling center staff, can always assist the TAM team in a more general advisory capacity, even in situations where they cannot disclose case-specific information.

Duties Based on Undertakings

Sections 42 and 43 of the Third Restatement (American Law Institute, 2011) describe other legal duties that could be relevant in certain TAM cases. These sections state that a person (e.g., TAM team member) who assumes responsibilities to provide services to another (in the case of TAM teams, to implement a case management strategy to mitigate the risk of physical harm) should presume that they have a duty to provide reasonable care in the undertaking if (a) the failure to exercise such care increases the risk of harm beyond that which existed without the undertaking, or (b) the person to whom the services are rendered (or another person) relies on the TAM team member exercising reasonable care in the undertaking. These duties (also referred to as "gratuitous undertakings") are adapted from earlier editions of the Restatement of Torts and have been utilized by many courts over the years, including having been applied in cases involving colleges and universities (see cases cited in Nolan, Randazzo, & Deisinger, 2011). These duties will likely continue to be accepted and utilized widely by courts as outlined in the Third Restatement of Torts.

In the context of actions taken by TAM team members, it could be (and likely will be) argued that a team's actions to assess and manage risks perceived to be posed (by subjects of concern) would fall within the scope of duties based on undertakings. To meet the likely standards of liability, the team's actions would have to either increase the risk of harm (beyond that which existed without the team's intervention) or the team's actions would have to be relied upon to the detriment of an injured person. One can imagine a scenario in which an injured person claimed that statements made or actions taken by the TAM team gave the (subsequently) injured person a "false sense of security" that resulted in the injured person being more vulnerable to an attack— since the injured person relied upon the TAM team for protection and therefore did not take protective actions of their own.

Of course, each case would be argued based on its unique set of facts and several elements would have to be satisfied before liability would attach. However, team members should be aware of the range of potential legal duties that may attach when working with their campus TAM teams and must be sure to undertake threat assessment and management activities in a professional manner and to perform them well.

Standards of Care

This section will focus on how TAM-related standards of care are likely to be developed in the litigation context in the United States. Team members in those states in which a campus TAM team is required by law (currently, Virginia and Illinois) should have no trouble explaining to administrators why TAM teams should be created and supported by their institutions. Virginia Code § 23-9.2:10 (2008) was enacted after the April, 2007 shootings at Virginia Tech and requires public higher education institutions in Virginia to establish a threat assessment team that will educate the campus community regarding behavior that may pose a threat to the community and to implement policies and procedures for the reporting of such behavior and the assessment of individuals whose behavior may present a threat. Similarly, Illinois Statute 110 ILCS 12/20(b) (2009), enacted after the February, 2008 shootings at Northern Illinois University, requires each Illinois institution of higher education (public and private) to develop a campus threat assessment team. The Restatement of Torts (American Law Institute, 2011) duties described above provide (in general) that, where an affirmative duty to avoid a risk is imposed by a special relationship, an actor (e.g., TAM team member) has an obligation to exercise "due care." This raises the question of the definition of "due care" in the context of campus threat assessment and management. There is no nationwide, universally applicable statute that defines due care in this context The Virginia statute lists, in general terms only, activities that TAM teams should perform in Virginia. Beyond that limited legal guideline, the TAM team "standard of care" issue is relatively wide open. Whether a TAM team's actions in a particular case met a broadly defined standard of care would be subject to debate. In the context of litigation, that debate is likely to be played out by the competing opinions of expert witnesses. Therefore, team members should be familiar with the range of resources that experts would likely reference as defining the standard of due care.

In regard to the elemental question of whether institutions of higher education should have threat assessment teams, there is little room for debate. Many of the campus safety reviews and reports that have been done (especially those conducted in the wake of the 2007 Virginia Tech shootings) contain recommendations to the effect that campuses should create and implement threat assessment teams on campus. Several of these reports are summarized in "The IACLEA Blueprint for Safer Campuses (IACLEA Special Review Task Force, 2008), a document published by the International Association of Campus Law Enforcement Administrators. The

Blueprint synthesizes several reports done regarding the Virginia Tech shootings as well as several general reviews of campus safety, and contains numerous recommendations for campus safety from the International Association of Campus Law Enforcement Administrators (IACLEA). Campus safety officials and TAM team members should review the campus safety-related recommendations noted in the Blueprint to assess whether their campus safety operations are consistent with best and promising practices. On the specific topic of Threat Assessment Teams, the Blueprint recommends that "[i]nstitutions of higher education should have a behavioral threat assessment team that includes representatives from law enforcement, human resources, student and academic affairs, legal counsel, and mental health functions. Specifically, campus public safety should be included on the team." In litigation, competent experts would likely testify that this recommendation, based as it is on consideration of several campus safety review reports, represents a consensus as to what institutions of higher education should be doing as part of efforts to prevent and mitigate risk for violence on campus. Further, as more institutions of higher education develop and implement threat assessment and management processes, the presence of such campus teams becomes a part of customary practice in the industry. Such customary practices may be used as evidence of the standard of care. While the "reasonable care under the circumstances" guideline remains the technical standard in most cases, evidence of customary practices can be persuasive to help define reasonable care. As noted in The Law of Torts, § 164 (Dobbs, 2001), "On the issue of negligence, a safety custom is often relevant because it reflects the judgment and experience of many people and thus directly suggests how a reasonable person might behave under the circumstances, on the theory that customary behavior is usually not negligent, or on the more specific ground that, under some circumstances, customary behavior tends to prove the proper balance of risks and utilities…[A] safety custom in a negligence case is relevant evidence tending to show what does or does not count as reasonable care." Therefore, customary practice strongly indicates that the applicable standard of care requires colleges and universities to have TAM teams.

This position would also be supported by a publication approved by the American National Standards Institute ("ANSI"), known as "A Risk Analysis Standard for Natural and Man-Made Hazards to Higher Education Institutions" (ASME Innovative Technologies Institute, LLC, 2010). This document outlines a "methodology to identify, analyze, quantify, and communicate asset characteristics, vulnerabilities to natural and man-made hazards, and consequences of these hazards on the campuses of colleges and universities." The Standard recommends "that Threat Assessment teams be put into place on campus to help identify potential persons of concern and gather and analyze information regarding the potential threat posed by an individual(s)."

In light of this recommendation, team members and campus administrators should recognize that courts have often either allowed testimony to the effect that standards promulgated by voluntary standards organizations (such as ANSI) represent the standard of care in an area of practice, or have allowed such standards into evidence as support for the standard of care. Voluntary standards do not have the force of law; however, they can be persuasive evidence of the standard of care, especially given the deliberative, consensus-driven, process by which recognized guidelines are typically created. There is ample case law to this effect (see cases cited in Nolan, Randazzo, & Deisinger, 2011), so it is likely that courts would similarly permit reference to the TAM team recommendation in the ASME-ITI/ANSI Risk Assessment Standard in the event of litigation related to threat assessment teams.

In addition to recommending the use of TAM teams within institutions of higher education, the ASME-ITI/ANSI Risk Assessment Standard also "provides resources for implementing Threat Assessment teams on campus." The ASME-ITI/ANSI Standard states that "the following resources or equivalent may be helpful in conducting a risk assessment" and lists the following:

- Plummer and Randazzo, *Implementing Behavioral Threat Assessment on Campus: A Virginia Tech Demonstration Project* (Virginia Polytechnic Institute and State University, 2009);
- Deisinger, Randazzo, O'Neill, and Savage, *The Handbook for Campus Threat Assessment & Management Teams* (Applied Risk Management, 2008);
- The Virginia Tech Review Panel Report, August 2007 (http://www.vtreviewpanel. org/report/index.html).

Such resources would not define the standard of care exclusively or conclusively. However, they would likely be cited as persuasive in the event of TAM-related litigation, because they are relied upon and recommended in the ASME-ITI/ANSI standard. Therefore, team leaders and members should determine whether their threat assessment teams are following practices consistent with those described in the ASME-ITI/ANSI-cited resources. Threat assessment teams should follow practices that are most responsive to the needs of their particular campuses and the cases in which they are involved, but if a team's practices differ substantially from the general approaches outlined in commonly cited resources (such as those cited in the ASME-ITI/ANSI Standard) the team should be able to articulate how a differing approach is more appropriate, given the unique needs of its campus.

CONCLUSION

Managing situations involving individuals who may pose a threat of violence or significant disruption is a challenging and risky business. However, some risk in this area cannot be avoided, as the current standard of care (at least in the United States) dictates that colleges and universities must have a campus threat assessment process involving a multidisciplinary team. Given this reality, campus leaders should assure that their campus communities know about and feel comfortable consulting with their TAM teams, that their teams follow best and promising practices informed by the evolving science of the field, that misconceptions about privacy and disability laws do not impede their teams' work, that institutional policies and procedures support rather than impede the work of their teams, that their teams follow optimal documentation practices, and that their institutions are positioned to balance appropriately the statutory rights of persons of concern against campus safety needs. Campus leaders that address these issues will have gone a long way toward reducing the risk of harm on their campuses and minimizing legal liability in this sensitive area.

APPENDIX: A CASE STUDY

Note that all identifying information, including case facts that might identify the parties or institution, has been changed to protect the privacy of those involved.

INITIAL REPORT

The student of concern, Marla Smith, first came to the attention of one of her university professors, Dr. Jason Lewis, who relayed his concerns to the campus Threat Assessment and Management (TAM) team. Dr. Lewis told the team that Ms. Smith had been successful academically in the first three years of her undergraduate program but that, within in the first few weeks of her senior year, her behavior had started to raise concern among several of his colleagues in the Political Science Department. Dr. Lewis indicated that Ms. Smith was a major in political science and was engaged in an honors thesis under his supervision. Dr. Lewis said that he had worked closely with Ms. Smith throughout the previous year and was very familiar with her. He said that he became concerned when he started hearing from two other professors that Ms. Smith was becoming verbally abusive and aggressive to other students in her classes and to those professors in meetings in their offices. She had gone so far as to make a veiled threat to one professor, Miriam Jones, during a meeting in her office, where Ms. Smith told Professor Jones she should "stop harassing me in class or you'll be sorry." Professor Jones mentioned this to Dr. Lewis because she was aware that Dr. Lewis had worked with Ms. Smith for over a year. Professor Jones told Dr. Lewis she found the comment to be "chilling" and that she was now somewhat fearful about having Ms. Smith in her class.

SCREENING/ INFORMATION GATHERING

After receiving this report, the TAM team screened the case to decide whether the report suggested an emergency or imminent situation. If a report that the team receives suggests an emergency or imminent situation, the team notifies campus police or local law enforcement immediately to contain the situation. In this case, the team reviewed the initial report and decided it did not suggest an imminent situation, so they did not need to notify campus police or local law enforcement.

For this team, the next step was to screen the case to determine whether a full threat assessment inquiry was warranted. To do so, they used the screening questions below. If they answered no to all of these questions, they would refer the case to the CARE team, another committee that handled lower-level student concerns. But if they answered yes to any one of the questions, the TAM team would conduct a full threat assessment inquiry.

Screening Questions

1. Has there been any mention of suicidal thoughts, plans, or attempts?
2. Has there been any mention of thoughts/ plans of violence? Or fear of violence from a potential target or third party?
3. Does the person have access to a weapon or is he or she trying to gain access? (In addition to whatever behavior has raised concern and led to a report to the TAM team.)

In this case, the TAM team answered yes to Screening Question 2. Based on the report the TAM team received, it seemed that there had been a possible threat of violence (although several team members pointed out that no one knew for sure what Ms. Smith meant by "you'll be sorry" and that they would have to speak with Ms. Smith directly at some point to find out.) The TAM team also answered yes to Screening Question 2 because they felt there was fear of violence from a potential target—citing Professor Jones's comments to Dr. Lewis that she was somewhat fearful of having Ms. Smith in her class. Based on these answers, the TAM team conducted a full threat assessment inquiry.

CONDUCTING A FULL THREAT ASSESSMENT INQUIRY

To conduct the full threat assessment inquiry, the TAM team first developed a list of all of the people, departments, and offices within the university—and other sources outside the university—that team members felt might have some information about Ms. Smith. Team members then volunteered to each take a few sources from the list to call, talk to, or ask for information regarding Ms. Smith and how she seemed to be doing.

Included on the list was Ms. Smith herself. The TAM team discussed whether to interview Ms. Smith, and most felt that it was important to talk with her and hear her side of the exchange with Professor Jones, as well as to ask her about her other confrontations with other students and faculty members. Once it was decided that someone should

talk with Ms. Smith, the team then discussed who should have that conversation with her. The team looked to see whether there was anyone they could identify that Ms. Smith might see as an ally or someone she might regard as being supportive of her. The team settled on Dr. Lewis as someone they wanted to include in the interview and also identified Emily Larson, the campus deputy police chief, who was a regular member of the team, to participate in the interview out of potential safety concerns. Because Ms. Smith had reportedly become aggressive and hostile in several recent conversations, the team felt that the deputy would be an important addition because she was adept at handling difficult conversations and skilled at defusing situations to prevent escalating hostility. Dr. Lewis and Deputy Larson agreed that it would be best to talk with Ms. Smith at the start of the inquiry so that she would hear from them that her behavior was raising some concerns— rather than hearing this at second or third hand from those whom the team planned to interview. At the conclusion of this initial case staffing meeting, the TAM team compiled a list of action items—people to talk with and other information sources to search—and each team member was given a portion of the list to complete. The team adjourned and agreed to talk by phone within the next day or two, after they had gathered this information—or sooner if any team member developed information that merited prompt attention.

CHECKING SOURCES AND FINDING INFORMATION

Team members were tasked with gathering information about Ms. Smith, her current situation, and her current behavior from various sources. The sources generally focused on information about the four components or factors that contribute to acts of targeted violence: information about the subject (i.e., person of concern), information about the target (e.g., recipient of a threat or anyone who feels unsafe), information about the subject's environment (i.e., the setting—and whether those around the person of concern may support or encourage violence), and information about any precipitating events (e.g., recent or impending losses, failures, humiliations, or jeopardy events—such as a tenure decision or child custody hearing). Using that framework, the TAM team members learned the following in their discussions with and searches of those sources:

Subject: From Ms. Smith's other professors, the team learned that she has been confrontational with other students in nearly every class session this semester, which two professors who previously taught Ms. Smith described as "highly uncharacteristic" and "not at all like her." Interviews with the professors who taught Ms. Smith in her junior year described her as a capable and friendly student who generally contributed well in class. None recalled confrontational or aggressive behavior from Ms. Smith.

In the interview with Ms. Smith, the interviewers described that she was defensive about her behavior and claimed she never acted aggressively toward anyone else but was merely defending herself against aggression from other students and faculty members. She said she did not remember students or faculty being so aggressive toward her in previous years, but she certainly was not going to take it. When asked what she meant by "not going to take it," Ms. Smith explained that she felt she had the right to stand up for herself and defend herself verbally. When asked about her veiled threat to Professor Jones, that she'd "be sorry," Ms. Smith said she meant that she would file a formal complaint against Professor Jones for harassment.

Checks with other university offices and external sources yielded some additional information about Ms. Smith: She was not of record with the student conduct office. Residence Life staff members were not aware of any complaints or issues involving Ms. Smith. A check with national criminal databases showed she had no prior arrests, restraining orders, or any registered weapons. A check with the campus police department yielded no incident reports involving Ms. Smith, although the campus police chief said that last year Ms. Smith stopped by the university police department a few times to talk with him about pursuing a career in federal law enforcement and seemed very interested in doing so. A check with the university's counseling center yielded no information; the counseling center could not acknowledge whether Ms. Smith was a patient there or not. A check with Disability Services showed that Ms. Smith was not known to that office. A check with the registrar showed a current GPA of 3.25 and a solid academic record throughout her time at the university. Her tuition payments were also current.

Target: Professor Jones confirmed the veiled threat and reiterated that she did tell Dr. Lewis that she felt "somewhat unsafe" about having Ms. Smith in her class but that she was not exactly sure why.

She also said she felt badly about saying that about a student but that "in this day and age you can't be too careful." None of Ms. Smith's other professors indicated that they felt unsafe because of Ms. Smith, although several described her behavior as "increasingly erratic." The chair of the Political Science Department later contacted the chair of the TAM team after she heard about the situation with Ms. Smith and demanded that Ms. Smith be removed from all political science courses and expelled from the university because she had threatened a member of her department. She said that if Ms. Smith were not immediately expelled, she, the department chair, would speak directly with the university president and have the TAM team reprimanded.

Environment: Checks with Residence Life revealed Ms. Smith had a roommate. Team members debated about whether to talk with Ms Smith's roommate because they did not want to alarm her or cause tension between the two. Team members instead asked the Residence Life director to have one of the resident advisors check with Ms. Smith's roommate in a general inquiry about how things were going in their living situation now that they were several weeks into the school year. The resident advisor reported that Ms. Smith's roommate seemed relieved to have a chance to talk with someone about Ms. Smith because she has been very concerned about her and did not know what she should do. She said that she knew Ms. Smith for over two years and that they had always been friends, but that this year she seemed very different. She was very aggressive in their conversations and seemed very anxious about a lot of academic and social things that never bothered her before. She also said that Ms. Smith rarely slept and would often pace around the room at night or spend hours on the computer, sometimes talking to herself. She said she was worried about Ms. Smith but had not told anyone because she did not want to get her friend in trouble. She added that she did not know why Ms. Smith would be acting so strangely because Ms. Smith told her she was on Lexapro, a new medication she was taking for depression, and she saw her take it pretty often, so she believed her. She said that Ms. Smith was also taking better care of herself, as she had recently stopped smoking and had gotten some generic Chantix pills while she was in Mexico over the summer, which she was taking to help her stay off cigarettes. The resident advisor asked the roommate if she felt safe and she said she did, but that she would be sure to call campus police if she had any concerns about safety and would tell the resident advisor if she noticed anything new or concerning about Ms. Smith.

Finally, an Internet search of major social media sites and a Google search of Ms. Smith's name, Professor Jones' name, the university's name, and a search on Ms. Smith's personal email address and mobile phone number revealed some limited information. Ms. Smith had a Facebook page but it had a privacy setting, so that only her Facebook friends can view her page. One of the friends listed was her roommate. There were a few comments from Ms. Smith on several online articles on the university newspaper's website, all from this academic year. The tenor of the comments was fairly aggressive and demeaning of the articles' authors, but there were no threats. No other results were found.

Precipitating events: Through its interviews, the TAM team was not able to identify any precipitating events coming up for Ms. Smith—or recent losses or failures that she may have experienced. The TAM team acknowledged that the insistence from the Political Science Department's chair that Ms. Smith be expelled introduced an unpredictable factor into the information they were reviewing in that the team could not know how the department chair would interact with Ms. Smith; and whether decisions or communications from the department chair could further exacerbate the concerning behavior already seen in Ms. Smith.

EVALUATING WHETHER THE PERSON/SITUATION POSES A THREAT

To analyze the information that the team had gathered, team members met by phone to share the various bits of information they had learned through their interviews and other research. Then, as a group, they answered the key investigative questions recommended in *The Handbook for Campus Threat Assessment & Management Teams* (Deisinger et al., 2008), which come from the original US Secret Service investigative questions recommended for use by law enforcement in protective intelligence and threat assessment investigations (Fein & Vossekuil, 1998). These questions are as follows:

1. What first brought the person to the team's attention? Do those conditions or situations still exist? Does the person of concern feel that he or she is being addressed?

    The team first became aware of Ms. Smith because she had been verbally aggressive and confrontational with fellow students and faculty members, leaving one professor "somewhat fearful." These conditions still exist because Ms. Smith contends that she has not been the aggressor but instead has been acting in self-defense in all of those interactions, saying that those individuals acted aggressively toward her first.

2. Have there been any communications suggesting ideas or intent to attack others?

    Ms. Smith told Professor Jones to "stop harassing [her] or you'll be sorry." The comment made Professor Jones "somewhat fearful." Ms. Smith contends that she meant she would file a formal harassment complaint against Professor Jones and did not mean she would harm her.

3. Has the person shown inappropriate interest in campus/workplace/school attacks or attackers; fixation on weapons; other mass violence or terrorism; obsessive pursuit, stalking or pursuit of others?

    None identified.

4. Has the person engaged in any attack-related behaviors?

    Not that the team has learned of thus far. The team agrees to follow up with Ms. Smith's roommate on this question if she will agree to talk again.

5. Does the person have the capacity to carry out an act of targeted violence?

    There is no record of Ms. Smith having a registered weapon. Ms. Smith's roommate said Ms. Smith has never mentioned weapons to her and believes she would know if Ms. Smith got one.

6. Is the person experiencing hopelessness, desperation, or despair?

    The clinical psychologist on the team noted it does not seem that Ms. Smith is currently experiencing desperation, but she may be experiencing increasing anxiety.

7. Does the person have a trusting relationship with at least one responsible person?

Ms. Smith appears to have a trusting relationship with her honors thesis advisor, Dr. Lewis.

8. Does the person see violence as an acceptable, desirable, or only way to solve problems?

Some team members opined that her veiled threat to Professor Jones means that Ms. Smith sees violence as at least a potential solution to her problems. Other team members disagreed, saying that they believed Ms. Smith's explanation that she would resort to formal grievance procedures if she felt Professor Jones was still harassing her but that she would not resort to physical violence.

9. Is the person's conversation or "story" consistent with his or her actions?

Ms. Smith's perception of the interactions where she has been described as aggressive are nearly the opposite of the others in those interactions. Ms. Smith does not deny her behavior, but denies that she is the one who initiated, saying instead that she only acted aggressively after others had acted aggressively toward her first.

10. Are other people concerned about the person's potential for violence?

Professor Jones said that Ms. Smith's comments made her "somewhat fearful" and described them as "chilling." Others asked whether they are concerned about Ms. Smith's potential for violence have said they do not think she would engage in violence.

11. What circumstances might affect the likelihood of violence—increase it or decrease it?

The psychologist on the team expressed concern that Ms. Smith appeared to be sleeping so little, was experiencing anxiety, and was taking two new medications— one of which did not seem to have been prescribed for her (the Chantix she told her roommate she purchased in Mexico). The

psychologist further noted that possible side effects of Lexapro and Chantix both include increased aggression and/or suicidal thoughts—and the two drugs may also have some interaction effect if Ms. Smith is in fact taking both. The warning labels for both medications instruct patients to immediately notify their doctor if they experience those side effects.

12. Where does the person exist along the pathway to violence—if at all?

The team members agreed that it was difficult to say if Ms. Smith had an idea to do harm to others, self, or both. All agreed that even if she had an idea to do harm, they had not uncovered any information suggesting she was taking steps to carry out the plan.

MAKING THE ASSESSMENT

Assessment Question 1: Does the person pose a threat of violence to others, to self, or both?

Based on the entirety of information they were able to learn about Ms. Smith and her current situation, the team did not feel that Ms. Smith was on a pathway to violence or that she posed a threat of violence to others or to herself at the time of their assessment.

Assessment Question 2: If the person does *not* pose a threat, is he or she otherwise in need of assistance or intervention?

Even though the team members did not feel that Ms. Smith posed a threat of harm to herself or others, they all agreed that without some intervention or referral for services, Ms. Smith's behavior would continue to disrupt the academic and living environments of the university. The clinical psychologist on the team specifically felt that the aggressive behavior seen in Ms. Smith could be the result of the new antidepressant she was on (Lexapro) if the dosage was not correct, or it could be the result of an interaction between the Lexapro and Chantix if Ms. Smith was in fact taking the Chantix. Therefore the team felt that some plan to inform Ms. Smith's treating psychiatrist of the behavior they were seeing, refer Ms Smith to any other necessary resources, and continue to monitor her and her situation would be necessary.

INTEGRATED CASE MANAGEMENT PLANNING

Because Ms. Smith's aggressive behavior toward faculty members and fellow students had violated the university's student code of conduct, the team recommended that the university require Ms. Smith to adhere to a behavioral contract with the university as a way to defer a conduct charge. The behavioral contract set forth specific behavioral and other conditions the Ms. Smith would have to meet in order to maintain her enrollment and agreed to put the student conduct charge on hold to see if Ms. Smith could conform her behavior to those expectations going forward. If she failed to do so, the conduct charge would be reinstated and Ms. Smith would face the typical penalties, which could include suspension or expulsion. The conditions to which Ms. Smith agreed to adhere in the behavioral contract included stopping all aggressive and "self-defense" behavior (as she saw it); agreeing to have the team share its observations about Ms. Smith's behavior with her treating psychiatrist; seeing a university counselor weekly for ongoing monitoring of her medication; and a clause that if she ever felt she needed to "defend herself" in an interaction with faculty, students, or staff, she was instructed to immediately leave the interaction and seek out Dr. Lewis for guidance. The team offered to Professor Jones to transfer Ms. Smith to a different class and to provide Professor Jones with campus security escorts if she wanted them. Professor Jones declined both offers. The team also reached out to Ms. Smith's roommate to ask her to share any ongoing or new concerns with her resident advisor in the event she observed any.

Outcome: When the psychiatrist heard the team's concerns and observations about Ms. Smith's aggressive behavior, she immediately changed the dosage of the Lexapro and instructed Ms. Smith to stop taking the generic Chantix. Within a few weeks, Ms. Smith's behavior returned to the normal behavior that she had shown in her previous three years. The team checked in periodically with Ms. Smith, Professor Jones, Dr. Lewis, and the roommate to make sure that Ms. Smith continued to adhere to the behavioral contract conditions. She completed her senior year successfully and graduated on schedule.

KEY POINTS

A threat assessment team operates effectively when it facilitates a systematic process that:

- Enables centralized awareness of developing concerns through an active outreach program
- Conducts a thorough and contextual assessment of the situation
- Implements proactive and integrated case management plans
- Monitors and reassesses the situation on a longitudinal basis
- Staffs the process with an effective and relevant multidisciplinary team
- Conducts all of these practices in accordance with relevant laws, policies, and standards of practice

---

REFERENCES

American Law Institute (2011). *Restatement of the law (third), torts: Liability for physical and emotional harm.* Washington, DC: Author.

ASME Innovative Technologies Institute. (2010). *A risk analysis standard for natural and man-made hazards to higher education institutions.* Washington, DC: Author.

Association of Threat Assessment Professionals. (2006). *Risk assessment guideline elements for violence: Considerations for assessing the risk of future violent behavior.* Los Angeles: Author.

Calhoun, F. S., & Weston, S.W. (2003). *Contemporary threat management: A practical guide for identifying, assessing and managing individuals of violent intent.* San Diego, CA: Specialized Training Services.

Corcoran, M. H., & Cawood, J. S. (2003). *Violence assessment and intervention: The practitioner's handbook.* New York: CRC Press.

De Becker, G. (1997). *The gift of fear: And other survival signals that protect us from violence.* New York: Dell.

Deisinger, G., Randazzo, M., O'Neill, D., & Savage, J. (2008). *The handbook for campus threat assessment & management teams.* Boston: Applied Risk Management.

Delworth, U. (1989). *Dealing with the behavioral and psychological problems of students.* New Directions for Student Services, no. 45. San Francisco: Jossey-Bass.

Dobbs, D.B. (2001). *The law of torts.* Eagan, MN: West Group.

Drysdale, D., Modzeleski, W., & Simons, A. (2010). *Campus attacks: Targeted violence affecting institutions of higher education.* Washington, DC: U.S. Secret Service,

U.S. Department of Homeland Security, Office of Safe and Drug-Free Schools, U.S. Department of Education, and Federal Bureau of Investigation, U.S. Department of Justice.

Dunkle, J., Silverstein, Z., & Warner, S. (2008). Managing violent and other troubling students: The role of threat assessment on campus. *Journal of College and University Law, 34*(3), 585–636.

Fein, R., & Vossekuil, B. (1998). *Protective intelligence and threat assessment investigations: A guide for state and local law enforcement officials.* Washington, DC: U.S. Department of Justice, Office of Justice Programs, National Institute of Justice.

International Association of Campus Law Enforcement Administrators. (2008). *Overview of the Virginia Tech tragedy and implications for campus safety: The IACLEA blueprint for safer campuses.* West Hartford, CT: Author.

Jaeger, L., Deisinger, E., Houghton, D., & Cychosz, C. (1993). *A coordinated response to critical incidents.* Ames: Iowa State University.

Jed Foundation. (2008). *Student mental health and the law: A resource for institutions of higher education.* New York: Author.

Leavitt, M., Spellings, M., & Gonzalez, A. (2007). *Report to the president on issues raised by the Virginia Tech tragedy.* Washington, DC: U.S. Department of Health and Human Services, U.S. Department of Education, and U.S. Department of Justice.

Meloy, J. R. (2000). *Violence risk and threat assessment.* San Diego, CA: Specialized Training Services.

Mohandie, K. (2000). *School violence threat management.* San Diego, CA: Specialized Training Services.

Nolan, J. J. & Moncure, T. M. (2012). The legal side of campus threat assessment and management: What student counselors need to know. *Journal of College Student Psychotherapy, 26*, 322–340.

Nolan, J. J., Randazzo, M. R., & Deisinger, E. R. (2011). Campus threat assessment and management teams: What risk managers need to know now. *URMIA Journal*, 105–122.

O'Neill, D., Fox, J. A., Depue, R., & Englander, E. (2008). *Campus violence prevention and response: Best Practices for Massachusetts Higher Education. Report to the Massachusetts Department of Higher Education.* Stoneham, MA: Applied Risk Management.

Pollard, J. W., Nolan, J. J., & Deisinger, E. R. D. (2012). The practice of campus-based threat assessment: An overview. *Journal of College Student Psychotherapy, 26*, 243–276.

Randazzo, M. & Plummer, E. (2009). *Implementing behavioral threat assessment on campus: A Virginia Tech demonstration project.* Blacksburg, VA: Virginia Polytechnic Institute and State University Press.

U.S. Department of Education. (October 2007). *Balancing student privacy rights and school safety: A guide to the Family Educational Rights and Privacy Act for colleges and universities.* Washington, DC: Author.

Virginia Tech Review Panel. (2007). *Mass shootings at Virginia Tech, April 16, 2007: Report of the Review Panel presented to Governor Kaine, Commonwealth of Virginia.* Richmond, VA: Author.

Vossekuil, B., Fein, R., Reddy, M., Borum, R., & Modzeleski, W. (2002). *The final report and findings of the Safe School Initiative: Implications for the prevention of school attacks in the United States.* Washington, DC: U.S. Department of Education and U.S. Secret Service.

8

Threat Assessment in Schools

KRIS MOHANDIE

ethal school violence incidents, while not new,
became a particular focus of threat assessment
professionals in the early 1990s—a concern that continues to the present day. While the United States has
been the apparent leader in terms of the phenomenon, noteworthy events have occurred in many countries including Russia, Germany, Finland, England,
Canada, China, and Afghanistan. This chapter will
outline the fundamentals of school violence threat
management: categories of potential perpetrators,
evolving patterns of violent offending on campuses,
dynamics of violent individuals who target schools,
essential threat assessment variables, practical
aspects of threat assessment in school environments,
interviewing techniques with at-risk subjects, threat
assessment teams, and threat management strategies. A short history of noteworthy events traces the
evolution of school violence threat management as a
contemporary international concern.

NOTEWORTHY EVENTS

The first major US school violence incident occurred
May 18, 1927, in Bath, Michigan, and resulted in the
deaths of 45 people, including 38 children and the
offender. The perpetrator was treasurer of the local
school board and upset about taxes that had been
levied to pay for the school, nursing his grudge for
nearly five years prior. He used explosives to kill most
of the victims, having spent the better part of spring
booby-trapping the school buildings under the guise
of performing electrical contracting work. The subject
murdered his wife prior to leaving for town to perpetrate

his carnage and burned down all the buildings on his
farm. He left a message painted on a fence rail at his
property: "Criminals are made, not born." Ultimately,
upon returning to the scene, he killed himself and two
additional victims after detonating a second round of
explosives in his car. Fortunately a malfunction kept
more than 500 pounds of explosives from detonating,
or he would have killed every student and staff member
in this 250-student school (Mohandie, 2000).

The arrival of regularly occurring, modern-day
mass homicide began August 1, 1966. College
student Charles Whitman used the tower at the
University of Texas, Austin, as his shooting platform,
killing 16 of his 45 victims before finally dying in
a hail of gunfire. His victims included his wife and
mother, who were killed at a separate location before
the school campus shooting. Premonitions of his
violent intentions were documented by a university
psychiatrist several months preceding the incident,
when Whitman disclosed his violent fantasy in which
he often thought about going up on the tower with a
deer rifle and shooting people (Lavergne, 1997).

General recognition of the need for school-based
threat assessment coincided with the Columbine
High School incident of April 20, 1999: it marked
the culmination of a number of events that had
occurred throughout the United States during the
1990s. This extensively planned mass homicide by
two teenage perpetrators who ultimately committed
suicide resulted in the deaths of 12 fellow students
and a teacher. This event shattered the illusion (and
shared denial) that school violence was an isolated

problem confined to rural communities within America. It was as if the United States, and perhaps much of the industrialized world, wearily sighed in acceptance that school violence could happen anywhere, and acknowledged a collective responsibility to do a better job of identifying the risks and intervening prior to such events.

Russia's terrorist-perpetrated Beslan School siege of September 2004 underscored the fact that campus violence was not exclusively the domain of lone, disenfranchised adult subjects or disaffected teenagers acting alone or in pairs (Meloy, Hempel, Mohandie, Shiva, & Gray, 2001); but that schools could be targeted by organized groups of individuals—violent true believers (Meloy, Mohandie, Hempel & Shiva, 2001)—with a sociopolitical agenda. Approximately thirty Chechen separatists, including several female offenders, violently took over a school in Beslan, holding over a thousand hostages. The incident concluded with a violent and bloody tactical intervention by Russian forces and the deaths of approximately 334 hostages, including 186 children (actual casualties and fatalities are estimated given misinformation from official sources). This is the world's worst incident of school violence.

The terrorist attacks on US soil of September 11, 2001, seemed to diminish the frequency of completed campus violence events for several years, at least partially owing to a widespread and heightened sensitivity to issues of violence risk. The symbol of a disconcerting return to a "normal" pattern of school violence occurred on April 16, 2007. Mentally disordered college student Cho Seung-Hui killed 32 people (students and several professors) and wounded 17 others at Virginia Polytechnic Institute and State University in two separate events occurring approximately two hours apart. Following this incident—which had apparently been planned for months—the subject committed suicide. He even took time between the events to send a video to a New York news outlet, documenting his angry and paranoid motivation. This particular event, which culminated in the most US fatalities in a campus violence incident since Bath, Michigan, in 1927, highlighted failures within the university to adequately address the subject's earlier problematic behavior, which had been reported by fellow classmates and an instructor; legal loopholes that allowed him to purchase a firearm despite having been declared mentally ill and suicidal by a judge; misunderstandings about privacy issues pertaining to at-risk students;

and gaps in the system that allowed court-mandated psychological treatment to be left unconfirmed.

Finland had two noteworthy events within a year. The first occurred November 7, 2007, at Jokela High School, resulting in the deaths of two staff members and six students and the suicide of the 18-year-old student offender. The offender posted, in English, dozens of YouTube videos, many of them articulating his homicidal and suicidal fantasies and intentions, disdain for humanity, self-hate and depression, admiration for the Columbine offenders, and footage showing him shooting his firearm. It was later discovered that he had been communicating through cyberspace with an American would-be offender who was ultimately arrested just prior to perpetrating a school violence event near Philadelphia—a phenomenon referred to as "virtual pairing" (J. R. Meloy, personal communication, December, 2007). A second Finland offender targeted his college campus on September 23, 2008, mimicking his predecessor with YouTube postings that showed him engaging in target practice (with stated homicidal fantasies), making threats in English such as "you will die now," and saying "goodbye." In this situation, the offender was reported to police based upon his cyberspace activity, but after interviewing him, authorities mistakenly concluded that they did not have enough information to take action. The unsuccessful police intervention likely accelerated his violent trajectory, because the next day he perpetrated his mass homicide, killing 10 people and committing suicide. It is noteworthy that both Finnish shooters participated in a cyberspace social network (and likely had some online contact with one another in yet another virtual pairing), revolving their activities around YouTube and the Finnish social networking site IRC-Galleria, intended for those interested in school shootings. This community—which included members from Finland, Germany, and the United States—exchanged videos related to school shootings.

UNDERSTANDING WHY

Analysis of many campus extreme violence events has led to the identification of some common themes among the offenders. Externalization of blame and the offender's need to communicate about his or her grievance and punish those whom he or she holds responsible for the associated suffering seem to be central, whether the foundation for that issue is accurate or delusionally based. Ultimately violence as a potential solution emerges, often in response to some life dilemma or precipitating event. The stated or underlying internal process may be personal, ideological, or religiously themed, with many recent events appearing to be multidetermined. Justification and rationalization harden the idea, and cognitive constriction of thought, inadequate problem solving, and poor coping occur for a variety of reasons, including acute stress or a lifelong pattern of habitual responding. The moment of decision (as perceived by the offender) arrives, and a conscious choice is made to pursue the violent idea. Preparations for the violence unfold, which may be immediate or longer-term. At this "operational" stage, weapon seeking, acquisition, and rehearsal occur. Without intervention (either happenstance or purposeful), the subject or subjects will engage in violence.

Many of the common patterns observed among school violence offenders mirror the commonalities of suicidal individuals as observed by Shneidman (1996): (1) solution-seeking, (2) cessation of consciousness, (3) unbearable psychological pain, (4) frustrated psychological needs, (5) common emotion of hopelessness/helplessness, (6) cognitive state of ambivalence, (7) perceptual state of constriction, (8) common action is escape, (9) common interpersonal act is communication of intent, and (10) consistency of lifelong styles. Violent actions, fantasy, and planning offer a grandiose, omnipotent antidote to counteract feelings of hopelessness and helplessness in homicidal (and sometimes concurrently suicidal) individuals.

This may not be all that unexpected, since the natural course of many mass murderers is suicide after the offense (Meloy et al., 2001). Suicide is often considered by the violent subject prior to settling on directing it outward or after discarding the inward option; instead, he elects to punish those he believes have driven him to it.

CYBERSPACE AND SOCIAL NETWORKING

The ever-increasing cyberconnection element merits consideration. Had the Internet been available in 1927, the Bath, Michigan, offender likely would have opted for this venue rather than his fence rail to convey his parting message. Many offenders have a profound narcissistic aspect to their personalities, and the Internet provides an ideal medium to reinforce certain core beliefs infused with themes of control, entitlement, and attention seeking, such as: "I am so important that naturally everyone wants or should listen to me," "You must listen to me," and "I am

entitled to be heard." Social media and cyberspace appeal to the narcissistic personality structure that underlies many of these offenders.

The Internet has stimulated the evolution of the "pronoid pseudocommunity," a phenomenon developed and described by Meloy (Meloy & Mohandie, 2009), which combines Goldner's (1982) concept of pronoia—the delusional belief that others are saying nice things about you, which exists as a counterpoint to paranoia—with Cameron's (1943, 1959) notion of the paranoid pseudocommunity. The subject believes that he or she is among a community of believers with whom he or she is mutually attached and identified (Meloy & Mohandie, 2009), with the Internet instantly and readily providing this virtual community. The Internet allows subjects to form attachments to ideas or ideologies that may replace genuine attachment to an actual group, allowing the individual to become much more grandiose and omnipotent in his or her beliefs. A simple Google search of a variety of deviant ideas will quickly validate that there is a virtual support group somewhere in cyberspace for just about anything. Cyberspace validates potential offenders for their violent ideas and justifications, reinforcing whom to hate and fear, and perhaps stoking behavioral escalation. It thus disinhibits aggression and allows the offenders' ideas to germinate, take stronger root, and develop more fully than ever before.

CAMPUS VIOLENCE—A RANGE OF BEHAVIOR

Campus violence includes a range of problematic behavior from threats and intimidation to single and mass homicide (Deisinger et al., 2008). In fact, some of the "lesser" forms of violence may serve as preludes to more lethal violence. These lesser forms include stalking, bullying, assaults, property damage, sabotage, vandalism, sexual victimization, arson, and cyberspace-based pursuits and harassment.

CATEGORIES OF VIOLENT OFFENDERS

To be effective, school-based threat assessment professionals must appreciate that threats come from a variety of sources. Type 1 events are perpetrated by individuals who have no connection to the campus; they target the campus for their own idiosyncratic reasons—the Beslan incident described above is an example of a terrorist motivation to select a school as a target. Other type 1 events have involved disturbed individuals who targeted a campus for delusional reasons. Type 1 events are challenging because with them, there may be less information available to campus personnel—information that might enable them to anticipate and prevent an attack, Instead, threat management must rely heavily on target hardening strategies such as security systems, campus police and security personnel, and access control systems to reduce accessibility to would-be perpetrators or convey that they will be interrupted if they attempt to carry out their violent plans. Occasionally, astute investigators or community members might become aware of reconnaissance or suspicious interest in a school by a subject, leading the violent pathway to be discovered and disrupted. In other situations, the subject may begin to communicate inappropriately with campus personnel, leading to assessment and intervention by proper authorities. The important point is that outsiders can and do target schools, and threat assessment professionals must be prepared to identify and stop these individuals.

Type 2 events are perpetrated by subjects who are customers or service recipients of the school, such as students, individuals coming on campus to make use of resources such as libraries or health services, or even parents and guardians of students. The Texas Tower incident as well as the Columbine, Virginia Tech, and Finland incidents are all type 2 events.

Type 3 incidents are employee-related events, caused by employees or former employees of the school and occasionally loved ones striking up the cause for their partner. These are classic workplace violence scenarios in which the offender strikes back at his or her campus employer in a violent way. An example of this is the University of Alabama incident of February 12, 2010, in which three professors were killed and three others wounded by Amy Bishop, another professor. The offender, a married mother of four, was reportedly upset over having been denied tenure and borrowed the gun used in the offenses.

In an example of a loved one taking up the cause, Clay Duke took a school board hostage on December 14, 2010, likely with the intent of mass homicide and/or suicide by cop (Mohandie, Meloy, & Collins 2009) prior to being shot by police. At the outset of the incident, he walked calmly into the room armed with a pistol and painted a "V" on the wall, his homage to the vengeance-oriented movie *V for Vendetta*. He was at least partially motivated by his wife's termination from the school district, but he also had a litany of other antigovernment complaints and sentiments.

Type 4 events are domestic violence-related incidents perpetrated by subjects who are current or former romantic partners of a student or staff member. The campus is selected because of its convenience to the offender in locating his or her victim. Type 2, 3, and 4 risk events offer the greatest opportunity for threat assessment and disruption of violence because there is usually information available about the subject, including leakage (defined and described below).

FOUR ASSESSMENT FACTORS—ESSENTIAL PRINCIPLES OF THREAT ASSESSMENT

Four categories of information inform threat assessment: (1) warning signs or leakage, (2) risk factors, (3) stabilizing factors, and (4) precipitating events. Threat assessment in schools begins with identification of a potential problem. Warning signs consist of behavior and statements sufficient and reasonable to cause concern that there might be a risk for violence. These may include verbal statements such as threats to physically harm made by an individual of concern; bizarre statements or behavior that suggest that the individual is delusional, paranoid, or psychotic; obsessions with themes of blame, desperation, or concerning behaviors such as threatening gestures, violent drawings or writings (beyond the context of an assignment), or weapons possession on campus (Mohandie, 2000). Meloy and O'Toole (2011) define leakage as communication of intent to harm a target to a third party; they suggest eight warning behaviors: (1) pathway warning behavior, (2) fixation warning behavior, (3) identification warning behavior, (4) novel aggression warning behavior, (5) energy burst warning behavior, (6) leakage warning behavior, (7) directly communicated threat warning behavior, and (8) last resort warning behavior. Meloy et al. (2012) further elaborate upon these supraordinate patterns of accelerating risk.

Pathway warning behavior is defined as any behavior that is part of the research, planning, preparation, or implementation of an attack (Meloy & O'Toole, 2011; Meloy et al., 2004). This may include information seeking about weapons and their acquisition, as noted in the Virginia Tech shooting fact pattern.

Fixation warning behavior is any behavior that indicates an increasingly pathological preoccupation with a person or a cause (Meloy & O'Toole, 2011), as occurred in the Florida school board hostage taking and thwarted shooting. Clay Duke was obsessed with the wrong he perceived his wife as having suffered, various paranoid ideas pertaining to the government-sponsored media, as well as the power of the wealthy in America.

Fixation may also include stalking as a warning behavior, and there are four commonly observed patterns of stalking: intimate stalkers, who target a current or former intimate; acquaintance stalkers, who pursue an individual they know, such as a coworker, classmate, health care provider, or former friend; public figure stalkers, who victimize someone they've never met but learned about through their public visibility, such as an actor, politician, school leader, or highly visible local celebrity—a well-known college athlete, for example; and private stranger stalkers, who stalk someone they have never met who has the misfortune of being in the same environment and thus accessible to the stalker, such as another student attending the school with whom the stalker has never had any kind of relationship (Mohandie, Meloy, McGowan, & Williams, 2006). Violence is possible with all types of stalkers; thus each case requires a unique evaluation of the variables enhancing or reducing risk within each. However, findings from group data indicate that intimate stalkers are the most violent, with a 74% violence rate. Acquaintance stalkers have a 50% violence rate, public figure stalkers have a 2% violence rate, and private stranger stalkers have a 36% violence rate (Mohandie et al., 2006). It may be that the 2% figure is an underestimate for campus-based local public figures owing to accessibility differences and other variables inherent in this victim pool. The Virginia Tech offender reportedly stalked and harassed several female victims in a private stranger pattern: they did not know him and were targeted, at least partially, because of their proximity to him. Stalking is very common as a warning sign within campus environments, with the most commonly observed pattern that of being stalking by a prior intimate.

Another form of fixation that is often observed in the more serious cases is aggression immersion, whereupon the offender repetitively exposes himself to violently themed media, revealing a potentially problematic underlying violent fantasy life (Meloy & Mohandie, 2001). Many offenders become preoccupied with violently themed movies, music, video games, and other media that are viewed repetitively and/or intensely, becoming part of how they further develop their fantasies of revenge. Their themes support violent acting out, such as the need for revenge,

and provide scenarios for such an individual to replicate. Inquiries in specific cases should include assessing recent or long-term interest in such material and whether it supports this dynamic. Many offenders—including the subjects from Virginia Tech, Finland, and Columbine—engaged in this aggression immersion before committing their offenses. Movies that have reflected this dynamic include *Old Boy* (Virgina Tech), *Falling Down* (Pearl, Mississippi), *A View to a Kill* (Jokela, Finland), *Natural Born Killers* (Columbine), and *V is for Vendetta* (Florida School Board shooting).

Identification warning behavior refers to any behavior that indicates a psychological desire to be a "pseudocommando," (Meloy & O'Toole, 2011) and have a "warrior mentality," to be closely associated with weapons or other military or law enforcement paraphernalia (Meloy, Hempel, & Richards, 1999), to identify with previous attackers, or to identify oneself as an agent advancing a particular cause or belief system. The Virginia Tech shooter demonstrated this feature in his choice of attire, statements, posturing, and props (the hammer he held was imitative of the *Old Boy* murder weapon) memorialized in the self-made videos that he created prior to the tragic incident.

Novel aggression warning behavior includes acts of violence unrelated to attack behavior committed for the first time. Such behaviors test the ability of the subject to actually do a violent act. When it comes to the forecasting of behavior, it is often said that the best predictor of future behavior is past behavior. Nearly all school violence homicide incidents are the first known murders perpetrated by the offender, and at some point offenders engage in the new escalation of behavior for the first time. Thus school threat assessment professionals must examine the subject's history, particularly recent history, for evidence that the person is escalating or capable of escalating. Assaults, harm to animals, arson, and rehearsed violence with inanimate objects (which are fantasized to be human targets) exemplify this issue. Luke Woodham, the teenage school shooter from Pearl, Mississippi, sadistically killed his dog Sparkle in an act of novel aggression days before he killed his mother and then two students at his high school on October 1, 1997.

Energy burst warning behavior is an increase in the frequency or variety of any noted activities related to the target. This was demonstrated by the Texas Tower offender Whitman, who made multiple visits to the site of the mass homicide before the actual shooting, while the Virginia Tech shooter engaged in several visits to the shooting range in the weeks prior to the event.

Leakage warning behavior is the communication to a third party of an intent to do harm to a target. This is one of the more commonly observed warning behaviors and was evidenced most prominently by the Finland shooter in his posting of multiple YouTube videos, many of which contained threats to do harm to others.

Directly communicated threat warning behavior involves the communication of a direct threat to the target or law enforcement beforehand. This occurs occasionally; however, many offenders recognize that directly threatening the target may reduce their chances of success. Nonetheless, such behavior does occur; in any case directly communicated threats should be taken seriously and investigated thoroughly. Sometimes offenders cannot contain their homicidal impulses in service of the operational viability of their criminal mission, thus affording authorities the opportunity to derail their efforts.

Last resort warning behavior involves increasing desperation or distress through declaration in word or deed by the would-be offender. In these communications or behaviors, it is evident that the offender views himself as running out of time or acts as if the end were near. Imminence is conveyed in thought or action. Most offenders will demonstrate this in one way or another. On March 21, 2005, the 16-year-old school shooter from Red Lake, Minnesota, killed his grandfather (a sergeant with the local police department) and his grandfather's girlfriend at his house; then he drove the grandfather's police car to his school and murdered seven others, finally committing suicide. He wrote on his MSN website prior: "16 years of accumulated rage suppressed by nothing more than brief glimpses of hope, which have all but faded to black. I can feel the urges within slipping through the cracks, the leash I can no longer hold."

Another methodology with which to review a behavioral trajectory is to analyze five factors related to the subject's behavior and/or communications: organization, fixation, focus, violent action imperative, and time imperative (Mohandie & Duffy, 1999). *Organization* refers to the extent to which an identified at-risk subject demonstrates the ability to sequence his or her actions as evidenced in written, verbal, or other behavior, and whether there are well-understood central themes of motivation.

If the subject is capable of sequencing, and able to clearly articulate his or her motivational themes, the risk for well-orchestrated, planned predatory attack is higher. If such an individual is disorganized in word and deeds and themes are unclear, risk may still exist but the offenses are more likely to take the form of impulsive and less predictable attacks. *Fixation* occurs when the subject is invested in an important issue or agenda, usually suffused with blame and the need for retaliation, but themes of omnipotence or misguided delusional missions might also be important. Fixation indicates energy that may fuel an attack and thus is a risk-enhancing variable. *Focus* indicates whether the subject has identified a potential target or set of targets at which to direct this energy vs. an individual or group who have yet to settle upon a direction. Focus increases risk. *Violent action imperative* occurs when the subject states or demonstrates through behavior a willingness to use violence or other unacceptable means to resolve an issue. *Time imperative* reflects urgency or an inferred or stated deadline for acting out. Both of these last variables signal increased violence risk potential.

CAMPUS SAFETY: A "WE" RESPONSIBILITY

Students, faculty and administrators, parents, and concerned community members should be encouraged to observe and report warning behaviors of individuals who might present a threat to others in the campus community, including if they might be at risk to themselves. Zero-tolerance policies should be thoughtfully developed; for example: "the school district has a zero tolerance policy against potential safety threats, takes potential threats seriously, investigates thoroughly, and will take actions appropriate to the situation" (Mohandie, 2000). This sample policy mandates an investigation and actions, but does not define specifics which could result in overreaction, given the reality that all threats are not created equal, and cases differ (Mohandie, 2000). What is mandated is to address the issue. It is useful to promote "see something, say something" outreach campaigns, to create a culture of shared responsibility for campus safety, and to provide clear options for reporting potential concerns with at least one anonymous reporting method. This outreach should target students, parents, staff members, and even outside community members who might become privy to warning sign information (Hoffman, Schuh, & Fenske, 1998).

RISK FACTORS

Risk factors are historical or other variables that have a known or presumed relationship to enhanced risk in a subject. These may include warning signs, but ordinarily refer to other facts that investigators learn about the subject during the course of investigation. These could include prior violence, weapon accessibility, research, seeking and acquisition, preparation, and practice. Social influences may also be valuable, including family instability, family violence and abuse, bullying, peer encouragement for acting out, and identification with deviant antisocial organizations—all variables that may model, justify, and reinforce violence as a problem-solving strategy. Psychological issues include command hallucinations, delusions, depression and hopelessness, poor impulse control, suicidality, paranoia, rigidity and a high need to control others, chronic anger, and various personality disorders—factors that undermine coping and narrow the field of potential problem-solving choices. Developmental issues can also be important: child and adolescent subjects are often inherently impulsive, less likely to contemplate and weigh options, and be more influenced by peer factors. Teens are more likely than adults to perpetrate in pairs. Substance abuse and dependency may also be part of a risk-enhancing picture, although seldom will an offender be intoxicated *during* acts of predatory, preplanned violence, as this diminishes the sense of omnipotent control and power that they seek. Rather, substance abuse is yet another red flag to poor coping resources in the individual.

STABILIZING FACTORS

Stabilizing factors are variables that may diminish risk in particular cases. Participation, identification, and membership in prosocial groups like churches, sports, or community service groups may reflect identification with ideas and values that are incompatible with violence. Supportive families or friends that encourage prosocial problem solving, prevent access to weapons, and model nonviolent solutions to problems may also help mitigate risk. For those subjects with mental health issues, competent treatment at an appropriate level of care may serve to mitigate risk as well. Potential targets may stabilize or enhance their own risk depending upon their behavior, including adherence to good safety and security procedures.

The school, for example, may have strong security and good campus access control to prevent outside offenders from breaching its perimeter.

THREAT ASSESSMENT TEAMS

Threat assessment teams (TATs) have been used successfully to help school districts and colleges manage violence risk; they represent a best practices approach to campus violence threat management. Teams are multidisciplinary and typically consist of an administrative-level educator (principal, assistant principal, dean), mental health consultant, campus-based security or law enforcement officer, and school legal counsel (internal and/or external). Individuals with potential role conflicts that could interfere with the primary purpose of the threat assessment team should not participate as team members except as sources of potential collateral information or external support sources. This would include individuals with loyalty conflicts such as parents or guardians, union representatives of an involved employee at risk, team members who may have been the victims of the alleged threat situation, and mental health professionals who already have a therapeutic relationship with the involved subject (Mohandie, 2000).

During intervals when they are not managing at-risk individuals who are exhibiting warning signs, TAT members may organize and initiate training in warning sign recognition and problem reporting for members of the campus community, help develop campus policies and procedures for school safety, and seek out and arrange training to support their own critical roles.

TATs typically convene when there is an identified problem; their task is to seek appropriate information and resources to manage a potential threat and bring it to its logical conclusion (Mohandie, 2000). Once a problem is reported, members of this team typically initiate and/or monitor the threat assessment investigation, seek and review additional information, apply their varied specialized expertise, advise decision makers, determine essential information, evaluate and recommend options for reducing risk, conduct appropriate follow-up, and document the process. Many campuses that do not have formally identified teams often do this in an *ad hoc* fashion.

Subgroups of the threat assessment team often assume a primary role during initial information gathering, particularly in cases that may first appear less serious. However, at some point a full convening (by conference call or in person) of the team may be necessitated by circumstances. Legal consultation supports the privilege of TAT communications and allows for consideration of important legal issues and statutes.

Documentation is the proof that issues were considered, safety and privacy were valued, and personnel were being "reasonable" in their efforts. Each time the TAT meets or a team member consults, there should be documentation of the date, who was present, how the meeting was conducted (telephonic, in-person, Skype, etc.), and issues that were the focus of review. Issues that were considered important, concerns that were ruled out, and follow-up on trailing action items should be documented. This file should be treated as a confidential file and secured in a manner that limits accessibility as much as possible to those who "need to know." One goal is to limit the subject's potential access in order to protect information sources and methods, while another is to avoid giving the subject something new to obsess about or formally grieve.

INVESTIGATIVE STRATEGIES

School threat assessment is only as good as the investigative steps and procedures that inform and support it. In addition, investigations must take into account legal constraints, as discussed in Chapter 5 of this volume, on legal issues in threat management. Collateral sources of information are important to develop intelligence about risk-enhancing variables as well as potential stabilizers. Human sources of information include potential victims, complainants, classmates, coworkers, family members, friends, associates, and significant others of the subject. Decisions about whom to interview should take into account the likelihood of the source giving feedback to the subject (which may or may not be desirable in a particular case), privacy concerns, and how likely it is that they will provide useful information that offsets any of these or other risks. Records may also be sought, including public records, school transcripts, disciplinary histories, and employment. School work assignments—particularly art and writing—might reveal disturbing content the subject has included beyond the context of the original assignment.

The subject's cyberspace presence should be thoroughly assessed, including personal websites, blogs, and online social networking sites like Facebook, YouTube, and Twitter. Emails sent by the subject are often informative. Many of these cyberspace sources are public or easily accessed using human sources, and the data are often rich. It may also be fruitful in certain cases to seize computers or other technology for accessing the Internet, like smart phones and iPads. These devices may shed light on important web surfing patterns that reveal interest in past violent events, information seeking about weapons or explosives, and attempts to purchase such items online.

Search warrants may facilitate access to more personal and potentially relevant information such as weapons in the subject's possession, books or movies, writings, drawings, and diaries that belie violent fantasy or unfolding plans. Video equipment or devices and homemade videos should be seized if they exist, for they could contain a prepared (or developing) statement related to a planned event or reveal past rehearsing of an operational plan for an attack.

In some cases information about past mental health treatment—including prior evaluations, hospitalizations, or medication—may be available. Often these rich sources of information require the subject (and/or guardian) to consent to their release. However, there are many occasions where this information may be known to police, found in a public record, or even discussed or scanned and posted online by the subject.

Investigation related to weapon access, possession, and interest is critical, particularly as it relates to firearms and explosives; but other weapons may be selected by offenders, such as poisons, knives, or exotic improvised devices. Threat assessment professionals should keep an open mind. How familiar is the subject with various weapons, and does the subject appear overly interested or stimulated by weapons? Weapon availability and access checks through traditional databases that may exist as part of gun licensing are an important basic step. Questions to explore include whether the subject has been practicing with his or her weapons; if so, how recently and how often? Has there been any attempt to modify or adapt weapons? Has the subject sought out new weapons, gone to gun shows (in America one can buy a gun at a gun show and leave no record), have there been new purchases, is there stockpiling of ammunition, or purchasing of special ammunition that is more lethal, like slug rounds instead of buckshot for a shotgun? Has the individual engaged in carrying and concealing weapons? Is there any Internet trail leading to gun sales websites or ebay for weapons parts? Do phone records reveal calls to gun dealers, shooting ranges, or sources of weaponry? Has the subject purchased any clothing that could be part of developing a "costume" for a violent episode? Who within the subject's circle of life has weapons that could potentially be stolen or "borrowed" by the potential offender?

Proactive law enforcement derived techniques may also be employed. Informants close to a subject of concern may be sought, or undercover operations targeting the subject may be developed. Source development may make use of friends, acquaintances, teachers, and family who are similarly concerned about the subject's potential, or who might simply be willing to occasionally offer a "status check" for the good of everyone involved. However, consideration should be given to assess their loyalty and the risk that they may share information with the subject. In some cases this may be desirable, if it is deemed helpful, for the subject to believe he or she is being monitored as a component of risk assessment. Such proactive techniques may be reserved for more difficult cases and subjects perceived as higher risk. Surveillance might also be used with certain subjects to track and document their movements, or it may, on some occasions, afford the opportunity for authorities to be notified and step in to interrupt them if they are suspected of moving to imminent violent action while the surveillance is occurring.

INTERVIEWING THE SUBJECT

Some school threat assessment involves indirect assessment of behavioral information without actually interviewing the subject. Obviously, the subject is a rich source of information (via self-report and behavioral observations during interview) about his or her motivations, self-control, relevant history, suicidal impulses, fantasies, intentions, and potential behavior—thus he or she will often be interviewed. But an important first question is: Should an interview be done? This question should be answered on a case-by-case basis, but more often than not a determination will be made that much useful information could be revealed by talking to the subject. Generally once an interview is scheduled or conducted, it is officially revealed that there is an investigation. This information in and of itself may affect the risk in the situation and should be calculated as a factor in the threat assessment equation. The attention and opportunity to air grievances with a third party may provide an alternative to violence for the subject. In other cases, it may escalate the subject for a variety of reasons, including the subject's resistance to control and authority, influencing perceptions that fuel desperation and hopelessness, and conveying that if violent action is not taken by the subject it will be interrupted and they will miss their opportunity for acting out violently.

The timing of the interview is important; it is usually preferred to have solid knowledge of the known facts prior to conducting it. This allows for veracity checks and enables investigators to address areas of which they would not otherwise be aware. Further, the interviewer may get only one opportunity to question the subject, so it is best to make the interview count. Realistically though, it may not always be possible to precede an interview with a solid investigation because of time constraints and the genuine urgency of unfolding, dynamic situations. If this is the case, a follow-up interview might be arranged to address information that is further developed.

Decisions must be made about who will do the interviewing: should it be campus police, security, a mental health professional, human resources, legal counsel, or some combination of these? Circumstances will dictate these choices; with cases perceived as more risky, weapons involved, or outside threats, most likely the choice will lean toward a law enforcement-driven interview. When mental health professionals are used, it should be clearly understood and communicated to all parties that the interview is for threat or risk assessment purposes, part of an investigation, and not confidential. Appropriate releases should be prepared and signed, with relevant legal issues incorporated. (See Appendices 1 and 2 for examples of releases).

The location of the interview is important to consider. Generally for college cases, more serious cases, cases where the subject has already been banned from the campus, and outsider-involved situations (type 1), it is preferred to conduct the interview off campus so as to avoid elevating risk by bringing a potential offender back on campus or sending a mixed message. Hotel conference rooms are sometimes utilized. On other occasions, subjects may be interviewed at their residences: this presents potential safety risks to an interviewer, including access to weapons by a subject; on the other hand, it may afford the opportunity to personally inspect the residence (with permission or warrant). In a recent threat assessment case, the author interviewed an 11th-grade student of concern at his residence and was able to view the student's bedroom as part of the assessment, noting that a used gun practice target hung on the wall.

Safety is a paramount consideration for all interviews; the known facts of a given situation and common sense should drive safety planning. For some cases, law enforcement should conduct the interview; in others, it may be other professionals with security or law enforcement standing nearby. On yet other occasions, the interview might be conducted by a pair of professionals (see Chapter 27, this volume, on interviewing the violent true believer).

Gender, age, and cultural/language decisions might also affect the choice of interviewer. To enhance the building of rapport, some thought should be given to appropriate matching of an interviewer with respect to these issues or any others that appear important.

There are occasions where an individual of concern is in jail, prison, or some other custodial facility, particularly if pending release. In these cases, access to the subject may be difficult or the school may wish to minimize the subject's perception of any ongoing campus investigation that could inflame hostile impulses or obsessions. In these circumstances, a suitable proxy might be developed, whereby someone on the staff of the institution might be recruited to ask questions of the subject and provide this information to a liaison at the school.

The interview should be scripted beforehand for content areas and lines of questioning. This prevents important issues from being overlooked. It also conveys to the subject that the interviewer has done her or his homework and may improve the chances of getting truthful responses. This presupposes that the interviewer is well versed in the minutiae of the case facts. The purpose of the interview is to develop, discover, confirm, or disconfirm information relevant to answering various predetermined questions: could this person become dangerous, violent, self-destructive, or destructive? What is the meaning of past behavior and statements? There should be clear scripting to answer questions the subject might ask, or to respond to scenarios the subject might present, such as a refusal to be interviewed, insisting that he or she be allowed to record the interview, or asking pointed questions as to where the interviewer obtained the information being presented. The

interviewer must decide how any known deception will be handled and what the criteria will be for ending the interview. Adequate time should be allotted, generally at least two hours and up to four hours. Breaks should be offered, and the subject should know that she or he is free to go or take a break. The interviewer should take extensive notes of the interview, as verbatim as possible. This supports the benefit of two interviewers, so that one may take primary responsibility for notes while the other is able to interact and speak more freely with the subject. This raises the question about the potential advantages of audio- or videotaping the interview. That has not been a standard procedure for the author's threat assessment interviews (although it is fairly routine in other forensic assessment situations). Many subjects—given that they are not in custodial settings with unfolding civil or criminal proceedings—may balk at consenting to this. Further, this issue could also be complicated by the fact that many cases involve minors, whose guardians might not consent to an interview being recorded. Pushing the issue may end the interview before it has begun.

GENERAL INTERVIEW TOPICS

The interview should begin with an explanation of the purpose, the role of the interviewer (whether police, security, mental health, etc.), and the fact that it is part of an investigation and not confidential. The subject should be told that he or she can take a break anytime and may end the interview at any point if he or she so chooses. If it is a law enforcement interview, any admonitions that are necessary, given the particular context of the investigation, should be performed. The tone should be one of respect and professionalism; this is particularly important, since many potential offenders are hypersensitive to issues of respect and often identify disrespect as one of the motives for their problematic behavior.

Subjects should be asked about their versions of the events leading up to the behaviors of concern. If they omit important details that are relevant to specific risk questions (threats, stated intentions to harm others or themselves, etc.), these items should be asked about at a later point during the interview. Subjects should be asked if they have ever thought about hurting themselves or others, weapon accessibility and possession, past violence, as well as other incidents or issues of concern that may have surfaced during the investigation.

The author will often ask questions about known risk factors and stabilizers. It is important to ask about subjects' expectations regarding outcome; that is, how they think the school or authorities are going to respond. This allows risk assessment of the subject's ability to realistically anticipate the fallout from his or her behavior. If a subject is not able to consider, for example, that he or she might be expelled from school and has the unrealistic belief that their acting out will be allowed to continue, this would likely increase the identified risk in the situation. Additionally, a series of "what if's" might be explored to assess the subject's anticipated responses under a range of possible scenarios. This line of questions also allows the interviewer to assess variables such as cognitive rigidity, reality testing, and overall flexibility. Questions such as, "what do you think is going to happen next?" "What if that doesn't happen?" "What do you think the school's options are here?" and "What if _____ happens, how will you handle that?" are useful to adapt for a variety of campus threat assessment scenarios. Furthermore, it is helpful to inquire how significant others or parents might react to the fallout with questions like, "How will you deal with your parents and what do you think your parents will do?"

INTEGRATING THE DATA

Ultimately the interview data will have to be integrated with other known information on the case. Decisions will have to be made about what will be deemed credible among the subject's many statements and other collateral information. The format of the feedback could be verbal or written. Risk assessment or investigation seeks to answer the following overall questions: Is the individual moving on a path toward violent action? Is there evidence to suggest movement from thought to action? Additional questions may include the following: (1) Are others concerned by observed behaviors (subject discussed plan/threat with others, others are afraid)? (2) Does the at-risk individual comply with risk-reduction steps? (3) Does the person have the ability (access, means, capacity, and opportunity) to become violent? (4) Is there evidence of intent (specificity of plan, action taken toward plan)? and (5) Has the subject crossed thresholds (engaged in attack-related behaviors, broken rules) that indicate elevated risk? (Borum, 2000).

LEVELS OF RISK

An important principle of threat assessment is that all threats are not created equal. After an appropriate investigation, it may be determined that the risk is high, medium, or low or some other finding expressed on another continuum of violence potential. The threat assessment professional should specify, if possible, what the exact risk might be. For example, in one situation it might be determined that the subject will make additional threats, while in another it may appear that the subject will become assaultive. The assessment might identify high risk for lethal violence such as homicide or mass homicide, or it could be determined that no threat occurred or that no threat is posed. In communicating the results of threat or risk assessments, it is helpful for team members to have a common language and for the risk assessment findings to include appropriate qualifications (Monahan & Steadman, 1996). Campus threat assessment situations are rarely as simple as "threat or no threat"; thus a dichotomous system is not usually helpful. One system (Mohandie, 2000) categorizes risk across five levels: (1) high risk for violence, qualifies for immediate arrest or hospitalization, usually reserved for the imminently dangerous individual (self and/or others); (2) high risk for violence, does not qualify for immediate arrest or hospitalization which involves situations of apparent danger looming off a future horizon under a given set of conditions; (3) insufficient evidence for violence potential, evidence for the repetitive or intentional infliction of emotional distress upon others, a situation of the repeat harasser or intentional intimidator; (4) insufficient evidence for violence potential, evidence of the unintentional infliction of emotional distress upon others, describing a circumstance of an isolated set of behavior ultimately determined to not be purposeful nor threatening but may have involved a miscommunication or isolated lapse of judgment; and (5) insufficient evidence for violence potential, no evidence of emotional distress upon others, a situation that may stem from a false report, a misunderstanding, or a misperception. Ultimately it should be recognized that the threat assessment finding is for a particular time period and given set of known conditions. Considering the dynamic nature of most human behavior, violence potential may escalate or diminish based upon variables in play. Thus risk assessments should be modified as may be appropriate based upon new information or behavior.

THREAT ASSESSMENT ERROR

This brings up an important point: there can be error in threat assessment. One error is the false positive, where it is determined that the person is a risk when in fact no risk exists. The false negative is the opposite case, wherein it is found that no risk is present, only to have the individual engage in violence. Both types of errors have inherent problems, with the false negative being the most problematic. Yet false positives may result in stigma and negative consequences for the individual wrongly deemed a risk, and there may be liability and credibility consequences for the organization perceived as having made that mistake. Thus it is important to balance safety concerns in risk assessment work while considering privacy and well-being issues for the subject. Obviously safety is the most important issue, but the rights of the individual are a very close second. Because of this, when possible, it is preferable to introduce interventions that involve not only limit setting and safety planning but might also provide needed interventions for the subject. This is an ethic or value that has a place in many threat assessments, given that many of the subjects are juveniles or young adults with the potential for positive redirection.

Sources of error include failure to investigate, reliance upon second- or third-hand information, inadequate investigation, lack of timeliness in responding, failure to gauge the accuracy of information, disregarding complaints, overreacting to events (failure to respond at a level merited by the situation), and use of the process for internal political agendas.

OTHER CONSIDERATIONS

It is important to distinguish the risk assessment from traditional work fitness evaluations. In a given case—for example, involving a school employee—both assessments could be conducted. However, these are different processes, with threat assessment having a very narrow purpose and the work fitness a broader, more diagnostically related assessment of the individual's ability or fitness to fulfill essential work responsibilities. Threat assessments may be informed by diagnostic processes and issues, but the rendering of a diagnosis is seldom the ultimate goal.

This raises the issue of the use of psychological testing and structured professional judgment in school-based threat assessments. Generally there are occasions where standard tests and evaluative procedures such as a Minnesota Multiphasic Personality Inventory-2 (MMPI-2), MMPI-A, Psychopathy Checklist-Revised (PCL-R), the Psychopathy Checklist: Youth Version (PCL:YV),

or other measure might be administered or available as an aspect of the assessment. These measures may at times offer useful information to support the presence of risk-enhancing or stabilizing variables; however, they were not specifically designed for such assessments. The Workplace Assessment of Violence Risk (WAVR-21) developed by White and Meloy (2010) is a structured professional judgment measure for adults based on 21 coded items related to targeted workplace violence risk. This measure—and others like it for adolescents, such as the Structured Assessment of Violence Risk in Youth (SAVRY) (Borum, Bartel, & Forth, 2002)—can often help organize risk assessment information and may have the added benefit of having been developed specifically for violence risk assessment.

It is critical that mental health professionals who are asked to serve as consultants and/or to conduct threat assessments adhere to the evaluative role; they should not undertake the evaluation or consultation if they are providing treatment to the subject. Otherwise the inherent conflict of interest and divided loyalty issues may cloud the professional's judgment and impair his or her ability to assess the threat objectively. Threat assessment by mental health professionals requires a competent, objective, informed, and impartial perspective.

CASE EXAMPLE

The subject, a 21-year-old university student, became the focus of a threat investigation when he reportedly blogged about his anger and frustration, suicidal impulses, and interest in firearms, in tandem with making classmates uncomfortable with verbal tirades that were unrelated to class material (his childhood trauma) but touched upon similar themes. Some of his classmates dropped the classes and two professors complained about him monopolizing class time and making other students uncomfortable. Ultimately he was suspended pending a threat assessment. He was being enabled or supported (depending on the perspective) by one professor, who tried without success to get him to conform his conduct to the school environment. It was determined that he had possessed guns in the past, but no longer did, having relocated from another state and left them behind. His parents were unable to control his behavior, and he was unwilling to seek counseling to address his anger and other issues. The school mandated a threat assessment by a forensic psychologist, who determined that the student had suicidal impulses but denied homicidal fantasies or intentions. The student was heavily invested in continuing his higher education. At the same time he did not understand or care that his behavior influenced others negatively and felt that the school was required to tolerate his behavior, which he justified. It was determined that he had been subject to a restraining order by another college because of harassing behaviors directed toward members of that campus community. It was assessed that there was some risk for violence, directed toward himself and potentially others, but not imminently so, and that there was clear risk for him to continue to distress, intimidate, and harass others. The WAVR-21 was coded and supported the moderate to high risk nature of this case. The university did not want him to continue as a student based upon these risk concerns and the fact he had violated school policy by creating a hostile campus environment. The anticipation that he would be separated from the university was considered an important potential trigger for escalation, and an agreement was reached with the student to leave the school voluntarily. This remedy allowed him to apply to other campuses and thus preserved his hope and dream of continuing his education; if he had been expelled, he would have been denied admission to other schools of interest. While one might view this option as passing the buck, it resulted from balancing the risks and benefits of the available options and generated an acceptable solution to a serious case. However, one mistake was made: the negotiated settlement omitted including a clear stay-away part of the agreement. When he showed up on campus to "visit" friends, this issue was addressed. To date, this case continues to be monitored, partially in cyberspace but also through the emails he occasionally sends to various collateral information sources.

THREAT MANAGEMENT AND INTERVENTION

Intervention should match the level of apparent threat. Effective threat management strives for optimal solutions that reduce risk, but in many cases teams are forced to choose the lesser of evils. Figure 8.1 is a flowchart of intervention considerations that match apparent risk. Intervention options are presented, hierarchically arranged by level of invasiveness: (1) incarceration (jail or prison); (2) arrest; (3) hospitalization and other forms of institutionalization; (4) restraining/protection

order; (5) referral of subject to outpatient counseling; (6) administrative actions including suspensions, expulsions, and terminations; (7) various physical security measures to harden the target and reduce accessibility, such as deactivating security cards and confiscating keys, removing IDs, posting photographs of banned individuals, and increasing security officer or campus police presence; (8) leveraging the subject's social network to influence positive behavior and reduce acting out; (9) informing the subject about potential boundaries or consequences, including behavioral contracting; and (10) informing potential victims of appropriate personal safety and security measures.

Palarea and Van Horn (2010) organize threat assessment interventions into five categories: (1) organizational control, (2) social control, (3) psychological control, (4) physical control, and (5) legal control. School threat assessment professionals may consider each category of intervention in a given case as appropriate.

Given the dynamic process of unfolding cases, an important observation to keep in mind is that cases do not usually end but rather become dormant. This necessitates the creation of mechanisms for monitoring the episodic nature of risk, including subject escalation, de-escalation, institutionalization, involvement in legal proceedings, and release over time. School threat assessment teams might determine that periodic status checks and reassessments may be precipitated by new behaviors, anticipated events, and circumstances that could serve as triggers for escalation, or they might simply decide that there will be a proactive check-in after a particular time period whether or not there seems to be activity in the case. In higher-risk school threat assessment cases, there should be someone assigned to track, update, and reassess the risk. Information seeking varies by case and could include school or employment status; current events and problems; victim, coworker, or classmate reports; and public and source supplied intelligence.

Threat assessment is intervention and intervention is assessment; effective school-based threat assessment calculates the impact of the process upon the situation. Violence risk may be managed, but one can rarely guarantee threat prevention. The process is effective if it reduces uncertainty, diminishes access to victims by a would-be attacker, hardens targets, and restricts weapon accessibility.

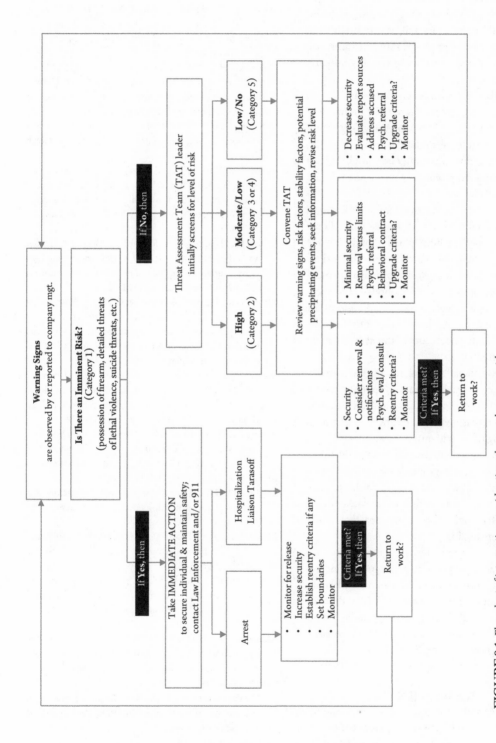

FIGURE 8.1 Flow chart of intervention considerations that match apparent risk.
Copyright Mohandie, 1997–2011. Reprinted with permission.

KEY POINTS

- Campuses must recognize that they are vulnerable to violent attacks from individuals within and those not affiliated with the school. Denial of this reality enhances risk and interferes with the opportunity for early detection.

- Schools need an accessible and visible system in place to encourage reporting of apparent risk situations. A "see something, say something" ongoing expectation for all members of the campus community is helpful. At least one anonymous reporting mechanism should be available.

- Threat assessment teams are a critical part of school-based threat assessment. These teams are multidisciplinary and include appropriate administrative decision makers (deans or principals/vice-principals), mental health professionals, campus-based security or police, legal counsel, and appropriate specialists for particular situations (outside counsel, private security, threat assessment consultants).

- Effective threat assessment considers appropriate collateral information, applies effective subject interviewing techniques (including safety provisions), and balances information seeking needs with privacy concerns.

- All threats are not created equal, and threat assessment findings should be communicated in a specific way that addresses the level of risk, the dynamic nature of human violence potential, and information gaps that might limit the findings.

- Threat management may target multiple variables as appropriate to a given case, including administrative, legal (criminal and civil), law enforcement, mental health, and social resources. Follow-up and periodic status checks may address the fluctuations in cases that may enhance or diminish risk.

REFERENCES

Borum, R. (2000). Assessing violence risk among youth. *Journal of Clinical Psychology, 56,* 1263–1288.

Borum, R., Bartel, P., & Forth, A. (2002). *Manual for the structured assessment of violence risk in youth (SAVRY).* Tampa: University of South Florida.

Cameron, N. (1943). The paranoid pseudo-community. *American Journal of Sociology, 49,* 32–38.

Cameron, N. (1959). The paranoid pseudo-community revisited. *American Journal of Sociology, 65,* 52–58.

Deisinger, G., Randazzo, M., O'Neill, D., & Savage, J. (2008). *The handbook for campus threat assessment and management teams.* Boston: Applied Risk Management.

Goldner, F. H. (1982). Pronoia. *Social Problems, 30,* 82–91.

Hoffman, A. M., Schuh, J. H., & Fenske, R. H. (1998). *Violence on campus: Defining the problems, strategies for action.* Gaithersburg, MD: Aspen Publishers.

Lavergne, G. M. (1997). *A sniper in the tower: The Charles Whitman murders.* Denton: University of North Texas Press.

Meloy, J. R., Hempel, A. G., Gray, T. B., Mohandie, K., Shiva, A., & Richards, T. C. (2004). A comparative analysis of North American adolescent and adult mass murderers. *Behavioral Sciences and the Law, 22,* 291–309.

Meloy, J.R., Hempel, A. & Richards, T. (1999). Offender and offense characteristics of a nonrandom sample of mass murderers. *The Journal of the American Academy of Psychiatry and the Law, 27,* 213-225.

Meloy, J. R., Hempel, A. G., Mohandie, K., Shiva, A., & Gray, T. B. (2001). Offender and offense characteristics of a nonrandom sample of adolescent mass murderers. *Journal of American Academy of Child and Adolescent Psychiatry, 40,* 719–728.

Meloy, J. R., Hoffman, J., Guldimann, A., & James, D. (2012). The role of warning behaviors in threat assessment: An exploration and suggested typology. *Behavioral Sciences and the Law, 30,* 256–279.

Meloy, J. R., & Mohandie, K. (August 12, 2009). Violent and suicidal: Contemporary trends. Anaheim, CA: Association of Threat Assessment Professionals.

Meloy, J. R., Mohandie, K.,,, Hempel, A.G. & Shiva, A. (2001). The violent true believer: Homicidal and suicidal states of mind. *Journal of Threat Assessment, 1,* 1–14.

Meloy, J. R., & O'Toole, M. E. (2011). The concept of leakage in threat assessment. *Behavioral Sciences and the Law, 29,* 513–527.

Mohandie, K. (2000). *School violence threat management: A practical guide for educators, law enforcement, and mental health practitioners.* San Diego, CA: STS Publications.

Mohandie, K., & Duffy, J. (1999). First responder and negotiation guidelines with the paranoid schizophrenic subject. *FBI Law Enforcement Bulletin,* December, 8–16.

Mohandie, K., Meloy, J. R., Collins, P. (2009). Suicide by cop among officer involved shooting cases. *Journal of Forensic Sciences, 54,* 456–462.

Mohandie, K., Meloy, J. R., Green McGowan, M., & Williams, J. (2006). The RECON typology of stalking: Reliability and validity based upon a large sample of North American stalkers. *Journal of Forensic Sciences, 51,* 147–155.

Monahan, J., & Steadman, H. J. (1996). Violent storms and violent people: How meteorology can inform risk communication in mental health law. *American Psychologist, 51,* 931–958.

Palarea, R. & Van Horn, D. (2010). From assessment to management: designing case specific management plans. Presentation to Association of Threat Assessment Professionals Annual Conference, Anaheim, CA, August.

Shneidman, E. S. (1996). *The suicidal mind.* New York: Oxford University Press.

White, S., & Meloy, J . R. (2010). *WAVR-21 training manual, 2nd ed.* San Diego, CA: Specialized Training Services.

APPENDIX 1

OPERATIONAL CONSULTING INTERNATIONAL, INC.
P.O. BOX 88
PASADENA, CALIFORNIA 91102-0088
(626)666-6139

INFORMED CONSENT AND AUTHORIZATION

We _____,_____,_____ have been informed and understand that minor _____ is participating in a risk assessment, which may include interviewing, other background reviews, psychological testing, and review of collateral information to assess statements, behavior, and safety related concerns being raised by _____ ("the school"). The school has obtained the services of Operational Consulting International, Inc. (including its representative, licensed psychologist Dr. Kris Mohandie) to conduct this risk assessment. I understand this interview is not confidential and I am not the client of Dr. Mohandie or Operational Consulting International, Inc. (OCI). I acknowledge and understand that the client in this situation is the school and that risk-relevant information (including conversations, statements, behavior, and information obtained from this interview, parents, and other sources including background reviews, cyberspace and the internet(including social networking sites), other interviews, and any other sources) from this process may be shared in any form (verbal and written), including electronic, with the following individuals: _____ and others from school administration that may be deemed appropriate for disclosure such as school legal counsel, principal, and campus based law enforcement and any others that may be deemed appropriate for disclosure. As a component of this risk assessment, school representatives have provided OCI and its representatives with a description of the conduct and/or statements that have led to questions on the part of your school about whether you might pose a substantial threat to your own safety or to the well-being and safety of others, materially disrupt, substantially disorder, or invade the rights of others related to the educational environment. If you have not been told by the school what actions have led to these questions, please inform the OCI representative Dr. Mohandie.

I understand that I will not be provided any feedback by OCI or its representatives about this assessment. Any feedback which might be provided to me will be at the discretion of the school, and as such any requests for such feedback must be directed to their representatives. It is up to them what information from this assessment they may release, if any.

Although the school is OCI's client, not you, OCI nevertheless is observant of the duty to conduct this assessment with fairness, impartiality, and objectivity. Because this assessment is being conducted at the request of the school, you do not have doctor-patient or psychotherapist-patient privilege in your communications with Dr. Mohandie or any other OCI representative. However, OCI and its representatives will make an effort to respect your privacy by disclosing to the school only the minimum information necessary to satisfy the purpose of this referral. OCI will make a good faith effort to restrict the disclosure of private information to the minimum necessary to satisfy the purpose of the examination and to support any findings, conclusions, and recommendations. If the findings, conclusions, opinions, or recommendations are challenged in an adjudicative forum, OCI may make full disclosure of all information as may be necessary or required by law.

I understand that, other than as noted above, discussion and/or assessment/interview results will remain confidential and in the custody of Operational Consulting International, Inc. (OCI, Inc.), stored in compliance with legal and professional regulatory record keeping requirements (which are usually a minimum of seven years or longer past the age of majority, prior to appropriate destruction). Exceptions to confidentiality and privilege are the usual situations mandated by law, and professional reporting responsibilities and obligations (potential danger to self or others, serious threats to physically harm, child and elder abuse, other legally mandated circumstances such as a court order, national security mandated disclosures per the Patriot Act, or any other mandated or allowable exceptions). In cases of serious threats to physically harm others, for example, it is required that the intended victim and the police be notified, and in cases of potential danger to self, disclosures may occur in order to help keep you safe.

Consistent with the provisions of state and federal law, I understand that the school will be advised to maintain any written report provided to it by OCI and its representatives in a confidential file separate from other school records such as cumulative files, and that the information should be made available only to persons who have a bona fide need to know the information included any reports. I expressly acknowledge that OCI and its representatives have no control over how the school uses the report once it receives it. I understand that the information used or disclosed pursuant to this authorization may be subject to re-disclosure and no longer protected under federal law. I expressly release OCI and its representatives from any liability for that redisclosure. However, I also understand that federal or state law may restrict re-disclosure of HIV/AIDS information, mental health information, genetic testing information and drug/alcohol diagnosis, treatment, or referral information.

With respect to the reported results of this risk assessment which will be communicated to the school as noted, the school may choose not to rely on the findings, in whole or in part, when deciding on how to respond to their concerns in relation to your school status. However, your school may rely entirely on the risk assessment report in determining your school status. Thus, depending on any risk assessment conclusions and recommendations reached concerning your safety, statements, and behavior, and depending on your school's consideration of these conclusions and recommendations, the results of this examination could have a significant impact on your school status. Regardless of any conclusions and recommendations, your school still may choose to address the behavior that formed the basis for its referral in accordance with its policies and procedures.

You do not need to sign this authorization. However, your refusal will mean that the risk assessment will not take place. This fact may very well have implications for your continued school status, but this is a determination that will be made by your school. Your freedom to decline participation in this risk assessment is a matter for you to determine directly with your school, and/or your attorney, as appropriate.

You may revoke this authorization in writing at any time. If you revoke your authorization, the information described above may no longer be used or disclosed for the purposes described in this written authorization. However, any use or disclosure already made with your permission cannot be reversed. Unless otherwise notified, this authorization will expire 180 days from the date of signature below. To revoke this authorization, please send a written notice, stating that you are revoking this authorization, to:

Kris Mohandie, Ph.D.
Licensed Psychologist
Operational Consulting International, Inc.
P.O. Box 88
Pasadena, CA 91102
(626) 666-6139

I agree and consent to participate in this process under these aforementioned conditions. I authorize OCI and its representatives to use and disclose any risk assessment findings and opinions to the school for the purpose of assessing statements, behavior, and safety related concerns being raised by the school. These findings could include addressing your risk to materially disrupt the educational environment, or substantially disorder, or invade the rights of others.

(Note: if you do not have adequate time to review this form or if you require additional time to consult with an attorney or other advisor, you may reschedule this assessment for a later time by checking the box below, initialing it, and immediately informing Dr. Mohandie.)

☐ I require additional time to consult with my attorney or other advisor. Initial here:

☐ I have read, understand, and agree to the terms of the informed consent and authorization.

Printed Name of Minor _____

Signature of Minor _____ **Date** _____

SIGNATURE OF PARENT/LEGAL GUARDIAN: _____
RELATIONSHIP TO MINOR: _____ **DATE:** _____
PRINT PARENT/LEGAL GUARDIAN'S NAME: _____
SIGNATURE OF PARENT/LEGAL GUARDIAN: _____
RELATIONSHIP TO MINOR: _____ **DATE:** _____
PRINT PARENT/LEGAL GUARDIAN'S NAME: _____

I hereby warrant that I am the parent and/or legal guardian of _____ ("Minor"), one of the individuals who signed the foregoing authorization, and that I have caused said Minor to execute said authorization.

SIGNATURE OF PARENT/LEGAL GUARDIAN: _____
RELATIONSHIP TO MINOR: _____ **DATE:** _____
PRINT PARENT/LEGAL GUARDIAN'S NAME: _____

NOTICE

The Privacy Rule via HIPAA protects all *"individually identifiable health information"* held or transmitted by a covered entity or its business associate, in any form or media, whether electronic, paper, or oral. The Privacy Rule calls this information *"protected health information (PHI)."* OCI, Inc. and its representatives, as noted throughout this document, have informed you about how your PHI will be used and the extent of, and limits to, the disclosures you have agreed to. If you are concerned that we have violated your privacy rights, or you disagree with a decision that has been made about access to your records, you may contact Kris Mohandie, Ph.D. You may also send a written complaint to the Secretary of the U.S. Department of Health and Human Services. The person listed above can provide you with the appropriate address upon request.

APPENDIX 2

OPERATIONAL CONSULTING INTERNATIONAL, INC.
P.O. BOX 88
PASADENA, CALIFORNIA 91102-0088
(627) 666-6139

INFORMED CONSENT AND AUTHORIZATION

I _____, have been informed and understand that I will be participating in a risk assessment, which may include interviewing, other background reviews and interviews, and review of collateral information to assess work, performance, and safety related concerns being raised by my employer (the company). The company has obtained the services of Operational Consulting International, Inc. (including its representative licensed psychologist Dr. Kris Mohandie) to conduct this risk assessment. I understand this interview is not confidential and I am not the client of Dr. Mohandie or Operational Consulting International, Inc. (OCI). I acknowledge and understand that the client in this situation is the company and that risk relevant information (including conversations, statements, behavior, and information obtained from this interview and other sources including background reviews, cyberspace and the internet(including social networking sites), other interviews, and any other sources) from this process may be shared in any form (verbal and written), including electronic, with company management, security, human resources, legal counsel and any others that may be deemed appropriate for disclosure. As a component of this risk assessment, your employer has provided OCI and its representatives with a description of your conduct and/or statements that have led to questions on the part of your employer about your ability to effectively perform your duties and to perform them without posing a substantial threat to your own safety or to the well-being and safety of others. If you have not been told by your employer what actions on your part have led to these questions, please inform the OCI representative Dr. Mohandie.

I understand that I will not be provided any feedback by OCI or its representatives about this assessment. Any feedback which might be provided to me will be at the discretion of your employer, and as such any requests for such feedback must be directed to your employer. It is up to them what information from this assessment they may release, if any.

Although your employer is OCI's client, not you, OCI nevertheless is observant of the duty to conduct this assessment with fairness, impartiality, and objectivity. Because this assessment is being conducted at the request of your employer, you do not have doctor-patient or psychotherapist-patient privilege in your communications with Dr. Mohandie or any other OCI representative. However, OCI and its representatives will make an effort to respect your privacy by disclosing to your employer only the minimum information necessary to satisfy the purpose of this referral. OCI will make a good faith effort to restrict the disclosure of private information to the minimum necessary to satisfy the purpose of the examination and to support any findings, conclusions, and recommendations. If the findings, conclusions, opinions, or recommendations are challenged in an adjudicative forum, OCI may make full disclosure of all information as may be necessary or required by law.

I understand that, other than as noted above, discussion and/or assessment/interview results will remain confidential and in the custody of Operational Consulting International, Inc (OCI, Inc.), stored in compliance with legal and professional regulatory record keeping requirements (which are usually a minimum of seven years or longer, prior to appropriate destruction). Exceptions to confidentiality and privilege are the usual situations mandated by law, and professional reporting responsibilities and obligations (potential danger to self or others, serious threats to physically harm, child and elder abuse, other legally mandated circumstances such as a court order, national security mandated disclosures per the Patriot Act, or any other mandated or allowable exceptions). In cases of serious threats to physically harm others, for example, it is required that the intended victim and the police be notified, and in cases of potential danger to self, disclosures may occur in order to help keep you safe.

Consistent with the provisions of state and federal law, I understand that my employer will be advised to maintain any written report provided to it by OCI and its representatives in a confidential file separate from other personnel information and that the information should be made available only to persons who have a bona fide need to know the information included any reports. I expressly acknowledge that OCI and its representatives have no control over how my employer uses the report once it receives it. I understand that the information used or disclosed pursuant to this authorization may be subject to re-disclosure and no longer protected under federal law. I expressly release OCI and its representatives from any liability for that re-disclosure. However, I also understand that federal or state law may restrict re-disclosure of HIV/AIDS information, mental health information, genetic testing information and drug/alcohol diagnosis, treatment or referral information.

With respect to the reported results of this risk assessment which will be communicated to your employer as noted, your employer may choose not to rely on the findings, in whole or in part, when deciding on how to respond to their concerns in relation to your employment status. However, your employer may rely entirely on the risk assessment report in determining your employment status. Thus, depending on any risk assessment conclusions and recommendations reached concerning your safety, performance, and work related behavior, and depending on your employer's consideration of these conclusions and recommendations, the results of this examination could have a significant impact on your current employment. Regardless of any conclusions and recommendations, your employer still may choose to address the behavior that formed the basis for its referral in accordance with its policies and procedures.

You do not need to sign this authorization. However, your refusal will mean that the risk assessment will not take place. This fact may very well have implications for your continued employment, but this is a determination that will be made by your employer. Your freedom to decline participation in this risk assessment is a matter for you to determine directly with your employer, your labor representatives, and/or your attorney, as appropriate.

You may revoke this authorization in writing at any time. If you revoke your authorization, the information described above may no longer be used or disclosed for the purposes described in this written authorization. However, any use or disclosure already made with your permission cannot be reversed. Unless otherwise notified, this authorization will expire 180 days from the date of signature below. To revoke this authorization, please send a written notice, stating that you are revoking this authorization, to:

Kris Mohandie, Ph.D.
Licensed Psychologist
Operational Consulting International, Inc.
P.O. Box 88
Pasadena, CA 91102
(626) 666-6139

I agree and consent to participate in this process under these aforementioned conditions. I authorize OCI and its representatives to use and disclose any risk assessment findings and opinions to my employer for the purpose of determining my ability to safely and effectively perform my essential work functions.

(Note: if you do not have adequate time to review this form or if you require additional time to consult with an attorney or other advisor, you may reschedule this assessment for a later time by checking the box below, initialing it, and immediately informing Dr. Mohandie.)

☐ I require additional time to consult with my attorney or other advisor. Initial here:

☐ I have read, understand, and agree to the terms of the informed consent and authorization.

_____   _____

Signed   Name   Dated

_____

Printed Name

NOTICE

The Privacy Rule via HIPAA protects all *"individually identifiable health information"* held or transmitted by a covered entity or its business associate, in any form or media, whether electronic, paper, or oral. The Privacy Rule calls this information *"protected health information (PHI)."* OCI, Inc. and its representatives, as noted throughout this document, have informed you about how your PHI will be used and the extent of, and limits to, the disclosures you have agreed to. If you are concerned that we have violated your privacy rights, or you disagree with a decision that has been made about access to your records, you may contact Kris Mohandie, Ph.D. You may also send a written complaint to the Secretary of the U.S. Department of Health and Human Services. The person listed above can provide you with the appropriate address upon request.

9

Mass Casualty Homicides on Elementary School Campuses

Threat Management Lessons Learned from Bath, Michigan, to Newtown, Connecticut

KRIS MOHANDIE AND J. REID MELOY

The tragedy of Newtown, Connecticut, on December 14, 2012, sent a shock wave throughout the United States and indeed the rest of the civilized world. With our hearts sensitive to the enormity of the loss of these young lives and the unbearable grieving of the parents and families of the victims, we would like to provide a preliminary examination of mass casualty events where elementary-age children were specifically targeted on school or school-like campuses, such as day care centers. Commonalities, lessons learned, and ideas for future prevention, early identification, and disruption of these events are discussed.

MASS CASUALTY EVENTS

Bath, Michigan

On May 18, 1927, the United States experienced its most lethal incident of school violence at Bath Consolidated School (student population 250) in Bath, Michigan: 38 elementary school children, two teachers, a retired farmer, the town postmaster, and the school superintendent were killed by explosives. The offender, 55-year-old Andrew Kehoe, was a local farmer who served as treasurer of the school board. He was infuriated by the new taxes that had been levied to pay for the five-year-old school, his spring 1926 defeat in a local political race (county clerk), and a pending foreclosure on his property (he received notice in June, 1926). He apparently sought to punish the citizens of Bath. His wife suffered from tuberculosis, and Kehoe had stopped making his mortgage payments. A neighbor noticed that he had stopped taking care of his property for approximately a year and wondered whether he might be contemplating suicide. He spent the better part of spring 1927 booby trapping the school with explosives he had been acquiring and hiding around his personal property. School administrators were led to believe that Kehoe was doing odd jobs to save the school the expense of hiring an electrician. Fortunately a malfunction kept more than 500 pounds of explosives from detonating or he would have killed every person on the campus of this school. After the initial explosions, he responded to the scene of the crime; other people responding to the emergency assumed he was also rendering assistance, and it was at this point that, using his firearm, he detonated the remaining explosives inside his car, killing two more victims in the process. It was later discovered that prior to coming to the school, Kehoe had burned down all the buildings on his farm and murdered his wife. He left a message to the community painted on his property fence: "criminals are made, not born" (Ellsworth, 1927). Various speculative diagnoses have been assigned to Kehoe, ranging from manic depression by a group of medical scientists a few days after the bombing to psychopathy in a recent study of the case (Bernstein, 2009).

Dunblane, Scotland

Armed with four guns, 43-year-old Thomas Hamilton walked to Dunblane Primary School on March 13, 1996, and burst into the gymnasium where 29 children were attending class. He systematically killed 16 children and their teacher and then shot himself. Another teacher and a dozen other students were wounded during the rampage. Five- and six-year-old children were sitting in circles playing when he began his assault. It appeared that he had timed his assault to coincide with a major school assembly, which he believed was being held in the gymnasium. Hamilton was an avid gun collector and disgraced scoutmaster, known as "Mr. Creepy" to the boys in this small community, as he seemed to be obsessed with filming young boys with their shirts off. His fixation with young boys led him to be dropped from and banned by the Boy Scouts. Twenty years subsequent to this, he was still seething with anger over this rejection; during the weeks prior to the mass homicide, he had been turned down as a volunteer by Dunblane Primary School. A week prior, he wrote a letter to the media and Queen Elizabeth II complaining about a campaign by the police and Dunblane teachers to ruin his reputation (Douglas & Olshaker, 1999; Meloy et al., 2012).

Cleveland Elementary School, San Diego

On January 29, 1979, Brenda Spencer, 16 years old, opened fire on the Cleveland Elementary School—located across the street from her house—wounding eight children and a police officer before killing the principal and a custodian who were attempting to protect the children. A chronic drug abuser, poorly supervised by her father, she had told a friend two days earlier, "I am going to do something big." Spencer had been caught burglarizing the school one year prior, was sent to probationary diversion, and received counseling. Her counselor opined at the time that there were indicators of suicidality. Spencer had received a .22 rifle and several hundred rounds of ammunition as a gift from her father several days prior to the shooting, and made her decision to kill the night before while watching *Battlestar Galactica* on television. She was taken into custody and, after several hours of dialogue with police negotiators, was asked about the motivation for her acts; her reply was "I don't like Mondays." This comment was picked up by the news outlets and led to the creation of a popular song by the *Boomtown Rats*, aptly titled *I Don't Like Mondays*.

Stockton, California

Patrick Edward Purdy, 25 years old, opened fire on January 18, 1989, in an attack lasting several minutes on Cleveland Elementary School in Stockton, California; he killed five Southeast Asian children and wounded 29 more before killing himself with a single shot to the heart with a pistol. As a diversionary tactic prior to opening fire, Purdy parked his car and set it ablaze with a Molotov cocktail in a Budweiser bottle before sneaking onto school property.

Purdy had been a student there from kindergarten through third grade. The demographic had changed since that time; what was once a primarily Caucasian neighborhood and school was now predominantly made up of Southeast Asian refugees whom he apparently hated—more than 600 of the 980 students were recent immigrants of Southeast Asian ancestry. Purdy reportedly hated almost everyone, but especially people in positions of authority and Southeast Asians. He often bragged about his father's Vietnam War experience and how his father had killed "gooks." He frequently made hostile racial comments to coworkers about the influx of Southeast Asians into the United States, and was angry about their large representation in the industrial arts courses that he was taking at a local community college. He complained that these immigrants were taking all the jobs and resented having to compete with them. Just prior to the mass murder, Purdy told another resident of the El Rancho Motel, "The damn Hindus and boat people own everything" (Green, cited in Fox & Levin, 2012, p. 188). He apparently fantasized about becoming a soldier like his father, but the withdrawal of US forces from Vietnam when he was just a boy precluded this channeling of his homicidal impulses. He was armed with a 9 mm handgun and an AK-47 rifle. He displayed symbols reflective of his extremist leanings: he had carved the words "freedom" and "victory" into the butt of his AK-47 and wrote on the camouflage shirt he wore over his military jacket the words, "PLO," "Libya," and "Death to the great Satin [sic]."

Four days before the event, Purdy told his half-brother that he would soon make headlines. For about five years prior, he had drifted through Connecticut, Nevada, Florida, Oregon, Tennessee, and Texas, working a variety of short-term jobs as laborer, security guard, and welder. He had been repeatedly arrested for various offenses in the past: in Los Angeles for soliciting a sex act from an undercover police officer, possession of hashish, possession of a dangerous weapon, receiving stolen property, and being an accomplice to a robbery. In 1987, he was arrested for indiscriminately firing a

9 mm pistol in the El Dorado National Forest. He was also charged with resisting arrest for kicking a deputy sheriff and shattering the window of the patrol car with his feet. While in jail awaiting trial, he attempted to commit suicide by hanging and cutting his own wrist with one of his fingernails.

Mr. Purdy lived in a room at a nearby motel (about two miles away) for weeks prior to the massacre; many of his final plans seem to have been made there, where evidence of military obsession and fantasy rehearsal was found. It appears that he spent hours in this room, manipulating hundreds of toy soldiers, tanks, jeeps, and weapons in simulated attacks. Investigators found more than a hundred plastic toy soldiers arrayed about the room, along with toy jeeps and tanks, in what appeared to be an imaginary battle scene. As an additional factor, it appears that Purdy may also have tracked other acts of school violence that targeted elementary schools within the year preceding his mass homicide (Fox & Levin, 2012).

Oklahoma City Federal Building

The Oklahoma City bombing was a terrorist attack on the Alfred P. Murrah Federal Building in downtown Oklahoma City on April 19, 1995. It was the most lethal act of domestic terrorism and the greatest loss of life on American soil to a terrorist event until the September 11, 2001 attacks: 168 people were killed, including 19 children under the age of six, and more than 680 people were injured. The blast destroyed or damaged 347 buildings within a 16-block radius, 86 cars, and shattered glass in 258 nearby buildings. The primary offender, combat-decorated Gulf War veteran Timothy McVeigh, was enamored of the "Patriot Movement" and inspired by extremist philosophy from the writings of William Pierce and others. He sought to retaliate against the government for what he saw as the conspiracy that led to the tragic events at Waco and Ruby Ridge, hoping that he would establish himself as the first hero of the "Second American Revolution," a war he hoped to initiate through the bombing (Meloy, Hoffmann, Guldimann, & James, 2012). Extensive planning, target reconnaissance, materials acquisition, and preparation were involved in this autonomous cell terrorist attack—he drove the truck alone, but his cohort Terry Nichols helped him construct the bomb the day before, and the third member of the cell, Michael Fortier, eventually testified against McVeigh for a reduced sentence. He also identified with imagery and ideas from the Star Trek series, justifying his killing of the innocent through their association with the "evil empire," and identified himself as a Klingon, a member of the fictional warrior race in the series.[1] McVeigh was charged, convicted, and ultimately executed for his role in the attacks, and Nichols was sentenced to life imprisonment.

McVeigh reportedly gave conflicting statements regarding his awareness of the presence of the day care center. On the one hand he stated he was not aware of it and, had he been, he might not have selected that location. Later, however, he contradicted this statement and justified his killing of children in the bombing: "I didn't define the rules of engagement in this conflict. The rules, if not written down, are defined by the aggressor. It was brutal, no holds barred. Women and kids were killed at Waco and Ruby Ridge. You put back in [the government's] faces exactly what they're giving out" (Michel & Herbeck, 2001, p. 225). According to Dr. Meloy, the forensic psychologist for the US government during the criminal trial (personal communication, January, 2013), McVeigh was likely aware of the presence of children, "due to line of sight to the daycare from the truck underneath the approach to the building—lots of kids in full view." McVeigh had also made a number of reconnaissance drives by the building in the months preceding the attack.

Jewish Community Center, Los Angeles

On August 10, 1999, Buford Furrow, a racially motivated anti-Semitic offender associated with the Aryan Nations, traveled from Washington State and ultimately attacked the Jewish Community Center (a children's day care center) in Los Angeles, California. He had probed the boundaries of at least two other Jewish institutions (Museum of Tolerance and University of Judaism) and determined that they were not soft enough targets—their security was too stringent. He killed a Filipino worker for the US Postal Service while making his escape and wounded three children, a counselor, and a receptionist at the day care center. When he turned himself in, he told the police, "This is a wake-up call for America." Furrow had nurtured a romantic interest in the widow of Robert Mathews (deceased member of a late-twentieth-century US white nationalist militant group known as The Order, who was killed at Whidbey Island during a police operation on December 8, 1984) and married her in 1995.

They separated after six months and she divorced him three years later, perhaps partly because he had demanded her complete submission as his wife. In July, prior to the assault, he had tried unsuccessfully to reconcile with her. Furrow had an extensive psychiatric history, including civil commitment for both suicidal and homicidal threats (Puckett, 2000), and was arrested for assault while he was in a psychiatric hospital. He had a bachelor of science degree in engineering, and had worked for both Boeing and Northrop.

Mountain View Elementary School, Anchorage, Alaska

On May 1, 2001, a 33-year-old man armed with a filet knife went onto the campus and attacked four children (aged 8 to 11) while they waited in the playground area for breakfast, which was provided for low-income students. With the perpetrator in pursuit, the children fled to the inside of the building. Mumbling something to the effect of "taking people back to God," the perpetrator continued to strike them, stabbing them in their necks, until he was cornered by teachers using a snow shovel. Shortly after that police officers (trained in active shooter response) arrived and apprehended the subject using less lethal munitions. He reportedly threatened the interveners and made a number of religiously themed statements that made no sense but implied a psychotic "mission." As he was taken away, he reportedly rambled incoherently. He had been loitering around the campus for several days and even brandished a knife at students, but no reports of trespassers or unusual behavior had been made to school authorities prior to this event. Fortunately, owing to the rapid response and intervention, there were no fatalities and the children, despite serious injuries, were quickly treated and released. The subject had been arrested 13 times since 1994 on charges including assault, stalking, criminal trespassing, and driving while intoxicated. He reportedly used a mental health center as his official address.

Beslan, North Ossetia

The Beslan School siege started on September 1, 2004, the first day of school, with the taking of over 1,100 hostages, most of them children. The assailants were a group of heavily armed Islamic separatist militants, mostly Ingush and Chechen, in the town of Beslan, North Ossetia, an autonomous region of the Russian Federation. The first day of school in this area is traditionally the day of highest attendance, with parents and relatives often accompanying their children. The terrorists demanded recognition of the independence of Chechnya at the UN and Russian withdrawal from Chechnya. On the third day of the standoff, Russian security forces entered the building with tanks, incendiary rockets, and other heavy weapons: at least 334 hostages were killed as a result of the crisis, including 186 children, with a significant number of people being injured or reported missing. To date, this remains the world's most lethal episode of school violence.

It is uncertain exactly how many terrorists stormed the school, but there were multiple groups, including one female who was reportedly a surviving widow of a terrorist and another who was a veteran of other terrorist events. During the initial takeover, the offenders quickly exerted control, confiscated mobile phones, and insisted that victims speak in Russian. When a father tried to explain to other victims, using the local regional dialect, what was being demanded of them, a hostage taker asked him if he was finished, then shot him to death. Another dissenter was also shot and left to bleed to death. A group of 15 to 20 male adult victims perceived by the hostage takers as strongest were taken into a separate room, where explosives were detonated; survivors of this attack were reportedly executed.

Ultimately "secret" negotiations between government and militant leaders took place. As a result of the tactical assault, nearly all of the estimated 32 hostage takers were killed, although substantial innocent life was also lost, mostly children. Some of the deaths were attributed to the detonation of explosives by the hostage takers as well as from firearms, but others may have been inadvertent casualties of the tactical assault by authorities. Much criticism was leveled at the Russian government for its handling of the incident.

Nanping School, China, and Other Events

The first of a cluster of Chinese school attacks occurred at Nanping City Experimental Elementary School on March 23, 2010, in the city of Nanping, Fujian Province. The offender used a knife to kill eight children and seriously wound five others. The offender, Zheng Minsheng, was a few weeks away from his 42nd birthday and had previously worked as a community physician. He had a good reputation among the factory patients he treated, but his relationship with his employers had deteriorated over the course of several years. In 2009 he quit, and at the beginning of 2010 he gave up hope of finding another job and became depressed. He reportedly had a history of mental illness, which was disputed at his trial. He told police that he perpetrated the attack because he thought "life was meaningless." He also apparently stated that he perpetrated the attack after being rejected by a romantic interest and suffering "unfair treatment" from the woman's wealthy family. His failures in both love and work were the two major reasons reported for his depression (Steinmuller & Fei, 2011). He was found guilty and executed on April 28, 2010. Given media control in the People's Republic of China, news reports of these events may not be entirely reliable.

More elementary school massacres occurred in different parts of China over the next several months. They all appeared to be perpetrated by mentally disturbed men, individuals with personal grievances, or those reacting to changes in Chinese society. In China, owing to strict gun-control laws, knives are the weapons of choice in violent crimes.

Just a few hours after the execution of Zheng Minsheng, another knife-wielding man, aged 33, attacked Hongfu Primary School in neighboring Fujian Province, in Leizhou, Guangdong, and wounded 16 students and a teacher. The offender had been a teacher at a different primary school in Leizhou and was also sentenced to death in June 2010.

On April 29 in Taixing, Jiangsu, 47-year-old Xu Yuyuan went to Zhongxin Kindergarten and stabbed 28 students, two teachers and one security guard. Unlike the other killers, he was from a wealthy family. Many people spoke of his bad temper, he often gambled, and he was accused of sexual harassment and domestic violence. Following an accusation of fraud, he was terminated by his employer. He had accumulated substantial debts, and a week before the massacre a creditor slapped him during an argument.

On April 30, Wang Yonglai used a hammer to attack preschool children in Weifang, Shandong, causing head injuries; he then used gasoline to commit suicide by self-immolation. As a farmer, he had been involved in a property dispute stemming from a government finding that his village committee had issued building permits without proper authorization. As a result, his new home had been torn down, causing him to lose substantial assets.

On May 12, 2010, Wu Huanming, aged 48, killed 7 children and 2 adults and injured 11 other persons with a cleaver at a kindergarten in Hanzhong, Shaanxi. He later committed suicide. He reportedly had been the landlord of the school and had been involved in an ongoing dispute with the school administrator over when the school would vacate his building.

On August 4, 2010, Fang Jiantang, 26 years old, slashed more than 20 children and staff with a large knife, killing 3 children and 1 teacher, at a kindergarten in Zibo, Shandong Province; 3 other children and 4 teachers were taken to the hospital. In Minhang District, Shanghai, 8 children, all aged four or five, were injured when an employee at a child-care center for migrant workers attacked them with a box cutter.

In September 2011, a young girl and three adults taking their children to nursery school were killed in Gongyi, Henan, by 30-year-old Wang Hongbin, who was armed with an axe. He was a local farmer who reportedly suffered from schizophrenia. "Revenge against society" (*baofu shehui*) was the most commonly claimed motivation for all the killers (Steinmuller & Fei, 2011).

Social changes, a failure to adequately address needs for the treatment of mental illness, and especially a contagion or copycat effect (Cantor, Sheehan, Alpers, & Mullen, 1999) were all factors that likely played a role in the plethora of school attacks in China during 2010. Reportedly, parents asked local government and school officials to address their serious concerns about safety, and an emergency panel was created by the education ministry. There was an attempt by the state media to minimize news about the attacks so as to prevent copycat crimes and panic. Efforts were made to increase school security by providing pepper spray and metal pitchforks to security personnel. Following the Chenpeng school attack, the Chinese government began posting security guards in schools throughout the country. All schools were scheduled to receive a security guard by 2013.

Chenpeng Village Primary School, China

On December 14, 2012—the same day as the Newtown massacre—36-year-old villager Min Yongjun stabbed 24 people, including 23 children and an elderly woman, in a knife attack at Chenpeng Village Primary School in Wenshu Township, Guangshan County, Henan Province, China. The attack began as the children were arriving for classes; the victims were between 6 and 11 years of age. The event was partially captured on security video cameras.

It appears that the offender first attacked an elderly woman, aged 85, who lived next to the school, after he had entered her house; he then stole one of her knives. Shortly thereafter, he pursued the children with the knife and slashed them, many on their heads. Although none of the victims was fatally wounded, several were reported to have had fingers or ears cut off during the attack. Given the manner of the wounds inflicted, it was surmised that his goal was to maim and disfigure the victims. Min Yongju was captured at the scene and taken into police custody. He was reported to have a long history of seizures and may have been influenced by the 2012 Mayan Doomsday prophecy, something that was also of interest to a local cult.

Sandy Hook Elementary, Newtown, Connecticut

On Friday, December 14, 2012, at approximately 9:30 a.m., Adam Lanza, age 20, fatally shot his mother, Nancy Lanza, age 52, at their Newtown home. Investigators later found her body, clad in pajamas, in her bed with four .22 caliber gunshot wounds to her head. Lanza then drove to Sandy Hook Elementary School. At about 9:40 a.m., using his mother's Bushmaster XM15-E2S rifle, he shot his way through a locked glass door at the front of the school. He was wearing black clothing, earplugs, and an olive green utility vest that contained multiple ammunition magazines for the Bushmaster.

Principal Dawn Hochsprung and the school psychologist were meeting with other faculty members when they heard gunshots. They rushed to the source of the sounds then encountered and confronted Lanza, who shot and killed them both. Ms. Hochsprung may have turned on the school intercom to alert others in the building. A nine-year-old boy said he heard over the intercom the shooter say, "Put your hands up!" and someone else say "Don't shoot!" while people yelled amid many gunshots. He, his classmates, and teacher took refuge in a closet in the gymnasium. Diane Day, a school therapist who was at the faculty meeting, heard screaming, followed by more gunshots. Natalie Hammond, lead teacher in the meeting room, pressed her body against the door to keep it closed. Mr. Lanza shot Ms. Hammond through the door, wounding her in a leg and arm—injuries for which she was later successfully treated.

In a first-grade classroom, Lauren Rousseau, a substitute teacher, was shot in the face and killed.

Fifteen of the sixteen students in her class were killed; a six-year-old girl was the sole survivor. The girl's family pastor said that she survived the mass shooting by playing dead and remaining still until the building grew quiet and she felt it was safe to leave. She ran from the school, covered in blood, and was the first child to escape the building. When she reached her mother, she said, "Mommy, I'm okay, but all my friends are dead." The child described the shooter as a very angry man.

The events in another first-grade classroom remain uncertain, with varying accounts attributed to the surviving children. Teacher Victoria Soto was reported to have attempted to hide several children in a closet and cupboards. As the offender entered her classroom, Ms. Soto reportedly told him that the children were in the auditorium. Several of the children then came out of their hiding place and tried to run for safety and were shot dead. Soto put herself between her students and the shooter, who then fatally shot her. Six surviving children from Soto's class crawled out of the cupboards after the shooting and fled the school. They and a school bus driver took refuge in a nearby home. As reported by his parents, a six-year-old boy in Soto's class fled with a group of his classmates, who escaped through the door when the offender shot their teacher.

Anne Marie Murphy, a teacher's aide who worked with special-needs students, shielded six-year-old Dylan Hockley with her body, trying to protect him from the bullets that killed them both. Paraprofessional Rachel D'Avino, who had been employed at the school and had been working with special-needs students for a little more than a week, also died trying to protect her students. School nurse Sally Cox, aged 60, hid under a desk in her office; she described hearing the door open and seeing Mr. Lanza's boots and legs facing her desk from approximately 20 feet away. He remained standing for a few seconds before turning around and leaving. She and school secretary Barbara Halstead, after calling 911, then hid in a first-aid supply closet for four hours. A custodian, Rick Thorne, ran through the hallways, alerting classrooms. First grade teacher Kaitlin Roig, age 29, hid 14 students in a bathroom and barricaded the door, telling them they must be completely quiet to remain safe. School library staff Yvonne Cech and Maryann Jacob first hid 18 children in a part of the library the school used for lockdown in practice drills. But on discovering that one of the doors would not lock, they had the children crawl into a storage room and barricaded the door with a filing cabinet. Music teacher Maryrose Kristopik, 50, barricaded her fourth-graders in a tiny supply closet during the rampage. Mr. Lanza arrived moments later, pounding and yelling "Let me in," while the students in Ms. Kristopik's class quietly hid inside.

Two third graders, chosen as classroom helpers, were walking down the hallway to the office to deliver the morning attendance sheet as the shooting began. Teacher Abbey Clements pulled both children into her classroom, where they hid. Laura Feinstein, a reading specialist at the school, gathered two students from outside her classroom and, after they heard gunshots, hid with them under desks. Ms. Feinstein called the school office and attempted to call 911 but was unable to connect because her cell phone did not have reception. She hid with the children for approximately 40 minutes before law enforcement came to lead them out of the room.

Mr. Lanza stopped shooting between 9:46 and 9:49 a.m., after firing 154 rounds in less than five minutes. He reloaded frequently during the shooting, sometimes firing only 15 rounds from a 30-round magazine. He shot all of his victims multiple times and at least one victim, a six-year-old boy, was shot 11 times. He shot mostly in two first-grade classrooms near the entrance of the school, killing 14 in one room and 6 in the other. The student victims were 8 boys and 12 girls, between six and seven years of age; the 6 adults were all women who worked at the school. After realizing that he had been spotted by a police officer who had entered the building, Lanza killed himself with a shot to the front of the head from a handgun. In a moment of brilliance, the surviving children in the school were told to hold each other's hands and close their eyes as they were escorted outside.

A large quantity of unused ammunition was recovered inside the school, along with three semiautomatic firearms, the .223-caliber Bushmaster, a 10mm Glock, and a 9mm Sig Sauer P226. A 30-round magazine was recovered with the rifle. Outside the school, an Izmash Saiga-12 combat shotgun was found in the car Lanza drove to the school. At Lanza's home, there were three additional firearms: a .45 Henry repeating rifle, a .30 Enfield rifle, and a .22 Marlin rifle.

All of the weapons were legally owned (Kellerman et al., 1993) by Lanza's mother, who was a gun enthusiast and often took her two sons to the shooting range. Their home was about five miles from the school. The offender had attended Sandy Hook for a brief time—entering there as a six-year-old in first grade—as well as several other schools before being home schooled starting in the ninth grade and receiving his GED. Later he briefly attended Western Connecticut State University. He was first diagnosed with "sensory integration syndrome" as a young boy and then later diagnosed with Asperger's syndrome[2] in middle school. He appeared to have severe emotional and psychological problems; his mother placed him in various programs and schools to attempt to treat his condition, finally reverting to her sole care for his mental health. Lanza's father, Peter Lanza, a General Electric executive, had left when the boy was 9 years old, and the parents divorced when he was 17. Lanza ceased all contact with his father a year later. Prior to the crimes he spent hours in the basement playing violent first-person video games ("Call of Duty"). He reportedly had conflicts with his mother over his use of time and may have had an unusual interest in the military—a military uniform was found in his bedroom and he deeply admired one of his mother's brothers, James Champion, a retired Kingston police officer and veteran. Forensic evidence subsequent to the crime indicated that Lanza had developed an interest in the mass murder at Northern Illinois University in February 2008, when Steven Kazmierczak killed 5 and injured 21 people. Search warrants and related affidavits were released on March 28, 2013. The New York Times reported, "Adam Lanza lived amid a stockpile of disparate weaponry and macabre keepsakes: a pair of rifles, 11 knives, a starter pistol, a bayonet, 3 samurai swords. He saved photographs of what appeared to be a corpse smeared in blood and covered in plastic" (Kleinfield, Rivera, & Kovaleski, 2013).

LESSONS LEARNED

Although our sample of cases is nonrandom and small ($n = 13$), we think it represents those individuals who have perpetrated mass casualty events at the elementary school level over the past century. A Wikipedia search of primary school assaults across the world indicates that there have been approximately 109 incidents since July 26, 1764, when four Lenape Indian warriors entered the Enoch Brown Elementary School in Franklin County, Pennsylvania, and killed and scalped 9 or 10 of the 12 children present. The next attack did not occur for over a hundred years. The Wikipedia citation (http://en.wikipedia.org/wiki/List_of_attacks_related_to_primary_schools) defines such mass casualty events as "attacks on school property or related primarily to school issues or events."

Since the event in Bath, Michigan, there have been about 88 worldwide incidents of attacks on primary schools. The Wikipedia data, however, should be treated with caution, since the definition of *mass casualty* is unclear and the citations are typically not drawn from primary-source historical material but rather from secondary source news reports or historical footnotes. We offer the following comments as preliminary opinions drawn from our analysis of our relatively small sample.

Offender Commonalities

These offenders were nearly all adult outsiders (with the exception of Brenda Spencer) who seemed to fit into one of several sometimes overlapping categories: psychotic individuals with a delusional agenda, those with personal grievances that caused them to target a school, and those with a sociopolitical agenda, namely terrorists (autonomous cells and large groups), utilizing the location to make a statement and potentially destabilize the existing power structure. There was a high prevalence of type 1 subjects (with no real connection to the school) along with some type 2 offenders (individuals like Purdy and Lanza would technically fit into this category, although it had been more than 15 years since either had attended the respective schools), and there was one apparent type 3 (Andrew Kehoe, the treasurer of the school board) (Mohandie, 2000).

The offenders appear to have been similar to those who perpetrate mass murders (Meloy, Hempel, Gray, Mohandie, Shiva, & Richards, 2004), with the possible exception of the terrorists at Beslan: many evidenced a military and weapons preoccupation (pseudocommando or warrior mentality) (Dietz, 1986; Hempel, Meloy, & Richards, 1999; Knoll, 2010a, 2010b) and an obsession with violence; they identified and tracked other perpetrators of mass casualties. Psychologically they often exhibited extreme detachment, chronic unresolved anger, interpersonal isolation, and a sense of having been victimized; they were easily offended and apt to perceive mistreatment by others. In addition to being homicidal, they tended to also be suicidal, often killing themselves rather than submitting to arrest. A number of them also demonstrated likely psychotic thought processes, as often seen in mass murderers who target strangers (Hempel et al., 1999). Generally speaking—with the exception of

the ideologically motivated offenders (Beslan and Oklahoma City cases)—they acted alone.

Warning behaviors (Meloy, Hoffman, Guldimann, & James, 2012)—acute, dynamic accelerating behavioral patterns that likely signal increasing risk of violence—were often demonstrated by the offenders, including pathway, fixation, identification, energy burst, leakage, and last resort warning behavior (see Meloy et al., this volume, Chapter 3). Fixations (i.e., pathological preoccupations) were variable in frequency and intensity, but included racial and sociopolitical agendas as well as personal grievances and overvalued ideas that were often delusional.

The behavioral pattern of bifurcation seen in some mass homicides (Hempel et al., 1999) was also represented in the selected cases. It appears that the initial violence, usually a homicide, was part of an unfolding and imminently lethal plan. The pattern of violence was predatory (instrumental): proactive, driven by fantasy, non-time limited in sequence, directed by cognition and perhaps initiated by emotion, which was then transformed into an action plan that was mentally and usually behaviorally rehearsed in some fashion (Meloy, 2004, 2006).[3] This is in contrast to affective (reactive, emotional or defensive) violence, which was not in evidence in any of these cases during the behavioral sequence leading to the casualties; however, there may have been a sequencing from predatory to affective violence once the killing began.

Noticeably absent were any direct threats to intended targets (MacDonald, 1968; Warren et al., this volume, Chapter 2). While there may have been communications, would-be offenders are usually in enough control to realize that if they did telegraph their intentions to the intended target, it would interfere with the consummation of their violent intent. Subjects will "leak" statements to third parties (Meloy & O'Toole, 2011), often of an ominous or indirect nature. This often reflects the presence of homicidal thinking along with the cognitive load (Sweller, 1988) it creates and the dynamic undercurrent of power that is sought, which sometimes compels expression.

Target Selection

It appears that most subjects selected the schools as a target based on convenience and availability, high visibility, maximum shock value and dramatic effect, attention and notoriety, and the symbolic value of attacking those most innocent, vulnerable, and incapable of defense. Selection for this group of offenders usually has multiple determinants. The major psychodynamic in these cases may be pathological narcissism: the desire for recognition through infamy and the gratification of overdetermined and chronic anger toward others for mistreatment—if not a full-blown paranoid state of mind. An often overlooked emotion in these cases, which may provide an undercurrent fueling the act, is envy: the wish to destroy the goodness in others (Klein, 1975) or the goodness represented by the innocence of children. The media coverage of high-profile events likely stimulates copycat acts (Cantor et al., 1999) among other unstable or angry subjects who are seeking to channel their grievances and homicidal impulses. This seemed particularly evident in the multitude of Chinese cases occurring between 2010 and 2012.

THREAT MANAGEMENT ISSUES

Prevention or Risk Mitigation

Mental health care. Complete prevention of these events is impossible—even totalitarian regimes with much less personal freedoms have not been immune—but it is possible to reduce the frequency of these catastrophic acts of mass violence. Proactive and comprehensive public mental health services accessible at a moment's notice to facilitate outreach, intervention, and involuntary hospitalization are key to reducing the pool of individuals with untreated psychotic and other mental illnesses—and fixed ideas or delusions that may justify violent problem solving, diminish impulse control, and increase poor judgment. Service providers must be competently trained in the indicators of extreme violence, and *local* medical systems must receive the legal and financial support necessary for these external controls, including greater flexibility to involuntarily hold individuals of concern. This approach is epidemiologically sound, since it does not attempt to specifically identify individuals at risk for mass murder—an impossible task given its extremely low base rate—but instead identifies through known risk factors the pool of individuals who might present a risk of targeted violence and treats them accordingly. A useful analogy is the impossibility of identifying those individuals who will have a myocardial infarction (heart attack), therefore cardiologists and allied medical professionals attempt to treat risk factors for such events in the general population and have

succeeded in decreasing various cardiac diseases over the past 40 years in the United States. The loophole in mental health care leaves out the patients who refuse voluntary psychiatric treatment, and do not seek it out, yet are *not* at imminent risk of violence toward self or others. Such individuals cannot be involuntarily treated, want no help, yet may present a risk over time for violent behavior given a precipitating event. Preventive detention for mental health reasons in the United States has largely been reduced to very short-term hospitalization, usually less than 72 hours, for those at imminent risk of danger to self or others. In other countries, such as the United Kingdom, protection of the public welfare can also be utilized as a reason for involuntary treatment, affording an opportunity for greater gains in public safety.

Education and awareness. Community education and a sense of shared responsibility for safety from these and other events requires greater public attention and private situational awareness. In this regard, the "see something, say something" campaigns, first initiated in New York City following the 9/11 attacks, are a helpful venue for this message, along with a supporting network of staff (mental health and law enforcement) who can then field in a timely fashion the investigations generated by such campaigns.

Gun control. Over a thousand individuals were killed by a firearm in the United States between the Newtown disaster in December, 2012 and the time of this writing in February 2013. Most of these cases were single-victim homicides or suicides. Thoughtful gun control is critical, meaning careful screening, universal registration, and repeated demonstrated competency in use.[4] While certain countries—namely China—have had significant clusters of these tragic events without the use of firearms, the death toll in these events would likely have been higher if the offender had used a handgun or long gun. Limited or nonexistent access to a high-capacity firearm not only reduces the practical ability of the subject to carry out such an act, but also reduces the anticipatory fantasy that may motivate planning and preparation. Such fantasies are extremely gratifying, since they compensate for an often blighted social and occupational existence (Meloy et al., 2001, 2004) and facilitate the subject's identification with previous mass murderers. For a moment in time the offender can actually look forward to being omnipotent—a stark contrast to his or her usual quotidian existence. Removing ease of access also creates the potential to generate gun traces and tracks on potential offenders and gives opportunity for lesser penal code statutes to be used as tools of behavioral control. Thoughtful gun access restriction would strive to (1) reduce access to the unstable, (2) eliminate weapons that increase killing efficiency and lethality, (3) enable the removal of firearms from deteriorating people in a broader sense, and (4) facilitate proactive investigations as to whether or not prohibited individuals possess or can access a firearm.[5] Enhanced background checks limit access, improve police investigations, and convey a greater sense of community safety.

Armed guards and other security. The idea of posting armed guards or police on campuses has also been suggested as a method of prevention. This solution, while costly, would certainly dissuade some offenders and potentially allow for engagement prior to lethal attacks.[6] It becomes critical to address three issues while contemplating such a solution: (1) the cost of coverage while such individuals are on break, out on sick leave, or patrolling other areas of a campus or school district; (2) the need for high-level training to make sure that such staff can competently use and safely possess firearms while on campus; and (3) the fact that their presence may unduly increase perceptions of vulnerability and fear among children.

Basic physical security issues—cameras and surveillance systems, gate control and campus access, and identification methods—must balance deterrence and reassurance and also deal with parental resistance, the fact that most adults do not want to send their children to a fortress reminiscent of a prison. The school should be a warm environment for the children, but appear to the offenders to be an undesirable place for them to consider perpetrating their crimes. Violence must be a less acceptable alternative for the offender and the public at large.

Disruption

Disruption is central to threat management and relies on the identification of potentially at-risk individuals, usually in the late stages of a pathway to violence. While mass casualty events may be perpetrated by insiders such as former students, parents, or staff members, most are inflicted by outsiders. It is important for students, staff, and parents to be vigilant for apparently unstable outsiders and report them to the authorities and the school's threat assessment team (Mohandie, this volume, Chapter 8).

More likely though, community members will subsequently provide the essential information to police. Law enforcement will need to work proactively to investigate the subject's ability to pose a risk to the school and work closely with the school to harden the target. Creative use of legal and civil strategies (Mohandie & Hoffmann, this volume, Chapter 5) to reduce risk in cases that do not qualify for immediate arrest and hospitalization will be critical to establish boundaries and contain the individual of concern. In particular, if the offender is not somehow institutionalized post-intervention, the potential for escalation must be considered and planned for. Monitoring—including surveillance, online postings, the use of informants and even undercover operations—may be important in other cases. The philosophy of *need to know* should be replaced with the belief in *need to share*. This eliminates the risk of a silo effect: different individuals may know different details, but if information is not exchanged, the totality of violence risk cannot be accurately assessed and managed.

CONCLUSION

When it comes to mass casualty and other lethal events, the goal is threat prevention but the reality is threat management. Sandy Hook Elementary School had a closed, locked campus, utilized emergency procedures, and—through the heroics and clear thinking of multiple individuals under conditions of chaos and confusion—greater loss of life was averted but tragedy nonetheless occurred. The offender reportedly utilized his high-powered rifle to shoot his way through the barriers. Would the posting of an armed security guard have prevented him from targeting the campus? Would such a guard been able to defend the school? In some situations these factors dissuade, deter, and interrupt offenders, but not always. Would the tragedy have been averted if the offender had not been easily able to obtain the weapons from his home? If he had not had access to an assault-type weapon, would there have been fewer casualties? If he had not apparently been trained in the use of such a weapon, would more lives have been spared? If he had received appropriate treatment for his mental health conditions, would he have decided on this plan of action? Could something have been done to bring attention to and manage his interest in violence, weapons, and destruction?

Preventing mass casualty events on elementary school campuses—events of extremely low frequency but high impact that inflict trauma on entire populations—means addressing the complex and multifaceted social, political, group, familial, organizational, individual, and other factors that fail when these tragedies occur. While the issue is complex, there is an obligation to seek innovative solutions and improve upon established protocols, question cherished principles that may require modification, and be reasonable yet firm; our children are our most precious resource and deserve nothing less. In the end, however, our schools are still among the safest places in our communities.

NOTES

1. McVeigh actually signed himself in as "Timothy Klingon" in a motel the night before the bombing.

2. There is no evidence that any of the autistic disorders are linked to predatory or instrumental violence (Murrie et al., 2002; Jones et al., 2010). However, secondary aspects of autism—such as certain empathic deficits, social isolation, and personality characteristics that are maladaptations to the neurobiological condition, such as paranoia—could contribute to violence risk.

3. A good example is the McVeigh case: he felt tremendous anger over the deaths in the Branch Davidian compound on April 19, 1993; but then, over the next two years, he developed a methodical plan to bomb the Murrah building and evidenced little emotion toward anyone (Meloy case files).

4. On February 14, 2013, Oscar Pistorius allegedly killed his girlfriend, Reeva Steenkamp, in Pretoria, South Africa. Mr. Pistorius reported that he owned a 9mm pistol; when asked how often he went to a shooting range, he said, "Just sometimes when I can't sleep." He posted a tweet on Nov. 27, 2012, concerning a false alarm at his home: "Nothing like getting home to hear the washing machine on and thinking it's an intruder to go into full combat recon mode into the pantry!" (New York Times, Feb. 15, 2013, p. A6).

5. It is argued by the National Rifle Association in the United States that gun control will lead to abolition of the right to bear arms. There is already gun control in the United States; the debate is how much. The individual's right to bear arms for traditionally lawful purposes, guaranteed by the Second Amendment to the US Constitution and embedded in the American culture, has already been affirmed by the US Supreme Court in District of Columbia v. Heller 554 U.S. 570 (2008).

6. The devil, however, is in the details. Should armed guards or police officers be armed with AK-47s or M-16s? If not, can an armed person adequately respond to a semi-automatic assault rifle with a handgun? Perhaps an H&K MP5 fully automatic 9mm machine gun should be considered by the school protectors to overcome any conceivable firepower advantage by a would-be offender.

KEY POINTS

- There have been over a hundred attacks on elementary or primary schools worldwide since the mid-eighteenth century.
- The attackers are usually adult outsiders and are quite similar to other mass murderers; their attacks are virtually always predatory or instrumental. They do not "snap."
- They are either psychotic, have a personal grievance, or are trying to advance an ideological agenda. The last group typically do not attack alone.
- Psychologically they often exhibit extreme detachment, chronic unresolved anger, interpersonal isolation, and a sense of having been victimized; they are easily offended and apt to perceive mistreatment by others.
- Prevention is impossible but risk mitigation is achievable.
- Mental health care, community education and awareness, firearms regulation, and enhanced security are central elements to mitigate the risk of such crimes.
- Disruption in the later stages of a pathway to violence can be accomplished through vigilance and the sharing of information with those who can and will intervene.

REFERENCES

Bernstein, A. (2009). *Bath massacre: America's first school bombing.* Ann Arbor: University of Michigan Press.

Cantor, C., Sheehan, P., Alpers, P. & Mullen, P. (1999). Media and mass homicides. *Archives of Suicide Research, 5,* 283–290.

Dietz, P. (1986). Mass, serial and sensational homicides. *Proceedings of the NY Academy of Medicine, 62,* 477–491.

Douglas, J. & Olshaker, M. (1999). *Anatomy of motive.* New York: Scribner's.

Ellsworth, M.J. (1927). *The Bath school disaster.* Bath School Museum Committee.

Fox, J. A., & Levin, J. (2012). *Understanding serial and mass murder,* 2nd ed. Thousand Oaks, CA: Sage.

Hempel, A., Meloy, J. R., Richards, T. (1999). Offender and offense characteristics of a nonrandom sample of mass murderers. *Journal of the American Academy of Psychiatry and the Law, 27,* 213–225.

Jones, A., Happe, F., Gilbert, F., Burnett, S., & Viding, E. (2010). Feeling, caring, knowing: Different types of empathy deficit in boys with psychopathic tendencies and autism spectrum disorder. *J Child Psychology and Psychiatry, 11,* 1188–1197.

Kellerman, A. L., Rivara, F. P., Rushforth, N. B., Banton, J. G., Reay, D. T., Francisco, J., ... Somes, G. (1993). Gun ownership as a risk factor for homicide in the home. *New England Journal of Medicine, 329,* 1084–1091.

Klein, M. (1975). *Envy and gratitude and other works, 1946-1963.* New York: Free Press.

Kleinfield, N., Rivera, R., & Kovaleski, S. (March 29, 2013). Newtown killer's obsessions, in chilling detail. *New York Times,* p. A1.

Knoll, J. (2010a). The "pseudocommando" mass murderer: Part I, the psychology of revenge and obliteration. *Journal of the American Academy of Psychiatry and the Law, 38,* 87–94.

Knoll, J. (2010b). The "pseudocommando" mass murderer: Part II, the language of revenge. *Journal of the American Academy of Psychiatry and the Law, 38,* 262–272.

MacDonald, J. (1968). *Homicidal threats.* Springfield, IL: Charles C. Thomas.

Meloy, J. R. (2004). Indirect assessment of the violent true believer. *Journal of Personality Assessment, 82,* 138–146.

Meloy, J. R. (2006). The empirical basis and forensic application of affective and predatory violence. *Australian and New Zealand Journal of Psychiatry, 40,* 539–547.

Meloy, J. R., Hempel, A. G, Gray, T. B., Mohandie, K., Shiva, A., & Richards, T. C. (2004). A comparative analysis of North American adolescent and adult mass murderers. *Behavioral Sciences and the Law, 22,* 291–309.

Meloy, J. R., Hempel, A .G., Mohandie, K., Shiva, A., & Grey, T. B. (2001). Offender and offense characteristics of a non-random sample of adolescent mass murderers. *Journal of the American Academy of Child and Adolescent Psychiatry, 40,*719–728.

Meloy, J. R., Hoffmann, J., Guldimann, A., & James, D. (2012). The role of warning behaviors in threat assessment: An exploration and suggested typology. *Behavioral Sciences and the Law, 30,* 256–279.

Meloy, J. R., & O'Toole, M.E. (2011). The concept of leakage in threat assessment. *Behavioral Sciences and the Law, 29,* 513–527.

Michel, L., & Herbeck, D. (2001). *American terrorist: Timothy McVeigh & the Oklahoma City bombing.* New York: Regan Books.

Mohandie, K. (2000). *School violence threat management: A practical guide for educators, law enforcement, and mental health practitioners.* San Diego, CA: STS Publications.

Murrie, D., Warren, J., Kristiansson, M., & Dietz, P. (2002). Asperger's syndrome in forensic settings. *International Journal of Forensic Mental Health, 1,* 59–70.

Puckett, K. M. (2000). *The lone terrorist.* Counterterrorism Division, Federal Bureau of Investigation. Washington, DC.

Steinmuller, H., & Fei, W. (2011). School killings in China. *Anthropology Today,* 27:10–13.

Sweller, J. (1988). Cognitive load during problem solving: effects on learning. *Cognitive Science, 12,* 257–285.

10

Contemporary Research on Stalking, Threatening, and Attacking Public Figures

JENS HOFFMANN, J. REID MELOY, AND LORRAINE SHERIDAN

This chapter describes the current state of the science concerning stalking, threatening, and attacking public figures. Much of the contemporary systematic research started after the assassination attempt on US President Ronald Reagan in 1981, which also led to the development of an interdisciplinary approach to the prevention of this form of targeted violence (Coggins, Pynchon, & Dvoskin, 1998). The studies of public figure attacks have had a sustained and powerful influence on the general evolution of threat assessment methodology (Fein & Vossekuil, 1998), inspiring research and threat assessment models in different countries (Meloy, 2011; Meloy, Sheridan, & Hoffmann, 2008).

But there is an even longer tradition in psychiatry and criminology focusing on the victimization of public figures. For more than a century and a half, scientific reports on unusual behavior toward public figures have appeared in the literature constellated around our contemporary terms, such as *stalking, public figure attacks,* and *pathological fixations*. In 1838 the French psychiatrist Esquirol—the man who coined the term *erotomania*—published a case study on celebrity stalking. He described a male who was following an actress throughout Paris. Notwithstanding her repeated rebuffs, this stalker remained convinced that the actress was in love with him. Esquirol confronted his delusion by brusquely asking, "How could you believe she loves you? You are not handsome. You possess neither rank or fortune." The stalker answered poetically, hinting that his delusion of a mutual relationship may have served

to overcome his solitude: "All that is true, but love does not reason, and I have seen too much to leave me in doubt that I am loved" (cited in Mullen, Pathé, & Purcell, 2009, p. 94).

More than half a century later, the Austro-German psychiatrist Richard von Krafft-Ebing, arguably the father of forensic psychiatry, noted that women of all ages can be fascinated by successful actors, singers, or athletes, so much so that they overwhelm these individuals with love letters (Krafft-Ebing, 1912). The German Eugen Bleuler, one of the most influential psychiatrists of the early twentieth century, found mental illness to be a possible trigger for violent attacks against public figures. "If the mentally ill thinks that he cannot help himself anymore with legal means, he acts in self-defense, shooting his enemy or attempting a nonserious attack on a high-ranking figure because he wants to enforce an 'unprejudiced' investigation" (Bleuler, 1943, p. 501).

Around that same time the French psychiatrist Gaëtan Gatian de Clérambault (1921, 1999) described a Frenchwoman who was stalking the British King George V, delusionally believing that the sovereign was in love with her. She pursued him from 1918 onward, paying several visits to England. She frequently waited for him outside Buckingham Palace and once saw a curtain move on one of the palace windows. Surely this was a signal from the king! She claimed that all Londoners knew of his love for her, but alleged that he prevented her from finding lodgings in London, made her miss her hotel bookings, and was responsible for the loss of her baggage containing money and portraits of him. Such doubts as she had never persisted for long. She vividly summarized her passion for him: "The king might hate me, but he can never forget. I could never be indifferent to him, nor he to me" (cited in Enoch & Ball, 2001, p. 21).

CONTEMPORARY RESEARCH ON DIFFERENT KINDS OF PUBLIC FIGURE FIXATIONS

Dynamics vary depending on the domain of public figures being pursued (Hoffmann, 2009). There seems to be a difference if the target of unwanted contact or approach behavior—or even a violent attack—is a politician, a celebrity, a member of a royal family, the head of an international company, or a religious leader. The following sections give an overview of studies on stalking, threatening, and attacking different kinds of public figures from this perspective.

Politicians

Politicians are the best researched samples, with arguably the highest number of published studies focusing upon their victimization by stalkers and attackers. They may more frequently be the target of violent attacks when compared to other public figures (Fein & Vossekuil, 1997; Hoffmann et al., 2011). Since politicians often have the power to decide how to spend the public's money, they are continuously tempted to support research that advances their own self-interests. More than a century ago, for example, a study on assassinations was commissioned to find ways of preventing such attacks (MacDonald, 1911). But the last 25 years of research in this field have witnessed substantial progress.

Stalking and unusual contact or approach behavior. Politicians have recently been surveyed to detail their experiences with unusual contact and stalking behavior (James, Farnham, & Wilson, Chapter 20, this volume). In Sweden, 74% of the members of Parliament reported having been subject to harassment, threats, or violence. In Australia, 93% of the politicians in the state of Queensland reported having experienced threats, harassment, and other concerning behaviors, and 15% had been subjected to at least one attempted or actual assault. In the United Kingdom, 80% of the members of the House of Commons had experienced harassing and intrusive

behaviors. A survey of Canadian politicians found that 30% had suffered harassment, with 87% believing their harassers to be suffering from a mental disorder (Adams et al., 2009).

One of the most influential studies on threatening and otherwise inappropriate letters to politicians was published by Dietz and colleagues more than twenty years ago (1991b). They found that letter writers who threatened a member of the US Congress were less likely to approach the politician personally. In a number of studies addressing threatening and harassing contacts to members of the US Congress, several risk factors for problematic approach behavior could be identified (Scalora et al., 2002a,b; Scalora, Zimmerman, & Wells, 2008). For instance, subjects who display mental illness symptoms tied to the target or to a personal motive pose a heightened risk of problematic approach behavior. The same holds for subjects with recent life stressors or prior arrest records. Furthermore, the likelihood of problematic approach behavior is significantly heightened by the perceived level of personal relevance of the issue presented by the subject, especially if help-seeking requests or other demands are made. Looking at risk factors within contact behavior, subjects who made multiple contacts through multiple modalities, such as phone calls and letters, were more likely to present a higher risk—factors related to *intensity of pursuit.* If threats emerged as part of an escalating pattern of problematic communications, an approach was less likely to occur. Further research has elaborated upon the differences between letter writers and email writers to members of the US Congress and the associated implications for problematic approaches (Scalora, Chapter 13, this volume).

In a Dutch survey study, one third of the questionnaires were returned; 33% of these reported stalking. The politicians surveyed said that they had been stalked primarily for reasons that had to do with their work as a politician (Malsch, Visscher, & Blaauw, 2002). The motives of the stalkers often centered around certain topics that were currently being managed (or arguably mismanaged) by the government—a perceived injustice or specific decisions made. Often the stalkers formulated suggestions about how to deal with these topics, but almost half the politicians reported being threatened by the stalker (46%). The average age of these stalkers was 48 years and the majority were males who lived alone. A female politician mentioned receiving hundreds of faxes in a week from one person. It was also reported several times that certain stalkers were motivated by a wish for recognition. Two politicians reported that they had offered the stalker an opportunity to talk about her or his grievances and feelings of injustice, and that this had helped; the stalking had stopped. In a sample of Dutch celebrities analyzed by the same research group, a direct confrontation with the fixated person had an opposite effect and intensified the stalking (Malsch et al., 2002).

Violent attacks. In a study of 14 attacks on German public figures between 1968 and 2004, the vast majority of the victims (86%) were politicians (Hoffmann et al., 2011). In a research project on assassinations of public figures in the United States, at least 63% of the sample were politicians (Fein & Vossekuil, 1999). Compared with other public figures, politicians appear to have the highest risk of being attacked with violent intent.

James and colleagues (2007) studied 24 nonterrorist attacks on European politicians and found a high proportion of psychotic offenders. Cases examined involved attacks on elected politicians between January 1990 and December 2004. Attacks occurred in Austria, France, Germany, Italy, the Netherlands, Sweden, Switzerland, and the United Kingdom. Five of the attacks involved fatalities (21%) and eight involved serious injuries (33%). The average age of the attackers was 39 years. Five of the assailants were women (21%). In all cases except one, the attacker acted alone. In 10 cases (42%) there was evidence that the assailant was a loner or social isolate. Ten attackers were psychotic, four drunk, nine politically motivated, and one unclassifiable. The mentally disordered were responsible for most of the fatal and seriously injurious attacks. Most of them gave repeated warnings in the form of obviously disordered communications and approaches. In 19 cases (79%) the attack was either clearly planned or involved specific weapons suggesting planning. When planning occurred, it was usually only a matter of days, in contrast to the US attackers, who planned for a longer period of time before the attack. Attacks resulting in either death or serious injury were likewise associated with evidence of mental disorder, the presence of psychosis and delusional beliefs, the perpetrator being a loner, and the absence of a political motive. The authors concluded that recognizing the links to attacks on public figures of both delusional fixations and disordered communication could increase the frequency of earlier mental health interventions in cases of concern. This could prevent some of these attacks.

There are some case dynamics gaining special attention in the field of attacks on political figures, and are captured by the concepts of the "lone wolf" or "violent true believer" (Meloy, 2004; Meloy & Mohandie, Chapter 27, this volume; Simon, 2013). An ideologically-motivated attack on a politician was apparent in a 1968 German case in which a suicidal young man, loosely connected to the extreme right, shot a left-wing student leader (Hoffmann et al., 2011). More recently, in the year 2011 in Norway, Anders Behring Breivik, an offender who identified himself as a member of the Knights Templar—a twelfth-century corollary of the current term "special forces"—bombed government buildings in Oslo before committing a mass murder of adolescents (see a detailed case study on Breivik in Meloy, Hoffmann, Roshdi, Glaz-Ocik & Guldimann, Chapter 3, this volume). Also the concepts of different forms of targeted violence are not always as pure as they seem to be at first sight. In January 2011 in Arizona, a young man committed a mass murder, killing six people right after he tried to assassinate a female politician in the same event; he did assassinate a US federal judge. The distinction between fixation, psychiatric disorder, and ideological motivation is sometimes not as clear as researchers and commentators would like. The young man who committed the Arizona killings, Jared Loughner, was a diagnosed paranoid schizophrenic, but his delusions were defined by a nihilistic philosophy—that life is without objective, purpose, or meaning—and the government was controlling his freedom of thought and speech. He had been fixated on the congresswoman for four years following her perceived slight of him at an open forum when she did not answer his written question, "What is government if words have no meaning?"

Significant Results of Politician Research

- Politicians are often the target of threats and harassing behavior.
- Unusual communication and approach behaviors are normally not focused on relationship issues but rather on grievances and anger regarding political and social issues.
- Compared with other groups of public figures, politicians appear to have an elevated risk of being attacked.
- Fixation on the basis of romance or sexual attraction toward politicians is highly unusual. As Paul Begala, the political commentator,

once quipped, "Washington is Hollywood for ugly people."

- It is difficult to clearly demarcate psychiatric disorder and ideological motivation in some political attackers.
- Intensity of pursuit is a key variable in the assessment of approach risk to politicians.

Celebrities

In contrast to the media attention that celebrity stalking attracts, empirical research on this topic is rare. Only a single study on attacks on celebrities could be identified (Schlesinger & Mesa, 2008). However, the scientific literature does offer a moderate number of case studies. There are, for example, detailed analyses of the attempted bombing of pop singer Björk (Schlesinger, 2006) and the stabbing of tennis star Monica Seles (Hoffmann & Meloy, 2008).

An unusual clinical case study about a teenager with a fixation on a celebrity was offered by McCann (2001). He described a 14-year-old boy who came into psychiatric treatment with suicidal ideation.

Terry had developed a fixation on a male child actor who starred in several successful movies. Terry's fixation included repeated statements of his intent to travel to Hollywood to meet this actor to become friends. Terry would write numerous notes and letters to the actor....It was apparent that the public persona of this celebrity was an idealized portrayal of all that Terry felt lacking in his life; the star was attractive, popular, well liked, intellectual, and competent as portrayed in his movies. Terry's unrealistic expectation of friendship, although nonviolent in its intent, was clearly a compensatory fantasy-based union in which the child actor could help Terry overcome his feelings of rejection and inadequacy by joining into an idealized friendship. (p. 65)

A novel study design by Leets, de Becker, and Giles (1995) analyzed a sample of letters to an international celebrity and came to the following conclusion, which marked the difference between fans and stalkers of a public figure: "The reasonableness of expectations seems to be the most significant difference of those who would be called normal and those likely to pursue inappropriate, unwanted, intrusive or even hazardous encounters" (p. 120).

Meloy et al. (2008) labeled this belief "entitled reciprocity": a debt is believed to be owed by the celebrity to the stalker commensurate with the time and energy the stalker has devoted to the celebrity.

Stalking and unusual contact or approach behavior. The first study focusing on the stalking of celebrities was conducted by Dietz and colleagues (1991a). The group examined 1,800 letters sent to Hollywood celebrities, comparing those who pursued encounters with celebrities and those who did not. A vast majority of the writers put themselves in a positive relationship with the celebrity as a friend, spouse, or lover. The study revealed 15 factors associated with such pursuit, such as duration of correspondence of a year or longer or an expressed desire for face-to-face contact with the celebrity.

In Europe, two empirical studies could be identified which addressed celebrity stalking. In the Netherlands, 105 public figures who had experienced "repeated harassment originating from an obsession with the victim as a public figure" took part in a study that sought to determine some characteristics of public figure stalkers and their victims (Malsch, Visscher, & Blaauw, 2002). Celebrity agents and publishing house employees distributed questionnaires among clients whom they believed had been targeted by stalkers. Questionnaires were also mailed to members of the Dutch government. Thus the sample comprised politicians, writers, performing musicians, actors, and television and radio presenters. Among the 105 public figures who responded, 35 (33%) self-reported that they had been stalked. There was a difference between the frequencies of political (21%) and celebrity (38%) victims. Many of the stalkers were said to be mentally disordered, with 34% of the public figures reporting that their stalker had undergone psychiatric treatment. Most of the public figures questioned took the stalking very seriously, with the majority reporting to the police. The stalkers of those in the entertainment world were more likely to physically pursue their targets. Generally the celebrity stalkers were motivated by love, by an illusion that the public figure was in love with him or her, or by the intention to become famous themselves. Those public figures who more regularly appeared on television and radio had a greater chance of experiencing multiple stalking. The extent of media exposure may be an important risk factor. The same effect was not found, however, among politicians.

In Germany, a sample of 53 celebrities—most of them news presenters—was studied. The celebrities provided the study data by responding to questionnaires (Hoffmann, 2005; Hoffmann & Sheridan, 2008a). Among the sample, 79% reported having been stalked at some point in their careers. This is the first reported lifetime prevalence rate for stalking of public figures. Although this rate may be higher than in other public figure groups because television personalities would seem to be particularly frequent objects of stalkers, it is clear that celebrity status carries with it a heightened risk of being targeted as compared with the status of the private citizen. Although independent data sets must be compared with great caution, when examined against a German population sample (Dressing et al., 2005), the rate of stalking victimization for this celebrity group of news presenters was more than six times higher (79% vs. 12%).[1]

The celebrities were asked to record their longest period of harassment by one individual. The average length was 25 months, ranging from 1 month to more than 10 years. Although these were the most extreme stalking cases the television personalities reported, this number also fits well with findings from the general research on stalking. In their meta-analysis of 175 stalking studies, Spitzberg and Cupach (2007) found that the average case of stalking (the *mean*) lasted for 22 months or close to 2 years—although the *mode* (most frequent length of a stalking case) appears to be 1 month (Mohandie, Meloy, McGowan, & Williams, 2005). Only a minority (14%) of the stalked television personalities declared that they had been targeted just once. The majority had been the target of a stalker more frequently, most between two and five times in their careers (62%). Similarly, in the Dutch study of Malsch et al. (2002), 59% of respondents stated that they had been targeted more than once.

Letters sent by stalkers were suffused with themes of love and adoration. Almost half of the sample (43%) were physically approached by an obsessively preoccupied (fixated) individual. A quarter of the television personalities (25%) reported that this had happened on only one occasion, but a fifth (19%) had experienced multiple incidents. In virtually all cases the celebrity's workplace was the location of encounter on at least one occasion (96%). This high rate is easily attributable to the profession of the public figures: most worked regularly at a well-known television station, the location of which could be easily traced.

A study in the United States analyzed the largest celebrity stalker sample worldwide to date (Meloy, Mohandie, & McGowan, 2008). It consisted of 271 stalkers with an average age of 39 years, of whom 74% were males. The duration of the stalking of the celebrities averaged 26 months. As expected, there was a substantial rate of mental illness present in the sample: 27% were psychotic at the time of stalking, 17% had a psychiatric medication history, and at least 7% had attempted suicide; 29% were unemployed and the same number had a criminal history. The majority of the stalkers (52%) sought a relationship, and 20% sought help from the celebrity victims. Thirteen percent wanted to only communicate, whereas 8% insulted their targets and 6% offered help; only a minority (18%) made threats.

The study also attempted to predict a physical approach. Ten variables were identified. However, only two of those variables, escalation and police intervention, were significant predictors of an approach. These were (1) if the stalking escalated (in frequency or intensity), there was a ninefold increase in likelihood of an approach, and (2) if the subject was not reported to the criminal justice system or there was nothing more than a police report taken and no other police response, the likelihood of an approach decreased by almost half.

In some of the celebrity stalking studies reviewed, there was a marked distinction regarding the gender distribution of victimization as compared with most other stalking studies. Among the German female television personalities, 83% claimed they had been stalked, as did 74% of their male colleagues (Hoffmann & Sheridan, 2008a). In the Dutch study of public figure victims (Malsch et al., 2002), the percentage of male and female public respondents who reported incidents of stalking was similar. In the US sample, 58% of the celebrities were female, 31% were male, and 11% were unknown (Meloy et al., 2008). In many earlier studies of stalking, both among noncelebrity populations (Spitzberg, 2002) and within celebrity groups (Dietz & Martell, 1989), an average of 70% to 80% of all stalking victims were women. There may be a quantitative difference regarding the gender distribution of stalking victims in celebrity vs. noncelebrity stalking; the approximate gender parity among celebrity victims may also be a relatively new phenomenon given the findings of Dietz et al. (1991a) over twenty years ago.

Violent attacks. The research on celebrity stalking revealed some frequencies for physical violence. In the US sample, 2% of all stalkers attacked the celebrity upon whom they were fixated (Meloy et al., 2008). In no case did the physical attack require medical support. The frequency of violence in the German study was identical (Hoffmann & Sheridan, 2008a). Of the 42 television personalities who reported being stalked, one female presenter was physically attacked and strangled. In the Dutch study none of 35 stalked public figures were attacked (Malsch et al., 2002). Compare these figures to stalking in the general population—especially when the perpetrator was a former intimate partner—where the violence rate is at least 25 times higher (Mohandie, Meloy, McGowan, & Williams, 2005).

Two other studies gave some indication of the risk of violence for celebrities compared with other public figures. In the Exceptional Case Study Project (ECSP) on lethal or near-lethal attacks, public figures of all types were included in the sample (Fein & Vossekuil, 1997). However, film, sport, and media celebrities comprised only 19% of the cases. In a smaller sample of 14 violent nonterrorist attacks on public figures in Germany, there were only two incidents in which the public figure targets had a nonpolitical background (14%): one was an athletic star and the other was a television presenter (Hoffmann et al., 2011). In these two independent public figure attack samples from the United States and from Germany covering a similar time frame after World War II, there was almost an identical proportion of celebrities within each attack sample. We can say with caution that among public figures who are attacked, no more than one in five will be a celebrity figure.

Until now there is only one scientific study looking exclusively at attacks on celebrities or other disturbing and extremely destructive behavior directly related to celebrities. Schlesinger and Mesa (2008) analyzed 21 cases occurring worldwide after 1949. The sample included cases where the stalker killed or attempted to kill the celebrity with whom he or she was obsessed (11 cases); cases where the violence was displaced to a person directly connected to the celebrity (3 cases); and cases where the violence was displaced to an individual completely independent of the celebrity (3 cases). Four cases of celebrity stalkers who threatened, attempted, or committed suicide were also included as a separate group because their behavior was not homicidal but rather involved harming themselves. A direct homicidal attempt was made on 14 celebrity victims—5 died, 5 were injured, and 4 managed to escape the attack without injury—for a lethality rate of 36% and a casualty rate of 71%.

Schlesinger and Mesa (2008) found that the frequency of homicidal celebrity stalking has increased significantly since 1980. There were only 2 cases before 1980 and there have been 19 cases since. A majority of the offenders were male (76%) and one third had prior offenses (33%). Mental health problems were common in the sample: 52% had a psychiatric diagnosis, 57% had been in treatment, and 38% had been psychiatrically hospitalized. The investigators identified three "red flags" that appear to be useful indicators of a dangerous person: (1) all the stalkers were obsessed with their celebrity victims, and the level of obsession ("pathological fixation") was apparent to others in many cases, (2) almost every offender had unrealistic or delusional expectations of the celebrity ("entitled reciprocity"), and (3) almost half the offenders were angry about some personal behavior of the celebrity that seemed to have served as a trigger for the violent acting out.

Another rare form of violent attack on celebrities must be mentioned. In 2004 the Dutch artist Theo van Gogh was murdered by Mohommad Bouyeri, a young man with a radical Islamic background (Buruma, 2006). Theo van Gogh was well known for his critical and provocative work on some aspects of Islam. Although having been part of a radical group, his murderer resembled an ideologically motivated lone wolf attacker, which is more often found in attacks on politicians than celebrities (Biesterfeld & Meloy, 2008).

Significant Results of Celebrity Research
- Compared with the general population and other groups of public figures, celebrities seem to have an elevated risk of being victimized by stalking.
- The communication of stalkers with celebrities is often suffused with themes of love and adoration; a sense of perceived rejection likely plays a critical role in the genesis of hostility toward the celebrity who was once loved.
- Intensity of fixation is a central point of analysis in estimating the probability of an approach—evidenced by frequency of communication and multiple methods of communication.
- The general rate of physical violence is very low, probably because of enhanced security measures.
- There has been a rise in lethal or near lethal attacks on celebrities since 1980.

- A significant minority if not a majority of stalkers and attackers of celebrities are psychotic at the time.
- There is typically a linear and positive correlation between frequency of appearance and notoriety of the celebrity and the number of stalkers pursuing him or her.

Royalty

Systematic research on problematic approaches, threats, and attacks on royal personages is a rather new field as compared with the similar study of politicians and celebrities. The work began with the founding of the Fixated Research Group in the United Kingdom in 2002 (see also James, Farnham, & Wilson, Chapter 20, this volume). Seven leading researchers in the field of stalking from England, Australia, and the United States were invited to participate and submitted a proposal that the Home Office agreed to fund. The researchers' major task, which eventuated in eight years of study, was to analyze unusual contact, harassing behavior, and attacks on the British Royal Family.

Stalking and unusual contact or approach behavior. Most of the Fixated Research Group's studies were conducted on a sample of *randomized* files (n = 275) of inappropriate communications or approaches to members of the British Royal Family (James et al., 2009) drawn from a database of over 8,000 files compiled by the Metropolitan Police Service's Royalty Protection Unit over a period of 15 years. The three theoretical parameters were motivation, mental disorder, and communication/approach behavior. Within the study sample, 84% were suffering from serious mental illness. Different forms of behavior were associated with different patterns of symptomatology. Cases could be separated into eight motivational groups, which also showed significant differences in mental state. Relevant parameters for the differentiation of motivational groups were found in 90% of the cases. The motivational groups were delusions of royal identity (27%), amity seekers (17%) offerng their friendship or advice, counselors (11%), intimacy seekers (12%), sanctuary and help seekers (9%), those who held the belief that they were being royally persecuted (3%), querulants (6%) who were pursuing a highly personalized quest for justice and vindication, and the chaotic (15%) with unclear motivation. Marked differences in the intrusiveness of behavior were found among these groups.

Another of the group's published studies, which eventually numbered 10, analyzed factors associated with approach and escalation toward the British Royal Family (James et al., 2010). In a sample of those who engaged in abnormal communication (n = 132), those who approached (n = 79) were significantly more likely to evidence mental illness and grandiosity, to use multiple communications, to employ multiple means of communication, and to be driven by motivations that concerned a personal entitlement to the prominent individual.

Until now there has been only one study researching royalty other than the British Royal Family. A team from the Netherlands and the United States examined all 107 subjects referred to the Threat Assessment Unit of the Netherlands National Police Agency who engaged in disturbing communications or problematic approaches toward the Dutch Royal Family during the period 1995–2010 (Van der Meer, Bootsma, & Meloy, 2012). The majority of these subjects were male (68%), the average age was 48 years, and 71% were unemployed, while 70% percent had prior police records and 40% a prior record for violence; 75% had psychotic symptoms.

Thirty-two percent of the study subjects showed signs of "pathological fixation" and 36% showed "grandiosity." The most common primary motivations of all subjects for contacting the Dutch Royal Family were "seeking to bring attention to a perceived problem" (24%) and "claiming royal identity" (13%). All other motivations were far less common.

Statistical analysis explored differences among three subgroups: those who only communicated, those who only approached, and those who did both. Consistent with the public figure research in other countries, it was found that the last subgroup used multiple means of communication more frequently and made communications that were less threatening than those made by people who only communicated. Other differences that distinguished those who both communicated and approached from at least one of the other two groups were a history of property crime (theft, robbery, or burglary), property damage, not engaging in recommended psychiatric treatment, seeking attention to solve a perceived problem, and pathological fixation (Van der Meer et al., 2012).

Violent attacks. In a further study from the Fixated Research Group in Britain (www.fixatedthreat.com), all attacks on a member of the British Royal Family since 1778 for which there were public records were examined (James et al., 2008; Mullen et al., 2008). In the 23 attacks, there was evidence of psychotic illness at the time in 11 (48%) cases, with evidence of mental disorder in 4 additional ones. Eighty-three per cent of the attackers were male. Seven cases (30%) involved adolescent males. Only two attackers were known to be married. An interesting research question—yet to be studied—is change in the demographics and motivations of stalkers and attackers of royalty as the royal subject ages; in no other public figure domain is the target imbued with both status and power over the entire course of life.

Nine attackers had stalked their victims. Only two attacks resulted in serious physical injuries. In 1864, Prince Alfred, Queen Victoria's son, was shot and seriously injured. The attempted kidnap of Princess Anne in the Mall in 1974 left the princess unharmed but led to four people being shot and seriously injured. Minor injuries were sustained by King William IV when he was hit by a stone. Queen Victoria received a black eye and bruise to the head when attacked while riding in her carriage.[2] Thirteen cases (57%) involved firearms, a handgun in all cases except one. Of the 12 handguns, 6 (50%) were not loaded with live ammunition. Three cases involved knives, three involved stones, and one case involved a brass-headed walking cane. Purely political motivations, which can be clearly adduced in very few of these cases, seem to have been unusual. The objective of most attackers was to commit an outrageous act that would draw attention to their grievances.

It is unclear if this rather low frequency of severe targeted violence against the British Royal Family over centuries is typical for all royals in European countries or worldwide. There are several cases of assassinations of a royal figure in history that would be classified today as an act of targeted violence by a fixated person. For example, in 1898 the Italian anarchist Luigi Luccheni stabbed the Austrian Empress Elisabeth. The 25-year-old Luccheni was an unsteady character who had lived in different countries (Lombroso, 1899). Luccheni was heard to say, "I wanted to kill some great person, so as to get my name in the papers."

Significant Results from the Royal Family Research

- Most problematic contacts with royals are driven by prosocial motives, such as getting attention for a problem or seeking a relationship. Aggressive communication is the exception.

- Most problematic communicators and approachers are mentally ill.
- Communicated threats typically are associated with a lower risk of an approach, but all direct threats should be investigated.
- Delusions of royal identity are a common motive for contact and approach behavior.
- The general rate of physical violence is very low. Lethal or near lethal attacks are even rarer.
- Once again, the intensity of pursuit is a central aspect in assessing the risk of an approach.
- Fixation on a *cause* appears to be more dangerous than fixation on a person.
- A little researched but most aggressive group comprises those who approach the royal but do not communicate beforehand.
- The two royalty studies excluded those involved in explicit terrorist activity, either as lone actors or members of a group.

Corporate Figures

Little is known about the experiences of business executives, some famous, who become the victims of stalking, threats, or nonterrorist violent attacks. Systematic research is still needed. A small number of scientific papers offer some case studies (Fein & Vossekuil, 1997; Hoffmann & Sheridan, 2008b; Meloy & Mohandie, 2008; O'Toole et al., 2008).

An unsystematic case review came to the conclusion that fixations on business representatives take many forms, ranging from those rooted in the private realm, such as ex-partner and familial stalking, to stalking by delusionally driven individuals who incorporate the public image of a company figurehead into their fantasies (Hoffmann & Sheridan, 2008b). Prompted by the variety of personal and psychological characteristics and motivations of those who stalk, threaten, and attack corporate leaders, Hoffmann and Sheridan (2008b) proposed four dimensions to help discriminate among subgroups: endurance, relationship, psychopathology, and motivation. Every individual can be evaluated on each of these dimensions, a procedure that the authors have found to be helpful in understanding the dynamics of a corporate threat or stalking case.

Stalking and unusual contact or approach behavior. Based on our case experience in the field of threat assessment, individuals who harass company figureheads are motivationally similar to those who fixate on politicians (Hoffmann & Sheridan, 2008b).

To test this assumption, a study was conducted by a German research group, which analyzed inappropriate letters to German CEOs (Hoffmann, Gotcheva, & von Groote, 2008). The sample included 83 unusual or threatening letters from 75 writers. In a third of all cases the authors showed signs of mental illness. More often than not a fixation on a cause rather than on an individual was evident (Mullen et al., 2009). Typical letter topics were a desire for revenge (36%), frustration with the conduct of the company or the CEO (69%), and descriptions of perceived problems (43%). Threats and insults were found regularly (45%), and in most cases the duration of the contact behavior did not last very long. We concluded that the letters to CEOs are more similar to inappropriate communications to politicians than to celebrities.

Meloy and Mohandie (2008) examined in detail the stalking of two male corporate celebrity figures by two stalkers. They found similarities in both males regarding criminal and drug abuse histories, major psychiatric disorders, likely personality disorders, and histories of chronic failures in their ability to sustain work and form a stable sexual bond with another person—data quite similar to those regarding many public figure stalkers (Meloy, Sheridan, & Hoffmann, 2008). O'Toole, Smith, and Hare (2008) used the example of the abduction and murder of a Fortune 500 CEO to illustrate the presence of psychopathy in public figure stalking. In all three of these cases, a history of antisocial behavior and psychopathy in particular was prominent.

Violent attacks. The only study of public figure attacks that reported explicit violence toward corporate figures was conducted by the US Secret Service (Fein & Vossekuil, 1997, 1998, 1999). Three business executives were included in their total sample of 74 attacks. Compared with politicians, celebrities, and federal judges, the public figure group of business executives had the lowest risk for becoming the targets of an assassination (4%). Despite the small sample size, different dynamics could be detected when the motives underlying assaults were examined. In one of the three cases, a deluded woman killed her victim in an attempt to avenge a perceived wrong. In another case a business leader died because a criminal intended to profit from exploiting his status.

Significant Results of Corporate Figures Research

- Empirical research on stalking, threats, and attacks directed toward corporate public figures is very scarce.

- Dimensional analysis of endurance, relationship, psychopathology, and motivation has been useful in specific cases.
- The communications of fixated persons directed toward corporate figures are similar to the communications sent to politicians.
- The general rate of physical violence is low. The risk of nonterrorist lethal or near lethal attacks appears to be lower for corporate figures than for politicians and celebrities, but this is largely speculative.

Religious Leaders

Stalking, threats, and attacks on religious leaders are largely unstudied, especially from a threat assessment perspective. This is at odds with the impression formed by media reports that religious figures are repeatedly victims of attacks. Looking, for example, at Pope John Paul II's reign, a number of acts of targeted violence became public (Wikipedia, 2013). In 1981 he was shot and critically wounded by Mehmet Agca, a Turkish gunman, in St. Peter's Square. At trial Agca claimed to be the second coming of Christ. The Pope attributed his survival of the assassination to the Third Secret of Fatima and the Virgin Mary: the date of the assassination, May 13, was the date on which the Virgin Mary appeared to the three Fatima children. One year later, a mentally ill man tried to wound the pope with a bayonet. Two years after the Agca attack, the Pope met with him in private and they developed a friendship, which lasted until the Pope's death in 2005. Agca was released from prison on January 18, 2010.

As is the case with other public figures, it seems that well-known religious leaders are often part of the delusional worldview of the mentally ill. Research on unusual communications to public figures indicates that pathologically fixated individuals seem to foster religious delusions from time to time (Dietz et al., 1991a,b). One pristine area of research that has not been addressed is attacks on the papacy, although a number of historical accounts of the papacy are available (Norwich, 2011).

The frequency and intensity of stalking of religious leaders is also unknown, although forensic cases appear to be increasingly common:

The minister of a so-called Christian "mega-church" in the US was the target of an anonymous blogger who incessantly criticized him, his beliefs, and his lifestyle. When it became apparent, however, that his wife and home were being photographed surreptitiously and she had been followed in an unknown automobile, the case was opened as a criminal matter. A detective who was also a competent threat assessor investigated the case and was able to identify the blogger. He interviewed the target, informed the minister of the blogger's identity, and determined that there was no stalking case and no evidence of any criminal threats. The blogger subsequently civilly sued the detective and the city for violation of his US Constitutional right to privacy, and eventually sued the minister for libel (defamation) since the latter had referred to him as a "psychopath" in a newspaper article. During the initial case, it was revealed in a deposition that the minister had first been informed of the blogger's identity by his sister-in-law, who was frightened of him. Both cases were settled for an undisclosed monetary sum, however, in favor of the blogger.

Results of a Research Review of Fixations on Religious Leaders

- No systematic study on unusual communication and targeted attacks on religious leaders could be identified, either terrorist or nonterrorist in motivation.
- Case studies indicate that religious figures are sometimes killed or severely injured by the mentally ill. These may be similar to attacks on politicians.
- Attacks on the most widely known religious figure in the world, the Pope, have never been empirically studied and published.
- It is likely that stalking, threats, and attacks on religious figures are directly and positively correlated with the actual celebrity and symbolic significance of the public figure.

NEW CONCEPTS AND RESEARCH

New concepts and research have emerged that promote a better understanding in the field of threats, stalking, and attacks of public figures. This knowledge can be also transferred to protocols for assessing fixated persons. In the following section we will give an overview of the concepts of pathological fixation, grandiosity and entitled reciprocity, intensity of pursuit, and the role of psychosis in attacks.

Pathological Fixation

Emerging research points to the importance of *fixation*, an intense preoccupation with an individual, activity, or idea (Meloy, Sheridan, & Hoffmann, 2008c). Normal fixations are a part of everyday life and include such states as romantic love, parental devotion, intense loyalty, and adulation. Pathological fixations are obsessive preoccupations that typically result in *deterioration* of the subject's intimate, social, and occupational life (Leets et al., 1995; Mullen, Pathé, & Purcell, 2009; Mullen et al., 2009; Schlesinger, 2006). Such pathological fixations focus on a *person* or a *cause*, the latter an intensely personal grievance or quest for justice that inhibits effective social functioning and alienates others. Research in Europe indicates that fixation on a cause is related to risk of attack. In a study of all nonterrorist attacks on western European politicians between 1990 and 2003 (James et al., 2007; $N = 24$), 50% were fixated on a cause. In a study of attacks on the British Royal Family between 1778 and 1994 (James et al., 2008; $N = 23$), where the motivation could be discerned ($n = 19$), 63% of the subjects were fixated on a cause.

In a study on attacks on German public figures (Hoffmann et al., 2011; $N = 14$), a fixation was present in every case. Nine of the attackers (69%) revealed a heavy and pathological fixation that included obsessive preoccupations. The most common were fixations on a cause (64%) such as political issues, or delusionally based feelings of a threat against the attacker or other individuals. In the group of five cases (36%) with a fixation on a person, two of the offenders were stalkers; three, including one of the stalkers, also had several personal contacts with the victim before the day of the attack. In a study of individuals who problematically contacted and approached the Dutch Royal Family, a pathological fixation was present in 52% of the cases (Van der Meer et al., 2012); this was significantly ($p = .03$) associated with an approach but with a small effect size (phi = 0.26) when compared with those who only communicated.

Although it is difficult to make this distinction in the US Secret Service Exceptional Case Study (Fein & Vossekuil, 1998, 1999), 67% of the near lethal approachers, attackers, and assassins had a grievance; motivations that suggested a focus on a cause included avenging a perceived wrong, bringing national attention to a perceived problem, saving the country or the world, and bringing about political change. Fixation on a *cause* may be a mediating variable between problematic approach and intent to attack but must be empirically studied. Such fixations are distinguished from political extremism, which usually emerges in interactions among a group on the fringes of the normal political process and may not be as intensely personalized—although lone wolves may be the exception.

The nature of the fixations evident in abnormal communications directed toward public figures were first studied in the context of attacks against the British Royal Family and western European politicians (James et al., 2007, 2008). In attacks on European politicians, fixation—"pursuing an agenda of an idiosyncratic nature, usually but not always delusional in content, to an obsessive and irrational degree" (James et al., 2007, p. 329)—was significantly associated with death or serious injury, warning behaviors, the subject being a loner, psychosis, and delusion. All effect sizes were large (phi > 0.54). Fixations may predict certain subsequent behavioral pathways or escalations. The empirical question is why fixation on a cause contributes incrementally to risk of an attack on a public figure, apparently most relevant to politicians and government officials. In recent theorizing and research, fixation has now been classified as one of eight patterns of warning behaviors (Meloy et al., 2012; Meloy, Hoffmann, Roshdi, Glaz-Ocik, Guldimann, Chapter 3, this volume).

Grandiosity and Entitled Reciprocity

Grandiosity and entitled reciprocity have emerged as two important psychological characteristics of subjects who approach. They suggest both psychopathology in general and pathological narcissism in particular. Grandiosity, an exaggerated sense of self-importance evident in communications, was tested in a logistic regression model in a study of those who approached or did not approach members of the British Royal Family (James et al., 2010). A regression for a model comprising the single factor of grandiosity produced an area under the curve (AUC) of 0.74 (95% CI 0.65-0.82), and correctly predicted 73.7% of the cases—73.8% of the approachers and 73.6% of the nonapproachers. The effect size was moderate (phi = 0.47).

Dietz and Martell (1989) found in their study, more than two decades ago, that those who approached celebrities were significantly more likely ($X2 = 4.85$, $p < .03$) to evidence an excessive sense of self-importance or uniqueness (52%) than those

who did not approach (36%). If subjects who problematically approached members of the US Congress took a "special constituent role," it did significantly increase the risk of an approach (46% vs. 16%, $X2 = 7.77$, $p = .0053$). Also, in a study on unusual contact and approach toward the Dutch Royal Family, grandiosity was present in 36% of the subjects (Van der Meer et al., 2012) but did not predict an approach.

Grandiosity can be somewhat grounded in reality ("I am the most politically astute person in my district!") or delusional ("I am the duly elected representative of my district!"). In many cases, grandiosity among such subjects compensates in fantasy for real-life failures in both work and love. It is one facet of pathological narcissism, an aspect of personality that is quite apparent in stalkers (Meloy, 1998; Mullen et al., 2009) and is an abnormal variant of narcissism, most clearly defined by Rothstein (1980) as "a felt quality of perfection" (p. 4). Grandiosity is also apparent in the attack research, specifically the ECSP study. Fein and Vossekuil (1998, 1999) reported that in 38% of the principal incidents of near lethal approach, attack, or assassination ($N = 74$) there was evidence that attention/notoriety was a goal. Among the eight motives they cited for attacking, one can infer grandiosity, or the wish to achieve such importance, in five: to achieve notoriety/fame, to bring national attention to a perceived problem, to save the country or the world, to achieve a special relationship with the target, or to bring about political change.

A close female friend of Lee Harvey Oswald in Minsk between 1959 and 1962, prior to his assassination of President John F. Kennedy in 1963, reflected on his personality years later: "I could paint a portrait of him as someone who thinks too much of himself but doesn't work to become the person he wants to be.... The most important thing for Lee was that he wanted to become famous. Idea number one. He was fanatic about it, I think. Goal number one. Show that he was different from others, and you know, he achieved this goal" (Mailer, 1995, p. 321).

The psychiatric social worker at the Youth House in Manhattan where he was briefly placed as a young adolescent for chronic truancy recorded similar findings: "He acknowledged fantasies about being all-powerful and being able to do anything he wanted. When asked if this ever involved hurting or killing people, he said that it did sometimes but refused to elucidate on it" (Mailer, 1995, p. 365). She later wrote, "there is a rather pleasant, appealing quality about this emotionally starved, affectionless youngster which grows as one speaks to him." (Mailer, 1995, p. 365)

A particular sense of entitlement, "entitled reciprocity" (Meloy et al., 2008a, p. 5), is the belief that the public figure owes the subject time and attention because of the time and attention the subject has paid to the public figure. It is also an aspect of pathological narcissism and is related to grandiosity: the subject's importance demands that he receive the attention he deserves. In the British Royal Family study (James et al., 2010), three motivations together accounted for 71.8% of the cases where the communicators went on to approach—those with delusions of royalty, amity seekers, and intimacy seekers. Among all these motivations is the subject's belief, often delusional, that he is owed a debt of gratitude through blood ties, friendship, or love. Entitled reciprocity, however, has not been measured, but it may be an important predictor of resentment and perhaps aggression in certain subjects who are shunned by the public figure. This could develop over time when communications are not responded to, or it could be an acutely negative emotional reaction when a highly anticipated personal encounter with the public figure instead results in disappointment or the humiliation of being ignored. Here is an example of both grandiosity and entitled reciprocity in a letter to a Royal Family member in Great Britain:

Dear (royal family member)—God dam it. God dam *you*! (royal family member title)! You know that the Catholic Church is a cult, right? You do know that, don't you? Well, it is. And you shouldn't be worshipping the Virgin Mary. She's not the Queen of Heaven. I AM! I'm God's wife, and you better make room for me there now! How dare you make me grovel in the dirt. (royal family member), I'm your Heavenly Mother! And you best start respecting me as such with a whole lot of hugs and kisses (on the cheek), well wishes, and tender loving care, or you are going to die a very long death starting right now! Stick to the Word of God, (royal family member). (Meloy case

files from Fixated Research Group; www.fixat-edthreat.com)

Intensity of Pursuit

One of the most replicated variables concerning a problematic approach to a public figure across the domains of politicians, celebrities, and royalty is the intensity of the pursuit. This appears to be a supra-ordinate variable that can be measured by looking at the frequency and duration of communications (see early work by Dietz & Martell, 1989), the use of multiple means of communication (emails, texts, written letters, faxes, etc.), and communication to secondary targets, what Scalora et al. (2002a) referred to as "target dispersion." In a comparison of six samples of problematic approachers within these public figure domains, multiple communications/targets and multiple means of communication emerged as two behavioral clusters that significantly distinguished between communicators and approachers (Meloy et al., 2010). These clusters have been adopted by the US Capitol Police in their Threat Assessment Unit (Scalora, Chapter 13, this volume), and multiple means of communication was replicated in the Dutch Royal study as significantly associated with an approach at $p = .01$, but with a small effect size (phi = 0.28) (Van der Meer et al., 2012). It is likely that such an intensity of pursuit is also apparent in public figure attackers, but it has yet to be systematically studied. One could infer it from the intensity of research and preparation for the attack and the degree of pathological fixation on the target, but typically not on a direct communication with the target, since this is quite uncommon for attackers and assassins. They instead leak their intent to third parties, which constitutes one of the warning behaviors (Meloy & O'Toole, 2011; Meloy et al., 2012).

Mental Disorder, Attacks, and Assassinations

Research indicates the importance of mental disorder in a large proportion of nonterrorist subjects who attack public figures (Fein & Vossekuil, 1998, 1999; Hoffmann et al., 2011; James et al., 2007, 2008; Meloy et al., 2004; Schlesinger & Mesa, 2008; see table 10.1). The substantial presence of mental disorder contrasts with the recommendations that diminished the importance of mental disorder in the ECSP study (Fein & Vossekuil, 1999) but not their findings: 61% of their subjects had been evaluated

TABLE 10.1. PSYCHOSIS AT TIME OF ATTACK OR HISTORY OF SEVERE MENTAL DISORDER AMONG NONTERRORIST PUBLIC FIGURE ATTACKERS AND ASSASSINS IN EUROPE AND THE UNITED STATES

Fein & Vossekuil, 1999	US presidential and other attackers	43%
Hoffmann et al., 2011	German public figure attackers	42%
James et al., 2007	British Royal Family attackers	48%
James et al., 2008	Western European politician attackers	42%
Schlesinger & Mesa, 2008	US nonpolitical homicidal celebrity attackers	65%

Adapted from Van der Meer, B. B., Bootsma, L., & Meloy, R. (2012). Disturbing communications and problematic approaches to the Dutch Royal Family. *Journal of Forensic Psychiatry & Psychology, 23,* 571–589.

Reprinted by permission of Taylor & Francis, Ltd., http://www.tandf.co.uk/journals.

by a mental health professional, 43% had a history of delusions and were delusional at the time of their attack or near lethal approach, and 21% had a history of auditory hallucinations. However, Fein and Vossekuil (1999) made several very important points: (1) within the delusion the behavior toward the target may be quite rational; and (2) focusing upon the "thinking that leads a person to see assassination as an acceptable, or necessary action" (p. 332) is operationally much more useful than labeling or diagnosing the person with a particular mental disorder. Their position has been supported by a large meta-analysis of the relationship between psychosis and violence (Douglas et al., 2009), which found that studies coded at the level of the symptom had significantly higher effect sizes, particularly active positive symptoms (delusions, hallucinations, etc.), in studying the violence-psychosis relationship.

Psychosis and delusions at the time have also been found to be positively correlated with lethality risk (death or serious injury) in contemporary attacks on western European politicians (James et al., 2007; phi = 0.49), and delusional content strongly influenced the motivation, and thus the behavioral pathway, toward historical attacks on members of the British Royal Family (James et al., 2008).

Hoffmann et al. (2011) have found that the majority of the small universe of potentially lethal attackers of public figures in Germany (1968-2004) were psychotic at the time ($n = 9$). All but one of these attacks occurred since 1990 and were mostly directed at politicians. In the psychotic cases, the content of the delusions was directly connected to the motivation. All delusions evidenced a paranoid dynamic—an irrational fear of imminent assault— and a majority of these attackers were suffering from paranoid schizophrenia at the time of their assaults. From their delusional point of view, the attacks were

eminently rational and necessary to protect them or others from serious harm. This contributed to their determination to act with lethal intent, a likely correlate of the perceived lethality of the threat posed to them. For example, in one case a paranoid schizophrenic individual believed that the German state was torturing his mind. He thought that the chancellor and the minister of the interior were specifically responsible. He desperately wrote to other politicians asking for help. Then he noticed that the minister of the interior was coming to speak at an election rally close to where he lived. He went to the rally and shot the minister, wounding him in a life-threatening manner. The conscious albeit psychotic motivation for this assassination attempt was self-defense.

Moreover, studies from attacks on public figures in the United States (Fein & Vossekuil, 1998, 1999; Meloy et al., 2004), the United Kingdom (James et al., 2008), and western Europe (James et al., 2007) underscore the fact that serious mental disorder does not mitigate risk of a planful attack on a public figure. All studies indicate that despite the presence of mental illness, subjects can carefully plan an attack over the course of days, weeks, or months. And a motivational delusion may give the attacker a level of commitment and resolve that would be absent or at least hampered by some ambivalence if the motivation was more reality-based.

CASE STUDY

Anja, a 27-year-old woman, had a three-month-long romance with Dan. Dan was the personal assistant of Michael, a British film actor. During the relationship, Anja met Michael on a number of occasions. She had never met public figures before but did not appear to be star struck. She was invited to parties and other occasions where celebrities were present. Dan was rather wealthy and, during their brief relationship, Anja received jewelry and other expensive gifts. She spent most of her time at Dan's London penthouse apartment and drove one of the luxury sports cars available to Dan through his employment. Prior to this time, Anja had earned little more than the minimum wage.

Dan ended the relationship abruptly, shortly after he met his new girlfriend. Anja, however, was unwilling to accept the ending of the romance. When Dan invited her to come to his penthouse to remove her belongings, she pleaded with him to reignite the relationship. Dan refused. For the next three weeks, Anja sent Dan an average of 15 emails per day. She was unable to telephone him because he had changed his phone number. It turned out that Dan would purchase a new cell phone every time he began a relationship with a woman and would use only that phone to communicate with her. Anja also visited Dan's workplace and his home at least twice a day for three weeks. Security staff were alerted and escorted her off the premises. The content of Anja's communications expressed shock and a belief that the relationship had been without flaw, and she pleaded with Dan to take her back.

After the three-week period during which Anja emailed Dan, sent him cards and letters, and called at his home and workplace, he did not hear from her for several days. He assumed that she had given up, but that was not the case. Instead, Anja shifted her focus to Michael, Dan's celebrity employer. Anja now expressed, via letters and emails (to Dan's email account), her belief that Michael was in love with her. She stated that she had come to the realization that she and Michael should be together always. Anja wrote that she had experienced something of an epiphany and that her relationship with Dan had been ordained by fate to allow her and Michael to meet. Michael was married to Justine, another celebrity, with whom he had three small children. Anja detailed her belief that Dan and Justine had felt an electric charge pass between Anja and Michael, and sought to remove Anja from the scene before Anja and Michael could realize that they were fated to be together. Anja stated that Dan still loved her but that his first duty was to protect his employer. Anja said that she no longer felt any loving feelings for Dan and that she was "consumed with love" for Michael.

Michael *took the advice of security staff* and telephoned Anja, leaving a message on her voicemail. He said that Anja had got the situation wrong, that she needed to go and make a life for herself and not contact him, Dan, or anyone connected with them. He said that she was a very attractive woman—that

she was very pleasant and that she should have no problem finding someone right for her. Anja's interpretation of this message was not the one intended by Michael. She focused on the "very attractive" and "very pleasant" aspects. The remainder of the message she interpreted as the result of interference by Dan and Justine.

After three weeks of sending letters declaring love for Michael and suggesting meeting times and places, there was a second hiatus. Again it was assumed that Anja had given up and again this was not the case. Anja had been writing a 120,000-word story, which was delivered to Michael at his home address. The story described an ideal life for Anja and Michael in which Michael gave up his fame and they moved together to Hawaii, where Anja opened a perfume shop. At this point, Michael contacted an organization that employed a threat assessor psychologist. On the same day, Thomas, Anja's brother, sent an email message to Dan, asking him to call. Dan ignored this message for several days and then forwarded it to the threat assessor. The threat assessor telephoned Thomas, who expressed concern about his sister and agreed to meet the threat assessor. At this meeting, which was arranged on the same day, Thomas revealed that Anja had been printing pictures of Justine that she found on the Internet. Using these pictures, she made a photo story in which Justine was murdered by strangulation. At this point the police were informed.

A police officer visited Anja and spoke with her. He was not convinced that Anja presented a danger and decided that no follow-up was necessary. The threat assessor then met again with Thomas, who continued to worry about his sister. He said that Anja had always been an isolated person who was uncomfortable in social situations and had never had any close friends. He described her as having "autistic tendencies." He said that Anja had had a number of relationships with men but that they tended not to last long; she was "very clingy," quiet, and introverted. He said that Anja had been bullied at school. He had known her to be violent on a single occasion, when she pushed one of the bullies down two flights of stairs at school, injuring her. Anja refused to apologize, and changed schools.

Thomas agreed that Anja had a delusional fixation on Michael. He said that when Anja was 16, she had been fixated on their family doctor, a married man. She had written long stories about an ideal life for herself and the doctor and had spent lengthy periods sitting in the doctor's waiting room. The fixation ended abruptly, but it was not possible to establish how or why. The threat assessor contacted the police and asked for a meeting, which was granted. She summarized what Thomas had said and talked about erotomania. She explained that when an erotomanic realizes that the highly desired connection is not actually taking place, he or she may rationalize that this is the fault of a third party. In this case, it was evident that Justine was perceived as the primary obstacle to Anja's desires. In such cases, the perceived obstacle may be at physical risk. Although the threat assessor was not convinced that Justine was in any immediate physical danger, she felt that it was possible that Anja might act out violently after pursuing other pathways. The police agreed to speak with Anja again.

The threat assessor judged that Anja was likely to continue her campaign. She had engaged in a fairly diverse range of activities in order to try to make contact with the target. She genuinely believed that she and Michael were meant to be together and felt that Michael was suffering as she was. The threat assessor recommended a mental health remedy in the first instance followed by a legal remedy if necessary. She advised that media involvement be avoided as far as possible, as any publicity could serve to reinforce Anja's delusional beliefs. The target and his family were advised not to respond if possible. If, however, it became absolutely necessary for the family to respond to the offender, they were advised to do so without anger, a clear denial of Anja's beliefs, and a request for Anja to leave Michael and Justine alone. All parties were advised, however, that Anja would not be responsive to reason or rejection because she was convinced that she was doing no wrong and that her behavior was fully justified.

Thomas agreed to ask Anja about her feelings toward Justine. Anja stated that Justine was an evil woman who had entrapped Michael, keeping him as a slave, and that the children were not his. Anja said that Justine deserved to die; then Justine's spell would be broken and the world would realize what a terrible person she had been. The police officer was advised to follow this line of enquiry urgently. Anja told the police exactly the same thing. The police then charged her. Anja was shocked and could not understand why; she quickly rationalized that Justine had control over the police. Anja became the subject of a psychiatric assessment and was detained in a mental institution and medicated. After her release she immediately began once again writing to the media and to Michael,

stating her belief that she was the victim of persecution orchestrated by Justine. She was then rearrested.

Thomas continued to provide valuable help and was asked about Anja's interests. He said that the only real interest Anja had enjoyed in the past was her involvement with a church, which had ended when Anja had a falling out with one of the church leaders. The threat assessor contacted the church and discovered that the woman Anja had argued with had since moved on. The church's minister visited Anja and invited her back. She readily accepted and was warmly welcomed. The minister was fully apprised of the situation and decided to make Anja his priority. He organized all her free time around the church. He, along with Thomas, also convinced Anja to undergo mental health treatment. A follow-up meeting with Thomas revealed that Anja was continuing to write stories and letters, but she did not send them to Michael, simply keeping them instead. She maintained her beliefs but did not appear to be motivated to act on them. The threat assessor continued to be informed of developments. After a year, Anja developed a relationship with a fellow church member who was understanding of her delusions. To date she has not recontacted Michael or any of his associates.

CONCLUSION

We have reviewed the current state of the science of stalking, threats, and attacks on public figures. It appears that various target domains—politicians, celebrities, royalty, corporate leaders, and religious figures—show both similarities and differences in the motivation for problematic communications, attacks, risk of violence, and pursuit behavior. New concepts have emerged in both the theoretical and empirical research over the past few years, including the prevalence of mental disorder, grandiosity, fixation, entitled reciprocity, and the intensity of pursuit. These theoretical formulations, which in some cases have begun to be validated through empirical research, give guidance to an emerging specialty area of behavioral science and certain operational aspects of threat assessment.

NOTES

1. Television news anchors and presenters, unlike film actors, have direct eye contact with the viewer, are not pretending to be another character, and are specifically trying to establish an approachable and appealing object to whom the viewer can relate—all in the service of increased ratings. We think these subtle differences may drive the

frequency of pursuit of this particular group of celebrities, especially among those psychotic viewers who believe they have a special and idealized relationship with the news anchor or presenter (Meloy, 1998).

2. Murphy (2012) reports that there were no less than eight attempts on Queen Victoria's life during her 64-year reign.

KEY POINTS

- Public figure threat assessment has an old provenance and a new empirical grounding.
- A useful analysis identifies static and dynamic characteristics of subjects within various target domains, including politicians, celebrities, royalty, corporate figures, and religious leaders.
- Empirical research continues as a nascent development in the field, with a few replicated findings that are associated with problematic communications, approaches, and attacks.
- Direct threats continue to be uncommon among attackers of all public figures; but all direct threats should be investigated when communicated to a public figure.
- Data collection has generated new theory, and new theory has directed data collection.
- Certain areas of research remain unexplored, including both corporate and religious public figure threats, approaches, and attacks.
- There is no demographic profile of a public figure approacher or attacker; however, dynamic behaviors provide useful points of assessment in the determination of risk.

REFERENCES

Adams, S. J., Hazelwood, T. E., Pitre, N. L., Bedard, T. E., & Landry, S. D. (2009). Harassment of members of parliament and the legislative assemblies in Canada by individuals believed to be mentally disordered: *Journal of Forensic Psychiatry & Psychology, 20*, 801–814.

Biesterfeld, J., & Meloy, J. R. (2008). The public figure assassin as terrorist. In J. R. Meloy, J. Hoffmann, & L. Sheridan (Eds.), *Stalking, threatening, and attacking public figures: A psychological and behavioral analysis* (pp. 143–162). New York: Oxford University Press.

Bleuler, E. (1943). *Lehrbuch der Psychiatrie.* Berlin: Springer.

Buruma, I. (2006). *Murder in Amsterdam: The death of Theo Van Gogh and the limits of tolerance.* London: Penguin books.

Clérambault, G. G. de. (1921/1999). Passionate delusions: Erotomania, claiming, jealousy. In F. R. Cousin, J. Garrabé, & D. Morozov (Eds.), *Anthology of French language psychiatric texts* (pp. 475–492). Le Plessis-Robinson: Institut Synthélabo.

Coggins, M. H., Pynchon, M. R., & Dvoskin, J. A. (1998). Mental health consultation to law enforcement: Secret Service development of a mental health liaison program. *Behavioral Sciences and the Law, 16*, 407–422.

Dietz, P. E., & Martell, D. A. (1989). *Mentally disordered offenders in pursuit of celebrities and politicians.* Washington, DC: National Institute of Justice.

Dietz, P. E., Matthews, D. B., Van Duyne, C., Martell, D. A., Parry, C.D.H., ... Crowder, J. D. (1991a). Threatening and otherwise inappropriate letters to Hollywood celebrities. *Journal of Forensic Sciences, 36*, 185–209.

Dietz, P. E., Matthews, D. B., Van Duyne, C., Martell, D. A., Parry, C.D.H., Stewart, T., ... Crowder, J. D. (1991b). Threatening and otherwise inappropriate letters to members of the United States Congress. *Journal of Forensic Sciences, 36*, 1445–1468.

Douglas, K., Guy, L., & Hart, S. (2009). Psychosis as a risk factor for violence to others: A meta-analysis. *Psychological Bulletin, 5*, 679–706.

Dressing, H., Kuehner, C., & Gass, P. (2005). Lifetime relevance and impact of stalking in a European population: Epidemiological data from a middle-sized German city. *British Journal of Psychiatry, 187*, 168–172

Enoch, D., & Ball, H. (2001). *Uncommon psychiatric syndromes.* London: Arnold.

Fein R., & Vossekuil, B. (1998): Preventing attacks on public officials and public figures: A Secret Service perspective. In J. R. Meloy (Ed.) *The psychology of stalking: Clinical and forensic perspectives.* San Diego, CA: Academic Press, 176–194.

Fein, R. A., & Vossekuil, B. (1997). *Preventing assassination: A monograph.* Washington, DC: U.S. Department of Justice.

Fein, R. A., & Vossekuil, B. (1999). Assassination in the United States: An operational study of recent assassins, attackers, and near lethal approachers. *Journal of Forensic Sciences. 44*(2), S. 321–333.

Hoffmann, J. (2005). *Stalking.* Heidelberg: Springer.

Hoffmann, J. (2009). Public figures and stalking in the European context. *European Journal on Criminal Policy and Research, 15*(3), 293–305.

Hoffmann, J., & Meloy, J. R. (2008). Contributions from attachment theory and psychoanalysis to advance understanding of public figure stalking and attacking. In J. R. Meloy, L. Sheridan, & J. Hoffmann (Eds.), *Stalking, threatening, and attacking public figures: A psychological and behavioral analysis* (pp. 165–194). New York: Oxford University Press.

Hoffmann, J., & Sheridan, L. (2008a). Celebrities as victims of stalking. In J. R. Meloy, L. Sheridan, & J. Hoffmann (Eds.), *Stalking, threatening, and attacking public figures: A psychological and behavioral analysis* (pp. 195–213). New York: Oxford University Press.

Hoffmann, J., & Sheridan, L. (2008b). Stalking, threatening and attacking corporate figures. In J. R. Meloy, L. Sheridan, & J. Hoffmann (Eds.), *Stalking, threatening, and attacking public figures: A psychological and behavioral analysis* (pp. 123–142). New York: Oxford University Press.

Hoffmann, J., Gotcheva, B., & von Groote, E. (2008). A study of inappropiate letters to German CEOs. Unpublished research report. Darmstadt: Centre of Forensic Psychology, University of Darmstadt.

Hoffmann, J., Meloy, J. R., Guldimann, A., & Ermer, A. (2011). Attacks on German public figures, 1968–2004: Warning behaviors, potentially lethal and nonlethal acts, psychiatric status, and motivations. *Behavioral Sciences and the Law, 29,* 155–179.

James, D. V., Meloy, J. R., Mullen, P., Pathé, M., Farnham, F., Preston, L., & Darnley, B. (2010). Abnormal attentions towards the British Royal Family: Factors associated with approach and escalation. *Journal of the American Academy of Psychiatry and the Law, 38,* 329–340.

James, D. V., Mullen, P. E., Meloy, J. R., Pathé, M. T., Farnham, F. R., Preston, L., & Darnley, B. (2007). The role of mental disorder in attacks on British and European politicians 1990–2004. *Acta Psychiatrica Scandinavica, 116*(5), 334–344.

James D. V., Mullen P. E., Pathé M. T., Meloy J. R., Farnham F. R., Preston L., & Darnley B. (2008). Attacks on the British Royal family: the role of psychotic illness. *The Journal of the American Academy of Psychiatry and the Law, 36*(1), 59–67.

James, D. V., Mullen, P., Pathé, M., Meloy, J. R., Preston, L., Darnley, B., & Farnham, F. (2009). Stalkers and harassers of royalty: the role of mental illness and motivation. *Psychological Medicine, 39,* 1–12.

Krafft-Ebing, R. von. (1912). *Psychopathia sexualis.* Stuttgart: Verlag von Ferdinand Enke.

Leets, L., de Becker, G., & Giles, H. (1995). Fans: Exploring expressed motivations for contacting celebrities. *Journal of Language and Social Psychology, 14,* 102–123.

Lombroso, C. (1899). A study of Luigi Luccheni. *Appleton's Popular Science Monthly, 45*(11), 199–207.

Malsch M., Visscher M., & Blaauw, E. (2002). *Stalking van bekende Personen.* Den Haag: Boom.

McCann, J. T. (2001). *Stalking in children and adults. The primitive bond.* Washington, DC: American Psychological Association.

MacDonald, A. (1911). Assassins of rulers. *Journal of the American Institute of Criminal Law and Criminology, 2,* 505–520.

Mailer, N. (1995). *Oswald's tale: An American mystery.* New York: Random House.

Meloy, J. R., ed. (1998). *The psychology of stalking: Clinical and forensic perspectives.* San Diego, CA: Academic Press.

Meloy, J. R. (2004). Indirect personality assessment of the violent true believer. *Journal of Personality Assessment, 82,* 138–146.

Meloy, J. R. (2011). Approaching and attacking public figures: A contemporary analysis of communications and behavior. In C. Chauvin (Ed.), *Threatening communications and behavior: Perspectives on the pursuit of public figures.* Washington, DC: National Research Council, National Academies Press, 75–101.

Meloy, J. R., Hoffmann, J., Guldimann, A., & James, D. (2012). The role of warning behaviors in threat assessment: An exploration and suggested typology. *Behavioral Sciences and the Law, 30,* 256–279.

Meloy J. R., James, D. V., Farnham, F. R., Mullen, P. E., Pathé, M., Darnley, B. & Preston, L. (2004). A research review of public figure threats, approaches, attacks, and assassinations in the United States. *Journal of Forensic Sciences, 5,* 1–8.

Meloy, J. R., James, D. V., Mullen, P., Pathé, M., Farnham, F., Preston, L., & Darnley, B. (2010). Factors associated with escalation and problematic approaches toward public figures. *Journal of Forensic Sciences, 56*(1), 128–135.

Meloy, J. R., & Mohandie, K. (2008). Two case studies of corporate-celebrity victims: The stalking of Steven Spielberg and Stephen Wynn. In J. R. Meloy, L. Sheridan, & J. Hoffmann (Eds.), *Stalking, threatening, and attacking public figures: A psychological and behavioral analysis* (pp. 245–269). New York: Oxford University Press.

Meloy, J. R., Mohandie, K., & McGowan, M. G. (2008). A forensic investigation of those who stalk celebrities. In J. R. Meloy, L. Sheridan, & J. Hoffmann (Eds.), *Stalking, threatening, and attacking public figures: A psychological and behavioral analysis* (pp. 37–54). New York: Oxford University Press.

Meloy, J. R., & O'Toole, M. E. (2011). The concept of leakage in threat assessment. *Behavioral Sciences & the Law, 29*(4), 513–527.

Meloy J. R., Sheridan, L., & Hoffmann, J. (2008). Public figure stalking, threats, and attacks: The state of the science. In J. R. Meloy, L. Sheridan, & J. Hoffmann (Eds.), *Stalking, threatening, and attacking public figures: A psychological and behavioral analysis* (pp. 3–34). New York: Oxford University Press.

Mohandie, K., Meloy, J. R., McGowan, M. G., & Williams, J. (2005) The RECON typology of stalking: Reliability and validity based upon a large sample of North American stalkers. *Journal of Forensic Sciences, 51*(1), 147–155

Mullen, P. E., James, D. V., Meloy, J. R., Pathé, M. T., Farnham, F. R., Preston, L., & Darnley, B. (2008). The role of psychotic illnesses in attacks on public figures. In J. R. Meloy, L. Sheridan, & J. Hoffmann (Eds.), *Stalking, threatening, and attacking public figures: A psychological and behavioral analysis* (pp. 55–82). New York: Oxford University Press.

Mullen, P. E., James, D. V., Meloy, J. R., Pathé, M. T., Farnham, F. R., Preston, L., ... Berman, J. (2009). The fixated and the pursuit of public figures. *Journal of Forensic Psychiatry & Psychology, 20*(1), 33–47.

Mullen, P., Pathé, M., & Purcell, R (2009). *Stalkers and their victims*, 2nd ed. London: Cambridge University Press.

Murphy, P. (2012). *Shooting Victoria: Madness, mayhem, and the rebirth of the British monarchy*. New York: Pegasus Books.

Norwich, J. (2011). *Absolute monarchs: A history of the papacy*. New York: Random House.

O'Toole, M. E., Smith, S. S.. & Hare, R. D. (2008). Psychopathy and predatory stalking of public figures. In J. R. Meloy, L. Sheridan, & J. Hoffmann (Eds.), *Stalking, threatening, and attacking public figures: A psychological and behavioral analysis* (pp. 215–243). New York: Oxford University Press.

Rothstein, A. (1980). *The narcissistic pursuit of perfection*. New York: International Universities Press.

Scalora, M. J., Baumgartner, J. V., Callaway, D., Zimmerman, W., Hatch-Maillette, M. A., Covell, C. N., ... Washington, D. O. (2002a). An epidemiological assessment of problematic contacts to members of Congress. *Journal of Forensic Sciences, 47*, 1360–1364.

Scalora, M. J., Baumgartner, J. V., Callaway, D., Zimmerman, W., Hatch-Maillette, M. A., Covell, C. N., ... Washington, D. O. (2002b). Risk factors for approach behavior toward the U.S. Congress. *Journal of Threat Assessment 2*, 35–55

Scalora, M. J., Zimmerman, W. J., & Wells, D. G. (2008). Use of threat assessment for the protection of the United States Congress. In J. R. Meloy, L. Sheridan, & J. Hoffmann (Eds.). *Stalking, threatening, and attacking public figures: A psychological and behavioral analysis* (pp. 425–434). New York: Oxford University Press.

Schlesinger, L. B. (2006). Celebrity stalking, homicide, and suicide: A psychological autopsy. *International Journal of Offender Therapy and Comparative Criminology, 50*, 39–46.

Schlesinger, L., & Mesa, B. (2008). Homicidal celebrity stalkers: Dangerous obsessions with nonpolitical public figures. In J. R. Meloy, L. Sheridan, & J. Hoffmann (Eds.), *Stalking, threatening, and attacking public figures: A psychological and behavioral analysis* (pp. 83–104). New York: Oxford University Press.

Simon, J. (2013). *Lone wolf terrorism*. Amherst, NY: Prometheus Books.

Spitzberg, B. H. (2002). The tactical topography of stalking victimization and management. *Trauma, Violence & Abuse, 3*, 261–288.

Spitzberg, B. H., & Cupach, W. R. (2007). The state of the art of stalking: Taking stock of the emerging literature. *Aggression & Violent Behavior, 12*, 64–86.

Van der Meer, B. B., Bootsma, B., & Meloy, J. R. (2012) Disturbing communications and problematic approaches to the Dutch Royal Family. *Journal of Forensic Psychiatry & Psychology, 23*, 571–589.

Wikipedia (2013). Pope John Paul II. Available at: http://en.wikipedia.org/wiki/Pope_John_Paul_II#Assassination_attempts_and_plots

11

Intimate Partner Violence, Stalking, and Femicide

P. RANDALL KROPP AND ALANA N. COOK

Intimate partner violence (IPV) can be defined as any actual, attempted, or threatened physical harm against a current or former intimate partner. Such violence can be perpetrated by males or females, in heterosexual or same-sex relationships, and in the form of threatening or intimidating conduct, physical or sexual assault, abduction, and homicide. This form of violence is prevalent internationally and has devastating social, economic, and health impacts on society (Garcia-Moreno, Jansen, Ellsberg, Heise, & Watts, 2006; Tjaden & Thoennes, 1998). Acute and chronic consequences for victims include impaired social functioning, psychological distress, physical trauma, and death (Bonomi et al., 2006; Campbell, 2002; Campbell, Glass, Sharps, Laughon, & Bloom, 2007).

Owing to the seriousness and prevalence of this problem, professionals are commonly asked to address the risk of IPV or the safety of victims in criminal justice, civil court, health care, and postsecondary settings. Thus informal threat assessments in one form or another have existed in the field for decades, but systematic studies of IPV threat assessment technology are relatively few. That being said, the field has been expanding in the past 10 years. This chapter will review the existing literature addressing risk factors for IPV and the state of the art for threat assessment tools for this form of violence. Further, we will devote special attention to the topics of stalking and killing of intimate partners. While these issues are of course related to the more general problem of IPV, they require some unique considerations in conducting threat assessments. Finally, we will describe an IPV case study to illustrate a structured professional judgment (SPJ) approach to threat assessment in this context.

ISSUES

Defining Threat

Threat assessments can be compromised by vague language regarding the terms *threat* and *risk*. Unfortunately, the literature on IPV threat assessment is often equally vague in its definition of these terms (Kropp, 2008). Hart and colleagues (2003) described a risk as a "hazard that is incompletely understood" and "multifaceted, referring to the nature of the hazard, the likelihood that the hazard will occur, the frequency or duration of the hazard, the seriousness of the hazard's consequences, and the imminence of the hazard" (p. 2). Risk or threat is also inherently contextual—it depends on the specific circumstances of the case in hand. Thus the process of risk assessment should attempt to address this complexity and range of possibilities for violence. In practice, decisions about risk likely involve consideration of the imminence, nature (e.g., emotional, physical, sexual), frequency, and seriousness of the violence in addition to the likelihood that it will occur (Hart, 2001; Mulvey & Lidz, 1995)—the who, what, where, when, and how of violence. For example, a perpetrator could be at risk for long-term verbal intimidation of his ex-girlfriend under certain circumstances or for an imminent sexual femicide (killing of women) under other circumstances.

These are two rather different scenarios that present different implications for monitoring, supervision, treatment, and planning for victim safety. Thus vague statements such as "This individual represents a threat against his spouse," or simplistic statements about the probability of violence, are unhelpful if we cannot be specific as to what we mean by *threat*.

The Role of the Victim in Risk Assessment

IPV is targeted violence—that is, we typically know the identity of the individual or individuals at risk. The targeted victim will also typically have important knowledge regarding risk factors related to the perpetrator. It logically follows that an IPV threat assessment should include the potential victim's perspectives, especially given the unreliability of offenders' self-reported information (Kropp, 2008). Thus having access to the victim offers a potential advantage over situations where the potential victims are often unknown (e.g., sex offending, general violence). Most IPV risk assessment tools (which are discussed later in this chapter)—such as the Danger Assessment (DA) (Campbell, 1995), the Ontario Domestic Assault Risk Assessment (ODARA) (Hilton, Harris, & Rice, 2010), and the Spousal Assault Risk Assessment Guide (SARA) (Kropp, Hart, Webster, & Eaves, 1995, 1999)—emphasize the importance of including the victim's perspective. There is also some literature demonstrating that victims' estimates of their own danger are empirically related to recidivistic violence and risk ratings (Cattaneo, 2007; Gondolf, 2001; Whittemore & Kropp, 2001; Weisz, Tolman, & Saunders, 2000). It is important to remember, however, that victims' perceptions of risk are influenced by a number of psychological, social, economic, and health factors (Barnett, 2001) and therefore are not always accurate. For example, victims can also grossly misjudge the risk posed by their partners (Campbell et al., 2001; Kropp, 2008; Whittemore & Kropp, 2001). The important finding by Campbell and colleagues (2001) that victims underestimated their spouses' risk in 47% and 53% of actual and attempted femicides, respectively, is illustrative of this problem.

There are other potential complications with victim involvement in the threat assessment process. First, the whereabouts of the victim might be unknown or the victim might be reluctant to provide information for a number of reasons, including a distrust of the criminal justice system. Second, a victim could be reluctant to provide risk-relevant information and/or violence predictions owing to concerns about the confidentiality of the information. Third, a victim might also fear that participating in a threat assessment could increase the danger posed to her or him. Indeed, this is often a realistic fear; asking victims to participate in a threat assessment places them in a difficult position, especially if the assessment is going to be used to determine sanctions against the perpetrators. Thus threat assessment professionals in this field should have knowledge of the complicated victimology involved. They should recognize that while victims potentially have much to contribute to the assessment, their judgment and cooperation could be compromised by a number of factors. Indeed, the best IPV threat assessments should include consideration of victim-related issues, and some recent risk assessment tools have begun to build victim safety or vulnerability factors into the threat assessment process (Hilton et al., 2010; Kropp, Hart, & Belfrage, 2011).

Selecting Risk Factors

A number of comprehensive reviews on risk factors for IPV have appeared in the literature (Cattaneo & Goodman, 2005; Dutton & Kropp, 2000; Hilton & Harris, 2005; Riggs, Caulfield, & Street, 2000; Schumacher, Feldbau-Kohn, Slep, & Heyman, 2001; Vest, Catlin, Chen, & Brownson, 2002) and intimate partner homicide and femicide (Aldridge & Browne, 2003; Campbell, Sharps, & Glass, 2001). These reviews address a growing literature that, in the past 20 years, has seen hundreds of studies touching on risk issues. Importantly, there appears to be some consensus regarding the relevant risk factors. Commonly mentioned perpetrator risk factors include prior violence in intimate relationships, past antisocial behavior or attitudes, attitudes that support violence, prior threatening or stalking behavior, substance abuse, personality disorder, sexual proprietariness, homicidal or suicidal ideation, recent relationship problems, recent employment/financial problems, and minimization/denial of violent behavior. These risk factors have all appeared consistently in either or both of the empirical and professional threat assessment literatures.

Some have argued that it is problematic to consider risk factors with solid theoretical or intuitive appeal but limited empirical support with respect to their relationship with recidivistic violence (Hanson & Morton-Bourgon, 2004; Hilton et al.,

2010). Others, however, have pointed out that scientific methods might be inadequate to reliably capture rare or difficult to measure risk factors, such as homicidal/suicidal ideation or patriarchal attitudes (Douglas & Kropp, 2002; Hart, 1998; Kropp, 2008). A potential problem with the orthodox empirical approach is that it precludes practitioners from considering "commonsense" risk factors that should be addressed in risk management. For example, Kropp (2008) described the professional dilemma of whether or not to consider suicidal ideation as a risk factor for IPV. The factor lacks consistent empirical support—at least in terms of the traditional quantitative definition of *empirical*—but has been identified in many narrative and qualitative data reviews as an important risk factor for intimate partner femicide (see Watt, 2008). We argue that a delicate balance must be achieved between selecting risk factors using both the professional and empirical criteria. Too much emphasis on the former can lead to erroneous assumptions about what is and is not related to violence (Douglas & Kropp, 2002). However, qualified threat assessment professionals should also have some license to consider risk factors justified by sound theory or professional consensus, especially considering the practical and ethical barriers to conducting research in this field.

Managing Risk

Risk assessment should assist evaluators to identify risk management strategies. Ideally, it requires cooperation among various professionals working in different agencies, each with a different skill set and mandate. Evaluators should consider four basic kinds of risk management strategies: monitoring, treatment, supervision, and victim safety planning (Hart et al., 2003; Kropp, Hart, & Lyon, 2008).

Monitoring, or repeated assessment, is an essential aspect of effective risk management. The goal of monitoring is to evaluate changes in risk over time so that risk management strategies can be revised as appropriate. It is especially important to monitor dynamic risk factors—for example, relationship problems, employment problems, psychological distress—that could signal an escalation in short-term risk to the victim. Monitoring services may be delivered by a diverse range of mental health, social service, law enforcement, corrections, and private security professionals. Monitoring, unlike supervision, focuses on surveillance rather than control or restriction of liberties; it is therefore minimally intrusive.

Treatment involves the provision of rehabilitative services. The goal of treatment is to improve deficits in the individual's psychosocial adjustment. One important form of treatment is directed at mental disorder that is causally related to the individual's history of violence. Treatments may include individual or group psychotherapy; psychoeducational programs designed to change attitudes toward violence, such as batterer treatment programs; training programs designed to improve interpersonal, anger management, and vocational skills; psychoactive medications, such as antipsychotics or mood stabilizers; and substance abuse programs. Another important form of treatment is the reduction of acute life stresses, such as physical illness, interpersonal conflict, unemployment, legal problems, and so forth.

Supervision involves the restriction of the individual's rights or freedoms. The goal of supervision is to make it more difficult for the individual to engage in further violence. An extreme form of supervision is incapacitation, such as incarceration. However, in IPV cases, community supervision is much more common than institutionalization. Typically it involves allowing the perpetrator to reside in the community with restrictions on activity, movement, association, and communication. In general, supervision should be implemented at a level of intensity commensurate with the risks posed by the individual (Andrews & Dowden, 2006).

Finally, *victim safety planning* involves improving the victim's dynamic and static security resources, a process sometimes referred to as "target hardening." The goal is to ensure that, if violence recurs—despite all monitoring, treatment, and supervision efforts—any negative impact on the victim's psychological and physical well-being will be minimized. These services can be delivered regardless of whether the individual is in an institution or the community.

IPV THREAT ASSESSMENT INSTRUMENTS

A number of risk assessment tools or instruments have been described in the empirical literature, on the Internet, and in government documents and reports (Dutton & Kropp, 2000; Hilton & Harris, 2005; Kropp, 2008; Roehl & Guertin, 1998). Many of these instruments were designed by local correctional, police, or victim agencies, and the developers have reported little or no normative, reliability, and validity data; therefore they are not discussed in this chapter. It thus appears that there are six risk assessment instruments that currently hold the most promise: the Danger Assessment (DA), Domestic Violence Screening Inventory-Revised (DVSI-R), Ontario Domestic Assault Risk Assessment (ODARA), Domestic Violence Risk Appraisal Guide (DVRAG), Spousal Assault Risk Assessment Guide (SARA), and the Brief Spousal Assault Form for the Evaluation of Risk (B-SAFER). Each is described below in some detail.

Danger Assessment

The Danger Assessment (DA; Campbell, 1995) was developed by Campbell and colleagues in consultation with victims of domestic violence, law enforcement, victim safety workers, and other domestic violence experts. It was originally designed to assess the likelihood for spousal homicide, particularly femicide, and the original items were chosen from retrospective studies on homicide or near fatal injury cases (available at: www.dangerassessment.com).

The DA consists of two sections. The first is a calendar that asks potential victims to record the severity and frequency of violence in the past year (1 = slap, pushing, no injuries and/or lasting pain, through 5 = use of weapon, wounds from weapon). This part of the measure is intended to raise the awareness of the woman and reduce the minimization of the abuse. In one initial study, 38% of women who initially reported no increase in severity and frequency changed their response to yes after filling out the calendar (Campbell, Sharps, & Glass, 2001). The second section consists of a 20-item yes/no list of risk factors associated with intimate partner homicide. The woman can complete the instrument independently or with the assistance of professionals working in the health care, victim advocate, or criminal justice systems. The number of risk factors is then totaled, and cutoff scores associated with the levels "variable danger," "increased danger," "severe danger," and "extreme danger" are determined.

Campbell and colleagues (2001) summarized the results of 10 research studies conducted on the DA. In those studies, interrater reliability coefficients were in the moderate to good range ($r =$. 60 to .86). According to its authors, the DA has also been demonstrated to have strong test-retest reliability in two studies ($r =$. 89 to .94). Construct validity has also been reported, with the DA discriminating between battered women in an emergency department and nonabused controls (Campbell, 1995).

It has been found that the DA correlates strongly with other measures of abusive behavior such as the Index of Spouse Abuse and the Conflict Tactics Scale (Campbell, 1995). The DA is also associated with the severity and frequency of domestic violence (McFarlane et al., 1998).

Campbell and colleagues (2003) completed a multisite case control study to investigate the relative importance of various risk factors for femicide in abusive relationships. The study included many of the items from the original DA. The investigators interviewed 220 proxies of femicide victims along with 343 abused control women. All but one of the original 15 DA items was significantly associated with femicide, and the measure was subsequently revised to include additional risk factors that were not in the original version. Both the original and revised versions of the DA significantly discriminated between the femicide and abused control groups.

Limitations in the use of the DA include the lack of a formal user's manual, little information on interrater reliability, and the lack of predictive studies on the DA and life-threatening violence and femicide (Campbell et al., 2001; Hart & Watt, 2008). There is some indication that the measure might be prone to overidentifying cases deemed to pose an "extreme" danger for life-threatening violence (Hart & Storey, 2011). Overall, however, the DA appears to be a generally well-constructed measure that can be extremely helpful in raising threat awareness in victims.

Domestic Violence Screening Inventory–Revised

The Domestic Violence Screening Inventory (DVSI) was developed by the Colorado Department of Probation Services. It was designed to be a brief risk assessment instrument that could be completed with a quick criminal history review. The 12 social and behavioral factors it contains have been found to be statistically related to recidivism by domestic violence perpetrators on probation (Williams & Houghton, 2004). The authors also justified including the risk factors based on a thorough review of the literature, and they consulted judges, law enforcement personnel, lawyers, and victim advocates. The social factors include current employment and relationship status. The behavioral items essentially summarize the offender's history of DV and non-DV criminal history. A copy of the DVSI coding sheet is included in an appendix of the Williams and Houghton (2004) validation paper. The DVSI was validated on a sample of 1,465 male domestic violence offenders on probation who were selected consecutively over a 9-month period. Data on reoffending were collected in a 6-month follow-up period from a subsample of the victims ($N = 125$) of these perpetrators and from official records for all perpetrators during an 18-month follow-up period. The DVSI also appeared to have adequate concurrent validity, correlating strongly with ratings of risk to spouses on the Spousal Assault Risk Assessment Guide (SARA). Finally, Williams and Houghton reported statistically significant predictive validity for the DVSI using a prospective (follow-up) design, with an area under the curve (AUC) of .60 (r = .18, $p < .001$).

The Domestic Violence Screening Inventory-Revised (DVSI-R) (Williams, 2012) is a modified version of the DVSI (see Williams, 2008). Williams (2012) reported the results of a large-scale predictive study of 3,569 "family violence" perpetrators which indicated that the measure had significant predictive validity across various recidivism measures. He concluded that the DVSI-R is a "robust" measure that can be used reliably with different types of perpetrators and in different settings. Williams also concluded that both the numerical scores produced by the DVSI-R and the "structured clinical judgment" ratings appear to have an important role to play in using this instrument.

Ontario Domestic Assault Risk Assessment and Domestic Violence Risk Appraisal Guide

The Ontario Domestic Assault Risk Assessment (ODARA) is a 13-item actuarial instrument developed in Ontario, Canada (Hilton et al., 2004). The items were empirically derived from an initial pool of potential risk factors gleaned from police files on 589 domestic violence perpetrators. The study followed back the cases for an average of five years and coded the risk factors from archival information in several domains including offender characteristics, domestic violence history, nondomestic criminal history, relationship characteristics, victim characteristics, and index offence. Using setwise and stepwise logistic regression, the developers were able to reduce the item pool to 13. The resulting instrument, the ODARA, correlated well with the DA and the Spousal Assault Risk Assessment Guide (SARA—see later in this chapter), thus demonstrating adequate convergent validity. The instrument was also

able to significantly discriminate between recidivists and nonrecidivists (AUC = .77); the ODARA total score was also associated with the number, severity, and imminence of new assaults. One shortcoming of the study was that there were no homicide cases in the construction sample, and the authors have cautioned against using the ODARA for predicting homicide. There is also a need for further cross-validation studies to substantiate the precise probabilities associated with each ODARA score.

The developers of the ODARA have more recently reported on an actuarial tool designed for use in correctional settings where more historical information is available and there is concern about the severity as well as the imminence of domestic violence (Hilton et al., 2008). Thus the authors modified the ODARA by combining the original items with those of the Psychopathy Checklist Revised (PCL-R) (Hare, 2003). The combined instrument is named the Domestic Violence Risk Appraisal Guide (DVRAG). Hilton and colleagues (2008) reported relatively strong reliability and validity data, similar in magnitude to the ODARA findings. The authors have since published a comprehensive actuarial model for IPV risk assessment that includes the use of both the DVRAG and the ODARA (Hilton, Harris, & Rice, 2010).

This model represents a sound example of the prediction paradigm (Heilbrun, 1997) in violence risk assessment, and it is laudable for its emphasis on the empirical selection and application of risk variables; in this way it is suitable for those wanting to anchor their assessments with actuarial scores. Actuarial approaches have been criticized, however, for their lack of practical utility, their inability to consider the context of individual cases, their rigidity, and the potential lack of relevance to risk management considerations (Douglas & Kropp, 2002; Kropp, 2008; Litwack, 2001).

Spousal Assault Risk Assessment Guide and the Brief Spousal Assault Form for the Evaluation of Risk

The Spousal Assault Risk Assessment Guide (SARA) (Kropp et al., 1995, 1999; see Table 11.1) is a set of guidelines for the content and process of a thorough risk assessment. It comprises 20 items identified by a review of the empirical literature on wife assault and the literature written by clinicians who evaluate male wife abusers. The authors point out that the SARA is not a test. Its purpose is not to provide absolute or relative measures of risk using cutoff scores or norms but rather to structure and enhance professional judgments about risk. Since the SARA is not a formal psychological test, professionals other than psychologists can use it. The SARA assessment procedure includes interviews with the accused and victims, standardized measures of physical and emotional abuse and of drug and alcohol abuse, and a review of collateral records, such as police reports, victim statements, criminal records, and other psychological procedures. The SARA also serves as a guide for a comprehensive process of threat assessment that involves (1) gathering information, (2) coding risk factors, (3) formulating motivations for violence, (4) considering future risk scenarios, (5) devising risk management plans, and (6) offering summary judgments of risk.

The authors have evaluated the reliability and validity of judgments concerning risk for violence made using the SARA (Kropp & Hart, 2000). SARA ratings were analyzed in six samples of adult male offenders (total N = 2,681). Structural analyses of the risk factors indicated moderate levels of internal consistency and item homogeneity. Interrater reliability was high for judgments concerning the presence of individual risk factors and for overall perceived risk. SARA ratings significantly discriminated between offenders with and without a history of spousal violence in one sample (t = 27. 04, $p < .0001$), and between recidivistic and nonrecidivistic spousal assaulters in another ($r = .36, p < .0001$; or, AUC = .70). Finally, SARA ratings showed good convergent and discriminant validity with respect to other measures related to risk for general and violent criminality (Kropp & Hart, 2000).

Other independent studies have supported the validity of the SARA. Williams and Houghton (2004), in their evaluation of the DVSI, included the SARA in some of the analyses. Thus the results also supported the concurrent validity of the SARA, and the AUC for the SARA in the 18-month follow-up exceeded that of the DVSI (.65 versus .60, although the difference was not statistically significant). Similarly, Hilton and colleagues (2004) reported an AUC for the SARA of .64 in a five-year follow-back study. The authors concluded that in this study the SARA did not postdict violence as well as the ODARA. However, that conclusion was significantly limited by the fact the authors did not use the administration procedure recommended in the SARA manual. The authors employed the SARA solely as an actuarial instrument, which it is not, and they noted that the

"integrity" (p. 271) of the SARA scores could not be guaranteed because they were coded from archival data only. Finally, Kropp and Gibas (2010) provided a comprehensive review of the research literature on the SARA, summarizing nine studies that offer either reliability or validity data.

In response to calls from the field (particularly from law enforcement agencies) asking for briefer risk assessment tools to conduct time-limited assessments, the authors of the SARA developed the Brief Spousal Assault Form for the Evaluation of Risk (B-SAFER) (Kropp, Hart, & Belfrage, 2005, 2011). The B-SAFER consists of 10 risk factors, which were derived from the 20 SARA risk items using factor analysis, and five additional victim vulnerability factors chosen from the literature. Several studies now suggest that the B-SAFER can be a reliable, useful, and valid tool for police officers and other threat assessment professionals (Au et al., 2009; Belfrage & Strand, 2008; de Reuter et al., 2008; Kropp, 2008; Kropp & Belfrage, 2004; Soeiro & Almeida, 2010; Winkel, 2008).

The SARA and B-SAFER are examples of the structured professional judgment approach (SPJ) to violence threat assessment. Indeed, with the authors of the DA (Campbell et al., 2003) and DVSI-R (Williams, 2012) now recommending actuarial procedures, it appears that the SARA and B-SAFER are the only published IPV tools strictly adhering to the SPJ emphasis on the use of professional discretion in making threat judgments. The strengths of the SPJ approach include its flexibility, its emphasis on contextual factors, and its focus on violence prevention via risk management. However, critics have pointed out that some of the risk factors included in these instruments do not have strong empirical support (see discussion under "Selecting Risk Factors" earlier in this chapter), and that the complexity inherent in the discretionary approach requires users to have considerable training and experience (Sutherland et al., 2012).

INTIMATE PARTNER STALKING

Stalking may be defined as unwanted and repeated communication, contact, or other conduct that deliberately or recklessly causes people to experience reasonable fear or concern for their safety or the safety of others known to them (Kropp, Hart, & Lyon, 2002, 2008). The stalking of current and former intimate partners is a particularly common and potentially lethal form of stalking behavior (Campbell, et al., 2003; Kropp, Hart, & Lyon, 2002; Mohandie, Meloy, McGowan, & Williams, 2006; Mullen, Pathé, & Purcell, 2009; Norris, Huss, & Palarea, 2011; Palarea, Zona, Lane, & Langhinrichsen-Rohling, 1999; Rosenfeld & Lewis, 2005; Walker & Meloy, 1998). Indeed, the severe risk posed to former intimate partners by stalkers largely contributed to the genesis of the first antistalking laws in North America (Bernstein, 1993; Gill & Brockman, 1996). The threat assessment of intimate stalkers poses some special problems for professionals owing to the complex—often ambivalent—relationship between stalker and victim, the diversity of the problematic behavior, the persistence of the stalker, the extremely dynamic and rapidly changing nature of the risk, the often complicated psychopathology of the stalker, and the highly emotionally charged context in which the stalking occurs (Kropp, Hart, & Lyon, 2002). This complexity does not lend itself well to actuarial approaches predicated on the accuracy of historical predictors, and it may never be feasible to develop such a tool (Kropp, Hart, Lyon, & Storey, 2011). Indeed, to date there are no actuarial procedures for assessing risk for stalking behavior. It appears that most risk assessments in this field are still unstructured professional judgments, although this is in part because there were no guidelines or tools in this area until recently.

It is feasible to develop SPJ guidelines for stalking threat assessment because of the growing literature documenting stalking risk factors and management procedures (Kropp et al., 2011; Mullen et al., 2006), and two such sets of guidelines now exist: The Guidelines for Stalking Assessment and Management (SAM) (Kropp, Hart, & Lyon, 2008) and the Stalking Risk Profile (SRP) (MacKenzie, McEwan, Pathé, James, Ogloff, & Mullen, 2009). These are currently the only published stalking risk assessment tools, and both are well suited to assessing risk for the stalking of intimate partners.

Guidelines for Stalking Assessment and Management

The guidelines for Stalking Assessment and Management (SAM) were developed to assist criminal justice, mental health, and security professionals who work with stalkers and their victims. They were created in part using a systematic review of the existing stalking research—a process consistent with recommendations for guidelines in the field of health care (e.g., American

Psychological Association [APA], 2002). Consistent with an evidence-based, best practices model, the SAM helps users to exercise their best judgment; it is not a replacement for professional discretion.

The factors considered in the SAM are divided into three domains. "Nature of Stalking" includes 10 factors related to the pattern of stalking behavior. "Perpetrator Risk Factors" are 10 factors reflecting the psychosocial adjustment and background of the perpetrator. "Victim Vulnerability Factors" comprises 10 factors reflecting the psychosocial adjustment and background of the victim. These factors are summarized in Table 11.2. Users are also encouraged to document "other considerations," which are typically rare or unusual risk factors that are relevant to the case at hand. Users are then required to rate the relevance of each risk factor (i.e., the degree to which it is important for risk management plans), posit possible risk scenarios, and document recommended management strategies. Finally, users can offer their conclusions regarding case prioritization, risk for continued stalking, risk for serious physical harm, reasonableness of victim's fear, and whether immediate action is required. Further details regarding the development, content, and administration of the SAM can be found in its user manual (Kropp et al., 2008).

There have been two published studies reporting on the utility and validity of the SAM. Belfrage and Strand (2008) evaluated 230 SAM risk assessments conducted by police officers in two counties in Sweden. The results indicated that the police could easily code the SAM, as there was very little missing information in the assessments. The researchers also found strong positive correlations between the individual risk factors and total number of risk factors (in all three SAM domains) and overall SPJ judgments of risk (i.e., SPJ ratings); in other words, greater numbers of risk factors were associated with elevated judgments of risk. The authors concluded that the SAM was a useful tool for the police.

Storey, Hart, Meloy, and Reavis (2009) examined some of the properties of the SAM in a study of 62 male stalkers. The authors reported moderate interrater reliability between two trained raters who coded the files: ICC1 (single rater, random effects model, absolute agreement method) for presence ratings across the three domains of risk factors was 0.77 for "nature of stalking," 0.68 for "perpetrator risk factors," and 0.63 for "victim vulnerability

TABLE 11.1. RISK FACTOR RATINGS ON THE SARA

Domain	Rating	Critical
Criminal History		
1. Past assault of family members	●	
2. Past assault of strangers or acquaintances	●	
3. Past violation of conditional release or community supervision		
Psychosocial Adjustment		
4. Recent relationship problems	●	
5. Recent employment problems	●	
6. Victim of and/or witness to family violence as a child or adolescent		
7. Recent substance abuse/ dependence	●	●
8. Recent suicidal or homicidal ideation/intent	●	●
9. Recent psychotic and/or manic symptoms		
10. Personality disorder with anger, impulsivity, or behavioral instability	●	●
Spousal Assault History		
11. Past physical assault	●	●
12. Past sexual assault/sexual jealousy	●	●
13. Past use of weapons and/or credible threats of death	●	●
14. Recent escalation in frequency or severity of assault	●	●
15. Past violation of "no contact" orders		
16. Extreme minimization or denial of spousal assault history	●	●
17. Attitudes that support or condone spousal assault	●	●
Alleged (Current) Offence		
18. Severe and/or sexual assault	●	●
19. Use of weapons and/or credible threats of death	●	●
20. Violation of "no contact" order		

Note: ● = yes or present; ○ = possibly or partially present; blank = no or absent.

factors" (moderate agreement). The study showed some concurrent validity for the SAM risk factors, as total scores for the nature, perpetrator, and victim vulnerability domains all had significant positive correlations with traits of psychopathic personality disorder. Further, psychopathic traits were associated with a wide range of individual SAM risk factors (as measured by the SAM). For example, those subjects with relatively high psychopathic traits tended to show escalation in the frequency, severity, or diversity of their stalking; they were relatively unrepentant regarding their actions; and they tended to select victims with financial or employment problems. These correlations were in the predicted direction, as these risk factors have often been associated with the severity of future stalking (Meloy, Sheridan, & Hoffmann, 2008).

Building upon the study of Storey and colleagues (2009), Kropp and colleagues (2011) reported the results of an extended sample of 109 stalkers who were assessed using the SAM. Results indicated that interrater reliabilities for the SAM risk factors and total scores range from fair to good and that the structural reliability of the SAM is sound. Moreover, the SAM showed good concurrent validity when it was compared with two other measures of violence propensity: the Psychopathy Checklist Screening Version (PCL:SV) and the Violence Risk Appraisal Guide (VRAG). Overall, the data appear to support the reliability and validity of the tool, but certainly more research is needed on the ability of the SAM to help reduce stalking and violent behavior.

Stalking Risk Profile

The Stalking Risk Profile (SRP) (MacKenzie et al., 2009) was developed to help professionals in clinical settings assess and manage risk for stalking behavior. It is rooted in the stalker typology advanced by Mullen and colleagues and is based on years of thoughtful, programmatic clinical work and research with stalkers and their victims (Mullen et al., 2009; McEwan et al., 2011). It aims to help clinicians to identify areas of greatest risk to victims and stalkers, identify intervention targets, provide victim safety strategies, and provide practical feedback to law enforcement, courts, and tribunals (MacKenzie et al., 2009). The stated intent of the SRP is that it should be used by mental health clinicians with assessment skills and familiarity with antistalking legislation. It might therefore have more limited applicability for those professionals without mental health qualifications.

Like the SAM and other SPJ instruments, the SRP recommends a structured process for assessing risk and subsequently making management recommendations. The sequential process begins by asking the user to determine the stalker's motivation from a fixed typology: rejected, resentful, intimacy seeker, incompetent suitor, predatory, unknown. After determining the stalker type, the SRP requires the coding of specific risk factors. Finally, the professional is taken through a menu of potential management targets and strategies. Thus, the SPJ process appears to be similar to that of the SAM, but it differs in some important ways (e.g., the SAM employs scenario planning, whereas the SRP uses a motivational typology). The goals of the two instruments, however, appear to be similar and complementary.

To date there are no reported validity data on the SRP, but a number of studies are under way in Australia. McEwan and colleagues (2011) have indicated that the first published validity research is expected to be available in 2015. For now, the authors recommend that the SRP be used as best practices guidelines, much in the way that other SPJ instruments are currently employed.

INTIMATE PARTNER FEMICIDE

In conducting an IPV threat assessment, special consideration must always be given to the possibility of life-threatening violence, especially when the perpetrator is male and the potential victim is female. For example, intimate partner femicide (IPF)—the killing of women by their current or former intimate partners—is a pandemic problem (Krug, Dahlberg, Mercy, Zwi, & Lozano, 2002) and is the most common form of homicide perpetrated against women worldwide (Browne, 1987; Campbell, 1986; Daly & Wilson, 1988; Mouzos, 2000; Polk, 1994; Wilson & Daly, 1992). For example, in the United States, Canada, and the United Kingdom, intimate partner femicides account for 30% to 60% of all culpable homicides against women (Bureau of Justice Statistics, 2004; Dobash, Dobash, Cavanagh, & Lewis, 2004; Statistics Canada, 2003).

Femicide is certainly a form of IPV; threat assessments can therefore be informed by what we know about IPV risk factors in general. However, attempts have been made to identify risk factors that might differentiate life-threatening from non-life

threatening violence (Campbell et al., 2003; Dobash et al., 2004). In the best-controlled study of this sort, Campbell and colleagues (2003) reported that factors discriminating between the two groups included perpetrator's access to a gun and previous threat with a weapon; perpetrator's stepchild in the home; victim estrangement, especially from a controlling partner; victim leaving abuser for another partner; and the perpetrator's use of a gun in the assault. Stalking, forced sex in the relationship, and abuse during pregnancy also had some significance.

Although there are few controlled empirical studies examining the risk factors for intimate partner femicide, useful information can be gleaned from government reports (e.g., Websdale, Sheeran, & Johnson, 2001), crime statistics (e.g., Browne, Williams, & Dutton, 1999; Bureau of Justice Statistics, 1998; Daly & Wilson, 1988), coroner reports, interviews with survivors or family members (e.g., Bourget et al., 2000; Campbell et al., 2003; Dutton & Kerry, 1999; Morton, Runyan, Moracco, & Butts, 1998), and reports by domestic violence fatality review teams (e.g., Abrams et al., 2000). Some studies have focused on describing cases of IPF (e.g., Dawson & Gartner, 1998; Johnson & Hotton, 2003; Moracco, Runyan & Butts, 2003), whereas others have compared IPFs with cases of nonlethal IPV (e.g., Campbell et al., 2003; Kellerman, Rivara & Rushforth, 1993) or other types of homicide (e.g., Belfrage & Rying, 2004; Dobash et al., 2004). Some narrative reviews of this literature also exist (see Aldridge & Browne, 2003; Watt, 2008).

It is possible to find some commonly cited risk factors among the diverse sources listed above. Thus perpetrator factors of special relevance for femicide include (1) *proprietariness*—defined as a desire or entitlement regarding exclusive control of women—including concerns about sexual infidelity and strong beliefs about sexual ownership (Block, 2003; Campbell et al., 2003; Dobash et al., 2004; Easteal, 1993; Polk, 1994; Serran & Firestone, 2004; Websdale, 1999; Wilson, Johnson, & Daly, 1995); (2) *possession or availability of firearms* (Bailey et al., 1997; Campbell, et al., 2003; Kellerman et al., 1993), although this risk factor might be particularly relevant in the United States (see Aldridge & Browne, 2003; Belfrage & Rying, 2004); (3) *escalation in severity or frequency of IPV*, especially if past violence has included threats to kill, life-threatening methods such as stabbing or strangling, beating while pregnant, or forced sexual relations (Block, 2003;

Campbell, 1995; Campbell et al., 2003; Websdale, 1999); (4) *mental health problems*, especially severe personality disorder, depression, and suicidal or homicidal ideation and intent (Belfrage & Rying, 2004; Campbell et al., 2001; Dobash et al., 2004; Dutton & Kerry, 1999; McFarlane et al., 1999; Morton et al., 1998; Zawitz, 1994); (5) *stalking*, especially in context of a recent separation and when the stalking involves threats of harm, extreme jealousy, possessiveness, and proprietariness (Aldridge and Browne, 2003; Campbell, 1995; Campbell et al., 2003; Daly & Wilson, 1988; McFarlane et al., 1999); and (6) *recent separation or divorce*, especially within the first few months following estrangement (Aldridge & Browne, 2003; Belfrage & Rying, 2004; Block, 2003; Campbell et al., 2001; Daly, Wiseman, & Wilson, 1997; Dobash et al., 2004; Stout, 1993).

Other studies have identified characteristics or vulnerabilities of victims associated with risk for being killed by intimate partners. These factors include being socially disadvantaged, mental health vulnerabilities, prior IPV victimization, and substance abuse problems (Abrams et al., 2000; Campbell et al., 2003; Richie & Kanuha, 1997; Riggs, Caulfield, & Street, 2000; Santa Clara County Domestic Violence Council Death Review Committee, 2000; Sharps et al., 2001, 2003). Further, some have discussed characteristics of communities that might increase femicide risk, including poor availability, accessibility, appropriateness, coordination, and responsiveness of supportive and protective services (Abrams et al., 2000; Florida Domestic Violence Fatality Review Team, 1994; Santa Clara County Domestic Violence Death Review Committee, 2000; Watt, 2008; Websdale, 2003; Watt, 2008).

In summary, it is possible to organize the femicide literature into a threat assessment model for life-threatening IPV. Thus evaluators of perpetrator risk should consider three domains—acute conflict, capacity for serious violence, and severe disinhibition—when there is concern for life-threatening violence or femicide. These domains are illustrated in Figure 11.1.

First, evidence of an *acute conflict* exists when a perpetrator is seriously upset over such things as a recent separation, infidelity, or the initiation of a new relationship by his former partner, a child custody or access dispute, or ongoing litigation (e.g., regarding property). Important warning signs of such a conflict include stalking behavior, proprietary statements (e.g., "You belong to me" or "If I can't have

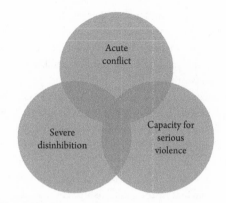

FIGURE 11.1 Model for threat assessment of life-threatening intimate partner violence.

you nobody can"), or conditional threats such as "If you don't come back then I will harm you." Second, evaluators should consider whether the perpetrator has shown a *capacity for serious violence*, evidenced by a history of using weapons or the use of high lethality methods such as strangulation. Finally, it is necessary to consider whether the perpetrator is experiencing *severe disinhibition* whereby his mental state is overriding natural inhibitions against life-threatening violence. Important examples of this include severe substance abuse, serious mental illness such as psychosis or major depression, and significant suicidal or nihilistic thoughts.

CASE STUDY[1]

The following case study is intended to illustrate an IPV threat assessment using the structured professional judgment (SPJ) approach.

Background

Mr. Wall (age 37) and Mrs. Wall (age 33) have been married for three years. Both Mr. and Mrs. Wall are from Lebanon. Mrs. Wall immigrated to the United States when she was seven years old. She performed well in school and went on to obtain her law degree from the University of Toronto when she was 26. Mrs. Wall has always been close with her family and had a pleasant upbringing. After graduation, Mrs. Wall began working at a large law firm in Toronto, Canada. She has been very successful in her position and provides the primary financial support for herself and her husband. The rest of her family reside in New York City.

Mr. Wall immigrated to Canada with his two brothers when he was 20 years old. He was raised in a traditional patriarchal household and, growing up, was obedient to both his mother and father. He had a relatively unremarkable childhood: His performance in school was average, he did not get into any significant trouble, and he had a stable mental health history as a youth.

Since coming to Canada, Mr. Wall has been employed intermittently by friends of his family but has been unable to maintain employment. Mr. and Mrs. Wall met through family friends just over three years ago and married soon after. Almost immediately after getting married Mr. Wall exhibited controlling behaviors in the relationship. He placed limits on Mrs. Wall's contact with her friends and family in New York and Toronto. She was not permitted to socialize with her coworkers or attend social events in their community. Mr. Wall would frequently berate her, telling her she was a "slut" and "unclean" and accusing her of infidelity. Mrs. Wall had typically tried to leave the room when he was yelling at her; many times she was unsuccessful, as Mr. Wall would block her way and on one occasion had physically forced her to remain on the couch while he screamed in her face.

Current Offense

Mr. Wall was first brought to the attention of authorities when Mrs. Wall called the local police in New York to report that her husband was harassing her and that she feared for her life. Mrs. Wall told the police that she had fled to New York three days earlier after her husband had tried to kill her. She reported that over the past several weeks Mr. Wall was acting "crazy." He refused to let her leave their home for work. When she would leave and go to work, he would call her repeatedly at her office crying and yelling for her to come home. When she returned home, he would scream at her and call her a "slut," accuse her of cheating on him, and state that she was "barren." He demanded to see her emails from work and mobile phone records to "prove" that she was seeing another man. A few nights before she left for New York he had taken her phone out of her hand, placed it in a pot of boiling water, and stated, "Try to get out now." Mrs. Wall stated that she was terrified about what her husband was going to do. She was not allowed to speak to anyone in her family, was unable to attend to her work regularly, and reported being unable to sleep or eat because of the stress.

When Mr. Wall discovered his wife had purchased a new mobile phone, he dragged her up to their bedroom by her hair and locked her in the closet. She remained in the closet for three days. He would bring her one meal a day and would repeatedly bang on the door screaming, "live like the pig you are, you slut." During the evenings he would bring her out of the closet, make her strip naked, and have her dance in the nude while he watched. On one occasion he threw her on the bed and told her: "spread your legs." When she refused he grabbed her by the throat and choked her yelling, "You do as I say" over and over until she lost consciousness. She told the police that he kept her awake every night by banging and yelling at the door every 15 minutes and flicking the lights on and off repeatedly.

Mrs. Wall said that she felt he was going to kill her, that it was only a matter of time. She planned to escape the next morning, at a time when she assumed that he would be sleeping. She reported escaping from the closet using one of the hangers to pick the lock and running to her car, then driving across the border to stay with her family in New York. She felt safe in New York and did not call the police about her husband. She said that on multiple occasions he told her that if she told anyone about "their business" he would kill her mother and sisters. Mrs. Wall knew her husband was aware of where her family lived because they had visited her parents on several occasions during their marriage.

When she arrived at her family's home she was relieved for a few days because she had not heard from Mr. Wall. However, one day prior to calling the police, Mr. Wall began calling her parents' house stating "I know she is there... I am coming for her." Mrs. Wall's father told Mr. Wall to stop calling and that Mrs. Wall did not want to speak with him. He had called the home approximately 60 times over a four-hour period. During several of the phone calls to her parents' residence Mr. Wall stated: "When you come home, you are going to pay for this." Mrs. Wall was scared and took this to mean he was going to kill her. Mrs. Wall decided to phone the police.

The New York police opened an investigation. Mrs. Wall provided the police with Mr. Wall's phone number as well as the phone number of one of Mr. Wall's brothers. When Mr. Wall spoke to the police over the phone, he denied ever having hurt Mrs. Wall. He said that she was angry with him for suggesting that she cut down on her work hours to focus on maintaining their home and getting pregnant. He also stated, "you know how women can be... they think a lesson learned is some kind of abuse." When asked why he was calling Mrs. Wall in the United

States, he began to cry and said, "I just miss her so much. I love her. I love her. I want her back home."

The police also spoke to Mr. Wall's brother. His brother reported that Mr. Wall had always had a "temper." He also told the police that his brother had often been kicked out of nightclubs and family events for getting into fights, although none of these fights ever resulted in police involvement. When asked why he thought Mr. Wall got in fights, he responded, "it is the booze; he has to stop drinking." His brother stated he had never suspected that Mr. Wall was abusive to his wife. He reported that they had a "happy marriage" and that he had never witnessed Mr. Wall even raising his voice to Mrs. Wall.

Assessment and Management of Risk: SARA and SAM

This case study has elements of both IPV and stalking. To thoroughly assess the risk of violence posed, both the SARA and SAM were used as guidelines to ensure relevant risk factors were considered. The authors of the SARA and SAM recommend that two or more guidelines be used if indicated by the nature of violence, as in the current case. Both instruments are applied using six systematic steps. For a full discussion of these steps, see the SARA and SAM user manuals (Kropp, Hart, Webster & Eaves, 1995; 1999; Kropp, Hart, & Lyon, 2008).

Step 1: Case Information

The perpetrator in the current case is Mr. Wall and the victim is Mrs. Wall. The pattern of violence has arisen since their relationship began, but the most recent violence occurred over the past several weeks.

Steps 2 and 3: Presence and Relevance of Risk Factors

The presence and relevance of risk factors of the SARA and SAM are provided in summary form in Tables 11.1 and 11.2, respectively. A factor is considered relevant (or "critical" on the SARA) if it is important to address in risk management. In formulating this case, it appears that motivators that contribute to Mr. Wall's risk for violence included his need for control, his extremely angry and negative attitudes toward women, and his obsessive jealousy regarding his wife. Disinhibitors that contribute to Mr. Wall's risk for violence include his lack of remorse, lack of empathy, and negative attitudes. Destabilizers that contribute to his risk for violence include his intimate and nonintimate relationship problems, his employment and financial problems, and—perhaps

TABLE 11.2. RISK FACTOR RATINGS ON THE SAM

Nature of Stalking	P	C	R	Perpetrator Risk Factors	P	C	R	Victim Factors	P	C	R
Communicates about victim				Angry	●	●	●	Inconsistent behavior	○	○	
Communicates with victim		●	●	Obsessed	●	●	●	Inconsistent attitudes	○	○	
Approaches victim				Irrational		○		Inadequate access resources			
Direct contact		●	●	Unrepentant	●	●	●	Unsafe living situation		●	●
Intimidates victim		●	●	Antisocial lifestyle				Problems caring for dependents			
Threatens victim		●	●	Intimate relationship problems	●	●	●	Intimate relationship problems	●	●	
Violent toward victim		●	●	Non-intimate relationship problems	●	●		Non-intimate relationship problems	●	●	
Stalking is escalating		●	●	Distressed				Distressed	●	●	●
Stalking is persistent		●	●	Substance use problems	●	●		Substance use problems			
Stalking involves supervision violations				Employment and financial problems	●	●		Employment and financial problems			

Note: ● = yes or present; ○ = possibly or partially present; blank = no or absent.

most significantly—his alcohol abuse. Additional contributors to Mr. Wall's risk for violence include Mrs. Wall's unsafe living situation and her extreme fear of her husband.

Step 4: Management Strategies

To manage Mr. Wall's risk for violence the following strategies are recommended. *Monitoring* tactics should include (1) interviews of Mr. Wall by both the Toronto Police Service and the New York Police Department to monitor his whereabouts and understanding of the seriousness of his behavior, (2) interviews with Mr. Wall's brother to determine Mr. Wall's current level of functioning regarding dynamic risk variables (e.g., jealousy, stress, financial problems, substance abuse, and so forth), and (3) regular contact with Mrs. Wall and her parents to monitor any contacts from Mr. Wall or other evidence of stalking and threatening behavior.

Supervision strategies should include remanding Mr. Wall into custody given the severe and imminent threats posed. If he is released to the community, Canada-US border restrictions should be imposed so as not to allow him to travel to the United States. If possible he should surrender his passport. Further, conditions not to contact or otherwise approach Mrs. Wall or her family should be in place, as should restrictions on Mr. Wall's use of alcohol and access to weapons. With respect to *treatment* strategies, Mr. Wall should be mandated or encouraged to attend IPV and substance abuse treatment programs. Finally, *victim safety planning* should involve providing Mrs. Wall with supportive counseling, helping her to find safe living conditions on her return to Canada (including the possibility of a shelter), and ensuring that her current living arrangements have adequate static security.

Step 5: Concluding Opinions

It is our opinion that this case is of high or urgent priority given the severity of the violence and threats made by Mr. Wall. He poses a high imminent risk for violence against Mrs. Wall and her parents in the form of assaults, threats, and intimidating behavior. There is also a relatively high risk for life-threatening violence toward the victims.

NOTE

1. This case study is based on a compilation of cases reviewed by the authors. Identifying details have been changed.

KEY POINTS

- Threat assessment in this field is complicated by several issues including difficulties in defining *threat*, determining the role of the victim in this form of targeted violence, selecting risk factors, and determining effective management strategies.

- There has been a proliferation in literature around IPV risk assessment in recent years, and there are now six risk assessment tools that have been discussed in the literature with some regularity: Danger Assessment (DA), Domestic Violence Screening Inventory-Revised (DVSI-R), Ontario Domestic Assault Risk Assessment (ODARA), Domestic Violence Risk Appraisal Guide (DVRAG), Spousal Assault Risk Assessment Guide (SARA), and Brief Spousal Assault Form for the Evaluation of Risk (B-SAFER).

- There are two primary models of risk assessment for IPV: structured professional judgment approaches (SPJ), such as the SARA and B-SAFER, and actuarial approaches, such as the ODARA and DVRAG. A case study using the SPJ approach was presented.

- Assessing threat in cases involving the stalking of current or former intimate partners presents some special challenges. To date, however, there are only two published risk assessment tools designed specifically for stalking situations: the Guidelines for Stalking Assessment and Management (SAM) and the Stalking Risk Profile (SRP). Both of these sets of guidelines show considerable promise in their application to IPV cases.

- There are also unique issues associated with threat assessment of life-threatening violence. While relatively few empirical studies have focused on this issue exclusively, much can be gleaned from qualitative research, fatality review analyses, and coroner reviews. A model of assessing risk for intimate partner femicide was presented, focusing on a perpetrator's capacity for severe violence, acute conflict, and severe disinhibition.

REFERENCES

Abrams, M. L., Belkap, J., Melton, H. (2000). *When domestic violence kills: The formation and findings of the Denver metro domestic violence fatality review committee.* Denver, CO: Project Safeguard.

Aldridge, M. L., & Browne, K. D. (2003). Perpetrators of spousal homicide: A review. *Trauma, Violence and Abuse, 4,* 265–276.

American Psychological Association. (2002). Ethical principles of psychologists and code of conduct. Washington, DC: Author.

Andrews, D. A., & Dowden, C. (2006). Risk principle of case classification in correctional treatment: A meta-analytic investigation. *International Journal of Offender Therapy and Comparative Criminology, 50,* 88–100.

Au, A., Cheung, G., Kropp, R., Yuk-chung, C., Lam, G.L.T., & Sung, P. (2009). A preliminary validation of the Brief Spousal Assault Form for the Evaluation of Risk (B-SAFER) in Hong Kong. *Journal of Family Violence, 23,* 727–735.

Bailey, J. E., Kellerman, A. L., Sommes, G. W., Banton, J. G., Rivara, F. P., & Rushforth, N. P. (1997). Risk factors for violent death of women in the home. *Archives of Internal Medicine, 157,* 777–782.

Barnett, O. (2001). Why battered women do not leave: Part 2. External inhibiting factors—social support and internal inhibiting factors. *Trauma, Violence & Abuse, 2*(1), 3–35.

Belfrage, H., & Rying, M. (2004). Characteristics of spousal homicide perpetrators: A study of all cases of spousal homicide in Sweden 1990–1999. *Criminal Behavior and Mental Health, 14,* 121–133.

Belfrage, H., & Strand, S. (2008). Structured spousal violence risk assessment: Combining risk factors and victim vulnerability factors. *International Journal of Forensic Mental Health, 7*(1), 39–46.

Bernstein, S. E. (1993). Living under siege: Do stalking laws protect domestic violence victims? *Cardozo Law Review, 15,* 525–567.

Block, C. R. (2003). How can practitioners help an abused woman reduce her risk of death? *National Institute of Justice, 250,* 4–7.

Bonomi, A. E., Thompson, R. S., Anderson, M., Reid, R. J., Carrell, D., Dimer, J. A., Rivara, F. P. (2006). Intimate partner violence and women's physical, mental, and social functioning. *American Journal of Preventive Medicine, 30,* 458–466.

Bourget, D., Gagne, P., & Moamai, J. (2000). Spousal homicide and suicide in Quebec. *Journal of the American Academy of Psychiatry and the Law, 28,* 179–183.

Browne, A. (1987). *When battered women kill.* New York: Free Press.

Browne, A., Williams, K. R., & Dutton, D. G. (1999). Homicide between intimate partners: A 20-year review. In M. D. Smith & M. A. Zahn (Eds.), *Homicide: A sourcebook of social research* (pp. 149–164). Thousand Oaks, CA: Sage.

Bureau of Justice Statistics (2004). *Homicide trends in the United States.* Washington, DC: U.S. Department of Justice.

Bureau of Justice Statistics, U.S. Department of Justice. (1998). *Violence by intimates: Analysis of data on crimes by current or former spouses, boyfriends, and girlfriends.* Washington, DC: JCJ-167237.

Campbell, J. C. (1986). Nursing assessment for risk of homicide with battered women. *Advances in Nursing Science, 8,* 36–51.

Campbell, J. C. (1995). Prediction of homicide of and by battered women. In J. C. Campbell (Ed.), *Assessing dangerousness: Violence by sexual offenders, batterers, and child abusers* (pp. 96–113). Thousand Oaks, CA: Sage.

Campbell, J. C. (2002). Health consequences of intimate partner violence. *Lancet, 359,* 1331–1336.

Campbell, J. C., Glass, N., Sharps, P. W., Laughon, K., & Bloom, T. (2007). Intimate partner homicide: Review and implications of research and policy. *Trauma, Violence, & Abuse, 8,* 246–269.

Campbell, J. C., Sharps, P. & Glass, N. (2001). Risk assessment for intimate partner homicide. In G. F. Pinard and L. Pagani (Eds.), *Clinical assessment of dangerousness: Empirical contributions* (pp. 137–157). New York: Cambridge University Press.

Campbell, J. C., Webster, D., Koziol-McLain, J., Block, C., Campbell, D., Curry, M. A., …Laughon, K. (2003). Risk factors for femicide in abusive relationships: Results from a multi-site case control study. *American Journal of Public Health, 93,* 1089–1097.

Cattaneo, L. B. (2007). Contributors to assessments of risk in intimate partner violence: How victims and professionals differ. *Journal of Community Psychology, 35*(1), 57–75.

Cattaneo, L. B., & Goodman, L. A. (2005). Risk factors for reabuse in intimate partner violence: A cross-disciplinary critical review. *Trauma, Violence, & Abuse, 6*(2), 141–175.

Daly, M., & Wilson, M. (1998). An evolutionary psychological perspective on homicide. In M.D. Smith & M. Zahn (Eds.), *Homicide: A sourcebook of social research* (pp. 58–71). Thousand Oaks, CA: Sage.

Daly, M., Wiseman, K. A., & Wilson, M. (1997). Women with children sired by previous partners incur excess risk of uxoricide. *Homicide Studies, 1,* 61–71.

Dawson, M., & Gartner, R. (1998). Difference in the characteristics of intimate femicides: The role of relationship state and relationship status. *Homicide Studies, 2,* 378–399.

De Reuter, C., de Jong, E., Reus, M., & Thijssen, J. (2008). *Risk assessment in perpetrators of relational violence: A comparison of RISc and B-SAFER.* Netherlands Institute of Mental Health and Addiction.

Dobash, R. E., Dobash, R. P., Cavanagh, K., & Lewis, R. (2004). Not just an ordinary killer—just an ordinary guy. When men murder an intimate women partner. *Violence Against Women, 10,* 577–605.

Douglas, K., & Kropp, P. R. (2002). A prevention-based paradigm for violence risk assessment: Clinical and research applications. *Criminal Justice and Behavior, 2,* 617–658.

Dutton, D. G., & Kerry, G. (1999). Modus operandi and personality disorder in incarcerated spousal killers. *International Journal of Law and Psychiatry, 22,* 287–300.

Dutton, D. G., & Kropp, P. R. (2000). A review of domestic violence risk instruments. *Trauma, Violence & Abuse, 1,* 171–181.

Easteal, P. W. (1993). *Killing the beloved.* Canberra: Australia Institute of Criminology.

Florida Domestic Violence Fatality Review Team (1994). *Florida fatality review project.* Available at: http://www.fdle.state.fl.us

Garcia-Moreno, C., Jansen, H., Ellsberg, M., Heise, L., & Watts, C. H. (2006). Prevalence of intimate partner violence: Findings from the WHO multi-country study on women's health and domestic violence. *Lancet, 268,* 1260–1269.

Gill, R., & Brockman, J. (1996). *A review of Section 264 of the Criminal Code of Canada.* Ottawa: Department of Justice, Canada.

Gondolf, E. W. (2001). *Batterer intervention systems: Issues, outcomes, and recommendations.* Thousand Oaks, CA: Sage.

Hanson, R. K., & Morton-Bourgon, K. (2004). *Predictors of sexual recidivism: An updated meta-analysis.* Ottawa: Public Safety and Emergency Preparedness.

Hare, R. D. (2003). *Hare Psychopathy Checklist—Revised (PCL-R),* 2nd ed. Toronto: Multi-Health Systems.

Hart, S. D. (1998). The role of psychopathy in assessing risk for violence: Conceptual and methodological issues. *Legal and Criminological Psychology, 3,* 123–140.

Hart, S. D. (2001). Assessing and managing violence risk. In K. S. Douglas, C. D. Webster, S. D. Hart, D. Eaves, & J. R. P. Ogloff (Eds.), *HCR-20 violence risk management companion guide* (pp. 13–25). Burnaby, British Columbia: Mental Health, Law, & Policy Institute, Simon Fraser University, and Department of Mental Health Law and Policy, Florida Mental Health Institute, University of South Florida.

Hart, S. D., & Storey, J. E. (2011). *An examination of the danger assessment as a victim-based risk assessment instrument.* Paper presented at the 4th International Congress on Psychology and Law, Miami, Florida.

Hart, S. D., & Watt, K. (2008). Danger assessment instrument. In B. L. Cutler (Ed.). *Encyclopedia of psychology and law* (pp. 185–186). Thousand Oaks, CA: Sage Publications, Inc.

Hart, S. D., Kropp, P. R., & Laws, D. R. (2003). *Risk for sexual violence protocol (RSVP).* Burnaby, British Columbia: The Mental Health, Law, & Policy Institute, Simon Fraser University.

Heilbrun, K. (1997). Prediction versus management models relevant to risk assessment: The importance of legal decision-making context. *Law and Human Behavior, 21,* 347–359.

Hilton, N. Z., & Harris, G. T. (2005). Predicting wife assault: A critical review and implications for policy and practice. *Trauma, Violence, & Abuse, 6*(1), 3–23.

Hilton, N. Z., Harris, G. T., & Rice, M. E. (2010). *Risk assessment of domestically violent men: Tools for criminal justice, offender intervention, and victim services.* Washington, DC: American Psychological Association.

Hilton, N. Z., Harris, G. T., Rice, M. E., Houghton, R. E., & Eke, A. W. (2008). An in depth actuarial assessment for wife assault recidivism: The domestic violence risk appraisal guide. *Law and Human Behavior, 32,* 150–163.

Hilton, N. Z., Harris, G. T., Rice, M. E., Lang, C., & Cormier, C. A. (2004). A brief actuarial assessment for the prediction of wife assault recidivism: The ODARA. *Psychological Assessment, 16*(3), 267–275.

Johnson, H., & Hotton, T. (2003). Losing control: Homicide risk in estranged and intact relationships. *Homicide Studies, 7,* 58–84.

Kellerman, A. L., Rivara, F. P., & Rushforth, N. B. (1993). Gun ownership as a risk factor for homicide in the home. *New England Journal of Medicine, 329,* 1084–1091.

Kropp, P. R. (2008). Intimate partner violence risk assessment and management. *Violence and Victims, 23*(2), 202–222.

Kropp, P. R. & Belfrage, H. (September 2004). *the brief spousal assault form for the evaluation of risk: B-SAFER.* Paper presented at the 2nd International Conference—Toward a Safer Society. Edinburgh, Scotland.

Kropp, P. R., & Gibas, A. (2010). The spousal assault risk assessment guide (SARA). In R. K. Otto & K. D. Douglas (Eds.), *Handbook of violence risk assessment* (pp. 227–250). New York: Taylor & Francis.

Kropp, P. R., & Hart, S. D. (2000). The spousal assault risk assessment (SARA) guide: Reliability and validity in adult male offenders. *Law and Human Behavior, 24,* 101–118.

Kropp, .P. R., Hart, S. D., & Belfrage, H. (2005). *The brief spousal assault form for the evaluation of risk (B-SAFER).* Vancouver, BC: Proactive-Resolutions.

Kropp, .P. R., Hart, S. D., & Belfrage, H. (2011). *The Brief Spousal Assault Form for the Evaluation of Risk (B-SAFER),* 2nd ed. Vancouver, BC: Proactive-Resolutions.

Kropp, P. R., Hart, S. D., & Lyon, D. R. (2002). Risk assessment of stalkers: Some problems and possible solutions. *Criminal Justice and Behavior, 29,* 590–616.

Kropp, .P. R., Hart, S. D., & Lyon, D. R. (2008). *Stalking assessment and management (SAM).* Vancouver, BC: Proactive-Resolutions.

Kropp, P. R., Hart, S. D., Lyon, D. R. & Storey, J. E. (2011). The development and validation of the guidelines for stalking assessment and management. *Behavioral Science and the Law, 29,* 302–316.

Kropp, P. R., Hart, S. D., Webster, C. D., & Eaves, D. (1995). *Manual for the spousal assault risk assessment guide,* 2nd ed. Vancouver, BC: British Columbia Institute on Family Violence.

Kropp, P. R., Hart, S. D., Webster, C. D., & Eaves, D. (1999). *Spousal assault risk assessment guide (SARA)*. Toronto: Multi-Health Systems.

Krug, E. G., Dahlberg, L. L., Mercy, J. A., Zwi, A. G., & Lozano, R. (Eds.). (2002). *World report on violence and health*. Geneva: World Health Organization.

Litwack, T. R. (2001). Actuarial versus clinical assessments of dangerousness. *Psychology, Public Policy, and Law, 7*, 409–443.

MacKenzie, R. D., McEwan, T. E., Pathé, M., James, D. V., Ogloff, J.R.P., & Mullen, P. E. (2009). *Stalking risk profile: guidelines for the assessment and management of stalkers*. Melbourne: Centre for Forensic Behavioral Science.

McEwan, T. E., Pathé, M., & Ogloff, J.R.P. (2011). Advances in stalking risk assessment. *Behavioral Science and the Law, 29*(2), 180–201.

McFarlane, J., Soeken, K., Campbell, J. C., Parker, B., Reel, S., & Silva, C. (1998). Severity of abuse to pregnant women and associated gun access of the perpetrator. *Public Health Nursing, 15*, 201–206.

McFarlane, J. M., Campbell, J. C., Wilt, S., Sachs, C. J., Ulrich, Y. & Xu, X. (1999). Stalking and intimate partner femicide. *Homicide Studies, 3*, 300–316.

Meloy, J. R., Sheridan, L., & Hoffmann, J. (Eds.). (2008). *Stalking, threatening, and attacking public figures: A psychological and behavioral analysis*. New York: Oxford University Press.

Mohandie, K., Meloy, J. R., McGowan, M., & Williams, J. (2006). The RECON typology of stalking: Reliability and validity based upon a large sample of North American stalkers. *Journal of Forensic Sciences, 51*(1), 147–155.

Moracco, K. W., Runyan, C. W., & Butts, J. D. (2003). Female intimate partner homicide: A population-based study. *Journal of American Women's Medical Association, 58*, 20–25.

Morton, E., Runyan, C. W., Moracco, K. E., & Butts, J. (1998). Partner homicide-suicide involving female homicide victims: A population-based study in North Carolina, 1988–1992. *Violence & Victims, 13*, 91–106.

Mouzos, J. (2000). *Homicide encounters: A study of homicides in Australia, 1989–1999*. Canberra: Australian Institute of Criminology.

Mullen, P. E., Mackenzie, R., Ogloff, J.R.P., Pathé, M., McEwan, T., & Purcell, R. (2006). Assessing and managing risks in the stalking situation. *Journal of the American Academy of Psychiatry and Law, 34*, 439–450.

Mullen, P. E., Pathé, M., & Purcell, R. (2009). *Stalkers and their victims*. 2nd ed. New York: Cambridge University Press.

Mulvey, E. P., & Lidz, C. W. (1995). Conditional prediction: A model for research on dangerousness to others in a new era. *International Journal of Law and Psychiatry, 18*, 129–143.

Norris, S. M., Huss, M. T., & Palarea, R. E. (2011). A pattern of violence: Analyzing the relationship between intimate partner violence and stalking. *Violence and Victims, 26*(1), 103–115.

Palarea, R. E., Zona, M. A., Lane, J. C., & Langhinrichsen-Rohling, J. (1999). The dangerous nature of intimate relationship stalking: Threats, violence, and associated risk factors. *Behavioral Sciences and the Law, 17*, 269–283.

Polk, K. (1994). *When men kill: Scenarios of masculine violence*. New York: Cambridge University Press.

Richie, B. E., & Kanuha, V. (1997). Battered women of color in public health care systems. In M. Baca Zinn, P. Hondagneu-Sotelo, & M. Mesner (Eds.), *Through the prism of difference* (pp. 121–129). Boston: Allyn and Bacon.

Riggs, D. S., Caulfield, M. B., & Street, A. E. (2000). Risk for domestic violence: Factors associated with perpetration and victimization. *Journal of Clinical Psychology, 56*, 1289-1316.

Roehl, J., & Guertin, K. (1998). *Current use of dangerousness assessments in sentencing domestic violence offenders*. Pacific Grove, CA: State Justice Institute.

Rosenfeld, B., & Lewis, C. (2005). Assessing violence risk in stalking cases: A regression tree approach. *Law and Human Behavior, 29*, 343–357.

Santa Clara County Domestic Violence Council Death Review Committee (2000). Final report: 2000. Unpublished manuscript.

Schumacher, J. A., Feldbau-Kohn, S., Slep, A.M.S., & Heyman, R. E. (2001). Risk factors for male-to-female partner physical abuse. *Aggression and Violent Behavior, 6*, 281–352.

Serran, G., & Firestone, P. (2004). Intimate partner homicide: A review of the male proprietariness and the self-defense theories. *Aggression and Violent Behavior, 9*, 1–15.

Sharps, P., Campbell, J. C., Campbell, D., Gary, F., & Webster, D. (2003). Risky mix: Drinking, drug use, and homicide. *National Institute of Justice, 250*, 8–13.

Sharps, P. W., Koziol-McLain, J., Campbell, J., McFarlane, J., Sachs, C., & Xu, X. (2001). Health care providers' missed opportunities for preventing femicide. *Preventive Medicine, 33*, 373–380.

Soeiro, C., & Almeida, I. (2010). *Spousal Assault Risk Assessment and Police Intervention: Application to the Portuguese Population*. Paper presented at the 10th Annual International Conference—Toward a Safer Society. Edinburgh, Scotland.

Statistics Canada (2003). *Homicide in Canada, 2003, 24*(8), 1–23.

Storey, J. E., Hart, S. D., Meloy, J. R., & Reavis, J. A. (2009). Psychopathy and stalking. *Law and Human Behavior, 33*, 237–246.

Stout, K. D. (1993). Intimate femicide: A study of men who have killed their mates. *Journal of Offender Rehabilitation, 19*, 81–94.

Sutherland, A. A., Johnstone, L., Davidson, K. M., Hart, S. D., Cooke, D. J., Kropp, P. R., … Stocks, R. (2012). Sexual violence risk assessment: an investigation of the interrater reliability of professional judgments made using the risk for sexual violence protocol. *International Journal of Forensic Mental Health, 11*(2), 119-133.

Tjaden, P., & Thoennes, N. (1998). *Stalking in America: Findings from the national violence against women survey.* Washington, DC: National Institute of Justice.

Vest, J. R., Catlin, T. K., Chen, J. J., & Brownson, R. C. (2002). Multistate analysis of factors associated with intimate partner violence. *American Journal of Preventative Medicine, 22*(3), 156–164.

Walker, L. E., & Meloy, M. J. (1998). Stalking and domestic violence. In M.J. Meloy (Ed.), *The psychology of stalking: Clinical and forensic perspectives.* (pp. 139–161). San Diego, CA: Academic Press.

Watt, K. A. (2008). Understanding risk factors for intimate partner femicide: The role of domestic violence fatality review teams. In A. C. Baldry & F. W. Winkel (Eds.), *Intimate partner violence prevention and intervention: The risk assessment and management approach.* New York: Nova Science.

Websdale, N. (1999). *Understanding domestic homicide.* Boston: Northeastern University Press.

Websdale, N. (2003). Reviewing domestic violence deaths. *National Institute of Justice, 250,* 26–31.

Websdale, N., Sheeran, M., & Johnson, B. (2001). *Reviewing domestic violence fatalities: summarizing national developments.* Minneapolis: Minnesota Center Against Violence and Abuse.

Weisz, A. N., Tolman, R. M., & Saunders, D. G. (2000). Assessing the risk of severe domestic violence: The importance of survivors' predictions. *Journal of Interpersonal Violence, 15,* 75–90.

Whittemore, K. E., & Kropp, P. R. (August, 2001). *The victim's impact in spousal assault risk assessment.* Paper presented at annual meeting of the American Psychological Association, San Francisco, California.

Williams, K. R. (2008). Domestic violence screening instrument (DVSI). In B. L. Cutler (Ed.), *Encyclopedia of psychology and law* (pp. 240–242). Newbury Park, CA: Sage.

Williams, K. R. (2012). Family violence risk assessment: A predictive cross-validation study of the domestic violence screening instrument-revised (DVSI-R). *Law and Human Behavior, 36*(2), 120–129.

Williams, K., & Houghton, A. B. (2004). Assessing the risk of domestic violence reoffending: A validation study. *Law and Human Behavior, 24*(4), 437–455.

Wilson, M., & Daly, M. (1992). Who kills whom in spouse killings? On the exceptional sex ratio of spousal homicides in the United States. *Criminology, 30,* 189–215.

Wilson, M., Johnson, M. E., & Daly, M. (1995). Lethal and non-lethal violence against wives. *Canadian Journal of Criminology, 37,* 331–362.

Winkel, F. W. (2008). Identifying domestic violence victims at risk of hyper-accessible traumatic memories and/or re-victimization through validated screening: The predictive performance of the Scanner and the B-SAFER. In A. C. Baldry and F. W. Winkel (Eds.), *Intimate partner violence prevention and intervention: The risk assessment and management approach.* Hauppauge, NY: Nova Science.

Zawitz, M. W. (1994). *Violence between intimates.* Washington, DC: US Bureau of Justice Statistics.

12

The Assessment of Anonymous Threatening Communications

ANDRÉ SIMONS AND RONALD TUNKEL

Much has already been written about the evaluation of persons exhibiting concerning behavior and of the characteristics of threatening, problematic, or disturbing communications. In the wake of many high-profile and tragic events, substantial attention has been rightfully devoted to the identification of preattack behaviors to better guide threat assessment and safety professionals in the effort to disrupt acts of quickly unfolding but catastrophic violence. The many differences between those who make threats of violence and those who pose threats of violence have similarly been well established (Borum, Fein, Vossekuil & Berglund, 1999; Calhoun, 1998; Calhoun & Weston, 2003; Dietz et al., 1991a, b; Meloy, 2000). The landmark Exceptional Case Study Project by the U.S. Secret Service (Fein & Vossekuil, 1999) and the equally impactful Safe School Initiative by the Secret Service and the US Department of Education (Fein et al., 2002; Vossekuil et al., 2002) demonstrated that offenders who committed acts of targeted violence rarely issued a direct communicated threat to their intended target prior to attacking. This finding was recently supported by the Bureau of Alcohol, Tobacco, Firearms and Explosives' (ATF) Bomb Data Center, which reported that between January 2004 and June 2012 there were 1,559 explosives-related events (including actual bombings, hoax devices, recoveries, and suspicious packages) reported at educational facilities in the United States. According to the Bomb Arson Tracking System (BATS), only 41 had communicated a threat associated with the event, representing

2.6% of all events. In the 323 cases where actual bombs were discovered, only one case had a communicated threat associated with it, representing a mere 0.3% (R. S. Simpson, personal communication, July 9, 2012). There is a pragmatic rationality to these findings in that a direct threatening communication generally and logically sparks a predictable response, which invariably generates increased law enforcement attention, enhanced security countermeasures, and additional barriers between the offender and the target. All of these reactions are ultimately undesirable to a dedicated attacker and counterproductive to an authentic plan of violence.

Yet, research and experience have also demonstrated that sometimes an individual making an *inappropriate physical approach* to a public figure will directly communicate intentions to the target prior to attempting the approach. As recently described by Meloy (2011), some researchers have found that 21% to 41% of offenders who were focused on public figures engaged in preapproach direct communications (Dietz et al., 1991a,b; Scalora et al., 2002a,b; Meloy et al., 2008). Additionally, there is some evidence (Dietz et al., 1991a; Scalora et al., 2002a, b) to suggest that offenders who provide identifying information in communications may be more apt to attempt inappropriate physical approaches to public figures such as members of Congress. To further complicate matters, there is strong evidence to indicate that threatening communications between intimate or former intimate partners may be correlated to subsequent acts of violence (see discussion below).

Attempting to predict the intentions and abilities of a threatener can be a daunting task. The fact remains that federal, state, and local law enforcement agencies remain obliged to respond in some fashion to *all* threatening communications that come to their attention. As noted by Meloy et al. (2008), "the operational position is clear: All communicated threats should be initially taken seriously because any particular individual may act subsequent to his threat" (p. 6). Faced with a communicated threat, law enforcement agencies must quickly and accurately ascertain the probability of violence or problematic approach, identify the author, and move swiftly in order to protect the targeted individual or institution.

In this context, anonymous threatening communications (ATCs) represent a unique and growing challenge for investigators and safety professionals. A traditional threat assessment often relies on a holistic review of an offender's personal, historical, contextual, and clinical factors (Monahan et al., 2001)—information that is typically absent or masked in an ATC. The writers[1] predict that ATCs will become more common, problematic, and time-consuming in the coming years. The overwhelming majority of threatening communications received at the FBI's Behavioral Analysis Unit (BAU) for assessment each year are anonymously authored and delivered. An increasing number of threats feature anonymous online communications by technology-savvy offenders using Mixmaster or TOR encryption layers to obfuscate their identities. Privacy-enhancing cascading remailer services mask a threatening offender's email headers and assigned Internet protocol addresses, stymieing law enforcement efforts to trace the source of the threat. While historically rare, a burgeoning trend observed by the BAU involves anonymous threateners who strike at academic institutions using blitzkrieg campaigns of remailed bomb threats to force evacuations and paralyze day-to-day operations. The recent targeting of colleges and universities in several countries, some of which have received literally hundreds of anonymized emailed bomb threats, is a troubling example of how ATCs continue to present a complex and persistent issue for campus safety and law enforcement agencies.

The writers have also observed offenders' continued use of more rudimentary but exceedingly disruptive white powder ATCs. Several hundred white powder ATCs have been delivered in recent years to schools, day care facilities, churches, and government offices throughout the world. These letters create profound anxiety, drain precious first responder resources, and cost taxpayers millions of dollars (Robbins, 2012). Nearly every time a white powder ATC has been discovered, the targeted business, school, or facility was forced to shut down as frightened occupants, often children, were rushed outside for testing and decontamination.

The law enforcement investigator assigned to such an ATC case has the daunting task of determining the credibility of the threat, deploying sound and defensible mitigation strategies, and prioritizing already stretched resources toward both investigative and protective objectives. The prospect of coordinating multiple evacuations, screening for bombs or hazardous materials, addressing community anxieties, and simultaneously searching for an anonymous threatening offender are just a few of the many challenges the "lucky" investigator will face in an ATC case.

Many researchers and practitioners who have addressed the topic of threatening communications have focused on the stylistic or linguistic variables that may hold predictive value for a subsequent problematic approach or for an act of targeted violence (Smith, 2008; Fitzgerald, 2005; Dietz et al., 1991a,b; Fein & Vossekuil, 1999; Miron & Douglas, 1979; Scalora et al., 2002a,b; Schoeneman et al., 2011; Schoeneman-Morris, et al., 2007; Smith & Shuy, 2002; Tunkel, 2002). These valuable works have shaped the identification of factors to be considered and remain essential components of every assessment of a threatening communication. As the promising field of automated text analytics continues to grow and develop, calculations of factors represented in thematic content analysis, computerized word pattern analysis, and word count strategies (Chung & Pennebaker, 2011; Parker et al., 2004; Smith, 2007) may one day become standard variables to support the professional threat assessor in his or her evaluation. In the meantime, investigators and security professionals will remain dependent on the consistent and efficient application of a sound threat assessment protocol to identify the appropriate responses.

The writers as investigators and threat assessors assigned to the BAU struggled to find substantial literature describing the group *process* for assessing an ATC. One can turn to several outstanding publications to find guidance on conducting threat assessments of persons of concern (Corcoran & Cawood,

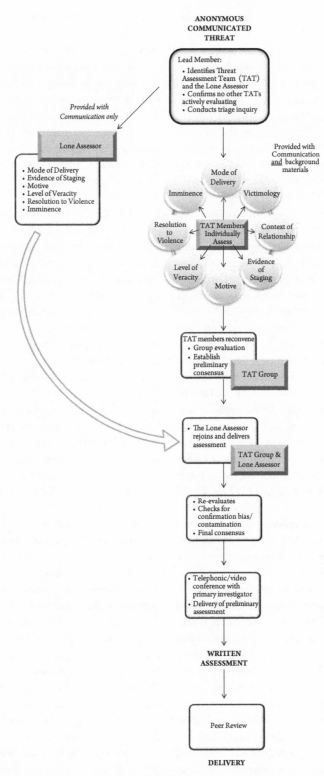

FIGURE 12.1 FBI Behavioral Analysis Unit procedure and process for evaluating anonymous communicated threats. (Special thanks to Stephanie J. Gaines for her assistance in creating Figure 12.1.)

2003; Deisinger et al., 2008; Dunn, 2008; Fein et al., 1995; O'Toole, 2000; Randazzo & Plummer, 2009; Van Dreal & Speckmaier, 2011; Vossekuil et al., 2002) along with some limited examples concerning the steps involved in the evaluation of threatening communications (Calhoun & Weston, 2003; Fitzgerald, 2005; Napier & Mardigian, 2003; Rugala & Fitzgerald, 2003). We imagine that our own beginnings in threat assessment may mirror those of others; namely, discovering the ample research and literature concerning *what* factors to consider in an ATC assessment but also desperately seeking nuts-and-bolts guidance as to *how* to conduct the assessment and apply the body of knowledge in an operational setting. We further suspect that many threat assessment team (TAT) members and law enforcement investigators, thrust into the position of evaluating anonymous threatening letters, emails, or telephone calls, ask "Where do I begin?" and are met with the unsatisfying and frustrating answer, "The only way to learn it is to do it."

The paucity of information regarding the group process of assessing ATCs likely results from the fact that each assessment is necessarily individualized by the spectrum of contextually specific variables surrounding victims, offenders, and the communication. While every evaluation must be approached in appreciation of situational and environmental idiosyncrasies, the routine application of a sound threat assessment *protocol* to be used in each case should remain a priority for every new (or existing) TAT. Identifying these general procedural steps for use in analyzing ATCs—including many steps that have been used for years by the writers and others at the BAU—is the goal of this chapter.

The specific assessment factors that are considered within the offered protocol are heavily based on the work of researchers and practitioners within the field of threat assessment, to whom the writers remain exceptionally grateful. Building on this body of knowledge, we offer an operationally oriented, synthesized, and "road-tested" practitioner's guide honed from lessons learned and mistakes made. As this is a functional model, the efficacy and accuracy of the protocol is naturally limited and has not been validated through empirically controlled studies to demonstrate that outcomes were accurately predicted through use of the described process. The BAU is currently gathering outcomes for documented, adjudicated ATC cases, a collection process that may better inform the development of

this framework. Despite these limitations, the writers suggest that a structured, balanced, and deliberate approach such as the one described here remains a crucial consideration for any threat assessment team. A haphazard or disorganized approach invites the potential for incomplete or inaccurate assessments. The writers recommend that assessors who are charged with the evaluation of inappropriate communications consider this protocol or develop their own process in order to standardize each assessment of an ATC. (see Figure 12.1).

THE BAU PROCESS FOR ASSESSING ATCS

Federal, state, and local law enforcement agencies routinely request the BAU's assistance in the evaluation of ATCs. Recognizing that resources and staffing levels may vary, every ATC should be evaluated by a team, not just an individual investigator or threat assessor. Having multiple evaluators representing diverse disciplines with specific training in threat assessment generates a more robust, useful, and arguably more defensible evaluation.

In analyzing ATCs, the BAU typically offers operationally driven recommendations and observations in the effort to guide the appropriate allocation of law enforcement resources through the prioritization of investigative leads and the strategic application of protective measures. It bears repeating that *all communicated threats should be carefully assessed and treated seriously.*

When a request for an ATC assessment is received at the BAU, a team member is designated as the *lead member* in the inquiry. The lead member is responsible for collecting and distributing relevant data; selecting team members to participate in the assessment, both core members and *ad hoc* specialists; evaluating the ATC; facilitating the group assessment; coordinating the subsequent consultation with the primary investigators; and generating the written assessment for the requesting agency. Although the TAT will work collaboratively to assess the threat, the lead member will ultimately be the person responsible for ensuring that the analysis accurately reflects the observations and recommendations of the TAT in compliance with agency guidelines.

Before starting the threat assessment process, the lead member should make every effort to determine if another threat assessment professional or TAT is actively analyzing the ATC. Redundant or competing assessments issued by multiple TATs can create problems for the investigation, particularly if divergent or contrasting opinions are generated. Absent extraordinary circumstances, the BAU will generally decline to evaluate a threatening communication if another TAT or threat assessment professional is actively assessing the evidence or has very recently analyzed the communication of concern.

The writers suggest that communicated threat collection and data tracking may help to avoid occasions of redundancy or competing assessments. Each TAT or law enforcement agency should consider developing a mechanism for cataloguing and tracking received and assessed threatening communications. The tracking of ATCs can enhance an agency's ability to recognize patterns in communications, such as escalations in frequency and severity or potential shared authorship in a series of threat letters. The Communicated Threat Assessment Database (CTAD) serves as the repository for threatening communications received at the BAU for analysis (Fitzgerald, 2007). In 2012, the CTAD was merged with the FBI's Anonymous Letter File (ALF) in the Laboratory's Questioned Documents Unit. BAU analysts and investigators can now access nearly 6,500 separate threat communications for pattern analysis, comparison, and tracking. One of the first steps for any incoming ATC is to conduct a database survey of the CTAD and ALF for any communications that feature similarities of style, content, or delivery. BAU crime analysts also track and gather outcomes of threatening communication cases in order to generate operationally relevant statistics that inform the BAU assessment process. The collection and maintenance of these communications will serve as the raw data to drive future research projects within the BAU.

CONFIRMATION BIAS AND THE "THE LONE ASSESSOR"

Of all the duties borne by the lead member, none may be as important as ensuring the integrity of the threat assessment process. Any threat assessor must be aware of the possible influence of confirmation bias, generally defined as the seeking or interpreting of evidence in ways that are partial to existing beliefs (Nickerson, 1998). This problematic tendency to view information through the lens of a preconceived hypothesis can be mitigated in scientific settings through the use of double-blind or randomized controls. In the operational threat assessment world, investigators often have preliminary leads or logical theories as to

who may have authored the ATC and may even hold opinions as to the offender's propensity for violence. Although this information is often crucial to understanding the context and environment in which the ATC appears, threat assessors must remain vigilant for the effects of any possible contaminating influences regarding the identity, motivations, and intentions of the threatening anonymous author.

A proposed remedy for the potential impact of confirmation bias and contamination is the use of a "sanitized" TAT member or *lone assessor*. This individual, assigned to the TAT, remains insulated from the investigative findings, suspect information, or the investigator's theories that frequently accompany a request for an ATC assessment. The lone assessor is provided with a copy of the ATC only, with no additional context or accompanying investigative reports. The lone assessor evaluates the communication strictly within the "four corners of the document" and engages the group at the end of the process. This insulated individual enhances the purity of the threat assessment process and may act as a counterbalance to any possible influences of confirmation bias. If staffing and schedules allow for this flexibility, the writers suggest that the lone assessor be designated at the beginning of each threat assessment process, rotating the duty through the TAT with each new incoming ATC.

THE TRIAGE QUESTIONS

After designating the lone assessor, the lead member should seek to gather the crucial background and contextual information that will inform the analysis conducted by the remaining core participating TAT members. The writers favor the use of "key questions" similar to those that were promoted by the talented team that generated the Safe Schools Initiative (Vossekuil et al., 2002). These threat "triage" questions represent a focus on the minimal amount of information a TAT should possess before initiating the process of an ATC assessment. The triage questions may also assist the lead member to gauge the urgency of the situation, which can guide internal TAT case management prioritization. The writers recommend that the following questions be considered when first examining an ATC:

1. How was the communication delivered?
2. How many communications have been received and by whom? During what time frame?

3. Is this a single, isolated communication, or part of a series sent to the same victim(s)?

4. Are there indicators of a possible relationship or prior contact between the victim and the offender (if knowable)?

5. When did the victim receive the communication, and when was it reported to law enforcement?

6. According to the anonymous threatening offender, when will the undesirable threatened act occur?

7. Is it feasible for the offender to carry out the threatened act? (e.g., "I will destroy the earth…" vs. "The next time you leave work I will be there waiting.")

8. Who are the targets, named and implied, of the threatening communication?

9. Who are other persons or organizations named or referenced within the communication, and what is their relationship to the primary targeted victim?

10. What is the significance of any named or referenced locations or dates?

11. What steps or measures did the author take to conceal his or her identity?

12. What details are available concerning the recipient's victimology (defined by the BAU as a comprehensive analysis of a victim)?

13. What details are available concerning any personal or professional issues and conflicts experienced by the targeted recipient(s)?

14. What is the victim's assessment of the ATC, both for level of concern and authorship?

15. What specific analysis (or combination thereof) will most benefit the primary investigating agency (e.g., assessment of concern for violence, threat, and/or risk management strategies; target hardening strategies; unknown offender characteristics; investigative suggestions; media strategies; etc.)?

After the lead member collects as much information as possible related to the threat triage questions, these facts should be organized and provided without filters to the TAT members. As noted, the information derived from the triage inquiry is deliberately withheld from the lone assessor, who will analyze the ATC and remain insulated from any background or investigative information.

Once the triage information is distributed, individual TAT members should independently analyze the ATC. This is not the time for collaborative, dynamic discussion but rather the appropriate stage for a deliberate and thoughtful application of the threat assessment process as described below. As each individual team member explores the communication, certain variables and factors are recommended for in-depth examination.

MODE OF DELIVERY

The writers suggest that TAT members first consider the mode of delivery, which can often yield insight into the offender's abilities, dedication, level of sophistication, and commitment to the threatened act. Described by Meloy et al. (2008) as *means*, the intensity of an offender's desire to remain anonymous will likely be evidenced in the chosen mode of delivery. While obvious methods of delivery include U.S. Postal Service and email, less frequently observed channels may include voice-disguised telephonic threats, online blog postings, text messages, or strategically placed items with ominous or frightening meanings (e.g., a bullet left on the victim's pillow or an ice pick stuck into the front deck of a victim's residence).

In ATCs, offenders obviously construct their threats to minimize the risk of identification, presumably to avoid the negative consequences of law enforcement contact or simply the potential for personal embarrassment. When considering the level of concern for significant or imminent violence or approach as indicated by the mode of delivery, the writers attempt to address the following questions:

- How important is it for the threatener to remain unknown?
- How sophisticated was the mode of delivery (e.g., anonymized rerouter versus throwing a note tied to a brick through a window)?
- How many different channels of delivery were utilized (e.g., email, fax, letter, phone)?
- Did the delivery of the threat involve the offender's physical approach or intrusion into the private space of the targeted victim?
- How much effort and energy was needed to deliver the threat via the chosen channel?
- How much risk did the author take when he or she delivered the threatening communication?

In addressing these questions, it is important to recognize how combined levels of *energy* and *risk taking* should draw the attention of evaluating TAT members. Drawing upon previous research concerning the importance of an offender's "intensity of interest" and use of multimodal communication channels (Dietz et al., 1991a; Fein & Vossekuil, 1999; Scalora et al., 2002a,b; Schoeneman et al., 2011; Schoeneman-Morris, 2007), the writers suggest examining the mode of delivery through these lenses. In the experience of the BAU, an offender's demonstrated risk taking and energy in the delivery of the communication may be intertwined concepts that hinge on the brazenness displayed, the author's skill or comfort in overcoming or circumnavigating any physical security boundaries, the amount of prerequisite research or surveillance that enables delivery; and the relative amount of energy and effort that is expended in the process of physically delivering the communication.

The level of an offender's invested energy may often quickly be assessed through examination of the recipient address used in mailed or emailed communications. For instance, an offender who sends a threatening letter to an easily obtained, generic, and/or outdated public address at the target's place of business may have dedicated relatively little effort in researching the target's background, being either unwilling or unable to locate a personal or residential address for the targeted victim. Compare this with the offender who vigorously conducts concentrated or persistent research to identify the victim's residential address, then drives to the location and hikes in to personally deposit a carefully prepared package on the victim's front porch. The latter has clearly invested higher levels of both energy and risk taking, exposing himself to possible identification and capture in the act of delivery. Reflecting the previously cited works related to intensity of effort, the writers would offer that expressions of elevated energy and risk taking in an ATC should be considered as problematic indicators of potential significant or imminent violence or approach.

VICTIMOLOGY AND THE CONTEXT OF THE RELATIONSHIP WITH THE AUTHOR

Given that an ATC may yield limited information about the author, it is crucial to gather as much information concerning the victim recipient as possible.

While logical investigative questions will undoubtedly probe for conflicts and disputes with possible subjects in the victim's life, a more holistic approach to assemble the full picture of the victim's private, professional, and social life is also recommended. Understanding why the offender chose to anonymously threaten this particular victim in this specific manner is obviously a key issue that can only be considered once a full victim profile is obtained. The BAU commonly refers to the process of analyzing a victim's personality and lifestyle as developing the "victimology." Some of the core considerations for the assessment of the victim include the following:

- Identifying the victim's current, former, and recently developed intimate, professional, familial, social, and casual contacts, including those established or maintained online
- Identifying the victim's daily habits, travels, activities, and work
- Identifying any potential conflicts within the victim's life, including professional and personal disputes or other circumstances that may possibly contribute to an offender's real or perceived hostility toward the victim
- Determining whether the victim is involved in any illicit or illegal activities which could expose the victim to threats or acts of violence
- Finding out whether the victim is involved in any political or social activities, the views and philosophies of which could engender strong feelings of antagonism or opposition in others
- As appropriate, seeking to understand stressors in the victim's life, including social/relational; financial; occupational; academic; mental or physical health issues; chemical/substance dependencies, etc.

By gathering this information, the writers suggest that the TAT can begin to understand the motivation behind the ATC and why the offender selected this particular victim recipient.

If knowable, the context of the relationship between the victim recipient and the threatening offender may play a significant role in the threat assessment. Research and experience (Brewster, 2000; Calhoun & Weston, 2003; Meloy & Gothard, 1995; Palarea et al., 1999; Tjaden & Thoennes, 1998) has shown that threatening communications issued between intimate partners and former intimate partners may in fact be highly correlated to a subsequent attack of physical violence. Accordingly, in cases involving threatening communications between intimate or former intimate partners, the writers frequently default to a higher level of concern for significant and imminent violence.

Of course, with ATCs it may be difficult to determine if the offender is a current or prior intimate partner. Even though an anonymous offender may omit his or her identifying information, a threat assessor may be able to derive information from the text of the ATC to develop insights related to knowledge, access, and influence, suggestive of intimate or prior intimate contact. TAT assessors should therefore probe to ascertain the following:

- Does the offender demonstrate the ability and willingness to surveil or closely observe the victim?
- Does the offender have the ability and willingness to be in close physical proximity to the victim?
- Does the author demonstrate knowledge of the victim's history, behaviors, opinions, affiliations, obligations, habits, future plans, and/or actions, particularly noting behaviors or facts not publically available or widely disclosed?
- Does the language rise to the level of disgust, betrayal, or contempt for the victim, suggestive of feelings often noted in intimate partners whose relationships have degenerated into irreconcilability? Does the author degrade or dehumanize the victim?

LINGUISTIC STAGING

The Times is a paper which is seldom found in any hands but those of the highly educated. We may take it, therefore, that the letter was composed by an educated man who wished to pose as an uneducated one, and his effort to conceal his own writing suggests that that writing might be known, or come to be known, by you.

SIR ARTHUR CONAN DOYLE, *The Hound*

of the Baskervilles, 1902/1994, pp.46–47

In the case referenced here, Sir Author Conan Doyle had Sherlock Holmes, his great fictional detective, wisely deduce that the anonymous mailer of a cut-and-paste threatening letter was not an uneducated malefactor, as the communications might lead the target to believe, but in fact an educated subject close to the victim. Gratefully, he also provided us with an apt introduction to this next factor of an ATC analysis: the consideration of whether or not the threat features *linguistic staging*.

The concept of staging as a form of crime scene behavior has long been noted in the history of the BAU, when John E. Douglas, one of the original luminaries in the discipline of criminal personality profiling, and Corrine M. Munn, his coauthor, used the term to describe "when someone alters the crime scene prior to the arrival of the police. There are two reasons why someone employs staging: to redirect the investigation away from the most logical suspect or to protect the victim or the victim's family" (Douglas & Munn, 1992, p. 251). Our other esteemed colleagues and mentors, Hazelwood and Napier (2004), expanded the concept of staging and its definition to include "the purposeful alteration of a crime or crime scene in an attempt to mislead investigators and frustrate the criminal justice process" (p. 745). The BAU notes the evolutionary aspect of some of the terms and concepts used in this discipline and generally describes staging as the intentional manipulation of physical evidence by the offender at a crime scene or purported crime scene in order to redirect an investigation away from the offender and/or mischaracterize the nature of the event and its true motivation.

The ATC itself can in many ways be considered the "crime scene" and assessors should be alert for signs of *linguistic staging*, a term first used by one of the writers in a 2002 assessment of a threat to disrupt an international political summit through a series of terrorist acts. The TAT assessor should consider if there are signs that the author is manipulating the crime scene. What is his or her motive for this manipulation? And, as with traditional crime scene analysis, can linguistic staging sometimes suggest someone close to the victim or target?

Several strategies can assist in answering these questions. For instance, one basic technique borrowed from statement analysis (discussed in detail later) is to examine a threatener's use of pronouns. Pronouns can often suggest ownership and accountability and may telegraph who is present or absent in a statement. An author's omission of pronouns may suggest a lack of commitment of a subject to a statement, and pronouns may be less likely to appear in deceptive narratives (Knapp et al., 1974; Newman et al., 2003). What has often been noted by the

BAU in threatening communications is the use of the pronoun *we* by a lone author, as if to instill credibility and fear through the invocation of a large and mysterious group that has the ability to monitor the target and subsequently carry out the threatened violence (Tunkel, 2002). Monitoring the author's use of pronouns may reveal areas where he or she may inadvertently slip into the first person (I, my) from the second person (we, our), oftentimes deeper into the communication. Generally that slippage suggests that original suspicions of potential staging may be correct and that the threat does not come from a group. The invocation of a large group has also been noted in communications from more than one subject; however, what is more often the case is that a smaller group of subjects, if not simply a pair, is responsible.

This amplification may be an attempt by the offender to *convince* the reader that this group exists, rather than actually *conveying* a truthful aspect of his identity (Rabon, 1996). The BAU generally views an author's attempt to inflate his or her numbers through the use of plural personal pronouns as a compensatory action more commonly observed in false threats with low credibility. The effort by an anonymous author to convince the reader of his or her dangerousness is often further demonstrated by the classic admonition, "This is not a hoax!" or the equally frequent, "This is not a joke!!" These pleadings and assurances often appear at the end of an ATC and seem to represent the anonymous author's "final push" to convince the reader of the seriousness of the threat. The writers generally consider any attempt by an anonymous author to bolster his or her dangerousness as another example of a compensatory act. It is likely a byproduct of the offender's own recognition that the ATC, lacking credibility of ability and intent, requires enhancement.

Another way the anonymous threatener may attempt to mislead the readers is through the intentional misspelling of words or inclusion of glaring grammatical errors, commonly referred to as downgrading or "dumbing-down" the language. Linguistic staging of this kind may imply a higher degree of criminal mindfulness, suggestive of a more sophisticated offender who fears being recognized and deploys the countermeasure of deliberately inserting de-intellectualized verbiage. One of the most notorious apparent examples of downgrading may have occurred shortly after the September 11, 2001, terrorist attacks against the United States, when the country was again victimized through a series of envelopes mailed to media outlets and the US Senate, containing the anthrax bacterium. The unknown subject wrote in one of his communications:

> 09-11-01
> THIS IS NEXT
> TAKE PENACILIN NOW
> DEATH TO AMERICA
> DEATH TO ISRAEL
> ALLAH IS GREAT

This language, used so close in time to the previous month's attacks, could lead a reader to assume the author to be an agent of a foreign terrorist group. However, the misspelling of penicillin (*PENACILIN*) was conspicuous and appeared intentional. This subject's weapon of choice was anthrax; would not his or her use of this deadly and uncommon weapon suggest a familiarity and comfort level with the substance? Would not this same offender necessarily possess above average scientific knowledge and concurrently the ability to correctly spell a commonly known antibiotic to neutralize the bacterial agent of interest? This misspelling was an immediate clue to assessors that intentional downgrading might be in play; in fact, subsequent developments in laboratory analysis eventually enabled the FBI, through the use of molecular genetics, to biogenetically trace the substance back to its original parental sample stored in a flask, created and controlled by Dr. Bruce Ivins, an American citizen. Ivins was an employee of the US Army Medical Research Institute of Infectious Diseases (USAMRIID), who committed suicide as he was nearing indictment by a federal grand jury. An outside multidisciplinary scientific panel of mental health and systems professionals recently supported the Department of Justice's determination that Ivins was responsible for the anthrax mailings, likely acting from various motives related to personal grievance, faulty ideation, and emotional stress (Saathoff et al., 2010; Schouten & Saathoff, this volume, chapter 16).

The BAU has used the term *contraindicator* to describe what appears to be biographical information deliberately inserted into an ATC to mislead the reader (Fitzgerald, 2005). Contraindicators often appear in the opening or early lines of a communication as if to frame the overall reading of the document in the deceptive light. For example, the BAU analyzed a communication from an anonymous offender who threatened terrorist acts against a university. The subject described himself as "a native from Europe" in the second line of his communication, then later correctly used the colloquial plural pronoun *ya'll*. Near the end of the communication the offender described the violence that would happen to "these *fellow* American bastards and idiots." No subsequent act of violence occurred, reflecting the writers' experience that an anonymous offender who inserts contraindicators may view the preservation of his or her anonymity as a priority over other concerns or motives. The writers generally consider that an ATC author's concern for his or her own safety, well-being, and anonymity may reflect his or her primary desire to avoid negative consequences. This awareness and appreciation of future consequences may subsequently serve as a potential inhibitor to dramatic or catastrophic acts of targeted violence.

Not surprisingly, linguistic staging often appears in ATC cases involving self-victimization. ATC authors who self-victimize often do so to draw attention or to extricate themselves from difficult personal or professional situations. Again, the traditional hallmarks of linguistic staging tend to cue assessors to the possibility of self-victimization: a mysterious and powerful group is invoked, capable of surveilling the target at any time; "insider" details are referenced; sometimes complimentary information about the victim is provided; and occasionally the scheme does not make sense or appears to be taken directly from infamous crimes or the media. Often with self-victimization cases, the ATC is discovered in an area not readily accessible to the public or even skilled intruders. The BAU has long noted that cut-and-paste communications—where the letters have been cut out of printed materials such as magazines and newspapers—are rarely seen in legitimate extortionate communications and are most often associated with self-victimization or staging.

In one noteworthy case of self-victimization, an editor of a local newspaper had reported receiving cut-and-paste ATCs, and fire had been set to his detached garage on multiple occasions. The ATCs threatened death unless the editor stopped writing for the newspaper. He lived with his wife and son in the targeted residence and it was a frightening situation for the family and local authorities. Given the suspicion of staging and the thought that the offender was either one of the victims or someone very close to them, the BAU determined that the likelihood of

a serial arsonist or stranger to the family targeting their house was low. Law enforcement investigators remained concerned that the author would fulfill his pledge to kill the editor. The BAU suggested that the linguistic staging observed in the statement mitigated the potential threat to the editor. The author's masquerade indicated that self-preservation and avoidance of identification were the top priorities. The investigation then shifted away from the outside actor and focused on the editor himself, who ultimately admitted to starting the fires and creating the communications. The self-made threats and fire sets apparently served to provide a noble reason to remove himself from stressful employment and life situations.

In self-victimization cases such as these, the recognition of linguistic staging can serve to refocus an investigation away from the unknown random actor who targets and terrorizes the community. For the threat assessment professional evaluating an ATC, this valuable insight can assist in the prioritization of investigative and protective resources. In another case investigated by one of the writers, a female received a package bomb correctly addressed to her place of employment. The return address on the package featured the name of a fictitious company. The first and last names of the victim were misspelled, adding an "e" to her name, Stacy (*Stacey*) and changing one of the vowels of her last name from a "u" to an "o." This could appear at first blush to be a simple spelling mistake. However, when properly assessed, these misspellings could be viewed as glaring examples of staging. An offender harboring such a profound grievance with this woman—a low-risk victim with no obvious ties to illegal, illicit, or terrorist activities—who took the time to construct and correctly address a package bomb in an attempt to kill her, would likely know the correct spelling of her name. The victim's husband, later identified as the perpetrator and convicted of sending the bomb to his wife, had correctly assumed that he would be considered as an initial suspect.

The writers have anecdotally observed, especially in cases of threatened school violence and "hit lists," that the offender may sometimes include his or her own name in the communication as a target or at least tangentially noted. Given the intense community pressure that typically follows the discovery of a hit list, a TAT member recognizing this and other potential signs of staging in an ATC can assist to quickly diffuse an urgent situation.

MOTIVE

As the TAT assessor progresses with his or her analysis, shades of suggested motives behind the ATC often begin to appear, indicating whether the threat is expressive or instrumental (Meloy, 2000). The BAU has traditionally referenced a number of potential motives, including the following: *financial gain*, through some extortionate scheme; *revenge* on or *punishment* of the victim for some real or perceived grievance held by the offender; *instilling fear and anxiety* in the victim; *relief* from the stress of underlying emotions such as anger, sexual frustration, unrequited love, fear, jealousy, or other feelings of inadequacy; *manipulating or forcing the victim to take a desired action*, such as with communications from extremist or terrorist groups; *excitement* gained by being the cause of fear and activity resultant from the threat; *attention* received by someone in the chain of events following the threat, often seen in self-victimization cases; and in rare cases, to *telegraph or warn* of a future violent act (O'Toole, 2000; Tunkel, 2002). Occasionally the motive behind an ATC is unclear and analysis suggests that the communication is the product of a mentally disordered offender.

The latter cause was readily noted in a series of anonymous communications sent to a Catholic church in New Jersey. The local police requested BAU assistance because the church had a school on its grounds and the police chief was concerned about a potential school attack by the anonymous author. The notes were mailed from Florida and one was written on a photocopy of a book jacket from a library in a small resort town. One anonymous communication, written on a postcard, was filled with odd signs and rambling writing in very small print, with letters being written over one another. The margins were filled with equally bizarre and nonsensical verbiage and symbols. This style of writing and the virtual word salad it communicated was a strong indicator of a potential thought disorder. There were gender markers suggestive of feminine authorship, and dates were given indicating when the author might have begun experiencing delusions. The BAU offered a threat assessment and unknown author characteristics, including the gender and possible age range of the anonymous author. The BAU also believed that the author likely had some direct connection to the library. The police in Florida quickly identified the author, a local female who suffered from a profound thought disorder and frequently visited the library.

She was subsequently assessed as not posing a threat of significant or imminent violence.

Establishing the likely motive in an ATC can be a challenge for the threat assessor. Motives are not always crystal clear in a communication that is deceptive in nature, and assessors may not always fully understand an offender's goal or grievances. If the motive is elusive, one helpful way to reframe the analysis is to ask, "What is the profit, both material and psychological? What is the gain to the offender?" When the motive is unclear and the profit or gain to the offender remains a mystery, the BAU will often consider the amount of attention and energy focused on specific topics featured within the content of each paragraph or section of an ATC. By identifying the topics and themes that dominated the author's attention during the construction of the ATC, and the ranking of frequency of appearance of these topics and themes, a TAT assessor can likely deduce the probable goal (e.g., *the offender is jealous of the victim's popularity, family, wealth, etc., and wants to exact revenge by humiliating and controlling the victim*). This informs the overall assessment as the primary motive is frequently something other than the heralding of an impending threatened act.

LEVEL OF VERACITY

As observed by Adams and Jarvis (2006; Adams, 1996) statement analysis can be a useful tool for investigators in examining subjects' written or spoken language; it can help to assess veracity and look for areas of possible deception, purposefully missing information, concealed themes, or other areas of sensitivity that should be followed up on in subsequent inquiry. This technique focuses on the structured and careful examination of an author's word choices to discern the motivations and sources behind the disclosure. Using probabilistic guides based on generalized and idiosyncratic patterns, the analyst attempts to develop interview strategies that may eventually be useful and are based on the known author's reflections of authentic memories or fabricated disclosures of imagination. A central question addressed by the analyst is: Does the disclosure reflect the author's best attempt at recollection or does the disclosure reflect a location of origin other than authentic memory (Kohnken, 2004)?

All BAU members have received training in statement analysis and use these techniques in the course of their duties. Although statement analysis is traditionally applied in the context of reviewing solicited written statements, the BAU suggests that it has value in conducting assessments of ATCs. Areas that are given particular attention include the following: the use of pronouns, including first, second and third person and their plurals; using the passive voice (*someone will be killed*) versus active tense (*I will kill you*), with the passive voice potentially suggestive of a lack of commitment to the threatened act; deviations from the subject's normal communication habits; evidence of editing or missing time in statements; signs of equivocation, such as the use of words like *basically, essentially,* and *maybe,* suggestive of ambivalence or a lack of commitment to a threatened act; changes in language (*her bedroom... her bedroom... the bedroom*) possibly reflecting a reluctance to assert ownership; providing apparent unnecessary information to relay the story; providing sensory and spatial details usually associated with veracity; and examining whether or not the statement is rich in detail (Adams, 1996; Adams & Jarvis, 2006; Sapir, 1987; Rabon, 1996; Rudacille, 1994; Pennebaker, 2011).

In assessing veracity, threat assessors should borrow lessons from statement analysis and pay particular attention not only to the quantity but also the quality of the offered details. An offender who unintentionally provides erroneous or flawed details may demonstrate a lack of ability to complete the threatened act. For instance, a threatener who suggests omnipotent abilities to harm a victim "anytime, anywhere" yet uses outdated addresses or vague references to the victim's daily movements clearly does not demonstrate current "eyes on" surveillance of the victim. The BAU has assessed cases where offenders fail to provide accurate bona fides of surveillance, which compromises their claims of omnipotent control and diminishes their overall veracity. In several cases, perhaps in an attempt to compensate for a perceived deficiency, offenders have sought to bolster their credibility by claiming to be former military special operators. Invariably these false claims yield mistakes in the unique terminology associated with these specialized groups such as, "*I passed Green Beret tryouts,*" as opposed to correctly writing, "*I went through Assessment and Selection and then went to the Q-course.*" A threat assessor who carefully screens an ATC for both quantity and quality of detail may discover these discrepancies and errors, which ultimately can inform the assessment of the offender's abilities and veracity.

Threat assessors should be mindful of the limitations of statement analysis as applied to threatening communications, since ATCs are often deceptive in nature, concern future intent, and are frequently designed to coerce or intimidate. The offender has likely put energy and effort into crafting words designed to meet these goals. In an ATC, the chosen words may therefore not reflect the pure version of a first narrative of a purported memory, which is the more traditional platform for the application of statement analysis principles and techniques. Most of the successful uses of statement analysis in the BAU have involved assessing narratives of *past* events and recollections rather than gauging the sincerity of expressed future intentions. At the very least, however, statement analysis forces the assessor to slow down his or her reading and meticulously scrutinize every word in the communication. This process can be likened to "really *listening* with your *eyes.*" The type of painstaking rumination of each word, line, and sentence that statement analysis demands may be its ultimate value in its application to threatening communications.

RESOLUTION TO COMMIT VIOLENCE

While infrequent, threat assessors evaluating an ATC should recognize that a threatening author may pass the point of peaceful return and become fully committed to the threatened violence. Identifying indicators of this "graduation" is a difficult and crucial task. An anonymous author who is determined to act on his or her threats may be likened to an Olympic ski jumper who has trained for the event, assembled and prepared his or her equipment, then ascends to the starting gate before launching down the ramp, hurtling toward the inevitable jump. There is no turning back.

De Becker (1997) provided a valuable model for describing the thought process leading up to a decision of violence with his concept of JACA: the offender's perception of his *justification* for violence, his ability to consider *alternatives* to violence, his acceptance and views of the *consequences* of his actions, and his *ability* to carry out the violence. This useful framework may be one lens through which to review an ATC.

For the offender, there is a magnitude to this decision for violence, perhaps unlike any he or she has ever made. At risk could be his or her reputation, finances, freedom, and life itself. The gain for the offender may be the emotional profit of redress or feelings of satisfaction not attainable through socially acceptable or legally sanctioned means. The writers have observed that this decision is of such magnitude and focus to the offender that it will likely be echoed in the language of the ATC. The writers suggest that the offender's *resolution to commit violence* will often become manifest in detectable ways and may be evident in the offender's language in the following manner:

1. *Justification.* In one case assessed by the BAU, an anonymous offender wrote: *"Your actions cannot be tolerated. It is a disgrace. For this reason, I am going to kill you. This is because you tried to assert authority over me and my family. You have committed a wrongful act and you will pay for it."* This example highlights the aspect of *justification* (De Becker, 1997), wherein an offender's psychological rationalizations occasionally enable him or her to find internal sanction and validity of sufficient degree to self-authorize the use of violence. An anonymous author who feels justified in using violence may display a sense of entitlement or a grandiose perception of enhanced position that often invokes moral righteousness as cause for action. An anonymous author's display of justification was observed by the BAU in February 1997 when convicted serial bomber Eric Rudolph mailed letters to various news organizations within hours of the bombing at the Otherside Lounge in Atlanta. Rudolph claimed "the Army of God" as responsible for the last two bombings. Rudolph implied in his writings that he had the duty, right, and moral obligation to use violence to oppose abortion and defend unborn children. His intricate and vigorous justifications for his actions permeated his anonymous letters, including his statement that *"THE MURDER OF 3.5 MILLION CHILDREN EVERY YEAR WILL NOT BE TOLERATED."*

2. *Commitment of energy and effort.* As noted above in the discussion concerning mode of delivery, the assessor should consider whether the ATC features a degree of *commitment* to the offender's plan as evidenced in time, money, energy, and activity spent on it. Does the author provide accurate descriptors of the target—his or her appearance, descriptions of the residence or any children—suggestive of recent surveillance? As research and experience suggest, suspicious activity (e.g., feelings of being followed; items left for them to find at work or home; vandalism to property or breaches of security) noted by a victim may often be of far greater concern than the receipt of an anonymous threatening communication (Calhoun, 1998). Therefore an anonymous author's descriptions of these activities should alert threat assessors to the possibility of active planning and preparation in furtherance of a physical approach or an act of violence.

3. *Abilities.* All offenders who commit themselves to violent acts believe that they have the ability to complete the acts (De Becker, 1997). This prerequisite self-confidence serves as the baseline foundation that is occasionally evidenced in an ATC. The writers extrapolate that an anonymous author's demonstrated or perceived skill and ability should be considered as a risk-enhancing factor in the assessment of the author's overall resolution to violence. Again, in the case of Eric Rudolph, anonymously authored letters featured accurate knowledge, familiarity, and competence regarding explosives (with several specific details suggestive of veracity). In his communications, Rudolph wrote, *"YOU MAY CONFIRM THE FOLLOWING WITH THE F.B.I. THE SANDY SPRING'S DEVICES— GELATIN-DYNAMITE-POWER SOURCE 6 VOLT D BATTERIES BOX, DURACELL BRAND, CLOCK TIMERS. THE MIDTOWN DEVICES ARE SIMILAR EXCEPT NO AMMO CANS."* As his letters portended, Rudolph would bomb and kill again.

A more global yet nuanced inquiry into an offender's ability lies in assessing the anonymous author's levels of intelligence and organization, essential characteristics that serve as the foundation for the design and execution of the threatened act. For instance, the writers frequently observe ATCs featuring sloppy, disjointed construction, multiple errors in grammar, and impulsive methods of delivery. Would this author simultaneously possess the ability, maturity, patience, sophistication, and intelligence to secrete multiple explosive devices on remote timers in hidden locations throughout a community? While possible, this profound dichotomy of behavior and incongruence could alert the assessor to a potential hoax threat.

4. *Lack of resiliency.* An anonymous author who is resolved to violence may include indicators in the ATC that his or her coping mechanisms have been overwhelmed. Words implying hopelessness, fatigue, and a compromised ability to sustain normal functioning may suggest that the anonymous author has lost the will to seek alternatives to violence. As the end game nears, the assessor may note a degree of *resignation* in the offender's language, which may then be conveyed by apparent relief in the verbiage of the ATC. This factor is especially noted in cases where there is a series of communications.

5. *Contempt.* As noted above in the section on victimology, assessors should be vigilant for language that suggests not only disgust but also strong *contempt* for the victim. This level of contempt seems to be a component of an untenable relationship and may fuel an offender's sense of superiority and hostility toward his target. Associative language may appear, for example, in this way: *"Watching you on television makes me want to vomit; as far as I am concerned you are subspecies and not even worth the cost of the bullet I will use to end your wretched life."* Often such degrading and violent language may reflect contempt and demonstrate the companion emotion of *envy*: not only do I want what you have, but I want to destroy you too.

6. *Consequences.* *"I don't care if the cops come to my house and shoot me or I'm executed in the chair, I will get my revenge."* As noted earlier, the BAU suggests that an offender's desire for self-preservation may indicate that future consequences remain important to him or her. At the other end of the spectrum, an ATC that features acceptance of even the most dire consequences, such

as death or incarceration, may suggest a progression toward violence (De Becker, 1997). Language evidencing sincere suicidal ideation (e.g. *"my days are nearing an end"*) should also be considered as threat-enhancing.

7. *Inevitability.* *"When the Court rejected my last appeal, you left me with no alternative but to take matters into my own hands."* There is no other remedy, and the offender has lost the ability to perceive any redress of his grievance. This concept resonates "last resort" warning behaviors (Meloy et al., 2012) as well as the violent action and time imperatives (Mohandie, 2000; Turner & Gelles, 2003). An anonymous threatening author who uses language indicating the violent act will occur, and that nothing can intervene to interrupt the progression toward the act, is demonstrating the perceived inevitability of violence.

IMMINENCE IN THREATENING COMMUNICATIONS

Related to an offender's resolution to commit violence, the concept of imminence in threat assessment should be of great interest to the evaluating professional; he needs to gauge not only the potential of a violent act but also the urgency for deployment of any appropriate countermeasures. Meloy et al. (2012) describe imminence as implying "an increasing probability of the act occurring within a specific time-frame. As such, it is a further variable which may influence both concern level and, within a given concern level, necessary speed of interventional response" (p. 259). Mohandie (2000) and Turner and Gelles (2003) have also described a "time action imperative" that may or may not be present within a threatening communication, suggesting that the offender is no longer willing to delay the act of violence.

Many threat assessment professionals routinely guide the allocation of law enforcement resources via the prioritization of investigative actions and/or protective measures. While nearly every law enforcement agency has the ability to temporarily maintain a "high alert" status for a perceived threat, no agency or unit can reasonably sustain that level indefinitely. Mining the ATC for indicators to justify an escalation or reduction in response remains a critical function of the threat assessment process.

In evaluating ATCs for signs of imminent action, the BAU considers several factors, including:

- Does the ATC feature evidence of the author's evaporating patience or intolerance for delay (e.g. "I can't take it any longer—this has to end now!")?
- Does the ATC suggest that the offender perceives his or her "window of opportunity" for an attack to be rapidly closing, owing to circumstances such as deteriorating health, pending arrest/incarceration, or decreased access to the targeted victim(s)?
- Does the offender's writing suggest any indication of a "last resort" (Meloy et al., 2012) or "violent action imperative" (Mohandie, 2000; Mohandie & Duffy, 1999), whereby the offender has lost the ability to recognize, perceive, or pursue any alternatives to violence? Faced with the vanishing prospect of nonviolent options, does the offender demonstrate "desperation or distress" (Meloy et al., 2012) in writing, (e.g., *"I will kill you because you have left me with no other choice! If I can't have you, no one else can!!"*)
- As observed by the writers, some communications have featured signs that both logistic and psychological preparations for violence were nearly completed and the violent act was fast approaching. Threat assessors may therefore wish to remain alert for the following such indicators within ATCs: cleansing/purifying of all narcotics or alcohol (e.g., *"Haven't had a drink since Friday. Total effort needed"*); reckless sexual or financial behaviors in excess of the offender's norms and in blatant disregard of future consequences; or preparation and delivery of a manifesto, video will, or other "legacy token" designed to claim credit for the attack and articulate the motivation behind the violence.

In assessing ATCs, threat professionals should be vigilant for the above characteristics suggestive of a potentially imminent act. Rapid reactions and immediate interventions to protect the target may be required if these indicators are detected.

THE CONSULTATION

After each TAT member independently applies the factors described above to the ATC, the TAT group should convene for the purpose of generating a group threat assessment. The goal of the group TAT is to synthesize the individual assessments and provide a collective opinion as to the level of concern for *significant* violence and for the *imminence* of a violent act. The BAU avoids characterizing assessments as predictions of violence risk and instead refers to levels of concern. The concept of "concern" vs. "risk" is nuanced yet important, as it reflects the impact of operational interventions and recognizes the potential of incomplete information (Scalora et al., 2002a; S. Hart, personal communication, May 2011).

To arrive at the collective assessment of concern, the TAT group session should be facilitated to encourage dynamic discussion, debate, and review. The lead member acts as facilitator, encouraging each TAT participant to reveal, justify, and defend his or her individual assessments for group consideration. This part of the collaborative process may be likened to the ancient parable of the blind men and the elephant, reflecting the natural limitations of individual assessments and the power of a consultative group setting. As the story goes, three blind men encounter an elephant for the first time. In their attempt to describe this creature to each other, one blind man speaks of feeling two big trees without branches. The second, who felt the wagging tail, likened the elephant to a swinging straw fan. The third felt the trunk and thought it similar to a snake. Failing to integrate their individual analyses of the elephant, each blind man's assessment remained incomplete and inaccurate. Further applying the metaphor to the assessment of ATCs, imagine the enormousness of the challenge if each blind man were actually touching the same small part of the elephant, with all the other parts missing or unavailable for assessment. In addressing ATCs, the TAT is often faced with the same scenario: a need to form the most holistic and accurate threat assessment picture using limited or incomplete information. In the TAT group setting, the collective opinion, assembled from shared individual assessments, remains the most powerful method for assessing ATCs and articulating concerns of significant and imminent violence. Recognizing the inherent value found in a collaborative "tribal wisdom," any professional debate or disagreement is to be embraced rather than avoided, as diverse perspectives can provoke new investigative directions that were previously hidden or masked. While a group consensus is desirable, it is occasionally unattainable. The divergent views should be shared with the primary investigative agency, as the discussion surrounding the disparity may yield additional avenues of inquiry.

After the TAT group has reached consensus or near consensus on the levels of concern, the lone assessor rejoins the TAT group session. The lone assessor has applied the concepts related to mode of delivery, evidence of staging, motive, level of veracity, resolution to violence, and imminence to the ATC. Issues related to victimology and the context of the relationship, as well as any background investigative information, have not been included in the lone assessor's evaluation. Before learning of the group's conclusions, the lone assessor delivers his or her observations regarding the levels of concern, which have been determined without any contaminating background or suspect information. Once the summary is delivered and the lone assessor has shared his or her analysis, the TAT members can reinitiate discussion to determine if the group consensus is validated or challenged by the lone assessor's evaluation. Special attention should be dedicated to cross-checking the TAT group's initial conclusions against the observations of the lone assessor to minimize possible effects of confirmation bias or other contaminating information. The lead member again facilitates this discussion with an orientation toward achieving group unanimity. This process is designed to stimulate and enhance interrater reliability and create a more complete, robust, and defensible assessment.

The BAU often delivers the summary of the preliminary group assessment to the requesting agency via a telephone or videoconference call. The personal interaction between the TAT and the requesting investigators represents the next-to-last stage of the assessment, where final questions can be addressed and observations by the group can be shared. The BAU typically offers a summary of the threat-enhancing characteristics, the threat-mitigating characteristics, any identified buffers and stabilizers, along with trip-wires for escalation that, when noted, should prompt enhanced responses from responsible law enforcement agencies. After the threat assessment regarding significance and imminence is completed, the BAU typically offers additional threat management strategies that describe unknown author characteristics, protect the victim recipient, and mitigate potential concerns of violence. The BAU also routinely offers behaviorally based investigative suggestions, including interview and media strategies designed to elicit truthful disclosures and identify the responsible author(s).

The final step of the process is to provide a written summary of the communicated threat assessment to the primary investigating agency. The authors strongly encourage TATs to memorialize each assessment in writing, in accordance with individually established organizational guidelines as maintained by each TAT's respective agency and general counsel. Appropriate *caveats* regarding limitations of the assessment and suitability for use in administrative or judicial proceedings should be constructed in cooperation with each TAT's general counsel. The lead member should draft the written assessment, completely and precisely reflecting the conclusions of the TAT. Before delivering the assessment to the primary investigators, the lead member should provide the written draft assessment to the participating members of the TAT for peer review. This ensures the accuracy of the assessment and is a crucial component in the delivery of a document that may be utilized in administrative or judicial proceedings. Once the TAT peer review is completed, the written assessment is delivered to the primary investigators. The assessment serves as a foundation on which to build an effective and appropriate threat management strategy.

The BAU remains available to provide assistance in the assessment of ATCs and other matters involving targeted violence. Agencies wishing to enlist the assistance of the BAU should contact the nearest FBI field office or legal attaché and request contact with the field office's National Center for the Analysis of Violent Crime/BAU coordinator.

CONCLUSION

The writers as investigators and threat assessors assigned to the FBI's BAU have offered one methodology for the evaluation of anonymous threatening communications. No one process or method will apply in every circumstance given the contextual complexities that arise in each assessment. However, the writers suggest that having an established framework that "sets the stage" for each threat assessment team's evaluation will enhance the team's ability to detect the rare but problematic signs of significant and imminent violence as expressed in an ATC.

ACKNOWLEDGMENT

The information and recommendations contained herein reflect current procedures used by the BAU in many, but not necessarily all, cases. They do not necessarily reflect procedures adopted by the FBI as a whole, and may continue to evolve over time.

KEY POINTS

- Threat assessment teams may consider designating a "lone assessor" to insulate the process against confirmation bias, enhance interrater reliability, and create a more robust and defensible analysis.
- In the analysis of ATCs, threat professionals should focus on assessing the offender's ability to engage in *significant and/or imminent* violence. The offender's chosen mode of delivery may telegraph the level of energy and effort that has been invested and provide insight to inform the assessment.
- A victimological study of the recipient of an ATC, including an analysis of the context of the relationship between the victim and the author, is critical to assessing the level of threat posed to the victim.
- Some concepts from statement analysis may assist the threat professional in assessing an ATC. However, the real value may lie in its inherent intense focus on language and content.
- Identifying efforts by the ATC offender to deliberately obfuscate his identity and motive can assist in revealing key and authentic characteristics of the offender.
- Consistent application of a standardized threat assessment process such as the one offered here will help TATs to generate operationally useful and sound guidance in the investigation of ATCs.

NOTE

1. To minimize confusion, the writers of this chapter are referred to as "the writers" throughout. The individual who writes an ATC is referred to as "the offender," "the author," or "the threatener."

REFERENCES

Adams, S. H. (1996). Statement analysis: What do suspects' words really reveal? *FBI Law Enforcement Bulletin*, October, 12–20.

Adams, S. H., & Jarvis, J. P. (2006). Indicators of veracity and deception: An analysis of written statements made to police. *Speech, Language and the Law, 13*(1), 1–22.

Borum, R., Fein, R. Vossekuil, B., & Berglund, J. (1999). Threat assessment: Defining an approach for evaluating risk of targeted violence. *Behavioral Sciences and the Law, 17*, 323–337.

Brewster, M. P. (2000). Stalking by former intimates: Verbal threats and other predictors of physical violence. *Violence and Victims, 15*(1), 41–54.

Calhoun, F. (1998). *Hunters and howlers: Threats and violence against federal judicial officials in the United States, 1789-1993.* Arlington, VA: US Marshals Service.

Calhoun, F., & Weston, S. (2003). *Contemporary threat management: A practical guide for identifying, assessing, and managing individuals of violent intent.* San Diego, CA: Specialized Training Services.

Chung, C., & Pennebaker, J. (2011). Using computerized text analysis to assess threatening communications and behavior. In C. Chauvin (Ed), *Threatening communications and behavior: Perspectives on the pursuit of public figures* (pp. 3–32). Washington, DC: National Academies Press.

Corcoran, M. H., & Cawood, J. S. (2003). *Violence assessment and intervention: The practitioner's handbook.* Boca Raton: CRC Press.

De Becker, G. (1997). *The gift of fear.* Boston: Little, Brown.

Deisinger, G., Randazzo, M., O'Neill, D., & Savage, J. (2008). *The handbook for campus threat assessment and management teams.* Stoneham, MA: Applied Risk Management.

Dietz, P., Matthews, D., Martell, D., Stewart, T., Hrouda, D., & Warren, J. et al. (1991a). Threatening and otherwise inappropriate letters to members of the United States Congress. *Journal of Forensic Sciences, 36*, 1445–1468.

Dietz, P., Matthews, D., Van Duyne, C., Martell, D., Parry, C., Stewart, T., et al. (1991b). Threatening and otherwise inappropriate letters to Hollywood celebrities. *Journal of Forensic Sciences, 36*, 185–209.

Douglas, J. E., & Munn, C. M. (1992). The detection of staging and personation at the crime scene. In J.E. Douglas, A.W. Burgess, A.G. Burgess, & R.K. Ressler (eds.), *Crime classification manual* (pp. 249–252). New York: Lexington Books.

Doyle, A. C. (1902/1994). *The hound of the Baskervilles.* New York: Book of the Month Club.

Dunn, J. (2008). Operations of the LAPD Threat Management Unit. In J. R. Meloy, L. Sheridan, & J. Hoffmann (Eds.), *Stalking, threatening, and attacking public figures* (pp. 325–341). New York: Oxford University Press.

Fein, R., & Vossekuil, B. (1999). Assassination in the United States: An operational study of recent assassins, attackers, and near-lethal approachers. *Journal of Forensic Sciences, 44*, 321–333.

Fein, R., Vossekuil, B., & Holden, G. (1995). *Threat assessment: An approach to prevent targeted violence* (Publication NCJ 155000). Washington, DC: U.S. Department of Justice, Office of Justice Programs, National Institute of Justice.

Fein, R., Vossekuil, B., Pollack, W., Borum, R., Modzeleski, W., & Reddy, M. (2002). *Threat assessment in schools: A guide to managing threatening situations and to creating safe school climates.* Washington, DC: U.S.

Department of Education, Office of Elementary and Secondary Education, Safe and Drug-Free Schools Program and U.S. Secret Service, National Threat Assessment Center.

Fitzgerald, J. R. (2005). *Forensic linguistic services at the Behavioral Analysis Unit-1*. Quantico, VA: FBI Academy and the National Center for the Analysis for Violent Crime.

Fitzgerald, J. R. (2007). The FBI's communicated threat assessment database: History, design, and implementation. *FBI Law Enforcement Bulletin*, February, 6–9.

Hazelwood, R., & Napier, M. (2004). Crime scene staging and its detection. *International Journal of Offender Therapy and Comparative Criminology*, 48(6), 744–759.

Knapp, M. L., Hart, R. P., & Dennis, H. S. (1974). An exploration of deception as a communication construct. *Human Communication Research*, 1, 15–29.

Kohnken, G. (2004). Statement validity assessment and the "detection of the truth." In, P. A. Granhag & L.A. Stromwall, (Eds.). *The detection of deception in forensic contexts* (pp. 41–63). Cambridge: University Press.

Meloy, J. R. (2000). *Violence risk and threat assessment*. San Diego, CA: Specialized Training Services.

Meloy, J. R. (2011). Approaching and attacking public figures: A contemporary analysis of communications and behavior. In C. Chauvin (Ed.), *Threatening communications and behavior: Perspectives on the pursuit of public figures* (pp. 75–101). Washington, DC: National Academies Press.

Meloy, J. R., & Gothard, S. (1995). Demographic and clinical comparison of obsessional followers and offenders with mental disorders. *American Journal of Psychiatry*, 152(2), 258–263.

Meloy, J. R., Hoffmann, J., Guldimann, A., & James, D. (2012). The role of warning behaviors in threat assessment: An exploration and suggested typology. *Behavioral Sciences and the Law*, 30(3), pp. 256–279.

Meloy, J. R., Sheridan, L., & Hoffman, J. (2008). Public figure stalking, threats, and attacks: The state of the science. In J. R. Meloy, L. Sheridan, & J. Hoffman (Eds.), *Stalking, threatening, and attacking public figures* (pp. 3–34). New York: Oxford University Press.

Miron, M., & Douglas, J. (1979). Threat analysis: The psycholinguistic approach. *FBI Law Enforcement Bulletin*, September, 5–9.

Mohandie, K. (2000). *School violence threat management*. San Diego, CA: Specialized Training Services.

Mohandie, K., & Duffy, J. (1999). First responder and negotiation guidelines with the paranoid schizophrenic subject. *FBI Law Enforcement Bulletin*, December, 8–16.

Monahan, J., Steadman, H., Silver, E., Appelbaum, P., Robbins, P., Mulvey, E., ... Banks, S. (2001). *Rethinking risk assessment: The MacArthur study of mental disorder and violence*. New York: Oxford University Press.

Napier, M., & Mardigian, S. (2003). Threatening messages: The essence of analyzing communicated threats. *Public Venue Security*, September/October, 16–19.

Newman, M. L., Pennebaker, J. W., Berry, D. S., & Richards, J. M. (2003). Lying words: Predicting deception from linguistic styles. *Personality and Social Psychology Bulletin*, 29(5), 665–675.

Nickerson, R. S. (1998). Confirmation bias: A ubiquitous phenomenon in many guises. *Review of General Psychology*, 2(2), 175–220.

O'Toole, M. E. (2000). *The school shooter: A threat assessment perspective*. Quantico, VA: Critical Incident Response Group, FBI Academy, National Center for the Analysis of Violent Crime.

Palarea, R., Zona, M., Lane, J., & Langhinrichsen-Rohlin, J. (1999). The dangerous nature of intimate relationship stalking: Threats, violence, and associated risk factors. *Behavioral Sciences and the Law*, 17, 269–283.

Parker, T., Shaw, E., Stroz, E., Devost, M. G., & Sachs, M. H. (2004). *Cyber adversary characterization: Auditing the hacker mind*. Rockland, MA: Syngress Publishing.

Pennebaker, J. W. (2011). *The secret life of pronouns: What our words say about us*. New York: Bloomsbury Press.

Rabon, D. (1996). *Investigative Discourse Analysis*. Durham, NC: Carolina Academic Press.

Randazzo, M., & Plummer, E. (2009). *Implementing behavioral threat assessment on campus: A Virginia Tech demonstration project*. Blacksburg: Virginia Polytechnic Institute and State University.

Robbins, D. (2012, May 17). White powder costs millions in first response. Associated Press. Available at: http://www.bigstory.ap.org.

Rudacille, W. C. (1994). *Identifying lies in disguise*. Dubuque, IO: Kendall/Hunt.

Rugala, E., & Fitzgerald, J. R. (2003). Workplace violence: From threat to intervention. *Clinics in Occupational and Environmental Medicine*, 3, 775–789.

Saathoff, G., Defrancisco, G., Benedek, D., Everett, A., Holstege, C. P., Johnson, S. C., ... White, J. C. (2010). Report of the expert behavioral analysis panel. Available at: http://www.dcd.uscourts.gov/dcd/sites/dcd/files/unsealedDoc031011.pdf.

Sapir, A. (1987). *Scientific content analysis*. Phoenix, AZ: Laboratory for Scientific Interrogation.

Scalora, M., Baumgartner, J., Zimmerman, W., Callaway, D., Mailletteer, M., Covell, C., ... Washington, D. O. (2002a). Risk factors for approach behavior toward the U.S. Congress. *Journal of Threat Assessment*, 2, 35–55.

Scalora, M., Baumgartner, J., Zimmerman, W., Callaway, D., Mailllette, M., Covell, C., ... Washington, D. O. (2002b). An epidemiological assessment of problematic contacts to Members of Congress. *Journal of Forensic Sciences*, 4(6), 1360–1364.

Schoeneman-Morris, K., Scalora, M., Chang, G., Zimmerman, W., & Garner, Y. (2007). A comparison of email versus letter threat contacts toward members of the United States Congress. *Journal of Forensic Sciences, 52*, 1142–1147.

Schoeneman, K., Scalora, M., Darrow, C., McLawsen, J., Chang, G., & Zimmerman, W. (2011). Written content indicators of problematic approach behavior toward political officials. *Behavioral Sciences and the Law, 29*, 284–301.

Smith, S. (2008). From violent words to violent deeds: Assessing risk from FBI threatening communication cases. In Meloy, J. R., Sheridan, L., & Hoffman, J. (Eds.), *Stalking, threatening, and attacking public figures* (pp. 435–455). New York: Oxford University Press.

Smith, S., & Shuy, R. (2002). Forensic psycholinguistics: Using language analysis for identifying and assessing offenders. *FBI Law Enforcement Bulletin*, April, 16–21.

Tjaden, P., & Thoennes, N. (1998). *Prevalence, incidence, and consequences of violence against women: Findings from the National Violence against Women survey.* Washington, DC: Department of Justice, National Institute of Justice, and Center for Disease Control.

Tunkel, R. (2002) Bomb threat assessments. *FBI Law Enforcement Bulletin*, October, 6–7.

Turner, J., & Gelles, M. (2003). *Threat assessment: A risk management approach.* Binghamton, NY: Haworth Press.

Van Dreal, J., & Speckmaier, M. (2011). Level 2 student threat assessment team operations. In J. Van Dreal (Ed.), *Assessing student threats: A handbook for implementing the Salem-Keizer system* (pp. 93–98). Lanham, MD: Rowman & Littlefield.

Vossekuil, B., Fein, R., Reddy, M., Borum, R., & Modzeleski, W. (2002). *The Final Report and Findings of the Safe School Initiative: Implications for the Prevention of School Attacks in the United States.* Washington, DC: U.S. Department of Education, Office of Elementary and Secondary Education, Safe and Drug-Free Schools Program and U.S. Secret Service, National Threat Assessment Center.

13

Electronic Threats and Harassment

MARIO J. SCALORA

The Internet has had a pervasive and comprehensive impact across all levels of society, transforming the daily activities of millions of individuals who access it. The Internet and other computer-mediated communication technology (e.g., Twitter posts, texting) have become increasingly important in many facets of life, especially related to instantaneous communication and social interaction. With this technology's global span, users encounter an unlimited number of opportunities for social networking and developing personal and professional networks almost instantaneously. Such opportunities exist at all hours of the day and night, far outnumbering comparable offline opportunities. These technologies—with their vast volume of users and an almost endless supply of potential victims—also provide a new venue for criminal activities such as cyberstalking.

The National Institute of Justice (2012) defines cyberstalking as the use of technology to stalk victims. In general, for most criminal activities, a victim and offender must converge in physical proximity in time and space to produce an elevated risk of victimization. However, contrary to this premise, the physical intersection in time and space of the victim and offender is not a necessary element in creating opportunities for online victimization. Anyone with access to the Internet can cheaply and easily deliver messages to a target group as well as interact with other like-minded individuals within a range of formats. Given the relative ease of dissemination, these electronic media sources are fertile ground for the proliferation of harassing and threatening messages (Allen et al., 2009; Matusitz and O'Hair, 2008). In some cases, these communications can be utilized to recruit disenchanted individuals who are open to violent or disruptive ideologies (Blazak 2001; Moghaddam, 2005). In the case of less extreme behavior, Internet communications have also facilitated the growing issue of cyberstalking and harassment across an array of venues. The purpose of this chapter is to detail various aspects of cyberstalking and harassment activity, including the psychological and behavioral aspects of such behavior that differentiate it from other forms of stalking and harassment typically encountered by threat assessment professionals. In addition, a review of the relevant threat assessment literature and its application to the growing presence of computer-mediated communications will follow.

LIMITED RESEARCH

Despite the pervasive impact of Internet-based communications, research in this area has been limited. However, early research noted the nature of aggression in computer and electronic interactions. Wallace (1999) asserted that online behavior is mediated by numerous features, including the degree of perceived anonymity, which leads to increased disinhibition and lowered behavioral constraints. Wallace also noted that such behavior was facilitated by the perceived absence of any monitoring and managing of inappropriate behavior as well as the ease of finding like-minded persons with common interests, which may reinforce inappropriate beliefs or behavior. Early research showed that electronic communications (e.g., via email or Internet postings) contained a higher level of aggressive language—as indicated by name-calling, swearing, insults, and hostile comments—than communications taking place in face-to-face exchanges (e.g., Kiesler & Sproull, 1986). Additional research found that online aggressiveness was more likely if members were involved in group forums as opposed to private email (Thompsen & Ahn, 1992). Research has also found that anonymity (whether actual or perceived) contributes to increased aggressive language as a result of lowered inhibition (e.g., Siegel, Dubrovsky, Kiesler, & McGuire, 1986). In addition, the ease of quick replying may contribute to verbally aggressive language (Wallace, 1999).

EPIDEMIOLOGY

Cyberstalking and harassment obviously take place within the broader context of other stalking and harassment behavior. Tjaden and Theonnes' (1998) large-scale epidemiological study of stalking estimated that approximately 1.4 million men and women are stalked annually in the United States, with lifetime prevalence ranging from 2% of men to 8% of women. More recently, Baum, Catalano, Rand and Rose (2009) surveyed over 65,000 adults aged 18 and over in the United States. Based on their results, the researchers estimated that approximately 3.4 million Americans were stalked in the preceding 12 months and an additional 2.4 million who did not meet the fear standard were harassed. Research indicates that although purely online stalking is infrequent, computer-mediated communications are frequently used in the course of general stalking (Alexy, Burgess, Baker, & Smoyak, 2005; Sheridan & Grant, 2007; Spitzberg & Hoobler, 2002; Baum et al., 2009). In fact, Baum et al. (2009) found that approximately one-fourth of victims reported experiencing cyberstalking or electronic monitoring, predominantly through email and instant messaging technologies. Concerning prevalence, the National Intimate Partner and Sexual Violence Survey (2010) indicated that 12.9% of female and 12.3% of male stalking victims surveyed experienced unwanted emails or messages. Finn's (2004) study of 339 college students found that approximately 10% to 15% of students reported receiving repeated email or Instant Messenger messages that "threatened, insulted, or harassed," and more than half of the students received unwanted pornography. Such messages originated from a variety of sources, including strangers, acquaintances, and significant others.

SOCIAL NETWORKING

During the last decade, one form of computer-mediated communications, namely social networking sites (SNSs) such as Facebook, have woven their way into our global social fabric. While sharing many features with existing computer-mediated communications (e.g., email, instant messaging, and blogging), SNSs are unique in their integration of these features on individualized pages ("profiles") that publish the user's personal information and activities. Although this creates a valuable social networking and communication tool, SNSs also have various features that leave them vulnerable to abuse. To start, research indicates that users disclose a substantial amount of personal information on SNSs (Tufekci, 2008; Kolek & Saunders, 2008). Likewise, their integrated communications modalities are not necessarily separated from the information-seeking and monitoring features. Further, since the major SNSs (Linked In, Facebook) have existed only briefly, the creation of social norms for mediating appropriate use is still in progress. Because of these qualities as well as the risks associated with computer-mediated communications in general (e.g., anonymity), users of SNSs face a potentially heightened risk of harassment and stalking despite the attraction of their integrated communication and information access capabilities.

Another computer-mediated communication that has exploded in its use is the highly interactive Twitter. Twitter posts (Tweets)— given their significant increase in use —have come to the recent attention of threat assessment professionals for a variety of reasons. Because of the spontaneous nature of their communication, Tweets heighten the perception of users' availability to the audience. As with other computer-mediated communications, such posts are also likely to draw emotional and threatening language. While preliminary unpublished data collected by this author indicate that threatening language within Tweets is not likely predictive of approach unless coupled with other activity/contacts, the prevalence of such communications still poses significant challenges to threat assessment professionals. One such challenge involves the practice of retweeting/forwarding tweets to share information or encourage others' reactions.

While the increased presence of computer-mediated communications related to cyberstalking and harassment is undeniable, a review of the relevant threat assessment and targeted violence literature is worthwhile to guide threat assessment and management efforts.

RELEVANT THREAT ASSESSMENT AND TARGETED VIOLENCE LITERATURE

Stalking and harassment are known for courses of conduct that are not restricted to any single behavior. Victims frequently portray their perpetrators' pursuits as encompassing a range of distressing behaviors. Research estimates that about three fourths of stalkers use multiple methods to communicate with or harass their targets (Mohandie, Meloy, McGowan, & Williams, 2006; Mullen, Pathé, Purcell, & Stuart, 1999); and between two thirds and half of victims report being subjected to at least one unwanted behavior each week (Baum et al., 2009; Mohandie et al., 2006). Additionally, a review of 1,005 case files from law enforcement and security agencies has revealed that 37% of stalking cases evidence escalation (Mohandie et al., 2006).

Relevant to computer-mediated communications, a significant number of stalking cases involve a considerable amount of direct and indirect communication with the victim. Spitzberg (2002) described *mediated contacts* as those communications that occur through technological or indirect means (e.g., email, telephone, Internet, etc.). In a meta-analysis of over one hundred stalking studies (before 2002), Spitzberg (2002) found that over 25% of cases involved electronic contact with the victim. Similarly, a large national victimization study of stalking in the United States revealed that two thirds of victims reported unwanted telephone calls and one third reported mail (traditional or electronic) from their pursuers (Baum et al., 2009). Meta-analytic and case study approaches estimate that between a half and two thirds of stalking cases exhibit physical approach of the target (Spitzberg, 2002; Mohandie et al., 2006). Perpetrators intruded on the victims' interactions with others in 28% of cases (Spitzberg, 2002).

Among a range of behaviors that can occur as a result of stalking behavior, Spitzberg and Cupach (2007) described hyperintimate behaviors that may typically occur during courtship (e.g., ingratiation, bids for relationship escalation, etc.) that are taken to excessive levels. Often these behaviors reflect boundary violations because of their intensity or inappropriateness in the context of the relationship. Across studies, over half of cases, on average, involved exaggerated expressions of affection (Spitzberg, 2002). Likewise, between one fifth and one fourth of cases, on average, evidenced sexualized behavior and ingratiation, while more than 40% included bids for relationship escalation (Spitzberg, 2002). Large-scale studies of victim and police reports have found that packages and/or gifts were received in 12% of cases (Mohandie et al., 2006; Baum et al., 2009). Finally, in over 40% of cases investigated by security and law enforcement personnel, expressions of love and/or desire for a relationship constituted the predominant content of communications (Mohandie et al., 2006).

Surveillance behaviors involve attempts to either overtly or covertly seek information and/or monitor the target. Research indicates that in approximately one third of cases perpetrators engage in physical following, lying in wait, or watching (Spitzberg, 2002; Baum et. al., 2009). Mohandie et al. (2006) found that half of stalking cases obtained from law enforcement/security agencies exhibited some degree of surveillance-type behaviors, but less than 10% obtained private information. Less is known about the use of multimedia and Internet technologies to monitor victims, since these behaviors can be done without the victim's knowledge. Only 7.8% of a large national sample of stalking victims reported being monitored by electronic equipment such as video cameras and global positioning systems (Baum et al., 2009). This figure is likely higher at present.

Spitzberg and Cupach (2007) described invasion behaviors that violate normatively prescribed personal and legal boundaries, such as the theft of information, breaking and entering into a person's premises, and trespassing. In his meta-analytic research, Spitzberg (2002) found that approximately one quarter of cases involved invasion-type behaviors. For example, 29% of cases, on average, included information theft (Spitzberg, 2002). Finally, Baum et al. (2009) indicated that over half of victims surveyed reported some degree of interference with their financial accounts.

In addition to threatening activity, harassment and intimidation can be understood as encompassing a variety of socially aggressive tactics to annoy, bother, or otherwise distress a target. These behaviors can include attempts to sully the reputation of another through rumors, irritatingly persistent low-level behaviors (e.g., defamatory or insulting website or SNS posts), and socially aggressive behaviors that do not reach the level of threat or violence. Among a large national sample of stalking victims, over 35% reported that their perpetrators spread rumors about them (Baum et al., 2009), with 31% of studies, on average, reporting such reputational harassment (Spitzberg, 2002).

Within the stalking literature, persistent activity may signify a risk for future violence. For example, an examination of campus attacks revealed that approximately one third of subjects had come to the attention of others, including law enforcement, and nearly one fifth had engaged in stalking behaviors prior to the violent incident (Drysdale, Modzeleski, & Simons, 2010). Finally, persistent cases without violence can still cause a considerable amount of social and emotional harm to victims. In this regard, early identification and appropriate intervention could aid campus security personnel in effectively managing problematic cases before significant economic, social, emotional, or physical harm occurs.

Given the range of problematic behaviors described above, the presence of threats within stalking and harassment remains an area of concern. Estimates of the occurrence of threats in stalking cases range between 30% and 60% (Spitzberg, 2002; Baum et al., 2009; Mohandie et al., 2006; McEwan, Mullen, & Purcell, 2007). Based on over a thousand cases, Mohandie et al. (2006) found that perpetrators expressed an average of five threats—with a range from one to one hundred. Using a large sample of victims from a national telephone survey, Baum et al. (2009) found that 43% of perpetrators expressed one or more threats of violence to their victims. More often threats appear to be direct (73%) and expressed to the target, but nearly one fourth are made to the targets' close contacts, family, or friends (Mohandie et al., 2006). Research has found that threats are less characteristic of public figure stalkers (Mohandie et al., 2006) and more characteristic of the rejected relational subgroup of stalkers (MacKenzie, James, McEwan, Mullen, & Ogloff, 2010).

A prior intimate relationship between the stalker and victim has been consistently shown to positively correlate with higher rates of violence (Harmon, Rosner, & Owens, 1998; James & Farnham, 2003; McEwan et al., 2009; Meloy & Boyd, 2003; Meloy, Davis, & Lovette, 2001; Meloy, 2001; Mohandie et. al., 2006; Morrison, 2008; Mullen, Pathé, & Purcell, 2000; Sheridan & Davies, 2001; Thomas, Purcell, Pathé, & Mullen, 2008). One study demonstrated that a prior intimate relationship alone predicted violence toward both persons and property with a 90% sensitivity and 97% specificity (Meloy, Davis, & Lovette, 2001). While most incidents of violence within stalking appear to be minor, James and Farnham (2003) found that prior intimate relationships were also associated with more serious forms of stalking-related violence. In fact, ex-intimate partner stalkers were substantially more likely to have engaged in stalking-related homicide (James & Farnham, 2003).

Within the threat assessment literature, one of the major predictive factors for problematic approach is intensity of effort (Meloy, 2011). Intensity of effort is usually measured by frequency of contact, duration of contact, multiple means of contact, and multiple contacts with other figures (target dispersion), and is associated in the research with the presence of serious mental disorder (James et al., 2008; Scalora et al., 2002b). Research on targeted violence and stalking suggests that physical approach may escalate risk owing to proximity to the victim (Scalora et al., 2002a,b; 2003; James et al., 2010, 2011). Given the ease of physical approach in the community setting, persistence may be better demonstrated by multiple approaches or communication with a target. Similarly, physical following and multiple methods of contact are qualities frequently associated with the persistent pursuit of stalkers (Marquez & Scalora, 2011; Mullen et al., 2009). As will be explained further, in assessing the presence of computer-mediated communications, the presence of electronic communications related to cyberstalking and harassment should be evaluated with the other behaviors and communications of concern from the subject. As indicated above, electronic communications are rarely the sole mode of threatening or harassing behavior of concern within a problematic campaign of this sort.

On a related note, a warning behavior that carries significant importance from an operational perspective is "leakage" of intent to harm a target, whether vague or specific, to third parties (Meloy and O'Toole, 2011). Leakage is one of the warning behaviors noted earlier and is characteristic of both assassins of public figures and mass murderers (Meloy et al., 2004). Leakage is also evident in communications to third parties and electronically via the Internet. An operational implication in evaluating electronic communications of concern is to search additional Internet sources for potential leakage of planning or intent to do harm. Particularly with younger subjects of concern who are adept with electronic communication, checking personal websites or social network pages enables searching for recent activity, declarations, or shifts in emotions. As suggested by the literature summarized in this chapter, in assessing Internet postings of concern, one should look for:

- The subject of concern posting across sites and communication modes (e.g., website comments, blogs, Facebook walls, emails) pertinent to the grievance raised
- Posts escalating in their rhetoric and emotion in chronological time
- Messages/postings encouraging violence

For example, a college student reported that another student (a 21-year-old male student) made several troubling email communications with veiled threats, including "You're going to get yours," and subsequently sent a text stating, "You're a dead man." The victim reported the concerning communications to police. As part of their investigation, detectives performed an immediate search of Internet activity by the subject, which indicated that he posted a picture on his Facebook page of himself posing with a shotgun stating, "Need to take care of business," within an hour of sending the threatening text.

In another example, a subject was found to have posted across multiple websites and blogs the following (with obscenities removed), related to a public figure, over the course of three days:

- "Any violence directed at [target] would be well deserved."
- "All I have to say is F___ YOU....I hope you die you f____ bastard. I hope I can be there to watch you die slowly."
- Links to personal websites in which the subject expressed anger over difficulties in his personal life (i.e., unemployment and lack of benefits) and his perceiving the public figure as responsible.
- Subsequent posts noting intent to travel to the city where the public figure resided.

When interviewed by threat assessment professionals, the subject admitted to the postings and demonstrated his efforts to travel to confront the public figure (i.e., purchase of a rail ticket). Although he denied violent intent, the subject admitted to feeling significant anger toward the targeted public official and admitted to blaming the official for his own difficulties. The subject also admitted to having planned to angrily confront the target while armed.

McEwan and colleagues (2007) noted that even though earlier studies found a limited relationship between threats and violence, this was likely due to the heavy reliance on samples of public figure victims. Researchers have argued that threats are less likely to precede violence in public figure contexts because they can cue early intervention from law enforcement and security personnel (e.g., Meloy, 2001; Fein & Vossekuil, 1999). More recent studies examining a broader context of stalking perpetration have found positive correlations between threats and violence (Brewster, 2000; Harmon, Rosner, & Owens, 1998; James & Farnham, 2003; Meloy, Davis, & Lovette, 2001; Morrison, 2008; Roberts, 2005; Rosenfeld & Harmon, 2002; Sheridan & Davies, 2001; Sheridan & Roberts, 2011; Thomas, Purcell, Pathé, & Mullen, 2008). Evidence suggests that the relationship between threats and stalking violence is stronger for intimate partners (Brewster, 2000; McEwan et al., 2009).

Length of pursuit may also relate to risk of violent activity. McEwan and colleagues (2009) observed that the risk factors for stalking varied by the length of pursuit. Brief pursuits were more likely to involve single and young perpetrators who engaged in fewer communications. Moderate pursuits (12 weeks or more), on the other hand, were more likely to involve older, single, intimacy-seeking perpetrators who more commonly sent unsolicited material to their victims (McEwan et al., 2009). Highly persistent perpetrators were also more likely to be intimacy-seeking acquaintances and more frequently issued threats (McEwan et al., 2009). Additional research has revealed that the risk factors of persistence differ by stalking sample types and mode of measuring persistence. In particular, James et al. (2009) demonstrated that persistent communication with public figures occurred more with telephoning, whereas persistent approach occurred more with rambling and confusion but not with chaotic and resentful motivations. Both persistent communication and approach to public figures were positively associated with fixation and target dispersion (James et al., 2009). Similarly, moderately to highly persistent pursuits (based on length) in a general forensic sample of stalkers were positively associated with resentful motivation, written communications, stalking by proxy, threatening language, and being female (James et al., 2009). Written communications and threats were also associated with protracted pursuits in the forensic sample of stalkers studied by Purcell, Pathé, and Mullen (2002).

RECENT STUDIES IN ELECTRONIC THREAT AND HARASSMENT

Our targeted violence research team has performed studies involving targeted harassment or threatening activity involving electronic communications sent to political figures. Increases in media focus on congressional activities and Congress' supervision of executive activities has made politicians more visible to the public. This, alongside their greater accessibility, heightens their risk for harassment (Scalora et al., 2002a,b). As suggested above, electronic communications should be viewed in the context of all behaviors demonstrated by the subject. Even when threats are present, electronically communicating subjects are not as likely to approach *unless* communication was part of a campaign with other forms of communication (Schoeneman-Morris, Scalora, Chang, Zimmerman, and Garner, 2007; Schoeneman, Scalora, Darrow, McLawsen, Chang, & Zimmerman, 2011).

Research has also indicated that some content risk factors within communications (electronic or otherwise) predict an approach (James et al., 2007, 2008; Mullen et al., 2009; Schoeneman-Morris, Scalora, Chang, Zimmerman, & Garner, 2007), including:

- Personalized motive (e.g., request for assistance, addressing a personal grievance)
- Expressing intent or plans to approach
- Language regarding justified violence tied to above

Schoeneman-Morris, Scalora, Chang, Zimmerman, and Garner (2007) compared 301 cases involving written letters and 99 cases involving emails directed to members of the US Congress. They found that letter writers were more likely than emailers to show indicators of serious mental illness, to contact multiple targets, and to use multiple methods of contact aside from writing letters (e.g., telephone calls, faxing, etc.). Letter writers were also found to be more likely to engage in problematic approach behavior toward their target than were emailers. Emailers were more likely than letter

writers to focus their correspondence on government concerns, to display disorganization in their writing, and to use obscene language. Emailers tended to be focused on one governmental issue and one target and appeared to spend less overall effort on their contact behaviors. Letter writers presented as less rational and more willing to put a lot of effort behind their contact behaviors. Letter writers were also found more likely to be engaging in higher-risk behaviors, or behaviors that have been shown in the research to be risk factors for problematic approach. In summary, the presence of electronic communication was not predictive of approach unless communication was part of a campaign with other forms of communication.

In a related study, Schoeneman, Scalora, Darrow, McLawsen, Chang, and Zimmerman (2011) again compared letter writers and emailers to determine whether these two groups were associated with differential risk factors for engaging in problematic approach behavior toward their targets. In their analyses of 326 letter writers and 120 emailers, these investigators found some differences and some similarities in the factors related to future approach. Both letter writers and emailers who approached their targets were more likely than their corresponding non-approachers to exhibit indicators of serious mental illness and threat-control override symptoms, to engage in prior contact with the target, and to use multiple methods of contact other than letter writing. The authors also found that letter writing and emailing approachers were more likely to emphasize personal themes (e.g., help seeking, entitlement claims, etc.) and to have made significantly more contacts with their targets overall. In contrast, letter writers and emailers who approached were more likely than letter writers who did not approach to show evidence of agitation and to make demands in their correspondence and less likely to focus on target-oriented themes (e.g., insulting, degrading, racist, sexist language, etc.). This study further demonstrates that the risk factors for approach found in letter-writing and emailing subjects are consistent with the previous literature that identified risk factors for all contactors without segregating cases by method of contact.

In an effort to assess the influence and presence of extremist rhetoric in threatening and harassing communications toward politicians, Cacialli (2011) examined sample of 506 individuals who engaged in threatening or otherwise inappropriate contact with members of the US Congress. It was hypothesized that significant predictors of problematic approach behavior would include (1) similarity between inappropriate contact with politicians and extremist group literature and writings, (2) the temporal proximity to violent or otherwise criminal actions and notable anniversaries of such groups, (3) detailed specification of a plan to engage in problematic approach behavior, and (4) self-focus. The results indicated that a detailed specification of a plan to engage in problematic approach behavior was strongly predictive of actually engaging in problematic approach. Furthermore, high self-focus was significantly related to problematic approach between persons. Neither temporal proximity to notable acts of extremist violence nor similarity to known extremist group writings was found to be associated with problematic approach in this sample.

CONCLUSION

The research is slow to catch up with the rapidly evolving and accessible electronic communication media. While the exploding array of computer-mediated communications allow for instantaneous outreach and networking, they also provide newer opportunities for threatening and harassing behavior, including that from individuals with more extremist views and related grievances. Further, because such computer-mediated communications often occur within multiple platforms that are often viewed by audiences and within interactive contexts, the threatening content sometimes found therein may result in an inordinate amount of concern relative to other communications. Although preliminary research findings suggest that such electronically mediated communications are more likely to contain threatening content that is often shared with a wider audience, such communications *alone* are not predictive of problematic approaches. However, the caution that all threats must be taken seriously still applies, given that the presence of threatening and near threatening activity is related to disruptive and violent activity (Fein & Vossekuil, 1999; Meloy, 2011). To guide threat assessment and management activity, the research to date suggests that threat assessment professionals should focus on the pattern and nature as opposed to the modality of communications in assessing the risk entailed by threatening and harassing electronic communications. The nature and pattern of contacts must also be evaluated in the context of how the

correspondence relates to other contact behaviors as part of a *chain of events signaling intent from ideation to action*. Rarely does the content in a single piece of correspondence alone signal approach behavior in the case of a person with a persistent grievance toward a target. In other words, all communications should be evaluated within the behavioral context of the campaign of communications, with particular attention to the following:

- The pattern of communications, particularly if indicative of an escalation of language pertinent to the grievance displayed
- Intensity of effort as measured by frequency of contact, duration of contact, multiple means of contact, and target dispersion
- Intensity of focus upon a specific target across the campaign of communications
- Potential leakage of intentions of harm or plans of harmful activity either in communications to the target or to third parties (e.g., via various computer-mediated communications)
- The presence of relevant content factors (including, for example, personalized motive, expressing intent or plans to approach, and language regarding justified violence)

Despite the guidance offered by the preliminary data, additional research is necessary to assist threat assessment and management efforts in response to the growing impact of computer-mediated communications. Research is still needed to continue to assess the predictive value of risk factors for problematic approach pertaining to the range of communication strategies (e.g., SNS activity, blog postings, Twitter postings). Given the lack of face-to-face contact with such electronic communications, the question arises as to whether more persons suffering from mental illness will access such platforms to ventilate and promote their grievances. Continued focus is also necessary to investigate the impact of extremist rhetoric justifying and encouraging violent activity. Computer-mediated communications continue to provide an easily accessible platform for a growing array of disenchanted and disgruntled individuals. Given the highly interactive and public nature of such electronic communications, additional research is needed to assess whether such electronic purveyance of extremist rhetoric may incite or facilitate the violent actions of others.

KEY POINTS

- Electronic communications are significantly impacting the nature of harassing and stalking behavior confronted by threat assessment professionals.
- Although more research is needed, threat assessment professionals should focus on the pattern and nature rather than the modality of communication in assessing the risk entailed with threatening and harassing electronic communications.
- The available research suggests that electronic communications in isolation from other contact behavior and activity do not predict problematic approach or violent behavior.
- Therefore, all communications should be evaluated within a behavioral context of the campaign of contact behaviors, including:
  - The pattern of communications
  - Intensity of effort
  - Intensity of focus upon a specific target
  - Potential leakage of intentions
  - Presence of relevant content language predictive of approach activity

REFERENCES

Allen M., Angie, A., Davis, J., Connelly, S., Mumford, M., & O'Hair, H. D. (2009). Virtual risk: The role of new media in violent and nonviolent ideological groups. In & R. Heath & H. D. O'Hair (Eds.), *Handbook of risk and crisis communication* (pp. 446–470). New York: Routledge.

Alexy, E. M., Burgess, A. W., Baker, T., & Smoyak, S. A. (2005). Perceptions of cyberstalking among college students. *Brief Treatment and Crisis Intervention, 5*(3), 279–289.

Baum, K., Catalano, S., Rand, M., & Rose, K. (2009). *Stalking victimization in the United States* (Report No. 224527).Washington, DC: United States Department of Justice, Bureau of Justice Statistics.

Blazak, R. (2001). White boys to terrorist men: Target recruitment of Nazi skinheads. *American Behavioral Scientist, 44*(6), 982–1000.

Brewster, M. P. (2000). Stalking by former intimates: Verbal threats and other predictors of physical violence. *Violence & Victims, 15*(1), 41–54.

Cacialli, D. O. (2011). Predicting problematic approach behavior toward politicians: Exploring the potential contributions of control theory. *Dissertation Abstracts International: Section B: The Sciences and Engineering, 71*(9-B), 5782. (UMI No. AAI3412850)

Drysdale, D., Modzeleski, W., and Simons, A. (2010). *Campus attacks: Targeted violence affecting institutions of higher education.* U.S. Secret Service, U.S. Department of Homeland Security, Office of Safe and Drug-Free Schools, U.S. Department of Education, and Federal Bureau of Investigation. Available at: http://www.ed.gov/admins/lead/safety/campus-attacks.pdf

Fein, R. A., & Vossekuil, B. (1999). Assassination in the United States: An operational study of recent assassins, attackers, and near-lethal approachers. *Journal of Forensic Sciences, 44*, 321–333.

Finn, J. (2004). A survey of online harassment at a university campus. *Journal of Interpersonal Violence, 19*(4), 468–483. doi:10.1177/0886260503262083

Harmon, R. B., Rosner, R., & Owens, H. (1998). Sex and violence in a forensic population of obsessional harassers. *Psychology, Public Policy, and Law, 4*(1/2), 236–249.

James, D., & Farnham, F. R. (2003). Stalking and serious violence. *Journal of the American Academy of Psychiatry & the Law, 31*, 432–439.

James, D. V., McEwan, T. E., MacKenzie, R. D., Meloy, J. R., Mullen, P.E., Pathé, M. T.…Darnley, B. J. (2010). Persistence in stalking: A comparison of associations in general forensic and public figure samples. *The Journal of Forensic Psychiatry & Psychology, 21*(2), 283–305.

James, D. V., Mullen, P. E., Meloy, J. R., Pathé, M. T., Farnham, F. R., Preston, L., & Darnley, B. (2007). The role of mental disorder in attacks on European politicians 1990-2004. *Acta Psychiatrica Scandinavica, 116*(5), 334–344.

James, D. V., Mullen, P. E., Meloy, J. R., Pathé, M. T., Preston, L., Darnley, B.,…Scalora, M. J. (2011). Stalkers and harassers of British royalty: An exploration of proxy behaviours for violence. *Behavioral Sciences & the Law, 29*(1), 64–80.

James, D. V., Mullen, P. E., Pathé, M. T., Meloy, J. R., Farnham, F. R., Preston, L., & Darnley, B. (2008). Attacks on the British royal family: The role of psychotic illness. *Journal of the American Academy of Psychiatry and the Law, 36*(1), 59–67.

Kiesler, S., & Sproull, L. S. (1986). Response effects in the electronic survey. *Public Opinion Quarterly, 50*, 402–413.

Kolek, E.A., & Saunders, D. (2008). Online disclosure: An empirical examination of undergraduate Facebook profiles. *NASPA Journal, 45*(1), 1–25.

MacKenzie, R. D., James, D. V., McEwan, T. E., Mullen, P. E., Ogloff, J.R.P. (2010). Stalkers and intelligence: Implications for treatment. *Journal of Forensic Psychiatry & Psychology, 21*(6), 852–872.

Marquez, A., & Scalora, M. J. (2011). Problematic approach of legislators: Differentiating stalking from isolated incidents. *Criminal Justice and Behavior, 38*(11), 1115–1126.

Matusitz, J., & O'Hair, H. D. (2008). The Internet and terrorist networks. In D. O'Hair, R. Heath, K.

Ayotte, & J. Ledlow (Eds.), *Terrorism: Communication and rhetorical perspective* (pp. 383–407). Cresskill, NJ: Hampton Press.

McEwan, T. E., Mullen, P. E., & MacKenzie, R. (2009). A study of the predictors of persistence in stalking situations. *Law and Human Behavior, 33*(2), 149–158.

McEwan, T. E., Mullen, P. E., MacKenzie, R. D., & Ogloff, J.R.P. (2009). Violence in stalking situations. *Psychological Medicine, 39,* 1469–1478.

McEwan, T. E., Mullen, P. E., & Purcell, R. (2007). Identifying risk factors in stalking: A review of current research. *International Journal of Law and Psychiatry, 30,* 1–9.

Meloy, J. R. (2001). Communicated threats and violence toward public and private targets: Discerning differences among those who stalk and attack. *Journal of Forensic Sciences, 46*(5), 1211–1213.

Meloy, J. R. (2011). Approaching and attacking public figures: A contemporary analysis of communications and behavior. In C. Chauvin & Board on Behavioral, Cognitive, and Sensory Sciences (Eds.), *Threatening communications and behavior: Perspectives on the pursuit of public figures* (pp. 75–101). Washington, DC: National Academies Press.

Meloy, J. R., & Boyd, C. (2003). Female stalkers and their victims. *Journal of the American Academy of Psychiatry & the Law, 31,* 211–219.

Meloy, J. R., Davis, B., & Lovette, J. (2001). Risk factors for violence among stalkers. *Journal of Threat Assessment, 1*(1), 3–16.

Meloy, J. R., Hempel, A. G., Gray, B. T., Mohandie, K., Shiva, A., & Richards, T. C. (2004). A comparative analysis of North American adolescent and adult mass murderers. *Behavioral Sciences & the Law, 22*(3), 291–309.

Meloy, J. R., & O'Toole, M. E. (2011). The concept of leakage in threat assessment. *Behavioral Sciences & the Law, 29*(4), 513–527.

Moghaddam, F. M. (2005). The staircase to terrorism: A psychological exploration. *American Psychologist, 60*(2), 161–169.

Mohandie, K., Meloy, J. R., Green-McGowan, M., & Williams, J. (2006). The RECON typology of stalking: Reliability and validity based upon a large sample of North American stalkers. *Journal of Forensic Sciences, 51*(1), 147–155.

Morrison, K. (2008). Differentiating between physically violent and nonviolent stalkers: An examination of Canadian cases. *Journal of Forensic Sciences, 53*(3), 742–751.

Mullen, P. E., James, D. V., Meloy, J. R., Pathé, M. T., Farnham, F. R., Preston, L., ... Berman, J. (2009). The fixated and the pursuit of public figures. *Journal of Forensic Psychiatry & Psychology, 20*(1), 33–47.

Mullen, P. E., Pathé, M., & Purcell, R. (2000). *Stalkers and their victims.* Cambridge, UK: Cambridge University Press.

Mullen, P. E., Pathé, M., Purcell, R., & Stuart, G. W. (1999). Study of stalkers. *American Journal of Psychiatry, 156,* 1244–1249.

Purcell, R., Pathé, M., & Mullen, P. E. (2002). The incidence and nature of stalking in the Australian community. *Australian and New Zealand Journal of Psychiatry, 36*(1), 114–120.

Roberts, K. A. (2005). Women's experience of violence during stalking by former romantic partners. *Violence Against Women, 11*(1), 89–114.

Rosenfeld, B., & Harmon, R. (2002). Factors associated with violence in stalking and obsessional harassment cases. *Criminal Justice and Behavior, 29*(6), 671–691.

Scalora, M. J., Baumgartner, J. V., Zimmerman, W., Callaway, D., Hatch Maillette, M. A., Covell, C. N ... Washington, D. O.(2002a). An epidemiological assessment of problematic contacts to members of Congress. *Journal of Forensic Sciences, 47,* 1360–1364.

Scalora, M. J., Baumgartner, J. V., Zimmerman, W., Callaway, D., Hatch Maillette, M. A., Covell, C. N ... Washington, D. O. (2002b). Risk factors for approach behavior toward the U.S Congress. *Journal of Threat Assessment, 2*(2), 35–55.

Schoeneman, K. A., Scalora, M. J., Darrow, C. D., McLawsen, J. E., Chang, G. H., & Zimmerman, W. J. (2011). Written content indicators of problematic approach behavior toward political officials. *Behavioral Sciences & the Law, 29*(2), 284–301.

Schoeneman-Morris, K. A., Scalora, M. J., Chang, G. H., Zimmerman, W. J., & Garner, Y. (2007). A comparison of email versus letter threat contacts toward members of the United States Congress. *Journal of Forensic Sciences, 52* (5), 1142–1147.

Sheridan, L., & Davies, G. M. (2001). Violence and the prior victim-stalker relationship. *Criminal Behaviour and Mental Health, 11,* 102–116.

Sheridan, L. P., & Grant, T. (2007). Is cyberstalking different? *Psychology, Crime & Law, 13*(6), 627–640.

Sheridan, L., & Roberts, K. (2011). Key questions to consider in stalking cases. *Behavioral Sciences & the Law, 29*(2), 255–270.

Siegel, J., Dubrovsky, V., Kiesler, S., & McGuire, T. (1986). Group processes in computer-mediated communications. *Organizational Behavior and Human Decision Processes, 37,* 157–187.

Spitzberg, B. H. (2002). The tactical topography of stalking victimization and management. *Trauma, Violence, and Abuse, 3,* 261–288.

Spitzberg, B. H., & Cupach, W. R. (2007). The state of the art of stalking: Taking stock of the emerging literature. *Aggression and Violent Behavior, 12,* 64–86.

Spitzberg, B. H., & Hoobler, G. (2002). Cyberstalking and the technologies of interpersonal terrorism. *New Media & Society, 4*(1), 71–92.

Thomas, S.D.M., Purcell, R., Pathé, M., & Mullen, P. E. (2008). Harm associated with stalking victimization. *Australian and New Zealand Journal of Psychiatry, 42,* 800–806.

Thompsen, P. A., & Ahn, D. (1992). To be or not to be: An exploration of E-prime, copula deletion and flaming in electronic mail. *Et Cetera: A Review of General Semantics, 49,* 146–164.

Tjaden, P., & Thoennes, N. (1998). *Stalking in America: Findings from the national violence against women survey* (Report No. 169592). Washington, DC: National Institute of Justice and Center for Disease Control and Prevention.

Tufekci, Z. (2008). Can you see me now? Audience and disclosure regulation in online social network sites. *Bulletin of Science Technology Society, 28*(1), 20–36.

Wallace, P. (1999). *The psychology of the Internet.* New York: Cambridge University Press.

14

Computer Modeling of Violent Intent

A Content Analysis Approach

ANTONIO SANFILIPPO, LIAM MCGRATH, AND ERIC BELL

A speaker's language is the window to his intent. Diverging attitudes to the use of violence of groups or individuals who otherwise share the same ideological goals are reflected in the language communication strategies that these groups/individuals adopt in advocating the pursuit of their cause (Smith, 2011; Smith et al., 2008). The identification of language use factors that are highly correlated with a speaker's attitude to violence enables the development of computational models of violent intent. These models can help recognize violent intent in written or spoken language and forecast the likely occurrence of violent events (Sanfilippo et al. 2011) and help to identify changing communication outreach characteristics across radical groups (Sanfilippo & McGrath, 2011). The goal of this chapter is to review recent approaches to modeling violent intent based on content analysis and demonstrate how the ensuing models can be used to assess ebbs and flows of sociopolitical contention in the public dialogue. The chapter is organized into four sections. First we review some recent efforts on modeling radical rhetoric to detect and forecast violent intent. Then we focus on one of the efforts reviewed, which leverages insights from frame analysis to characterize and provide a detailed description of the approach. In the final part of the paper, we demonstrate how the frame analysis approach to modeling violent intent can be used to characterize the ebbs and flows of sociopolitical contention in social media content.

MODELING RADICAL RHETORIC TO DETECT VIOLENT INTENT

Social movements are often characterized by radical groups and individuals that, while sharing the same ideological goals, adopt opposite practices to the use of violence. For example, compare Central al Qa'ida (AQC) and al Qa'ida in the Arabian Peninsula (AQAP) with Hizb ut-Tahrir in Jordan (HuTJ) and the Movement for Islamic Reform in Arabia (MIRA). The four groups all advocate the establishment of a theocratic state ruled by Shariah law. However, while AQC and AQAP together have been implicated in over 85 attacks that have resulted in the loss of human lives, there is no evidence that HuTJ and MIRA have engaged in terrorist violence (Smith, 2011). The ability to estimate the propensity of a group or individual to engage in violent behavior is essential in establishing a framework for threat assessment that can save lives.

Several approaches have recently been developed that rely on content analysis to detect a group's or individual's propensity for violent behavior. Content analysis is a methodology in the social sciences that uses textual interpretation through categorical annotation to study the content of communication (Krippendorff, 2004). The assessment of violent intent through content analysis involves the identification of categories of meaning that are correlated with the expression of violent behavior or lack thereof. Inferences are then drawn from the occurrence of such categories in the text(s) analyzed to estimate the likelihood of the communication source to engage in violent behavior.

Categories for the analysis of violent intent can vary considerably in complexity. Pennebaker (2011) uses the occurrence of function words to characterize texts authored by terrorist groups (AQC and AQAP) as compared with nonterrorist radical groups (HuTJ, MIRA). For example, texts from terrorist communication sources contain a statistically significant higher number of personal pronouns, while texts from nonterrorist communication sources contain a statistically significant higher number of articles. Function words can also be grouped into higher-order variables, such as the variable *status*, which measures the presence of "we" words and "you" words and the absence of "I" words.

Some violent intent category schemes are shaped in terms of specific theoretical approaches to social and political analysis. Hermann and Sakiev (2011) and Walker (2011) base their analysis of violent intent on characteristics of leadership. Hermann and Sakiev evaluate leadership styles along seven dimensions—control, power, conceptual complexity, self-confidence, task orientation, distrust of others, and in-group bias—to detect terrorist rhetoric. Walker examines the violent propensity of leaders in terms of their overall political philosophies and views on how best to achieve them. For example, Walker's findings indicate that terrorists have a deterministic view of the political universe, believe that they exert greater historical control on world events, are less accepting of risk, and are more prone to choose conflict over cooperation as compared with nonterrorist groups.

Other approaches to violent intent modeling focus on communication strategies. For example, Sanfilippo et al. (2011) combine insights from frame analysis, which examines how communication sources try to influence audiences and how audiences respond and theories that explain the emergence of violence in terms of moral disengagement, the violation of sacred values, and social isolation in order to model violent intent. For example, communicative strategies that involve feelings of moral disengagement (such as hate and disgust) and focus on religion and military topics tend to be more highly correlated with texts from terrorist sources.

All the approaches reviewed above use some form of automated language analysis or text mining to annotate text with the categories that have been chosen to detect violent intent. This is a somewhat recent development. Traditionally, content analysis—where content categories are defined out of sets of words based on explicit rules of coding—has relied on manual annotation, including those analyses focusing on the assessment of violent intent (Conway et al., 2011; Smith et al., 2008; Suedfeld & Brcic, 2011; Winter, 2011). As compared with automated methods, manual annotation is less prone to error when carried out by highly trained annotators, but it tends to be less consistent, more time- and cost-intensive, and ultimately impractical with large datasets.

A COMPUTATIONAL MODELING APPROACH TO VIOLENT INTENT

Most of the approaches reviewed in the previous section, whether relying on manual or automated annotation, focus on assessing how relevant a given set of content categories is to the detection of violent intent by measuring how strongly correlated each category is with documents known to be from terrorist/nonterrorist communication sources. From an operational perspective, we are interested in using the content categories analyzed to establish whether and to what extent new communications from unknown sources express violent intent. This task can be accomplished by building a computerized classification model using the content categories that indicate violent intent to establish the violent intent potential of new communications from unknown sources. There are two main reasons for adopting a computational modeling approach. First, we need to evaluate the accuracy with which the chosen content categories help detect documents from terrorist and nonterrorist sources in a systematic fashion against large test datasets. Second, we need to enable the automatic detection of communications that express violent intent in large data streams, where manual processing is too labor-intensive to be realistically applicable. In this section we describe a computational approach to modeling violent intent that satisfies both requirements. This approach relies on the coexpression of rhetoric and action features in discourse. It combines insights from frame analysis (Benford & Snow, 2000; Entman, 2004; Gamson, 1992; Goffman, 1974) and theories that explain the emergence of violence with reference to moral disengagement (Bandura, 1999), the violation of sacred values (Tetlock et al., 2000), and social isolation (Navarro, 2009) in order to develop a predictive computational approach to radicalization and violent intent.

Frame Analysis

The objective of frame analysis is to understand the communicative and mental processes that explain how groups, individuals, and the media try to influence their target audiences and how target audiences respond. Since Goffman's initial exploration (Goffman, 1974), frame analysis has become an important analytical framework for the study of social movements. The introduction of frame analysis in social movement theories was facilitated by the renewed interest in the social psychology of collective action during the early 1980s (Gamson et al., 1982). A series of seminal papers that rebuilt Goffman's initial insights within the study of collective action and with a more solid theoretical basis (Gamson, 1988) provided the initial impetus. In the next two decades, frame analysis grew very quickly to become a main component in social movement theory (Benford & Snow, 2000; McAdam et al., 2001; Noakes & Johnston, 2005; Snow et al., 1986; Wiktorowicz, 2004).

Two main perspectives have emerged on collective action frames. Gamson (1988) focuses on social-psychological processes that explain how individuals become participants in collective action in terms of identity, agency and injustice:

- *Identity*: ascertain aggrieved group with reference to shared interests and values
- *Agency*: recognize that grieving conditions can be changed through activism
- *Injustice*: identify individuals or institution to blame for grievances

Benford and Snow (2000) concentrate on the relationship between social movement entrepreneurs and their potential constituencies as borne out through:

- *Diagnostic frame*: tell new recruits what is wrong and why
- *Prognostic frame*: present a solution to the problem suggested in the diagnosis
- *Motivational frame*: give people a reason to join collective action

Entman (2004) provides yet another characterization of collective action frames in terms of frame functions and foci:

- Substantive frame functions
  - Define effects or conditions as problematic
  - Identify causes
  - Convey moral judgment
  - Endorse remedies or improvements
- Substantive frame foci
  - Political events
  - Issues
  - Actors

Sanfilippo et al. (2007, 2008) provide an integration of these three theories of collective action frames using a natural language semantics approach based on speech act theory (Austin, 1962; Searle, 1969). Frames are analyzed as speech acts that convey a

- communicative *intent*
- identify a frame *promoter*
- may identify a frame *target*
- specify one or more *issues*

This characterization equally leverages the various ways in which collective action frames have been treated in the literature:

- The notion of a frame *promoter*, used by Benford and Snow, corresponds to the result of Gamson's *identity* frame function and overlaps with Entman's notion of *actor*.
- Communicative *intent* is implicit in the framing task classification provided by Gamson (*injustice, identity, agency*), Benford and Snow (*diagnostic, prognostic, motivational*), and Entman (*substantive frame functions*).
- Frame *target* partially overlaps with the result of Gamson's *injustice* frame function.
- The category *issues* is used by Entman.

The frame categories *intent* and *issues* are divided into subcategories to provide a clearer mapping to the existing frame notions and facilitate identification. Intent subcategories include *accept, accuse, assert, believe, correct, criticize, emphasize, explain, impute, judge, negate, reject, request, support, urge*. The issue subcategories are *economy, politics, social, law, military, administration, environment, security, religion*. For each frame category or subcategory, a specific set of guidelines is identified to reduce the level of subjective uncertainty in the assignment of frame annotations to text segments. For example, the identification of the *intent* subcategory *urge* in a text is established through the occurrence of specific word meanings from WordNet (wordnet.princeton.edu), (e.g., *urge#1, urge on#2, press#2, exhort#2*). The full communicative intent ontology comprises 15 subcategories covering some 10,000 word meanings from WordNet. The viability of the resulting annotation scheme was tested through interannotator agreement. A set of four human annotators expressing judgments about some 1,800 frame ratings achieved an average kappa score of 0.70 (see Sanfilippo et al., 2007, for further details).

Sanfilippo et al. (2007) also show how an automatic annotation process can be developed to identify frame categories in unstructured text (i.e., text that has not been previously annotated) using text mining techniques (Feldman & Sanger, 2007). This process combines a variety of language analysis capabilities including grammatical sentence analysis, named entity recognition, temporal resolution, and the assignment of appropriate domain codes to words so as to relate words (e.g., *terrorist*) to issues (e.g., *security*). A sample output of the frame extraction process described is shown in Figure 14.1. The accuracy of this automatic annotation process was measured using agreement with four human annotators (kappa score) and precision and recall metrics— see (4), (5) and (6) below and related notes for an explanation of the precision and recall metrics. The average kappa score between the automated annotator and the human annotators was 0.52. The average precision/recall (F1 measure) for frame detection was 74%. See Sanfilippo et al. (2007) for further details.

Extending Frame Analysis

Sanfilippo et al. (2008, 2011) extend the frame analysis approach to violent intent detection using theoretical insights that explain the emergence of violence as a function of moral disengagement (Bandura, 1999), the violation of sacred values (Tetlock et al., 2000), and social isolation (Navarro, 2009); they also integrate action frames germane to the emergence of protest, violence, and contention.

Moral disengagement occurs when people choose and urge others to engage in inhumane conduct (e.g., genocide) to achieve a goal believed to be morally right (e.g., the Nazi idea of racial-biological purity). Moral disengagement is expressed by communicative acts such as attributing blame to the victim and conveying hatred, disgust, and fear of the victim. The violation of sacred values occurs when ideals of love, honor, justice, and religion come under secular assault and people struggle to protect their private selves and public identities from moral contamination. The violation of sacred values is linguistically marked by the co-occurrence of military and religious terms, which signals the propensity for armed struggle under the apprehension that religious freedom is under secular attack. Within a terrorist context, social isolation results from the requirement that a recruit cut off ties to family, friends, and others who are not part of the organization. It is widely regarded as a key factor promoting radicalization (Navarro, 2009). Social isolation is marked by the occurrence of events conveying abandonment, confinement, withdrawal, and isolation.

The resulting annotation scheme, called Frames in Action (Sanfilippo et al., 2011), has 160 categories covering some 13,000 word meanings from WordNet. Events are organized in three tiers: 31 event categories linked to 120 event subcategories comprising some 4,000 verb meanings. Issues are organized into 9 categories subsuming some 8,000 word meanings. Figure 14.2 provides an abridged representation of the Frames in Action annotation scheme.

Building the Computational Model

Following Sanfilippo et al. (2011), we used the Frame in Action (FA) annotations to build a violent intent classifier that identifies messages from terrorist sources. We start with a training dataset that includes document subsets for each of the categories of interest: violent vs. nonviolent rhetoric. We then used machine learning techniques to infer a multinomial Bayesian text classifier that identifies the categories of interest in terms of the FA annotations assigned to the documents in the training dataset.

| Yesterday, khairat el-Shater blamed the group's poor performance in the parliamentary elections on the government. (UPI) - Egypt. *Saturday, December 03, 2005.* ... | ⟹ | PROMOTER
C-INTENT
TARGET
ISSUES

EVENT_DATE
PUBLISH_DATE | =
=
=
=

=
= | khairat el-Shater
CRITICIZE (blame)
government
POLITICS: 50%, LAW: 25%,
ADMINISTRATION: 25%
02/12/2005
03/12/2005 |

FIGURE 14.1 Sample input/output of the automated frame extraction process.

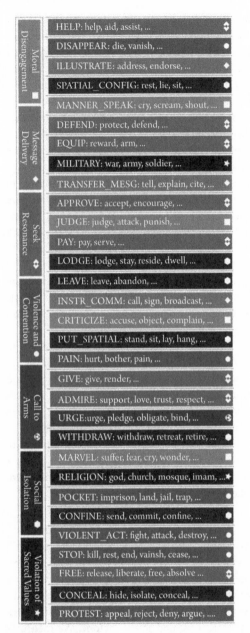

FIGURE 14.2 Partial representation of the *Frames in Action* annotation scheme.

Source: Sanfilippo, A., McGrath, L., & Whitney, P. (2011). *Violent frames in action: Dynamics of asymmetric conflict*. Reprinted by permission of Taylor & Francis, Ltd., http://www.tandf.co.uk/journals.

The training dataset includes documents authored by four groups: Central al Qa'ida (AQC), al Qa'ida in the Arabian Peninsula (AQAP), Hizb ut-Tahrir (HuT), and the Movement for Islamic Reform in Arabia (MIRA) (Smith 2011; Smith et al., 2008). AQC and AQAP are known for their extremist violence. HuT and MIRA share the same ideology and goals with AQC

and AQAP but have not engaged in terrorism. We divide the document collection in two subsets: documents from terrorist sources (AQC, AQAP) and documents from nonterrorist sources (MIRA, HuT).

Using the automated FA annotator described in the previous section, we mapped each document subset into a set of annotations. We then calculated the relevance of each annotation feature in distinguishing the two document subsets (terrorist vs. nonterrorist) using information gain (Mitchell, 1997, Ch. 3). In text classification, the information gain of a feature measures the decrease in information entropy (i.e., less uncertainty) in assigning a document to its correct class (e.g., terrorist or nonterrorist) when the feature is given vs. absent. Features that have higher information gain help build more accurate classifiers (Yang & Pedersen, 1997). We selected all FA features whose information gain was greater than zero and used the document annotations relative to the feature selected (57 out of the original 160 FA features) to train a multinomial Bayesian classifier capable of recognizing terrorist and nonterrorist documents using the Weka machine learning software (Witten et al., 2011).

Within a multinomial Bayesian classifier, a document is represented by a vector of attributes indicating the number of times each feature occurs in a document (McCallum & Nigam, 1998). The probability that a document D belongs to a class C—$p(C|D)$—is computed as the product of the probability of a document given its class—$p(D|C)$—and the probability for the class divided by the probability of the document, according to Bayes rule (1).

$$p(C|D) = \frac{p(D|C) * p(C)}{p(D)} \qquad (1)$$

The probability of a document given its class—$p(D|C)$—is derived as the product of the probabilities of the features occurring in the document, as shown in (2), where

- N is the number of FA features in document D.
- $n_1, n_2, \ldots, n_k$ is the number of times feature i occurs in document D.
- p_i is the probability of obtaining the feature i from sampling the documents in category C.

$$p(D|C) = N! * \prod_{i=1}^{k} \frac{p_i^{n_i}}{n_2!} \qquad (2)$$

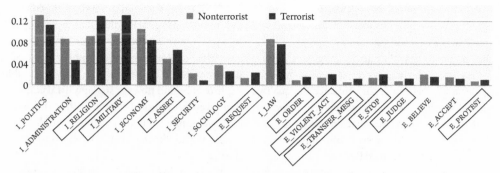

FIGURE 14.3 Probabilities relative to the terrorist and nonterrorist classes.

For example, suppose that there were only two features in our category scheme, I_RELIGION and I_LAW, and the *terrorist* class has $p(\text{I\_RELIGION}|terrorist) = 75\%$ and $p(\text{I\_LAW}|terrorist) = 25\%$. Suppose further that the document D has only three annotations: (I_LAW, I_RELIGION, I_LAW). Then the probability of D given the class *terrorist* would be calculated as shown in (3) (see Witten et al. (2011) pp. 97–98, for additional details).

$$p\big(\{\text{I\_LAW},\text{I\_RELIGION},\text{I\_LAW}\}|terrorist\big)$$
$$= 3! * \frac{0.25^2}{2!} * \frac{0.75}{1!} = \frac{9}{64} \qquad (3)$$

I for each category C (i.e., terrorist, nonterrorist), the probability p_i of obtaining the feature i from sampling from all documents in C is estimated by computing the relative frequency of the feature i in the text of all training documents for C. Figure 14.3 shows the probabilities estimated for 18 of the 57 selected FA features from the two document datasets described earlier in this section—documents from radical terrorist groups (AQC and AQAP) and documents from nonterrorist radical groups (HuT and MIRA). The accuracy of the multinomial Bayesian classifier defined by these feature probabilities was evaluated using tenfold cross-validation—training on 90% of the data and evaluating on the remaining

10%, each time selecting a random 90% to 10% split, and then averaging the evaluation results across the 10 runs. Evaluation was carried out using as metrics precision (4), recall (5), and F1 score (6). Precision and recall are defined in terms of true positives (TPs), true negatives (TNs), false positives or "false alarms" (FPs), and false negatives or "misses" (FNs).

$$Precision = \frac{TPs}{TPs + FPs} \qquad (4)$$

$$Recall = \frac{TPs}{TPs + FNs} \qquad (5)$$

$$F1 = 2 * \frac{precision * recall}{precision + recall} \qquad (6)$$

The evaluation results for the violent intent classifier described above are provided in Figure 14.4. The average precision and recall score (F1) is 85% for the detection of instances of the terrorist class and slightly over 70% for the detection of instances of the nonterrorist class. These are very good results, especially when we take into account that the precision score for the nonterrorist class, which displays comparatively lower accuracy, is still over 76%. Moreover, we are primarily interested in the detection of the terrorist class (where the model achieves higher accuracy), since our primary motive is to detect violent intent and

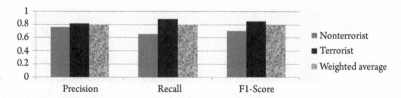

FIGURE 14.4 Evaluation results obtained through tenfold cross-validation for the multinomial Bayesian classifier assigning documents to the terrorist and nonterrorist classes.

ultimately to use violent intent indicators to assess sociopolitical contention in social media content, as discussed in the next section.

In conjunction with human judgment, automated predictive analytics as implemented through computer modeling can greatly enhance the quality of decision making. Computer models give us awareness of plausible outcomes that are easily missed through manual inspection, especially in processing large amounts of data. Guided by insight and creativity, the human as the ultimate decision maker can examine the results of modeling to select the best hypotheses to pursue.

Currently the detection of the terrorist class in the model is slightly skewed in favor of recall (89%) as compared with precision (82%). More precisely, the model's error rate can, on average, be expected to comprise 18% false positives and 11% misses. We think that this is a desirable balance as opposed to one where recall is lower than precision, especially in facing a high-stakes task such as the detection of terrorist communications. Automated predictive analysis is always open to error. However, while errors that emerge as false positives can be detected and discarded through manual inspection, this is not the case with false negatives. It is therefore much safer to filter out messages that have wrongly been identified as conveying violent intent rather than missing an equal or higher number of messages from violent sources.

FRAMING SOCIOPOLITICAL CONTENTION IN SOCIAL MEDIA: ANALYZING TWITTER POSTINGS TO DETECT VIOLENT INTENT

Having established that the violent intent model based on FA annotation performs at an acceptable level of accuracy (85% for the terrorist class), we proceeded to apply the model to new documents. Our aim was to evaluate documents in terms of FA annotations to:

1. Detect when sociopolitical contention rises
2. Identify contributing factors and their relative impact
3. Capture variation across communication sources

Of particular interest is the application of violent intent models to social media content. Social

media have been shown to serve as effective channels in furthering sociopolitical change; they therefore provide an excellent resource in the analysis of such change. For example, by applying the violent intent model to Twitter postings, we may be able to capture ebbs and flows in sociopolitical contention in a given geopolitical region. To test this hypothesis, we applied the violent intent model we had developed to Twitter postings related to the Arab Spring.

We examined about 300,000 Twitter postings about Syria, Egypt, Tunisia, and Libya for the period December 2010 through March 2012. We then processed these postings using the FA annotation pipeline. About 44,000 of the harvested postings, between 12,000 and 10,000 for each of the four countries under analysis, yielded FA annotations. We then measured the occurrence of top frame features used in detecting terrorist rhetoric to assess ebbs and flows in sociopolitical contention in Twitter postings, as shown in (7), where $|F_{ij}|$ is the number of times FA feature i occurs in message j and $p\,(F_i)$ is the probability with which Fi identifies violent rhetoric in the multinomial Bayesian net model of violent intent. While the stylistic nature of the texts were used to train the violent intent model (formal speeches and interviews vs. tweets), the FA features used to measure sociopolitical contention in Twitter postings were not inherently linked to a specific narrative style and, as discussed below, provide useful and relevant insights.

$$contention(message_j) = \sum_{i=1}^{n} |F_{ij}| * p(F_i) \qquad (7)$$

Since we were interested in violent intent characteristics of communication sources, we used only the probabilities of FA features that were more highly correlated with terrorist documents (i.e., the features marked by a surrounding rectangle in Figure 14.3). For ease of exposition, we show only results for the top 10 FA features that are more highly correlated with violent intent: the issues I_MILITARY, I_RELIGION, E_ASSERT, and the events E_JUDGE, E_ORDER, E_PROTEST, E_REQUEST, E_STOP, E_TRANSFER_MESG, E_VIOLENT_ACT.

Figure 14.5 provides an example of the analytical insights emerging from the application of the FA violent intent model to Twitter postings for Libya. We observed three peaks in sociopolitical

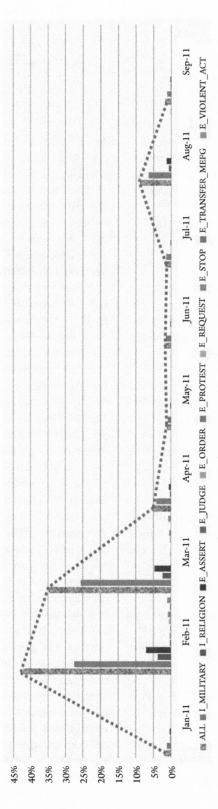

FIGURE 14.5 Application of the FA violent intent model to Twitter postings for Libya.

contention as the sum of all (normalized) FA feature probabilities by month.[1] These peaks correspond to the major uprising events as reported in the media:[2]

- *February 2011*: The beginning of protests in Benghazi (2/16/11) and the first casualties among protesters (2/18/2011).
- *March 2011*: The first major counterattack by Gaddafi in Zawiyah (3/5/2011), culminating in air attacks on the civilian population, which led to the implementation of a no-fly zone (3/8/2011) by Britain and the United States.
- *August 2011*: The establishment of the rebel interim government in Tripoli (8/26/22).

The most prominent features in characterizing the peaks of sociopolitical contention are the issues I_MILITARY, I_RELIGION, and the event E_ASSERT. This suggests that the contentious rhetoric dominating the public discourse is primarily focused on the violation of sacred values (e.g., suppression of basic liberties) and dominated by "prognostic" frames (e.g., telling people how to fight oppression). The additional frames complement this general orientation through "diagnostic" communication strategies (e.g., E_JUDGE, E_PROTEST, E_REQUEST), and actions of message delivery (E_TRANSFER_MSG) and violence (E_VIOLENT_ACT).

Strong correlations between peaks of sociopolitical contention and decisive events in charting the development of the Arab Spring are observed with the other three countries for which Twitter data were harvested and analyzed:

- Tunisia
  - The strongest spike in contention coincides with the intensification of the protests in early January 2011, culminating in the fleeing of Ben Ali to South Arabia.
- Syria
  - The first contention peak in March 2011, when Syrian security forces start killing protesters.
  - The second peak in August 2011 coincides with the massacre in Hamas, where 109 people are killed by Syrian security forces.

- Egypt
  - The first peak coincides with the first large protest against Mubarak on 1/25/2011.
  - The second peak in February 2011 occurs at the same time as the brutal crackdown on Tahrir Square in Cairo (2/2/2011) and the following resignation by Mubarak (2/11/2011).

As for the Libyan data, the FA features I_MILITARY, I_RELIGION and E_ASSERT were dominant in characterizing peaks of contention.

The results shown in Figure 14.5 emerge as the aggregate of postings from different communication sources. A characterization of the individual communication sources can help us understand whether and to what extent the violent contention expressed has diverse characteristics and how these characteristics evolve over time. In principle we could provide such an analysis for each communication source. However, in practice this can be unwieldy because of the high number of communication sources. For example, the 12,102 Twitter postings for Syria we analyzed come from 3,531 users. Fortunately, in order to have a comprehensive picture of the situation, an analysis of each user is not necessary. Of the 12,102 Twitter postings from Syria, about 50% were generated by less than 4.2% of users, each with 12 or more postings. Users with higher number of postings are those who start discussion threads and influence others (trend initiators/setters), while users with fewer postings tend to be followers (trend adopters/consumers). An analysis of top users therefore offers a representative view of changes in levels of contention expressed across the board.

Figure 14.6 provides an analytical example of 10 communication sources, whose messages present elements of violent contentions, with ≥47 postings from the Twitter data for Syria. These represent less than 0.3% of users but account for over 13% of postings. The graph on the left side of Figure 14.6 provides a reading of the level of violent contention expressed in the posting for each top user. An example of the individual rhetorical characteristics relevant to violent contention is provided for two users (User60 and User355) in the graph on the top right side of Figure 14.6.[3] The bottom right graph in Figure 14.6 exemplifies the evolution of rhetorical characteristics of one of the users relevant to violent contention through time.

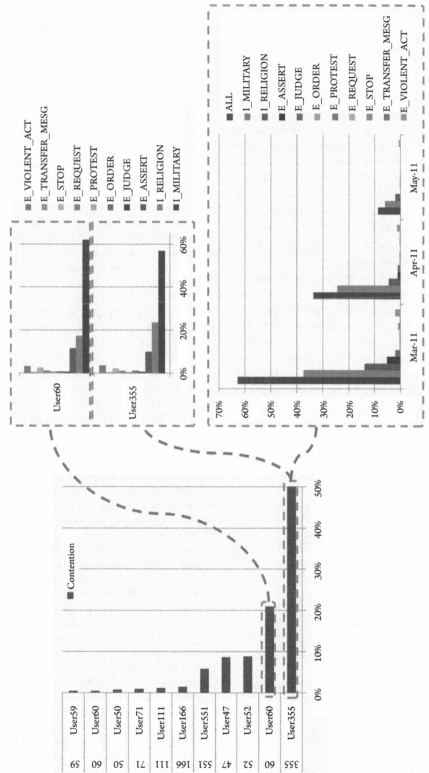

FIGURE 14.6 Analysis of top users (users with ≥50 postings) from the Twitter data for Syria.

CONCLUSIONS

Content analysis provides an effective methodology for examining the intentions of communicative sources to detect their propensity to engage in violent behavior. This methodology can be used to build computational models of radical rhetoric intent that enable the detection of violent intent in written and spoken language and the evaluation of how accurate such detection can be expected to be. Because the expression of violent intent often coincides with or precedes violent acts, models of radical rhetoric help us understand and predict the occurrence of violence. The ability to detect the likelihood of a communication source to engage in violent behavior is therefore essential in establishing a framework for threat assessment that can save lives. In this chapter, we have described a computational approach to modeling violent intent based on content analysis that achieves these objectives and shown how the emerging capabilities can be applied to social media content to capture changes in contention in the public discourse that signal the impending occurrence of political violence. The approach presented is based on a Bayesian classification model that detects contention and its characteristic components. This model can be easily extended to provide a dynamic view of how patterns of contention can be expected to develop in the future, using what we know about past and present pattern of contention and machine learning techniques that enable the creation of a dynamic Bayesian network from timed training data (Ghahramani, 1998; Murphy, 2002).

ACKNOWLEDGMENTS

This work was supported by the Technosocial Predictive Analytics Initiative, a research program at the Pacific Northwest National Laboratory (http://predictiveanalytics.pnl.gov).

KEY POINTS

- Content analysis helps detect violent intent in human communication.
- The results of content analysis enable the development of data-driven computational models of violent intent.
- Computational models of violent intent that are data driven can be evaluated to establish their expected margin of error in terms of false alarms (false positives) and misses (false negatives).

- Computational models of violent intent can be applied to new messages to assess whether and to which extent they express violent intent and establish what the predominant indicators of violent intent are.
- The assessment of violent intent via computer modeling helps us understand and predict the occurrence of violence.

NOTES

1. Since we have grouped Twitter postings by month, onsets preceding the emergence of peaks of contention are less visible than they would have been with a more granular grouping (e.g. by week).
2. Event time-line source: http://www.guardian.co.uk/world/interactive/2011/mar/22/middle-east-protest-interactive-timeline
3. The names of Twitter users have been changed to protect their privacy.

REFERENCES

Austin, J. (1962). *How to do things with words*. Oxford, UK: Oxford University Press.

Bandura, A. (1999). Moral disengagement in the perpetration of inhumanities. *Personality and Social Psychology Review, 3*, 193–209.

Benford, D., & Snow R. (2000). Framing processes and social movements: An overview and assessment. *Annual Review of Sociology, 26*, 611–639.

Conway, L., Gornick, L., Houck, S., Hands Towgood, K., & Conway, K. (2011). The hidden implications of radical group rhetoric: Integrative complexity and terrorism. *Dynamics of Asymmetric Conflict, 4*(2), 155–165.

Entman, R. (2004). *Projections of power: Framing news, public opinion, and U.S. foreign policy*. Chicago: University of Chicago Press.

Feldman, R., & Sanger, J. (2007). *The text mining handbook: Advanced approaches to analyzing unstructured data*. Cambridge, UK: Cambridge University Press.

Gamson, W. (1988). Political discourse and collective action. In B. Klandermans, H. Kriesi, & S. Tarrow (Eds.), *International Social Movement Research* (Vol. 1, pp. 219–244). London: JAI Press.

Gamson, W. (1992). *Talking politics*. New York: Cambridge University Press.

Gamson, W., Fireman, B., & Rytina, S. (1982). *Encounters with unjust authority*. Homewood, IL: Dorsey Press.

Ghahramani, Z. (1998). Learning dynamic Bayesian networks: In C. Lee Giles, & M. Gori (Eds.), Adaptive processing of sequences and data structures. *Lecture Notes in Computer Science* (Vol. *1387/1998*, pp. 168–197). Berlin/Heidelberg: Springer-Verlag.

Goffman, E. (1974). *Frame analysis: An essay on the organization of experience*. London: Harper and Row.

Hermann, M., & Sakiev, A. (2011). Leadership, terrorism, and the use of violence. *Dynamics of Asymmetric Conflict, 4*(2), 126–134.

Krippendorff, K. (2004). *Content analysis: An introduction to its methodology,* 2nd ed. Thousand Oaks, CA: Sage.

McAdam, D., Tarrow, S., & Tilly, C. (2001). *Dynamics of contention.* New York: Cambridge University Press.

McCallum, A., & Nigam, K. (1998). A Comparison of event models for naive Bayes text classification. In *AAAI/ICML-98 Workshop on Learning for Text Categorization* July 26–27, 1998, Madison, Wisconsin, (pp. 41–48). Technical Report WS-98-05. Palo Alto, CA: AAAI Press.

Mitchell, T. M., (1997). *Machine learning.* New York: Mc-Graw-Hill.

Murphy, K. (2002). *Dynamic Bayesian networks: Representation, inference and learning.* PhD thesis. Berkeley: University of California.

Navarro, J. (2009). Unmasking terrorists—Two critical characteristics! Key signs which point to potential terrorist activity. *Psychology Today,* December 31 [Online]. Available: http://www.psychology-today.com/blog/spycatcher/200912/unmasking-terrorists-two-critical-characteristics

Noakes, J., & Johnston, H. (2005). Frames of protest: A road map to a perspective. In H. Johnston & J. Noakes (Eds.), *Frames of protest: Social movements and the framing perspective* (pp. 1–29). Lanham, MD: Rowman and Littlefield.

Pennebaker, J. (2011). Using computer analyses to identify language style and aggressive intent: The secret life of function words. *Dynamics of Asymmetric Conflict, 4*(2) 92–102.

Sanfilippo, A., Cowell, A. J. Tratz, S., Boek, A., Cowell, A. K., Posse, C., & Pouchard, L. (2007). Content analysis for proactive intelligence: Marshaling frame evidence. *Proceedings of the 22nd AAAI Conference,* Vancouver, BC, Canada.

Sanfilippo, A., Franklin, L., Tratz, S., Danielson, G., Mileson, N., Riensche, R., & McGrath, L. (2008). Automating frame analysis. In H. Liu, J. Salerno, & M. Young (Eds.) *Social Computing, Behavioral Modeling, and Prediction,* 239–248.

Sanfilippo, A., & McGrath, L. (2011). Social predictive analytics and terrorism deterrence. *IEEE Intelligent Systems, 26*(4), 87–91.

Sanfilippo, A., McGrath L., & Whitney, P. (2011). Violent frames in action. *Dynamics of Asymmetric Conflict, 4*(2), 103–112.

Searle, J. (1969). *Speech acts.* Cambridge, UK: Cambridge University Press.

Smith, A. (2011). The relationship between rhetoric and terrorist violence: Introduction to special issue. *Dynamics of Asymmetric Conflict, 4*(2), 85–91.

Smith, A., Suedfeld, P., Conway, L., & Winter, D. (2008). The language of violence: Distinguishing terrorist from non-terrorist groups using thematic content analysis. *Dynamics of Asymmetric Conflict, 1,* 142–163.

Snow, D., Rochford, B., Worden, S., & Benford, R. (1986). Frame alignment processes, micromobilization and movement participation. *American Sociological Review, 51*(4), 464–481.

Suedfeld, P., & Brcic, J. (2011). Scoring universal values in the study of terrorist groups and leaders. *Dynamics of Asymmetric Conflict, 4*(2), 166–174.

Tetlock, Ph., Kristel, O., Elson, B., Green, M., & Lerner, J. (2000). The psychology of the unthinkable: Taboo trade-offs, forbidden base rates, and heretical counterfactuals. *Journal of Personality and Social Psychology, 78,* 853–870.

Walker, S. (2011). Anticipating attacks from the operational codes of terrorist groups. *Dynamics of Asymmetric Conflict, 4*(2), 135–143.

Wiktorowicz, Q. (2004). Introduction: Islamic activism and social movement theory. In Q. Wiktorowicz (Ed.), *Islamic activism: A social movement theory approach* (pp. 1–31). Bloomington: Indiana University Press.

Winter, D. (2011). Scoring motive imagery in documents from four Middle East opposition groups. *Dynamics of Asymmetric Conflict, 4*(2), 144–154.

Witten, I., Frank, E., & Hall, M. (2011). *Data Mining: Practical Machine Learning Tools and Techniques,* 3rd edition. Burlington, MA: Morgan Kaufmann.

Yang, Y., & Pedersen, J. (1997). A comparative study on feature selection in text categorization. *Proceedings of the 14th International Conference on Machine Learning,* 412–420.

15

The Use of Threat Assessment in Tactical Operations

Reverse Engineering the Method

JAMES BIESTERFELD

Threat assessments have been utilized by strategists since the first Cro-Magnon leader wanted to secure his cave from the clan located over the ridge. As we have previously seen, methods have changed over the centuries as technologies have improved, but essentially the same aspects are in play in conducting threat assessments.

The basic questions presented to any threat manager are these: "What are you trying to protect?" And "What are you afraid of?" Again, as technologies improve, threat managers are faced with increasing problems in identifying the threats arrayed against them and the complexity of the individual, facility, or property they must protect.

While the stability of such basic questions and the fluidity of technology are well known, this also means that the enemy, our adversaries, must also take into consideration these changes in developing a strategy as to how to effectively attack their chosen target and do with it what they intend to do. What planners sometimes neglect is the fact that the enemy implements and conducts its own assessments, a counterstrategy to our work, or a form of reverse engineering.

In the world of corporate espionage, a competitor wishes to obtain the product of its competition in order to "reverse engineer" the device or product, thereby saving millions of dollars of research and development costs; it then can bring the product to market and deny the originator due credit as the inventor and developer.

By way of example, in the late 1990s a major European automobile manufacturer sent observers to the Detroit Auto Show to look over its products and to see what its competitors were offering. To their dismay, these observers saw one of their prototype vehicles, still at least a year away from production, sitting on a dais with someone else's logo on it as an offering for the upcoming model year.

Shocked by what had been seen, it was plainly evident to this European manufacturer that by stealing this design, the competitor had gotten at least a year's lead and edged it out of the marketplace. This cost the manufacturer more than $50 million in research and development costs.

The first manufacturer then purchased one of these copied cars and reverse engineered it. While there were subtle differences in the cosmetics of body styling, the internal components proved to be virtual copies of its original design. As a result, an investigation ensued—quietly, so as not to bring the matter to the attention of the media—wherein the "internal spy" was identified. This individual then identified the "external spy" or "handler." When confronted, the handler produced documentation establishing a paper trail back to the competitor who had commissioned the initiation of the espionage effort against my client (Biesterfeld, 1998).

In this instance, the company had a product to protect from conception to production. To do this, it developed policies, procedures, and physical security methods to a specific end. The competitor had to identify those methods and procedures and develop countermeasures to defeat them. In essence, the competitor had to either place its spy inside the target organization or suborn an existing employee who had placement and access to the information they required, including the ability to transmit that data to the handler. The competitor had to reverse engineer the entire threat assessment process in order to successfully initiate and complete its plan.

TACTICAL OPERATIONS

In the world of tactical operations, there are significant differences between the law enforcement community and the special operations (military) community. Their specific missions vary widely depending on situation, complexity and political considerations.

Law enforcement reaction teams, generically referred to as Special Weapons and Tactics (SWAT) teams, are the final option for heavily armed or barricaded suspects within the United States and elsewhere and are formed by all levels of government (municipal, county, state, and federal). Such tactical teams first appeared in the early 1970s, after the advent of terrorist groups in the United States and other countries—especially in the aftermath of the Munich Olympic massacre of Israeli athletes in 1972, when no such response existed.

Military special action units have existed in one form or another almost since the establishment of armies. Specifically identified commando units saw a great deal of development and use in World War II within paratroop and other military units. The First Special Service Force was established in 1943 in the United States and was a joint American and Canadian venture. It was originally tasked to be used as elite ski troops in Scandinavia, but this mission was terminated and they were ultimately used as special mountain troops. It was this unit that was the foundation for the US Army Special Forces, formed by President John F. Kennedy.

Now we see significant differences in the use of these forces. Law enforcement SWAT teams are typically used in small-scale situations involving one or two armed persons barricaded with or without hostages. They are composed of an assault team and snipers and are deployed at the discretion of the chief of police, sheriff, or other executive authority. Their effort is to minimize the use of violence in order to keep destruction and loss of life to an absolute minimum. Further, their training for such eventualities typically consists of possible scenarios against generic targets. They are able to train against known potentials such as school takeovers or attacks against government buildings. It is in these cases that the threat assessment process may be used to its best advantage and afford the SWAT units the ability to know their target well. Their drawback is that they function only in response to an event; also the team must likely spend a great deal of time cordoning the action and preparing its plan; it does not act offensively against a known or planned target or respond force on force from the outset of the action.

Military special-purpose forces, on the contrary, tend to be used for more proactive (offensive) operations against an identified target. In January 1945, selected troops from the 6th Ranger Battalion, the Alamo Scouts, and Philippine guerrillas launched a raid against the Japanese-held Cabanatuan prisoner of war camp to free US POWs. In this case, the raid was conducted after intelligence reports indicated that withdrawing Japanese Imperial troops would massacre the POWs rather than leave them or move them with the withdrawal. Within the space of a few days, the Rangers had to conduct reconnaissance of the target, develop a plan, and execute that plan.

This was a classic situation of the reverse engineering of the threat assessment process that the Japanese had conducted in establishing their camp. The camp itself was situated on a broad open plain with no appreciable cover for an attacking force. The compound was actually four compounds within the perimeter: one was used to house the prisoners and the other three for quartering Japanese soldiers assigned to the camp, working areas, and a motor pool. Towers provided elevated observation posts for the guards to survey both the inside and outside areas of the camp. The guards were selected troops under a competent commander, all dedicated to their jobs. Given the nature of technology at the time and the temporary nature of such camps, the Japanese had done a credible job in establishing their camp.

Once the 6th Rangers were given the mission, the reverse engineering began. Critical was "on the ground" information on the camp. The Rangers had basic information from aerial reconnaissance photos and observations as well as anecdotal information from local villagers. To fill in the gaps, the army's Alamo Scouts were sent into the area to obtain the necessary information. This required the Alamo Scouts to infiltrate almost 30 miles behind Japanese lines without detection, get to the camp, conduct their collection activities, and return to their own headquarters with their information.

Captain Robert Prince developed the assault plan for the nighttime raid. His task was further complicated in two ways: the need to skirt a Japanese infantry battalion that was bivouacked a few miles from the camp and to integrate Philippine guerrillas—who would play an absolutely critical role in preventing the Japanese battalion from reinforcing the camp guards—into the operation. The plan itself, based on all available information, was simple in concept: The Rangers would assault the camp from three sides, killing or disabling the Japanese soldiers there. They would then enter the prisoner compound and move all the POWs out the main gate to a rally point nearby, from which they would march back to friendly lines. Simultaneously, the Philippine guerillas would engage the Japanese infantry from ambush and prevent them from aiding the camp guards (Breuer, 1994).

The raid went off flawlessly, resulting in the rescue of over 500 POWs with only 2 Rangers killed and 7 wounded—none seriously. The Philippine guerrillas suffered no deaths and only a few minor casualties. The Cabanatuan raid is considered the most complex and successful raid ever conducted by the US military and is a classic example of using the threat assessment process against an adversary.

ELEMENTS THAT ARE ALWAYS CONSIDERED IN TACTICAL PLANNING

First and foremost is *mission*. What is the objective of the exercise? What must be accomplished? This must be clearly defined for the operators.

Second, what is the *target*? Is it a location, a campus, an individual or group of individuals? Knowing this will help to determine the number of operators needed for the mission and the nature and extent of the equipment.

Third, what is the *location* of the target? What are its environs and how will its location affect the operation?

Fourth, what is the *geography* of the location? Terrain aspects can influence travel time, methods of travel, and other aspects of movement.

Fifth, what are the *assets*? That is, who are we sending in to complete the operation and what is their opposition? During my years as a surveillance operator in western Europe, we would prebrief before we began an operation. One of the oft repeated statements remains in my memory: "The population is at best insecure and at worst hostile." This simple statement would apply to virtually any situation for either side. What are the threats? Who is providing security? What is the nature of the law enforcement arm in the area of operations and what is its effectiveness? Who will provide our operators' security? What about support personnel? Who are they and what are their contingencies?

Sixth, what is the *essential plan* of the operation? How do the operators get to the target and back (if that is a consideration) and how will the operators complete the job on site?

Seventh, what is the *ingress and egress plan*? How will the operators get inside the target and then, once the operation is completed, how will they get out of the target and away?

Eighth, who is issuing the *operations order* (op order) to the operators? This order will provide all of the information necessary for the conduct of the operation.

Finally, ninth—who is issuing the *"Go"* order? This will launch the operation and send the operators into harm's way. General George S. Patton's words are typically whispered into the ears of special operators: "No plan survives first contact with the enemy." Any plan must allow for flexibility if and when something goes awry, so that the operators are not locked into a plan that is so rigid that if something does go wrong, they will simply die in place, a mission failure.

CASE STUDY: THE MUMBAI ATTACKS, 2008

These situations outlined above are but some small examples about the need for reverse engineering of the threat assessment process that we, in the modern world, rely on to keep ourselves, our families, our employers, and even our governments safe and protected. But let us take this aspect of "good guys and bad guys" to a modern extreme and apply it again. Let us look back on the attack on Mumbai, India, on November 26, 2008. Mumbai (Bombay), with a population of over 20 million people, is India's commercial and entertainment capital and the provincial capital for Maharashta. The city has the potential to be a tactical nightmare, as most of it occupies a peninsula. This played a major role in the terrorists' attack sequence.

On November 26, 2008, ten terrorists arrived in the bay east of Mumbai on a fishing boat they had hijacked earlier. Having placed their equipment on small rubber boats, the terrorists used these to reach the beach; they then began to move into the city, dividing themselves into two-man teams for the initial assault. Following is a timeline of the assault:

Time Line

9:30 p.m., November 26:

The attackers arrived by boat. Each carried a backpack with ammunition, explosives, cell phones, AK 47s, knives, and GPS devices. They also carried high-energy food, water, and drugs to keep them going.

9:30 to 10:40 p.m.:

The attack begins at the Chatrapati Shivaji railway station, where 52 people were killed.

9:30 p.m. onward:

Other attackers targeted the Leopold Café before moving in on the Nariman Jewish center and the Taj Mahal and Oberoi Trident hotels.

10:40 p.m.:

The bombs carried by the attackers caused serious problems across Mumbai. Of 10 devices, 7 exploded. Two of these had been put in taxis, one at a gas station, one at the train station, and others at a flower garden in front of the Taj Mahal Hotel.

November 26 to 29:

The battle against the attackers continued. No one knows whether the attackers, who were not planning a suicide mission but were prepared to die, had anticipated such a long siege.

Intercepted messages between the controllers and the attackers at Nariman House said, "Do not saddle yourself with the burden of hostages. Immediately kill them." Other messages told the attackers to set fire to the buildings. After three days, the sieges were finally ended by Indian commandos (Gardham, 2009).

As could be seen by the response to the initial attack, the Indians were woefully unprepared for such an assault. The attackers used a classic diversion tactic to keep the Indian police and military off balance in order to reach their intended targets and lengthen their time line before the Indians were able to respond effectively.

The methods used by the attackers reflect a concept known as "battle buddies" and is commonly used by US Special Operations Forces. This, again, demonstrates that terrorists continue to study their adversaries and use the latest methods and tactics.

In their attack, the terrorists landed their rubber boats near the harbor in the eastern central part of the city. Once on land, they formed their teams and began to move south and east. As can be seen in the time line, their initial attacks involved public places with high traffic. Certainly this was done to not only maximize casualties but to also create the greatest amount of chaos and confusion possible, both for the general population and for the first responders. This undoubtedly aided the terrorists in their movement through the city. And they kept moving. This must have been a critical part of their strategy, for it did not allow law enforcement or the military to force the attackers to ground and end the attacks. In point of fact, for each assault made at the various locations, law enforcement had to send a separate response component.

In the United States, for example, police response to critical situations is predictable. We have trained literally thousands of police officers and have questioned these tactics: The officers are on patrol, when suddenly their radio dispatcher declares, "Shots fired!" at a specific location. Who responds? Everybody. When they arrive on the scene, they see panic, confusion, and casualties. Suddenly, the dispatcher comes over the air, "Shots fired!" and identifies a different location some distance away. Now what? The responders break off a couple of units—unsure if the two incidents are related—and send these officers to the other location. When these units arrive on scene, they are again met with casualties, panic, and confusion. Then again, the dispatcher comes over the radio, "Shots fired!" at a third location.

"If you know your enemy's capabilities as well as you know your own, you will never be defeated in one hundred engagements."

SUN TZU, *The Art of War*

As one can see, this develops into an impossible situation for the responders, as their assets are spread out and reduced in functionality with each new incident; all the while, the incidents are not clearly connected, nor are they being properly assessed by the intelligence assets of the law enforcement agency involved. The collateral effect on the responders is frustration, confusion, and fatigue, which continue to impact their collective response.

Thus as the "battle buddy" teams attack targets of opportunity, either by design or not, the responders continue to move to each incident independently, finally getting the idea that a significant terrorist attack is under way but continuing to respond in a reactive and inept manner. This became very expensive for the Indian security forces when the chief of their counterterrorism division was killed by the attackers. It is unknown if he was targeted for assassination or whether he was simply at the wrong place at the wrong time.

Capabilities

The terrorists had a complement of 10 personnel. These men were in plain clothes and each carried the following (Indian 37th Court, 2008):

1. AK 47 assault rifle, pistol, and knife
2. Two backpacks/slingpacks containing
   a. Ammunition
   b. High-energy food
   c. Drugs (amphetamines)
   d. Water
   e. Grenades/bomb
   f. Cell phone

The Indians have, as a nation, approximately 2.4 million police, special-purpose police, military police, and paramilitary police throughout the country. Although exact figures are unavailable, one might estimate during the Mumbai attacks a total law enforcement capability from all sources at somewhere around 12,000+ personnel. Training for these various elements ranges from good to nonexistent.

Armament also varied for the responders. Some had modern AK-47 assault rifles while many had World War II-vintage Enfield bolt-action rifles; some were unarmed.

Once the terrorists had achieved their primary targets (The Taj Mahal Hotel, the Oberoi Hotel, and the Nariman House) the real fight was on. The terrorists deployed, as best as can be determined, four personnel to the Taj Mahal Hotel and two each to the Oberoi Hotel and the Nariman House. Two others were freelancing and their ultimate target was not determined.

As with any terrorist attack, the initial momentum is always with the terrorists, since the attack occurs at a time and place of their choosing. In this case, the ultimate goal of the terrorists appears to have been killing as many people as possible before they themselves were killed by security/police responders. Once the targets were achieved, the terrorists set about their grisly duties.

Evidence from the scene indicates that the terrorists were in almost constant telephonic contact with their handlers in Pakistan. Audio recordings of these conversations were made by Indian intelligence officials *for three days* before someone decided that these calls were not a good idea and the cellular service was cut off by Indian law enforcement agencies.

Yet before this occurred, the Pakistani handlers used their control to urge their attackers to do as much damage as possible, kill as many as possible, and sacrifice their lives dearly to achieve their goal. According to one of the intercepted calls, the death of the attackers was an essential part of the plan (HBO, 2010).

At the Taj Mahal Hotel, two of the terrorists simply entered the lobby and opened fire, killing nine at the outset. They then proceeded through the ground floor and were joined by two other terrorists. As they made their way through the hotel, they received frequent calls from their handler—identified only as Brother Wasi—who pushed them into completing their tasks and provided encouragement for their martyrdom.

The police response was confused and chaotic. Local police officials had requested the support of commando units, but their arrival did not occur for many hours, leaving the local police—who had *never* received training for any kind of terrorist attack, let alone the multipronged complex attack that they were involved in at this time—in an almost catatonic condition for response. A few officers, however, did manage to get into the security room of the Taj Mahal Hotel, where the monitors for the closed circuit television system were located. These officers were able to provide invaluable information as to the movement of the terrorists in the hotel. However, once the terrorists had set a fire inside the hotel, the officers were forced to retreat or be caught in the flames. After that, it was a waiting game.

The one good piece of news was what happened to the other two-man team who had not gone to ground. These two, including Muhammed Kasab—the sole surviving terrorist—were driving through the city making their way toward another target when they ran into a police roadblock. The police, thankfully, were ready for these two and a gun battle ensued, causing the terrorists' vehicle to crash into a pole. Kasab's partner was killed in the battle, while Kasab was only wounded. Kasab was immediately taken to a hospital, where he received initial treatment and was then subjected to police interrogation.

Twenty-one-year-old Kasab was the third of five children of an impoverished family from a small village in Pakistan. Kasab left home in his teens to seek his own path but soon fell into a life of petty theft. He and some partners apparently wanted to obtain firearms to conduct more profitable thefts but did not know how to use them. It was then that Kasab saw a recruitment poster for the Lashkar e Tayyiba (LeT) and decided to join them in order to obtain weapons training. What he did not apparently expect was the religious indoctrination that turned him into a "violent true believer" (Meloy, 2011) and ardent jihadist. Kasab's capture afforded Indian police and intelligence personnel the opportunity to find out more about the planning, recruitment, command and control, and execution of LeT in this particular attack (Indian 37th Court, 2008).

The attack was carried out, leaving over 150 people dead and hundreds more wounded. The question is how the terrorists managed to get to that point. Attacks that are this sophisticated are not made on the spur of the moment. They take planning, preparation, and many matters that must be considered and planned for it the attack is to be successful.

So, let us recap this attack:

1. Ten males hijack a fishing boat and murder the crew.
2. They sail to the bay at Mumbai, grab gear, get into small boats, murder the ship's captain, and float to shore.
3. They achieve landfall, proceed to initial targets, and commence to kill everything that moves.
4. They move to their primary targets, where the siege begins, ending almost three days later.

In the threat assessment process, we have distinct divisions of labor that will assess the nature of the threat and inspect physical security, technical security, IT security, personal security, and so on. Terrorist organizations also have distinct divisions of labor to accomplish their goals. For them, however, the effort is to defeat the opponent's threat assessment process, which is designed to protect any organization or individual.

For example, in the major motion picture *Taken*, the filmmakers demonstrate this division of labor concept. The "bad guys'" first division of labor was the "spotter" at the Paris airport: in this case, the spotter was a Sky Cap who would evaluate young women as they left the airport. When he saw a potential victim, the spotter would give a nod to a character called Peter, who would approach the victim, initiate a conversation, share a cab, and in general play the role of a charming young man. His purpose was to collect intelligence on the potential victim: traveling alone, staying where, background, and so forth. Then came the "snatch team," housing team, and on and on.

Terrorist organizations must develop their attack plans by essentially reverse-engineering the threat assessment process to find any additional "holes" in the protection program or to at least identify the "weak link" that might allow a successful attack.

The Indians had apparently not done a great deal of assessing except for the hotels—which have been lucrative targets in the past—but their efforts, apparently, were not heavily supported by law enforcement and the presence of private security. Regardless of whatever security there may have been, LeT wanted this attack to go well; therefore planning was essential. Here, again, the division of labor becomes apparent.

Senior members of LeT—Indian investigators have identified at least 32 people (from attackers to support personnel) as part of the plot—began planning for this attack months in advance.

The beginning of the planning cycle started with senior members of LeT sitting down and deciding what kind of attack they wanted to mount, what targets were to be attacked, how many attackers would be involved, what equipment and transportation would be needed, logistics, communications, and other sundry concerns.

Fleshing out the plan into something that could be executed was another matter entirely. Funding the operation was a critical part of this preparation. LeT receives funding through donations, criminal activity, and—if rumors are to be believed—from Pakistan's Inter-Services Intelligence, or ISI.

In Kasab's interrogation, he stated that money was a prime motivator for him and that "A few hundred thousand" was paid to his father in return for his participation (Shrivastava, 2009). The other attackers' families were also probably compensated for their participation. Weapons, explosives, communications equipment, and other gear were either purchased or donated to the operation. Training for the attack team was provided at LeT training camps in Pakistan. It was conducted in phases, each more sophisticated than the previous one, including religious indoctrination and philosophy. Team members were forbidden to speak to each other during the course of their training so as to further strengthen the control of the overseers and mission control personnel.

Target selection is essential so that a flow plan can be developed to aid in the dynamic nature of the attack. Selecting Mumbai was easy, since it had been a favorite target in the past. Additionally, Mumbai was a commercial and financial center for the entire country and served as headquarters for many foreign businesspeople and tourists.

But what to attack? Thus began the arduous task of collecting sufficient data to provide planners with specific targets within the city. Attacking the Nariman House (Jewish Chabad House) fit with the anti-Israeli tone of most Islamic extremist groups, and it was near the other two principal targets. According to the Mumbai website, the Oberoi and Taj Mahal Hotels were listed as the first and second choices among the 357 hotels in Mumbai. Additionally, the Taj Mahal Hotel was a landmark building and an attack there would attract a lot of attention.

As with any assessment, actual surveillance was key. LeT sent out collectors to Mumbai to identify and validate the targets. Indian authorities identified Fahim Arshad Mohammad Yusuf Ansari and Sabauddin Ahmed Shabbir Ahmed Shaikh as the people responsible for this effort. Additionally, the Indian authorities identified US national David Headley, born Daood Sayed Gilani, of Pakistani descent, as a major player in the collection effort. Headley, a former Drug Enforcement Administration informant and drug dealer, had been arrested by US authorities and cooperated with the government in speaking about his role in the Mumbai attack (Rotella, 2011). (It was Headley who directly implicated Pakistan's ISI in the planning and preparation of the Mumbai attack.)

The job of the collectors was to move about the city, conducting "light" surveillance of potential targets for the attack team. Once those potential targets had been identified, the planning group evaluated each target for its potential and proximity to other targets, thus creating a list of those targets from which to make a final selection.

Now began the intense surveillance of each target and associated acquisition of information. The intelligence collectors had to determine how well each target was protected and to identify their vulnerabilities. Does this sound familiar? A great deal of information about anything can be gleaned from the Internet—such a marvelous resource. During threat assessments, the assessors also cull the Internet to see what information can be easily obtained. The attackers do the same. By searching Taj Mahal Hotel, one can find 11,700,000 results from a single search engine; over 1,300,000 results on the Oberoi and 637,000 results for the Nariman Mumbai. Enormous amounts of information as well as images are there for the taking by both attackers and defenders.

Yet when all is said and done, one must still go and look at the ground. Information is two-dimensional; it is only through seeing locations in three dimensions that one can get a full picture of that location. Ansari, Shaikh, Headley, and probably others engaged in an intensive surveillance of the primary targets—Taj Mahal Hotel, Oberoi Hotel, and Nariman House—as well as a similar intense surveillance of the rail terminus, hospital, theater, and restaurants that made up the secondary or deception targets. The latter would draw all of the law enforcement and other responder resources away from the primary targets, allowing the attackers to gain easy access to them.

As we have seen, each one of the secondary targets was a location that had more than one entrance, was well known, and contained a lot of people. While there were uniformed officers present, not all were armed and none were well trained to respond to a serious incident. While there is no hard evidence to support this theory, it is widely believed that there were other targets along the "route of advance" taken by the attackers that might have been assaulted as opportunity permitted but that were not attacked for reasons that will never be known.

The collectors were tasked with identifying these primary, secondary, and perhaps even tertiary targets for the attack team. Let us put ourselves in the place of the collectors and ask how we would accomplish our mission of identifying the targets, and determining how the attacks could take place with the greatest potential death toll and prolongation of the attack.

Selection of the Taj, Oberoi, and Nariman House targets was likely made by the planning committee because the Taj is an iconic location used by foreigners and is an older facility with many nooks and crannies; the Oberoi is also somewhat iconic, used by foreigners, and it is a high-end facility. The secondary targets were likely identified and selected by the collectors. The collectors, with the known exception of Headley, lived locally in Mumbai and had a reasonable familiarity with the city. Once assigned their task, the collectors had to visit each location and evaluate each as a potential target. The train station was of some concern, since it is a large facility with a huge flow of pedestrian traffic moving through it. As a public transportation hub, it had a significant police presence, as many such locations have. Unfortunately for the Indian police, not all of their officers were armed and most lacked training in the use of firearms or tactical deployment (Chudwin, 2009).

This lack of training and preparation on the part of the Indians was of course to the terrorist collectors' advantage. They would have easily been able to enter the train station, loiter for extended and repeated collection efforts, and probably photograph or videotape the train station without interference.

Collection against the hospital might have been slightly trickier, since it has a smaller flow of pedestrian traffic and there is a heightened sense of awareness among the staff. Still, a single collector could easily have infiltrated the facility. This author, under contract, has successfully infiltrated a number of such facilities in the United States, conducting vulnerability tests for private clients to determine such facilities' accessibility by intelligence collectors vis-à-vis a direct attack.

Consider the simplicity of simply walking into the train station in the middle of a multitude of travelers. You are essentially invisible in the crowd. This is a skill, not just a happenstance. The collectors' ability to disappear in a crowd is a key element of their collection effort.

Now, you are inside and you begin your effort by simply walking about, making observations. You locate all of the entrances, both public and restricted. Are the doors controlled electronically or with guards? What are the doors made of? Will explosives be necessary to breach the doors for ingress or egress? How do the passengers directly access the boarding platforms? How open are they? Are they a viable target?

You continue your walk. Where are police and security personnel? Are they mobile? Are they static? They are likely a combination of both. Note the locations of the static posts. What kind of law enforcement personnel are present? Are any or all of them armed? What is their attitude? Are they alert? Do supervisors closely monitor their personnel? When do they change shifts? Do they move personnel on the static posts frequently? Are they bored? Do they commonly interact with the civilian travelers? Do they have communications? Radios? Cell phones? What frequencies are being used? Is there a control room for the communications support?

What about vendors? How many shops are their inside the station? How many kiosks? When do they open and close? How are they staffed? Are they busy, or do they have time to simply observe the passing crowd?

What about the transportation other than rail? Bus stops? How many are there, or is this a terminus location for buses as well? Are buses always present or are there periods of no activity at the stops? What about the taxi stands? Are they sequestered in a specific area? Are they monitored or controlled by law enforcement/traffic enforcement personnel? Do the drivers congregate during slack periods? Are there slack periods, or is there a constant flow of travelers?

What about the technical security? Is there controlled access onto the boarding platforms? Are there closed circuit television cameras? Where are they located? Are they fixed or pan/tilt/zoom? Where is the monitoring room?

How close is law enforcement support? Do they maintain a SWAT-type presence nearby? How long would it take for such a force to respond to an event at the train station?

Such an intense surveillance would be conducted over days or weeks of effort. It is the meticulous work of the collectors that provides planners with the data to develop an attack plan. Yet each target requires similar effort.

The train station, as large as it is, is one target. The example of the Leopold Restaurant is another. Here we have a much more confined space with a flow of customers coming and going. The fact that it catered to foreign customers and tourists was an attraction for the collectors and planners. This surveillance was twofold. First, collectors would have to observe the location from outside the structure. What is the building made of? What is the street traffic like, both pedestrian and vehicular? Is there a police or security presence outside the building?

Once the outside observation has been conducted or in concert with it, inside observation must occur. This is easily done, since going in and enjoying a meal is what they are in business to have people do. Collectors can then take note of the same attributes of the train station: entrances, access controls, placement of the tables, kitchen, and restrooms, among other things.

Again, this will take place over an extended period of days to weeks, at different times of day, to develop a "feel" for the normal operation of the location. Striking the target at an optimal time would provide a higher body count and additional confusion, allowing the attackers to continue their operation.

Perhaps the most difficult target for the terrorists to assess would have been the Nariman House. Renamed Chabad House by the Jewish owners, the structure had been purchased by the Chabad Trust of India two years prior to the attacks; it was a five-story building used to provide support and sleeping accommodations to Jews traveling through the area.

Because of their narrow type of support activity, access to the Chabad House was controlled better than that to other locations. It is unclear whether the collectors were able to get inside the structure to assess the interior. No direct evidence has been developed to support such an activity on the part of the collectors, but it is possible that they could have gained at least some level of access. It is also likely, again not directly substantiated, that the collectors were able to gather other information (e.g., floor plans and interior photographs) from public resources that may have been used in lieu of direct observation of the interior.

After the completion of the collection operation, the collectors had to whittle down their information to a concise, readable report accompanied by maps depicting the area and the targets. Timings, landing zones, transportation methods, and recommendations for equipment and armaments had to be part of the report, all geared toward defeating the established security protocols of the Indian government.

According to the Indian After-Action Report, the collectors provided very detailed maps and instructions, which were given to the assault force for use in the attacks. This information was absolutely vital to the planning, preparation, and execution of the attack. It can be assumed that these maps and collected information drove the planning, preparation and training for the attack (Indian 37th Court, 2008).

"NO PLAN SURVIVES FIRST CONTACT WITH THE ENEMY"

This quotation from Field Marshal von Moltke has been used throughout modern history. It has been attributed to Karl von Klauswitz and even General George S. Patton. In essence, it is a more eloquent way to say: "Whatever can go wrong, will go wrong," commonly known as Murphy's law.

Modern military and tactical planners are painfully aware that they will never be able to prepare for every possible contingency their forces might encounter. In the attack on Mumbai, this concern is very evident due to the level of control that the LeT handlers in Pakistan attempted to exert over the attacking force throughout the attack.

It is obvious that the LeT handlers did not trust their minions to carry out the plan or believe that they had the ability to make changes or hard decisions during the execution of the attack. Further, the handlers had to continuously cajole their fighters into conducting their operations and to remind them of the requirements of their faith: to die in the completion of the attack. Both sides suffered from Moltke's observation.

For the Indians, the ever-present specter of complacency seemed to have found a home. The preparation for any such complex terrorist attack was virtually nonexistent. There has been little evidence that any formal *protective* threat assessments were ever conducted on the significant targets in Mumbai. Although the Indians field large numbers of law enforcement and paramilitary officers, their training is minimal and their antiterrorist training in this situation was virtually nonexistent. Few if any of the law enforcement officers had ever trained with live ammunition (Chudwin, 2009). When the attack began, the response was chaotic; officers at the scene typically did not engage the terrorists but simply tried to run away with the mass of civilians. There did not seem to be any cogent response to the attackers, no established chain of command for the event, and there was no emergency management system in place to deal with the catastrophe. Even the commander of the counterterrorism office—instead of establishing a command post and directing events— donned body armor, joined the troops, and was then killed in an ambush on his vehicle.

The Mumbai attack was the terrorist debacle that all law enforcement professionals fear the most. However, as threat assessment professionals, what does this significant terrorist event mean to us and the way in which we perform our tasks?

First and foremost, it demonstrates the need for threat assessments at all levels in modern society. Preparation for the worst is something that is often ignored in hopes that it will not occur and that it can be dealt with when it happens. Whether the protection is necessary for a home, a school, or infrastructure, it is essential to identify vulnerabilities to a variety of threats.

Second, no matter how well one plans, one cannot prepare for all contingencies. Threats and vulnerabilities tend to be fluid. New technologies result in new threats and vulnerabilities. Terrorist groups and intelligence agencies spend enormous amounts of time and effort developing new ways to access areas that are typically denied. Cybersecurity is one of those growing areas of concern, as has been seen all too often in recent years. The best that can be hoped for is to make access to sensitive areas so difficult that an enemy will decide that they are too difficult to attack.

Third, the threat assessment process and profession are not static. Ongoing professional study and analysis are required as technologies change or improve. This is especially so in the matter of cybersecurity. Threat assessment professionals must also try to anticipate future methods of attack, no matter how esoteric or arcane. The enemy is not restricted in methods or planning. So we also must not be restricted. Sun Tzu's quotation regarding "knowing your enemy" must rest firmly in our lexicon. The more one knows, the less one fears. We will not be able to stop all attacks, but we can certainly deter and mitigate some of them and their effect on those we want to protect. The philosophy of threat assessment is becoming a part of our security lexicon.

KEY POINTS

- Study: Take a few minutes every day to study some aspect of our profession or an incident that may have impacted the assessment process.
- Find a niche: The threat assessment genre has become so vast that specialties must be developed. Cybersecurity, physical security, and technical security are some. Find your niche and become the subject matter expert.

- Tell others: Clients, peers, subordinates, or students. Teach others about the threat assessment process and how it can benefit them.
- Practice: Use downtime to practice your skills. Pick a location and run your own assessment of it, paying particular attention to your subject matter expertise. Once done, tear your effort apart to see where you did well or could improve.
- Network: Find other threat assessment professionals, either in associations or independently, with whom you can network. Compare skills, resources, and perhaps work together in future efforts.

REFERENCES

Biesterfeld, J. (1998), Cyber-stalking case (names withheld), From the case files of Sovereign Executive Services.

Breuer, W. (1994). *The great raid on Cabanatuan.* New York: Wiley.

Chudwin, J. (2009), Lessons of Mumbai—Tactical/gear issues, Draft Article, November.

Court Investigators et al. (2008), "Final form/report," (Under Section 173 Cr.P.C.) in the Court of Addl. Ch. M.M., 37th Court, Esplanade, Mumbai, November, pp. 3–4.

Court Investigators et al. (2008), "Final form/report," (Under Section 173 Cr.P.C.) in the Court of Addl. Ch. M.M., 37th Court, Esplanade, Mumbai, November, pp. 9–10.

Court Investigators et al. (2008), "Final Form/Report," (Under Section 173 Cr.P.C.) in the Court of Addl. Ch. M.M., 37th Court, Esplanade, Mumbai, November, p. 15 ff.

Gardham, D. (2009). *The Telegraph,* United Kingdom, November. London: Telegraph Media Group.

HBO Documentary Films. (2010). *Terror In Mumbai.* New York, NY.

Meloy, J. R. (2011). Violent true believers. *FBI Law Enforcement Bulletin,* July, pp. 24–32.

Shrivastava, S. (2009), *The World Reporter: News Opinion & Analysis,* November, New York, NY.

Rotella, S. (2011). David Headley, witness in terror trial, ties Pakistani spy agency to militant group. *The Washington Post-Online,* May 23, 2011.

16

Insider Threats in Bioterrorism Cases

RONALD SCHOUTEN AND GREGORY SAATHOFF

Modern organizations face security risks that are both varied and continuous. Most of these risks—including industrial espionage, cyberattacks, and acts of physical violence—arise from external sources. While these are of great consequence, few nefarious acts have the potential for harming organizational operations, security, and morale more than insider threats: those that arise internally from a member of the organization.

This chapter addresses insider threat, with specific attention to the potential for such threats in the life sciences. It does so using as an example the largest and most prominent case of bioterrorism on American soil, the 2001 anthrax mailings. These attacks, referred to as Amerithrax, resulted in the most comprehensive and costly investigation in the history of the FBI. Ultimately, the US Department of Justice (Rugala & Isaacs, 2002) concluded that the attacks were the work of Bruce Ivins, Ph.D., a civilian microbiologist who headed the anthrax vaccine program for the U.S. Department of Defense at the US Army Medical Research Institute of Infectious Diseases (USAMRIID). Ivins committed suicide in July 2008, just prior to his expected indictment. While some continue to dispute his guilt or see the events as part of a larger conspiracy, the evidence indicates that he carried out the attacks and acted alone, without any ties to outside groups.

This chapter focuses on lone actors such as Ivins. Importantly, these lone actors may have vulnerabilities that make them susceptible to recruitment for espionage. Detailed discussion of individuals associated with state or nonstate entities engaging in espionage or other nefarious activity is beyond the scope of this chapter and is best left to chapters on counterespionage. Our discussion of the Amerithrax case includes a review of lessons learned from the analysis of the case by the Expert Behavioral Analysis Panel (EBAP), on which both of the present authors served (EBAP & Saathoff, 2011). While a single case does not define the entire universe of potential insider threats, that case nevertheless serves as an exemplar of individual and organizational risk factors that resulted in tremendous human, financial, and institutional consequences.

DEFINITION AND SCOPE OF THE PROBLEM

Defining Insider Threat

Building upon the definition of insider threat offered by Schultz (2002), we can define insider threat in the biological sciences as the deliberate misuse of systems, laboratory facilities, or biological agents by those who are otherwise authorized to have access to them. Misuse can include (1) theft of materials with intent to transfer them to a third party, cause harm to the organization and the research program, or to use the materials in an attack; (2) interference with research efforts by sabotage or tampering with materials; or (3) making legitimate laboratory facilities available for use by others for illicit purposes.

The Scope and Nature of the Insider Threat in the Life Sciences

The memory and impact of the anthrax mailings loom large more than a decade after they occurred. Some reject the findings of the U.S. Department of Justice (Rugala & Isaacs, 2002) and continue to argue that they did not constitute an insider attack but rather were the work of an outside group, a government project gone awry, or a larger conspiracy or coverup. Others have suggested that, even if the anthrax mailings were the work of an insider, it was the first and only example of such misuse. They argue that the possibility of recurrence is minimal, and the cost of protecting against another attack is excessive in terms of dollars spent and the possible chilling effect on research of increased security measures and scrutiny of scientists. In light of these arguments, it is worth reviewing the evidence for the existence as well as scope of any such problem.

Prior to 2001, the use of biological agents in North America to cause harm to others was infrequent, at least according to publicly available information, but not unknown. In his seminal work on bioterrorism and biocrimes over a hundred-year span, Carus (1998, 2001) identified a total of 180 confirmed cases worldwide involving alleged actual or threatened use of biological agents by terrorists, criminals, or covert state operators. In identifying the motives of the various perpetrators, Carus divided them into three groups: terrorists, criminals, and other/uncertain. Criminals were considered to be those who had motives of financial gain, revenge, or nonpolitical considerations. Only one case, involving the group Dark Harvest, was explicitly motivated by a desire to make a political statement. The contamination of restaurant salad bars with *Salmonella* by the Shree Rajneesh cult in The Dalles, Oregon, in 1984, while a terrorist act, was a politically motivated attempt to incapacitate local residents in order for cult-supported candidates to win an election. The motivation in other cases included murder of specific individuals and acts of revenge within personal or workplace relationships.

Carus identified 33 cases of actual acquisition of biological agents by nonstate actors. In 11 of these cases, the agents were obtained through ordinary channels from biological supply houses. This is still possible today, even after the tightening of the regulation of biological agents over the last two decades, pursuant to the Biological Select Agents and Toxins (BSAT) regulations, as many pathological agents are not on the BSAT list. In four cases reviewed by Carus, the materials were stolen from a research or medical laboratory. Of these, three involved individuals who had legitimate access to the materials as part of their work. The fourth involved the efforts of the Weather Underground movement to persuade a laboratory technician at USAMRIID to provide anthrax spores. Interestingly, 23 of the cases described by Carus involved perpetrators with medical training, many of whom used their positions to acquire and utilize the biological agents in question. The mastermind behind the Shree Rajneesh attacks, for example, was a registered nurse who worked with a trained laboratory technician to culture *Salmonella typhimurium* for use in the attacks.

It is well established that the majority of threats to organizations, from thefts to acts of workplace violence and terrorism, are posed by outsiders rather than insiders (Kosal, 2006; Schouten, 2008). In their study of insider threats in the nuclear industry, discussed in more detail below, Hoffman and associates concluded that while the greatest insider threats to nuclear facilities were posed by those in collusion with outsiders, the risk posed by those conspiring with other insiders or who acted alone could not be ignored (1990). It is worth noting that Hoffman and associates had to look outside the nuclear industry to find examples of insider threats, as none had been realized within that industry.

Publicly available materials relied upon in this chapter indicate that the known incidence of insider threats is low in the nuclear industry and life sciences, but that does not mean that the risks associated with such attacks can be ignored. Risk is defined as the probability of an event multiplied by the severity of its impact ($R = P \times I$). Thus, an event that is likely to come to pass but poses limited threat of harm (e.g., shoplifting in a retail establishment) is considered to be high risk. Similarly, an event of low probability but potentially devastating consequences, like misuse of nuclear and biological materials or facilities, must also be considered high risk.

Biological agents, more so than nuclear materials, lend themselves to misuse by both insiders and outsiders. Unlike nuclear materials, biological agents are self-replicating, and only a small amount of such an agent is necessary to initiate production. In addition, even small quantities of biological agents or toxins may cause illness or death. Because limited quantities are necessary, theft and concealment of usable quantities is easier and less detectable than is the case for nuclear materials. And while skill in microbiology and specific equipment are necessary to successfully culture and produce substantial quantities of these agents, those skills and the requisite equipment are increasingly available.

In considering the level of risk posed by insider threat in the life sciences, the range of consequences of such an event must be considered, including morbidity and mortality, psychological distress, and financial costs.

The human costs of a biological attack are obvious. Amerithrax, for example, was a relatively small-scale attack. The actual number of letters mailed is unknown; only five were recovered. Nevertheless, the attacks resulted in the deaths of 5 people and infection of at least 17 others who survived with various long-term sequelae.

The psychological impact of traumatic events varies by the characteristics of the event and the perpetrator(s). Intentional human-made disasters have a greater psychological impact than natural disasters or unintentional human-made disasters (e.g., an act of terrorism has a greater impact than an industrial accident). Intentional acts of violence, for which the motivation is unknown or difficult to comprehend, have a greater impact than those in which the purposes are apparent (e.g., robbery) (Holloway & Fullerton, 1994). For example, at the time of the 2001 anthrax attacks in the United States, the uncertain motivation for the attacks added to the sense of vulnerability among potential target populations.

Biological agents have unique characteristics that result in social disruption and psychological consequences beyond those seen in attacks with conventional weapons. These include fears that contamination will spread into the community far beyond those initially affected, with coworkers, family, and friends serving as potential vectors. Unlike chemical agents and some biological toxins that have more immediate effects, it is often difficult to distinguish those who have been exposed and infected from uninfected individuals. Symptoms of illness may be unclear and confused with routine infections and psychosomatic symptoms associated with anxiety and fear. This lack of clarity results in false alarms, anxiety among worker populations and their families, and disruption of normal activities, including work (Baum, 1986).

Releases of biological agents and toxins, as well as chemical agents, pose a substantial risk of overwhelming first responders and the health care system, as demonstrated by the 1995 sarin gas attacks in Tokyo by the Aum Shinrikyu cult. The attacks on the Tokyo subway killed 13 and affected hundreds, including over 6,000 people who had not been exposed to the gas but presented themselves to hospitals for emergency evaluation and treatment of symptoms that were psychosomatic in origin, overwhelming the medical response capability. In total, 6,583 people are documented to have claimed injury from attacks perpetrated by Aum Shinrikyo (Danzig et al., 2011; Kyodo News Service, 2010).

Fear and anxiety are increased further when those exposed are unfamiliar with the source or cause of the injury. For this reason, biological, chemical, radiological, and nuclear attacks are likely to cause greater fear and disruption than attacks with conventional weapons. The *perception* of exposure to such materials alone can result in psychological symptoms, social disruption, and—as occurred in the Japanese subway sarin attacks—litigation. Even when later disproved, the perception of exposure can be enough to create symptoms.

The Amerithrax attacks demonstrated the human as well as the economic impact of actual bioterror attacks. The Brentwood postal facility in Washington, DC, the Hart Senate Office Building, and the American Media, Inc., publishing offices in Boca Raton, Florida, were all contaminated with anthrax. As noted above, the human costs were high in spite of the relatively small scale of the attacks. A total of 22 people are known to have been infected, 11 with cutaneous and 11 with inhalational anthrax. Five of those exposed died, all due to inhalational anthrax. Twenty of those infected (91%) worked for the US Postal Service and are presumed to have been unintended targets of the perpetrator (Callahan, 2001). As a result of the mailings to Senators Daschle and Leahy, the Hart Senate Office Building and several other Capitol Hill buildings were shut down for 14 weeks for decontamination. The cleanup efforts are estimated to have cost US taxpayers over $25 million (Heyman, 2002).

Hoaxes, which are common in the wake of actual events, can have a psychological impact that rivals that of actual attacks. There were numerous examples of these after the terror attacks of September 11, 2001. Miami police had to evacuate six downtown buildings after anonymous callers reported that they had planted explosives inside. In Wilmington, Delaware, five buildings were evacuated for the same reason. An anthrax hoax at the Connecticut Department of Environmental Protection on October 11, 2001, resulted in the evacuation of the building and shut down a portion of downtown Hartford. It was estimated to have resulted in $1 million in lost employee productivity alone (Mahony, 2002). The costs of police and fire response, lost sales, requests for medical services, and decreased productivity in the extended community were not included in that estimate.

There is a lack of consensus as to the level of risk of an insider attack with biological agents. While a review of publicly available unclassified documents suggests that the frequency of misuse of biological agents by insiders has been low, there is ample evidence of the physical, psychological, and economic consequences of acts of terrorism and possible exposure to biological agents and toxins. In combination with the ready availability of the skills and equipment necessary to work with these materials and the small quantities needed to begin to develop a stock of the agents, the misuse of biological agents and toxins must be considered a high risk.

Motivations and Characteristics of Insider Threats

A fundamental challenge in assessing and managing insider threat is determining which of an organization's employees, all of whom have presumably been hired because they have the knowledge, skills, and abilities (KSA) to be productive within the organization, are at risk for such an act. In some cases, individuals harbor malicious intent prior to joining the organization and may pursue employment for the specific purpose of carrying out a planned action. In other, even more perplexing cases, individuals with the requisite KSA join the organization for legitimate purposes but subsequently develop the intent to exploit their facilities' weaknesses in order to perpetrate acts that can result in fatal outcomes. Ivins, who devoted his career to developing anthrax vaccines to protect American troops, would appear to fall within this latter group. Other examples include former FBI Supervisory Special Agent Robert Hanssen and former CIA Counterintelligence Officer Aldrich Ames, both of whom turned against their country and spied for Soviet and Russian intelligence.

The characteristics and motivations of insider threats vary, as studies have shown. Insiders may be purely lone actors motivated by identification with a belief or cause or by idiosyncratic beliefs that in some cases are rooted in a major mental illness or severe personality disorder. They also may be part of smaller or larger groups, some of which may be sponsored by outside entities.

Hoffman and associates (1990) conducted a study of insider crimes for the US Department of Energy. Owing to the absence of examples from inside the nuclear industry, they examined 62 cases from other fields and divided the insider threats into three categories:

1. Individuals who were conspiring with outside state or nonstate groups
2. Individuals who were conspiring with other insiders
3. Individuals who were acting for personal reasons

Their research indicated that emotional disturbance, including anger at the employer, was more prevalent in group 3. While 68% of those in group 3 were motivated by financial gain, that motivation was more common among those conspiring with outsiders (85%) or other insiders (92%). Other motivations for the lone insiders included anger at the employer, emotional disturbance, or "idiosyncratic" (e.g., a fantasy of being a hero by discovering the crime).

Elsewhere, we have suggested that the lone insider group may be further divided into five subgroups with varied motivations, none of which are mutually exclusive (Schouten & Saathoff, 2010).

1. Disgruntled individuals seeking to cause harm
2. Disgruntled individuals seeking to demonstrate the capacity to do harm or to cause actual harm
3. Individuals attempting to demonstrate weakness in the system in order to encourage better security (e.g., altruistic hackers)
4. Individuals seeking to demonstrate their own ability and prove their worth to an organization, community, or other individuals
5. Those attempting to test the bounds of science and their ability through unauthorized experimentation

Terrorism was a factor in only 2 of the 62 cases examined by Hoffman and associates. In both of those, they determined that while ideology played a role, the insiders were acting for monetary gain as well.

Literature in the field of financial fraud suggests that three factors contribute to the problem of insider threat in that area: pressure, opportunity, and rationalization (Albrecht, Williams, & Wernz, 1995). Albrecht and colleagues refer to this as the "fraud triangle." Among the pressures to commit fraud, they include financial problems, pressures related to "vice," and work-related pressures. Financial pressures include greed, high personal debt, high medical bills, living beyond one's means, poor credit, personal financial loss, and unexpected financial needs. Vice-related pressures include gambling debts, drug and alcohol abuse, and expensive sexual relationships. The work-related pressures described by Albrecht and colleagues include a desire to "get even" with the employer or someone else, job dissatisfaction, getting little recognition for one's work, fearing loss of one's job, being overlooked for a promotion, and feeling underpaid. Under one or more of these pressures, the insider takes advantage of the opportunity to commit fraud, often intending to do it "just this once." However, the combination of initial success and ongoing pressures leads the perpetrator to rationalize his or her action and progress to an ongoing pattern of fraud.

In examining why insiders may shift from using their KSA for good to malevolent ends, Clark and James (1999) noted that perceptions of unjust treatment by employers often provide a core rationalization for the activity. James and Taylor (2010) propose a model for understanding "negative" or "dark side" creativity. At the heart of the model they suggest is an individual with some form of personality disturbance who exhibits a "motivational complex" that includes one or both of the following: (1) negative feelings toward the employer or the outside world (e.g., resentment, frustration, anger) or (2) pathologically positive goals for him or herself (e.g., fulfillment of grandiose notions of his or her ability, desire for fame or attention, financial gain). An individual such as this, who has both the technical or domain skills to pursue an illicit act and the creative knowledge and skills necessary to develop a plan for the act, can function within the workplace for years, perhaps forever, without acting on his or her impulses. As James and Taylor suggest, however, a situational trigger like a personal crisis, world events, or professional reversals or crises, may lead such an individual to take action.

Ivins provides a good example for this model. Evidence from the case indicates the presence of a personality disturbance that included fluctuation in mood, substance abuse, fear of abandonment and attempts to avoid it, obsession with organizations and individuals who rejected him, a pattern of criminal behavior, and a history of violent fantasies, threats, and acts aimed at revenge against those whom he felt had betrayed or abandoned him. His motivational complex included both negative-outward (depression, anger and resentment toward individuals and his employer) and positive-inward emotions (a desire to be restored to professional prominence, attempts to impress those who had left or rejected him, hopes for financial gain). He had excellent domain skills in the field of microbiology. In addition, Ivins was a creative person, both in his work as a researcher and in his personal life, where he was a musician, poet, performer, screenwriter, juggler and practical joker, not to mention an inventive liar. Ivins possessed most of these characteristics throughout his adult life, yet he continued to do work that earned him the Department of Defense's Outstanding Civilian Employee Award in 2003. His illegal behaviors may be explained by the occurrence of several situational triggers in rapid succession, including personal stressors, psychiatric symptoms, the terrorist attacks of 2001, and threats to close down his vaccine program.

PROTECTING AGAINST INSIDER THREAT

Given the potential harm that can come from the misuse of biological agents and toxins, there is great incentive to find ways of not only detecting and responding to these events when they occur but also of preventing them from occurring in the first place. The desire for a tool that would make it possible to predict who might pose a risk of insider threat in bioterrorism—a prospective profile of perpetrators—is strong, as it is in the areas of workplace violence, attacks on public figures, and other crimes of violence. As in these other fields, however, the reliability and validity of any such prospective profile will be doubtful.

The problems with prospective profiles are well known and widely recognized by experts in the fields of workplace violence (American Society of Industrial Security, 2005; Association of Threat Assessment Professionals, 2005; Rugala & Isaacs, 2002), campus and school shootings, (Drysdale, Modzeleski, & Simons, 2010; Vossekuil,

Reddy, & Fein, 2000), and targeted violence against protectees of the US Secret Service (Fein & Vossekuil, 1999).

A fundamental difficulty with the profiling approach to any of these problems is the same as that encountered with attempts to predict infrequent events like insider threats and acts of violence, including suicide. With all efforts to predict such low-incidence phenomena, even a highly sensitive test will result in a high level of false positives—that is, many individuals will be falsely identified as being at risk (Rosen, 1954). This is problematic from a manpower standpoint where, as is the case with researchers in the field of biological agents and toxins, the pool of those possessing the requisite KSA is relatively small.

As we discuss below, there are risk factors for insider threat that have been derived from cases in various fields of endeavor. Such a list of risk factors has questionable predictive validity as a prospective screening device for several reasons. First, there is the false-positive problem outlined above. Second, and perhaps more importantly, without knowledge of the base rate of a given risk factor or combination of risk factors in the population of concern, it is impossible to determine their validity for screening purposes. This is not a problem for the more obvious and accepted risk factors, such as history of a felony, membership in a terrorist organization, or illegal substance abuse. "Profiles" that contain such items as a history of depression, bipolar disorder, anxiety, "loner," introvert, and alcohol abuse are of much less value because (1) they may be common, particularly so among individuals in a given field, such as academic research; (2) the base rates of the presence of those factors among target populations is unknown, and (3) they are accepted as risk factors on the basis of face validity without any scientific evidence that they are present in individuals truly at risk and not in those who do not pose a risk. Indeed, suggestions of psychological screening as part of personnel reliability programs for life science researchers often elicit skepticism among those researchers. They express concern that such screening will detect psychological problems and eccentricities believed to be common among academics and will be used as the basis for unjustifiably excluding otherwise qualified, safe, and reliable individuals from working in the field. This could dissuade qualified individuals from applying for such positions, with both manpower and productivity implications, and set the stage for disability discrimination suits initiated by individuals who had

been excluded on the basis of a perception of mental illness or other disability.

Finally, in addition to the false-positive problem, reliance upon unproven profiles creates a problem with false negatives (i.e., mistakenly ruling out true positives because they do not exhibit the risk factors on the list). This is a particular problem where an individual passes the initial screening, develops valid risk factors later in his or her work life, but is presumed to be safe because he or she did not "fit the profile" at the time of hire.

Identified Risk Factors

The limited number of insider threat bioterrorism cases available for study makes it worthwhile to consider identified risk factors for insider threat in other fields. Although not a focus of this chapter, it is instructive to look at the classic paradigm for insider threat of espionage through an analysis of 60 years of prior cases, completed by Herbig (2008).

From concerns relating to communism in the 1950s to the 9/11 attacks, one major focus has been individuals with potentially divided loyalties regarding foreign nations or ideologies. From a demographic standpoint, white males have committed most acts of espionage against the United States during the last six decades. However, the percentage of women, minorities, and foreign-born individuals—as well as those with advanced graduate degrees—who have engaged in espionage has increased, as women and minorities have had more access to higher education and international travel has led to globalization. There has also been a "graying" of American spies since 1990, with almost half being over the age of 40. Interestingly, the percentage of individuals who possess no security clearance and yet are able to engage in espionage has increased from 20% before 1980 to 37% since 1990.

The 2008 study also examined motivations and found that the most common motivations to spy against the United States include greed, divided loyalties, and disgruntlement. Smaller numbers of spies related that ingratiation, coercion, thrills, and recognition/ego served as motivators. Although they did not necessarily lead directly to espionage, potential vulnerabilities for recruitment included the following (Herbig, 2008):

- Weak allegiance to the United States
- Foreign influence
- Foreign preference

- Sexual behaviors
- Personal conduct
- Financial considerations
- Alcohol consumption
- Drug involvement
- Psychological conditions
- Criminal conduct
- Handling of protected information
- Outside activities
- Use of information technology systems

The financial sector within the United States is also vulnerable to insider threat. According to the Software Engineering Institute at Carnegie Mellon University (CERT), more than 80% of financial threats are planned in advance and executed during working hours by insiders. Fully a third had been described as "difficult" by management and 17% had been described as "disgruntled." Although approximately a quarter of cases involved people who were in financial difficulty at the time, financial gain was a motive in more than 80% of the cases. Notably, revenge was a motive for almost a quarter of those who perpetrated malicious acts (Cummings et al., 2012).

Theft of intellectual property is a form of insider threat that poses a significant risk to the US economy. Although the FBI notes that "many people experience or exhibit some or all" characteristics that it lists and that "most people will not cross the line and commit a crime," the Bureau instructs employers to examine three separate areas in considering vulnerability to insider threat: personal factors, organizational factors, and behavioral indicators.

Similar to the findings of espionage research noted earlier, the FBI notes the following personal factors as being significant with regard to financial fraud: greed or financial need, divided loyalty, disgruntlement, ingratiation, coercion, thrills, and recognition/ego. In addition, it includes motivators such as a desire to help the "underdog" or a particular cause, compulsive and destructive behaviors, and family problems.

Work carried out as part of the Department of Defense Personnel Security Research Center (PERSEREC) has demonstrated the utility of a personality screening protocol, the Shedler-Westen Assessment Procedure (SWAP), in identifying and detecting individuals at risk of security breaches (Shedler & Westen, 2007). This process involves an extended clinical diagnostic interview that generates

Dispositional Indicators of Risk Exposure (DIRE) scores. Research to date has demonstrated three personnel security risk factors: psychopathy, malignant narcissism, and borderline personality organization (Lang & Schechter, 2011).

Importantly, in addition to personal risk factors, the second area of risk focus is the organization. Lack of training, time pressure, poor identification of sensitive materials, and perceptions that physical security is lacking can make an organization vulnerable to insider threat (Federal Bureau of Investigation, 2012). The Expert Behavioral Analysis Panel's analysis of the Amerithrax case similarly found a number of organizational factors that allowed Ivins to exploit the USAMRIID environment, which gave researchers access to laboratories on weekends and late at night when others were not there. Notably, in the weeks leading up to the anthrax mailings, Ivins' hours in the hot suites during late nights and weekends increased dramatically in a pattern that was not seen before or after. His time in the laboratory during the weeks leading up to the attacks was not only unusual for other scientists but also unprecedented for him. Although he was later unable to explain why he would dramatically increase his time in the laboratory during this period, this unusual behavior did not, at the time, raise concerns among colleagues and supervisors. In the months following the attacks, Ivins repeatedly swabbed his office area for anthrax and cleaned the area without reporting these behaviors, in clear violation of policy and procedure.

While risk factors may predispose an individual to insider threat, behavioral indicators are observable findings that should raise suspicions among colleagues and supervisors and indicate the need for further investigation. Behavioral indicators of increased risk of intellectual property theft listed by the FBI include transfer of proprietary material away from the office without authorization or need, interest in matters outside one's regular scope of duties, unnecessary copying of proprietary materials, remote access of the computer network at odd times, changes in work hours without authorization, disregard for information technology policies, short trips to foreign countries, unreported and/or suspicious foreign contacts, feeling overwhelmed by life stressors, and unusual interest in coworkers (Federal Bureau of Investigation, 2012).

In the case of Ivins, the Expert Behavioral Analysis Panel found that the laboratory environment at USAMRIID was susceptible to the serious threat that he posed. As emphasized in a report on insider cyberthreat, insider threats arise from a combination of characteristics of the insider perpetrator and his or her work environment:

> There is a complex interplay of personal and cultural or environmental factors which, over time, funnel an individual toward insider actions and that an understanding of this critical pathway has implications for personnel screening, monitoring, case management, and training. We also know that predisposing traits and situational factors are only part of the problem. What might be called acute situational stressors such as marital or family problems, episodes of substance abuse, disappointments at work, threatened layoffs, or other stressful life events can trigger an emotional reaction leading to impaired judgment and reckless or vindictive behavior (Anderson, Bozek, Longstaff, Meitzler, & Skroch, 2000, pp. 82–83).

Just as there are dynamic environmental factors that can increase the likelihood of an insider attack, there are also temporal factors regarding the evolution of the perpetrators during the course of their careers. Whether it is an individual like Ivins or a group such as Aum Shinrikyo, methods and motives can evolve over time. A recent analysis of the Japanese Aum Shinrikyo cult reveals how such destructive groups can indoctrinate scientists over time, evolving from the use of weapons for assassination toward broader and indiscriminate mass attacks (Danzig et al., 2011).

LEARNING FROM BIOTERRORISM: THE AMERITHRAX CASE

At least five sealed letter-size envelopes containing powdered anthrax spores were postmarked on September 18 and October 9, 2001. The first set was addressed to media outlets in New York and Boca Raton, Florida. Twenty-two known individuals were infected, with half contracting inhalational anthrax and the others suffering skin infections. Five of those who suffered inhalational anthrax died.

The anthrax attacks became the focus of the largest investigation in FBI history, referred to as Amerithrax, and gave rise to novel scientific advances, including the new discipline of microbial

forensics. Initial suspicions that the attacks were the work of a foreign terrorist group and an extension of the 9/11 attacks were refuted when the spores were traced to US sources. While a number of scientists both inside and outside of government were considered as possible suspects, the investigation focused on Dr. Steven Hatfill starting in 2002. As a result of a perfect storm of media demands, unreliable sources, and felt pressure to demonstrate that progress was being made, Hatfill's name was released as a person of interest (Willman, 2011). As a result, Hatfill filed a series of defamation suits against media outlets and the federal government. The suit against the federal government was settled for $5.8 million in 2008.

Years prior to the settlement of the Hatfill defamation claim, the FBI investigative team had increasingly turned its attention to Dr. Bruce Ivins. At the time of the attacks, Ivins was a 55-year-old microbiologist employed at the US Army Medical Research Institute for Infectious Diseases (USAMRIID). He was a codeveloper of the anthrax vaccine administered to US military serving in the Gulf War.

Keeping in mind our earlier discussion of negative creativity, risk factors, and risk indicators, it is useful to examine some of Ivins' personal characteristics. His personal and professional history is compelling and reveals a number of serious markers of potential for insider threat in that he experienced (1) significant homicidal rage, (2) periods of suicidality, and (3) the abuse of prescription drugs and alcohol. It is beyond the scope of our chapter to provide a full review of Ivins' case, which is provided in greater detail within the authors' Expert Behavioral Analysis Report as well as in recent books by David Willman and Jean Guillemin (EBAP & Saathoff, 2011; Guillemin, 2011; Willman, 2011). With the benefit of microbial forensics, it was established that the strain of anthrax in the letters came from the flask that, according to Ivins' own admission, was solely within his possession and control. Coworkers, family, and friends professed to be unaware of Ivins' secret life of obsessive revenge, late-night drives, and history of illegal behaviors including homicidal planning. When he was finally involuntarily hospitalized for dangerousness to self and others in July 2008, Ivins admitted in a phone call to his therapist that he did in fact require hospitalization for his imminent suicidality and homicidality. Unfortunately, his suicide shortly following his release from that hospitalization prevented the adjudication of the case within the federal court system.

After a year-long review of the extensive documentation related to the case, including Ivins' mental health records, which had been provided to the panel by order of Chief Judge Royce Lamberth of the U.S. District Court for the District of Columbia, the Expert Behavioral Analysis Panel developed its report and submitted it under seal in August 2010. Seven months later Judge Lamberth authorized release of a redacted version of the report, which included findings and recommendations. While it is not our intent to provide a comprehensive summary of the report for this chapter, a brief review of the case's salient issues and key findings will be valuable from the standpoint of offering greater insight into insider threat.

Familiarity played a significant role in the evolution of the threat Ivins posed, as it led to complacency and a decrease in vigilance within the laboratory environment. This lesson is at the heart of the insider threat problem and distinguishes it from more traditional outsider threat. Simply put, the collegial bonds that form among teams of professionals can become shields, obscuring and obstructing the necessary vigilance required within organizations that require a high degree of personnel reliability. This familiarity can cause a supervisor to be blind to pathology and illicit behavior, going so far as to ignore specific threats and indicators of risk rather than to identify and confront the insider.

Ivins, as a trusted insider, posed a serious threat in the arenas of substance impairment, suicidality, and homicidality. Over and above the determination by the US Department of Justice that Ivins was solely responsible for the anthrax mailings postmarked in September and October 2001, he had (1) violated basic biosafety policies and procedures during a period when he was abusing alcohol and sedative-hypnotics; (2) threatened to kill himself with substances including anthrax, required involuntary hospitalization for suicidality, and ultimately took his life with an overdose of acetaminophen; and (3) planned to kill others through the purchase of bomb-making materials, cyanide, and firearms. In addition, he poisoned a bottle of wine that he took to a former colleague and developed a list of enemies with the intent to kill them. He admitted his homicidality when he was involuntarily hospitalized because of his plans to kill others.

Multiple points of failure contribute to insider threat risk. In the case of Ivins, points of failure that allowed his risk to be realized included his treating clinician, the workplace overall, and his supervisors. Ivins revealed his suicidality, homicidality, and substance impairment to individuals who were responsible for separate scientific, professional, and psychiatric domains. Ivins' medical records documented his criminal behaviors, yet they were never reviewed, despite multiple written releases of information issued by Ivins. Had they been reviewed, the information they contained would have prevented his hiring in December 1980. In addition, the failure of one of his psychiatrists to be familiar with Ivins' medical records – which would have illustrated his criminal behavior – and the failure of a USAMRIID senior supervisor to respond to Ivins' threatening behavior are also examples of point failures. Finally, the failure of medical authorities to follow up on required communications authorizing Ivins' return to work in May 2005 is also an example of a point failure both within and across Ivins' domains.

Motivated insiders do not necessarily restrict themselves to specific weapons. Insiders with scientific expertise in one weapon may gain and maintain expertise and develop plans for using other weapons. Ivins acquired many threat agents and developed plans for their use. Although his expertise was with a select biological agent (anthrax), Ivins' substantive threats prior to and following the anthrax letter mailings also included chemicals (poisons), explosives, and firearms. Ivins' comfort in planning and using these various agents underlines the importance of motivating factors rather than professional expertise alone. His expressed plan to poison a female colleague in the 1970s and a female subordinate in 2000 utilized positions of trust as a way to commit murder by stealth, a common feature in other poisoners who exploit existing trusted relationships in order to kill without confrontation (Saathoff, 2011). As a microbiologist, his weapon of choice appeared to be anthrax. However, after losing access to the hot-suite laboratory areas, he resorted to firearms as a means of harming others, going so far as to arrange for a Glock pistol to be brought to him after his own firearms and bulletproof vests had been confiscated following an FBI search of his home.

Assessment of insider threat requires an understanding of the insider's workplace culture. An insider will exploit his or her workplace environment in order to identify and utilize existing gaps in security. Hence an understanding of the workplace is essential to understanding how the insider operates within that habitat. Workplace culture includes not only physical but also social and interpersonal relationships that bond the insider with colleagues, while at the same time shielding the insider from detection. Colleagues explained away Ivins's unusual and at times stealthy behaviors as "Bruce just being Bruce." While USAMRIID culture provided freedom for inquiry for conscientious scientists, that same workplace environment was permissive for Ivins in that, in the weeks leading up to the anthrax mailings, it allowed him to conceal his unusual behaviors. These included unusual spikes in weekend and nighttime hours in the hot suites, physical stalking and cyberstalking of subordinates, photographing himself handling anthrax in a manner that violated standard biosafety procedures, and substance impairment reflected by incoherent emails to colleagues.

Insiders develop their workplace culture over a period of months and years, often transcending existing professional, social, and personal boundaries. Effective insiders evolve over time and their behaviors affect numerous domains in ways that cannot necessarily be predicted at the time of their hiring. Because it included educational and employment records, emails, medical records, and FBI interviews of colleagues, friends and family members, Ivins' investigative file was large and complex. Although he admittedly suffered from mental illness requiring treatment, the investigative review of Ivins' case revealed that psychiatric symptoms were just one of a number of areas of concern. The Expert Behavioral Analysis Panel had the advantage of being composed of professionals with expertise in medicine, psychiatry, law, medical toxicology, and systems management, and thus was able to bring a diverse range of expertise to the analysis of the problem.

Risk factors for insider threat can develop over time. Although Ivins had engaged in revenge-related behaviors since his days as a college and graduate student, his behaviors were variable and dependent in part on his experience at home and at work. As his personal and professional frustrations increased, so too did his use of alcohol and need for medications, which included sedative-hypnotics, antidepressants, and antipsychotics. This deterioration in his behavior and habits emphasizes the importance of programs to identify and mitigate stressors for scientists who are already employed, and also for maintaining strategies to ensure the reliability of personnel at the time of hiring. The proactive development of wellness programs within facilities would offer therapeutic vigilance for scientists and others who work with biological agents and toxins. Such programs could constitute an investment in maintaining productivity while also decreasing threat.

INSIDER THREAT AS A HARD PROBLEM: THE CHALLENGE OF SHIFTING OUR FOCUS FROM OUTSIDER TO INSIDER

Insider threat is a hard problem; that is, its difficulty is matched by its importance (Muresianu, 2010). In addition, insider threat presents a conundrum not only because its very identification is difficult, but also because its solution has serious consequences. For example, the discovery of a bank vice-president's embezzlement is, on the one hand, a positive step toward justice for the perpetrator but, on the other hand, poses a publicity nightmare that may well shake the confidence of investors and customers. Another example could be the existence of a child sexual predator who remains a high-profile leader within a respected institution. In such cases, one might argue that a stance of willful blindness would be a calculated risk in that it could offer the best hope for preserving the institution. In this admittedly cynical perspective, the failure to acknowledge insider threat could be a solution rather than a problem, as it would arguably represent the lesser of two evils.

When the American scientist and visionary Vannevar Bush wrote about the threat of biological weapons in 1949, his rhetoric focused on the taboo nature of the threat, with the implicit assumption that an external enemy would be loath to unleash biological agents into the environment (Bush, 1949). Fifty years later, Nobel Laureate Joshua Lederberg cited Bush's assessment of the nature of the threat:

> Without a shadow of a doubt, there is something in man's makeup that causes him to hesitate, when at the part of bringing war to his enemy by poisoning him or his cattle and crops or disease, even Hitler drew back from this. Whether it is because of some old taboo ingrained in the fiber of the race...the human race shrinks and draws back when the subject is broached. It always has, it probably always will. (Cited in Lederberg, 1999, p. 6)

Lederberg reflected on the emergence of the bioterrorism threat by referencing Vannevar Bush and the changes that have taken place in the twenty-first century. Underlining the fact that it is indeed a "hard problem," he stated "there are no panaceas here, but little thought has yet been given towards the most elementary measures that could have some benefit" (Lederberg, 2004, p. 16). Using the anthrax attacks as an illustration of the seriousness of the problem, Lederberg described the insidious nature of bioterrorism with the realization that "Biowarfare agents were accessible to individuals and terrorist groups with no discernible launching from a sovereign state" (p. 17).

Perhaps the greatest obstacle to understanding the problem of insider threat is *seeing* it in the first place. The problem will remain invisible as long as we search in the wrong place. Unfortunately, when it comes to insider threat, cultural denial is the norm. It is admittedly much easier to focus on both the outsider and external security measures (i.e., guns, gates, and guards). These perimeter measures, while important, have little or nothing to do with effective personnel reliability measures aimed at ensuring that only safe, reliable, and trustworthy individuals have access to materials and information that require the highest level of protection.

Although we are accustomed to scanning the horizon in search of outsider threat, the true challenge lies within; it requires a paradigm shift in the form of willingness to attend to insider, not just external, threats. We can again return to Dr. Ivins as an example. The authors of the Expert Behavioral Analysis Panel Report found that supervisory denial of the problem can supersede existing personnel reliability measures. Indeed, just days after the US Department of Justice's financial settlement in the Hatfill case was announced and in the final days of his work at USAMRIID, when a subordinate complained of Ivins' verbal threats to shoot and kill others, Ivins' supervisor did not notify security or ask for an assessment of the scientist. Rather, the supervisor advised the subordinate to merely "hide in the hot suites," saying that Ivins no longer had access to those laboratories because of his earlier behavior, which had violated basic standards of biosafety. Whether the supervisor's refusal to acknowledge the problem and take action constituted willful blindness or contrived ignorance is difficult to know for certain (Luban, 1999). We do know that the subordinate's serious report about Ivins' behavior in the laboratory on July 7, 2008, was essentially ignored and left for others to face two days later. Ivins'

repetition of his threatening statements and behavior in an evening group therapy session required the two therapists present to take action by requesting an assessment for civil psychiatric commitment, which was obtained the following day (EBAP & Saathoff, 2011).

The problem is hard not only because of the cultural denial and the challenge to look at ourselves and our coworkers, but also because of the potential long-term damage to the workplace from insider threat. Such events constitute an existential threat to an organization, and can damage its core. Whether an insider's criminal behavior occurs in a government or private laboratory, the confidence of taxpayers and stockholders can be shaken, and ultimately can lead to the destruction of the corporation or government agency through withdrawal of support or increased scrutiny and regulation that can damage morale and productivity. Because the threat of dissolution is very real, exposing the problem can seem more dangerous than the actual threat itself. The organization may actually reinforce the very problem of cultural denial, which is so corrosive in the first place.

In addition to the antecedent cultural complacency and devastating aftermath, the investigative process involved in addressing insider threat is a great challenge that is often painful to those innocent employees unaccustomed to the increased vigilance and decreased transparency that accompany an investigation. Because of the rarity of these events, any member of a laboratory workforce is unlikely to experience more than one serious investigation of insider threat during his or her career. Because it is such a foreign experience, often anathema in a collaborative environment of colleagues, an investigation can be polarizing and disruptive of the essential team processes necessary to the functioning of an effective laboratory. When, as in the Ivins case, the perpetrator names numerous colleagues as probable perpetrators while maintaining close relationships with those same colleagues, the resulting atmosphere becomes not only polarizing but also toxic.

The process of inquiry in science requires transparency. Unfortunately this process is subverted by the stealth required by the insider perpetrator. In a laboratory unaccustomed to scrutinizing colleagues, the perpetrator can exploit that environment. Certainly a culture of denial allows for the type of insider crimes that require stealth and duplicity.

In the arena of Chemical, Biological, Radiological, Nuclear and Explosive (CBRNE) weapons, the most vexing challenge is that senior scientists have few peers who can monitor—much less understand—the complexities of criminal behavior in a laboratory. Because few are privy to the most advanced areas of classified scientific research, the scientist perpetrator who records a secret formula or equation is difficult to detect, whether he or she scribbles it on the back of an envelope or texts into a mobile phone.

CONCLUSION

History and logic inform us that insider threats in the life sciences are real and pose a high risk by virtue of their demonstrated devastating impact, if not their frequency. Assessment and prevention of insider threats of bioterrorism require an appreciation of the personal and organizational risk factors outlined above, which are associated with such threats in the life sciences and elsewhere. The Amerithrax case provides important lessons that can be generalized to assessing and managing insider threats related to bioterrorism and other areas.

KEY POINTS

- The problem is real and serious, if not common.
- Biological agents and toxins have unique qualities that increase the seriousness of their impact and the ease with which they can be stolen and concealed.
- Risk factors for insider threat can develop over time in individuals who were safe, reliable, and trustworthy earlier in their careers.
- Motivations for insider threat include negative factors such as dissatisfaction with the employer due to anger and perception of unfair treatment, revenge, financial pressures, and resentment toward individuals, groups, or the world at large.
- Motivations for insider threats also include positive factors in the form of pathological self-interest, such as the fulfillment of grandiose notions of one's ability, desire for fame, attention, and financial gain.
- Risk factors may undermine the desire to realize an insider threat until a situational trigger appears and the opportunity for action presents itself.

- Organizational risk factors for insider threat include complacency, failure to follow and utilize security policies and procedures, and a lack of willingness to address behavioral problems and other risk factors.
- The management of insider threat risk requires comprehensive personnel reliability measures that are commensurate with the level of risk posed by the information, materials, and equipment to which personnel have access.
- The assessment and management of insider risk should be based on established risk factors and behavioral indicators, as opposed to prospective profiles, in order to avoid problems with both false positives and false negatives.
- Institutional cultures that emphasize collective responsibility for safety, wellness, and security offer the best protection against the deterioration in personnel health and behavior that can increase the risk of insider threat.
- Those who assess insider threats should expect to encounter institutional and individual resistance from supervisors and coworkers who are unable to accept that someone with whom they work and associate has turned against them and the organization.

REFERENCES

Albrecht, W. S., Williams, T. L., & Wernz, G. W. (1995). *Fraud: Bringing light to the dark side of business.* Burr Ridge, IL: Irwin.

American Society of Industrial Security. (2005). *Workplace violence prevention and response guideline* (p. 18). Available at: http://lamontwatson.com/wp-content/uploads/2013/03/Item_1635E-WPV_GDL.pdf

Anderson, R. H., Bozek, T., Longstaff, T., Meitzler, W., & Skroch, M. (2000). *Research on mitigating the insider threat to information systems-# 2* (No. RAND-CF-163-DARPA). Santa Monica, CA: RAND. Available at: http://www.dtic.mil/cgi-bin/GetTRDoc?AD=ADA386077

Association of Threat Assessment Professionals. (June 10, 2005). *Violence risk assessment guideline: Standard considerations for assessing the risk of future violent behavior.* Huntington Beach, CA: Association of Threat Assessment Professionals.

Baum, A. (1986). Toxins, technology, disaster. In G. R. VandenBos & B. K. Bryant (Eds.), *Cataclysms, crises, and catastrophes* (pp. 9–53). Washington, DC: American Psychological Association.

Bush, V. (1949). *Modern arms and free men*. New York: Simon and Schuster.

Callahan, M. V. (December, 2001). Perspectives on low technology endospore biological munition production. Paper presented at a National Academy of Science Special Meeting, Washington, D.C.

Carus, W. S. (1998). Biological warfare threats in perspective. *Critical reviews in microbiology, 24*(3), 149–155.

Carus, W. S. (2001). *Bioterrorism and biocrimes: The illicit use of biological agents since 1900*. Washington, DC: Center for Counterproliferation Studies, National Defense University.

Clark, K., & James, K. (1999). Justice and positive and negative creativity. *Creativity Research Journal, 12*(4), 311–320.

Cummings, A., Lewellen, T., McIntire, D., Moore, A., & Trzeciak, R. (2012). *Insider threat study: Illicit cyber activity involving fraud in the U.S. financial services sector* (CMU/SEI-2012-SR-004). Available at the Software Engineering Institute, Carnegie Mellon University website: http://www.sei.cmu.edu/library/abstracts/reports/12sr004.cfm

Danzig R., Sageman M., Leighton T., Hough L., Yuki H., Kotani R., & Hosford Z. M. (July 20, 2011). *Aum Shinrikyo: Insights into how terrorists develop biological and chemical weapons*. Washington, DC: Center for a New American Security.

Drysdale, D. A., Modzeleski, W., & Simons, A. B. (2010). *Campus attacks: Targeted violence affecting institutions of higher education*. Washington, DC: U.S. Secret Service, U.S. Department of Homeland Security, Office of Safe and Drug-Free Schools, U.S. Department of Education, and Federal Bureau of Investigation, U.S. Department of Justice. Available at http://www.fbi.gov/publications/campus/campus.pdf

Expert Behavioral Analysis Panel & Saathoff, G. B. (2011). *The Amerithrax case: Report of the Expert Behavioral Analysis Panel*. Redacted version. Vienna, VA: Research Strategies Network. Available at https://www.researchstrategiesnetwork.org/images/docs/Document_Interior_062711_Redacted.pdf

Federal Bureau of Investigation. (2012). *The insider threat: An introduction to detecting and deterring an insider spy*. Available at: http://www.fbi.gov/about-us/investigate/counterintelligence/the-insider-threat

Fein, R. A., & Vossekuil, B. (1999). Assassination in the United States: An operational study of recent assassins, attackers, and near-lethal approachers. *Journal of Forensic Sciences, 44*, 321–333.

Guillemin, J. (2011). *American anthrax: Fear, crime, and the investigation of the nation's deadliest bioterror attack*. New York: Times Books.

Herbig, K. L. (March, 2008). *Changes in espionage by Americans: 1947–2007*. Defense Personnel Security Research Center, Technical Report 08–05. Available at: http://www.fas.org/sgp/library/changes.pdf

Heyman, D., Achterberg, J., & Laszlo, J. (2002). *Lessons from the anthrax attacks: Implications for U.S. bioterrorism preparedness*. CSIS Report.

Hoffman, B., Meyer, C., Schwarz, B., & Duncan, J. (1990). *Insider crime: The threat to nuclear facilities and programs*. Santa Monica, CA: Rand Corporation. Available at: https://www.ncjrs.gov/pdffiles1/Digitization/147423NCJRS.pdf

Holloway, H. C., & Fullerton, C. S. (1994). The psychology of terror and its aftermath. In R. J. Ursano, B. G. McGaughey, & C. S. Fullerton (Eds.), *Individual and community responses to trauma and disaster* (pp. 31–45). Cambridge, UK: Cambridge University Press.

James, K., & Taylor, A. (2010). Positive and negative creativity (and unintended consequences). In D. H. Cropley, A. J. Cropley, J. C. Kaufman, & M. A. Runco, (Eds.), *The dark side of creativity* (pp. 33–56). New York: Cambridge University Press.

Kosal, M. E. (2006). Terrorism targeting industrial chemical facilities: Strategic motivations and the implications for U.S. security. *Studies in Conflict & Terrorism, 29*(7), 719–751.

Kyodo News Service. (December 20, 2010). Police final tally confirms 6,583 fell victim to 8 Aum-related crimes. *Japan Today*. Available at: http://www.religionnews-blog.com/25531/final-police-tally-confirms-6583-f ell-victim-to-8-aum-related-crimes

Lang E., & Schechter, O. (July 2011). Human Reliability/Insider Threat Technical Exchange (conference presentation). Ft. Belvoir, Virginia.

Lederberg, J. (Ed.). (1999). *Biological weapons: Limiting the threat*. Cambridge MA: MIT Press.

Lederberg, J. (2004). Psyche at risk, psyche as armor: Biodefense as primary prevention. In R. J. Ursano, A. E. Norwood, & C. S. Fullerton (Eds.), *Bioterrorism: Psychological and public health interventions* (pp. 16–17). Cambridge, UK: Cambridge University Press.

Luban, D. (1999). Contrived ignorance. *Geo. LJ, 87*, 957.

Mahony E. H. (June 5, 2002). Anthrax hoax case falters. *Hartford Courant*. Available at: http://articles.courant.com/2002-06-05/news/0206050199_1_faryniarz-h oax-s-perpetrator-hoax-victim

Muresianu, J. (April 10, 2010). Available at: http://socialscience.fas.harvard.edu/hardproblems

Rosen, A. (1954). Detection of suicidal patients: An example of some limitations in the prediction of infrequent events. *Journal of Consulting Psychology, 18*(6), 397.

Rugala, E. A., & Isaacs, A. R. (Eds.). (2003). *Workplace violence: Issues in response*. Critical Incident Response Group, National Center for the Analysis of Violent Crime, FBI Academy.

Saathoff, G. (2011). Poisoners and their relationship to victims: the need for an evidence-based understanding. In C P. Holstege, T. Neer, G. Saathoff, & R. B. Furbee

(Eds.), *Criminal poisoning: Clinical and forensic perspectives* (pp. 13–18). Sudbury, MA: Jones and Bartlett.

Schouten, R. (2008). Workplace violence and the clinician. In R. I. Simon & K. Tardiff (Eds.), *Textbook of violence assessment and management* (pp. 501–520). Washington, DC: American Psychiatric Publishing.

Schouten, R., & Saathoff, G. (2010). Biosurety in the post-9/11 era. *Microbial Forensics,* 2nd edition (pp. 221–238). Elsevier.

Schultz, E. E. (2002). A framework for understanding and predicting insider attacks. *Computers & Security, 21*(6), 526–531.

Shedler J., & Westen D. (2007). The Shedler-Westen assessment procedure (SWAP): Making personality disorder diagnosis clinically meaningful. *Journal of Personality Assessment, 89*(1), 41–55.

Vossekuil, B., Reddy, M., & Fein R. (2000). *Safe school initiative: An interim report on the prevention of targeted violence in schools.* Washington, DC: U.S. Secret Service.

Willman, D. (2011). *The mirage man: Bruce Ivins, the anthrax attacks, and America's rush to war.* New York: Bantam Dell Publishing Group.

17

Threat Assessment of Targeted Honor-Based Violence

HENRIK BELFRAGE AND LINDA EKMAN

Honor-based violence can be defined as any "actual, attempted or threatened physical harm, including forced marriages, with honour as the motive" (Belfrage, 2005). In its most extreme form it is manifested as murder of a family member (most often a woman or girl) or an intimate partner of a family member, because of the perpetrator's belief that the victim has brought dishonor upon the family (e.g., Welchman & Hossain, 2005). The perceived dishonor is most often the result of one of the following behaviors or the suspicion of such behaviors: (a) dressing in a manner unacceptable to the family or community, (b) wanting to terminate or prevent an arranged marriage or desiring to marry by own choice, (c) engaging in sexual acts outside marriage or having a nonsexual relationship perceived as inappropriate, or (d) engaging in homosexual acts (e.g., Chesler, 2009). Honor-based violence can also occur within social groups, where the victim has violated the group norms and dishonored the group in some way.

According to the United Nations, approximately 5,000 women and girls lose their lives in honor killings around the world each year, usually at the hands of their own family members (www.unfpa.org). The problem seems to exist particularly in countries in the Middle East and South Asia as well as in Africa and the Balkans. However, studies suggest that honor killings are accelerating in North America and may correlate with the numbers of first-generation immigrants (Chesler, 2009). In Europe, where cases are reported from all countries, Great Britain seems to have the highest number of honor killings, approximately one every month (The Foreign & Commonwealth Office, 2004).

There is some debate about the motivation for honor killings. In describing honor killings in North America, Chesler (2009) argues that "the common denominator in each case is not culture but religion," while others state that honor killings are about patriarchy, not religion (e.g., Sever & Yurdakul, 2001). To these authors the problem seems to have its roots in both religion and patriarchy, since the problem basically can be described as men's reputation in the eyes of other men—a view sometimes rooted in religion and sometimes in patriarchy. This is supported by Macey (1999), who argues that a combination of culture, religion, and patriarchy must be considered in this context. However, it is important to keep in mind that perpetrators of honor-based violence have cultural and religious attitudes that are not considered representative of any religion or culture worldwide. Additionally, we like to stress that irrespective of the explanation we choose for the existence of honor-based crimes, the severity of the problem must be acknowledged and taken seriously.

In honor-based cultures, it is only men who can be regarded as honorable, and their honor depends to a great extent on the actions of the female members of their families. It is particularly important for the men to have control over the female family members' sexuality (Akpinar, 2003).

Honor-based crimes include not only murder and violence. One important part of honor-based violence, for example, is forced marriage and the threat of a forced marriage. Between 2003 and 2005, for example, 518 forced marriages were recorded in London (The Foreign & Commonwealth Office, 2004). In Sweden, based on information from surveys, it is estimated that approximately 70,000 adolescents feel that they are not entitled to choose their partners freely, and 8,500 fear being subjected to a forced marriage (The Swedish National Board for Youth Affairs, 2010).

In a recent Swedish study of honor-based violence, it was found that as many as 84% of the victims were women, most often daughters of the perpetrators. The second most common victim group consisted of present and former wives, but there was also a small group (16%) consisting of males who were mainly unaccepted boyfriends of the offenders' daughters. The overall picture was that cases with suspected honor-based criminality usually are assessed as high risk. The risk was particularly high when the victims were daughters (Belfrage et al., 2012a).

THE NEED FOR A DIFFERENT APPROACH IN ASSESSING THE RISK FOR HONOR-BASED VIOLENCE

Undoubtedly there are few other crimes as complicated to investigate and understand as honor-based crimes. Law enforcement usually deals with individuals who commit crimes that are considered unacceptable by most other people, particularly when the victims are women and girls. Such perpetrators are often viewed as psychopaths, mentally ill, or evil. But in dealing with honor-based criminality, the planning and execution often involve multiple family members, usually without personality disorders or major mental disorders; it can include mothers, sisters, brothers, cousins, uncles, and grandfathers of the victim, whose actions are considered good or necessary. Since entire families and sometimes even social communities are involved, investigations often have to include different authorities and sometimes several countries.

Very common risk factors among violent offenders in correctional populations are previous violence, anti-social attitudes, personality disorders and substance abuse (Webster, Douglas, Eaves, & Hart, 1997). Assessors will typically find none of these

in dealing with perpetrators of honor-based violence. Thus common risk instruments for violence, rooted in broader groups of violent offenders, will undoubtedly focus on risk factors of little or even no interest in this context and miss others that might be crucial, such as forced marriages.

Three high-profile cases of honor killings in Sweden came to play a particularly important role in our understanding of the need for a somewhat different approach in assessing risk in honor-based violence cases. The various insights gained from these cases are described below.

PELA

Swedish-Kurd Pela Atroshi was just 19 years old when she was shot to death during a visit to the family hometown in the northern part of Iraq in June 1999. The family moved to Sweden in 1995, and Pela adapted quickly to the Swedish lifestyle, which led to conflicts with her parents. In January 1999 Pela left home permanently; but she missed her family and eventually returned home, later agreeing to an arranged marriage in Kurdistan.

When the Atroshi family arrived in Iraq, Pela was killed by two of her uncles in front of her mother and younger sister. The Iraqi court sentenced her father and one of the uncles to five months' probation because their motives were "honorable." However, when the uncles came back to Sweden, they were arrested, eventually convicted for murder, and sentenced to life in prison. The Swedish court stated that since the murder was obviously planned in Sweden, the uncles could be prosecuted in Sweden.

A couple of years later, the first author of this chapter interviewed one of the uncles as part of a risk assessment in the Swedish correctional system, in the course of which he gained access to very detailed and extensive material; everything from the Iraqi police investigation and the whole legal process had been translated into Swedish. It was obvious from the material that the uncles and the father were very clear about the murder and displayed attitudes supporting honor-based violence when they were in Iraq, probably because they knew that they did not have much to fear in terms of the sentence. In Sweden, however, they firmly denied having committed the crime and also denied having any attitudes or values supporting honor-based violence. This was considered somewhat surprising, since it would seem likely that if an attitude is so important that one is prepared to kill even one's own flesh and blood, one should also readily admit to it and defend it if challenged. However, in our experience, denial is very common, probably because the perpetrators involved understand that attitudes in support of honor-based violence are totally banned and unacceptable in western societies and will not gain them any sympathy in the courts.

What was evident in the Pela case was that neither the uncles nor the father displayed many of the traditional risk factors, such as previous violence, antisocial attitudes, substance use problems, or personality disorders. Thus using a traditional risk assessment instrument might not be the optimal way to identify the risk among presumptive perpetrators of honor-based violence.

FADIME

Fadime, a 25-year-old woman of Kurdish origin from Turkey, had migrated to Sweden as a 7-year-old with her family. She was shot to death by her father on January 21, 2002. Because she had not complied with her family's wishes to marry her cousin, she had received death threats for years from her father and brother. Instead of her cousin, she had fallen in love with a young Swedish man. Additionally, she had given testimony to the Swedish Parliament, where she explained the patriarchal cultural tradition of her upbringing, whereby female sexuality was relegated to male control according to the code of honor and shame. She also emphasized the fact that her family needed more help to integrate into Swedish society (see Akpinar, 2003).

Fadime's speech in the Swedish parliament upset her family; she was banned by her father and brother from coming home and threatened with death if she did so. The Swedish police took her case very seriously, and she lived far from her hometown in an apartment unknown to her parents. However, because she was feeling very isolated and longed to see her mother, she secretly visited her hometown one day. Somehow her father found out and shot Fadime dead at the mother's and sister's apartment.

One of the most important lessons learned from the Fadime case was that these victims are extremely vulnerable. Victims of honor-based violence are commonly young females who sometimes have to live isolated and hidden away from all their family, relatives, and friends; because of their loneliness, they can often act in ways that compromises their safety. It is therefore of great importance to incorporate and analyze victim vulnerability factors in carrying out risk assessments in this context.

ABBAS

Abbas Rezai, a 20-year old refugee from Afghanistan, was living alone in the north of Sweden. In 2005, on the Internet, he came in contact with a 16-year old girl, also from Afghanistan, who was living with her family in the south of Sweden. They eventually fell in love, which was totally unacceptable to her family. She was already promised and forcibly engaged to another man chosen by her family; moreover, Abbas came from a family considered by the girl's family to be of low status.

The young girl eventually fled from her family and hid with Abbas in northern Sweden. The girl's family searched very intensively for her and reported her missing to the police. After a couple of weeks the young couple made a mistake: they contacted the Swedish social authorities. They told staff at the social services about their situation and that they were convinced that the girl's family would kill them both if they were found. The staff at social services listened to their story and immediately contacted the girl's family by phone, asking them if it was true that they posed a risk to their child and her boyfriend. The family explained that all this was an unfortunate misunderstanding, and that they just wanted the young couple to come home so that they could all celebrate their upcoming engagement. Despite protests from the young couple the authorities then arranged for their travel back home. Abbas told all his friends that he was convinced that he would never survive this trip.

In order to make sure that everything was all right, a couple of social workers escorted the young couple to the door of the family's apartment. The social workers noted that the family did not look happy in welcoming the youngsters, so they actually stood outside the apartment door for almost five minutes and listened in case something should happen before they left. Later, in the same apartment, Abbas was subjected to the most horrific murder anyone can imagine. The family beat him with an iron rod and a baseball bat, poured boiling oil in his throat, scalped him, and stabbed him in his buttocks and all over the body. The mother, father, and son were all tried for murder, but from the start the teenage son claimed full responsibility for the crime; he said that he was the only one involved in the murder and that the act had nothing to do with honor. The daughter survived but has been living in a shelter, unknown to her family, for many years.

There were important lessons to be learned from this case as well. As in several other honor cases, the involved families convinced the youngest family member to take responsibility for the crime, since young people face less extensive judicial sanctions and comparatively short periods of institutionalization. The most important lesson, however, probably involved the naïveté of the authorities. Social services were heavily criticized for the way they handled this case. The authorities, however, pointed out that they were unfamiliar with honor-based violence and unable to assess risk adequately in cases like this. They had never received any training in this very complex area, and this was true. The authorities were in great need of training and education on how to act and assess risk in cases involving suspected honor-based violence.

The aftermath of this case was that the son eventually changed his story, now pointing the finger at his parents. The case was reopened in 2011, after which the father and mother were convicted of murder and sentenced to 10 years in prison.

THE STRUCTURED PROFESSIONAL JUDGMENT APPROACH TO RISK ASSESSMENT

A common approach to risk assessment is Structured Professional Judgment (SPJ). Decision making is assisted by guidelines developed to reflect the "state of the art" with respect to scientific knowledge and professional practice (Borum, 1996). These guidelines attempt to define the risk being assessed, recommend what information should be considered as part of the evaluation and how it should be collected, and identify a set of core risk factors and sometimes victim vulnerability factors that, according to the scientific and professional literature, should be weighed as part of any reasonably comprehensive assessment. SPJ guidelines help to improve the consistency and usefulness of decisions and certainly improve the transparency of decision making (Kropp, Hart, & Lyon, 2008; Belfrage et al., 2012b). The use of SPJ guidelines also permits evaluators to consider the uniqueness of the case at hand.

Since 2005 Swedish law enforcement has taken an SPJ approach in carrying out threat and risk assessments in cases involving suspected honor-based violence. The PATRIARCH, Draft Version (Belfrage, 2005), to our knowledge the only risk assessment instrument in this context, was developed from a SPJ approach and mandated for use by the Swedish police in cases of honor-based violence. The process of developing this checklist, the way it has been revised and modified over the years, and the experiences from its use in practice are described in detail in Belfrage et al. (2012a).

THE PATRIARCH

The PATRIARCH, Draft version[1], is a checklist comprising empirical factors that have proven to be of importance in this particular context and assembled with professional integrity and responsibility. A literature search of important risk factors was conducted with particular focus on the following areas: general violence, targeted violence, spousal violence, stalking, and honor-based violence. Additionally, experts in the field were consulted and asked to comment on previous drafts of the PATRIARCH. It was tested in practice for several years and modified after experience and feedback. Finally, a prospective study was conducted, where an important finding was a significant correlation between number of risk factors and vulnerability factors in the PATRIARCH and the level of risk assessed by the police (Belfrage et al., 2012a). The factors in the PATRIARCH seem to capture risk in this particular context (Table 17.1).

As can be seen in Table 17.1, the PATRIARCH consists of 15 factors: 10 risk factors and 5 victim vulnerability factors. The latter have proven to be of significant importance in all contexts of targeted violence. Contemporary SPJ guidelines in the contexts of stalking (Stalking Assessment and Management, or SAM) (Kropp, Hart, & Lyon, 2008), and spousal assault (Brief Spousal Assault Form for the Evaluation of Risk, or B-SAFER) (Kropp, Hart, & Belfrage, 2010) both incorporate victim vulnerability factors. The importance of these factors is also accentuated by the fact that many victims of honor-based violence are young girls who have had to leave and hide away from their families and friends with the same subcultural values. These girls are often extremely isolated and lonely and struggle to have a consistent attitude and behavior toward their presumptive perpetrators. The five victim vulnerability factors are basically the same as those in the B-SAFER (Kropp, Hart, & Belfrage, 2010).

The risk factors are a combination of traditional risk factors for targeted violence with support in previous research on targeted violence ("violent threats or thoughts," "violent acts," "escalation," and "personal problems") and factors more specifically directed at

TABLE 17.1. THE PATRIARCH, DRAFT VERSION,—CHECKLIST FOR THE ASSESSMENT OF RISK FOR PATRIARCHAL VIOLENCE WITH HONOR AS MOTIVE

Risk Factors N,P,Y	Victim Vulnerability Factors* N,P,Y
1. Violent threats or thoughts	11. Inconsistent behavior and/or attitude
2. Violent acts	12. Extreme fear
3. Honor based violent acts	13. Inadequate access to resources
4. Arranged marriages or engagements	14. Unsafe living situation
5. Escalation	15. Personal problems
6. Attitudes that support honor violence	
7. High degree of insult	
8. Origin from an area with known subcultural values	
9. Lack of cultural integration	
10. Personal problems	

Other considerations?

Summary risk rating:

  — *Imminent (acute) risk? (N,P,Y)*

  — *Long term risk? (N,P,Y)*

  — *Risk for severe/fatal violence? (N,P,Y)*

Specify risk (scenarios?):

Safety plan (consider how actions might generate threats):

---

* The victim vulnerability factors are drawn from the B-SAFER.
Source: Kropp, Hart, and Belfrage (2010). Reprinted with permission.

honor-based violence ("previous honor-based violence," "arranged marriages or engagements," "attitudes that support honor-based violence," "high degree of insult," "origin from an area with known subcultural values," and "lack of cultural integration").

Some of the above mentioned risk factors may seem somewhat surprising (e.g., "personal problems") and controversial (e.g., "origin from an area with known subcultural values" and "lack of cultural integration"). None of these risk factors are causal by nature. On the contrary, personal problems and lack of cultural integration generally do not have anything to do with risk of honor-based violence. However, in some cases and in some contexts, these factors have been judged important to consider in assessing risk in honor-based cases. Generally, honor-based violence is characterized by well-planned acts, often with more than one perpetrator involved. In some cases, though, the perpetrator is acting alone and is motivated by very irrational personal beliefs. These perpetrators have generally been found to have personal problems such as unemployment, substance abuse, and/or mental health problems. Thus, the purpose of this risk factor is to ensure that the assessor considers whether one or more of the presumptive perpetrators might have such problems. Such information can contribute in an important way to a risk assessment, particularly

if the assessor comes to the conclusion that a family/clan does not pose a threat to a presumptive victim but that a single person does.

The risk factor "lack of cultural integration" does not mean that people who adhere to their culture of origin are not integrated and therefore at risk of committing honor-based violence. The essence here is whether presumptive perpetrators have any understanding of, and respect for, the culture in the country in which they are living and whether their beliefs are in conflict with fundamental human rights (e.g., the right to choose one's own partner).

The most important risk factor here is "arranged marriages or engagements." A number of scholars argue not only that forced marriages are a type of honor-based crime in themselves, but that they are also the precursors to or results of other types of honor-based violence (e.g., Reddy, 2008; Welchman & Hossain, 2005). Forced marriage may lead to ongoing marital rape because of the lack of consent to the marriage. Once she is married, a woman's attempts to escape from a forced marriage are often the catalyst for further violence, including "honour killing" (Siddiqui, 2005). Forced marriage may also be used to prevent women from exercising a range of autonomous behavior or actions, such as attempting to choose their own partners (Chakravarti, 2005).

"Attitudes that support or condone honor-based violence" might be seen as somewhat self-evident or arbitrary. Some readers might argue that this is what this whole problem is all about. And, to a large extent we are prepared to agree. The reason this risk factor is included in the PATRIARCH is that it is so important to carefully consider the involved persons' attitudes. It is well known that a person's attitudes to a great extent trigger his or her behavior. In our experience, it is commonly quite easy to get a good picture of the attitudes involved in a case, whether the victims or the alleged perpetrators are interviewed. We have defined "attitudes that support or condone honor-based violence" as subcultural or personal beliefs and values that encourage, excuse, justify, or minimize abusive, controlling, and violent behavior (e.g., forced marriages).

OTHER CONSIDERATIONS

A checklist such as the PATRIARCH can never be claimed to be perfect or to include all risk and vulnerability factors that appear in every single case. One has to remember that all factors in the PATRIARCH are drawn from the literature and from various professionals' experiences, where data are considered on a group level. Each case is, however, unique, and it is therefore important to encourage users to consider alternate or other possible case-specific factors in using the checklist. To have space for "other considerations" is important not only for practical usefulness but also for reasons of principle, since this clearly differentiates the PATRIARCH from being an actuarial risk instrument, with scores, cutoffs, and norms.

SUMMARY RISK RATINGS

Finally, the evaluator should make a summary risk rating in terms of low, medium, or high risk. Again, it is important to keep in mind that the PATRIARCH should not be used in an actuarial manner. That is, evaluators should not attempt to quantify and combine algorithmically judgments of risk that are made using the PATRIARCH. There is no magic formula for calculating risk. It might be both possible and reasonable for an evaluator to judge a case as "high" on the presence of a single risk factor, or "low" on the presence of several risk factors. The important thing is that the evaluator has formed a structured base for his or her decisions without leaving out evidently important risk and victim vulnerability factors.

Evaluators summarize their opinions of risk for several reasons. First, and of utmost importance, a summary risk rating can act as a formal base upon which one can make decisions regarding protective actions. In Swedish law enforcement, for example if an assessment is made using the PATRIARCH or any other SPJ assessment tool and the summary risk is "High acute risk for severe violence," there is an increased possibility of motivating higher-level protection beyond just supportive measures from the police.

Summary risk ratings are also of great importance for research and evaluation purposes. These ratings make it possible for researchers to carry out studies on how various risk and victim vulnerability factors might influence summary risk ratings—for example, if some of the factors are more important than others or some factors have a tendency to initiate specific protective actions. All such research efforts aim to improve the instrument and thus the protection of future victims of honor-based threats.

It is also becoming increasingly important that evaluators document their risk assessments so that they can be followed up and evaluated in the future. In many authorities and jurisdictions around the world, it is mandatory not only to carry out risk assessments in various contexts but also to document the method used. One important reason for this is that morbidity and mortality review boards must have access to risk assessments in situations where a worst-case scenario has come about in order to learn something from it.

In thinking in terms of "summary risk," it is important to consider various "risk scenarios" and sometimes to discuss these with the victims. One common outcome in these cases is that young victims who are not behaving in an "honorable" way suddenly "disappear" and end up in their former home country. Many of them are subjected to forced marriages and thus the possibility of repeated rape and abuse. The authors have seen several cases where families try to lure back young victims who have left home by informing them of some serious illness or impending death in the family. It is extremely important to consider a variety of possible scenarios in these cases, not only because so many of the victims are young and vulnerable but also because there are usually several rational perpetrators involved who often carefully plan and then carry out their crime.

The summary risk rating in the PATRIARCH is done in three steps: first, determine whether the case is of low, medium, or high risk; second, determine whether there is an acute risk, long-term risk, and/or risk for severe/lethal violence. Finally, the assessor should think of a safety plan or engage someone else who deals with victim safety. This is the main reason for risk assessments: to understand whom to protect and how. In this context it is extremely important for an evaluator to keep in mind that a safety plan in itself might contribute to a rapidly changed risk. For example, there are a number of cases where schoolteachers or social workers have contacted a family suspected of treating their children badly, with the unforeseen result that the child is only subjected to larger risks and sometimes immediately taken out of the country.

The PATRIARCH is intended to be used as a tool for the evaluator in order to lead him or her to focus on things and circumstances that in previous cases have proven to be important. A completed PATRIARCH rating sheet should not be considered a final product. The next step is usually to communicate the risk orally or in written form to others; the PATRIARCH can then serve as a structure within which the most important risk factors in the case can be discussed. Finally, the evaluator can recommend protective measures or carry them out—if that is part of the evaluator's profession. The PATRIARCH should normally never leave the threat assessor's desk. It is basically a working tool or an aide memoire.

THE VALIDITY OF THE PATRIARCH

In a prospective study of 56 cases of honor-based violence in Stockholm, there was a significant correlation between the number of risk factors and vulnerability factors in the PATRIARCH and the level of risk assessed by the police (Belfrage et al., 2012a). This indicates that the factors in the PATRIARCH measure what it is intended to measure. Additionally and probably of greater importance, the Swedish National Council for Crime Prevention (2012) conducted a study of all cases of honor-based crimes handled by Swedish law enforcement in 2009 with more than one perpetrator involved ($N = 117$). They made a comparison of all cases where the PATRIARCH had been used (34%) with other cases where the PATRIARCH had not been used. They found that the police did more comprehensive investigations when they used the PATRIARCH (collected more information, interrogated more

witnesses, and so on) and that the victims received significantly more protective measures. Of the cases where the PATRIARCH was used, 25% of the cases were judicially solved, compared with just 8% when the PATRIARCH was not used. These significant differences remained even when controlled for type of criminality (i.e., the differences could not be explained by speculations that the PATRIARCH was used only in particularly severe cases and therefore generated more comprehensive investigations).

CASE EXAMPLE

In the case example below we describe how the PATRIARCH can be used in practice and provide some recommendations on how to approach suspected victims of honor-based violence.

Sara—A Victim of Honor-Based Violence

Sara, who is of Iraqi origin, immigrated to Sweden together with her parents and two siblings at the age of 10. The family settled in the suburb of a larger Swedish town. Sara's father started his own business as a car dealer; the mother was a housewife. Sara has described her family as a normal one, with good relationships, living according to the Iraqi culture but in Sweden. Sara has described her life as lacking in freedom and independence, with no privacy because of her father's control over her.

When Sara was 14 years old and entering puberty, her father expressed concern about the possibility that Sara might become involved with young men. She had started a "chat" on the Internet and the father suspected that she wanted to "pick up men." Sara felt pressured by her father and tried to commit suicide as a result. Later the same year Sara attended a school meeting with her father. While at school the father spoke to a friend of Sara's who told him that Sara had a boyfriend. Sara's father was furious and they headed home. As they entered the house the father yelled at Sara, calling her a whore and saying that he would kill her. Sara did not understand what was going on and tried to assure him that she did not have a boyfriend. The father would not listen to her but grabbed her head and banged it on the wall repeatedly. He then pulled her hair back while he used his knee to kick her torso several times. As Sara slumped to the floor he began to strangle her—only stopping when Sara's mother intervened. Sara's mother and younger siblings were in the hallway when the assault took place, the mother shouting abuse at Sara as well. Sara could not breathe after the attack and was taken by car to the closest hospital. On the way to the hospital Sara's father told her not to divulge to anyone that he had caused her injuries. If she did so, he would kill her. At the hospital, the younger sister approached the staff, saying that Sara needed help; the reason given was that she had fallen over and hurt herself. Sara was admitted to hospital and stayed for two days suffering from fractured ribs, damage to the lung tissue with fluid in the pleural sacs, and a hematoma on her head. The doctors treating Sara contacted the police, realizing that her injuries could not have been caused by a fall. The parents were in Sara's room as the police arrived. When asked by the police, Sara agreed to be questioned in her parents' presence. Sara then told the police that she had been attacked by a stranger outside her house. The next day two social workers came to the hospital to see Sara. Again the parents were present as the social workers asked Sara whether everything was all right at home, and Sara answered that everything was fine within the family.

A few days after Sara was discharged from hospital she left for Iraq together with her mother and two younger siblings. The family had been planning the trip but it was carried out much earlier than expected. While in Iraq, Sara found herself spending most of her time indoors in the house where they were staying. Her cousins treated her as if she had done something shameful. Uncles came to visit and Sara found that they would talk about her and not address her directly. They would speak about another girl who was close to the family who had disappeared, saying that the girl's father had done a good job, unlike Sara's father who should have finished the job better. Sara stayed in Iraq for one year. Her mother was pregnant with her fourth child and could not travel back earlier, Sara was told, although she was well aware that the trip to Iraq was her family's way of regaining control over her. When Sara was back in Sweden and school, she saw her school counselor and spoke about how her father was treating her. Since their return from Iraq, the father was very cold to Sara. She had to return home directly after school, not mix with any people who were not close friends or related to the family, and on no account have any contact with boys. Sara also spoke about threats she had received from her father. On various occasions the father had been so angry with Sara that he had threatened to kill her. One example

was when Sara wished to join a local gym. Her father forbade her saying, "What would the people say if they saw you there?! You just want people to speak badly about us. If we get a bad reputation it's because of you. Stop this or I'll kill you. You will disappear! You are shameful!"

The second situation leading to death threats was stimulated by Sara's cell-phone bill. If her bill was very high, the father would conclude that she had been calling "someone," meaning a male. And if that was the case, he said he would kill her. The third situation involved a planned marital engagement between Sara and a cousin from Iraq. Sara was called by her friend in Iraq who congratulated her on her engagement. Sara questioned her mother, who confirmed that she was engaged to be married to her cousin. Sara expressed her objections—she did not want to marry her cousin. Sara's mother simply responded; "It's time you pull yourself together—you've had a boyfriend!" Her father was furious about Sara's objections to the engagement, saying "Either you agree to this or you go to Iraq and I'll kill you there. I'll do anything to maintain my reputation." As Sara began to tell her school counselor about her home situation, she was uncertain how much she wanted to involve the authorities in her life. She hoped that her mother would be on her side and convince the father that she did not have to marry her cousin. As time passed, Sara realized that this was probably not going to happen. When she gave her first statement to the police, she was reluctant to tell the full story, being vague and not answering questions adequately. Not until she was taken into care according to the Child Protection Act did she relax and speak about the abuse she had suffered a few years earlier and the death threats she faced at home. She was happy in her care home and had a warm connection with the care family. Unfortunately, something happened that prevented her from staying with that family; she was therefore placed in another home and finally moved to an apartment of her own. The situation was not ideal for Sara. She had to travel for over an hour to get to school and could meet with her designated person from social services only every few weeks. As time passed, Sara began to feel lonely. She had met and started a relationship with a young man, but she was living alone and missed her family terribly. Sara began to contact her mother and siblings and even visited the house on a few occasions. The visits went well, there were no threats or attempts to keep her there, and Sara did not tell social services and the protective police assigned to her case that she was in touch with her parents. One day, Sara's younger sister called Sara telling her that their father was very ill. Sara, distraught, rushed home to see him, only to find that he seemed his usual self. She prepared herself to leave but the father asked her to stay as it was a special religious feast day. In the police reports she said that she did not dare leave the house and disobey her father at that point. The family visited some friends and then came home to their house. Sara spent time with her mother and sister, as they usually did in the evening. Suddenly Sara's younger sister told Sara that she had heard that Sara was to travel at 6 a.m. the following morning. Sara immediately understood that they were planning to take her to Iraq and that she was in great danger. She managed to send a text message to her boyfriend, who called the police. The police arrived at 4 a.m. the next morning. There was no evidence to suggest that the family had planned to go abroad; no suitcases, passports, or tickets in sight. Sara was taken, very calmly, back to her safe house, where she started to doubt whether there really was a trip planned for her.

At this point, a risk assessment was made using the PATRIARCH as an SPJ instrument. The information to make an assessment was gathered from the police registers, police reports, and interrogations with all of the people involved, as well as background information such as previous criminality and income. Also included in the investigation was the verdict in the Care of Young People Act, which included statements from the parents and from Sara regarding their different viewpoints on her engagement and future schooling. An interview was conducted with the counselor from social services dealing with Sara in order to have as much relevant information as possible to assess the situation in an appropriate way. At this point the police personal safety officers had already had previous contact with Sara, so any additional questions that needed to be answered were put to Sara through them.

The context and case description were summarized in the PATRIARCH as follows:

> 17-year-old girl, wanting to live more freely and choose her own partner. Conceived norm/rule breaking: Believed to have had a boyfriend. Has also spoken to police and social services. Forced into engagement with her cousin from Iraq. Father is head of family in the clan. All the other family apart from an aunt lives in Iraq.

The risk and victim vulnerability factors that were perceived to be present were:

1. *Serious violent threats or thoughts*: Yes. The father had repeatedly threatened to take Sara's life.
2. *Violent acts:* Yes. Sara was severely assaulted in 2007. Sara's father also had a verdict of assault against a car mechanic in an argument over payment.
3. *Honor-related violent acts:* Partly. Sara knew of a close family friend whose daughter disappeared and it was understood by all that she had been murdered. (This risk factor was coded as "partly" because the killing was not within Sara's own family.)
4. *Arranged marriages or engagements:* Yes. Sara's family had arranged an engagement against Sara's will.
5. *Escalation:* Yes. The assessor regarded the situation as escalating since Sara was presumably to be taken to Iraq the following morning.
6. *Attitudes that support honor-based violence:* Yes. Both parents justified the use of violence toward Sara because of her alleged relationship with a young man. The mother minimized Sara's injuries and the father's abuse. Attitudes expressed by the family in Iraq assessed as supportive of honor violence. There was extensive control of Sara's contact with other youngsters to ensure that she did not enter into relationships with men and thereby compromise the family's reputation.
7. *High degree of insult:* Yes. The assumed relationship was considered an insult to the family's honor, compounded by involvement of the police and social services. Sara had lived away from the family for several months, which meant that she was not under her family's control, which is also considered an insult to the family's honor.
8. *Origin from an area with known subcultural values supporting honor violence, forced marriage, or genital mutilation:* Yes. Iraq has subcultures where honor violence is prevalent.
9. *Lack of cultural integration.* Yes. The parents were not willing to let their children participate in age-appropriate activities such as meeting peers after school or joining a gym.

10. *Psychosocial problems:* No. No identified problems.
11. *Inconsistent behavior and/or attitude toward family/perpetrator:* Yes. Sara was in contact with her family while living in a sheltered home and minimized the risks regarding her safety with them.
12. *Extreme fear of family/perpetrator:* Yes. Although Sara was inconsistent and kept in touch with the family, she was extremely fearful of the family and of the father in particular. A telling example was when she visited home the last evening; she did not dare to leave although she wanted to.
13. *Inadequate access to resources:* No. Sara had communicated her need for protection to her school counselor, to social services, and to the police.
14. *Unsafe living situation:* No. Sara's physical living situation was adequate in terms of safety.
15. *Personal problems that might influence management strategies:* Partly. We know that Sara has previously tried to commit suicide, which could be a relevant vulnerability factor to consider when Sara is under such strain.

Risk for Honor-Based Violence If There Is No Intervention

Imminent risk? High

Long-term risk? High

Risk for severe/fatal violence? High

Specify risk (scenarios)? The risk is high that Sara will return to her family. The risk is high that Sara will be taken out of the country and forced to enter into marriage or that she will be killed in the name of honor.

Safety plan: Build a strong relationship with Sara. Ensure that she gets enough professional help and support to cope with her loneliness and conflicting emotions. Provide her with a living arrangement where she has company day and night.

What Happened Next?

Sara was taken back to her safe house and started doubting whether her parents really were planning to take her to Iraq. She felt lonely and depressed. She felt that she could not live without her family; although

she realized the risk she took, she chose to go back and live with them. A few weeks later came the court trial of the father's abuse several years earlier. Although she was living at home, Sara had been in touch with her lawyer and with her assigned support person. The plan was that after the hearing, Sara would go straight to a shelter, and from there a long-term arrangement would be established involving the original family with whom Sara had stayed and liked. At the trial, Sara could not bear to accuse her father of the abuse and left the courtroom shattered. The recorded testimony she had given earlier was played in court and the father was convicted of abuse and sentenced to a year in prison. Sara was taken to the shelter as planned, but she pleaded with the police officers to take her home instead. They refused and urged her to wait at the shelter with the staff until her supportive counselor arrived. Sara left immediately after the police left the shelter and went back to her parents' house. Within a week, the family then left the country and Sara could not be located. Sara's lawyer pressured her father, saying that she wanted to speak with Sara, her client. Sara then called the lawyer from Iraq, said she was fine, and when prompted said that she was married.

Since then, Sara has sent emails to an organization in Sweden dealing with victims of honor-related violence, asking for their help. She explained that she was forced into marriage and that it was like being raped every night. The Swedish authorities' response to the case was that they would not begin an investigation while Sara was in Iraq because it would jeopardize her life. Experts among the police say that Sara could be fetched home discreetly, and efforts to locate her in Iraq and help her back are being made.

CONCLUSION

Experience from working with risk assessments in honor-related cases has taught us that it is necessary to have a basic understanding of the honor context in order to carry out an adequate risk assessment. It is also important for the victim's safety to be ensured by experts who understand the complex feelings that the victims are experiencing. The majority of victims of honor crime are very young, often adolescents, and acclimated to a close family with several members. They have a very hard time being alone. They often miss their families and choose to return to them although they know that they face great danger by doing so. In the long term, victim rehabilitation should include group meetings where victims can meet others in the same situation so as to share experiences, stimulate identification with others, and alleviate feelings of loneliness. Learning new skills and building self-esteem has enabled young girls to cope better with their sense of loss after having left their families.

Owing to the complexity of these cases, authorities must cooperate, using similar tools in assessing risks and other needs. For example, police should receive information from the social authorities if they plan any interventions in a case, since such interventions might drastically change the risk. And, vice versa, social authorities should benefit from law enforcement information about any previous honor-related violence in a particular case.

We are still sometimes greeted with hesitancy by professionals within various authorities who are asked to intervene in suspected honor-related cases. They feel insecure about the concept of "honor" and don't want to stigmatize a group. The argument usually is, "all people have the right to their culture of origin." We agree, as long as these cultural beliefs are not in conflict with fundamental human rights. If they are, society is obliged to intervene.

NOTES

1. The finalized version of the PATRIARCH is currently being completed together with Professors Kropp and Hart and will be published during Fall 2013.

KEY POINTS

- Honor-based violence is often manifested as violence, or threats of violence, toward a family member (most often a woman or girl), because of the perpetrator's belief that the victim has brought dishonor on the family.
- Perpetrators of honor-based violence have cultural and religious attitudes that are not considered representative of any religion or culture worldwide.
- Honor-based crimes include not only murder and violence but also forced marriages and threats of forced marriages.
- Since honor-based criminality often involves multiple family members, usually without personality disorders or major mental disorders, traditional violence risk instruments are generally of limited use in this context.

- The PATRIARCH is intended to be used as a tool by evaluators in order to lead them to focus on facts and circumstances that in previous cases of honor-based violence have proven to be important.
- In multiple studies with the Swedish police, the PATRIARCH has shown good validity and has helped to significantly improve police investigations.

REFERENCES

Akpinar, A. (2003). The honour/shame complex revisited: Violence against women in the migration context. *Women's Studies International Forum, 26*, 425–442.

Belfrage, H. (2005). *PATRIARCH. Draft Version. Checklist for the assessment of risk for patriarchal violence with honour as motive. User manual.* Sundsvall Forensic Psychiatric Hospital, Sundsvall. Available at: (www.lvn.se/rpk)

Belfrage, H., Strand, S., Ekman, L., & Hasselborg, A-K. (2012a). Assessing risk of patriarchal violence with honour as a motive. Six years experience using the PATRIARCH checklist. *International Journal of Police Science and Management, 14*, 20–29.

Belfrage, H., Strand, S., Storey, J. E., Gibas, A. L., Kropp, P. R., & Hart, S., D. (2012b). Assessment and management of risk for intimate partner violence by police officers using the spousal assault risk assessment guide (SARA). *Law and Human Behavior, 36*, 60–67.

Borum, R. (1996). Improving the clinical practice of violence risk assessment: Technology, guidelines, and training. *American Psychologist, 51*, 945–956.

Chesler, P. (2009). Are honour killings simply domestic violence? *Middle East Quarterly, Spring,* 61–69.

Chakravarti, U. (2005). From fathers to husbands: Of love, death and marriage in north India. In L. Welchman & S. Hossain (Eds.), *Honour: Crimes, paradigms and violence against women* (pp. 308–331). London: Zed Books.

Kropp, P. R., Hart, S. D., & Belfrage, H. (2010). *Brief spousal assault form for the evaluation of risk (B-SAFER), version 2: User manual.* Vancouver, BC: Proactive Resolutions.

Kropp, P. R., Hart, S. D., & Lyon, D. R. (2008). *Stalking assessment and management.* Vancouver, BC: Proactive Resolutions.

Macey, M. (1999). Religion, male violence, and the control of women: Pakistani Muslim men in Bradford, UK. *Gender and Development, 7*, 48–55.

Reddy, R. (2008). Gender, culture and the law: Approaches to "honour crimes" in the UK. *Feminist Legal Studies, 16*, 305–321.

Sever, A., & Yurdakul, G. (2001). Culture of honor, culture of change: A feminist analysis of honor killings in rural Turkey. *Violence Against Women, 7*, 964.

Siddiqui, H. (2005). "There is no 'honour' in domestic violence, only shame!" Women's struggles against "honour" crimes in the UK. In: Lynn Welchman and Sara Hossain (Eds.), *Honour: Crimes, paradigms and violence against women* (pp. 263–281). London: Zed Books.

The Foreign & Commonwealth Office (2004). *Young people & vulnerable adults facing forced marriage.* Practice guidance for social workers. London: Author.

The Swedish National Board for Youth Affairs (2010). *Free to choose.* Stockholm (Report in Swedish).

UNFPA—United Nations Population Fund. *Violence against women and girls.* Available at: http://www.unfpa.org

The Swedish National Council for Crime Prevention (2012). *Polisens utredningar av hedersrelaterat våNewld.* Rapport 2012:1 (in Swedish).

Webster, C. D., Douglas, K., Eaves, D., & Hart, S. D. (1997). *HCR-20: Assessing risk for violence* (version 2). Vancouver, BC: Mental Health, Law, and Policy Institute, Simon Fraser University.

Welchman, L., & Hossain, S. (2005). *Honour crimes, paradigms, and violence against women.* London: Zed Books.

18

Fundamentals of Threat Assessment for Beginners

MARY ELLEN O'TOOLE AND SHARON S. SMITH

Assessment of threatening behavior is done every day around the world in corporations, educational institutions and government agencies. In a perfect world, every person tasked with doing threat assessments for an organization would receive extensive training and experience from a variety of experts. However, it is not a perfect world, and the experience and knowledge base of some threat assessors is developed primarily through on-the-job training. When this happens, the responsibility of analyzing and assessing human behavior can seem overwhelming and intimidating, and the person doing the assessment might default to opinions based on gut feelings, personal biases, and myths or assumptions about violent behavior.

This chapter is designed to give the lay assessor an overview of the fundamental concepts and principles of threat assessment and human behavior and the type of information to consider in determining whether someone in his or her organization is contemplating carrying out an act of targeted violence.

We also offer a caution and reminder to all who do this kind of work: Threat assessment itself is a high-risk profession. It is fraught with uncertainty, limited details, and in some instances urgency for an immediate response. The repercussions that may stem from a wrong assessment or simply a lack of response to a threat can be great. Threat assessors will want to work with those who have a wide and varied background in human behavior and assessing and responding to threats; they must also be prepared to make some very tough and timely decisions

about threatening situations if the circumstances require it (O'Toole, 2011).

INTRODUCTION

One of the worst mass shootings in US history occurred in Aurora, Colorado, in the early morning hours of July 20, 2012. Twenty-three-year-old James Holmes, a doctoral student in neuroscience at the University of Colorado, was accused of killing 12 people and injuring another 58 as they sat in a local movie theater watching the premiere of the movie *The Dark Knight Rises*. According to witnesses, Holmes had a ticket and walked into the theater along with the other moviegoers. It appears that initially he did not draw attention to himself. After the film began, Holmes reportedly got up and left the theater. A short time later a lone man walked into the front of the theater dressed in tactical clothing and protective gear. This individual was heavily armed with multiple weapons including an AK-47 assault rifle. Witnesses report that this individual threw a canister of gas into the audience and then began shooting into the crowd. When the shooter was finished, he calmly exited the theater by the same door through which he had entered (Harlow & Payne, 2012; Watkins & Ford, 2012).

James Holmes was arrested without incident outside the theater, reportedly standing near his car next to the door from which he had just left the theater. He reportedly would later tell police he was the Joker, a character from the Batman series. Investigators would learn during the interview that Holmes had booby-trapped his apartment with a maze of explosives and flammable liquids, which, according to experts, were designed to detonate when someone walked through the front door of his apartment. (Harlow & Payne, 2012 ; Watkins & Ford, 2012).

Haunting questions repeat themselves after cases like this: "Why?" "What would motivate someone to carry out such a violent act against innocent persons?" "Were there warning signs along the way?" "Did he just snap?" These questions are the essence of threat assessment.

- What is the threat?
- Who is this person and is he or she capable of carrying out an act of violence?
- What are the indicators that threat assessors (TAs) should look for to determine whether this person is on a path to violence?
- What can be done before the incident to eliminate or mitigate the threat now and in the future?

As the investigation in Aurora continues, much more information will be forthcoming about the suspect and his behavior days, weeks, months, and possibly years before this shooting. This information will be pieced together to provide valuable insights into his motives, the warning behaviors (Meloy et al., 2012), circumstances leading up to the shooting, and what behaviors were missed that might have indicated what he was planning to do.

Fortunately, shootings like these are rare events, but they underscore the importance of threat assessment; and more specifically, what to look for and how to interpret known precursor behaviors observed in people who are thinking of acting out aggressively or violently against an individual or a group.

THREAT ASSESSMENT

Threat assessment is not an exact science. However, the ability to analyze behavior in terms of implications for future dangerousness has come a long way in the last 20 years. All threats are not created equal and most people who threaten do not carry out their threats (O'Toole, 2000). However, while the majority do not carry out their threats, a significant minority do (Smith et al., 2012). This fact underscores how important it is for threat assessment professionals to evaluate all available information thoroughly in order to determine the level of risk posed by an individual (Fein & Vossekuil, 1998, 1999).

The Association of Threat Assessment Professionals (ATAP) is an international organization of professionals involved in the research, training, and application of threat assessment principles and concepts. In a 2006 overview of the discipline, they provided a concise and clear definition of threat assessment: "Threat assessment is defined as the determination of the level of targeted violence risk posed by an individual or group toward a specific target" (ATAP, 2006; see also Borum et al., 1999).

Threat assessment is a method of assessing low base violence risk directed at a specific target. A low base rate for violence means that this type of violence does not occur often (Meloy & O'Toole, 2011; Smith et al., 2012). A base rate is different from a frequency: base rates indicate how often a particular behavior occurs in a group over a specific period of time. Frequency does not control for the group. Threat assessment is a dynamic process involving the analysis of available fact patterns and the interpretation of behaviors observed in these patterns (Meloy et al., 2012). A thorough threat assessment requires an in-depth evaluation of the person's background, lifestyle, personality, and observable behaviors, which can range from nonthreatening to concerning, threatening, or even dangerous. The purpose of the threat assessment is to ultimately neutralize or eliminate an immediate threat with appropriate levels of intervention, and to design strategies to facilitate successful and long-term resolutions (Drysdale et al., 2010). Zero tolerance for threats in one's organization does not mean a single sanction. In threat assessment, every situation is different, and every person must be treated fairly and with sensitivity using a threat assessment model that allows for variation in behavior and different types and degrees of intervention (O'Toole, 2000).

VIOLENCE RISK ASSESSMENT

Violence risk assessment within the context of threat assessment is:

a process of identifying behaviors that may signal an individual's preparation to commit a violent act, assessing those behaviors in the context of that person's past history of behavior and other known incidents of violence that have demonstrated those behaviors, quantifying the level of risk from this behavioral information by using professional judgment and objective, appropriate tools to provide a balanced assessment, and presentation of that assessment to the requestor of the assessment, in such a way, as to qualify the opinion and its limitations appropriately (ATAP, 2006).

IDENTIFYING THE MISSION OF YOUR THREAT ASSESSMENT PROGRAM

As simplistic as this might sound, defining the purpose of your threat assessment program will help to clarify the background and expertise of the professionals who should be involved with the program: the exact role of the assessors; how and when they will become involved in a threat; how the threat will be managed, evaluated, and resolved; and how strategies for intervention will be developed and implemented. A multidisciplinary team can bring a wide range of expertise to the threat assessment process, ensuring that single-focus and single-sanction resolutions are avoided (Van Brunt, 2012). Having a member of law enforcement on a threat assessment team can be very helpful. Although not every case involving threatening behavior will rise to the level of having law enforcement intervention, most will; therefore it is important to include a member of law enforcement on the team. Law enforcement officers, more than any other professionals, do risk assessments every day in the course of their work, whether it is going to a domestic dispute situation, making a traffic stop, or interviewing someone about a case. They are used to making fast, reliable decisions on limited information and they know where and how to immediately retrieve critical pieces of information (weapons ownership, outstanding warrants, etc.) that can provide that one piece of information which will set the course for the right resolution. This skill set can be very useful when there is concern that a threat of violence may be high and immediate action must be taken to intervene and de-escalate the threat.

TRIBAL WISDOM VS. GROUPTHINK

In the FBI's Behavioral Analysis and Behavioral Sciences Units, highly trained and experienced FBI agent analysts use a consultative and collaborative process to analyze and assess threats. This type of team approach allows for in-depth discussions, the exchange of ideas, and differences of opinion, which increase the likelihood that all the subtleties of a case

are identified and factored into the assessment. This ensures that the final opinions and recommendations will be comprehensive and fact-based. It is very difficult, and in some cases impossible, for a threat assessor working alone to identify and interpret each and every behavioral variable in a case; and then to make sure that the assessment captures the totality of the circumstances. With only one set of eyes reviewing the case, it is almost certain that important details will be missed. It is the details in threat assessment that can make a significant difference in concluding whether someone poses a real threat.

Differences of opinions should be encouraged during the threat assessment consultation process so that best approaches and resolutions will be identified (Van Brunt, 2012). When a group begins to take on a "groupthink" mentality, where members are encouraged and maybe even bullied into aligning their opinions and observations with the majority of the group, the process is no longer dynamic, open, and transparent, and the conclusions and recommendations can look more like boilerplate than a customized assessment (Van Brunt, 2012).

LOOKING FOR PATTERNS OF BEHAVIOR

As part of their threat assessment model, FBI agent/analysts are trained to look for patterns of behavior in a person's background in order to determine if they are more or less likely to act out aggressively or violently. Human beings are very complicated, and it can be difficult to identify patterns or even where to look for these patterns—particularly if someone is attempting to keep his behavior concealed or hidden. Ideally, assessors will want to have examples of behaviors in as many aspects of the assessed person's life as possible. There are six main areas of a person's life to be assessed: personal life, professional/occupational life, social life, family life, private life, and secret life (O'Toole, 2011); each of these can contain different types of information and even contradictory information, as well as different behaviors, interests, associates, and intentions. Obtaining information from as many of these areas as possible can help assessors identify both overt and hidden or secretive patterns of behavior, including concerning, threatening, and dangerous behaviors which will be critical to their threat assessment.

THE SHELF LIFE OF A THREAT ASSESSMENT

Threat assessments have limited shelf lives. In fact, their accuracy and subsequent value can diminish quickly and significantly over a short period of time for a variety of reasons, including the threatener's use of drugs, both prescription and over the counter, new stressors in his or her life, interpersonal problems, flare ups from untreated medical and/or mental health conditions, the influence of the media or other external stimuli, and unanticipated triggering events. For these reasons a priority for threat assessment teams must include outreach plans to monitor individuals once they have left, voluntarily or involuntarily, the workplace or educational institution; these activities help to determine if there is a deterioration in their thinking and behavior and whether the likelihood of their acting out has increased. Depending on the circumstances, these outreach plans could include working with law enforcement so they can follow through with a wellness check on the person, or even conduct record checks to make sure they know if this person has begun to take steps to put a plan in place. The team can design ways to continue some type of link via regular phone contacts or home visitations for a period of time. Teams can introduce a mental health professional into the situation in order to monitor the person to see if there is escalation of behavior or deterioration in the person's everyday functioning. They can identify a family member or friend who understands the situation and can provide ongoing support. If there is a concern that a person poses a threat to act out violently, there needs to be a safety net in place to monitor his or her behavior. This is particularly important if that same person, voluntarily or involuntarily, leaves the corporation, university, or school. The threat of violence does not abate because the threatener is no longer associated with his or her organization. In fact, this separation can be a trigger, causing the threatener to deteriorate and the threatening behavior to escalate.

In one case of school violence, a young man was suspended because he had claimed to want to shoot up the school on a scale greater than Columbine. Following his suspension, he was schooled by a visiting teacher. Without close monitoring, this young man's behavior devolved to the point where he was able to put together a plan to return to his school with multiple lethal firearms. His family was not in a position to provide a support system he could rely on, and they were not aware of how threatening his behavior was becoming. In addition, he was isolated from people at school, some of whom had previously been supportive of him. During the months following his suspension, this student designed a detailed plan to carry out a school shooting—a plan he was able to execute without being found out. Multiple people were killed and many more were injured as a result.

PROTECTIVE INHIBITORS AND BUFFERS AGAINST VIOLENCE

Threat assessments should not be based only on those of the threatener's behaviors, personality traits, and characteristics that support an opinion that he or she is likely to act out violently. Assessors also must consider and factor into their assessment those variables that can mitigate the likelihood of an act of violence. These variables include personality traits and characteristics, lifestyle behaviors, and social behaviors identified as protective inhibitors. They include such things as a high level of intelligence, an easygoing disposition, high-functioning interpersonal skills, effective social and problem-solving skills, good performance in school and at work, a viable family and social support network, a positive relationship with at least one other adult person, access and receptivity to treatment as evidenced by treatment in the past, spiritual or religious beliefs opposing violence, physical injuries or limitations, and a lack of resources (ATAP, 2006; Van Brunt, 2012).

TRIGGERS

Triggers are events and circumstances in others' lives that can increase the likelihood of their acting out violently or can strengthen their commitment to their plans. Triggers can include problems with work, feelings of rejection and abandonment, worsening psychosis or other mental health issues, recent failures or perceptions of failure, involvement in civil court or criminal court proceedings, anger management issues, lack of a support system or dissolution of same, financial problems, and drug and/or alcohol abuse (ATAP, 2006; Van Brunt, 2012).

In identifying triggering events and circumstances, the assessor should understand that these events may occur weeks, months, even years *after* the threatener first began entertaining violent or aggressive fantasies about hurting or killing people. In other words, his thoughts and fantasies of violence can often precede the triggering events, which may just reinforce his intentions (ATAP 2006; Van Brunt, 2012).

INJUSTICE COLLECTOR

In the FBI's research on school and university shootings, the term "injustice collector" is used to refer to people who see injustices in many or most of the things that happen to them. Injustice collectors can misperceive the smallest slights and turn them into major events, and they can accumulate these injustices for years and add to them day after day. An injustice collector's response to these injustices—real or perceived—can be extremely disproportionate to the original grievance. This tendency toward extreme or excessive overreaction can often be seen in their history and prior interactions with others, even over insignificant issues (O'Toole, 2000; 2011).

WARNING BEHAVIORS

After a case of the magnitude of the Aurora, Colorado, shooting, it is not uncommon to hear professionals say that the perpetrator must have "snapped." This implies that the shooter's behavior was an unexpected and spontaneous act occurring out of the blue and without any warning. The snap theory implies a type of emotionally and mentally spontaneous combustion from which no one is exempt, holding that if and when someone snaps, the consequences can be dire. Subscribing to the snap theory would be a terrible mistake, because it completely contradicts the premise of threat and risk assessment for violence. Most importantly, research on such horrendous acts as mass murder indicates that perpetrators do not snap—they decide, plan, and prepare (Meloy et al., 2004).

Warning behaviors as defined by Meloy et al. (2012) are observable patterns that can precede an act of violence. It is essential for threat assessors to be able to correctly identify and interpret these warning behaviors in a work environment or a school or university setting. Being knowledgeable about warning signs and what they are should not be limited, however, just to threat assessment teams. Training in learning to identify these behaviors should be part of a threat assessment awareness program and be provided to a wide range of people within the organization. Educating others with descriptions of these behaviors puts additional eyes and ears in the workplace to help spot concerning, threatening, or dangerous behaviors that may otherwise be missed or overlooked. Training on these behaviors, moreover, should include at least two cautions: (1) reporting procedures should allow for the confidentiality of the reporting parties as well as the person they are concerned about; and (2) the reporting parties should

only report the behavior but not screen it or evaluate it. The trained threat assessment person should make that evaluation in the context of other information he or she has about the threat and the person posing the threat. Warning behaviors within the context of threat assessment are described below (Meloy et al., 2012; Chapter 3, this volume).

1. *Pathway warning behavior*—any behavior that is part of research, planning, preparation, or implementation of an attack (Calhoun & Weston, 2003; Meloy et al., 2012; Meloy & O'Toole, 2011).
2. *Fixation warning behavior*—any behavior that indicates an increasingly pathological preoccupation with a person or a cause (Meloy et al., 2012; Meloy & O'Toole, 2011; Mullen et al., 2009).
3. *Identification warning behavior*—any behavior that indicates a psychological desire to be a "pseudo commando," (Dietz, 1986), have a "warrior mentality," closely associate with weapons or other military or law enforcement paraphernalia (Hempel et al., 1999; Meloy & O'Toole, 2011) and/or identify with previous attackers, or identify oneself as an agent whose purpose is to advance a particular cause or belief system (Meloy et al., 2012).
4. *Novel aggression warning behavior*—acts of violence unrelated to attack behavior that are committed for the first time. Such behaviors test the ability of the subject to actually do a violent act (Meloy et al., 2012; Meloy & O'Toole, 2011).
5. *Energy burst warning behavior*—an increase in the frequency or variety of any noted activities related to the target (Meloy et al., 2012; Meloy & O'Toole, 2011).
6. *Leakage warning behavior*—the communication to a third party of an intent to do harm to a target (Meloy et al., 2012; Meloy & O'Toole, 2011).
7. *Directly communicated threat warning behavior*—the communication of a direct threat to the target or law enforcement beforehand (Meloy et al., 2012; Meloy & O'Toole, 2011).
8. *Last resort warning behavior*—increasing desperation or distress through declaration in word or deed (Meloy et al., 2012).

One of the most powerful warning signs is leakage. Leakage can be covert or clearly overt, written or verbal. In some cases, the leakage has been as ambiguous as telling a coworker not to come to work the next day as something "big" was going to happen. It can be as clear and direct as a student posting an online video about his or her intended actions (Meloy & O'Toole, 2011; O'Toole, 2000, 2012). In both cases, however, it is directed at third parties, not the intended target(s). The key is that we recognize leakage and take it seriously; and that we train others to recognize it and know how to report it, rather than disregarding it as a joke or merely an inappropriate comment.

In a collaborative research effort by the US Secret Service, the FBI, and the US Department of Education on targeted violence occurring in colleges and universities, "preincident behaviors" were identified in 31% of the 272 incidents that were analyzed. Researchers reported that verbal and/or written threats to cause harm to the victim were noted in 13% of the cases. These threats were identified as both "veiled" and "direct" and had been conveyed to either the victim or a third party about the victim. In 19% of the cases, stalking/harassing behaviors were noted prior to the violent incident. These cases included prior romantic relationships as well as nonromantic relationships. The stalking or harassing included some type of contact with the victim or the victim's family as well as acts of vandalism. In 10% of the cases studied, there were "physically aggressive acts" directed at the target prior to the actual incident. These acts of aggression also included threats and intimidation with the use of a weapon (Drysdale et al., 2010).

Other concerning behaviors included paranoid ideas, delusional statements, changes in the person's personality or performance, disciplinary problems, depressed mood, suicidal ideation, nonspecific threats of violence, increased isolation, 'odd' or 'bizarre' behavior, and interest in or acquisition of weapons (Drysdale et al., 2010).

EVIDENCE OF ESCALATION

A threat assessment is a dynamic process—the assessment can change based on new information received about the situation and the threatener. Being able to correctly recognize observable behaviors that can suggest an escalation toward violence is critical. Some of these behaviors include an increase

in stalking or approaching behaviors; the identification of multiple victims or previous victims; an increase in aggressive behaviors; the offender taking greater risks in his or her behavior; if sexual deviancy is involved, the behavior becoming more excessive and/or extreme; the offender appearing to be learning from previous mistakes; cease-and-desist warnings or imposed restrictions, whether formal or informal, becoming less and less effective with the threatener; and the threatener taking steps to execute violent plans, such as purchasing weapons or preparing a videotape or journal of his or her intentions (O'Toole, 2011).

Superficial Indicators of Normalcy

Movies, TV shows, books, and the Internet can collectively shape our ideas and opinions about who poses a threat and who does not. The characterization of someone who carries out an act of violence often focuses on one or two personality traits or life experiences; for example, he is a loner or he just broke up with his girlfriend, neither of which in itself is indicative of someone planning to act out violently. In the late 1980s and 1990s, when the phenomenon of school shooters began to emerge, a student's hair color was frequently a concern for many who thought that having purple or pink hair or an ominous appearance might suggest that the student was a potential threatener; that is, it was felt that a person's physical appearance served as a sign of potential intentions to act out violently. The same was true for students who dressed in a "Goth" style or showed a preference for trench coats. While some school shooters did favor unusual hair colors and some wore black trench coats, these behaviors have nothing to do with predicting whether a student intends to act out violently. The vast majority of students wearing trench coats or who have dyed colorful hair will never act out violently (O'Toole, 2000), and are likely only making a fashion statement.

HOW WE MISINTERPRET CONCERNING, THREATENING, OR DANGEROUS BEHAVIOR

Blind spots can prevent assessors and others in an organization from reporting things that might be indicative of concerning, threatening, or even dangerous behaviors. Some may think a particular behavior is odd or unusual but interpret it in the context of an ordinary or logical scenario. For example, in May

1927, the first case of mass killing involving a school occurred in Bath, Michigan. The offender, Andrew Kehoe, was a middle-age man who served on the school board and was a well-respected member of the Bath community. Over the course of six months, Kehoe carried hundreds of pounds of explosives into the school and meticulously placed them throughout the basement. People saw him in the building and realized that he was working in the basement, but never questioned what he was doing and why it was taking so long. Kehoe was also practicing with explosives around his farm, setting them off in different ways and in different places. His neighbors were aware of this and would later say they thought it odd that there were explosions coming from his property, but they ignored it because he was their neighbor and someone important in the community (Bernstein, 2009).

In the first author's experience working in the FBI's Behavioral Analysis Unit over a nearly 15-year period, there were four general reasons for problematic behaviors to be missed (O'Toole, 2011):

1. *Normalizing Behavior*: Finding a "normal" explanation for what is seen (Example: *"Neuroscience majors are just a little quirky"*).
2. *Rationalizing Behavior*: Excusing the behavior, minimizing it or explaining it away (Example: *"If I notify HR, he might lose his job, and he's basically a nice guy."*)
3. *Ignoring Behavior*: Pretending the behavior did not occur (Example: *"I've heard him on the phone talking about how cool he thought the Colorado shooting was, but it's none of my business."*)
4. *Icon Intimidation or Influence*: The view that because a person is iconic or has a position of trust and/or importance, he or she would not be capable of dangerous behavior (Example: *"A widely known, friendly, and respected coach would never molest children."*)

CASE STUDY

A high-profile middle-age businessman, whom we will call Thomas Hutton, had been receiving multiple communications off and on over a three-year period from a woman the authors identify as Elizabeth Moore. These communications included voice mails, faxes, and greeting cards. Over this three-year period,

Mr. Hutton's assistant had contacted Ms. Moore on several occasions advising her to cease and desist any and all contact with Hutton. The authors refer to Hutton's assistant as Paul.

Trained threat assessors were ultimately retained to review the case, including all of the communications as well as available background information known about Moore. The purpose of their review was to provide investigative as well as resolution strategies.

Moore's contacts with Hutton began when he was working at two different companies. Her contacts were described as sporadic. There would be two or three months with no contact and then Moore would start up again. It is not known what originally triggered Moore's stalking of Hutton. According to Paul, on several occasions he had returned greeting cards Moore had sent to Hutton, always with a note telling her to cease and desist from all contact. Paul indicated that when he did this, Moore would cease her communication for several months. On several occasions, Paul also called Moore and left her a voice message telling her to cease all calls and faxes to Hutton. After that, Moore would again suspend her behavior, but only for a short time.

Moore's telephone calls and faxes generally came into Hutton's office after hours or on the weekends. Her messages were frequently rambling and disjointed. On occasion, Moore left so many messages that she overloaded his voice mail, preventing him from receiving legitimate calls. In her voice mails and faxes, Moore indicated that she had a specific situation she needed to discuss with Hutton. However, she provided no details about this situation or why she needed to discuss it specifically with Hutton. In some of Moore's faxes she gushed with praise about what a wonderful person Hutton was, and how he was a role model for her and many others who worked in his industry. Moore made no direct threats to Hutton or his family.

As part of his current and past strategies, Hutton had attempted to block Moore's phone calls. However, this did not deter Moore. She found new numbers associated with Hutton and left new messages on those lines.

Law enforcement had been contacted early on, but advised Hutton that there was nothing they could do to help him.

Hutton indicated that he did not know an Elizabeth Moore and he did not think he had ever met her. However, Hutton recalled when he recently attended a local charity event, he observed a lone middle-aged woman staring at him and waving. He did not know this woman. She did not approach him. Moore later made a reference to having seen him at this event.

There were no records of Hutton's business ever dealing with Moore. And neither Hutton nor Paul recall Moore showing up at their offices. There was also no indication that she ever sent gifts, flowers, or packages to Hutton.

As the case evolved, Moore traveled to Hutton's home and actually interacted with his mother, who also lived there. Moore left a short note on the outside of the house near the front door. It contained only her name. On a separate day she left a note with just a casual greeting on the family's vehicle, which was parked on the street. Hutton's mother saw Moore leaving the note on the car and ordered her off of the property. She described Moore as glaring at her. As she walked away, Moore told Hutton's mother to tell her son that she was, in fact, the woman who waved at him at the charity event he had attended several weeks prior.

A security expert was hired to conduct public record checks of Moore and obtain as much background information on her as possible. In order to capture the most relevant background information about Moore, a customized comprehensive questionnaire was designed by the threat assessors for this case; it helped Hutton, Paul, and the security expert focus on the information that would be most meaningful for a threat assessment. This questionnaire was designed to elicit information about escalation behavior, warning behaviors, triggers, and other background information.

It was subsequently determined that Moore had no firearms registered under her name and did not own a vehicle or possess a current driver's license. She relied on public transportation. She lived in the same city as Hutton. It was unclear if she was currently employed or what her source of income was. She had no prior criminal record.

Assessment

Following is a synopsis of the opinions and strategies provided:

- (*Escalation*) Ms. Moore's behavior appeared to be escalating. She left two notes at and around Mr. Hutton's home: one on the family vehicle parked in front of his home and

one near his front door. While there were no threats contained in either of these notes, the fact that she had traveled to Hutton's home on two separate occasions was concerning.

- (*Triggering Events; Escalation*) Moore's behavior showed commitment. Public transportation from Moore's apartment building to Hutton's home required multiple transfers on bus and rail and then travel on foot. On two separate occasions, Moore traveled to Hutton's home, in spite of the distance, logistics, and time it took for her to get there. Making contact at his residence indicated that she was taking more risks to get closer to him and possibly his family. Hutton's address was not out in the public domain, so Moore had to be resourceful in locating where he lived. Moore's appearance at a public event that Hutton was attending indicated that she was capable of surveilling him without his knowledge. Later, by telling Hutton's mother that she was, in fact, the woman he saw at the event, she meant to intimidate.

- (*Triggering Events; Mental Health Issues*) Attempting to approach Hutton at his home despite multiple warnings to cease and desist her contact with him suggests aggressiveness and possible mental health issues. Moore ignored multiple requests from Paul made on behalf of Hutton to stop contacting him. She continued pursuing Hutton, finally making at least two visits to his home. Moore may believe that rules do not apply to her; therefore it is doubtful that she will restrict any future contacts because of a restraining order or other legal process even if she risks being arrested as a consequence.

- (*Mental Health Issues*) Assessors also advised that if Moore were brought into the criminal justice system, she would probably have to undergo some type of mental evaluation and interview; this would be important and could provide additional information about prior stalking behavior that did not result in a formal arrest.

- Moore's choice of a victim is also interesting. Because Hutton was a high-profile, successful businessman, he had the financial means, in dealing with Moore, to access resources that many people would not have, including hiring a security expert, threat assessors, and a highly reputable attorney. Such an aggressive approach to the situation, with these kinds of resources—which could result in a restraining order, being arrested, or even being prosecuted and going to jail—might cause many people to rethink their choice of a victim. Moore appeared oblivious to Hutton's power; in fact, his status might have actually fueled her behavior and made it more exciting for her to be in contact with him (Meloy et al., 2008).

- (*Escalation*) Trends in Moore's behavior suggested that she could be moving toward more dangerous confrontations with Hutton or someone in his family, whom she might see as getting in the way of her access to him. Based on her escalating behavior, the threat assessors raised the threat level to high.

- (*Resolution Strategies*) The overall strategy should be to get Moore into the criminal justice system as quickly as possible so as to give Hutton more control over the situation and to pursue additional legal action if necessary. It was explained that the key to a successful stalking prosecution in the future would be a prior conviction for stalking.

- (*Patterns of Behavior*) Hutton's family members should be briefed about Moore and her behavior and develop a plan to react if she appeared at or around the Hutton home again or at any location where family members might be. Threat assessors felt that it was likely Moore would attempt more personal contacts.

- (*Patterns of Behavior*) School administrators should be briefed about Moore because of the possibility that she might show up at Hutton's childrens' school. Moore demonstrated her ability to be resourceful in finding information, and this resourcefulness would enable her to find the location of the school if she wanted to.

- (*Patterns of Behavior*) Other people in Hutton's circle with whom he visits or works should also be briefed on the situation in the event that Moore should show up at other locations in an effort to see Hutton or interact with him.

- (*Resolution Strategies*) Pursuing legal action against Moore could anger her and cause her behavior to escalate. Therefore every effort should be made to monitor her behavior through the security expert as appropriate.

- (*Resolution Strategies*) Members of Hutton's staff should have no further contact with Moore, even if only to advise her to cease and desist. If additional communications—both calls and faxes—were to come from her, the assessors would evaluate them, looking for threats, warning behaviors, and evidence that Moore was becoming angry or irritated with Hutton.

- (*Resolution Strategies*) A certified letter drafted by an attorney and on his or her stationery should be mailed to Moore to officially advise her to cease and desist all communication with Hutton and his family. This letter should be extremely specific as to her behavior and the legal implications (without threatening an arrest). The letter should describe in detail the behavior she is being asked to stop.

- (*Resolution Strategies*) Local law enforcement should be contacted regarding the new developments in the case, and provided with a complete summary of the case to date in order to determine what additional information would be necessary to obtain a restraining order against Moore. The specificity of the wording in the restraining order is important, and Hutton should ensure that all restrictions were clearly delineated—how close she might come to Hutton and his family and what the consequences would be if she violated the order. The assessors felt that such detail and specificity were essential because Moore's behavior indicated that she had violated boundaries in the past and did not seem to be dissuaded by cease- and-desist warnings. She did not seem to see rules as applying to her. If there were any violation of the restraining order, there should be no second chances. Law enforcement should be contacted immediately.

ACKNOWLEDGMENT

This chapter reflects the views and the opinions of the authors and does not reflect the opinion or views of the FBI.

KEY POINTS

- This chapter provides a basic overview of fundamental concepts of threat assessment and considerations for establishing a threat assessment program.
- Threat assessors, particularly those who are new and/or inexperienced, should seek to work within a group context rather than on their own.
- Threat assessment involves identifying patterns of behavior including warning behaviors, triggering events, escalation, and the presence of mental health issues.
- Protective inhibitors are those factors that can work against the likelihood that a person might carry out a threat and should be considered an essential part of preparing a threat assessment.
- The threat assessment process should also include identifying appropriate resolution strategies designed to minimize the problem and not make it worse.
- Professionals working in this field should seek ongoing training as well as opportunities to work with and be mentored by more experienced professionals in order to expand their knowledge and understanding and to stay current with new research findings.
- Most people who make threats of violence do not carry out those threats, but a significant minority do. Therefore every threat must be evaluated with a process that is fair, objective, thorough, and timely.
- Sensational and high-profile cases of school, campus, and workplace violence can obfuscate a normally rational and tempered approach to threat assessment, especially for beginners in the field. Working with seasoned threat assessment professionals "who have seen it all" is critical.

REFERENCES

Association of Threat Assessment Professionals (ATAP) (2006). *Risk assessment guideline elements for violence: Considerations for assessing the risk of future violent behavior.* Available at: http://downloads.workplaceviolencenews.com/rage-v.pdf

Bernstein, A. (2009). *Bath massacre: America's first school bombing.* Ann Arbor: University of Michigan Press.

Borum, R., Fein, R., Vossekuil, B., & Bergland, J. (1999). Threat assessment: Defining an approach for evaluating risk of targeted violence. *Behavioral Sciences and the Law, 17,* 323–337.

Calhoun, T., & Weston, S. (2003). *Contemporary threat management.* San Diego, CA: Specialized Training Services.

Dietz, P. E. (1986). Mass, serial, and sensational homicides. *Bulletin of the New York Academy of Medicine, 62,* 477–491.

Drysdale, D., Modzeleski, W., & Simons, A. (2010). *Campus attacks: Targeted violence affecting institutions of higher education.* Washington, DC: Secret Service, U.S. Department of Homeland Security, Office of Safe and Drug-Free Schools, U.S. Department of Education, and Federal Bureau of Investigation, U.S. Department of Justice.

Fein, R., & Vossekuil, B. (1998). Preventing attacks on public officials and public figures: A Secret Service perspective. In J. R. Meloy (Ed.), *The psychology of stalking: Clinical and forensic perspectives* (pp. 176–191). San Diego, CA: Academic Press.

Fein, R., & Vossekuil, B. (1999). Assassination in the United States: An operational study of recent assassins, attackers, and near-lethal approaches. *Journal of Forensic Sciences, 44,* 321–333.

Harlow, P., & Payne E. (July 24, 2012). *Trap in Colorado's suspect's home had 30 homemade grenades, gasoline.* Available at: http://www.cnn.com/2012/07/24/justice/colorado-theater-shooting/index.html

Hempel A., Meloy, J. R., & Richards, T. (1999). Offender and offense characteristics of a nonrandom sample of mass murderers. *Journal of the American Academy of Psychiatry and the Law, 27,* 213–225.

Meloy, J. R., Hempel, A., Mohandie, K., Gray, T., Shiva, A., & Richards, T. (2004). A comparative analysis of North American adolescent and adult mass murderers. *Behavioral Sciences and the Law, 22,* 291–309.

Meloy, J. R., Hoffmann, J., Guldimann, A., & James, D. (2012). The role of warning behaviors in threat assessment: An exploration and suggested typology. *Behavioral Sciences and the Law, 30*(3), 256–279.

Meloy, J. R., & O'Toole, M. E. (2011). The concept of leakage in threat assessment. *Behavioral Sciences and the Law, 29*(4), 513–527.

Meloy, J. R., Sheridan, K., & Hoffman, J. (2008). Public figure stalking, threats, and attacks: The state of the science. In J. R. Meloy, L. Sheridan, & J. Hoffmann (Eds.), *Stalking, threatening, and attacking public figures: A psychological and behavioral analysis* (pp. 435–455). New York: Oxford University Press.

Mullen, P., James, D., Meloy, J. R., PathéNew, M., Farnham, F., Preston, L., …Berman, J. (2009). The fixated and the pursuit of public figures. *J Forensic Psychiatry and Psychology, 20,* 33–47.

O'Toole, M. E. (2000). *The school shooter: A threat assessment perspective.* Washington, DC: Federal Bureau of Investigation, U.S. Department of Justice.

O'Toole, M. E. (2011). *Dangerous instincts: How gut feelings betray us.* New York: Hudson Street Press.

Van Brunt, B. (2012). *Ending campus violence: New approaches to prevention.* New York: Psychology Press.

Watkins, T., & Ford, D. Evidence of calculation, deliberation in Colorado shooting, July 21, 2012. Available at: http://articles.cnn.com/2012-07-21/justice/justice_ colorado-theater-shooting_

PART III

Operations

19

The Los Angeles Police Department Threat Management Unit

JEFFREY DUNN

Those of us currently working in law enforcement do so in an era of reduced budgets and diminishing resources. As a rule, most police departments are operating with fewer personnel and less funding than in recent years past. Additionally, many agencies have adopted strategically oriented policing models such as comparative statistics (COMPSTAT) to identify crime trends within the community; this enables them to reallocate resources to target the problem areas. Although this is, overall, a highly effective policing strategy, it is largely reactive and necessarily focuses enforcement efforts at the precinct level rather than on that of specialized detective services. In recent years, large agencies such as the Los Angeles Police Department (LAPD) have reorganized their detective bureaus and reassigned dozens of detectives from specialized assignments to outlying precincts in order to address reduced deployment due to attrition from retirements and budget cuts. For many law enforcement agencies, these moves have resulted in a positive overall reduction of suppressible crimes, but at the cost of some highly specialized investigative services.

Most law enforcement agencies are not currently equipped to provide the long-term attention that these cases often require. Making threat assessment a priority within your organization is crucial.

MAKING THE CASE FOR A THREAT MANAGEMENT UNIT

A precipitating event is often required to bring attention to an issue that was previously not a consideration or priority. Despite decades of terrorist activities around the world, the US Department of Homeland Security was not empowered until *after* the 9/11 attack at the World Trade Center. Terrorism became a priority when it occurred on our watch, in our backyard. As of this writing, several subsequent acts of terrorism have been averted owing to the early detection and intervention afforded by the creation of the Department of Homeland Security and its associated task forces. The tragic events of 9/11 could have been avoided had priority been given to terrorist threat assessment and management *before* that horrific act occurred.

Similarly, the LAPD established the Threat Management Unit (TMU) largely in response to the political and media scrutiny given to the murder of television actress Rebecca Schaeffer by an obsessed, mentally ill fan named Robert Bardo. The investigation revealed that Bardo had made several attempts to personally contact Schaeffer through her manager and by traveling to the studio location where her television show was filmed. Studio security agents became familiar with Bardo but had no tools with which to manage his obsessive behavior. There were no laws at the time that addressed stalking behavior, and no means of reporting the problem to the police absent the commission of some other criminal offense. Lobbying by the entertainment industry, private security professionals, and prosecutors moved California lawmakers to adopt the United States' first antistalking law in 1990.

The TMU began as an ancillary function of the LAPD Mental Evaluation Unit (MEU). The MEU had previously been tasked with tracking LAPD contacts with mentally ill subjects and assisting patrol officers with the hospitalization of problematic individuals identified through enforcement-related activities.[1] Through this tracking process, an astute MEU detective noted that several Los Angeles area celebrities had similarly been targeted by delusional individuals seeking to make personal contact with entertainment personalities. These individuals tended to be very persistent and caused a great deal of anxiety for those targeted, but few engaged in enforceable criminal acts that would justify a meaningful arrest.

MANAGEMENT BUY-IN

Given the media attention to the Schaeffer case and the political climate following the creation of the stalking law, LAPD management was compelled to dedicate resources to the issue of long-term threatening behaviors. The LAPD initially created the TMU with the objective of providing a point of contact for the entertainment studios to facilitate direct reporting and a timely response to stalking behavior. Recognizing that long-term obsessive (stalking) behaviors do not necessarily translate to defined criminal offenses, the directive from LAPD management to the TMU gave wide latitude: to utilize a range of strategies to manage cases in order to prevent violence before it occurred. Herein lies the problem for today's law enforcement agency seeking to implement a threat management type of unit in the era of COMPSTAT-type policing models: How do you quantify effectiveness when the goal is prevention and interruption *before* the violent act occurs? The LAPD notes:

> Unless a specific crime has been committed, police agencies have historically remained uninvolved in such cases, leaving the victim to deal with his or her problem. However, by the time such cases escalate, some victims have experienced tragic consequences before police intervention could be initiated (Lane & Boles: *Threat Management Unit Guidelines*, March 2000, p. 1).

This quotation clearly states the need for a specialized law enforcement unit that is able to provide nontraditional law enforcement services to interrupt persons embarking on a path toward violence.

Although it is impossible to quantify the number of violent incidents averted owing to TMU intervention, there can be no doubt that the TMU's proactive and ongoing management strategies have saved untold lives and minimized risk to victims. Additionally, with respect to workplace violence investigations, Los Angeles' exposure to civil and financial liability has been greatly reduced. Although prevention does not often result in traditional or verifiable crime statistics for the purposes of a COMPSTAT-type review process, the dynamics of a given case can serve to foreshadow the potential for violence when there is no intervention.

LOS ANGELES FIRE DEPARTMENT WORKPLACE VIOLENCE INVESTIGATION

In July 2002, Christopher Sooy, a 38-year-old recruit firefighter, was flunking out of the Los Angeles City Fire Academy because of below-par physical performance. Sooy had been trying for several years to become a firefighter with the Los Angeles Fire Department (LAFD) and would soon be ineligible for recycle training because of his age. As the oldest in his recruit class, Sooy was often the subject of harassment from his classmates. He was single, a loner, and withdrawn from most of his peers. During a lunch conversation with another recruit, Sooy stated that he knew he was failing, and when his termination day came, he would return to the academy and "fucking massacre everyone." The concerned recruit reported the threat, but the training staff at the fire academy considered this to be an offhand comment made out of frustration; therefore they waited several days before reporting the statement to the city's threat assessment team.

Once involved, TMU detectives learned of additional risk-enhancing facts through interviews with Sooy's classmates and trainers; perhaps the most concerning was the fact that this was his third and last attempt at achieving his lifelong ambition of becoming a firefighter. Sooy was resentful of most of his classmates, but among the few recruits with whom he interacted, he spoke frequently of his fascination with firearms and his shooting exploits at the target range. Detectives discovered that Sooy was recently separated from his live-in girlfriend and that his family (support system) lived several hundred miles away. Computer queries confirmed that Sooy was something of a gun fanatic, with over a dozen tactical weapons registered to him, including five that would

FIGURE 19.1 Enlarged photograph depicting some of the firearms seized from Sooy's apartment. Pictured are several semi-automatic weapons including a Colt AR-15 assault rifle and a Russian-made SKS 7.62mm military assault rifle.

be defined as assault rifles under California's current ban. In consideration of these facts, TMU detectives prepared a search warrant for Sooy's residence, a small apartment within a multiunit complex in the affluent San Fernando Valley area of Los Angeles.

At the time of the apartment search, TMU detectives discovered a possible explosive device that required containment and notification to the LAPD Explosives Unit (bomb squad). Upon evaluating the device, the bomb squad determined it to be live and unstable; therefore the search had to be suspended, the neighborhood evacuated, and the device detonated at the scene. Several hours, and several displaced tenants later, TMU detectives were able to resume the search. Detectives additionally recovered five assault-type rifles, seven semiautomatic handguns, a shotgun, laser sights, dozens of military knives, throwing stars, and hundreds of rounds of ammunition with high-capacity magazines (clips). Sooy had also maintained an extensive library of *Soldier of Fortune* magazines. He was arrested and convicted of possession of an explosive device and making a criminal threat.

The Sooy case (see Figures 19.1 and 19.2) is also illustrative of the city's potential for liability if there

FIGURE 19.2 Left to right: TMU Detectives Rose Smith and Tammy Dougherty with the cache of weapons, ammunition, and high-capacity magazines (clips) discovered inside Sooy's small one-bedroom apartment.

is an initial failure of timely reporting and intervention. City managers (LAFD training staff and their superiors) were aware of a specific threat made by a desperate and disgruntled employee who was not only facing termination but also the shattering of his lifelong dream of becoming a firefighter. Clearly, Sooy had difficulty coping with the impending termination as evidenced by his threatening comments. Simple cursory interviews with Sooy's classmates would have also revealed a person experiencing a personal crisis: a failed intimate relationship and no obvious peer or family support system. The city's pre-employment background screening process should have revealed the extent of Sooy's firearms collection as well as the nature of the weapons (i.e., tactical or sport). When considered in totality, it is a pretty frightening scenario.

Had Sooy engaged in an act of workplace violence, the results could have proven catastrophic and the liability implications for the city are obvious; what did we know, when did we know it, and what did we do to prevent it? Initially, nothing. In violation of the city's own Workplace Violence Prevention Policy, the LAFD conducted no internal administrative investigation and waited several days to report the threat to the CTAT to initiate a formal criminal investigation.

But what if Sooy never engaged in an act of workplace violence and the matter was never reported to the CTAT? Significant liability issues still exist for all of the aforementioned reasons. If the unstable explosive device found inside of his apartment had inadvertently detonated and injured area residents, the same liability would still apply.

These are the issues that our police agency managers and company executives need to understand in order to prioritize threat assessment and prevention within our organizations. In an era of COMPSTAT-type statistical analysis programs, the Sooy case gets lost in translation: a potentially devastating, life-altering, catastrophic event involving an untold number of casualties averted = 1 crime report cleared.

The numbers don't tell the story.

OVERVIEW OF TMU RESPONSIBILITIES

With the passage of time, local and world events have reshaped the LAPD's view of the resources needed to address the variety of threat-related issues. Today, the TMU is responsible for investigating:

- Aggravated stalking cases, citywide
- Aggravated criminal threat cases, citywide

- All threats directed to the city's elected officials
- Workplace violence cases involving city employees and departments

TMU investigations all involve similar tasks and problems. The most significant of these is the process of threat assessment and implementing that assessment into a case management strategy. Because these responsibilities often involve individuals of interest to other similarly tasked entities, the TMU acts as an LAPD liaison contact for the security directors of the various entertainment studios, all elected officials for the City of Los Angeles, the FBI Behavioral Analysis Unit, California Highway Patrol Dignitary Protection Unit, US Capitol Police, US Secret Service, Central Intelligence Agency, and Naval Criminal Investigative Service (NCIS).

Ancillary responsibilities include training LAPD detectives at quarterly Major Assault Crimes (MAC) school classes, staffing the City of Los Angeles Threat Assessment Team (CTAT), and cohosting the annual National Threat Management Conference (ATAP).

TMU STAFFING AND CASELOAD

Present staffing of the TMU includes seven detectives and one officer in charge (OI); this represents a significant expansion from the original three detectives and one supervisor. All TMU detectives have a minimum of 15 years of law enforcement experience with backgrounds in domestic violence and sexual assault investigations and a familiarity with computer forensics. This experience translates well to threat assessment/investigation and the ability to develop a multifaceted case management strategy. Additionally, TMU detectives are routinely required to interact with traumatized victims. Having a background in domestic violence or sexual assault investigations prepares investigators for the victim-management issues that often arise in our cases.

All cases accepted by the TMU involve threats to individuals (specific or implied) and/or long-term obsessive behaviors that convey a threat to the person targeted. On average, the TMU handles 200 to 250 cases per year; each detective will be handling 10 to 15 active cases at any given time. As previously noted, the TMU is required to investigate all incidents of workplace violence involving Los Angeles city employees as well as all threats directed to the city's elected officials. One area where we may exercise some discretion on case assumption is with criminal threat investigations. Domestic violence cases, private sector workplace violence, most threatening phone call investigations, and cases involving a one-time threat will usually be handled by detectives at one of the LAPD's 21 geographic areas (precincts).

Specialized units are created to provide services on complex cases that go beyond the time and resources available to area detectives. With that in mind, the caseload must remain at a manageable level to let TMU detectives fully investigate and manage complicated issues. Stalking cases, by their very nature, are long-term, protracted problems that routinely require detectives to identify and corroborate many years of harassment and obsessive behavior, often involving unknown suspects. The supervisor's job is to make sure that TMU investigators have the time and resources needed to work their assignments. Often this becomes a balancing act, since some cases are much more involved than others. Again, numbers do not tell the whole story, and a detective working five active cases may be more affected than a peer who is handling twice that many. Regular unit meetings with case status updates will ensure that supervisors remain informed and that peer investigators are familiar with all active cases within the unit. Murphy's law ("If anything can go wrong, it will") seems to always come into play: cases will become active when the assigned detective is in court, sick, or on vacation. Having all unit detectives somewhat familiar with every active TMU investigation allows for a seamless case hand-off with no interruptions in service when the assigned investigating officer is unavailable.

ACCEPTANCE OF CASE REFERRALS

Cases may be referred to the TMU through a variety of sources:

Calls from the Public

Media coverage of TMU cases throughout the years has heightened public awareness of the unit and the cases we handle. We frequently receive calls from private security professionals and victims (real and perceived) seeking assistance on threat-related matters. In each instance, a TMU detective will conduct a preliminary telephonic interview to determine whether the case meets TMU criteria for handling. If so, an in-person meeting will be scheduled with the victim for a more detailed interview, discussion of case management options, and completion of appropriate

reports. If the case does not meet TMU's criteria for handling, the victim will be referred to the appropriate investigative entity.

Liaison Contacts with Entertainment Studios and Elected Official Staff

The TMU maintains a liaison with security staff from the various entertainment studios as well as administrative staff for each elected city official. The TMU acts as a point of contact for direct reporting of all threat-related matters.

District Attorney/City Attorney

Periodically, prosecutors from either the district or city attorney's office will contact the TMU seeking assistance on an aggravated case presented to them by another investigator. Depending on how far along the original detective is with the case, the TMU may elect to either assume the entire investigation or act as a consultant/resource to the assigned officer.

Los Angeles City Departments and the City Threat Assessment Team (CTAT)

The Los Angeles city policy on the prevention of workplace violence requires that all city departments report threats or incidents of violence affecting city employees in the workplace to the TMU for investigation.

Major Assault Crimes Units

Most cases are routed to the TMU through the Area Major Assault Crimes (MAC) units. Within each of the 21 geographic LAPD areas (precincts), there are detectives assigned to investigate various crimes connected to that jurisdiction. Crimes such as homicide, robbery, burglary, auto theft, and so on will typically be handled by in-house area detectives familiar with the crime trends in that portion of the city. Detectives assigned to the MAC units will typically investigate all assault-related cases, such as battery, sexual assaults, assaults with a deadly weapon, criminal threats, domestic violence, and stalking. Area MAC detectives often deal with an oppressive caseload that limits their ability to respond quickly and dedicate focused attention to any one investigation. Mindful of that, the TMU is committed to being a resource to area operations and specifically MAC units. Unfortunately, seven TMU detectives cannot possibly investigate every stalking or criminal threat report that occurs in a city as large as Los Angeles. For that reason, case assumption criteria for these types of investigations were established.

CRITERIA FOR CASE ASSUMPTION

Mandated

All cases involving threats to a City of Los Angeles elected official and all cases involving workplace violence affecting city employees.

Aggravated

Unlike the TMU, area MAC detectives often lack the flexibility to "drop everything" and focus all of their resources on a single case at a time of crisis. Stalking or threat investigations that involve escalating, violent behaviors requiring immediate law enforcement intervention to safeguard the victim will always meet the TMU criteria for handling. These are cases that go beyond threats (which mean little to the actual threat assessment process) and involve deliberate/directed travel, physical confrontations, destruction of property, and/or assaults.

Multiple Jurisdictions

In a fragmented metropolitan area as large as Los Angeles (3.832 million people), it is not uncommon for a victim to live in one jurisdiction and work in another. In many stalking cases, the suspects have contacted the victim at both home and work, generating crime reports with two different agencies or area MAC units. Same victim, same suspect, but different detectives working parallel investigations: a waste of resources. On cases such as these the TMU will assume responsibility and consolidate the investigation. This not only frees the area detectives from the case but also allows for better service to the victim.

Discretionary

As caseload permits, we will assume stalking or threat cases that may not otherwise meet the threshold for TMU assumption. The overall TMU caseload, however, must remain at a manageable level; we must be able to respond and dedicate resources to those critical cases requiring immediate intervention and hands-on management.

INTERVIEWING THE VICTIM

Once it has been determined that the TMU will assume responsibility for the case, it is vitally important that we reinterview the victim in order to understand the context of the suspect's behavior and any threats that have been made. It is not uncommon for a TMU detective to spend three or more hours reinterviewing the victim in order to get a complete understanding of the issues and identify case management options. A case example:

Several years ago a colleague investigated a domestic violence case in which the suspect had battered his wife inside their home. The police were called and the suspect was arrested owing to the wife's obvious injuries. As the officers led the suspect away in handcuffs, he turned to the victim and said, "Don't worry honey, I'll be out in a few days. We'll go back to Las Vegas to celebrate." Without knowing the context, this appears to be an innocuous comment, certainly not overtly threatening. During the follow-up interview with detectives, the victim advised that while they were vacationing in Las Vegas the year before, the suspect had beaten her so severely that she was hospitalized for three days. The husband's seemingly innocent comment was certainly a threat as far as the victim was concerned. By asking a few probing questions, the detectives proved the credible threat element of the criminal statute. Without understanding the context, the threat could have been missed and that additional charge would never have been sought.

The most critical aspect of an investigation is the preliminary interview and report, which are usually completed by desk or patrol officers who have the least amount of job experience. If important elements are missed or overlooked, evidence may be lost and the case may be assigned to the wrong entity or not receive the appropriate prioritization. Officers are typically trained to stick to the known facts and to complete the required information boxes on the report form. Unfortunately, victims are neither professional witnesses nor experienced investigators; they typically don't know what information to volunteer to assure proper documentation or case classification. For these reasons, TMU investigators will *always* reinterview victims and witnesses in their assigned cases. It is imperative that we understand the history of the victim/suspect relationship and the progression of the aberrant behavior that led to police involvement.

A by-product of this interview is the establishment of rapport and trust with the victim. Open communication and detective availability instill comfort and confidence. Often, we will enlist victims as participants in their own investigations; we ask them to maintain a log, obtain restraining orders and phone traps, and retain evidence such as emails and voice mail messages. A confident and involved victim is more likely to follow through with recommended security measures, evidence gathering, and prosecution. Another benefit derived from the interview is the opportunity to educate victims on the nature of threat investigations and law enforcement's limitations in protecting them. Police agencies simply cannot provide protection 24 hours a day, 7 days a week. The victim must take some responsibility for his or her own safety. With that in mind, detectives should identify risks and hazards and present the victim with security options and suggestions without making guarantees of safety. Promises of safety can lead to civil liability should the victim ultimately be harmed and the courts determine that a "special relationship" existed with the law enforcement agency. Consequently decisions about personal security rest with the victims and their degree of tolerance of the threatening behavior. Guarantees of safety aside, the following recommendations should be considered in all stalking and/or threat investigations:

- Cease all contact with the suspect, including all personal, telephonic or email communications.
- Contact law enforcement to report all incidents and press for assurance that the assigned detective is notified.
- Keep a detailed log of all incidents to include dates, times, locations, and witnesses to what occurred.
- Save all evidence, such as gifts, letters, notes, photos, voice mail, and text/email messages.
- Allow the police to conduct the investigation without third-party interference.

Security agents and personal attorneys should first consult with the investigating detective before acting. This will avoid the possibility of an inadvertent negative impact on the criminal investigation.

EVIDENCE GATHERING

Once we have reinterviewed the victim and witnesses and have identified the relevant issues, we can take the next logical steps in our follow-up investigation. Identifying and locating corroborating evidence will be a dictating factor when we formulate our case management options. Do we arrest and seek

prosecution or utilize other means of intervention? Without evidence or other corroboration, arrest and prosecution are not options.

Once we know the dynamics of the case, it becomes obvious what corroborating evidence will be needed:

- Retain all letters, notes and gifts sent by the suspect. Photograph perishables such as flowers.
- If the suspect is texting or calling the victim, we need the text or voice mail and the relevant telephone company records, which can be obtained via search warrant or subpoena.
- If the suspect is emailing the victim, we need to retain the original email and obtain identifying information from the Internet service provider (search warrant or subpoena). We may also want to seize the suspect's computer for forensic testing.
- If the suspect has assaulted the victim, photos of any injuries must be obtained as soon as possible, along with all medical records.
- Signs of property damage, vandalism, and graffiti must also be photographed and repair estimates obtained.
- If the suspect has stolen property from the victim, we need to search his residence and vehicle for the victim's belongings via a search warrant.

Search warrants are a fundamental tool in the investigation of stalking and threat-related cases. Telephone companies, Internet service providers, and financial institutions all require a search warrant or subpoena to release the information or records we seek. Unfortunately detectives are apt to avoid using them because of the required writing time. As a result, good evidence is often lost. In years past, detectives opted to use parole or probation searches, when available, as an alternative to obtaining a warrant to search a suspect's home or vehicle. However, recent court rulings have limited the scope of such searches. Failure to write an affidavit and seek a search warrant can jeopardize the investigation.

TMU detectives have streamlined the process by maintaining templates of the various search warrant formats on computer media. To an extent, this allows detectives to fill in the blanks with information specific to the case being investigated, thereby greatly reducing the writing time needed. The affidavit or support declaration will naturally differ from case to case depending on the location to be served and the evidence sought. The most important thing to remember about search warrants is that *if you don't ask for it, you won't get it.* An investigator must give a foundation for the evidence sought in the narrative of the affidavit. Also, the court's permission must always be sought to seize a suspect's computer.

Suspects often research their victims on the Internet, maintain notes and diaries, and post messages with incriminating content. This information is stored on the computer's hard drive and is powerful evidence for law enforcement.

THREAT ASSESSMENT

As law enforcement officers, we are first responders. Many times we are asked to assess a threat on a moment's notice as we are running out the door to respond to a crisis. We often do not have the luxury of time to consider all the nuances of a case before we initiate a preliminary management plan. With that in mind, there are a few factors that we need to identify quickly that will provide a solid foundation for our preliminary assessment.

How the Threat Was Communicated

Words by themselves never physically hurt anyone. Verbal threats may be symptomatic of an underlying grievance, but they have little influence on the assessment of risk for violence. A formulation originally made by Fein, Vossekuil, and Holden in their Exceptional Case Study Project (1995, p. 2) said it best:

> Many persons who make threats do not pose threats,
> Some persons who pose threats never make threats,
> Some persons who make threats ultimately pose threats.
> (Fein et al., 1995)

The message they convey is to not get caught up in focusing on the threat itself but rather the person, behavior, circumstances, and context behind the threat and the manner in which it was communicated.

I am blessed (or cursed, depending on the day) with having a teenage daughter at home. I cannot count the number of times that she has come out of her bedroom crying because one of her friends sent her a nasty text message or email. The drama of the moment is overwhelming, the word goes out, and all of her friends get caught up talking about it and taking sides. A few days later, the drama has passed and the two girls are best friends again. I have learned that teenage girls will often say the most vile, hateful, and hurtful things to each other in notes, over the phone, or on the computer—things that they would never say to one another face to face.

That is exactly how we view threats that are similarly communicated.

The moral of the story is that we need to know how the suspect communicated the threat to the victim. It is relatively easy to threaten someone from the comfort and anonymity of a computer keyboard or cell phone keypad. Even if suspects identify themselves, they are doing so within the relative safety and comfort of their own environment. It requires much more conviction and a much greater emotional investment to confront the target face to face, outside of the suspect's controlled comfort zone.

Consequently we become concerned when we see the communications progress from less personal modes of contact (voice mail, email, *mailed* letters) to more personal methods of contact, such as directed travel to the victim's home or office. Confrontations with the victim, family members, or staff are red flags in a threat assessment and a signal for investigators to consider intervention options to slow the building momentum.

What Is/Was the Relationship Between the Suspect and Victim

The closer the relationship between the victim and suspect (real or perceived), the more personal the grievance (or trigger), the greater the risk of violence. All who have experienced a divorce or the breakup of an intimate relationship know that these are traumatic personal events that can cause dramatic emotional turmoil. Usually one or both parties feel that they were wronged or treated unjustly and harbor some resentment or anger. In the case of a failed long-term relationship, lives have become intertwined and cannot be immediately untangled. Child custody, property splits, loss of mutual friends, and financial instability can all contribute to this emotionally charged scenario.

Compounding the risk is the familiarity of the suspect with the victim. He or she knows where the other lives, works, and socializes. The suspect knows what car the victim drives and what school the children attend. In a domestic case such as this, the suspect may literally know the victim's pattern or schedule 24/7.

Working within the Hollywood community, we sometimes see cases involving erotomanic delusions wherein a suspect truly believes that he or she is romantically involved with someone rich or famous. If that suspect were to feel slighted, rejected, or ignored by the victim, the same emotional risk-enhancing factors apply.

It is our experience at the TMU that threat/stalking cases involving former intimate partners have the greatest potential for violence and can be the most dangerous in terms of the suspect's behavior. Conversely, our experience, as well as the literature, supports the notion that the more removed or distant the connection between the victim and suspect, generally the lower the violence risk.

Suspect's History of Violence

Past performance is the best predictor for future behavior. If a person has engaged in violent activity in the past to solve a problem or resolve conflict, he or she is much more likely to act out violently in the future, given the right motivation or trigger.

After an almost 30-year career in law enforcement, I can safely estimate that I have been involved in over 100 incidents where I have used some degree of physical force to control a volatile situation. I recall in great detail my first fight as a new officer fresh out of the police academy. I can also describe my last altercation because it is still relatively fresh in my memory. I just cannot remember too much about the other 98 or so fights that I have been involved in. Why do you think that is?

I believe that the first time we use physical force (violence) to overcome adversity and exercise control, we cross some sort of psychological threshold. We learn to view physical force as an acceptable means to overcome resistance. The more we use it, the more emotionally comfortable we become with it. Eventually, using force to overcome conflict becomes a natural reaction—a conditioned response to adversity. For the most part I do not remember my other 98 fights because they had no emotional impact; they represented just another day on the beat.

Consequently I pay very close attention when I encounter a suspect with a pattern and/or documented history of violence. Rap sheets indicating prior arrests for various assaults, battery, domestic violence, resisting arrest, animal cruelty, and so on should be a cause for concern to the investigator. Your suspect has become comfortable in using physical force to influence behavior and overcome perceived challenges. Even more concerning is a situation in which these offenses are coupled with a history of restraining orders or probation violations; now we have an individual who is not only potentially violent, but also shows no impulse control and/or no regard for authority and the consequences of violating court-imposed boundaries.

Before any intervention or management strategy is considered, we need to know the nature of the victim/suspect relationship, how the threats were communicated, and any history of violence in the suspect's background—whether it involved the victim or not. These are the foundations on which we will build our threat assessment.

Threat assessment is an evolving process. Pertinent information should be added and considered as it becomes known. Often, an initial assessment will change significantly after the addition of a few pieces of critical information. Stabilizing and destabilizing factors need to be considered and weighed in the overall scenario. Issues such as the suspect's mental health history, physical health, living environment, financial stability, the presence of a family or friend support system, and any significant upcoming anniversary dates need to be identified and considered. These are critical components of a meaningful threat assessment process. The accuracy and reliability of any assessment is diminished in the absence of these pertinent data. As police officers, we are familiar with the adage that a person who is suicidal is also homicidal. A person who perceives that he or she has nothing left to live for because of health, financial, or relationship reasons can be a very dangerous person indeed. Conversely, a person who has good health, is embraced by family and friends, has a good job, and plans for the future has a great deal to lose if his or her threat is exposed or acted upon. These are important facts to consider in trying to determine the actual risk posed by the individual and can also help to identify case management options.

CASE MANAGEMENT

Detectives working the TMU recognize that every case is different. Every case needs to be evaluated independently and on its own merits. There is no "one size fits all" response to threat cases. If there were, the TMU and the threat assessment process would not be necessary. With that in mind, we must remain flexible and sometimes develop an "outside of the box" management strategy depending on the dynamics/specifics of the particular case at hand.

There are dozens of things to consider in mapping out a case management strategy. Above all, the victim's safety should be the paramount and overriding issue. The manner in which we intervene should be driven by the immediacy of the threat posed by the suspect.

What is equally important is a buy-in from the victims. They must take some ownership in whatever strategy is selected. After all, they have to live with the results or the consequences if the chosen strategy is not immediately effective. Detectives can save themselves a great deal of grief and second guessing by presenting the victim with management options that are appropriate to the case and explaining the pros and cons associated with each.

As an example, arresting a suspect for a misdemeanor offense may provide immediate relief for the victim while also sending a strong message to the suspect, given his history. On the other hand, a misdemeanor arrest will not normally result in lengthy incarceration and may further exacerbate the situation, depending on the case and suspect dynamics (arrest history, history of violence, etc.). Additionally, the victim may ultimately be called upon to testify and confront the suspect in court. Perhaps instead, a mental health intervention or restraining order would be a preferable first step. In any given case there may be two or three viable strategies, or a combination of strategies, that may prove effective in managing the suspect's behavior. By suggesting best options, explaining the pros and cons associated with each, and allowing victims to voice their comfort level with the suggested management plan, we make them stakeholders in their own investigations. That said, the victim alone should never dictate the course of the investigation. Unless a case is aggravated to the extent that an immediate arrest and prosecution is warranted, the management strategy may be progressive and involve increasing levels and methods of intervention based upon the response of the suspect.

INTERVENTION VS. NO INTERVENTION

When is it best to wait and watch, or confront the offender and risk exacerbating the behavior? This can be a difficult decision and should be based on consideration of the following factors:

The Proximity of the Suspect to the Victim

In Los Angeles we sometimes get celebrity cases where an obsessed fan from another part of the country or abroad is writing or emailing a victim. In these cases, arrest and extradition are extremely unlikely unless there are some serious felony allegations. We have no quality control over any "knock and talk" intervention that may be done by local law enforcement on our behalf. Restraining orders are enforceable from state to state but would require the victim to travel to the suspect's jurisdiction to testify in any subsequent prosecution, which in turn would be likely to result in minimal jail time if the subject were convicted. Any intervention we might choose has a cause and effect. In these cases, we may want to consider just monitoring the suspect's communications rather than risk losing good intelligence on his or her thoughts and activities. We may be able to stop the communication but we cannot stop the obsession. The last thing we want is for the suspect to go off radar then suddenly appear when the police and victim are unprepared.

How and Where the Suspect Contacts the Victim

With elected official and celebrity cases, very often the suspect's only point of contact is through the victim's management or administrative offices. Typically these environments have protocols in place for the review and screening of mail, phone calls, and so forth, without direct contact with the victim. As long as they are devoid of serious criminal elements, we may want to keep those cards and letters coming if the communication is providing us with useful information or insight about the suspect's activities or intentions. One designated office contact person should serve to field the suspect's calls, letters, or emails and maintain a log of the activity. By keeping the contact limited to one or two individuals within the office, escalation in the suspect's rhetoric or frequency of calls can be better detected.

Seriousness of the Crime

Just because an act may constitute a crime does not mean that we should always arrest. Low-grade misdemeanors and infractions such as trespass or annoying phone calls may be symptomatic of a developing stalking scenario, but alone they will not result in significant jail time. Here is where we need to evaluate our suspect; does she have multiple arrests and a history of violence? If so, arresting and releasing her a few hours later may have little deterrent effect and may exacerbate the problem. Conversely, an otherwise law-abiding person with few police contacts may respond favorably to any police intervention, and the few hours spent in lockup may be all that is needed to alter his behavior. Every suspect is different.

Evidence

Having a reported crime is one thing, proving it is something else. The follow-up investigation will determine whether sufficient evidence exists to support a criminal filing. Losing a case at filing or in trial can empower and embolden a suspect. One should know what can and cannot be proven in court before committing to an arrest.

KNOCK AND TALK

If a verbal warning is to be used as a deterrent in your case management strategy, there is no substitute for a face-to-face interview with the suspect. A knock-and-talk intervention is fundamentally a form of intimidation. The intimidation aspect is derived from the simple presence of law enforcement within the suspect's comfort zone. As children, we learned that bullies will continue to be bullies until a bigger kid comes along. Law enforcement knocking on a suspect's door is that bigger kid (figuratively speaking). With that in mind, where we choose to conduct the intervention should be determined by what gives us the most leverage or psychological advantage.

The Suspect's Home

Does the suspect live alone or with family members? We sometimes deal with delusional individuals who live with family members because of mental illness. Typically, these individuals have a great deal of time on their hands to watch television, write letters, send emails, and make harassing phone calls to victims. By interviewing them at home, we can often elicit the assistance of family members to monitor and control such suspects' actions. Additionally, getting inside of someone's home gives us a great deal of insight into a suspect's lifestyle and environment as well as possible clues to the level of his or her obsession with the victim (posters, magazines, notes, videos, computer printouts, etc.). A disordered individual can sometimes seem organized and functional during a brief telephone conversation. Seeing how they live is much more telling (Gosling, 2008).

If the suspect is married and is concealing stalking activity from his or her spouse, we may elect not to do the interview at home, saving the disclosure issue as leverage to help manage the case. As investigators we must do our homework. The more background information that is obtained on the subject, the better we can judge what location will give us the best opportunity for a successful intervention.

The Subject's Job Site

This option must be carefully considered. Embarrassing a suspect in front of peers and coworkers can inflame a situation rather than resolve it. Additionally, if the individual were to lose employment as a result of our intervention, we would only have added a risk-enhancing factor to an already potentially volatile matter. I recommend this as a last resort, when attempts to locate the suspect elsewhere have met with negative results.

The Police Station

Here is the intimidation factor again. It can be very sobering for an individual who has had few prior contacts with the police to deal with the cold environment of a police station. Conversely, this may have little effect on a career criminal who has a lengthy arrest history. We must know our suspect before committing to an intervention strategy.

RESTRAINING/ PROTECTIVE ORDERS

The use of restraining orders to manage suspect behavior is often a controversial issue. To be certain, restraining orders are not appropriate or effective in every case. In fact, there have been incidents when the service of a protective order has inflamed the situation. Obviously, some suspects are not suitable candidates for a restraining order because of a past violent history with the victim or severe mental health issues. However, it is our experience that the failure of a restraining order as a management tool is generally the result of either or both of the following factors.

Failure to Report Violations

Many times victims will not report what they consider to be minor infractions because of the "trivial" nature of the offense. In reality, this minor infraction may in fact constitute boundary probing by the suspect so as to test the victim's resolve and the police's response. If not reported appropriately, the lack of response can embolden a suspect. In those instances, we can expect the behavior to escalate in subsequent violations.

Police Complacency

When violations are reported but not quickly acted on by the police, the same lack-of-response dynamics apply. Advising a victim to obtain a restraining order without being prepared to act on the first violation is counterproductive to the case and could increase the risk to the victim. Detectives should view restraining orders as tools rather than deterrents. We are seeking to place legal parameters around behavior that would otherwise not be criminal. We expect the suspect to violate the order, with the advantage that we can now justify an arrest where none was possible before. Restraining orders fill a huge void in the state of California, where no anti-harassment laws exist. When used in this capacity, restraining orders can be a vital component of a case management strategy.

MENTAL HEALTH INTERVENTION

Perhaps the most useful but least utilized tool as it applies to stalking and most threat investigations is a mental health intervention. Most jurisdictions in the United States have statutes in place that allow sworn police officers to detain individuals involuntarily who have demonstrated that because of mental illness, they are a threat to themselves or others or are gravely disabled to the point that they cannot care for themselves. The subjects are generally admitted to a secure mental health care facility for a 72-hour psychiatric evaluation and risk assessment. On the basis of the findings, the treating physician in California may extend this hold for a period of up to 14 days and beyond, depending on the level of impairment and the potential risk posed to self or the community if released. Now consider the minimal detention time that same subject would have received for a low-grade misdemeanor arrest without ever addressing the overriding mental health issues. Additionally, nothing about this process precludes investigators from later, upon the subject's release from the hospital, seeking criminal charges. There have been many such cases wherein TMU detectives have arrested suspects immediately upon their discharge from a psychiatric facility.

Consider the Many Benefits Afforded by a Mental Health Intervention

- The subject has been detained, thereby providing the victim short-term relief and the opportunity to implement security measures or obtain a restraining order.
- The subject has been evaluated, diagnosed, and treated for the same mental health issues that contributed to the aberrant behavior.
- Detectives have been afforded time to prepare search or arrest warrants or to interview witnesses.
- The subject is exposed to ongoing treatment, monitoring, and periodic welfare checks through county mental health resources and social agencies.
- In California, subjects placed on involuntary psychiatric holds for danger to self or others may not own or possess a firearm for a period of five years from the date of hospitalization.

An important consideration for investigators is that privacy laws may preclude hospitals from sharing treatment information or patient diagnoses with investigating officers. That does not prevent us from sharing information with the hospital. We frequently attempt to speak directly with the treating physician so that we may explain the dynamics of our case and the subject's behavior. The more information that we can offer the attending staff, the better equipped they are to properly evaluate and treat the subject.

ARREST AND PROSECUTION

In aggravated threat and stalking cases where sufficient evidence exists to support a felony criminal filing, there can be no better long-term intervention than arrest, incarceration, and probation. Many useful management tools can be brought to bear as a result of a felony conviction.

While in custody, a suspect may receive diagnostic testing and treatment. Once released, the suspect's terms of probation or parole can require drug testing, anger management, psychological counseling, outpatient treatment, and periodic reports to the court to verify compliance. Additionally, the court can issue criminal protective orders on behalf of the victim to further restrict the suspect's activity. In extreme cases, the suspect may be required to wear an electronic monitoring device to prohibit movement beyond a prescribed area. California law requires a psychological evaluation for individuals who have been convicted of stalking and sentenced to prison (California Penal Code 646.9). Occasionally, a convicted stalker who has served his prison sentence will then be committed as a "mentally disordered offender" (California Penal Code 2960) and transferred to a secure forensic hospital for at least a year's treatment and evaluation.

The suspect must demonstrate that he or she is suitable for release into the community before being eligible for discharge. This sometimes leads to several years of additional detention and treatment for the same behaviors that led to the initial criminal investigation. Perhaps the greatest benefit of the various containment strategies is the empowerment of the victims to regain control of their lives. The luxury of time affords the opportunity for the victims to alter their lifestyles and become less accessible to the suspect.

In discussing prosecution, we must also address the relationship between the victim, detective, and prosecutor. In Los Angeles, the District Attorney's Office has established a specialized unit to "vertically" prosecute aggravated stalking and threat cases. Vertical prosecution means that the same deputy district attorney who files the case will continue to be involved in all aspects of the prosecution: bail and discovery hearings, preliminary hearings, trial, and sentencing. Simply put, there will be no handoff to another attorney who may be unfamiliar with the case. The ability to interact with the same prosecutor throughout the court process is a great benefit to the detective. Similarly, a victim experiencing the ordeal of testifying and the unfamiliarity of the legal process is often more confident in dealing with a consistent team of investigators and a prosecutor who can be contacted to deal with any questions or concerns. Many jurisdictions offer vertical prosecution for domestic violence cases. Stalking and threat cases share the same victim dynamics and should be given the same emphasis.

CONCLUSION

Within this chapter I have tried to clarify how the LAPD Threat Management Unit approaches threat assessment and evaluates case management options. Because every case is truly different, there is no possible way to cover all of the nuances or issues that may be encountered during a stalking or threat investigation. There are too many variables involving victim dynamics, suspect dynamics, and the relationships between the two. Simply put, there is no checklist or "one size fits all" formula to successfully manage these cases. If there were, there would be no need for specialized services. From the law enforcement perspective, successful case management comes from experience, a fundamental understanding of threat assessment

principles, in-depth familiarity with applicable laws, and knowing the available resources within your jurisdictional control. We cannot expect overburdened area detectives handling a crushing caseload of dissimilar investigations to be able to dedicate the time needed to manage these cases, let alone develop the needed expertise to do it well. With that in mind, I have tried to make the case for establishing specialized threat management-type units within the respective agencies, regardless of size. One must only consider the 2011 assassination attempt on Congresswoman Giffords and subsequent mass murder, or the Aurora, Colorado, theater rampage killings in 2012, both perpetrated by offenders with prior observable high-risk behaviors, to understand that one overlooked clue and one missed intervention opportunity can lead to catastrophic consequences. How many similar events have been averted because of timely intervention and proactive case management? We will never know. The numbers don't tell the story.

KEY POINTS

- There is no "one size fits all" response to threat investigations.
- Understand that the prevention and interruption of targeted violence will not often provide the "recap" numbers sought in COMPSTAT-type policing models.
- Stalking and aggravated threat cases require hands-on management strategies that are best suited for specialized units.
- Arrest and prosecution are just two of many tools available to law enforcement; often there are better options that will provide a more desired result.
- Every case is different and investigators should evaluate the merits of each case independently, utilizing the management tools that offer the best prospect for long-term resolution.
- Understand that a threat assessment is not based on the threat itself, but rather the behavior and background of the suspect and her or his relationship with the target.
- In all case management discussions, the safety of the victim is paramount and the overriding consideration.

REFERENCES

Fein, R., Vossekuil, B., & Holden, G. (1995). *Threat assessment: An approach to prevent targeted violence.* Washington, DC: U.S. Department of Justice, Office of Justice Programs, National Institute of Justice, Publication NCJ 155000.

Gosling, S. (2008). *Snoop.* New York: Basic Books.

Lane, J., & Boles, G. (2000). *Threat management unit guidelines.* Unpublished document.

20

The Fixated Threat Assessment Centre

Implementing a Joint Policing and Psychiatric Approach to Risk Assessment and Management in Public Figure Threat Cases

DAVID V. JAMES, FRANK R. FARNHAM, AND SIMON P. WILSON

The Fixated Threat Assessment Centre (FTAC) was established in the United Kingdom in 2006 to assess and manage the risk to dignitaries from isolated loners pursuing idiosyncratic quests or causes. The term *fixated* in its title refers to an obsessional preoccupation with a person, place, or cause that is pursued to an irrational degree (Mullen et al., 2009). FTAC grew out of a research project, and its structure and procedures were designed de novo to reflect the most up-to-date research in the area and incorporate the best practices found in other public figure threat assessment units in Europe and the United States. Its defining characteristic is that, although it is a police unit, it incorporates psychiatric staff from the country's National Health Service (NHS) as full-time personnel working alongside police officers.

FTAC is the first such unit in the United Kingdom. It is located within the Specialist Operations section of the Metropolitan Police Service and is based in London. It has a national remit and is commissioned jointly by the Office of Security and Counter-terrorism at the Home Office and by the Department of Health. Its establishment followed the recognition that, whereas well-established systems were in place to assess threats from terrorists and criminals, no such mechanisms existed with regard to problems posed by disturbed members of the general public who exhibit a pattern of stalking-type behavior toward public figures, with repeated attempts at communication and/or approach. Such behaviors may give rise to anxiety, fear or concern, and can result in disruption, embarrassment, the dissipation of policing resources, physical risk to the individual themselves, and occasionally violence to others. However, in contrast to groups whose motives are usually easy to understand and whose modi operandi follow predictable patterns, fixated loners are usually difficult to understand in terms of motivation, their actions are often unpredictable, and they do not fit easily into standard policing mechanisms for assessing and managing threat (Mullen et al., 2009).

The following account will cover the principles underlying FTAC's formation, its structure, and the fundamentals of its threat assessment and management procedures. This last will be illustrated by a case example. The particular issues with which we shall first deal are the role of psychiatry, the population model for prevention, the differences between threat assessment and risk assessment, the relation between stalking in the general population and inappropriate or threatening attention to public figures, and the meaning of risk.

UNDERLYING PRINCIPLES

The Role of Psychiatry

A principal conclusion of the Fixated Research Group (FRG), which undertook the research upon which FTAC was founded (www.fixatedthreat.com), is that the role of psychiatry is central to confronting the issue of threat from fixated individuals (James et al., 2007, 2008, 2009; Mullen et al., 2008). This went against the recent prevailing wisdom in sections of the threat assessment community in the United States (Meloy et al., 2011), where mental illness had been assumed not to be of operational importance. This may in part have been due to a misreading of the published findings of the Exceptional Case Study Project (Fein & Vossekuil, 1998, 1999); to the omission of findings about mental illness by Dietz and colleagues in their earlier, influential studies in this field (Dietz et al., 1991a,b); and to nonclinicians erroneously equating the presence or absence of mental illness with whether or not an individual met the arguably artificial legal definition of insanity, which has no medical significance. A more detailed discussion of these issues is available elsewhere (Mullen et al., 2009). However, it is important to state that asserting the importance of mental illness does not mean adopting the simplistic notion that someone must be mad to attack a political leader in a democratic country, or some idea that mental illness could act as a marker for potential assassins, when psychotic illnesses affect nearly 1% of the population (i.e., are relatively common) and assassins are extraordinarily rare. Rather, it provides an avenue for improving the assessment of cases of possible threat to public figures and for employing specific forms of management, as well as opening some possibilities for prevention and early intervention.

Most Attackers Are Mentally Ill

The central importance of mental illness has been well articulated by Dietz and Martell (2010, p. 344): "Every instance of an attack on a public figure in the United States for which adequate information has been made publicly available has been the work of a mentally disordered person who issued one or more pre-attack signals in the form of inappropriate letters, visits or statements." Some evidence for this is provided by the well-known Exceptional Case Study Project (Fein & Vossekuil, 1998; 1999). Its authors studied 83 cases involving 74 incidents in the United States, 45% of which were attacks or assassinations and 54% "near lethal approaches" (people apprehended with a weapon in the vicinity of possible victims); 61% of these individuals had a history of psychiatric problems, 43% of delusional ideas, and 10% of violent command hallucinations. This compares with a point prevalence of psychotic illness in general community samples of around 0.4% (Kirkbride et al., 2011).

In Europe, a study of attacks on politicians (James et al., 2007) found that death and serious injury were associated with psychosis, the presence of delusions, loner status, and the absence of a political motive. Similar findings were reached in an overlapping German sample (Hoffmann, Meloy, Guldimann & Ermer, 2011). To forensic psychiatrists trained in the United Kingdom, all this has a familiar historical ring. Mentally ill individuals featured prominently in historical attacks on the Royal Family (James et al., 2008), and delusionally driven individuals were responsible for the killings of Prime Minister Spencer Perceval in 1812 (Hanrahan, 2008; Wilson, 1812) and Edward Drummond, the private secretary to the prime minister, for whom he was mistaken, in 1843 (West & Walk, 1977). Edward Drummond was killed by Daniel McNaughten, whose name remains associated with the legal test of insanity in many Anglo-Saxon jurisdictions. McNaughten continues to have other more modern resonances. A chronically deluded man who had made threats over a prolonged period before making his homicidal attack, he is typical of many contemporary threat assessment cases. Public outrage that he was found not guilty by reason of insanity led to the creation of the McNaughten Rules, expressly to prevent similar defendants from being found legally insane in the future. They are unique in the criminal law, having their origins in neither statute nor case law but instead the Law Lords' responses to a list of hypothetical questions, including one related to threat assessment where "the accused knew he was acting contrary to law, but did the act complained of with a view, under the influence of insane delusion, of redressing or revenging some supposed act or injury, or of producing some supposed public benefit" (Hansard, March 6, 1843, vol. 67, p. 288).

By contrast, terrorist attacks on politicians in western countries are rare and the terrorist threat to most public figures is low. The modern terrorist's modus operandi generally involves random attacks on mass population targets rather than attacks on politicians. The last terrorist killing of a politician on the British mainland was as long ago as 1990 (Ian Gow by the Provisional IRA). In October 2012, the terrorist threat level from Irish Republicans on the British mainland was downgraded to "moderate," the second lowest level on a five-point scale (http://www.bbc.co.uk/news/uk-northern-ireland-20066672; see also https://www.mi5.gov.uk/home/the-threats/terrorism/threat-levels.html). This illustrates that the terrorist threat waxes and wanes according to political and social circumstances. The risk to public figures from mentally ill loners, however, remains more or less constant across time and country and is unlikely to change until major breakthroughs are made in the treatment of schizophrenia and related psychotic disorders. It is therefore reasonable to conclude that the most constant threat to public figures with which both protection services and threat assessment services have to deal is that from fixated loners, most of whom are mentally ill.

Most People Engaging in Concerning Behaviors in Relation to Public Figures Are Mentally Ill

Attacks on public figures are very rare, whereas concerning and threatening cases are relatively common. It is therefore appropriate to consider the base population of fixated loners from which these attackers emerge. In the United States, Takeuchi et al. (1981) observed that "approximately 90% of all persons the Secret Service presently consider dangerous gave some indication of mental disorder." This is reflected in the various studies of White House attenders (Hoffman, 1943; Sebastiani & Foy, 1965; Shore et al., 1985). In Europe, a study based on the examination of 5,000 police case files of inappropriate or concerning approaches or communications to the British Royal Family found evidence of serious mental illness in 84% (James et al., 2009). A similar study concerning 107 cases of disturbing communications and problematic approaches to the Dutch Royal Family found that 75% were psychotic and a further 11% were suffering from mood disorders (Van der Meer et al., 2012). The situation has been summarized thus: "The post-bags of public figures are overflowing with the writings of the floridly psychotic, and the residences and workplaces of the prominent are magnets for the mentally ill" (Mullen et al., 2009, p. 41). This situation is not new. Attempts by mentally ill people to approach and force their attentions on the famous have long been a problem for public figures, especially politicians and royal families. The nineteenth-century classifications of attackers of public figures described this in some detail (Laschi & Lombroso, 1886; Régis, E., 1890). The files of nineteenth-century English lunatic asylums contain examples of fixated behavior toward public figures that are barely distinguishable from cases encountered today (Poole, 2000). In *Sketches in Bedlam* (A Constant Observer, 1823; p. 164), the anonymous author notes that there is "a class of lunatic visitors who were...assiduous and troublesome in their visits to Buckingham House

and in their endeavours to gain admission there." In 1835, *The Intelligencer,* a Washington, DC, newspaper, commented: "It is a notorious fact that this city, being the seat of government, is liable to be visited by more than its proportion of insane persons" (cited by Hoffman, 1943, p. 571).

The problem is current, not simply historical, and is common across countries in the western world. In a survey of members of parliament in Sweden for the years 1998–2005, 74% had been subjected to harassment, threats, or violence and 68% of the perpetrators were deemed by their victims to be mentally ill (SOU, 2006). A survey of Canadian politicians found that 29.9% had suffered harassment, with 87.4% believing their harassers to be suffering from a mental disorder (Adams et al., 2009). A study of politicians in the Australian state of Queensland (Pathé et al., in submission) with a 48% response rate found that 93% reported suffering threats, harassment, and other concerning behaviors, and 15% had been subject to at least one attempted or actual assault. In 48% of cases, the politicians believed the perpetrators to be mentally ill. A survey of members of the UK House of Commons (James et al., in submission) with a 37% response rate found that, of the 239 MPs who responded to the survey, 80.3% (192) had experienced one of the forms of intrusive and harassing behaviors set out in the questionnaire; the victims believed the responsible individual to be clearly mentally ill in 40% of cases. Politicians are at greatly elevated risk of being harassed, the life time risks of being stalked in the general population being around 2% to 5% for men and 10% to 20% for women (Pinals, 2007, p. 11). The importance of fixation and mental illness in terms of risk to public figures is also clear from the work of those involved in threat assessment for the US Capitol Police (Scalora et al., 2002a,b, 2003), the US Secret Service (Phillips, 2006, 2007, 2008) and the Swedish Security Police (Mullen, Pathé, & Purcell, 2009, p. 207).

Mental Health and Protection of the Wider Public

The issue arises as to why psychiatrists should be involved in what are primarily protection issues. Questions have been asked in the British press as to why dignitaries should receive a special service in terms of threat assessment and management:

> Why should such special protection be accorded to the governing elite? Non-politicians face the

random, but real, danger of being hacked at with machetes, knifed, pushed under trains or otherwise mauled or done away with by severely disturbed patients released—or, rather, propelled—into the "community" by authorities which refuse to detain them (Wright, 2007).

This is a rather simplistic and inaccurate assessment of the situation. The experience at FTAC (James et al., 2010a) is that protection of the general public from harm at the hands of the mentally ill, which is arguably a core element of psychiatric practice, overlaps substantially with the protection of the prominent. The issue is well stated by Dietz and Martell in a 1989 report to the National Institute of Justice (Dietz & Martell, 1989):

> The persons most at risk of violence from the individual mentally ill person who pursues public figures are not the public figures or those that protect them—assuming they have the necessary security arrangements—but rather the private citizens who are the family members and neighbours of the mentally disordered subject (p. ii).

Psychiatrists Are Already Involved in the Problem

Public figures in the United Kingdom receive many thousands of bizarre, worrying, and threatening communications each year. The most worrying are referred to FTAC. Of 100 consecutive threateners dealt with by FTAC, 81% had previously been treated by psychiatric services and 57 had previously undergone compulsory admission to hospital. Of all those with a history of psychiatric treatment, 60% (49) remained notionally under the care (or "on the books") of a community mental health team (James et al., 2010a). In other words, psychiatrists are already involved, or have previously been involved, with many of the individuals concerned. This is particularly important in countries with comprehensive national health services, where all care is provided by an integrated system. However, it applies to any treating practitioner in that awareness of the significance of different forms of warning behavior and certain forms of delusional belief is important in the prevention of harm and disruption to public figures. In addition, the pursuit of idiosyncratic grievances and the writing of threatening letters may overlap with stalking behaviors toward victims in the general public. Forensic psychiatrists may be met with requests for consultation from colleagues about risk in such cases, they may be consulted by victims or their organizations, or they may receive requests from law enforcement and commissions for preparing reports for the courts.

A Mental Health Problem Benefits from a Mental Health Response

The participation of mental health personnel in public figure threat assessment and management is desirable in two respects. First, it aids the understanding of motivation, particularly where this is affected by some form of mental disorder, such understanding being essential to effective threat assessment. Second, it enables the diagnosis of mental illness and so opens the possibility of co-opting psychiatric services into the intervention response. The study of 100 individuals referred to FTAC found that 57 were admitted to hospital by local psychiatric services following FTAC intervention and 26 taken on by community psychiatric teams (James et al., 2010a). The importance of this is that, where mental illness is present, treatment of that illness may be the most effective way of lowering threat. It enables the resources of other agencies to be recruited into case management—in effect, a multiagency response, rather than the burden being carried by policing and protection services. Such interventions are easier in countries where the threshold for civil commitment is low. But even in those jurisdictions where dangerousness has to be demonstrated in order to permit detention, there will be many cases that will reach this standard.

Psychiatric services are far more likely to pay attention to referrals from other psychiatrists than those from the police, and the ability for threat assessment units to navigate the complexities of health care systems increases the range of their interventions. This is particularly so as the characteristics of the fixated are often such as to make them unwelcome as patients. They are by definition without insight, frequently paranoid, and resistant to psychiatric intervention and follow-up; querulant cases are also markedly litigious. In addition, a proportion of these individuals suffer from delusional disorders or schizophrenic illnesses that are sufficiently encapsulated to allow individuals to function effectively in many aspects of day-to-day living. In other words, they do not exhibit the gross behavioral disturbances that readily identify them to law enforcement personnel and oblige mental health services to provide care without the resistance that is inevitable in health systems where resources are overstretched.

A further potential barrier to using mental health disposals in threat management is the issue of information sharing and medical confidentiality. Whereas in most jurisdictions there are restrictions on the sharing of medical information with policing agencies, these can usually be overridden where there are concerns about a risk of serious harm. However, the power of information is often in its being provided to doctors by policing agencies rather than the reverse. It is our experience that the significance of inappropriate communications and approaches to the prominent is insufficiently appreciated by treating teams, who may erroneously regard such behaviors as innocuous or quaint unless the consequences are brought to their attention. The problem in some cases may simply be that those in charge of a patient's care are not aware of the specific verbal or behavioral threats that an individual makes between outpatient appointments; therefore they cannot evaluate the case accurately. Provision of information to psychiatrists provides them with the power to make better assessments and intervene more effectively.

Evidently there are many cases of mental disorder where direct psychiatric intervention is problematic and compulsory detention simply not possible. Case management by the threat assessment team will not be a one-off intervention but a process that may continue for many months. The general approach in such instances will be to put into place a network around the individual, which enables some stabilizing social interventions to be introduced and performs a monitoring role, providing early warning of any change or escalation in behavior. This can then prompt further intervention. Such provision is far easier to organize if there is a mental health component to the threat assessment team.

Prevention, Not Prediction: A Population-Based Approach

Niels Bohr, the Danish physicist, stated: "Prediction is very difficult: especially about the future." Accurate prediction is all the more difficult for behaviors such as violence against public figures, which have a low base rate. This can be illustrated by the following example. Suppose the police in a city of a million people were in possession of a surveillance camera that, 99% of the time, could correctly identify a dangerous fixated person bent on violence toward a public figure. How useful would this be? On the face of it, such a device would seem powerful. It has false-positive and false-negative rates of only 1% and an accuracy of 99%, much greater than any predictive tests currently available. Simple mathematical calculation reveals that, if 3 in 10 of the population were dangerous fixated individuals, then 97.7% of positive identifications would be correct. However, if only in 1 in 10,000 were dangerous individuals, the chance of a positive identification being accurate would be only 0.98%.[1] In other words, in the prediction of rare events, such a tool would be useless. Yet, current risk assessment tools could not hope to approach an accuracy of 99% and, given the complicated influences upon human behavior, they never will. In consequence, it is now the general consensus that prevention, rather than prediction, is the only realistic focus for threat assessment (Department of Defense, 2012; Fazel et al., 2012).

The most effective tools in aiding the identification of risk are compilations of "risk factors." These are factors that are statistically significantly more common in those who have engaged in the behavior concerned than in those who have not. When combined into an "instrument" or "tool," they comprise a structured aide-mémoire that helps the risk assessor make sure that all relevant factors are considered in the evaluation. Risk factors present in a given case also point to risk management opportunities. Such "risk instruments" are not risk assessments in themselves, nor are they oracles to which data are given and which then provide answers. Rather, they supplement and structure professional judgment. Risk instruments suffer from two drawbacks. The current state of risk assessment research is such that their power is limited, as described above. Second, they are based on group data. This means that, if there is an 80% chance of a person belonging to a particular risk group, then 80 in every 100 people with the profile in question will in fact belong to the risk group and 20 will not. It is not possible, however, to tell whether any given individual belongs to the 80% or the 20%. The potential value of such data in the individual case therefore needs to be seen in the context of these limitations.

At FTAC, our approach is to adopt a population solution to risk management. It is not possible to predict what any individual will do. However, through the use of risk factors, it should be possible to identify the group of fixated loners that is most at risk (say, arbitrarily, 5%) and from which dangerous behavior is most likely to arise. If one then intervenes and treats the risk factors in this entire group, adverse outcomes will be prevented without the need to know which individuals would have gone on to engage in the behavior in question. An analogy is the risk of heart attack. One cannot predict which individual will have a heart attack. However, one can identify factors that make a heart attack more likely, such as smoking, obesity, hypertension, and high blood cholesterol levels. One then treats everyone who possesses these risk factors—for instance, by smoking cessation therapy, weight loss, antihypertensive agents, and cholesterol-lowering drugs. This will prevent heart attacks without needing to predict which individuals would have had a heart attack if they had not had treatment. Likewise, if one found that a number of individuals exhibited risk factors for violence (say, intrusive persecutory delusions, a license to possess a firearm, substance abuse problems, poor anger control, and destitution with little left to lose), one would intervene to reduce these risks (say, by compulsory antipsychotic medication, removal of the license and firearm, treatment of substance abuse, anger management, and measures to increase social stability). This would lower the risk in the group as a whole without needing to predict which person would have become violent without such intervention. The fact that mental state items and social items are prominent among the risk factors means that risk assessment and management could be improved by the inclusion of mental health personnel in the threat assessment unit in order better to understand the issues, allow mental health interventions as part of management plans, and enable multidisciplinary community approaches.

Warning Behaviors

A behavioral policing approach involves detecting individuals who are on a "pathway to violence" (see Calhoun & Weston, 2003, p. 79). This involves the development of violent ideation in response to an underlying grievance, followed by researching and planning an attack, pre-attack preparations, probing and breaches, and finally the attack itself. The strategy is to watch out for those engaging in these forms of behavior and then to intervene. Whereas this should evidently be part of the policing approach, it places the intervention toward the end of the process, when an individual is already moving toward action. It misses the opportunity to intervene earlier

in the process in order to manage down the risk before a person enters upon the "pathway to violence." Risk assessment, by contrast, should concern not simply behavioral observation but assessment of a person's motivation and psychological state and his or her interaction with factors in the environment that make escalation more or less likely. This requires some psychological expertise.

Evidently, in order to be able to assess individuals as to whether they belong in a high-risk group, it is necessary for a threat assessment unit to have a mechanism through which it becomes aware of those individuals who require assessment. The FRG's study of attacks on European politicians (James et al., 2007) found that death and serious injury were significantly associated with the attackers having exhibited one or more warning behaviors in the period before the attack. Warning behaviors included posters, newspaper advertisements, attempted lawsuits against the government, chaotic deluded letters to politicians and the police, threatening letters, leafleting the public, telling friends of the intent to attack, and, in one case, attempted self-immolation in front of the eventual victim's place of work. Most of these behaviors were engaged in many times, usually over weeks, months or even years before the eventual attack. The passage quoted above, from Dietz and Martell (2010), summarizes the US research in this respect, concluding that every attack on a public figure was the work of a mentally disordered person "who issued one or more pre-attack signals in the form of inappropriate letters, visits or statements." A suggested typology of these warning behaviors, into which the "pathway to violence" has been incorporated, has been devised by Meloy and colleagues (2012; also see this volume, chapter 3).

Public Figures and Stalking

The field of public figure threat assessment in the United States has developed entirely separately from that of stalking in the general population, the former being influenced by a law enforcement perspective and the latter being primarily the province of academic forensic psychiatrists and psychologists. This leads to some confusion over nomenclature and the degree to which various behaviors overlap. FTAC's view of the background research is that inappropriate attention, harassment, stalking, and the making of threats can usefully be considered part of a constellation of behaviors, with the last three forming subsets of inappropriate attention (see Figure 20.1).

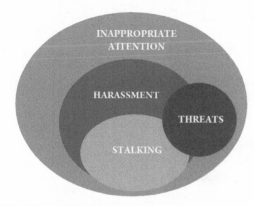

FIGURE 20.1 The constellation of inappropriate attention.

In consequence, broadly the same approach to risk assessment can be used in each, with supplementary considerations applied in the making of threats (see Warren, Mullen & McEwan, this volume, Chapter 2). Recent research finds that risk factors in public figure harassment and general public stalking are similar when former sexual partners are removed from the sample of general population stalkers. This has been established with persistence (James et al., 2000b) and with approach and escalation (McEwan et al., 2012). In addition, looking at US politicians, Hollywood celebrities, and the British Royal Family, a comparison of factors associated with escalation and problematic approach has found very similar results across studies with very different methodologies (Meloy et al., 2011). In other words, stalking and harassment remain stalking and harassment regardless of the public profile of the victim. This is of practical importance, as it indicates that research findings from one field will be relevant to the other; and it enables insights gained into the assessment and management of problem behaviors in one group of victims to be applied tentatively to the other.

The Differences Between Threat Assessment and Risk Assessment

Threat assessment and risk assessment both form part of the assessment process. Risk assessment, which is more familiar to clinicians, generally involves consideration of a case in a review setting, where there is little time pressure and a considerable amount of information about the case is available. Different types of risk can be considered, and the assessment results in a detailed formulation—including consideration of such issues as imminence, likelihood, severity, and mitigating and aggravating factors. Such an assessment identifies ways of reducing and managing risk, leading to effective intervention planning. Risk assessment is a process, not an event, and is repeated following intervention in order to assess its efficacy and in response to changed circumstances.

Threat assessment, by contrast, has a behavioral policing focus. It concerns the making of quick decisions in response to limited information in an operational, dynamic, real-time setting. It takes risk as a unitary concept and does not produce any form of nuanced judgment. Its purpose is to triage individuals into categories of high, medium, and low concern in order to determine the level of immediate response. Given that limited information is available, the concept of "risk" is not suitable and is replaced by that of "level of concern" (Scalora et al., 2002a).

At FTAC, the levels of concern (low, moderate, high) are carefully defined, both in terms of group criteria and of resultant level of resource allocation. High-concern cases require an urgent response and moderate a prompt response, whereas low concern cases do not require any further input. Allocation is based upon expertise, supplemented by an aide-mémoire of risk factors, the purpose of which is to ensure that all relevant factors have been considered. This aide-mémoire comprises 38 items grouped under 11 headings. Several of the items are psychological and therefore require some psychological expertise or training to understand and apply.

Threat assessment and risk assessment are undertaken at different points in the assessment and management cycle (see Figure 20.2).

What Is Risk?

FTAC has adopted a computerized version of the Stalking Risk Profile (SRP) (MacKenzie et al., 2009), public figure section, as the framework for risk assessment. The SRP is a manualized structured professional judgment tool that incorporates both international research findings and the clinical expertise accumulated by the Melbourne group in running a stalking assessment and management clinic for 10 years. It is structured around two fundamental concepts about risk: (1) risk is not a unitary concept and (2) risk is determined in part by motivation.

Risk assessment has been primarily concerned with the risk of targeted violence, particularly in the United States. However, risk is multidimensional.

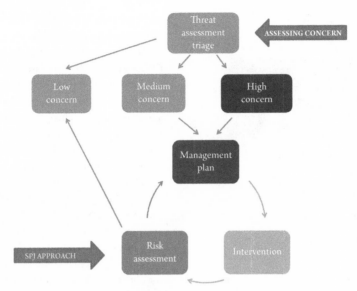

FIGURE 20.2 The threat assessment and risk management cycle.

Whereas death or serious injury to a prominent person is the most feared outcome, the base rate of serious violence is low. There are other domains of risk that need attention in formalized risk assessment. The public figure version of the SRP incorporates the following domains:

- Escalation—the risk that someone will increase the intensity of his or her activities or progress to more intrusive forms of behavior. The risk of change from communications to approach is particularly important to anticipate, given the disruption, distress to the individual,and concern about attack that progression to approach may engender.
- Disruption—impairment of the function of the individual or his or her agency, disruption or cancellation of public appearances, public or national embarrassment, and disruption caused by the resultant increase in expenditure on physical security.
- Persistence—the continuation of inappropriate behaviors despite injunctions to desist. Persistence is important because it is likely to increase problems in other domains.
- Psychosocial damage to the perpetrator—the obsessive actions of the perpetrator may lead to significant personal loss—of friends, family, employment and so on—as well as the acquisition of a criminal record and risk

to personal safety. Social isolation and the deterioration of a person's psychosocial position are important in that they increase risk in other domains by increasing desperation and decreasing social restraints.
- Violence—to public figures, their protection personnel, third parties and the general public.

It is essential to recognize that the risk factors for one domain may be very different from the risk factors for another. So, for instance, someone might present a high risk of disruption or of escalation but a low risk of violence. Risk in each domain therefore needs to be assessed separately.

Risk is also dependent on underlying motivation. At the simplest level, it is easy to understand that someone who is in love with a prominent figure would be likely to present different risks than someone who perceives such a figure as a threat to his life. The public figure SRP uses an adapted version of the Mullen classification of motivation (Mullen et al., 1999, 2009), which has been endorsed as the standard in the field of stalking and harassment by the Group for the Advancement of Psychiatry (Pinals, 2007). The relation of this classification to other public figure harassment topologies (Calhoun & Weston, 2009; Hoffmann & Sheridan, 2008; James et al., 2009; Phillips, 2006, 2007, 2009) is summarized in the SRP manual (MacKenzie et al., 2009, p. 71). The main groups of the Mullen classification as applied to the public figure arena are as follows:

- The resentful: those with a grievance against the public figure, often involving an idiosyncratic and highly personalized quest for "justice," not infrequently delusional in nature, or blaming the public figure for their persecution.
- Intimacy seekers: those with a perceived entitlement to an amicable relationship, whether through erotomania, morbid infatuation, grandiose pretensions, or claims to kinship.

Of the other groups, "incompetent suitors" (socially inept individuals seeking a sexual relationship) and the "predatory" (sexual predators planning a sexual attack) are less often encountered in public figure cases. The "rejected" (former sexual partners who are unable to accept the end of a relationship) are excluded, not because such persons are unusual in the lives of the prominent but because they have nothing to do with their public role. To the above are added two further categories for public figures: attention seekers and help seekers. Attention seekers include those who wish to make grand public statements or draw attention to themselves as part of a desire for self-aggrandizement, or those who hunger for notoriety in order to bolster their own feelings of self-worth. Help seekers comprise those who insistently request help from the public figure because they do not know to whom else to turn; such individuals are helpless and pleading, rather than angry.

FTAC'S OPERATIONS

Structure

FTAC is made up of staff from the Metropolitan Police Service and the National Health Service—nine police officers and four full-time forensic nurse specialists, with three consultant forensic psychiatrists and one consultant psychologist between them providing on-site supervision five days a week. FTAC is physically located within the Metropolitan Police Service's Protection Command. Its offices are in central London. Functionally, FTAC comprises three caseworker teams, each consisting of a forensic nurse specialist and two detective constables. Individual FTAC cases are allocated to caseworker pairs comprising a detective constable and a forensic nurse specialist. A named senior doctor or psychologist is responsible for supervising and managing risk assessment and management decisions within each FTAC team. Day-to-day case management of police staff is the role of the detective sergeant, who reports to the detective inspector. The unit is led by a detective chief inspector.

Responsibilities

The role of FTAC is the assessment and management of risks posed to prominent individuals, the places they work in, and the prominent organizations and events in which they are involved by isolated loners pursuing idiosyncratic quests or grievances to an irrational degree. The core constituency comprises members of the Royal Family, members of Parliament, members of the Scottish Parliament and the Assemblies of Northern Ireland and Wales, the mayor of London and ambassadors to the United Kingdom. The sites concerned include royal palaces, the Palace of Westminster (the UK Parliament), the Scottish Parliament, and the Assemblies of Northern Ireland and Wales, government ministries and the residences of government ministers, embassies, and buildings within the government security zone (including the headquarters of police and security services). Most referrals from core agencies originate from protective personnel, communications offices, or office staff. In a proportion of cases, the subject of the approach or communication is unaware of the issue.

The behaviors in question essentially comprise stalking, unwanted intrusion, harassment, threats, and persistent or querulant complaining. The risks that need to be evaluated and managed comprise violence to prominent individuals, their staffs and families, the general public, and police and security staff; distress to prominent individuals, their staffs, families, or protection personnel; disruption of events associated with the prominent person or their work and functioning; embarrassment to prominent individuals or police/protection staff; waste of resources associated with the prominent individual (such as office staff time); consumption of policing/protection time and resources; and risk to the safety of the isolated individual (e.g., by their actions in armed environments). The assessment of these risks depends upon achieving an understanding of the individual's motivation and mental state and an analysis of their behavior and their past for the presence of factors associated with particular forms of risk. Management of such cases depends on identifying risk factors that then also constitute opportunities for management intervention. Management plans often concern catalyzing and coordinating multiagency interventions from policing, health, and social agencies. Other than case assessment and management, FTAC acts as a consultation resource for other agencies. It takes part in the security planning for major national events and undertakes education, training and research. FTAC is concerned with the actions of lone individuals and does not assess or manage the risks presented by those in political, extremist, or protest groups. In the United Kingdom, the assessment of threat from isolated loners is dealt with separately from that from terrorists, unlike the situation in many other countries. There is a long history of antiterrorist policing in the United Kingdom dating back to the formation of the Special Irish Branch of the Metropolitan Police in 1883 in response to the Fenian threat. FTAC maintains operational contacts with relevant antiterrorism and security services but does not deal with terrorist cases.

Principles

Three principles are observed at all stages of assessing risk at FTAC in order that FTAC's decisions reflect best practice and are both defensible and reproducible and can reflect change.

- All referrals, once received, are subjected to the same standardized and formalized risk assessment procedures.
- All referrals are processed jointly by both police and psychiatric teams and the resultant decisions are formally signed off by both.
- All case processing follows a highly structured operating protocol and is recorded on a bespoke computerized database. The database functions as a flow line for case progression and is constructed in such a way as to ensure that all the relevant information is gathered, recorded, and considered; and that the same formalized risk assessment process is followed and thoroughly documented in all cases. Responsibility for completing individual database fields, and the deadlines for their completion, are exactly specified and are subject to online supervision.

Ethics

The health care members of FTAC are employed by the National Health Service, not by the police. Their place of work is a police unit and they are integral members of the team. The model is one of integration, not consultation or interagency working. However, the focus of the health care staff remains the health and welfare of individuals and of the general public. This model is possible because the interests of public protection overlap almost exactly with the interests of public health. In other words, interventions to assess, reduce, and manage the risk to prominent individuals from isolated loners coincide with the health interests of the isolated loners themselves. At one level, the entire FTAC operation could be conceived as a diversion scheme, identifying and directing into care severely disturbed people who have fallen through all the societal safety nets. The function of the unit is aided by the characteristics of mental health laws in England and Wales. Unlike the situation in many other jurisdictions, compulsory detention (civil commitment) does not depend uniquely upon dangerousness criteria but can be undertaken in the interests of the individual's health.

A further benefit of the joint staffing arrangement is the active facilitation of information sharing between agencies where appropriate, something which often bedevils multiagency working in other arenas. In the United Kingdom, medical information cannot be shared with policing agencies unless public interest criteria are satisfied—essentially a need to disclose to prevent serious harm. However, a doctor (and, by extension, the rest of the multidisciplinary team) may share information with another clinician or clinical team that has a legitimate interest in the care of the patient. FTAC's health care staff are funded by the Department of Health to provide a service to mentally disturbed individuals who present through inappropriate attention to public figures. As such, they have a legitimate reason to have access to confidential information. Of course they cannot share that information with their police colleagues unless there is a public interest in doing so. In the sort of cases with which FTAC deals, the necessary criteria are often satisfied. However, FTAC staff offer no details from medical files but rather their own processed conclusions, which are more relevant to operational needs. As already described above, the more useful and effective disclosures are often in the opposite direction, from police files to clinicians, and this, too, is facilitated by the joint approach at FTAC.

Activity

FTAC receives approximately a thousand referrals a year. Its activities can be considered in four main stages: referral mechanisms; initial threat assessment and case allocation; interventions, followed by further case and risk management; and case closure and follow-up. This division into sections is reflected in the structure of FTAC's computerized management database, which is integrated with its standardized operating procedures. The way in which FTAC works is illustrated below through a commented, anonymized case example.

CASE EXAMPLE

Referral

An email was sent to an MP by one of his constituents. It was copied to the prime minister. The writer, a man from the north of the country, gave his name and address and stated simply: "If you do not finally resolve this situation, then someone will have to die." The prime minister's office forwarded the email to FTAC, where it was picked up by the duty team of two detective constables and a senior psychiatric nurse.

Tens of thousands of bizarre communications are written to politicians and the Royal Family every year, both from within the United Kingdom and abroad, and many people attend sensitive sites behaving oddly, or evidently suffering from mental illness. FTAC would be swamped if it attempted to deal with all such cases. Instead, it ensures that the first filter (in effect, the first threat assessment) is conducted by those experiencing the primary contact in a manner specified by FTAC.

Communications offices are supplied with a checklist of criteria to help determine which cases should be referred. The relevant policing agencies and staff offices are similarly supplied with a checklist for approach cases. The criteria concern aspects of the subject's current and past behavior as well as his or her beliefs, motivation, emotional state, and declarations. The contents of the checklists are reviewed at intervals in the light of FTAC audit exercises and any relevant new research findings.

An individual FTAC caseworker (i.e., police officer or nurse) is designated as the single point of contact for each of the main referral agencies. This individual is responsible for giving regular training to correspondence offices about FTAC and about the suitability of cases for referral; he or she is also charged with giving feedback as to outcome in cases that have been referred. Given the high staff turnover in referring agencies, a regular program of liaison and training is essential. A rolling program of talks about FTAC's role and referral procedures is also undertaken for officers responsible for the security of buildings and for personal protection. Information about FTAC is supplied to MPs and their staffs, and talks are given as part of security training for new members and their staffs.

Audits of referrals are undertaken at approximately six-month intervals. Two forms of audit are undertaken: (1) examining referrals from a particular source and establishing the proportion that are inappropriately made and why; and (2) conducting an audit of a sample of cases that were *not* referred in order to establish whether contacts had occurred which should have been referred but were not.

In addition to referrals from relevant agencies, FTAC conducts daily searches of available police intelligence systems to identify cases that fall within its remit. With the explosion in the use of the Internet and social media, FTAC is finding it necessary to develop strategies for searching web pages, blogs, and social media sites.

Most referrals are made initially by telephone or email. Concerning communications are transmitted to FTAC by email, with letters and faxes sent as scanned attachments.

Initial Assessment

Initial information checks were carried out. The man was aged 53. The police database revealed that he had a previous conviction for assault against a neighbor six years earlier and was known to local police for various public order offences. His neighbors had made various allegations of harassment against him over the previous three years, but these had not led to his being charged. A check of the correspondence logs for the prime minister's office and Buckingham Palace revealed that he had written to the queen and the prime minister two years earlier complaining about mobile telephone masts in his neighborhood. The letters had not been seen as unusual, they had been given a standard response, and the original documents had not been retained.

A call to staff at the MP's constituency office established that the man in question had campaigned about a mobile phone (cell phone) mast in his road, which he believed was having injurious effects. He had written letters to the telephone company, the MP, and local newspapers and had then organized a petition. The MP was initially supportive and wrote three letters to the telephone company on his behalf. However, the man was not satisfied by the telephone company's response and his letters to the MP had become increasingly angry and personalized. Recently he had attended the constituency office without an appointment. The MP was not there at the time. The man had become angry and left. The constituency worker remarked that he had made the staff feel uncomfortable. The staff had told the MP about the incident over the telephone. They had not yet had sight of the email copied to the prime minister.

At this stage, the firearms register was consulted. (In the United Kingdom, the possession of firearms is very unusual and is strictly regulated. Hand guns and automatic weapons are banned. Limited other forms of firearm are permitted if a license has been granted—a process controlled and administered by local police forces. The details of all those licensed to possess firearms are kept in a centralized national register.) It transpired that the man had a license to possess a shotgun and was a member of a regional clay pigeon shooting club.

This information had been gathered within two hours of receiving the referral. The details had been entered into the FTAC work flow database. The next stage was to undertake an initial threat assessment, a triage of cases into low, moderate, or high concern.

Initial assessment of referrals involves consulting a standardized set of national policing databases, police systems in the area in which an individual resides, correspondence logs for the prime minister and the Royal Family, and open searching on the Internet. Health care information is not sought at this stage. Once the initial information trawl is complete, a case discussion ensues between the psychiatric nurse and the detective constable. Discussion of the case is supplemented by the formal consideration of an aide-mémoire of risk factors to aid in decision making as regards concern level. The FTAC list is based on consideration of the specialist literature and on its own research. It comprises 38 items under eight headings.

Allocation of Concern Level

The caseworkers considered the facts that they had established. A number of factors in the aide-mémoire were clearly present. The man was making a conditional and implied threat that he might kill an unspecified person if his demands were not satisfied. No time scale was specified. He had the means to carry out such a threat in that he possessed a shotgun. He appeared to have some idiosyncratic grievance of several years' duration, which he was now

personalizing in terms of the MP. Its precise nature was not yet clear, but it seemed to have something to do with mobile telephone masts, a subject that would not ordinarily be considered likely to inspire such rage. In addition, his behavior appeared very recently to have become more disturbed, given the incident at the constituency office and the gut reaction that he had occasioned in the staff. The initial assessment was that this case satisfied the definition in the FTAC operating policy as being of high concern until such time as it could be proved otherwise. This accorded with the caseworkers' subjective impression.

The caseworkers drew up an immediate management plan. This comprised five elements:

1. Local police should be contacted immediately to revoke the gun license and confiscate the shotgun.
2. Further information searches should be conducted straight away, in particular regarding the man's mental health history and current psychosocial status.
3. The MP should be approached urgently for more information and to warn him of the possible risk that the man might pose to him.
4. An image of the man should be obtained and circulated to the various places where he might turn up. (Images can be obtained by police from their own records or from the driving license agency or the passport agency.)
5. Local police should be primed to check the security of the MP's home.

As the case was deemed to be of high concern, the proposed management plan was put to the FTAC sergeant and to the consultant forensic psychiatrist responsible for that duty team, as the protocol specified. The plan was approved and the consultant suggested that, once these steps had been taken, the caseworkers should consider arranging a visit, in conjunction with local police, to interview the man at his home early the next morning. The initial assessment was recorded on the unit database together with the risk factors present, a formal explanation of the reason for choosing the particular concern level, and the details of the initial management plan. Supervision by the sergeant and the consultant of the plan was recorded, at which point this section of the management pathway was automatically locked down on the system.

The allocation of concern level is operationally defined and subject to strict supervision. Its purpose is to reach a rapid conclusion, based on the limited information available, as to the degree of response that the case warrants. The decision as to concern level must be made on the day that the case is referred and cannot be deferred until detailed information becomes available. Case management plans must be discussed with the consultant psychiatrist and formally recorded.

Implementation of the Immediate Management Plan

The management plan was put into operation. It was arranged with local police that the weapon would be removed that afternoon and they would then report straight back to FTAC on what they had discovered. They were to contact the MP's office to arrange an immediate view of his home security. Meanwhile, the nurse put the man's name into the National Health Service's register of general practitioner (GP, or family doctor) registration. (The details of the family doctor for every person in the country are centralized in a database that can be accessed by approved health service personnel.) The database showed the name, address, telephone number, fax number, and email of the man's GP. The nurse rang the surgery and left a message, then faxed through some introductory information about FTAC and its role for the GP to peruse.

The MP telephoned FTAC after a message had been conveyed to him through his office. He explained that the man had been to see him around 15 times over the last three years. The man's complaints had been around the siting of mobile phone masts. After a while, it transpired that the man's daughter had cancer and that the man had begun to blame this on the presence of the masts. He had originally evidently seen the MP as a source of help and support. But when the MP did not produce the expected results, the man began to blame him and accused him of colluding with the company that owned the masts. The MP had recently told the man that he could not help him any further. This had produced an angry reaction, and the incident at the constituency office seemed to have followed on from this.

The GP then rang and spoke to the consultant forensic psychiatrist. She confirmed that she knew the man and his family well. He had previously received treatment for depression and had been admitted to psychiatric hospital with a possible psychotic illness five years earlier. The man's obsession with the masts had been present for a number of years. When his daughter became ill, he had accused the company owning the masts of causing her illness, and he had no longer seemed amenable to reason. The GP had diagnosed him as being depressed and had tried to persuade him to take antidepressants, but the man had refused. The GP had made him an appointment to see the local community psychiatric team, but the man had not attended. He had recently taken to ranting at the GP in a paranoid fashion, describing how his MP and the telephone company were in league. Three months previously, his wife had left him and taken their daughter, telling the GP that she could no longer cope with the way his obsession had overtaken their lives. The GP had not seen him since.

At the end of the afternoon, the local police rang back. They had revoked the man's gun license, gone round to his address, and required him to surrender his shotgun.

The psychiatrist and the sergeant reviewed the case at the end of the day with the caseworkers. A considerable amount of information had been gathered from different sources in a short space of time. The man had grievances both against the phone mast company and the MP. It was not certain which might be the potential target; possibly both. He had lost his job, then his daughter, and then his wife; there did not appear to be much that he had left to lose. His behavior at the constituency office suggested that he was becoming overtly disturbed and was having difficulty in containing his anger. He appeared to believe that violence was justified and his email to his MP suggested that he was considering taking violent action and that this might be imminent. His gun had been removed but his current whereabouts were unknown. It was concluded that urgent intervention was necessary.

The man had not committed any criminal offense in that his email did not directly threaten an individual, nor did it fall within the definition of a malicious communication. So a criminal justice intervention at this stage was not possible. There was some discussion as to whether the telephone mast company ought to be warned about the man, but there was currently no information as to which office or which employees he might be focusing on. The most sensible course of action was to try to interview the man. It was decided that the psychiatrist and a police caseworker would travel north and that, with the support of members of the local police, an early-morning knock on the man's door would be undertaken. A risk assessment for the visit indicated that the police members of the team should wear stab-proof vests, and that the local police officers should remain at a distance in order not to occasion alarm. The local psychiatric service was made aware of the problem and the visit and agreed to send a psychiatric social worker to attend the visit. (Psychiatric social workers play a central role in civil detention under mental health legislation in England and Wales as "approved mental health professionals").

When a case is judged to be of high or moderate concern, an immediate management plan is drawn up and implemented and further information is sought, in particular from other agencies, including health care. In this instance the response had moved on from being an FTAC one to involving health care, local police, and the MP. The beginnings of a network response were being formed. A psychological understanding of the man and his motives was being established, and the beginnings of a more nuanced risk assessment were falling into place.

Interview

The next morning, while the FTAC team members were traveling to the address, the other team members in the office looked into the man's background. Open Internet searching produced several results. First, there were letters that he had written to the local newspaper five years earlier complaining about the masts, and other letters complaining about various other matters that had concerned him in his local community, such as the construction of a concrete skate-board ramp in his local park. Next, there were some postings on a conspiracy website with the name "Fighting Back." These set out his beliefs that the telephone masts were poisoning the local community and that the local council and the local MP were part of a conspiracy to hush this up for financial reasons. It then became apparent that the man had recently set up his own web page, entitled "The Mast Conspiracy." From its contents, the man's beliefs had been elaborated into a detailed, paranoid conspiracy theory, elements of which appeared clearly delusional. The latest of his bulletins on the website was entitled "A citizen's right to break the law." It put forward the contention that, where the government was

engaged in criminal activity that threatened the welfare of the entire nation, a citizen was entitled to use whatever levels of violence against the government might be necessary in order to correct the injustice. The website contained an open letter to the mast company in which the man stated that the masts were continuing to pass various beams into the brains of local people, causing brain tumors, and that he would not be responsible for his actions if the mast were not taken down by the end of that month. The letters contained vague threats to harm the MP. The website also gave further details about the man, who claimed to be a former member of an elite special forces group, a former policeman, and a lawyer. The man's grievances appeared to have developed into an all-absorbing querulant quest. The driver behind this was powerful in that he believed both that the company had injured his daughter and that the safety of the nation was at risk. His beliefs now incorporated delusional content and he appeared to have tipped into a paranoid psychosis. The traveling team now had a substantial number of issues to explore in their interview.

The team at FTAC attended the man's home. He was wary of the FTAC team but conversed politely with them, stating that, after the removal of his gun, he had been expecting a further visit. He recounted that he had been the victim of radiation poisoning from the telephone mast for several years. He had written to the telephone company and then his MP, and had recently become convinced that they were conspiring together to poison him. He stated that the MP was corrupt and was possibly taking bribes from the telephone company in order to avoid a proper investigation of his complaints. He told the assessing nurse that he had a degree in chemical engineering from Imperial College London, and had been employed by a large petrochemical company until three years earlier, when his employment was terminated after he repeatedly took time off to complain and demonstrate about the telephone mast, which he believed was responsible for his 10-year-old daughter's illness. His wife eventually left him, taking their daughter with her. He does not now have any contact with his wife or daughter. He had recently received a solicitor's letter explaining that his wife was filing for divorce. The man insisted to the visitors that he had no plans to harm anyone, despite his threats and the contents of his web page. He was simply upset at the turn of events and expressing his distress. He accepted the contact details of the members of the

FTAC team, provided his own telephone numbers, and agreed to continuing contact with a community police officer.

The FTAC team reached the conclusion that the man was suffering from a paranoid psychosis and that the beliefs variously expressed on his websites, to the MP and the GP, and in correspondence were undiminished. The community police officer and the psychiatric social worker were reassured by the visit. Some meaningful contact appeared to have been made with this individual. He had accepted continuing contact with FTAC and the local force. His beliefs about being a former policeman, a member of special forces, and a solicitor were probably delusional, but they involved a degree of support of policing institutions and deference to them. He had given assurances that he would not be taking any form of direct action. The psychiatric social worker, having heard this, stated that she could not see what all the fuss was about. However, the FTAC team held firmly to the view that the visit had simply confirmed the presence of factors indicating a high risk of violence. In terms of violence risk in the SRP, with the man classified as resentful in motivation, important risk factors were present. The first three of these are designated as "red-flag indicators," the presence of one such indicator being sufficient to put the individual into the high-risk category. In this case the man had fantasies about homicide, he was engaging in last-resort thinking, the psychotic phenomena that he described were invasive in nature, he had engaged in prior violence, and he had an affinity with weapons. The team decided that they should telephone the consultant psychiatrist on the local community psychiatric team and ask for an urgent assessment for compulsory detention under the Mental Health Act. A detailed report about the case was quickly typed and faxed to the psychiatric team.

This was a case in which assessment evolved rapidly as new information emerged. It illustrates the value of a face-to-face assessment of an individual in his or her own environment in gauging the degree of risk that a case presents. The presence of an FTAC psychiatrist enabled a detailed assessment of this man's mental state, allowing the psychiatrist to construct a detailed report for local psychiatric services which compelled action. Reference to structured forms of risk assessment prevented false reassurance at interview and added substantial weight to the argument for detention.

Continuing Assessment and Intervention Cycle

The local psychiatric team set up an early-morning home visit for the following day. However, overnight, the man appeared at the MP's home and threw a stone through the window, terrifying the MP's wife and young children. Police arrived quickly and arrested him for criminal damage. He was held in custody. FTAC was contacted and suggested that the man undergo a psychiatric assessment at the police station or at the local magistrates' court psychiatric diversion scheme. In the event, he was referred to the latter. FTAC staff attended the court with a copy of the FTAC report, which they provided to the court psychiatric team. The man was found to be irritable and paranoid and deluded in his belief that the MP had been bribed not to investigate the telephone company's irradiation of the public. He was admitted to the local psychiatric hospital from the court on a compulsory assessment order under the Mental Health Act.

FTAC's contacts with local police were sufficient to ensure that FTAC was informed of new developments in the case. The home visit and the information gathered through investigation were sufficient to give the court psychiatric team adequate grounds for detaining the man under the Mental Health Act.

In hospital, a diagnosis of a paranoid psychosis was confirmed. Antipsychotic medication was prescribed and, over the following month, although the man's core beliefs did not change, he was less preoccupied with them and no longer felt a compulsion to act. Against expectation, it was established that he had indeed been in the special forces and then a police officer, and that he had finally qualified as a solicitor. The FTAC team contacted the MP and tried to persuade him to press charges, as conviction for a criminal offense would be likely to increase the resources that the health care system deployed in the man's care. However, the MP declined to follow FTAC's advice, as he did not want to appear heartless in bringing the full weight of the law to bear on a mentally ill constituent for what was a comparatively minor offense.

After a month, acute pressure on beds within the psychiatric hospital led to the man's sudden discharge without any form of aftercare planning meeting, to which FTAC would have expected to be invited. A week later, having stopped his medication, the man returned to the MP's house, caused a disturbance, and was rearrested. FTAC was contacted by local police and suggested that he be reassessed in custody. FTAC faxed all available information to the assessing clinicians at the police station and the man was subsequently transferred to hospital on a treatment order.

Risk assessment and management is often a lengthy process, not a single intervention. Things that can go wrong do go wrong in underfinanced and overburdened care systems. It is often the case that several interventions need to be made before a case is brought successfully under control.

While these events were going on, case management was regularly and formally reviewed at FTAC by the team concerned under the supervision of the consultant forensic psychiatrist. After the second admission, FTAC requested that the treating psychiatric team organize a case conference on the ward, the aim being to assist the hospital team in thinking about the risks and how they might best be managed. At this meeting FTAC presented a completed SRP, which indicated that without intervention, there was a high risk of violence and of persistence, and that these risks were aggravated by psychosocial decline. The individual risk factors were discussed as treatment targets, and a treatment plan was drawn up. The management plan comprised four elements:

1. The first was treatment of psychotic illness with medication, in order to dampen the delusional beliefs, invasive experiences, and paranoid interpretations and to weaken the all-consuming preoccupation with the masts and the supposed associated conspiracies. Such treatment is central to what psychiatric services do. However, it was emphasized that a longer than average admission would be necessary, and careful assessment of the specific risks involved in the situation would need to be incorporated into decision making.

2. The second element concerned psychological maladaptations and vulnerabilities that would need to be made treatment targets once the psychotic symptoms had dampened down: cognitive distortions, problems with anger, and relinquishing the quest for justice (which had given him meaning in life and helped him to deal with loss). Such treatment requires the psychologist to arrange a modular program, much of it based on

cognitive behavioral therapy, drawing the patient in through a cost-benefit analysis and using the stages-of-change model as a framework (MacKenzie & James, 2011). This would need to begin in hospital and be continued after discharge, initially on a compulsory basis. This is a greater level of psychological input than most cases in general psychiatric practice require.

3. The man had been pushed towards a position of last resort by the psychosocial decline he had suffered secondary to his long campaign. He had lost his employment and with it his social status and financial security. He had lost his wife and child and had become socially isolated, with no personal support and no one to provide a commonsense reality check in terms of his wild ideas. Social work and occupational therapy input would be necessary to try to reverse this decline.

4. Discharge would need to involve an aftercare package with compulsory community treatment.

This plan was put into effect, and FTAC staff were invited to a discharge planning meeting four months later. By this stage, the man's condition had considerably improved, his risk scores on the SRP for violence had dropped to low, and his persistence scores to low to moderate. Discharge was agreed on; it involved a community treatment order, allocation of a community nurse and social worker to the case, and continuing psychological treatment sessions as an outpatient with supervision by the consultant psychiatrist. The psychiatric team were to contact FTAC if any problems arose, and the MP and prime minister's office were asked to report to FTAC if any more correspondence was received. At this point, FTAC's input was reduced to a mention of the case at its own weekly internal case review meetings and more detailed three-monthly reviews.

FTAC members often take part in multiagency and hospital case conferences about individual cases. Here, the psychiatric team had no issue with the diagnosis or the need for compulsory treatment. (Such is not always the case.) However, the nature of the man's behavior and querulant quest as well as the specialized risk assessment necessary were both matters of which the psychiatric team had little previous experience. They were grateful to have FTAC members offering expert advice.

FTAC continues to monitor cases until a sustained period of lowered risk is in evidence and a stable management plan bedded in. Once these conditions are in place, FTAC involvement is downgraded to discussion at the weekly continuing case reviews.

Three months after discharge, there had been no more correspondence from the man, he had not visited the MP's home or tried to contact him, and there had been no new website entries. He was cooperating with treatment and, while he retained some residual anger about the masts, was making an effort to become involved in other things. It had become apparent that he had been living for some time on his savings and had got into considerable debt. The social worker had arranged for a proportion of his debts to be written off and had helped him to sign up for the various state financial benefits to which he was entitled. The man had also instructed a solicitor to help him sort out matters between him and his wife. At six months, things had continued to improve. He was now in part-time work. He was having regular access to his daughter and he was on speaking terms with his wife, who remained somewhat cautious in her dealings with him. FTAC decided to continue quarterly reviews of the case.

FTAC's intervention in this case had catalyzed a multiagency response from local police, the health service, and psychiatric services. Specialized risk assessment had resulted in the seriousness of the problem eventually being recognized by the local psychiatric service. A management plan had been tailored to the risk factors present, and the importance of psychological therapies and of rebuilding social supports had been integrated into this. The need to protect the MP, and possibly others, against the threat from this individual had been met. The interventions had resulted in the individual receiving treatment for a serious illness and had helped him start putting his life back together. The intervention had been effective and had a good chance of providing a sustained solution. In other words, the interests of protection and of public health had both been met. This was a result that could not have been achieved by police and criminal justice intervention alone.

The Range of FTAC's Interventions

FTAC deals with a range of different sorts of cases requiring different types and levels of intervention, which a single case example cannot illustrate. FTAC will organize arrest and prosecution as part of a management plan where this is desirable. FTAC does not itself undertake criminal investigations, arranging instead for this to be done by local forces, just as FTAC psychiatrists do not take part in compulsory hospital detention. An appreciable minority of cases involve people from other countries, and FTAC liaises internationally with both police forces and mental health services as well as with other threat assessment units. It is also able to have people's arrival in the United Kingdom flagged up and to arrange to interview individuals at the port of entry.

More than half of referrals to FTAC are assessed as being of low concern. In such cases, FTAC's conclusions are reported to the referrer with an explanation as to the reasoning. Finding a case to be of low concern is a meaningful intervention in that it will allow policing agencies to stand down, thus saving resources, and it will alleviate anxiety on the part of the potential victims or those involved in their protection. It is also FTAC's experience that intervening in cases of low concern may actually result in an increase in the level of risk. This is a situation analogous to that found in sex offending (Bonta & Andrews, 2007) and offender rehabilitation (Bonta, Wallace-Capretta, & Rooney, 2000), in line with the risk-need-responsivity model. It is therefore important to identify the low-concern group in order to avoid the possibility of harmful interventions.

Following more detailed investigation, cases judged to be of moderate or high concern generally fall into one of three groups:

- Those that, after further investigation, can be designated as being of low concern.
- Those where immediate action results, usually within a few hours or days, of a definitive intervention. This will often constitute hospital admission or other forms of psychiatric care or sometimes arrest. It may often involve no contact with the individual concerned but rather the arranging of intervention by other statutory bodies by the FTAC office. With attenders at central London sites, it may involve interview on site by caseworkers. The typical case would be one of an acutely ill schizophrenic where FTAC's forensic nurse specialist can quickly orchestrate compulsory hospital detention by the relevant agencies.
- Cases that need more intensive or long-term management interventions. These broadly fall into two categories. Those where the mental

disorder is not severe enough to warrant or permit of psychiatric intervention and where no criminal charges can be brought. These require putting in place a network of various agencies to monitor the situation and provide early warning of change. Second, there are many cases where the person is mentally unwell but has a delusional disorder, leaving a broad range of cognitive and social functioning intact. Such cases are more difficult to fit within the constrained remit of mainstream psychiatric provision and do not exhibit the forms of disturbed behavior that encourage the use of compulsory detention powers. Such cases often involve complex and lengthy negotiations with local psychiatric services, and it may take a lengthy period to achieve eventual resolution.

Given the wide range of cases referred to FTAC, there is also a wide range in the lengths of time that cases may continue to be monitored by FTAC—from days to years.

The Efficacy of FTAC Interventions

FTAC conducted a study of 100 individuals that it assessed as being of moderate or high concern (James et al., 2010a); 86% were found to be suffering from psychotic illness. Compulsory admission to hospital was the outcome in 53% and voluntary admission in 4%, while 26% were taken on for management by community mental health teams or assertive outreach services. General practitioners engaged 4%; continued FTAC management alone was the outcome for 4%, whereas 2% were arrested and prosecuted, 2% disappeared and were untraceable in the United Kingdom, 1 was deported, and 4% underwent other outcomes. In brief, 57% were admitted to hospital as a result of FTAC intervention, with a further 26% receiving care from mental health services in the community. This amounts to 83% of 100 persons, with a further 4% receiving care from their GP, illustrating the efficacy of the intervention. However, it reflects an early period in FTAC's functioning, when it was dealing with an extant pool of psychotic cases, which it rapidly drained. Whereas the pool continues to be fed by streams of new psychotic individuals, the proportion of referrals to FTAC with obvious psychotic illness has declined, and the current psychiatric hospital admission rate is around 35%.

Of the 100 cases, 21% were classified at initial evaluation as being of high concern and 79% of medium concern. Reductions in concern level following FTAC interventions, taken at the end of year one, were as follows: high to low 11%; high to medium 10%; medium to low 69%; medium to medium 10%. In brief, 80% of the 100 had been managed down to a low level of concern by the end of the period considered. Those at medium concern after initial intervention remained active FTAC cases.

A follow-up study of 100 FTAC cases (James & Farnham, in submission) looked at inappropriate communications and approaches and compared figures for the two years before the FTAC intervention with the two years after, using a mirrored design, and also at the 12 months before the FTAC intervention and the 12 months after. The total number of inappropriate communications in the two years after the FTAC intervention compared with the two years before was reduced by 47%, and in the 12 months after compared with the 12 months before by 42%. Using before and after paired comparisons, there were significant reductions at two years ($p = .012$) and at 12 months ($p = .018$). With regard to approaches, the reductions for the mirrored periods were 68% for the two-year period and 77% for the 12-month period, the reductions being highly significant for both mirrored periods ($p = .000$). The number of incidents that required police call-out or police stop in the 2-year and 12-month periods before and after FTAC intervention were then investigated. Using paired tests, the differences between the periods were both highly significant ($p = .000$). The conclusion was that FTAC intervention was effective in reducing problematic communications and approaches and, in doing so, brought about a significant reduction in police time spent on lone individuals.

FTAC's Other Responsibilities
Event Planning

FTAC takes part in the forward security planning for major national events, such as the royal weddings, the papal visit, the diamond jubilee and the Olympics. This involves working with other agencies, both policing and medical, in different parts of the United Kingdom and further afield, in order to arrange for those with relevant fixations to be monitored more carefully during the relevant period and to educate agencies as to what they should be looking out for in terms of concerning ideas and behaviors. FTAC also has staff in operational control rooms during such events in order to advise on concerning individuals as they are spotted at events, and to aid in liaison with health agencies to enable rapid intervention.

Briefings

FTAC contributes specific briefing materials to aid in security planning for trips and events undertaken by prominent persons, and it contributes to formal reviews of the level of threat to individuals who are under personal protection.

Education, Training, and Public Profile

FTAC sees an important part of its role as educating other agencies about fixated loners. In part this is to encourage appropriate referral of cases to FTAC and to facilitate understanding and cooperation between relevant agencies. FTAC provides training modules for police and other agencies and academic presentations to professional bodies, as well as receiving visits from, and providing training for, policing and health care agencies from other countries.

FTAC has found it necessary, contrary to prevailing practice in this area, to adopt a public profile in order that the motives behind its joint policing and psychiatric interventions are not misunderstood and to improve the understanding of its function among professionals whom it may contact in the future. Its strategy involves the support of a website relating to the research upon which FTAC is based (www.fixatedthreat.com), cooperation with journalists from broadsheet newspapers, and the production of material for public consumption, such as this chapter. Its strategy excludes television or radio interviews with its staff or publication of the finer detail of its operating procedures.

Research

Academic research is integral to the FTAC process, and its behavioral science research informs operational policy at all stages. FTAC conducts audits of its own efficacy as well as satisfaction surveys of the policing and mental health agencies with which it works with on case management. FTAC's operational database is constructed so that the data can be automatically transferred into a statistical analysis package in order both to further the audit process and enable research into risk factors. FTAC staff regularly present to international specialist

conferences in the psychiatric and threat management fields.

Advice to Other Agencies

As a center of expertise in stalking and in querulant complainants, FTAC receives requests for assistance from other agencies, mainly police forces, in dealing with difficult cases that do not involve public figures. Its advice is limited to case analysis, threat assessment, and suggestions as to management. It does not take over lead responsibility for such cases.

Future Challenges
The Networked World

When FTAC began operations in 2006, the main ways in which people communicated with prominent figures involved paper. However, there are now few people under the age of 40 that use anything other than electronic media for communication. Research has shown that there are differences in the way in which emails and written letters are used (Schoeneman-Morris et al., 2007). The number of emails received by prominent figures has greatly expanded, presenting a problem in terms of filtering and analyzing content. In addition, individuals are communicating their beliefs and intentions through web pages, blogs, and social media such as Facebook. This is a source of warning behaviors that has yet to be tapped. Work in this area is likely to move from being reactive, in terms of responding to cases brought to its attention by others, to proactive, in searching of the Internet through developing protocols and strategies for looking for evidence of threat in cyberspace.

Querulants

Querulants exhibit a pattern of behavior involving the unusually persistent pursuit of a personal grievance in a manner seriously damaging to the individual concerned, and potentially also to those they blame for their situation or who get in the way of their idiosyncratic quest for "justice," in which they conflate the public interest with their personal aims (Mullen & Lester, 2006). Those fixated on a cause have been found to be of particular concern in violence toward public figures (James et al., 2011). This is, however, the endpoint on a road of persistent complaint and litigation, and the potential exists for interrupting this journey by recognizing the signs of progression at an earlier stage. Such cases are not uncommon in the work of MPs, and education in their identification is an achievable goal.

Lone Actors

The threat from isolated loners is separate from that of terrorist groups. There exists, however, the phenomenon of lone actor or self-starter terrorists, who engage in terrorist acts without being members of terrorist groups. The majority of such cases currently involve Islamic and right-wing extremism. Lone actor terrorists differ from fixated loners in a markedly lower prevalence of mental illness (as opposed to mental disorder). However, there is an overlap, with some psychotic loners acting on delusions colored by terrorist themes. There is also the question of whether the threat assessment approaches developed for isolated loners have relevance in the consideration of lone actors, a subject that needs further research.

CONCLUSION

When the Fixated Research Group began its work, concern in the protection of public figures was dominated by the issue of terrorism. The evidence of the importance of fixated loners in terms of attack and assassination has always been in the open, but had not been given the attention that it warranted. FTAC's contribution to threat assessment in the realm of public figures has been to help restore the balance. In conjunction with its Swedish counterparts, FTAC set up a new organization, the European Network of Public Figure Threat Assessment Agencies, which is concerned with assessing and managing threats from lone individuals. It comprises representatives from governmental policing, protection, and security agencies from 22 countries and holds annual conferences to exchange information and ideas. Since its foundation, the concept of threats from fixated loners has achieved widespread recognition and led to the adoption of FTAC principles by threat assessment agencies in other European countries.

NOTES

1. If one in 10,000 in a city of 1 million is a dangerous fixated person, then 99 out of 100 dangerous fixated people will trigger the alarm and 9,999 out of the 999,900 who are not dangerous fixated people will trigger the alarm. Therefore 10,098 people will trigger the alarm, of which 99 are dangerous fixated people. Therefore the chance of a person triggering the alarm being a dangerous fixated individual is 9 in 10,098 = 0.98% (i.e., less than 1%).

KEY POINTS

- Fixated loners are the main threat to public figures in western countries.
- Mental illness plays a central role in risk assessment and management.
- A population approach to threat assessment is necessary, with attention to warning behaviors.
- Structured aides-mémoire and specialized risk assessment tools constitute good practice.
- Joint working between policing and health agencies has considerable benefits in dealing with fixated loners.
- Long-standing grievances are common in fixated cases and should always be treated seriously.

Author note: In memory of Tom Kerrigan, who thought of the idea of FTAC.

REFERENCES

A Constant Observer (1823). *Sketches in Bedlam.* Sherwood: London.

Adams, S. J., Hazelwood, T. E., Pitre, N. L., Bedard, T. E., & Landry, S. D. (2009). Harassment of Members of Parliament and the Legislative Assemblies in Canada by individuals believed to be mentally disordered. *Journal of Forensic Psychiatry & Psychology, 20,* 801–814.

Bonta, J., & Andrews, D. A. (2007). *Risk-need-responsivity model for offender assessment and rehabilitation. Corrections User Report 2007-06.* Ottawa: Public Safety Canada.

Bonta, J., Wallace-Capretta, S., & Rooney, R. (2000). A quasi-experimental evaluation of an intensive rehabilitation supervision program. *Criminal Justice and Behavior, 27,* 312–329.

Calhoun, F.S., & Weston, S. W. (2003). *Contemporary threat management.* San Diego, CA: Specialized Training Services.

Calhoun, F. S., & Weston, S. W. (2009). *Threat assessment and management strategies.* Boca Raton, FL: CRC Press.

Department of Defense, Defense Science Board (2012). *Predicting violent behavior.* Washington DC: Office of the Undersecretary of Defense for Acquisition, Technology and Logistics.

Dietz, P., & Martell, D. A. (2010). Commentary: Approaching and stalking public figures—a prerequisite to attack. *Journal of the American Academy of Psychiatry and the Law, 38*(3), 341–348.

Dietz, P. E., & Martell, D. A. (1989). *Mentally disordered offenders in pursuit of celebrities and politicians.* Washington, DC: National Institute of Justice.

Dietz, P., Matthews, D., Martell, D., Stewart, T., Hrouda, D., & Warren, J. (1991a). Threatening and otherwise inappropriate letters to members of the United States Congress. *Journal of Forensic Sciences*, 36:1445–1468.

Dietz, P., Matthews, D., Van Duyne, C., Martell, D., Parry, C., Stewart, T., …Crowder, J. (1991b). Threatening and otherwise inappropriate letters to Hollywood celebrities. *Journal of Forensic Sciences*, 36, 185–209.

Fazel, S.,Singh, J. P., Doll, H., & Grann, M. (2012). Use of risk assessment instruments to predict violence and antisocial behaviour in 73 samples involving 24 827 people: Systematic review and meta-analysis. *British Medical Journal*, 345, e4692.

Fein, R.A., & Vossekuil, B. (1999). Assassination in the United States: An operational study of recent assassins, attackers and near-lethal approachers. *Journal of Forensic Science*, 44(2), 321–333.

Fein, R. A., & Vossekuil, B. (1998). Preventing attacks on public officials and public figures: A Secret Service perspective. In J. Reid Meloy (Ed.), *The psychology of stalking* (pp. 176–191). San Diego, CA: Academic Press.

Hanrahan, D. C. (2008). *The assassination of the prime minister: John Bellingham and the murder of Spencer Percival*. Stroud, UK: Stratton.

Hoffman, J. L. (1943). Psychotic visitors to government offices in the national capital. *American Journal of Psychiatry*, 99, 571–575.

Hoffmann, J., Meloy, J. R., Guldimann, A., & Ermer, A. (2011). Attacks on German public figures, 1968–2004: Warning behaviors, potentially lethal and nonlethal acts, psychiatric status, and motivations. *Behavioral Sciences and the Law*, 29, 155–179.

Hoffmann, J., & Sheridan, L. (2008). Stalking, threatening and attacking corporate figures. In J. R. Meloy, L. Sheridan, & J. Hoffmann (Eds.), *Stalking, threatening and attacking public figures: A psychological and behavioural analysis* (pp. 123–142). New York: Oxford University Press.

James, D. V., Farnham, F. R., Henley, S., Jones, K. L., Sukhwal, S., Carlisle, J., & Pathé, M. T. (in submission). *Harassment and stalking of members of the United Kingdom Parliament*.

James, D. V., & Farnham, F. R. (in submission). The effect of intervention by a joint police/NHS unit in reducing intrusive behaviour and police contacts in those targeting public figures: a follow-up study.

James, D. V., Kerrigan, T., Forfar, R., Farnham, F., & Preston, L. (2010a). The Fixated Threat Assessment Centre: Preventing harm and facilitating care. *Journal of Forensic Psychiatry and Psychology*, 21, 521–536.

James, D. V., McEwan, T. E., MacKenzie, R. D., Meloy, J. R., Mullen, P. E., Pathé, M. T., …Darnley, B. (2010b). Persistence in stalking: a comparison of associations in general forensic and public figure samples. *Journal of Forensic Psychiatry and Psychology*, 21, 283–305.

James, D. V., Meloy, J. R., Mullen, P., Pathé, M., Farnham, F., Preston, L., & Darnley, B. (2010c). Abnormal attentions towards the British Royal Family: Factors associated with approach and escalation. *Journal of the American Academy of Psychiatry and the Law*, 38, 329–340.

James, D. V., Mullen, P., Meloy, J. R., Pathé, M., Farnham, F., Preston, L., & Darnley, B. (2007). The role of mental disorder in attacks on European politicians, 1990–2004. *Acta Psychiatrica Scandinavica*, 116, 334–344.

James, D. V., Mullen, P., Pathé, M., Meloy, J. R., Farnham, F., Preston, L., & Darnley, B. (2008). Attacks on the British Royal Family: The role of psychotic illness. *Journal of the American Academy of Psychiatry and the Law*, 36, 59–67.

James, D. V., Mullen, P., Pathé, M., Meloy, J. R., Preston, L., Darnley, B., & Farnham, F. (2009). Stalkers and harassers of royalty: The role of mental illness and motivation. *Psychological Medicine*, 39, 1–12.

James, D. V., Mullen, P., Meloy, J. R., Pathé, M., Preston, L., Darnley, B… Scalora, M. (2011). Stalkers and harassers of British royalty: An exploration of proxy behaviors for violence. *Behavioral Sciences & the Law*, 29, 64–80.

Kirkbride, J. B., Errazuriz, A., Croudace, T. J., Morgan, C., Jackson, D., McCrone, P., …Jones, P. B. (2011). *Systematic review of the incidence and prevalence of schizophrenia and other psychoses in England*. Cambridge, UK: Department of Health Policy Research Programme: University of Cambridge.

Laschi, M., & Lombroso, C. (1886). Le dé lit politique. In *Actes du Premier Congrès International d'Anthropologie Criminelle*, Rome 1885 (pp. 379–389). Turin, Florence, and Rome: Bocca Frères.

MacKenzie, R. D. & James, D. V. (2011). Management and treatment of stalkers: Problems, options, and solutions. *Behavioral Sciences & the Law*, 29, 220–239.

MacKenzie, R. D., McEwan, T. E., Pathé, M. T., James, D. V., Ogloff, J.R.P., & Mullen, P. E. (2009). *The stalking risk profile: guidelines for the assessment and management of stalkers*. Melbourne: Stalk Inc. and Centre for Forensic Behavioural Science, Monash University.

McEwan, T. E., MacKenzie, R. D., Mullen, P. E., & James, D. V. (2012). Approach and escalation in stalking. *Journal of Forensic Psychiatry & Psychology*, 23(3), 392–409.

Meloy, J. R., Hoffmann, J., Guldimann, A., & James, D. V. (2012), The role of warning behaviors in threat assessment: An exploration and suggested typology. *Behavioral Sciences and the Law*, 30, 256–279.

Meloy, J. R., James, D. V., Mullen, P. E., Pathé, M. T., Farnham, F., Preston, L. F., & Darnley, B. (2011). Factors associated with escalation and problematic approaches toward public figures. *Journal of Forensic Sciences*, 56(S1), S128–S135.

Mullen, P. E., James, D. V., Meloy, J. R., Pathé, M. T., Farnham, F. R., Preston, L., & Darnley, B. (2008). The role of psychotic illness in attacks on public figures. In J. R. Meloy, L. Sheridan, & J. Hoffmann (Eds.), *Stalking, threatening, and attacking public figures: A psychological and behavioral analysis* (pp. 55–82). New York: Oxford University Press.

Mullen, P., James, D., Meloy, J. R., Pathé, M., Farnham, F., Preston, L., ...Berman, J. (2009). The fixated and the pursuit of public figures. *Journal of Forensic Psychiatry and Psychology, 20*, 33–47.

Mullen, P. E., & Lester, G. (2006). Vexatious litigants and unusually persistent complainants and petitioners: From querulous paranoia to querulous behaviour. *Behavioral Sciences and the Law, 24*, 333–349.

Mullen, P. E., Pathé, M., Purcell, R., & Stuart, G. W. (1999). Study of stalkers. *American Journal of Psychiatry, 156*, 1244–1249.

Mullen, P. E., Pathé, M., & Purcell, R. (2009). *Stalkers and their victims*, 2nd ed. New York: Cambridge University Press.

Pathé, M. T., Phillips, J., Heffernan, E., & Perdacher, E. (in submission). *The harassment of Queensland members of parliament: A mental health concern*

Phillips, R.T.M. (2006). Assessing presidential stalkers and assassins. *Journal of the American Academy of Psychiatry & the Law, 34*, 154–164.

Phillips, R.T.M. (2007). Celebrity and presidential targets. In D. A. Pinals (Ed.), *Stalking: Psychiatric perspectives and practical approaches* (pp. 227–250). New York: Oxford University Press.

Phillips, R.T.M. (2008). Preventing assassination: Psychiatric consultation to the U.S. Secret Service. In J. R. Meloy, L. Sheridan, & J. Hoffmann (Eds.), *Stalking, threatening, and attacking public figures: A psychological and behavioral analysis* (pp. 363–386). New York: Oxford University Press.

Pinals, D. A. (Ed.) (2007). *Stalking. Psychiatric perspectives and practical approaches.* New York: Oxford University Press.

Poole, S. (2000). *The politics of regicide in England, 1760-1850: Troublesome subjects.* Manchester & New York: Manchester University Press.

Régis, E. (1890). *Les régicidesdans l'histoire et dans le présent.* Paris: Maloine.

Sebastiani, J. A., & Foy, J. L. (1965). Psychotic visitors to the White House. *American Journal of Psychiatry, 122*, 679–686.

Shore, D., Filson, C. R., Davis, T. S., Olivos, G., DeLisi, L., & Wyatt, R. J. (1985). White House cases: Psychiatric patients and the Secret Service. *American Journal of Psychiatry, 142*, 308–312.

Scalora, M., Baumgartner, J., & Plank, G. (2003). The relationship of mental illness to targeted contact behavior toward state government agencies and officials. *Behavioral Sciences & the Law, 21*, 239–249.

Scalora, M. J., Baumgartner, J. V., Callaway, D., Zimmerman, W., Hatch-Maillette, M. A., Covell, C. N., ...Washington, D. O. (2002a). An epidemiological assessment of problematic contacts to members of Congress. *Journal of Forensic Sciences, 47*, 1360–1364.

Scalora, M. J., Baumgartner, J. V., Zimmerman, W., Callaway, D., Hatch-Maillette, M. A., Covell, C. N., ...Washington, D. O. (2002b). Risk factors for approach behavior toward the U.S. Congress. *Journal of Threat Assessment, 2*, 35–55.

Schoeneman-Morris, K. A., Scalora, M. J., Chang, G. H., Zimmerman, W. J. & Garner, Y. (2007). A comparison of email versus letter threat contacts toward members of the United States Congress. *Journal of Forensic Sciences, 52*, 1142–1147.

SOU (2006). *Jakten pa˚makten.* Stockholm: Staatens Offentliga Utredningar.

Takeuchi, J., Solomon, F., & Menninger, W. W. (Eds.). (1981). *Behavioral science and the Secret Service: Towards the prevention of assassination.* Washington, DC: National Academy Press.

Van der Meer, B. B., Bootsma, B., & Meloy, J. R. (2012). Disturbing communications and problematic approaches to the Dutch Royal Family. *Journal of Forensic Psychiatry & Psychology, 23*, 571–589.

West, D. J., & Walk, A. (1977). *Daniel McNaughton.* London: Gaskell.

Wilson, D. (1812). *The substance of a conversation with John Bellingham, the assassin of the late Right Hon. Spencer Percival, on Sunday May 17, 1812, the day previous to his execution, together with some general remarks.* London: Hatchard.

Wright, P. (2007). Editorial: This government's a 'fixated threat' to its own people. *Mail on Sunday,* 27 May.

21

Threat Triage

Recognizing the Needle in the Haystack

SHARON S. SMITH, ROBERT B. WOYACH, AND
MARY ELLEN O'TOOLE

Hospital emergency department workers are used to dealing with the bizarre. Still, on May 23, when a man with a "gruff voice" called the Clinton County Hospital emergency room threatening to kill some nurses, his call triggered alarm. Two days later, the same man phoned again, saying "there are going to be some dead nurses around there." A third call came five days after that. "Just 24 hours to go," he warned.

Was the caller serious? Or was he a prankster? Taking no chances, hospital employees called the Clinton County police, who conducted an investigation. But they could not identify a suspect. And so, a week after the third call, they closed the case.

On June 10 the emergency department received another chilling message: "Today you die," the now familiar voice said. Then, a week later, he sent a letter threatening to kill a doctor, a nurse, and a child as retribution for letting his wife and son die. Three more letters followed over the next two months. One included a newspaper article about a bombing and another an unspent .22 bullet. Again police officials investigated. Still they could not identify the threatener, nor could they corroborate information about the deaths of a mother and son at the hospital. So five weeks after the last letter was sent, they closed their case a second time. [1,2]

HISTORICAL PERCEPTIONS OF THE VALUE OF THREATS

Violence risk and threat assessment have traditionally relied on evaluating behavioral, historical, and dispositional variables along with membership in at-risk groups that are associated with violence (Meloy, Hoffmann, Guldimann, & James, 2012). These factors require knowledge of the identity of the person of interest (POI) for evaluation to occur. When the POI's identity is unknown and threatening or disturbing communications are present, law enforcement and private sector threat assessment teams may be forced to use those threats as the main and at times only source of information from which to make decisions about intervention and protection. But the perception of the value of threatening communications as violence and/or approach predictors has a varied history.

Prior to the studies of Dietz, Matthews, Van Duyne et al. (1991) and Dietz, Matthews, Martell et al. (1991) of threats to Hollywood celebrities and members of the US Congress respectively, the presence of communicated threats was assumed to be associated with an increased risk of approach behavior which then, because of proximity to the target, increased the potential for violence (Meloy, James, Farnham, et al., 2004). After Dietz's studies challenged these long-held beliefs, perceptions of a threat's predictive value diminished to the point that many regarded them as "dramatic but empty rhetoric" (Warren, Ogloff, & Mullen, 2012, p. 2) from individuals who would rant and then do nothing.

The Clinton County threats were not empty rhetoric. Six months after the last threat, a nurse who worked in the hospital's emergency room woke at 4:30 a.m. to find an intruder in her bedroom. After covering her eyes and mouth with duct tape, he tied her hands and legs with rope. Over the next few hours, he plied her with questions, pulling the tape off so she could answer, then taping her mouth shut again. During his time with her, he sexually assaulted her with the barrel of a gun. Finally, the intruder went to the bedroom where her six-year-old son was sleeping, placed a rope around the child's neck, and strangled him to death. After he left the house, the nurse untied herself and discovered her son's body. Seventeen days later, the threatener sent the hospital another letter boasting about the attack.

This case illustrates the frustrating reality for investigators in many threat cases. The police had investigated and closed the case twice without identifying a suspect or developing other clues. Until the break-in, the only tangible pieces of evidence in the case were the phone calls and threats. Even then, the threatener was not positively identified for two years.

PREDICTING APPROACH AND VIOLENCE USING LANGUAGE

Although the conventional wisdom has been that analyses of the form and content of threats offer no useful predictive information (Meloy, James, Farnham et al., 2004), this view has become nuanced because a growing body of literature shows that a significant minority of threateners do approach or become violent subsequent to threatening (Meloy, James, Farnham et al., 2004; Scalora, Baumgartner, & Plank, 2003; Smith, 2007; Warren, Ogloff, & Mullen, 2012). Recent research also indicates that the way people use language can have value for discerning their intent and future actions (Hermann, 2003; Smith, 2007, 2008; Young, 2001). If assessments of threatening communications can become more accurate, perhaps some tragedies like the Clinton County case can be averted. The issue then becomes one of identifying what factors in threats might be predictors.

The first author of this chapter was an FBI agent for 25 years, during the last 8 ½ of which she worked in the FBI's Behavioral Science Unit. Having studied psycholinguistics while getting her master's degree, she became interested in threat cases from local, state, and federal law enforcement agencies that had requested help from the FBI in identifying threateners and in assessing the likelihood that they might stalk or attack. As the new person sitting in on the consultations, she listened to more experienced agents pick communications apart while offering opinions on which linguistic factors increased or decreased the likelihood of stalking or violence. Over time, as she read research to inform her own evaluations, she realized that many of the factors that made intuitive sense were actually worthless as predictive factors. That motivated her to spend the next few years doing her own research to help law enforcement and threat assessment teams evaluate communications more accurately.

Smith's research (2007, 2008) found specific features of language use that would improve the accuracy of threatening communication assessments for approach and violence. From these she developed an algorithm or equation composed of nine weighted factors. One factor was the threatener contacting the target multiple times; the other eight involved elements in the threat itself (using conceptually complex language; expressions indicating paranoia; revealing religious prejudice; using a polite tone; mentioning love, marriage, or romance; indicating who the target is; giving the threatener's real return address; and specifying weapons). Her algorithm accurately assessed 70.8% of all case outcomes in her study and 92.9% and 93.2% of outcomes, respectively, in the low and high ranges of prediction scores. Of particular interest was one component of the algorithm—Conceptual Complexity—which Smith (2007, 2008) postulated may assist the threat assessor in detecting the type of thinking that precedes predatory (instrumental) violence (Meloy, 1988, 2006).

Conceptual Complexity reflects an individual's tendency to see the different parts or aspects of things (higher complexity) vs. seeing things in simpler terms (lower complexity). High-complexity thinkers consider the different factors that affect a problem, the different steps to or options for a solution, or the different points of view on an issue. A low-complexity thinker usually sees just one cause, the next step, the most available option, or his own point of view (Hermann, 2003; Suedfeld, Guttieri, & Tetlock, 2003).

Violent behavior can be classified as either predatory or affective (Meloy, 1988, 2006, 2012). Affective violence is a defensive response to an immediate perceived threat with a goal of self-protection. It is preceded by high levels of autonomic arousal typically expressed as anger or fear. In contrast, predatory violence is a planned, purposeful attack characterized by the absence of autonomic arousal and emotion. Both modes of violence are psychobiologically rooted and distinctive.

The potential value of Conceptual Complexity, coupled with other factors that research has shown to be predictive, is that it may offer a means of discerning the threatener's intent. Although Conceptual Complexity has both trait and state dimensions (Suedfeld, Guttieri, & Tetlock, 2003), linguistic measures of individual communications almost certainly tap primarily into the state, not the trait, dimension. In other words, the message reflects the complexity at which the threatener is operating when he or she writes the message, not the complexity at which the threatener normally works or the complexity of which he or she is capable. This is highly appropriate for threat assessment. "The central question concerning threat assessment and threat management is whether or not the subject poses a threat.... Posing a threat means that the individual is engaging in behavior to plan, prepare and implement an attack" (Meloy, James, Farnham et al., 2004, p. 1092). If a threatener has started to plan; and, in particular, if he or she has started to acquire resources or is near the implementation stage of an attack, his or her state of thinking may be more complex.

TURNING RESEARCH INTO A PRACTICAL TOOL

In October 2010, Social Science Automation, a text analysis company, set about turning Smith's (2007) research into a practical tool that could be used by threat assessors in law enforcement and the private sector. The goal was to create an Internet-based service that was readily accessible, easy to use, and as effective as possible. Because all but two of Smith's indicators (Real Return Address and Multiple Contacts) were linguistic variables intrinsic to the

communication, predictive factors could be gleaned from the message itself without any information about the threatener, the target, or the relationship between the two.

Threat Triage

Launched in October 2011, Threat Triage is a web-based software tool (www.threattriage.com) that uses Social Science Automation's proprietary content analysis engine (*Profiler Plus*) and a set of automated coding schemes to assess the linguistic characteristics of threatening messages. After assigning a unique ID to the message to be assessed, the user checks a box to report whether the threatener has contacted the target more than once and then types or pastes the threatening message verbatim into a box (Figure 21.1).

The user then clicks "Submit for Analysis," and an assessment of the message as high, moderate, or low risk is returned within seconds. The Threat Triage software calculates the probability that the message will be followed by targeted violence or approach based on the scores for six linguistic indicators and the additional indicator input by the user, all of which were found to be significant in Smith's (2007) research.

When cases are run through the Threat Triage software, one of the following three messages is returned:

- *High risk*: Based on the linguistic characteristics of this message, stalking or targeted violence by the threatener is likely. Research has shown that 2 of 3 cases in this scoring range resulted in approach or in some harmful action by the threatener. This scoring range represents the highest probability of threatener action that Threat Triage measures. However, threateners rarely do exactly what they threaten in communicated messages. Attempted acts may be to stalk, approach, or

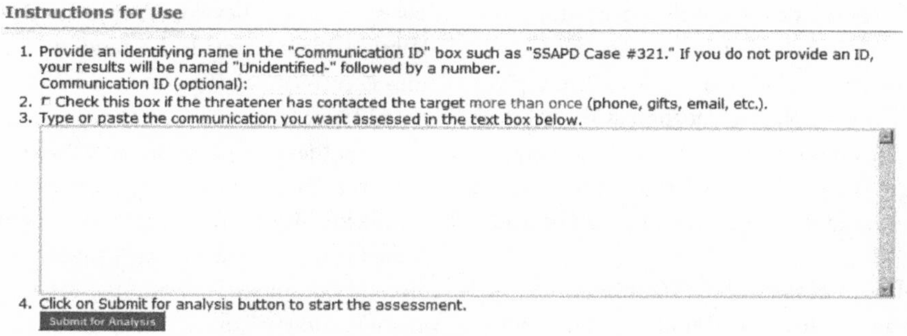

Instructions for Use

1. Provide an identifying name in the "Communication ID" box such as "SSAPD Case #321." If you do not provide an ID, your results will be named "Unidentified-" followed by a number.
   Communication ID (optional):
2. ⌐ Check this box if the threatener has contacted the target more than once (phone, gifts, email, etc.).
3. Type or paste the communication you want assessed in the text box below.

4. Click on Submit for analysis button to start the assessment.
   Submit for Analysis

FIGURE 21.1 Submitting messages for assessment in threat triage.

commit targeted violence against the stated target, against someone or something associated with the stated target, or even against a target not associated with the threatened target. Immediate safety precautions are recommended. Intervention by law enforcement may be appropriate.

- *Moderate risk*: Based on the linguistic characteristics of this particular message, the likelihood of stalking or targeted violence by the threatener cannot be discounted. Research has shown that action by the threatener occurs in 3 of 10 cases in this scoring range. Continued monitoring of the situation is strongly recommended.
- *Low risk*: Based on the linguistic characteristics of this particular message, stalking or targeted violence by the threatener is not likely. In our research, only 1 of 10 cases in the low-risk category resulted in action by the threatener. This category represents the lowest probability of threatener action measured by Threat Triage. Nonetheless, continued monitoring of the situation is recommended.

The accuracy of Threat Triage assessments depends on users correctly reporting whether the threatener has previously contacted the target. It also depends on having the verbatim text of the message. Thus messages that are delivered over the telephone or through nondigitized media must be entered precisely into the website text box. On the other hand, some aspects of the message, such as formatting, have no effect on the coding. Special coding routines inside Threat Triage even help the software interpret the linguistic conventions used in text messages or Internet postings (e.g., LOL).

On rare occasions, Threat Triage will fail to deliver an assessment. Although the tool is theoretically designed to work with messages of any length, shorter messages in particular are less likely to generate a score for Conceptual Complexity, which is a key indicator in the forecasting model. When no score for Conceptual Complexity is available, the equation at the heart of Threat Triage cannot calculate a risk probability for the message. As a result, Threat Triage returns a report to the user indicating that no assessment can be made.

From Research to Practice

Threat Triage is based on Smith's (2007) nine-variable forecasting model. However, to make the tool useful, readily available, and cost-effective, Threat Triage had to depart from the original model and methodology in some significant ways.

Most obvious are changes in the indicators upon which the forecasting model are based. One of the indicators in the original assessment model, for example, was Real Return Address. Whether the return address on a letter was accurate or not was known for most of the 89 test cases upon which Threat Triage was based because these were closed cases with known outcomes. For users of Threat Triage, however, this information is problematic. Most important, whether the return address is real will not be known in those cases for which Threat Triage is presumably most valuable (i.e., cases in which the threatener is not known or is misidentified). When this variable was dropped from the equation, however, it fundamentally changed the relationships among the remaining indicators.

Similarly, Smith's (2007) original research used two indicators (Conceptual Complexity and Paranoia) for which substitute measures had to be found. Although originally developed by Social Science Automation, the version of the Conceptual Complexity coding scheme that Smith used had been superseded by a more robust and stable version. Scores for this new version of Conceptual Complexity, which Threat Triage uses, highly correlate with the scores from the coding scheme used in Smith's original research ($r = .857$; $p < .01$). Similarly, in the original research, scores for Ambivalent Hostility (Paranoia) were generated with a coding engine developed by Robert Bechtel in association with Louis Gottschalk (the Psychiatric Content Analysis and Diagnosis system, or PCAD) (Gottschalk & Bechtel, 2001). However, using the PCAD version of Ambivalent Hostility (Paranoia) inside Threat Triage would have posed difficult technical challenges and also added to the cost. An alternative coding scheme, compatible with the Profiler Plus system, was developed to measure Paranoia. However, these scores had a modest although significant correlation with the original PCAD scores ($r = .513$; $p < .01$).

When these two new measures were combined in Threat Triage's original forecasting model, the results actually improved slightly compared with the results for the original coding schemes. The model correctly categorizes 78.6% of the cases in terms of whether action will or will not follow. This is slightly better than the 77.8% accuracy of the model using the original coding schemes and significantly better than the overall accuracy of Smith's model (70.8%). The improved performance is largely due to the more robust measure for Conceptual Complexity.

Tests of the new eight-variable model (i.e., the model without Real Return Address and with the alternative measures for Conceptual Complexity and Paranoia) uncovered the need for a final change to the original model. The variable indicating whether Religious Prejudice was expressed in the message no longer contributed meaningfully to the forecasting model. Dropping the Religious Prejudice variable once again slightly improved the success of the model. With Religious Prejudice included, the model successfully categorizes 76.7% of the 89 cases in terms of whether or not action followed. Without Religious Prejudice, the model successfully categorizes 78.6% of the cases.

Finally, in order to make Threat Triage accessible over the Internet, several new coding schemes had to be created to substitute for variables that had been hand coded in Smith's original research. Coding schemes were developed to measure whether (1) a victim was specified in the text; (2) the text referred to love, marriage, or romance; (3) the threatener used polite language in any part of the text; and (4) the message indicated a specific way in which the victim would be harmed. The development and use of automated coding schemes to measure these variables may seem significant. However, this change has the least impact on the forecasting model and methodology. Because all these indicators were operationalized as simply the presence or absence of the linguistic clue, automated coding could easily duplicate the hand-coding results for the 89 test cases. Not every instance of the linguistic behavior had to be correctly coded. Thus the ability to recognize novel ways of referring to such things as love, marriage, and romance were less critical. Human coders can recognize novel linguistic clues, so human coding will generally differ from automated coding when novel references are important. On the other hand, the use of automated coding schemes may make Threat Triage more accurate for assessing new messages. Given the all-or-nothing operationalization of these indicators, automated coding will usually be more accurate than hand coding. If the linguistic clues are rare or not featured prominently in the text, human coders can miss them because it is hard to maintain a high level of attention, especially when reading long texts.

The final Threat Triage forecasting model includes the following indicators:

- *Conceptual Complexity*—a scalar measure; the higher the score for Conceptual Complexity, the *more likely* it is that targeted violence or approach will occur.
- *Paranoia*—a scalar measure; the higher the score for Paranoia, the *less likely* targeted action or approach will occur.
- *Indication of the Victim*—a dyadic indicator; if the victim's identity is named or implied, targeted violence or approach *is less likely* to occur (a change in direction from Smith's model).
- *Mention of Love, Marriage, or Romance*—a dyadic indicator; if the message mentions love, marriage, or romance, targeted violence or approach is *more likely.*
- *Use of Polite Language*—a dyadic indicator; if any polite language is used in the message, targeted violence or approach is somewhat *less likely* (a change in direction from Smith's model).
- *Specification of Harm to Be Inflicted on the Victim*—a dyadic indicator; if any of a long list of violent actions or any of a diverse set of weapons are specifically mentioned, targeted violence or approach is *more likely* (a change in direction from Smith's model).
- *Whether the Threatener Has Contacted the Victim Before*—a dyadic indicator; if the threatener has contacted the target two or more times, targeted violence or approach is *more likely.*

TESTING THE EFFECTIVENESS OF THREAT TRIAGE

But how effective is Threat Triage at distinguishing between threats that pose a high risk and those that do not? The primary research done to date on Threat Triage has paralleled Smith's (2007) original research. Threatening messages associated with 89 of the cases that Smith used in her research[3] have been analyzed using probit regression and the new seven-variable model built into the Threat Triage software. All 89 messages were drawn from cases closed by the FBI's National Center for the Analysis of Violence Crime and had known outcomes. For those cases in which there were multiple communications, only the first

TABLE 21.1. THREAT TRIAGE'S ACCURACY FOR THE 89 TEST CASES

Observed Outcome	Predicted Outcome		
	No Action	Action	Percent correct
No action	62 (94%)	4 (6%)	
Action	15 (65%)	8 (35%)	
Overall correct			78.6% (70/89)

communication available to investigators was used in the analysis.

Predicting Targeted Violence Using the Original Cases

Not surprisingly, given that most threats are not acted upon, Threat Triage is better at identifying threats that pose a lower risk of targeted violence than those that pose a higher risk. Among the 89 cases used to design the system, 23 messages (26%) were followed by targeted violence or approach (some action) and 66 messages (74%) were followed by no action. When the seven-variable probit regression model used by Threat Triage is run on these cases, the model correctly identifies 94% of the cases in which no action occurs but only 35% of the cases in which targeted violence or approach (action) follows the message (Table 21.1). Overall, the model correctly classifies 78.9% of the cases.[4]

The 89 cases upon which Threat Triage is based are divided across the three risk categories as shown in Table 21.2. Almost half of the messages (46%) fall into the low-risk category, and of them, almost 90% were actually followed by no action. A far smaller number of messages (12) fall into the high-risk category, but two thirds of them (66.7%) were followed by targeted violence or approach of some kind. A little over a third of the cases (36 cases, or 40%) fall into the moderate-risk category. Roughly 69% of them were also followed by no action.

From a risk management perspective, these numbers tell an even more important story. They suggest that the risk of action following a low-risk message is still almost 10%, which means that the risk of action following such messages cannot be dismissed. However, if a message is assessed as being of moderate risk, the chance of action following the message rises threefold (from 10% to over 30%). In other words, for messages in the moderate-risk category, the likelihood that no targeted violence or approach will occur is substantial (69% of the cases). Nonetheless, the risk of violence for moderate-risk messages is more than triple the risk for the low-risk category. Most important, the risk of targeted violence or approach for high-risk messages is almost seven times greater than it is for low-risk messages (67% compared with 10%) and two times greater than it is for moderate-risk messages (67% compared with 31%). Thus, even though only two thirds of the cases assessed as high risk were actually followed by targeted violence or approach, the danger posed by them is far greater than for messages in the other risk categories.

Predicting Targeted Violence in New Cases

The apparent accuracy of Threat Triage in dealing with these 89 cases, of course, simply reflects its ability to fit the 89 cases used to calculate the probit regression equation used in the software. The

TABLE 21.2. DISTRIBUTION OF CASES ACROSS THE THREE RISK CATEGORIES

Risk Category	Observed Outcome		Total in Each Category
	No Action	Action	
Low risk	37 (90.2%)	4 (9.8%)	41 (46.1%)
Moderate risk	25 (69.4%)	11 (30.6%)	36 (40.5%)
High risk	4 (33.3%)	8 (66.7%)	12 (13.5%)
Total	66	23	89 (100%)

TABLE 21.3. THREAT TRIAGE FORECASTS FOR 24 NEW CASES

Risk Category	Observed Outcome		Total in Each Category
	No Action	Action	
Low risk	8 (88.9%)	1 (11.1%)	9 (37.5%)
Moderate risk	6 (66.7%)	3 (33.3%)	9 (37.5%)
High risk	1 (16.7%)	5 (83.3%)	6 (25%)
Total	15	9	24 (100%)

software was designed to fit these cases as well as possible. What about new cases? How accurate is Threat Triage in assessing the risk of violence in cases that it was *not* designed to fit?

Threat Triage continues to gather closed cases with known outcomes in order to further test and ultimately refine the Threat Triage model. Currently, Threat Triage has messages for 24 such cases. In general, these messages, like the original 89 messages, are the first communications available to investigators for the particular case. Although this is a small dataset from a statistical point of view, it can provide some insight into the likely ability of Threat Triage to accurately forecast targeted violence following messages it was *not* designed to fit.

The 24 new cases were run through Threat Triage through the standard submission process. Assessments of whether the messages were of high, moderate, or low risk were recorded, along with the actual outcome of each case. Table 21.3 shows the distribution of the 24 new messages across the three Treat Triage risk categories. It also shows, for each category, the number and proportion of cases in which targeted violence or approach actually did occur.

IMPLICATIONS FOR PREDICTING TARGETED VIOLENCE

When the first threat from the Clinton County Hospital case was run through the software—a case that was closed twice after brief investigations—Threat Triage assessed it as indicating a *high probability* that the threatener would approach or commit violence, a prediction that was tragically accurate. This suggests some implications for the field of threat assessment.

The reality of targeted violence is that a number of attackers do not communicate beforehand. Of those who do, some communicate only once while others communicate multiple times. Fein, Vossekuil, and Holden's research (1995) on assassinations of

public figures identified a pathway toward violence that a high-risk individual could take. "[I]n every case, assassination was the end result of an understandable process, involving the attacker's pattern of *thoughts*, *decisions* [italics added], behavior, and actions that preceded the attack" (p. 185). Perhaps the processes that impel threateners to put their thinking into words for the first time may be more suggestive of their true intent. Indeed, Smith's research (2007), which focused on assessing the first threat in each of the 96 cases in her database, found that *first* threats were predictive, even when risk-level assessments changed across the threats in individual cases with multiple communications. At the very least, the vacillations of predictive ratings of threats in cases with multiple communications suggest not only that escalation to action is not linear, but also that an assessment of any threat in the series as high or even moderate should be a red flag.

CONCLUSION

How do we discriminate between those who inappropriately communicate dramatic but empty rhetoric from those who communicate, then approach and harm? Traditional methods of evaluation have been informed by knowledge of the disposition as well as the behavioral and historical characteristics of the threat's author, but these factors are absent when the threatener is unknown. What factors then can help us more accurately identify planning and preparation for an approach or attack when few clues exist other than inappropriate communications?

If pathways "to violence can be analyzed according to behavioral, cognitive, and emotional evidence" (Meloy, Sheridan, & Hoffmann, 2008, p. 10), then inappropriate communications can contain language clues to the cognitive pathway toward predatory violence.

The cognitive aspect of the pathway includes the formulation of a grievance and the use of various psychological defenses such as denial and projection to blame the target, obsessional patterns of thinking that may contain unrealistic or delusional beliefs and expectations concerning the target, and certain other cognitive conditions that must be in place to warrant an attack: justification, a perceived lack of alternatives, and acceptance of the consequences of the attack. (Meloy, Sheridan, & Hoffman, 2008, p. 10)

A threat assessment model that taps into aspects of the complex thinking required to implement predatory (instrumental or intended) violence would be a valuable tool.

Factors in the model on which Threat Triage is built may offer the possibility of discerning cognitive processes consistent with predatory thinking at the time the communication is composed or spoken. When predatory intent is more accurately assessed, particularly from the first communication, then law enforcement and threat teams can become more effective in intervening and preventing tragedies like Clinton County.

ACKNOWLEDGMENT

ThreatTriage.com is a proprietary for-profit service owned and operated by Threat Triage LLC. Both Robert Woyach and Sharon Smith are beneficiaries of Threat Triage LLC.

NOTES

1 To protect the identities of all parties in case examples, all potentially identifying information has been deleted or changed, while the important facts of the case have been faithfully portrayed.

2 The opinions expressed in this book chapter are the authors, not those of the FBI.

3 Smith (2007) had a dataset of 96 closed cases, but only 89 cases were available to Threat Triage during development.

4 The assessment assumes a 0.5 cutoff. Thus it predicts that all cases with an estimated probability of action greater than 0.5 (50%) will be followed by action. It predicts that all cases with less than a 0.5 probability of action will be followed by no action.

KEY POINTS

- A growing body of literature shows that a significant minority of threateners do stalk, approach, or become violent subsequent to threatening.

- At the beginning stages of threat cases, the communicated threats may be the only information available from which to make an assessment of the likelihood that a threatener will stalk, approach, or harm. Threat assessors need to be cautious about relying solely on linguistic factors that make intuitive sense because many have proven to be worthless as predictors.
- Research indicates that the way people use language can have value for discerning their intent and future actions.
- If threateners have started to plan, and, in particular, if they have started to acquire resources or are near the implementation stage of an attack, their thinking may be more complex, and this may be reflected in the language they use in their threats.
- The language in both the single threat cases and the *first* threats in cases with multiple threats can be used to assess the likelihood that a threatener will act to stalk/approach or harm.
- Threat Triage, a web-based software tool, uses the linguistic characteristics of threatening messages to assess the likelihood of whether a threatener will act. It can be used in both identified and unidentified threatener cases absent any information about the threatener, the target, or the relationship between the two.

REFERENCES

Dietz, P. E., Matthews, D. B., Martell, D. A., Stewart, T. M., Hrouda, B. A., & Warren, J. (1991). Threatening and otherwise inappropriate letters to members of the United States Congress. *Journal of Forensic Sciences*, 36(5), 1445–1468.

Dietz, P. E., Matthews, D. B., Van Duyne, C., Martell, D. A., Parry, C.D.J., Stewart, T., Crowder, J. D. (1991). Threatening and otherwise inappropriate letters to Hollywood celebrities. *Journal of Forensic Sciences*, 36(1), 185–209.

Fein, R., Vossekuil, B., & Holden, B. (1995) *Threat assessment: An approach to prevent targeted violence* (NCJ 155000). Washington, DC: U.S. Department of Justice, Office of Justice Programs, National Institute of Justice.

Gottschalk, L. A., & Bechtel, R. J. (2001). *PCAD 2000: Psychiatric content analysis and diagnosis.* Available from GB Software at http://www.gb-software.com

Hermann, M. G. (2003). Assessing leadership style: Trait analysis. In J. M. Post (Ed.), *The psychological assessment of political leaders with profiles of Saddam Hussein and Bill Clinton* (pp. 178–212). Ann Arbor: University of Michigan Press.

Meloy, J. R. (1988). *The psychopathic mind: Origins, dynamics, and treatment.* Northvale, NJ: Jason Aronson.

Meloy, J. R. (2006). Empirical basis and forensic application of affective and predatory violence. *Australian and New Zealand Journal of Psychiatry, 40,* 539–547.

Meloy, J. R. (2012). Predatory violence and psychopathy. In: H. Hakkanen-Nyholm & J. Nyholm (Eds.), *Psychopathy and law* (pp. 159–175). London: Wiley-Blackwell.

Meloy, J. R., Hoffmann, J., Guldimann, A., & James, D. (2012). The role of warning behaviors in threat assessment: An exploration and suggested typology. *Behavioral Sciences and the Law, 30*(3), 256–279.

Meloy, J. R., James, D. V., Farnham, F. R., Mullen, P. E., Pathé, M., Darnley, B., & Preston, L. (2004). A research review of public figure threats, approaches, attacks, and assassinations in the United States. *Journal of Forensic Sciences, 49,* 1086–1093.

Meloy, J. R., Sheridan, K., & Hoffmann, J. (2008). Public figure stalking, threats, and attacks: The state of the science. In J. R. Meloy, L. Sheridan, & J. Hoffmann (Eds.), *Stalking, threatening, and attacking public figures* (pp. 435–455). New York: Oxford University Press.

Scalora, M. J., Baumgartner, J. V., & Plank, G. L. (2003). The relationship of mental illness to targeted contact behavior toward state and government agencies and officials. *Behavioral Sciences and the Law, 21*(2), 239–249.

Smith, S. S. (2007). From violent words to violent deeds? Assessing risk from threatening communications. *Dissertation Abstracts International, 68*(3), 1945B (UMI No. 3256532).

Smith, S. S. (2008). From violent words to violent deeds: Assessing risk from FBI threatening communication cases. In J. R. Meloy, L. Sheridan, & J. Hoffmann (Eds.), *Stalking, threatening, and attacking public figures* (pp. 435–455). New York: Oxford University Press.

Suedfeld, P., Guttieri, K., & Tetlock, P. E. (2003). Assessing integrative complexity at a distance: Archival analyses of thinking and decision making. In J. M. Post (Ed.), *The psychological assessment of political leaders with profiles of Saddam Hussein and Bill Clinton* (pp. 246–270). Ann Arbor: University of Michigan Press.

Warren, L. J., Ogloff, J. R., & Mullen, P. E. (2012). The psychological basis of threatening behavior. *Psychiatry, Psychology and Law,* May 1–15. Retrieved May 15, 2012 from http://www.tandfonline.com/doi/full/10.1080/13218719.2012.674716

Young, M. D. (2001). Building world view(s) with Profiler+. In M. D. West (Ed.), *Applications of computer content analysis* (pp. 17–32). Westport, CT: Ablex Publishing.

22

Domestic Violence Threat Assessment

Putting Knowledge and Skills into Practice

KEITH DORMOND

I have worked in the field of domestic violence and threat assessment for close to eight years as a detective with the Vancouver Police Department in Canada, and this chapter will focus on incidents of domestic violence in British Columbia. I am confident, however, that this chapter will have relevance to my national and international colleagues. Domestic violence is a universal problem; to be effectively addressed in any country, it requires agencies to work together, to share information, to support victims, and to hold offenders accountable. This chapter will focus on outlining how agencies can carry out an effective justice response to incidents of domestic violence in a way that increases the likelihood of victims remaining safe and offenders being held accountable for their actions.

Domestic violence is not a social problem that can be handled in isolation by the police, prosecutors, victim services, social services, and child welfare agencies. An effective response to domestic violence requires agencies to share information about victims and offenders in order to coordinate actions and assess and manage risk. Two domestic violence-related homicides that occurred in British Columbia in the last five years serve as vivid examples of the tragedies that can occur when agencies do not work together and miss opportunities for preventive intervention. The cases involved male offenders who were released on bail from the courts and went on to murder their families. The offenders were named Peter Lee and Allan Schoenborn; in both cases, the agencies that dealt with them believed that they

presented a risk to the victims but they failed to share information. Both cases prompted the government to draft reports that contained recommendations and initiatives designed to promote an effective justice response to domestic violence by encouraging information sharing and coordination between agencies. More specifically, the recommendations and initiatives closely followed the critical components of an effective justice response to domestic violence that were outlined in a 2008 report entitled *Keeping Women Safe: Eight Critical Components of an Effective Justice Response to Domestic Violence* (Critical Components Project Team, 2008). The eight components include:

1. Managing risk and victim safety planning
2. Offender accountability
3. Specialized victim support
4. Information sharing
5. Coordination and collaboration at all levels among relevant sectors
6. Domestic violence policy
7. Use of specialized expertise
8. Monitoring and evaluation

Managing risk and victim safety planning requires agencies to work together and coordinate interventions. Offender accountability consists of appropriate and consistent sentencing, consistent enforcement of court conditions, and accessible treatment for offenders of domestic violence. Specialized victim support consists of agencies working together to provide comprehensive, proactive, timely, and accessible support to marginalized groups. Information sharing involves agencies exchanging data on risk factors among themselves and with the victim—particularly in cases of high risk. Coordination includes collaboration among agencies and government sectors at all levels to provide resources and direction to adequately support a coordinated approach to domestic violence. Domestic violence policy includes adherence to a comprehensive justice system policy that promotes a consistent and informed approach to charging, prosecuting, and holding offenders of domestic violence accountable. The use of specialized expertise consists of dedicating justice system personnel and court time to domestic violence cases in order to promote a consistent approach. It also includes adequate funding for specialized training and the consideration of domestic violence courts. Last, monitoring and evaluation requires agencies to assess their effectiveness in carrying out the critical components and publicizing these results across all justice systems.

Since 1996, the Vancouver Police Department Domestic Violence and Criminal Harassment Unit (DVACH) has partnered with Family Services of Greater Vancouver (FSGV) to support victims of domestic violence and hold offenders accountable. DVACH and FSGV engage in all the components of an effective justice response to domestic violence to achieve these goals. DVACH and FSGV, for instance, actively engage in the first four components of an effective justice response through direct practice with offenders and victims; they engage in the last four components through participation in policy and evaluation projects as subject matter experts. In addition to these eight components, another component that is integral to an effective justice response to domestic violence is a common understanding of and language for critical risk factors and management strategies for domestic violence. Violence risk assessment tools utilized by DVACH and FSGV, such as the Brief Spousal Assault Form for the Evaluation of Risk (B-SAFER) (Kropp, Hart, & Belfrage, 2010), help to create this shared language by helping agencies to identify common risk factors of concern and appropriate risk management strategies. For close to eight years, I worked as a detective in the DVACH unit and utilized violence risk assessment tools such as the B-SAFER to assess and manage incidents of domestic violence and criminal harassment. In this chapter, I will review the two tragic domestic violence cases that illustrated the need for agencies to work collaboratively and systematically, much as DVACH and FSGV have done since 1996. In addition, I will utilize two case examples—in both of which I administered violence risk assessment tools—to demonstrate the effectiveness of such tools in helping to assess and manage risk as well as to foster collaboration.

On September 4, 2007, and April 6, 2008, in British Columbia, Canada, two domestic violence homicides occurred that caught the attention of the public, government, and community groups. Both homicides included the deaths of children at the hands of an estranged male partner; one case involved the murder of an intimate partner as well as that of her father and mother and the suicide of the perpetrator. The tragic element that made these cases stand out from other cases of domestic violence was the degree of violence and the multiple opportunities for preventive intervention that were not acted upon by child-serving, mental health, and criminal justice agencies.

On September 4, 2007, Peter Lee broke into the home where his son, his wife, and his wife's parents were sleeping; he then killed all of them before killing himself. At the time of the murder, Lee was on bail for attempting to murder his wife a few months earlier by driving their vehicle into a tree. Once he was released on bail, Lee breached his bail conditions by engaging in stalking behavior which was known to the police, his bail supervisor, the Crown (prosecution), and the Ministry of Children and Family Development (MCFD). All of these agencies believed that Lee posed a threat to his wife and family, but they failed to share information with each other and to develop a coordinated response (Representative for Children and Youth, 2009). The circumstances of the homicide that transpired on April 6, 2008, are just as tragic as those of the Lee case. As a result of having been charged with domestic violence, Allan Schoenborn had court-ordered "no contact" conditions with his common-law wife and three children, Kaitlynne, Max, and Cordon. In addition, the child welfare as well as the mental health and criminal justice systems were aware of incidents in which Schoenborn had exhibited violent behavior and symptoms of mental disorder such as delusions and erratic behavior, but they failed to share this information with each other. On April 6, 2008, Schoenborn was caring for his children. He put them to bed and then killed all three of them, claiming that he was protecting them from prostitution (Representative for Children and Youth, 2012).

Both the Lee and Schoenborn domestic violence homicides prompted government investigations and reports—including *No Private Matter: Protecting Children Living with Domestic Violence* (2009); *Honour Kaitlynne, Max and Cordon* (2012); and a *Domestic Violence Action Plan* (2010)—for the province of British Columbia. The common theme that ran through these documents was the need for an effective justice response to domestic violence, including the eight critical components mentioned earlier. In the fall of 2010, as part of the *Domestic Violence Action Plan*, the British Columbia Ministry of Public Safety and Solicitor General selected a risk assessment tool called the B-SAFER (Kropp, Hart, & Belfrage, 2010) as the standardized violence risk assessment tool for the province. This tool was selected since it provides the potential for agencies that work with families, offenders, and victims of domestic violence to share a common threat assessment process and structure.

USING THE B-SAFER

The B-SAFER, or Brief Spousal Assault Form for the Evaluation of Risk, is based on a structured professional judgment approach to assessing and managing violence risk. More specifically, it is a risk assessment tool that provides a set of guidelines for gathering and considering information for use by those making decisions about spousal assault risk (Kropp, Hart, & Belfrage, 2010). The 15 risk factors in the B-SAFER are divided into three sections: the first includes 5 risk factors related to the perpetrator's history of intimate partner violence (e.g., violent acts, violent threats or thoughts, violation of court order); the second includes 5 risk factors related to the perpetrator's history of psychological and social functioning (e.g., employment problems, substance use problems, mental health problems); and the third includes 5 risk factors related to the victim's ability or opportunity to engage in self-protective action (e.g., extreme fear of perpetrator, inadequate support or resources, unsafe living situation).

The B-SAFER also includes recommended strategies to manage risk factors that have been identified for spousal assault. These recommended risk management strategies include the following: (1) monitoring/surveillance, which involves evaluating changes in risk factors over time; (2) control/supervision, which involves restricting the activity, movement, or communication of the perpetrator; (3) assessment/treatment, which involves improving deficits in the perpetrator's psychosocial adjustment or functioning; and (4) victim safety planning, which involves improving the victim's physical security or self-protective skills.

To administer the B-SAFER, a user works through a four-step process in order to assess and manage the risk of violence. The first step involves identifying and gathering relevant case information through interviews, police reports, psychological and psychiatric reports, victim statements, perpetrator statements, and so forth. The second step involves coding the presence of risk factors and evaluating change in the risk factors over time. The third step involves determining which risk factors are the most relevant in the case and identifying risk management strategies that target them. Risk factors can be judged relevant if a user of the B-SAFER believes that they may influence the perpetrator's decisions to commit intimate partner violence by increasing the perceived benefits of violence, decreasing the perceived negative consequences, or disinhibiting the decision-making process (Kropp et al., 2010). Targeting risk management strategies at relevant risk factors consists of selecting management strategies from the four categories of risk management activities: monitoring/surveillance; assessment/ treatment; control/supervision; and victim safety planning.

The final step involves documenting judgments or conclusory opinions that address the case prioritization, risk for life-threatening and imminent violence, and the identification of likely victims of any future intimate partner violence (Kropp et al., 2010). *Case prioritization* is the level of intervention that is required to prevent the person from committing intimate partner violence. The levels are outlined as low, moderate, and high. The *risk for life-threatening violence* is the assessor's level of concern about future intimate partner violence that might result in life-threatening harm if there is no intervention. The levels are also outlined as low, moderate, and high. The *risk for imminent violence* is the assessor's level of concern about a person being an imminent risk to commit intimate partner violence if there is no intervention. Again the levels are outlined as low, moderate, and high. Finally, *likely victims of any future intimate partner violence* requires the assessor to identify all the parties who may be victims of future intimate partner violence, including current or former intimate partners, children, and family or friends.

THE FIRST CASE

I worked this case in the spring of 2011 and utilized the B-SAFER to assess risks posed and develop strategies to manage the risk that the offender presented to the victim. I have sanitized the case information by changing the names of the parties involved and other identifying information. The case involved a 20-year-old male named Bob, his on-again off-again 20-year-old girlfriend Karen, and their 2-year-old son, Peter. Both Bob and Karen had been involved in criminal activity in their teens. They considered themselves ex-girlfriend and ex-boyfriend, but Bob occasionally slept over at the home of Karen's parents. The MCFD was involved with Bob, Karen, and Peter owing to concerns about Karen's ability to take care of Peter. In addition, MCFD had concerns about Bob's criminal activity and associates, as they could potentially put Peter at risk for violence. In the spring of 2011, a supervisor from MCFD contacted the Vancouver Police Department, Domestic Violence and Criminal Harassment Unit where I was working at the time, and reported that they had concerns about the safety of Karen and Peter. The supervisor's main concern revolved around a tragic incident that occurred in the past involving Bob's family, which was related to his criminal activity.

In 2006 Bob lived with his mother, brother, and three sisters in a home in western Vancouver. Bob and his family immigrated to Canada from a "wartorn" country as refugees, and it was common knowledge among social service officials and the police that they had witnessed incidents of torture and murder at first hand. The police and social services agencies were constantly involved with Bob and his family because of his criminal behavior. This included his involvement with a youth gang that robbed and assaulted other youths, while also assaulting and threatening to kill his mother and entire family. In May 2006, Bob's associate, Jackson, became angry with him for providing information to the police about some of their crimes. Jackson rammed his vehicle into a car being driven by Bob's mother and forced it off a mountainous road and over a cliff. Bob was not in the vehicle at the time but his mother, two sisters, a brother, and Bob's girlfriend were in the vehicle and were all killed. Jackson was arrested, charged, convicted for the murders, and sentenced to life in prison. Bob declined

mentally and socially after most of his family was murdered; he continued to engage in a criminal lifestyle, which included robbery with firearms, assaults, and drug offenses. In addition, he was arrested under the Mental Health Act on several occasions after he threatened to kill himself, claiming that he could not live without his family and was overcome with guilt. In 2007, Bob met Karen, and in 2008 Peter was born.

In 2008, Bob was arrested and convicted for robbery with a weapon and incarcerated for two years. While Bob was in jail, his older brother, Derek, met Karen at a party and they ended up having sex. Once he was released from jail, Bob found out about this incident and assaulted his brother while they were both intoxicated. Bob also confronted Karen about sleeping with his brother and threatened to kill her and take their son away. In response, Karen threatened to remove their son and never let Bob see him again. Bob and Karen reconciled after these incidents, but they frequently argued about Karen's betrayal. On one occasion during an argument, Bob sent Karen a text message stating that he would "mess up your face so no else will want to be with you." Shortly after uttering this threat, Bob advised an MCFD worker that people were after him and that they wanted to harm Karen and Peter. Upon receiving this information, an MCFD supervisor contacted the DVACH unit as well as Bob's bail supervisor and mental health worker; they set up a meeting because of their concerns about Bob and/or his enemies who might harm Karen and Peter.

Prior to the meeting initiated by MCFD, I utilized the B-SAFER to assess Bob for the risk of intimate partner violence against Karen. In addition, I investigated Bob's claims that people were after him and his family. In the next section, I will discuss Bob's B-SAFER assessment and the outcome of my investigation into the threats from his criminal associates. I will then illustrate how I was able to utilize the structure and process of the B-SAFER in terms of risk factors and recommend risk management strategies to promote several components of an effective justice response to domestic violence.

Information Reviewed

As part of my risk assessment, I interviewed Bob, Karen, and the lead MCFD worker who was handling their file. I also reviewed several police reports in relation to Bob and Karen. After reviewing this information, I coded the presence of risk factors for domestic violence and identified those listed below as being relevant for Bob.

Identified Risk Factors

Violent threats and thoughts: Bob has a history of violent threats and thoughts toward Karen. On several occasions he threatened to kill her; in his most recent threat he stated that, "I am going to mess up your face so no one else will want to be with you."

Escalation: Bob's threats toward Karen have been escalating in frequency in the last few months. The incident that appeared to have contributed to this was Karen's threat to keep Bob from seeing his son.

Violent attitudes: Bob has exhibited violent attitudes toward Karen in the form of sexual jealousy about her being in a relationship with any other man. He has assaulted his brother for sleeping with Karen, and has threatened her as noted above.

General criminality: Bob was a member of a youth gang and has a history of engaging in criminal conduct, including robbery with a firearm, assaults, and drug-related offences. Bob was arrested, charged, and incarcerated for several of these offences. Upon being released from jail, he continued to associate with antisocial peers and engaged in criminal conduct likely in breach of his conditions of release.

Intimate relationship problems: Bob has exhibited problems in maintaining stable intimate relationships. His relationship with Karen has been characterized by multiple breakups and reconciliations as well as repeated infidelity on both of their parts.

Employment problems: Bob has a history of problems establishing and maintaining employment. He has never been gainfully employed, has never received government assistance, and according to his MCFD caseworker likely supports himself through criminal activity.

Substance use problems: Bob has a history of substance use problems in relation to cocaine and alcohol. In addition, he was prescribed medication for posttraumatic stress and depression after the death of his family and consumes these prescription drugs along with the street drugs.

Mental health problems: Bob has exhibited mental health problems. He exhibited disturbed and disorganized thinking during interactions with his MCFD caseworker. In addition, a few months after serving his two-year sentence for robbery and being released from jail, he was arrested under the mental health act on two occasions when he indicated that he wanted to kill himself.

Inconsistent attitudes and behavior: Karen has exhibited attitudes and behaviors that interfere with her ability and motivation to take self-protective action against Bob. For example, she has allowed Bob to sleep at her parents' home in the face of his threats and deteriorating mental health. Her rationale for these inconsistent attitudes and behaviors was that she felt sorry for him since he had a hard life.

Unsafe living situation: Bob and his criminal associates have easy access to Karen and her family because they know where they live. In addition, Karen continues to interact with criminal peers who also associate with Bob.

Based on the identified risk, I recommended the following risk management strategies:

Monitoring/surveillance: Face-to-face interviews with Bob and Karen.

Control/supervision: A review of his bail reporting conditions, specifically his attendance and behavior at bail meetings.

Assessment/treatment: A review of his compliance with attending forensic assessment and treatment appointments.

Victim safety planning: Placing a priority police response on Karen's home and ensuring that Bob would be able to have visitations with his son only when they were supervised by a social worker.

Assessment of Threat from Bob's Enemies

In addition to the risk factors that I identified for Bob, I investigated his claim that his son and Karen were in danger because his enemies were angry with him and wanted to take revenge on him through his family. This threat was of particular concern as one of his former criminal associates had murdered several members of his family two years earlier. After interviewing Bob and a reliable informant with intimate knowledge of his former and current criminal associates, I assessed this threat as low. In addition, evidence emerged suggesting that this threat was the result of Bob's deteriorating mental health as well as his attempt to gain custody of his son. Nonetheless, I advised the party with intimate knowledge of Bob's criminal associates to update me if she received any new information about this threat.

Meeting

A few days after I completed my assessment of Bob, I participated in a meeting with Bob's bail supervisor, his forensic psychologist, and his MCFD worker. In the early stages of the meeting initiated by MCFD, each agency provided an update on its dealings with Bob and its concerns. MCFD, for instance, indicated that they found Bob's behavior to be erratic: he was calm and rational at times and at other times his thoughts were disorganized. According to the MCFD worker, when his thoughts were disorganized, he talked about the enemies who were threatening his family. MCFD were very concerned about this threat based on the murder of Bob's family members several years earlier. Consequently they believed that his son was possibly at risk and needed to be taken into custody by their agency for protection. The bail supervisor indicated that Bob had attended most of his bail appointments but rarely said a word during their meetings. In addition, it was unknown where he lived, as his address had not been confirmed. The forensic psychologist indicated that Bob attended most meetings and was pleasant during these meetings, but it was unknown whether he was taking his medications.

When it came to the position of the police, I indicated that I utilized the B-SAFER to conduct a violence risk assessment. Also, I reviewed risk factors that were identified for Bob and the recommended risk management strategies. Once I presented this information, gaps in some of the risk management strategies that had been utilized for Bob became apparent to all the participants in the meeting. In addition, the risk that Bob posed to Karen and how this risk should be managed also became known. For instance, although he was attending bail appointments, Bob's behavior was not as restricted as it could have been, since his address was never confirmed and he was never challenged about his associates and how he supported himself. In addition, he was attending forensics for mental health assessment and treatment, but his mental health appeared to be deteriorating and it was unknown if he had been taking his medications. Once we collaboratively identified these gaps, the workers from bail and forensics took steps to address them, including visiting Bob's address and having him consume his medication in their presence. After this meeting, all the agency representatives maintained contact and exchanged relevant information. In addition, Bob was closely monitored and supervised, particularly by his bail supervisor and forensic psychologist; his risk of harming Karen was deemed to have been reduced.

Prior to the meeting initiated by MCFD, the risk that Bob presented to his former girlfriend and son was not being dealt with in a coordinated fashion. My utilization of the B-SAFER, however, helped to correct this situation by allowing each agency that was dealing with Bob to identify and comprehend the risk factors of concern, as well as the recommended risk management strategies. In other words, it allowed everyone to speak and understand the language of risk assessment and risk management. As a result, several critical components of an effective justice response to domestic violence were operationalized: managing risk, victim safety planning, and support; offender accountability; and information sharing and coordination. For instance, the identification of risk factors and risk management strategies for Bob that were rendered by the B-SAFER helped the different agencies to manage risk and victim safety planning collaboratively, hold Bob accountable for his actions, and share information.

DOMESTIC VIOLENCE CARD

When I utilized the B-SAFER in the case, I was a detective in the Vancouver Police Department DVACH unit and I had adequate training, experience, and time to administer the tool. Most uniformed patrol officers, however, do not have the same amount of time and training to conduct violence risk assessments in cases of domestic violence. This situation exists because patrol officers are generalists who respond to a wide variety of calls, including domestic violence, robbery, sexual assault, breaking and entering, and motor vehicle accidents, to name a few. Frequently, the number of calls that officers must respond to on a daily basis are high, and they have limited time to move from one call to the next. In addition, the need for patrol officers to be on the road responding to calls limits the amount of time they have to receive training in the area of domestic violence. This situation is a problem, since patrol officers must rely on unstructured professional judgment or their general training, experience, and instincts to identify domestic violence risk factors and then suggest appropriate risk management strategies. Because each officer is working from a different level of training and experience in domestic violence, the identification of risk factors of concern in police reports tends to be inconsistent. Hence, files of concern may not always come to the attention of prosecutors and members of DVACH, and appropriate risk management strategies may not be implemented.

In 2008, several members of DVACH—including a sergeant, two detectives and I—created a small laminated Domestic Violence Risk Factors card (see Appendix) for patrol officers loosely based on the B-SAFER in response to this problem. This card was created with approval of two authors of the B-SAFER, Stephen Hart and Randall Kropp. The card is two-sided, measures approximately 6 inches long by 4 inches wide, and can easily be placed in a police officer's shirt pocket or notebook. Thirteen domestic violence risk factors are outlined on the front of the card, along with a series of questions that patrol officers should consider. The headings for the risk factors include current status of relationship, history of violence, assaults/threats, weapons, children, abduction, strangulation, employment, criminal status, substance abuse, mental health, thoughts and plans for violence, and victim vulnerability. Bail conditions (including reporting to a bail supervisor, no contact with the victim; no going to the residence, workplace, or school of the victim; no possession of any weapons; and abstaining from consumption of drugs and alcohol—to name a few) are outlined on the back of the card. In addition, the back of the card includes phone numbers for women's shelters, transition houses, and referral agencies.

The card is not a replacement for the B-SAFER. It is a reference for officers who may have limited training and time to identify and outline risk factors of concern in their reports. Once these risk factors are identified in reports, members of DVACH and the Crown (prosecution) with training in threat assessment can identify cases that require follow-up investigation and risk management. The card serves as a screening and triaging tool for DVACH and the Crown. In the next section, I will review a case example in which I utilized the Domestic Violence Card in a patrol investigation. According to the authors of the B-SAFER, patrol officers in Sweden have successfully utilized the B-SAFER to assess and manage incidents of domestic violence (personal communication, R. Kropp, May, 2012). In Vancouver a limited number of patrol officers have been trained to utilize the B-SAFER, but the numbers are increasing as a result of "train the trainer" government initiatives. While I do have training in violence risk assessment and could have

used the B-SAFER, the time that I had to complete the report was extremely limited, so I utilized the Domestic Violence Card.

SECOND CASE EXAMPLE

As in the previous case example, I have sanitized the case by changing the names of the parties involved and other identifying information. This case involves an incident of domestic violence when I was dispatched to the scene with another officer. Because a limited number of officers were on shift and I was experienced in domestic violence investigations, I was assigned as the lead officer for the case. Upon our arrival at the scene, Jack, the suspect, had fled and Betty, the victim, was present with her son. The information that I relied on for my investigation and threat assessment was an interview with Betty and review of police reports. Betty indicated that she and Jack had been in a relationship for two years. They had a two-year-old adopted son and Jack had two children from a previous relationship. Jack was unemployed and received government social assistance for support. In his previous relationship, Jack had several times been charged with domestic assault and criminal harassment (stalking) of his wife. In one incident, Jack attempted to abduct his two children but returned them to their mother once the police were called. In his current relationship with Betty, Jack was charged with assaulting and criminally harassing her in the first year of their relationship. Jack, however, convinced Betty that he had changed, and she recanted her police statement and failed to show up in court. Consequently the charges against Jack were dropped.

Incident of Concern

In the course of the interview with Betty I also learned that she and Jack had been arguing about household bills. She told him that she was leaving him for good. She started to pack up her belongings and called her parents to help her with the move. It was at this point that Jack stated to her that he "would kill her if she left him and she was a no good slut." He also strangled her to the point of unconsciousness, punched her in the face, and kicked her body multiple times after she fell to the floor. Betty screamed for help and a neighbor called the police. Jack left the scene prior to the arrival of the police and could not be located.

Information Reviewed

After reviewing Betty's statement and several police reports in relation to her and Jack, I quickly outlined the following information in my report by utilizing the Domestic Violence Card:

Current relationship status: A pending separation is present as Betty has indicated to Jack that she will separate from him permanently. Also, when Jack assaulted her in the first year of their relationship and they separated, he stalked her through phone calls and visits to her home in breach of his conditions.

History of violence/abuse in relationship: In the most recent assault, Betty sustained injuries to her head, stomach, face, and legs that required medical attention. Previously when she had been assaulted by Jack, she sustained injuries including a dislocated shoulder and bruising to her face. She was hospitalized for 24 hours for these injuries.

Assaults/threats: Jack has assaulted Betty on a number of occasions and claimed that she was responsible for his behavior because she also assaulted him and he was just protecting himself.

Children witnessed abuse: Jack and Betty's two-year-old son was present during many incidents in which he assaulted her and MCFD has been involved with the family.

Abduction: In his previous relationship, Jack attempted to abduct his two children from his estranged wife.

Strangulation: Betty reported that Jack strangled her to the point of unconsciousness.

Employment: Jack has problems maintaining employment. He has been unemployed for over two years and receives government assistance for support.

Criminal status: Jack has been charged for assaulting and criminally harassing both his former and current partners. In addition, he has a history of contacting his victims in contravention of his court orders.

Thoughts and plans of violence: Jack has threatened to kill Betty on a number of occasions. In addition, he has escalated from threats to physical forms of violence, including strangulation. It is unknown at this time if he suffers from a mental illness.

Victim vulnerability: Betty recanted her police statement in a previous assault when Jack convinced her that he had changed. Betty is now adamant that she will separate from Jack for good and will follow through with charges.

Based on these risk factors, I stated in my report that I believed that the risk of Jack continuing to engage in domestic violence and criminal harassment against Betty was high due to his history of domestic violence and stalking, his escalation from threats to strangulation, and his history of breaching his bail conditions. Hence, I requested risk management conditions in accordance with *control/supervision* such as detaining him in custody until trial. I also recommended that if he were released, he should be released on stringent conditions in accordance with *control/supervision*, including reporting to bail, no contact with the victim, not going to her residence, not possessing any weapons, and abstaining from consumption of drugs/alcohol. Moreover, in accordance with the risk management strategy of *victim safety planning*, I recommended a panic alarm for Betty and police priority response (electronic flag on police system) to her home and day care of her child. I did not recommend any risk management strategies in the area of assessment and treatment as I had limited information about Jack's mental health or substance abuse issues that might be associated with his violence. In the area of *monitoring/surveillance*, I recommended that Jack report to a bail supervisor on a regular schedule so that his emotional and mental state could be monitored.

After reviewing my report and the risk factors present in Jack's background, the Crown agreed with my primary position that he be held in custody until trial. Consequently the prosecutor reviewed the risk factors in court with the judge and asked that Jack be held in custody. The judge acknowledged the risk factors of concern but believed that Jack could be managed in the community with stringent conditions. She released him on a bail surety (person who ensures Jack abides by conditions) one week later with the conditions that I requested. Once released, Jack criminally harassed Betty through phone calls and visits to her workplace and home. After breaching his conditions more than five times, Jack was held in custody until his trial.

My use of the Domestic Violence Card helped me to quickly and concisely identify risk factors of concern in my report. Consequently, when the report was reviewed by the Crown's counsel and members of DVACH, they were able to quickly assess the risk factors, determine that the risk was high, and devote resources to the case. The Crown, for instance, reviewed the risk factors of concern with a judge during a bail hearing and requested that Jack be held in custody until trial. In addition, DVACH assigned a detective and counselor to the file in order to support the victim and gather additional evidence to hold Jack in custody and ensure that he received the appropriate sentence. DVACH also installed a panic alarm at the home of the victim.

Many patrol officers in the VPD use the Domestic Violence Card; with limited training and time, they are able to identify risk factors of concern in their reports. As a result, Crown counsels and members of DVACH who review these files are able to quickly assess the risk factors identified in each case and determine which cases require additional assessment and risk management. Hence, like the B-SAFER, the Domestic Violence Card facilitates a common language to assess domestic violence risk factors among police, the Crown, victim services, and other agencies. Moreover, like the B-SAFER, it helps agencies to respond effectively and collaboratively to incidents of domestic violence.

CONCLUSION

When agencies do not share information or coordinate interventions in cases of domestic violence, tragedies like the murders discussed in this chapter can occur. These murders and other incidents of domestic violence indicate that an effective justice response to domestic violence requires agencies to work collaborative and systematically. More specifically, they point to a need for agencies to engage in the eight components of an effective justice response to domestic violence. Because domestic violence is a universal problem, these eight components are applicable throughout Canada and the rest of the world. I have sought to illustrate through case examples how violence risk assessment tools—including the B-SAFER and the domestic violence risk factors for patrol officers—can play an integral role in facilitating an effective justice response to domestic violence. Hence, like the eight components of an effective justice response, these risk assessment tools can be effectively utilized nationally and internationally to assess and successfully manage incidents of domestic violence.

ACKNOWLEDGMENT

I would like to thank Kelly Watt, Ph.D., for reviewing an earlier draft of this chapter.

APPENDIX

Domestic violence risk factors for patrol officers:

1. *Current status of relationship*: Are there past, recent, or pending separations? During separations has accused (ACC) stalked/harassed victim (VIC)? Displayed jealous behaviors?

2. *History of violence/abuse in relationship*: Has there been physical/ sexual/verbal/emotional/financial abuse and has abuse escalated in the past 12 months? Has VIC ever required medical attention?

3. *Assaults/threats*: Has ACC ever hurt, injured, or threatened to hurt VIC, family member, another person/pet? Does ACC use extreme minimization or denial of assaultive behavior?

4. *Weapons*: Has ACC ever used weapons against VIC/threatened to use weapons? Own a firearm or have plans to acquire a firearm?

5. *Children*: Have children witnessed the abuse by offender? Have children been abused? Has the Ministry of Children and Family Development been involved with the family?

6. *Abduction*: Has ACC ever abducted/ threatened to abduct children?

7. *Strangulation:* Has ACC ever strangled or bitten victim?

8. *Employment*: Has ACC employment history changed during the last 12 months? Does ACC have problems maintaining employment?

9. *Criminal status*: Is ACC currently before the courts? Has ACC ever violated a court order including Peace Bond or no contact?

10. *Substance abuse*: Is ACC currently using alcohol/drugs? Is substance abuse escalating? Does violence increase when ACC has been consuming?

11. *Mental health/suicide*: Does ACC have a mental illness? Has ACC ever expressed homicidal or suicidal ideas? Has ACC ever attempted suicide?

12. *VIC vulnerability*: Is VIC socially/ physically isolated, unwilling to leave home? VIC perception of personal safety? Cultural barriers to getting help?

KEY POINTS

- An effective justice response to incidents of domestic violence includes eight components: (1) managing risk and victim safety planning; (2) offender accountability; (3) specialized victim support; (4) information sharing; (5) coordination and collaboration at all levels among relevant sectors; (6) domestic violence policy; (7) use of specialized expertise; and 8) monitoring and evaluation.
- An additional component that is integral to an effective justice response is a common understanding and language for critical risk factors and management strategies for domestic violence. Violence risk assessment tools such as the Brief Spousal Assault Form for the Evaluation of Risk (B-SAFER) can help create this shared language by assisting agencies in identifying common risk factors of concern and appropriate risk management strategies.
- Since 1996, the Vancouver Police Department Domestic Violence and Criminal Harassment Unit (DVACH) in partnership with Family Services of Greater Vancouver (FSGV) has engaged in the eight critical components of an effective justice response to domestic violence. In addition, both agencies have utilized violence risk assessment tools such as the B-SAFER to identify risk factors of concern and appropriate risk management strategies.
- When agencies fail to work collaboratively and systematically, like the DVACH unit and FSGV, opportunities for preventive intervention may be missed and serious cases of domestic violence may occur. In British Columbia, two tragic incidents occurred in 2007 and 2008 that prompted the government to launch investigations, draft reports, and create a domestic violence action plan for the province. The theme that ran through all of these documents was that agencies increase the likelihood of responding effectively to incidents of domestic violence when they engage in the previously mentioned eight critical components. In addition, as part of the Domestic Violence Action Plan, the British Columbia government selected the B-SAFER as the standardized risk assessment tool for the province.
- Two case examples were presented to illustrate how the B-SAFER can help agencies to collaboratively engage in an effective justice response to incidents of domestic violence.

REFERENCES

Critical Components Project Team (April 2008). *Keeping women safe: Eight critical components of an effective justice response to domestic violence*. British Columbia, 2008. Available at: http://www.endingviolence.org/node/659

Kropp, P. R., Hart, S. D., & Belfrage, H. (2010). *Brief spousal assault form for the evaluation of risk (B-SAFER)*. Vancouver, BC: ProActive ReSolutions.

Representative for Children and Youth (2009). *Honour Christian Lee, no private matter: Protecting children living with domestic violence*. Vancouver: author.

Representative for Children and Youth (2012). *Honouring Kaitlynne, Max and Cordon: Make their voices heard*. Vancouver: author.

23

An Operational Approach to Prosecuting Stalking Cases

RACHEL B. SOLOV

There can be no justice until those uninjured by crime become as indignant as those who are.

SOLON: THE LAWMAKER OF ATHENS, *c. 500 B.C.*

Most prosecutors can't wait to be assigned their first homicide case; I was one of those. Murder is the ultimate crime, with the ultimate penalties and thus the ultimate challenge. For a prosecutor this is where the glory is found.

Or so I thought.

My first homicide case was a brutal murder where the defendant beat the victim on the head with a sledgehammer and strangled her. The defendant had displayed some stalking behaviors, although nothing that would have qualified as "stalking" under the California Penal Code. When the jury came back with guilty verdicts, I was satisfied that the right thing had happened and that this person would be sent to prison for the rest of his life without the chance of parole. But there was no joy and no celebration. The case redefined what justice meant to me. Yes, justice in the legal sense was served, but what does justice really mean when a mother, daughter, and sister is forever taken from this world in a senseless act of brutality? Isn't justice better served by doing whatever we can to prevent these unspeakable harms? I believe wholeheartedly that it is, and thus the genesis of my passion for prosecuting stalking cases was sparked.

In law enforcement generally and as prosecutors specifically, our role is traditionally reactive. A crime occurs and we respond to it by attempting to hold the offender accountable. Stalking cases are unique because we have the opportunity to intervene and prevent an even greater harm from happening. In this respect, the prosecution of stalking cases is proactive.

What follows is a nuts-and-bolts guide to the prosecution of stalking cases based on my almost 10 years' experience in dealing with these offenders. In some cases it is based on mistakes I have made along the way, and in others on lessons I have learned from some of the most brilliant minds in violence risk/threat assessment and management— too many to name here—to whom I owe a debt of gratitude. The views and suggestions offered in this chapter are my own and are not necessarily based on any position, policy, or practice of the San Diego District Attorney's Office. In the end, it is important to remember that every case is different and therefore you must use your own professional judgment in making what sometimes can amount to life-or-death decisions. My area of expertise is California, but stalking behavior exists all over the world; therefore I have attempted to write this chapter in such a way that the information can be applied in any jurisdiction.

THE GOALS

There are two primary goals in the prosecution of stalking cases. The number one goal is to keep the victim safe. First, you must assist the victim in making, in some cases, life-altering changes directed at keeping him or her physically safe. Second, you must constantly assess your own decision making through a filter of "do no harm." As prosecutors, we take an oath to uphold the US Constitution and the laws of the states in which we practice. Sometimes, however, the prosecution of an offender can cause an escalation that dramatically increases the risk to the victim because the penalty is not extreme enough or there is a risk of acquittal. In these cases, you may be forced to make the decision that the best way to keep the victim safe may, in fact, be a threat management plan and not a criminal prosecution. Intervention by the criminal justice system is the most severe and restrictive intervention strategy there is. Bringing a perpetrator into the criminal justice system can possibly trigger rage and shame in the perpetrator, which escalates the violence against the victim. Sometimes not prosecuting the suspect in lower-level stalking cases actually provides more protection to the victim. This is a difficult concept for a prosecutor to accept. By no means am I suggesting that stalkers should not be prosecuted. However, it is critical to educate yourself in the field of violence risk/threat assessment and management so that you can tell the difference between those cases requiring aggressive prosecution and those where a watch-and-wait approach is best.

The second goal in prosecuting stalking cases is to hold the offender appropriately accountable under the law. As prosecutors, we are sworn to seek justice and enforce the law. But justice and ethics require that we also seek to protect the rights of the defendant. Keep these two goals as your primary focus as you work these cases. It will force you at times to make decisions that may be contrary to what the average prosecutor might make, but remember that to prosecute these cases successfully, you must balance wearing two hats: the hat of a prosecutor and that of a threat assessor.

Some 3.4 million adults are stalked each year in the United States; 75% of them are stalked by someone they know (Baum et al., 2009). The relationship between the victim and the stalker will play a key role in potential plea bargains, punishment, and management post-release. A stalking case involving a former intimate partner will need to be handled very differently from a stranger or acquaintance stalking case.

Stalking is a crime in all states as well as under federal law; however, the elements and penalties vary dramatically. California was the first state to pass anti-stalking laws. Essentially, most stalking statutes can be distilled down to their simplest terms of prohibiting a course of conduct that includes a credible threat and causes various degrees of fear. Sometimes, there is a disconnect between stalking behavior and what will hold up in court as stalking under various penal codes. This can be very frustrating for victims, who feel that they continue to be victimized by receiving no protection or assistance from the law.

VERTICAL PROSECUTION AND SPECIALIZED STALKING TEAMS

Vertical prosecution is essential in dealing with stalking cases. This means that a single prosecutor handles a case from pre-issuance all the way through post sentencing. In most large prosecutors' offices, cases are handled in assembly-line fashion, with a different prosecutor handling each stage of the proceedings. This would mean that a stalking victim would be forced to interact with a new prosecutor every time he or she came to court, adding to the anxiety already being experienced. The victim would have to tell and retell his or her story multiple times. Additionally, the prosecutor probably would not have the training necessary to adequately handle these cases. Finally, because these cases are often long-term and complex, having a prosecutor with historical knowledge of the case and the stalker ensures that the appropriate penalties will be requested of the courts. So, in summary, vertical prosecution helps ease the burden on the victim while still holding the stalker appropriately accountable.

It is also helpful to have a team dedicated to stalking cases. The following model team has been very successful in my experience of prosecuting these cases:

1. An investigator who has law enforcement powers to assist in interviewing victims/ witnesses, collecting evidence, writing and obtaining search warrants and arrest warrants, and arresting stalkers.
2. A victim advocate trained in violence risk/ threat assessment who can help screen potential high-risk cases and assist victims through the court process as well as the safety planning process. Our victim advocate would review all patrol reports written for stalking, threats, and restraining order violations often before the agency's detective has received the case for follow-up. This effectively sped up the response time in getting critical safety planning information to the victim.
3. A prosecutor familiar with the legal nuances of stalking/threat cases and violence risk/ threat assessment.

By working together as a team, we can better recognize cases that law enforcement might not have seen as stalking cases and prevent them from falling through the cracks. This model also speeds up the response time in connecting with the victim and the assigned detectives. By becoming involved early, we can work together with law enforcement to divide some of the labor and make sure that the investigations are complete and charges can be filed at the earliest possible moment.

CASE EXAMPLE

In this case, the 22-year-old defendant dated the 19-year-old victim for about two years. The victim lived with her mother in an apartment and the defendant lived with them for part of the time they dated. Eventually, the victim's mother removed him because he was abusive to her daughter. Her daughter continued to date the defendant for a few more months, but ultimately ended the relationship because the abuse began to escalate. The defendant began to follow her, and he left her literally hundreds of threatening messages: getting her, beating her, and watching her like a hawk. She became so terrified that, except when she went to school and work, she stayed home behind closed doors, windows, and blinds. She changed both her school and work locations, which forced her to travel two hours by bus every day. Her mother called our stalking unit because she was terrified for her daughter and frustrated with law enforcement's response. Her daughter had gone to the local police station, but they would not take a report. She went to court to get a restraining order but the judge refused to issue it and made her cry. We agreed to meet with her daughter that afternoon.

After interviewing the victim and listening to the recorded messages she had, it became clear that she had not been able to articulate her situation properly to the police or the judge. We quickly filed a case and drafted an arrest warrant requesting $1 million bail. The warrant was signed by a judge and the investigator had the defendant in custody that night. This demonstrates the importance of having dedicated members of a stalking unit who are able to recognize dangerous situations and take swift action.

The defendant pled guilty and was initially sentenced to probation. Shortly into this probationary period, the city attorney's office notified us that he had been arrested for a misdemeanor domestic violence battery against a new victim. In our particular jurisdiction, the district attorney's office prosecutes felonies but has granted the city attorney the jurisdiction to prosecute misdemeanors. The city attorney's office forwarded the case to us in order to revoke the defendant's probation. In the new incident, there were no witnesses other than the victim and the defendant. However, what the victim described was strikingly similar to one of the incidents that the victim in our stalking case had described. Being highly familiar with the defendant's history was critical in proving the probation violation in a contested hearing that ended up with the defendant being sent to prison. This demonstrates the importance of implementing specialized stalking teams and the vertical prosecution of stalking cases.

RECOGNIZING THE STALKING CASE

Law enforcement, including prosecutors, often fail to recognize stalking cases. Any time a victim describes harassing behavior, you should consider whether this is a stalking case. Stalking cases often first present themselves as individual incidents that appear minor, but reveal themselves to be serious when considered as a whole. Additionally, it is common in the beginning for stalking victims to try to manage the situation themselves before involving law enforcement. You should always consider the fact that usually there will have been several prior incidents that occurred well before the reported activity. Further, if the victim has made more than one report, it is possible that the reports were taken in different jurisdictions and thus were not linked. It is important to get a complete picture of the case history to determine whether what appear to be minor nuisances actually add up to a serious stalking case. Common harassing behaviors may include the following:

1. Vandalism
2. Annoying, threatening or obscene phone calls, texts, or emails
3. Distributing private or embarrassing photos and/or information about the victim to friends, family or coworkers
4. Following, either in person or by using GPS technology
5. Sending unwanted letters or gifts
6. Repeatedly driving by or showing up at the victim's home or work location
7. Using social media to harass, threaten, or obtain information about the victim's activities

8. Stealing mail in an attempt to get intelligence on the victim's activities
9. Conducting surveillance on the victim or the victim's family or new significant other
10. Entering the victim's home when the victim is not there

Stalkers and victims present from all demographics, and stalking behaviors are as broad as the stalker's imagination and intelligence. Do not rely on law enforcement to put all the pieces of the puzzle together for you. It is critical for you to be as thorough as possible in this information-gathering stage. It is impossible to assess the seriousness of the stalking case accurately without getting a complete history of the behaviors and incidents.

PRE-FILING STAGE

There are several things you will want to do prior to filing charges.

First, gather all police reports and take the necessary steps to collect and preserve evidence. Be sure to have someone else collect the evidence, preferably law enforcement, so that you do not become a link in the chain of custody to get the evidence admitted in court. Law enforcement will sometimes have done much of this, but if not, it is important for the prosecutor to make sure that it is done. Ultimately, the responsibility for a successful prosecution lies with the prosecutor.

Collecting electronic evidence can be time-sensitive. Some phones save voicemail and text messages for only a limited period of time. It is important to make a recording of any voice messages and photograph or print text messages left by the stalker. Phone companies do not usually save call records or cell tower information indefinitely—in some cases they are saved for only for a matter of days. Many will not release information to you absent a subpoena or search warrant, which can take time to get; at a minimum, therefore, send the appropriate phone company a preservation letter. In the United States, this will require that they preserve this information for litigation at a later date.

Print out any email correspondence between the stalker and the victim. Make sure to print the expanded header that includes the Internet Protocol (IP) address information. Print out screen shots of any communications posted on social media sites such as Facebook, MySpace, or Twitter. Instruct the victim to preserve and save all evidence until it can be documented, recorded, and collected for use in the prosecution.

THE VICTIM INTERVIEW

The victim interview serves several purposes. First, it allows you to gather essential information. Second, it allows you to interact first hand with the victim in order to assess the victim's credibility. Third, it provides the opportunity to obtain information that is helpful in assessing the level of threat. This is important for safety planning with the victim as well as to assist in determining the appropriate settlement, sentence, and postrelease conditions to seek from the court. Finally, it provides an opportunity to discuss safety strategies with the victim. If available, a victim advocate trained in stalking and threat assessment can play a key role in the victim interview and safety planning process. Stalking victim handbooks can be helpful in providing important resources and safety information to the victim. However, if the handbook contains information regarding the elements of a stalking case, use caution in giving it to a victim whose credibility is suspect. The last thing you want to do is taint the integrity of the investigation or prosecution by providing the victim with the information he or she needs to fabricate a claim of stalking. The Stalking Resource Center is a good place to locate helpful materials on stalking. They can be located on the Internet at www.victimsofcrime.org/our-programs/stalking-resource-center.

Do not minimize the gravity of the situation in an attempt to make the victim feel better. The victim plays the most important role in his or her safety, and it is important for the victim to realistically appreciate the risks. Each case is unique. The tactics employed by the stalker and the risk to the victim cannot be generalized. Consider having the victim sign an advisal outlining some of these risks.

It is important to remember that restraining or protective orders can be very good tools for law enforcement in assessing risk. In some cases, restraining orders do work and compliance with such an order is very instructive in creating a threat management plan. However, always consider that in some cases restraining orders can escalate the level of violence and actually place the victim at greater risk of harm. A victim should never be told to get a restraining order. Instead, the process as well as the pros and cons of obtaining a restraining order should be discussed or provided to the victim. The victim should be advised that it is ultimately his or her choice whether to get a restraining order; if he or she does get one, a safety plan should be in place for when the stalker is served. These advisals not only assist the victim in making an educated decision, but also could protect you from civil liability if the restraining order causes the violence to escalate.

Some suggested questions for the victim interview are as follows:

1. Obtain background information regarding the parties and the relationship.
2. When did the harassment begin? Obtain dates, locations, and descriptions of each incident. It is usually easiest to go chronologically. Inquire if any other reports have been made to law enforcement; if so, obtain the report numbers.
3. Identify additional witnesses. Was anyone else present during any of the incidents? This can provide helpful corroboration.
4. Has the victim obtained or attempted to obtain a restraining/protective order? If not, it is important to find out why. Was it because the victim was afraid the restraining order would escalate the risk of violence? Or was it because the victim did not want to invest the time necessary to obtain one? Either answer is critical in assessing the level of fear felt by the victim.
5. Does the stalker:
   a. Have access to or a fascination with weapons?
   b. Have a history of violence?
   c. Have a history of restraining order violations?
6. Has the stalker been diagnosed with or display signs of:
   a. Mental illness?
   b. Substance abuse?
   c. Alcoholism?
7. Has the stalker made any threats, either verbal, written, electronically, or implied?
   a. What does the threat mean to the victim? This is especially important when the threat is implied or veiled. You need to be able to put the threat into the context of the victim/stalker relationship, whatever that relationship or lack of relationship may be.
   b. What is the victim afraid the suspect will do?
   c. Does the victim believe the stalker is capable of carrying out the threat? Why?

8. Has the victim made any changes to his or her life or routine as a result of the stalker's conduct? This is a good indication of the victim's level of fear.
9. When was the last time the victim had voluntary contact with the stalker? Why was the contact made? This is relevant to the victim's level of fear and credibility. Having regular voluntary contact with the stalker can be inconsistent with being afraid. If contact is being made, it is important to ask the victim why he or she is having contact. There may be a reasonable explanation.
10. Does the victim have any physical evidence? (For example, cards, gifts, emails, voicemails, photographs, text messages, etc.) If so, collect it.

These questions give you a good place to start to make a decision whether charges can be filed, as well as a beginning point to assess the risk and create a management plan. In this arena, your management plan will include gathering information to determine the appropriate bail to request, settlement strategies, sentencing arguments, and post-release conditions.

If the stalking has been long-term with a large number of incidents, it can be difficult for a victim to be an effective historian. Sometimes it can be helpful to have the victim create a chronology or outline of all of the incidents. Using a calendar can also help the victim to put the events in order and context.

CHARGING

Charging decisions are going to be based on your jurisdiction's laws and statutes; however, there are a few considerations that cross jurisdictional lines. Many times the stalking behavior can be broken down into separate and distinct violations of the criminal codes. The stalking charge then encompasses the entire course of conduct. Most jurisdictions prohibit punishing an individual multiple times for the same conduct. In other words, if an individual is sentenced for stalking, because the stalking comprises the individual crimes, that individual can be punished only for the stalking. However, there is the potential that when sentenced for each separate crime, the stalker's exposure will increase significantly. Consider whether it will be appropriate to seek the most amount of jail time possible and make your charging decisions accordingly.

Prosecutors are required to abide by a higher ethical standard than any other type of lawyer. This is critical to any legitimate criminal justice system because we have the power, almost with the stroke of a pen, to alter someone's life forever by taking away his or her liberty. Charges cannot and should not be filed if it is not believed that the charges can be proven beyond a reasonable doubt. The presence of proof beyond a reasonable doubt, however, does not always result in a conviction by a jury of 12 members of the community. Any trial lawyer knows there are many uncontrollable variables in a trial and that the outcome is never guaranteed. Stalking cases are not the venue for taking any chances. An acquittal places the victim at greater risk. He or she has been forced to engage with his or her stalker by testifying in court. This can agitate the stalker and escalate the level of risk. Further, an acquittal empowers the stalker by failing to hold him or her accountable. Last, most stalkers are intelligent, and even after a conviction their experience in the criminal justice system will have taught them how to better circumvent the law and continue to stalk.

BAIL AND PRETRIAL RELEASE HEARINGS

As a general practice, pretrial release should be avoided. The psychological wounds caused by the stalker stripping away the victim's sense of physical and emotional security can be more damaging than the scars left from a physical assault. Keeping the stalker in custody not only assists in assuring the victim's safety but also helps to begin to rebuild the victim's sense of security.

The bail schedule in San Diego provides for a minimum bail of $100,000 at the time of booking. At the time of arraignment, a prosecutor educated in violence risk assessment can make the appropriate arguments for the judge to set the bail even higher. It is not unusual for a judge to grant the prosecutor's request for bail of $1 million or higher. Defense attorneys often argue that bail in these amounts is similar to what is often set in homicide cases. The prosecutor needs to illustrate to the judge that our goal is to prevent the homicide and that, based on the risk factors present, the victim's safety demands that the stalker remain incarcerated.

Finally, always request a protective order be issued by the judge even if the victim already has another protective order. Judges do not take it lightly when defendants violate orders they issue in open court, so if the defendant violates the no contact order, it will be easier to hold him or her accountable. Additionally, proof that the defendant was served with and knew of the no contact order will be contained right in the court records of your case. Make sure that the victim has a copy of the order and the court minutes showing that the defendant was present when the order was issued. This will make it easier for the victim to get law enforcement to take action should the defendant violate the order.

RELOCATION

Temporary relocation, permanent relocation, or a combination of both may be necessary in certain cases. Temporary relocation might be appropriate in cases where the stalker is not yet in custody. Relocation may also be necessary even when the stalker is in custody if there are other individuals who can attack the victim on behalf of the stalker. Permanent relocation can be necessary in high-risk cases. In order for permanent relocation to be effective, there must be total cooperation, participation, and buy-in from the victim. Permanent relocation requires the victim to keep her new location hidden from friends and family. Steps must be taken to keep the victim's name and address out of databases, including the Department of Motor Vehicles, voter registration, and utility billing. It may require name and social security changes. Most states have programs and provisions in place for these situations. This is the most drastic step that can be taken to protect the victim, but it can be essential.

Sometimes a combination of temporary and permanent relocation must be used. In these cases, the victim will be placed in a temporary safe house or safe location until more permanent relocation can be facilitated.

CASE EXAMPLE

This defendant had prior convictions for robbery and burglary. The victim had been married to the defendant for seven years and they had a five-year old daughter. They were recently divorced. The defendant was angered when he learned that the victim had begun to date a coworker from the department store where she worked. The defendant called her, racked and fired a gun, and told her he had come close to killing her and her new boyfriend. Next he went to her workplace to confront her new boyfriend. Fortunately this man was not working at the time; however, store surveillance video showed the defendant walking through the store with a gun. Fearing that he would proceed to the victim's home next, a patrol officer was parked down the street from the victim's home. He observed the defendant drive toward the victim's house and made a traffic stop. The gun was found under the hood of the car. When interviewed, the defendant told officers that it did not matter how long they locked him up, he would kill his ex-wife when he got out of prison. He went on to explain that he would kill the victim in Mexico because his brothers were police officers in Tijuana and he would be able to get away with the murder. A few days prior to the preliminary hearing, the defendant's two brothers went to the victim's home, but she was not there.

In this particular case, the threat was immediate and the risk level was high. We quickly relocated the victim and her children to a temporary location until a more permanent relocation could be arranged. At a later date, she was completely relocated to a different city in a different state. In some cases, name and social security number changes are necessary. This is the only path to safety in such cases.

CASE SETTLEMENT

Almost all jurisdictions provide an opportunity or forum for settlement prior to trial. High-level stalking cases often necessitate an aggressive no-deals approach where the goal should be to lock the offender up for as long as possible. However, there is a need to carefully balance some important considerations. How long will the offender actually serve in custody? Based on the facts of your case and the criminal history of the offender, what sentence is a judge likely to impose? How long will post-release (i.e., probation or parole) supervision last? How stringent will post-release monitoring be? If the length of time in custody or the post-release supervision is not significant, consider the benefits of structuring a plea agreement at the early stages of the proceedings that provides for less than the maximum penalties, but accomplishes the goal of creating the safest environment possible under all circumstances. This approach is most successful before the victim testifies against the stalker.

In California, stalking can be charged as a felony or a misdemeanor and the elements are the same regardless of how it is charged. In appropriate cases, consider structuring a plea agreement where the defendant pleads guilty to a felony but has the opportunity to have the conviction reduced to a misdemeanor after a set period of time if he or she successfully completes probation conditions and has no probation violations. Often this provides an adequate incentive for the defendant to comply with probation and thus keep the victim safe.

Another tactic that has been successful is banishment. In California, courts have found that banishment—or prohibiting a defendant from being in a defined area, town or city—can be a legitimate condition of probation (*People v. Watkins* [1987] 193 Cal.App.3d 1686). Too broad a restricted area would likely be found to be unconstitutional; however, consider including such a restriction as part of the plea bargain. We have used this tool successfully to keep a stalker from entering the state of California, and in another case from entering the state of Nevada during their probationary period. If the stalker agrees to the condition as part of the plea bargain, he or she would have difficulty challenging the condition at a later date. Creativity can be an essential part of settling these cases in a manner that holds the stalker accountable, but also provides for the victim's long-term safety.

PRELIMINARY/ PROBABLE CAUSE HEARING

California provides for hearsay to be admitted at the probable cause hearing. In other words, a qualified law enforcement officer may testify to the victim's statement to that officer. The advantage is that the victim does not have to appear face to face with his or her stalker. This minimizes the trauma to the victim and does not give the stalker the opportunity to engage with or further the attachment to the victim.

When a victim gives multiple statements, it is not uncommon for minor inconsistencies to appear. These can be a result of the types of questions being asked, the person asking the questions, the way the questions are being asked, or the person preparing the report. It is normal for different parts of the experience to be foremost in the victim's mind at different times. The inconsistencies do not mean that the victim is lying. However, the more statements that exist, the more the defense can try to create confusion with minor inconsistencies.

From the prosecution's standpoint, the disadvantage of having a law enforcement officer testify to the victim's hearsay statements is the loss of the ability to see how the victim will testify or hold up under cross-examination—and, more importantly—the testimony will not be usable in later hearings if the victim becomes unavailable.

TRIAL

Trial tactics are unique to each jurisdiction and personal to individual prosecutors. However, there are a few issues that are worth noting.

Pro per Defendants

Pro per defendants, or defendants who choose to represent themselves, are very common in stalking cases. Despite how unfair and repulsive it may seem to allow a defendant to personally interact and cross-examine a stalking victim, in the United States a defendant has the constitutional right to represent himself or herself. When this occurs, if there was originally a defense attorney representing the defendant, you should immediately ask the judge to order the defense attorney not to provide any discovery directly to the defendant. You must prepare a complete new set of discovery, making sure that facts such as the victim's and witnesses' personal information (e.g., addresses, phone numbers, birth dates, social security numbers, and driver's license information) are properly removed.

Next, it is important to file *in limine* motions with the court to establish the ground rules of the defendant's conduct. Prior to any testimony, the court should establish where the defendant is allowed to walk and stand in questioning witnesses and addressing the jury. Additionally, if the defendant testifies, will it be in question-and-answer format or will he or she be allowed to testify in a narrative? This is important because it is much harder to object and keep improper evidence out if a defendant is allowed to testify in narrative form. Consider also informing the jury in *voir dire* that the defendant is exercising his constitutional right to act as his own attorney, this is his absolute right and his choice, and they should not have sympathy for him because he has no formal legal training. Last, prepare your victim and witnesses for the fact the defendant will be asking them questions. Remember, the court may revoke a defendant's *pro per* rights if the privilege is abused.

Evidence of Prior Crimes

It is a fundamental principle in criminal law that a defendant shall be convicted of his current offense, not based on his prior offenses. However, people generally act according to their nature, instinct, and wiring. Courts have found that perpetrators of some categories of crimes, including domestic violence, are essentially wired to commit domestic violence. Therefore the fact they have committed domestic violence in the past is relevant and compelling evidence that they are not being falsely accused in the present case. In these situations, the courts in fact allow you to use propensity evidence. This evidence can be very powerful and critical to gaining a conviction. However, use caution and be sensitive to the potential risk that a prior victim of the defendant's may be facing if brought to court and forced to re-engage with the defendant, as well as the trauma that may arise from reliving the abuse.

Presenting and Arguing the Stalking Case

Stalking is often a case of psychological trauma. Unlike most cases we prosecute, stalking cases often lack a tangible loss or physical injury that the jury can see. It is up to the prosecutor to paint the picture of the fear and agony the victim has experienced as a result of the stalker's behavior. What is it like to live your life looking over your shoulder, peering around corners, locking every door, closing all the blinds, and jumping at every noise? How exhausting is it to alter routines and routes, change phone numbers or email accounts, and guard details of your activities, plans, and whereabouts?

In one case, a victim was so terrified that she and her family installed cameras on her house and boarded up all the windows. A picture of the house boarded up provided the jury with tangible evidence of the fear the victim and her family lived with on a daily basis. Sometimes the stalking behavior has gone on for months or years. Consider outlining the incidents on a calendar to illustrate the number and frequency of the stalking incidents and give the jury a chronological perspective of the stalking. This also can assist the victim in sequencing the conduct when there are multiple acts that occurred over a long period of time.

Stalking cases often have strange dynamics. In many instances the stalker has a new girlfriend or love interest; however, he is still stalking his ex-intimate partner. At trial, he tries to argue that it was not him; or the victim is lying because he has moved on to another woman. What is evident in these cases is that the stalking behavior often has nothing to do with getting the ex-partner back. Rather, it is about exerting power and control over the ex, because as long as the ex is afraid for her safety, it is difficult for her to truly move on to someone else. As a prosecutor, you must be able to explain this dynamic to the jury.

SENTENCING AND POST SENTENCING ISSUES

A working knowledge and understanding of violence risk/threat assessment is essential at the sentencing stage in order to obtain the appropriate punishment. If a prosecutor asks for the maximum punishment in every case, he or she will lose credibility in the eyes of the court. It is important to understand violence risk assessment in order to articulate specific factors that support maximum punishment in the appropriate case. You must be able to separate the truly dangerous individual from those who can be successfully managed in the community.

The following conditions have been used to manage stalking offenders on probation:

1. Imposing the longest probationary term under the law. In California, the probationary term is usually three years. However, it may be as long as five years. Imposing a five-year probationary term gives us a better opportunity to monitor, as well as to impose restrictions and immediate custodial sanctions for violations.

2. Request a restraining order or protective order for the longest period allowed under the law. Some jurisdictions allow for permanent restraining orders, others for a set period of time. In California, stalkers can be served with a 10-year protective order as a sentencing condition.

3. Use GPS monitoring whenever possible. Technology is advancing at lightning speed. There are many types of GPS monitoring devices that can be used to make sure that the defendant is complying with protective orders and exclusion zones. However, the victim should be advised not to have a false sense of security when GPS devices are used. Often jurisdictions do not have the resources to monitor defendants 24 hours a day, so the usefulness of these devices is limited to proving violations of protective orders at a later date. There are GPS devices available now where the defendant/offender wears

the device and the victim has another device, similar to a cell phone, that alerts the victim if the offender enters an exclusion zone; then the device is cut off or allowed to lose its charge. The victim should be advised that technology is not foolproof.

A word on victim impact statements and restitution: Most jurisdictions afford the victim the opportunity to address the court at sentencing to deliver a victim impact statement. The delivery of such a statement can be empowering and part of the healing process for the victim, but it is not without risk. The mere fact that the victim has shown up for the sentencing can be interpreted by the defendant as a sign that the victim cares about him or her. It can also enrage the defendant if the defendant blames the victim for his or her situation. It can be one more event that ties the victim to the defendant in the defendant's mind. The same applies to any potential restitution the defendant is ordered to pay to the victim. The victim should be made aware of the options, along with the advantages and potential disadvantages, in order to make an informed decision.

The determination to sentence a stalker to prison or probation is often a delicate balancing act. While prison sentences result in longer incarceration, sometimes the supervision upon release is not as structured as it would be with probation. In some jurisdictions, offender management is stricter on a local level. Again, a good understanding of violence risk/threat assessment is critical in making this determination.

Building good working relationships across disciplines is paramount in effectively prosecuting and managing stalking cases. When a stalker is sent to prison, a good relationship with parole is the only way to have any effect on the defendant's supervision on release from prison. In one particular high-risk case, the defendant was sent to prison for the maximum term of three years and eight months despite a minimal criminal record. While in prison, the defendant sent letters to the judge proclaiming his love for the victim and stating that she and their children would be with him for eternity. In sending the letter to the judge, he was not violating the protective order because he was not contacting the victim. While his statements were certainly alarming, there was nothing about them that was actionable as a credible threat. His words were vague and ambiguous enough that no new charges could be filed. When it came time for his release, there was a high level of concern for the victim's and her children's safety. By contacting the assigned parole officer directly prior to defendant's release, parole was alerted to the high level of threat, and we were able to convince parole to monitor the defendant with a GPS device. We also had an arrest warrant ready to be entered immediately should defendant violate any parole condition. The defendant was strictly supervised for the entire period of parole and had no parole violations. When his parole period expired, he immediately violated the 10-year protective order that had been issued at sentencing and began to stalk the victim as well as the family law attorney handling her divorce. Because the case had been vertically prosecuted and there was a good working relationship with the local law enforcement agency where the victim lived, there was no delay in getting up to speed with the case history or the seriousness of the case. The defendant was quickly rearrested and prosecuted again and ultimately sent to prison—this time for a much longer period. This is also a good example of the life span that some of these cases have. There is no doubt that this defendant will continue to pose a risk to the victim and her children unless he remains confined to prison.

CIVIL SUITS

Some victims are not satisfied with the outcome of the criminal stalking case and pursue their stalker in civil lawsuits for actual damages and/or intentional infliction of emotional distress. Recently, this seems to be an avenue that some victim advocacy groups have been recommending. This can be a risky proposition and one that the victim should carefully consider before embarking on it. While it may help a victim to feel she has held the offender accountable, she is also continuing the engagement process through court hearings, which—in conjunction with any judgment for monetary damages—will provide the stalker with an official tie that binds the two, sometimes forever.

CIVIL LIABILITY

For the most part, a prosecutor receives absolute immunity and is protected from civil liability while acting within his or her official capacity. A prosecutor is acting in this official capacity when his or her conduct is an integral part of the judicial process or intimately associated with the judicial phase of the criminal process (*Falls v. Superior Court [Samaniego]*

[1996] 42 Cal.App.4th 1031, 1043-4). The following circumstances may create civil liability for prosecutors:

a. Failure to honor express or implied promises to warn or promises to protect. It is important to be very careful during your communications with victims and witnesses not to make any statements that can be perceived as a promise to protect or keep safe.

b. Making statements that minimize the actual danger to a victim or witness who detrimentally relies on the statements (*M.B v. City of San Diego* [1991] 233 Cal. App.3d 699).

c. Placing an unprotected victim or witness near someone who poses a foreseeable threat to the victim or witness. If the defendant is out of custody pending trial, or if there are concerns the defendant may have a third party act on his behalf, make appropriate arrangements for the victim's safety during any court hearings. If the victim is scheduled to testify, the defendant may be aware of what time she will be arriving at the courthouse. Consider providing a safe location for her to enter the building and wait until it is time for her to testify. It may be necessary and appropriate to have an armed investigator or police officer escort her to and from the courtroom.

d. Asking a citizen to perform an official function that involves a foreseeable risk of danger (*Walker v. County of Los Angeles* (1987) 192 Cal.App.3d 1393). In some stalking cases, obtaining the corroboration necessary to file charges can be difficult. Sometimes the only way to obtain such corroboration is with the assistance of the victim, who will try to provide photographs, recordings, or videotapes of incidents. When this occurs, it must be made clear to the victim that such activity is potentially dangerous, that he or she is under no obligation to assist, and that this should be done only from a position of safety and if the stalker is unaware of the victim's efforts to document the incident.

The prosecution of stalking cases requires passion and tireless dedication. There is often no margin for error. Your decisions truly can mean the difference between life and death. If you are not willing to rise to the challenge and accept the tremendous responsibility these cases impose, you should not prosecute these cases. At the end of the day, you may not collect any prosecutor-of-the-year awards; those are usually reserved for high-profile homicide prosecutions. However, you can rest assured in the knowledge that what you have done truly made a difference in someone's life. A good prosecutor can prosecute a murder, but a great prosecutor prevents a murder from ever occurring in the first place.

KEY POINTS

- The primary focus should always be the victim's short- and long-term safety.
- Vertical prosecution and dedicated stalking units/teams are key to the successful prosecution of stalking cases.

- It is important to build bridges across disciplines relevant to stalking cases, including but not limited to law enforcement, probation/parole officers, family law attorneys, psychologists/psychiatrists.
- Educate yourself in the area of violence risk/threat assessment and management. An organization such as the Association of Threat Assessment Professionals is a great place to start (www.atapworldwide.org).
- Be creative in your approach to the prosecution of stalking cases and be tenacious in your management of them.
- Look after your own safety. It is not uncommon for stalkers to redirect their focus, and the prosecutor makes an easy target.

REFERENCES

Baum, K., Catalano, S., Rand, M., & Rose, K. (2009). *Stalking victimization in the United States.* Washington, DC: Bureau of Justice Statistics. U.S. Department of Justice. NCJ 224527.

24

Building up a Threat Assessment Process at Universities

Experiences from Europe

JENS HOFFMANN AND KATHERINE TIMMEL ZAMBONI

Threat assessment in general and especially in a campus setting is a rather new field in Europe. For many decades if not centuries, the academic self-image was one of intellectual and moral superiority. Threats and violence seemed to belong to a world outside academia. Not too long ago, the idea of looking for potentially dangerous behavior within the university community would have been considered absurd in most European countries. The cases of aggression that must have been occurring all the while probably went unnoticed. There was simply no concept of physical violence in a university setting.

Without a doubt, the shooting at Virginia Tech in 2007 in the United States, where 33 people were killed and 17 injured, had a remarkable impact not only in the US but also internationally. Even in Europe, universities started to realize that lethal attacks, or even worse, mass killings might happen on their premises. In some places, working groups were established with the mission of creating concepts of how to deal with the problem of targeted violence in a campus setting. More often than not, the focus was too much on the most extreme forms of violence, namely mass murder cases, which led to a feeling of helplessness. Thus prevention seemed to be unachievable, especially as the concept of threat assessment and management (TAM) was largely alien at European universities at the time. Consequently the main activities of the working groups were frequently restricted to emergency planning in case a shooting should occur. This mirrored a dynamic that had already been reported at American campuses (Dietz, 2007). Apart from that, in some places there were discussions on whether to adopt general violence prevention approaches in a campus setting under the misconception that this was also the appropriate procedure to prevent rampage killings.

Another source of insecurity, especially in the German-speaking countries in Europe, was the fact that a number of shootings had occurred in secondary schools. Between November 1999 and February 2010, a total of 42 people died as a result of targeted violence in such schools (Hoffmann & Roshdi, 2013). Therefore, Germany is ranked second worldwide after the United States for the total number of school shooting incidents. The fear arose that such cases might ignite similar forms of targeted violence in universities. This may be the reason why, to the authors' knowledge, so far most of the TAM teams in Europe are located in the German-speaking countries of Switzerland and Germany.

Against the background of the new fear of targeted violence in a university setting since 2007, the two authors of this chapter were involved in setting up a number of TAM projects in academia in Germany and Switzerland. In this chapter, we describe our ideas, thoughts, and conclusions while referring to our work experiences in the academic field; we hope that some of this may be helpful to others who are launching a TAM program in a university setting. Of course, these concepts did not come out of the blue but were built on previous work by threat assessment experts in the United States (see also Deisinger et al.,

2008; Deisinger, Randazzo, & Nolan, Chapter 7, this volume).

At the same time, there are some notable differences between the organizational structures of European and US universities and their cultural embedding. First, campus law enforcement is by no means a rarity in the United States (Mohandie, Chapter 8, this volume), unlike in Europe, where a police presence at universities is practically unheard of. Another crucial difference is the gun culture. In contrast to the United States, in most European countries it is forbidden to carry a firearm, and usually the possession of guns is clearly restricted. Of course, this probably influences the number of firearm incidents that occur in educational settings. Such an effect was reflected in a study on international rampage killings at universities where a student or former student was the attacker (Rau et al., 2013). Of the 12 incidents that were identified in the decade from 2002 to 2012, the majority (58%) occurred in the United States, with 51 total fatalities; 32 of the latter were victims of the mass murder at Virginia Tech. During the same period, four incidents took place in Europe (33%), with 16 people killed. Thirteen of the latter were murdered in a single incident in the Azerbaijan.

THE STARTING POINT— EXPLAINING THE NEED FOR A THREAT ASSESSMENT PROCESS AT A UNIVERSITY

There are two elements that very often prompt a university to set up a TAM process. First, there is public attention surrounding a lethal incident that occurred at a university, especially when many people were murdered and the media coverage was extensive. Second, if the university was confronted with a threat or threatening behavior, it may not have known how to handle it properly and experienced the frustration that no outside organization, such as the police, would solve the problem for them. If only one of these two elements exists, then often only a formal and superficial violence prevention program is launched, and this rarely works properly. Another difficulty in Europe is that the concepts of targeted violence and threat assessment are not well known.

Here is an example of a successful starting point for a TAM team at a university where, in the aftermath of Virginia Tech, a working group for violence prevention was founded before a threatening case became the center of attention:

Just before the summer, an actual case happened—a former employee threatening former colleagues—that set the tone. Due to its actuality and the threats directed at members of the institution, the HSSE Unit (Health, Safety, Security and Environment) was involved. At a meeting, the discussion revealed that the threats had already been going on for a couple of years with varying degrees of severity, and a variety of remedial actions had been taken, unfortunately with no lasting effect. The number of threats against a couple of employees had increased, and there was a great fear that the former employee might show up on campus. It was obvious that all the heads expected support and advice from the HSSE Unit.

This was how a professional TAM team came to be established at this university. Presenting case studies proved to be very helpful in convincing the administration at that institution of the need for TAM. This advances the finding that acts of targeted violence are usually preceded by warning behavior, which can be potentially detected in a campus setting. We once gave a presentation about warning behavior at a university where a homicide had recently occurred. The audience became increasingly shocked as some of the participants began to talk about their previous worrying and frightening experiences with the offender, who was a student at their school. For the first time ever, because a number of different stories were now brought together, they saw a pattern of warning behavior that had been apparent before the attack, yet went unnoticed. As no TAM team was in operation at the time, there was no center where information from the different sources could have been combined to focus on a growing danger.

The case studies used to introduce the concept of threat assessment should be not only from the United States; this could create the impression that targeted violence in higher educational institutions is mainly a problem in North America and not in Europe. It is therefore important to do some research on recent cases in geographic and cultural proximity to the university in question, as this can raise awareness of the problem. For instance, in 2010, there was a case in France in the town of Perpignan where a mentally ill student, after behaving erratically for some time, stabbed an employee and wounded three others. And in the German town of Leipzig, in 2011, a female student was murdered with a hammer in her dormitory. The offender was a former student who had stalked her for two years.

As homicides at European universities are still very rare, the question that needs to be answered in discussing the issue with administration is why a university should set up a TAM process and how will it benefit. The answer is that there is a base rate for threats, stalking and violence in every community. The community at a university is very young, diverse, multicultural, and therefore a good "victim pool" (Meloy, 1987)—and most individuals who commit acts of violence are young males. What the administration needs to understand is that universities have a huge influence on the future paths of young lives, especially for those foreign students who come from distant countries and whose parents have high expectations for them. Failure to succeed in their academic careers then leads to frustration, humiliation, and desperation. If a university has a TAM program, it might be seen as an essential component and a sign of quality. Higher educational institutions may even promote TAM actively as a quality standard to highlight that their university is a safe place to stay and study, and therefore an institution that promotes academic freedom.

All too often, members of the administration have no idea how frequently threatening and other forms of problematic behavior occur at their universities. Anonymous online surveys can be very helpful in shedding some light on this issue. The results often convince the administration to support a TAM process. An anonymous survey at a German university, for instance, revealed that 19% of the respondents had been confronted directly or indirectly with threatening or problematic behavior (Hoffmann & Blass, 2012). The most frequent problems were cases of stalking (23%), suicide threats (22%), and threats of violence (18%).

SETTING UP
A TAM TEAM

Before initiating the TAM process, it is important to decide who should be part of the team. This is one of the most crucial decisions in the process, since the abilities, personal skills, and commitment of the team members will define the acceptance of the team and the whole threat management process. Members of such a multidisciplinary team should be representatives of administrative units which, based on their authority and competence, are able to handle

and manage future cases. Members of the core team should typically come from departments such as Safety and Security, Human Resources, psychological counseling services, legal services, and Student Affairs (see also Deisinger et al., 2008; Deisinger, Randazzo & Nolan, Chapter 7, this volume; Van Brunt, 2012).

It can be useful to distinguish between a core team and an extended team at an organizational level. The core team displays a greater continuity in collaborating on cases. It is responsible for establishing and constantly refining the TAM process and operations. Besides ad hoc case meetings, additional regular core-team sessions are also important to discuss fundamental topics. Members of the extended team are not involved as closely; they are called in for specific tasks. Representatives of the communications department or press office are typical examples of this. Here too, personal continuity proves effective in enabling the members of the extended team to have a basic grasp of threat assessment.

Although the TAM process requires direct support from the university's top-level administration, it can be a problem to include too many high-ranking people in the core TAM team. Their schedules are often very tight, so they lack the time for team meetings and casework. It may also be wise to avoid including in-house academic experts from the research departments on the core team, since they are often able to offer extensive knowledge on theoretical aspects of violence but may never have been actively involved in casework. Better candidates are members of the faculty or other university professionals with real-life case experience, such as clinical psychologists who are also actively practicing. The core team needs training from experienced threat assessment experts, which is not always easy to obtain in Europe. Sometimes a university tries to set up a TAM process by instructing the designated case managers to learn how to deal with casework purely from books or Internet research. Such an approach is doomed to fail.

ADDITIONAL
ORGANIZATIONAL
ASPECTS TO CONSIDER
IN A UNIVERSITY
ENVIRONMENT

The complex, non-hierarchical structures of a university, as well as attitudes of autonomy and independence, make any effort to comply with a program or set of measures more complicated. This often leads to inconsistent handling of difficult individuals.

Higher educational institutions differ from private sector companies in their process and culture. A university can be modeled as an ambidextrous organization (Tahar, Niemeyer, & Boutellier, 2011), a versatile organization that is able to blend two seemingly contradictory goals: efficiency as well as creativity and freedom. The administrative parts of the organization focus on efficiency, whereas the science and research units focus on creativity and freedom. They have different decision processes that lead to different reactions in the implementation of new concepts. This necessitates two types of approach, and the ability of the team members to adapt to the needs of the administrative and technical staff—as well as academia—without compromising the goal of threat management. The team is confronted by two predominant organizational logics: more extensive discussions explaining the reason for a specific measure and action among faculty on the one hand; and, on the other, strict adherence to management decisions in the administrative part of the organization.

OUTLINING A MISSION STATEMENT

It would be a mistake for a campus TAM team to focus solely on cases that could result in severe or lethal violence. As described in the research above, higher educational institutions are often confronted by cases of stalking or threats that may, for the most part, not be high-risk violence cases but are nevertheless incredibly frightening and inflict psychological damage on the victim. This is why campus threat assessment deals not only with the prevention of physical violence, but also, and much more often, with protection from it. Promoting a clearly worded statement to be disseminated within the university community is therefore a helpful step in the establishment of a TAM process. Here is an example from a German university (Technical University of Darmstadt, 2013):

Show courage! The Technical University of Darmstadt should be a safe place for everyone. The university has a policy of zero tolerance for violence! If you observe one of the following or any other threatening behavior at the university or hear about it from a reliable source, inform the threat management team immediately. Also

do so if you hear of any suicide threats from a member of the university.

- Any form of physical violence
- Any threat of violence, verbally or in writing, over the telephone or electronically
- Bringing or showing weapons
- Extreme expression of violent fantasies
- Sexual assaults
- Stalking

It is the duty and responsibility of every individual in the university to protect all members of the university from violence and threats.

Involving media relations in the process from the outset is also very helpful in creating awareness of TAM within the campus community. For example, the Swiss Federal Institute of Technology Zurich (2013) has included a TAM program in an existing campaign entitled "Respect." The campaign covers such unwelcome behaviors as sexual harassment, bullying, discrimination, and threats. It informs the members of the university that "if you feel that your personal integrity has been infringed upon, because someone is threatening you or even using violence, you can find help here," and it also provides a link to the TAM team and their contact data.

CREATING AWARENESS

Even if staff or students at universities recognize strange or threatening behavior, they often do not know whom to call (McElhaney, 2004). One of the core elements is a clear message to all members of the university as to how the chain of communication works. This is also the most difficult part of the process in a university environment, as the turnover is extremely high, not only because of new members joining the university or others leaving it, but also because functions in the academic field and the administration change from time to time. In addition, cultural backgrounds and values are often extremely diverse in higher educational settings. One of the key duties of the TAM team is to continuously inform and disseminate information about the team, telling people what to report and, most importantly, whom to contact.

Regular information events at the beginning of an academic year when the new students arrive, or when new professors or other members of staff are appointed, have proven effective. A special home page or reports on the Internet or in the university magazine can also keep the topic of TAM alive within the campus community. Regular courses and talks at the university held by representatives of the TAM team can help to establish contacts; these talks can cover subjects such as the de-escalation of problems or dealing with difficult people. In doing so, new areas that are frequently exposed include behaviors that overstep the mark. For instance, it is apparent that university libraries are regularly confronted by aggressive behavior, whether it is a question of escalating disputes over work stations or teaching material. Because they are often open at night and offer a warm place to stay, libraries tend to attract mentally ill or homeless people, which sometimes causes conflicts.

It is helpful for the TAM team to display creativity in generating awareness. At a German university, for instance, all the napkins at the canteen had the contact data of the TAM team printed on them, along with the pointer that victims of stalking or other threatening behavior could get help from the team. And in Switzerland, members of a TAM team committed themselves to giving several presentations to other university members to raise their awareness.

DESCRIPTION OF THE PROCESS

The development and documentation of a clear process is one of the most important building blocks of TAM; it clarifies the internal interfaces and responsibilities. The process begins with recognizing a potential case and ideally ends with a solution—or the clear assignment of continuous monitoring to a case manager. The assessment of the risk and agreement on a course of action are also key process components. It is important to discuss both at the team meetings: the different perspectives and skills facilitate a comprehensive assessment and consolidated approach. During the discussion, it is also clear that a common understanding needs to be created for the assessment of a risk.

Because a case has different gateway opportunities, the availability of TAM, and the various contacts—such as human resources, safety and security officers, the legal department, and the psychological service—should be pointed out to everyone associated with the university with the intent of raising awareness and enhancing media campaigns. It is also important to stipulate which cases are to be treated by TAM and which by existing functions (e.g., suicidal people or problems of personnel law). First and foremost, the TAM team should deal with threatening behavior and stalking. Suicidal people are mostly looked after by psychologists or other psychosocial contacts.

THE CASE MANAGER

A case manager is appointed for every case and all involved individuals and offices should be informed. All communications, both internally and externally, are to run through the case manager. It is his or her duty to assess and evaluate the incoming information and keep track of the case and any management interventions. Good case managers are good project managers; they can put themselves in various peoples' shoes and incorporate their differing perspectives into the assessment. The risk assessment is never carried out by a case manager alone, but is always discussed with at least one other team member, if not the entire team. The case manager proposes courses of action that are discussed with the team before being suggested to the people affected.

THE INTERNAL NETWORK

Depending on the size and spatial structure of the university, setting up an internal network can be a time-consuming job, but one of enormous importance. At universities, a great many functions are decentralized; therefore it is best to make a list of the different committees, commissions, and functions. All the members of the team can contribute to this by frequently updating the list with new functions and contacts. The department heads, equal opportunity officers, housing agencies, specialist societies, janitors, institute secretaries, social counseling offices, and many more need to be considered. Changes at universities occur constantly; this means that the dissemination of information and raising of awareness must be continuous. The TAM team can do its job only if it receives information about people who could pose a risk. It is critically important to inform as many members of the university as possible that the TAM team exists, and to remind them of this often, however time-consuming it may be.

Moreover, many universities in Europe have a large number of buildings scattered across town instead of a dedicated campus. Recognizing who might be the "eyes and ears" on site is central to establishing a TAM team. Who could spot suspicious and threatening behavior? These groups of people must be supplied with information so that they know what they need to report and when. They have to be able to trust that their information will be treated confidentially, the issue will be dealt with, and they will receive feedback on what happens.

THE EXTERNAL NETWORK

The interaction of the TAM team with external entities such as the police, the psychiatric service, and the judiciary works best if there is a common understanding of TAM and the possibilities available. In any case, the police are an important contact; universities in Europe usually do not have their own campus police. In the event of a threat or domestic disturbance, the police are brought in. It makes sense to foster a regular exchange with the local police, whether in workshops on TAM that the university can organize or within the scope of handling specific cases. Inviting the police to TAM team meetings can also reinforce cooperation and a common understanding. In order to establish a collaboration with the police, it has proven effective for the university administration also to contact the police command directly at the beginning of the process to underscore the importance of TAM. If there are then fixed contact people in both the police force and at the university, this creates an important interface for the TAM process.

Even with the best early warning system in place, however, the TAM team operates under the current law, and some cases will need to be monitored over a long period of time before a final solution can be achieved. The possibilities and boundaries of the legal system are important to know and need to be explained to the people affected by a case. In doing so, it is sometimes helpful for the university lawyers to foster contacts with entities from outside, such as authorities or lawyers serving people who have exhibited threatening behavior directed toward university members.

Psychiatric facilities are especially important for the external network. Frequently, people who exhibit threatening behavior also suffer from mental disorders, and a psychiatric intervention is often helpful to reduce aggression and alleviate the risk of violence. Regrettably, all too often mentally ill people who make threats are not particularly motivated to undergo a course of therapy; sometimes, owing to their mental disorder, they do not see any illness and thus fail to understand why treatment is necessary. The TAM team must sometimes make lengthy efforts to commit the threatening person into psychiatric care, even against his or her will.

In general, a useful strategy in cooperation with external bodies might consist in stabilizing the living conditions of the person making threats, be it finding accommodation for them or facilitating the funding of their final examinations. While simultaneously drawing the line at aggressive behavior, such a strategy reduces the probability of the threatening person ending up with a last-resort attitude, where an act of violence might appear as the only option.

THREAT ASSESSMENT AND MANAGEMENT AS AN ONGOING PROCESS

TAM is an ongoing process that never ends. It is in constant need of refinement. There will always be new ways of expressing threatening behavior. Only recently, for instance, new dynamics of aggressive forms of expression have been observed in the wake of the enormous spread of social media and mobile terminal devices for the Internet (see Scalora, Chapter 13, this volume). This means that procedures and strategies keep changing on a structural level and from case to case.

A willingness to learn and openness to new topics on the part of the core members of the team is a key prerequisite for TAM to continue as a living process. In doing so, TAM also needs to be understood as a discipline in its own right with professional know-how and tools that keep on developing. The members of the TAM team should therefore keep learning and seek contact with TAM peers from other universities or organizations, such as by attending conferences or exchanging information within professional groups like the Association of European Threat Assessment Professionals (AETAP).

One major success factor for a university TAM team, however, is more personal: experience during the setup and operations reveals that at least one or two dedicated people need to be available at the heart of the team; these individuals must invest time and energy to passionately bring the team forward. If this is not the case, the TAM process, in the long run, ossifies into a formal structure that tends to manage cases statically, and team members do not work actively to alleviate risk.

CASE STUDIES

The following two cases should provide an insight into the different forms of threatening behavior at universities. Depending on the case dynamics, different case management strategies will be useful. Universities are marked by very heterogeneous incidents, meaning that the TAM team must keep developing and working out new strategies in tackling these cases.

CASE STUDY 1: "THE ANGRY ACQUAINTANCE FROM THE PAST"

A young scientist had scored a major coup through a research project, which attracted a lot of attention. Television, radio, and newspapers reported on his work. Unfortunately, besides the positive media response, there was also a negative voice. An old acquaintance from his childhood began to send him personal, vitriolic email messages accusing him of having betrayed the common ideals of their youth, seeking only money, and grabbing the limelight. The scientist was taken aback by these accusations. First, he could not understand the harsh criticism in the slightest; second, he had only a superficial recollection of this acquaintance. All the same, he answered the email and tried to appease its author by referring to the good old days and noting in a conciliatory manner that the accusation must be a misunderstanding.

The tone of the subsequent response was even more acrimonious. The old acquaintance began to insult the young scientist openly and announce that he would come to the scientist's house or the university to make it clear to him what a bad person he was. Emails with aggressive or offensive contents began to arrive on an almost daily basis. Moreover, several scientific institutions contacted the young scientist asking him for a statement because they had received anonymous tips about cases of plagiarism in his work. The scientist was given the anonymous accusations to look at and found several identical formulations to those the acquaintance from his childhood had used in the emails.

At this point, the researcher contacted the TAM team at the university, complaining of trouble sleeping and a constant sense of danger. Every day, he was afraid to go home or to the university in case the old acquaintance should be lying in wait for him. Moreover, he feared that the smear campaign claiming that he was a plagiarist could harm his scientific career. Two members of the TAM team gave the initial assessment that a physical attack was not to be expected at that stage. To make him feel safer, they talked to the scientist about what he should do if the acquaintance from his childhood should ambush him. Furthermore, they suggested that he should not reply to any more emails and immediately report any incidents to the TAM team. He was assured that the university would not abandon him in the middle of the conflict.

The TAM team then internally discussed whether there was any merit to the accusations of plagiarism. After an examination of the anonymous allegations, however, this was rejected; there were no indications of any fraud in the discriminatory emails. The scientist's old acquaintance was subsequently sent an official letter, on behalf of the executive board, requesting he stop sending offensive email messages and cease his smear campaign without any solid evidence to back up the fraud accusation. The response was swift: the university should not get involved in private matters, and of course he would continue with his "illuminating" activities.

Meanwhile the TAM team had discovered that the email writer was employed at another university in a junior administrative position. In light of this, he was advised that the management of the university where he worked would be informed about his conduct if his defamatory statements and aggressiveness toward the scientist continued. This did not deter the author either, and he immediately sent a fresh series of malicious emails. The TAM team subsequently arranged for the administration at the writer's university to be contacted and asked for help. This offensive intervention evidently did the trick; there was no further aggression or libel directed at the scientist.

In this case, there were no visible signs of a risk of physical violence. Nonetheless, a university member was subjected to considerable psychological stress through threatening behavior. The case management of the TAM team endeavored to support the scientist with advice and guidance and thus alleviate the psychological stress. As a further strategy, official boundaries were drawn to curb the threatening behavior.

CASE STUDY 2: "THE DELUSIONAL SCIENTIST"

A concerned professor contacted the TAM team looking for help. He said that a female scientist from his group seemed to be confused and was no longer able to work productively. Various members of the institute had received peculiar emails, the research team felt uneasy, and the professor was looking for some advice. The psychologist from the TAM team was appointed as case manager since the team hypothesized that the scientist was suffering from paranoid delusions. In her opinion, the majority of the members of the institute were corrupt and she had to take action. In her emails, she stated that she had a mission to carry out: to protect the world from corrupt scientists who manipulate research data. She claimed that she had obtained this information from a higher authority based near Brighton, UK. The scientist's behavior had already started to change a number of months previously, and for a couple of weeks, some members of the staff at the institute had preferred to work from home so as to avoid coming into the department. They were worried because they had often been confronted by emails from this scientist describing her theories about corruption at the institute. She also called upon them not to sit back but to take a stand and do something about it. Moreover, she was also known to have done sports intensively until a couple of months previously, including karate and other martial arts, and expressed to colleagues an affinity for weapons, especially knives.

According to a close female colleague, these delusions had escalated. The scientist categorized people as good or evil and also tried to find supporters for her cause at the university. Over the previous few months, she had abandoned many friendships, seemed to be neglecting her husband and children, and was concerned only with the topic of corruption. She even posted messages on Facebook, such as, "Their cover is blown, corrupt scientists will suffer."

A meeting was arranged with the scientist. The psychologist from the threat management team and the professor who was her direct superior also took part. The psychologist wanted to assess and classify the behavior of this obviously mentally ill person more effectively in a direct meeting. Just to be on the safe side, a member of the security unit was placed in a neighboring office for the duration of the session. The conversation started calmly, but the scientist was unable to answer concrete questions constructively. As soon as she became mentally stressed, her behavior turned aggressive. It became clear that she had been suffering from psychosis for some time. Systematized delusions with paranoid content were symptomatic. This was also apparent in the emails she sent while at the institute. For safety reasons, not to mention her own well-being, psychiatric treatment needed to be arranged. However, this was primarily a matter for her relatives, since her behavior thus far—and the threats toward herself or others—were insufficient to forcibly commit her to a care facility. Therefore the psychologist contacted the husband and discussed the possibility of convincing her to undergo psychiatric inpatient treatment. The husband also seemed concerned and was very interested in improving his wife's medical condition; the marriage was under a lot of strain and the two children were also suffering. In the following

weeks, a series of events took place that subsequently seemed to be very helpful in finally forcing action: she verbally abused various people and ran through different buildings at the university as if by remote control. She also physically attacked someone in the canteen, who reported the incident to the police, who picked her up at her house. She then underwent a psychiatric examination and was admitted to the psychiatric hospital. The medical treatment and psychotherapy seemed to work. After eight weeks, she was discharged and her condition seemed stable as long as she took medication. She finally left the organization where she had been employed as her contract was due to expire.

An important learning aspect of the case is apparent: within a couple of weeks, a provisionally positive solution had been found that could not have been arranged without the interplay between the internal bodies (e.g., the TAM team) and external bodies such as the scientist's husband, the police, and psychiatric services. The various functionaries—the professor, human resources department, security staff—were able to gather all the relevant information, consolidate it, define the risk posed, and suggest possible strategies. The professor responsible for the scientist was very conscientious and interested in supporting her employee. There was confidence in the work of the TAM team, and the possibilities as well as restrictions in the legal system were known. Consequently all possible courses of action could be discussed realistically, both internally and externally, and safety was again gradually restored in the group.

KEY POINTS

- A key initial step in the introduction of a functioning threat assessment and management system is to convince the university board that such a process is important and useful.
- In doing so, a structure needs to be established gradually and systematically, with an internal and external network that continues to be refined and developed.
- One success factor is an interdisciplinary team that works with intrinsic motivation and has a proactive case understanding.
- It is important to focus not only on the prevention of serious violence but also on easier cases that cause fear and agitation.

REFERENCES

Deisinger, G., Randazzo, M., O'Neill, D., & Savage, J. (2008). *The handbook for campus threat assessment & management teams*. Boston: Applied Risk Management.

Dietz, P. (2007). *Prevention of campus threats and violence*. Paper presented at the Annual Meeting of the National Association of College and University Attorneys, June 29, 2007, San Diego, California. Available at: http://www.taginc.com/wp-content/uploads/2007/06/dietz-prevention-of-campus-threats-violence.pdf

Hoffmann, J., & Blass, N. (2012). Bedrohliches Verhalten in der akademischen Welt. Eine Studie zur Auftretenshäufigkeit von Stalking, Drohungen, Gewalt und anderem Problemverhalten an einer deutschen Universität. *Polizei & Wissenschaft, 2*, 38–44.

Hoffmann, J., & Roshdi, K. (2013). School shootings in Germany: Research, prevention through risk assessment and threat management. In N. Böckler, T. Seeger, P. Sitzer, & W. Heitmeyer (Eds.), *School shootings: International research, case studies, and concepts for prevention* (pp. 363–378). New York: Springer.

McElhaney, M. (2004). *Aggression in the workplace. Preventing and managing high-risk behavior*. Bloomington, IN: AuthorHouse.

Meloy, J. R. (1987). The prediction of violence in outpatient psychotherapy. *American Journal of Psychotherapy, 41*, 38–45.

Rau, T., Fegert, J., Hoffmann, J., & Allroggen, M. (2013). Zielgerichtete Gewalt von Studierenden an Hochschulen. *Das Hochschulwesen, 1–2*, 57–63.

Swiss Federal Institute of Technology Zurich (2013). *Respect Campaign*. Available at: http://www.respekt.ethz.ch/index_EN

Tahar, S., Niemeyer, C., & Boutellier, R. (2011). Transferral of business management concepts to universities as ambidextrous organisations. *Tertiary Education and Management, 4*(17), 289–308.

Technical University of Darmstadt (2013). *Threat management team homepage*. Available at: http://www.intern.tu-darmstadt.de/bedrohungsmanagement/index.de.jsp

Van Brunt, B. (2012). *Ending campus violence: New approaches to prevention*. New York: Routledge.

25

The Problem Behavior Program

Threat Assessment and Management in Community Forensic Mental Health

TROY E. MCEWAN, RACHEL D. MACKENZIE, AND
JENNIFER MCCARTHY

Threat assessment has attracted the concerted attention of forensic mental health clinicians and researchers only in the past two decades. Forensic mental health services have traditionally become involved in cases where offending occurs in the context of a mental illness and have primarily focused on treating the symptoms of the illness rather than dealing with issues of threat or risk. There are many reasons for this that are beyond the scope of this chapter, but a succinct overview is provided by forensic psychiatrist Anthony Maden, for those who are interested (Maden, 2007). In practice, the focus on mental illness and past offending means that mentally ill individuals who have not yet offended but may do so, those for whom mental illness is not the primary risk factor for offending, and those who do not suffer from psychopathology at all have been largely excluded from forensic mental health assessment and treatment. This practice disregards the majority of people who engage in difficult and problematic behaviors that may be associated with increased risk and who could potentially benefit from the expertise of forensic mental health clinicians.

This chapter describes the Problem Behavior Program (PBP) in Melbourne, Australia—a service that expands the scope of the traditional community forensic mental health service beyond the focus on psychopathology to other criminogenic needs. The PBP provides a recognizable referral point for clients of criminal justice and mainstream mental health agencies to access specialist forensic mental health services based on the nature of their *behavior* rather than the presence of mental disorder. Unlike the traditional forensic mental health model, expertise in threat assessment, as well as risk assessment more generally, is a central component of the PBP. Clients of this service are often people whose behavior has prompted concern about the potential for targeted or general violence even in the absence of criminal offending. Providing an avenue for comprehensive and evidence-based assessment, recommendations, and treatment of these difficult and sometimes frightening behaviors is the central purpose of the PBP.

WHAT ARE PROBLEM BEHAVIORS AND HOW ARE THEY RELATED TO THREAT ASSESSMENT?

Threat and risk assessments occur in a wide variety of contexts and in response to a range of perceived threats. Threats may be targeted and explicit but are more often inferred from the individual's other behaviors. Uttered threats, the presence of stalking, a history of violence, or a history of harmful sexual behavior or fire setting are all contexts that provoke concerns about the risk of future similar actions; in such cases a targeted threat assessment or a general risk assessment might be desired. Warren, MacKenzie, Mullen, and Ogloff (2005) have described these types of conduct as "problem behaviors"—actions that intentionally or recklessly cause harm to others and to the perpetrator. While in many cases such conduct is also criminal, the term *problem behavior* encompasses actions that are prosecuted as well as those that never come before a court (Warren et al., 2005). The problem behavior framework that underpins the PBP described in this chapter operates on two levels. In the individual case this framework presents a way of conceptualizing threatening or otherwise risky behaviors so as to make them more understandable and manageable. At the organizational level it is a model of service provision for clients who would otherwise find it difficult, if not impossible, to access interventions to ameliorate the risks associated with their behavior.

Problem behaviors are inherently complicated and involve a broad range of actions perpetrated by a diverse range of people with various motivations under various circumstances (Warren et al., 2005). All carry with them a perceived threat, or risk, and those tasked with assessing or managing that risk can often feel overwhelmed and confused by the complexity of the presentation. When applied to an individual case, the problem behavior framework is really a set of principles and a process of assessment that can be used to make these tasks more manageable. From the outset, such an approach is based on a health professional's perspective with the aim of being able to help the individual effect change in their behavior and circumstances. There is little interest in ascertaining the "truth" about what happened or acting as ersatz police officers or lawyers; rather, the aim of the assessment is to present the individual as a person within a social, psychological, and personal context so as to better understand their behavior (Warren et al., 2005). In doing so, the clinician using the problem behavior framework moves beyond a narrow focus on psychopathology to a wider perspective encompassing the developmental, social, psychological, and contextual roots of their behavior. Of course, the insights gained from this perspective can be of immense use to others involved in managing individuals who engage in problem behaviors, such as correctional and police services (Russell & Darjee, 2012).

The problem behavior framework takes a reductionist approach, assuming that complex human behaviors can be understood as the product of multiple contributory factors. In the broadest sense, individual factors such as personality attributes (attitudes, beliefs, and values), interpersonal and other skills deficits, and, in many cases, psychopathology, interact with the social milieu and context(s) in which the behavior occurs. Such contributory factors may have developed over time and be present throughout the individual's life or appear only in close proximity to the onset of the problem behavior. In undertaking a detailed assessment with an individual (as outlined later in this chapter), the clinician is attempting to elicit evidence of personal and situational factors that may predispose the individual to the behavior, precipitate its onset, and perpetuate it once it has begun. There is also an interest in identifying factors that may protect against the behavior occurring or lead to desistance from the behavior. Consequently the assessment also emphasizes times that the client has been able to refrain from the problem behavior and how he or she feels about engaging in treatment aimed at reducing the behavior. As might be evident, this framework is broader in scope than just a threat assessment. A structured threat or risk assessment often forms one part of the wider assessment of the problem behavior. A judgment of high or moderate risk informs decisions about whether the client should be offered interventions to reduce the problem behavior and the associated risks, and how immediately intrusive those interventions might need to be.

To identify personal and situational factors that might be relevant to the problem behavior it is necessary to have knowledge of the research literature pertaining to offending generally and to each type of problem behavior specifically. For example, being able to apply a problem behavior framework to a stalking situation means being familiar with the literature on psychopathology among stalkers, types of stalking risk, common motivations for stalking and associated attitudes and beliefs, and the types of behavioral and psychological risk factors for stalking that may be present. Any account of a problem behavior must be based on evidence and make reference to research findings to be of use in the subsequent treatment and management of the individual. It is beyond the scope of this chapter to provide a review of the research literature relevant to each type of problem behavior; suffice it to say that such knowledge is a prerequisite of using a problem behavior approach in conducting an individual assessment. This obviously poses problems when clients come from underresearched populations, such as female sexual offenders or Internet child pornography offenders. In these types of cases the same broad approach is taken, but conclusions are made more cautiously with explicit reference to relevant literature underpinning those conclusions where such exists (e.g., Gannon & Cortoni, 2010, in relation to female sexual offenders).

DEVELOPMENT OF THE PROBLEM BEHAVIOR PROGRAM

The PBP is one of a number of programs run by Forensicare, the publicly funded forensic mental health service in the State of Victoria, Australia. Forensicare is a statutory body with a statewide jurisdiction, providing forensic mental health services to a population of approximately 5.5 million people. The PBP is part of Forensicare's Community Forensic Mental Health Service (CFMHS), located in metropolitan Melbourne. While most clients of the service are from Melbourne (a city of just over 4 million people), PBP clients from regional and remote areas sometimes travel as far as 400 kilometers to attend an assessment. When Forensicare was established in 1998, the CFMHS consisted of a Mental Health Program (MHP), which worked with forensic patients released from a secure hospital, and a Psychosexual Treatment Program (PTP), which undertook assessment and treatment of high-risk sex offenders, some of whom required antilibidinal or psychiatric medication. With the advent of the community-based Sex Offenders Program within the State Department of Corrections, a review of the PTP purpose and function was conducted in 2002. This review identified an ongoing need for services for those who engaged in sexually problematic behaviors but were not subject to a legal order; and also identified a critical service gap for individuals presenting with other forms of "problem behavior." The CFMHS had been seeing stalkers and stalking victims since the late 1990s; in 2002, under the leadership of Professor Paul Mullen, specific research-oriented clinics were established to collect data on individuals who threatened or stalked (Warren et al., 2005). These clinics attracted considerable attention and requests for secondary consultations and presentence court reports quickly grew. There was also a clear need for an assessment and treatment pathway for adult deliberate fire setters, for whom no services existed despite periodic public attention due to high profile arson convictions.

In the face of this increasing demand, a structured governance mechanism for the non-sex-offender clients was needed. In January 2003, the Problem Behaviour Clinic (PBC) was established, incorporating the existing psychological and psychiatric assessment and treatment services for threateners and stalkers, and expanding them to fire setters, perpetrators of serious or repeated violence, those suffering from morbid jealousy, and querulous complainants. By 2004, demand for the PBC had increased to such an extent that the decision was made to amalgamate it with the sexual violence-focused PTP into a broader PBP. This decision was based on the premise that the target population of both programs shared certain similarities and included offenders or potential offenders characterized by the following factors: (1) they potentially posed a high risk of harm to the community, (2) their needs could not be met elsewhere, (3) their treatment needs were likely to extend beyond any statutory order, and (4) they showed some sign of willingness to engage in treatment and were likely to benefit from it.

Since 2004 the PBP has accepted an average of approximately 230 referrals per year. Of accepted referrals, 40% of clients have been referred by community-based probation services as a condition of a statutory order. The remaining referral sources include publicly funded adult mental health services (30%), self-referrals (7%), referrals from the private mental health sector (6%), youth mental health services (6%), and a range of other community and legal services (11%). Since the PBP began, 40% of clients have been referred for actual or fantasized violent behavior, 35% for problematic and harmful sexual behavior or fantasies of the same (e.g., child molestation, Internet child pornography, rape, exposure), 25% for stalking (including stalking involving violence or threats), 16% for making threats, 6% for fire setting, and 12% for a variety of other problematic behaviors. As is evident from the percentage figures, many clients present with multiple problem behaviors. The client group is diagnostically complex, with personality, psychotic, mood, and substance use disorders featuring prominently among those referred to the program. A small but significant number of clients do not present with any mental disorder.

Advantages and Challenges of the PBP Service Model

The PBP service model offers a number of advantages to clinical practice. The variety of presenting behaviors, legal status, and mental health diagnoses of clients seen within the PBP allows for the development of expertise in the assessment and treatment of a range of problem behaviors and their psychological, psychiatric, and social determinants. This clinical knowledge has been strengthened and underpinned by collaborations between clinicians and local academics to facilitate research into specific problem behaviors. The PBP service model provides a unique research opportunity as many individuals with similar problem behaviors accumulate in one location, providing a potential research pool that would otherwise be almost impossible to access. As a result, a significant proportion of international research into stalking and threatening originates in Melbourne. Since 2008, this has been aided by the colocation of the PBP and the Centre for Forensic Behavioural Science (a research center cosponsored by Forensicare and Monash University) in the same building. Problem behavior research to date has focused primarily on stalking and threatening; however, current research projects are under way investigating deliberate fire setting, Internet child pornography, sex offender risk assessment, intimate partner violence risk assessment, and the psychological correlates of violence. Work is also proceeding on an evaluation of the PBP examining both client outcomes and stakeholder experiences.

The PBP model also provides advantages when examined from a service delivery perspective. The program meets a critical service gap, seeing individuals who are at risk of engaging in criminal behavior but have not yet done so. Without the PBP, these clients would not be able to access specialist assessment and intervention unless they committed and were prosecuted for an offense. Even then their access to correctional rehabilitative services may be hampered by the presence of mental disorder or by a lack of services specific to their behavior. Acceptance into the PBP is also often a first step for clients toward establishing links with other key services such as mental health, community health, or other social services. By taking a lead clinical role in the management and treatment of high-risk behaviors, the PBP strengthens referral pathways to those services that may have previously been apprehensive about taking on such clients. The PBP's unique model of service delivery; the complex, high-risk behaviors that staff assess and treat; and the program's strong research links have all contributed to its strong national and international reputation.

While the PBP model clearly has a number of strengths, its implementation is not without challenges. Most notably, there is the delicate balance between managing the need for confidentiality in treating potential offenders and managing public interest and public safety. This is addressed in part by orienting the client from the outset of any assessment or treatment to the limits of confidentiality; that is,

that while their interests are paramount, if we believe their actions may place either themselves or others at risk, then action may need to be taken in the form of contacting police or potential victims. An ongoing process of regular threat and risk reassessment informs these types of decisions. Tension may still arise when there is disagreement between the PBP and other services or organizations, such as police or child welfare agencies, as to the nature of the risk posed by an individual; and therefore whether the best interests of the public outweigh the client's right to confidentiality. This can be particularly problematic when a breach of confidentiality has the potential to adversely impact on therapeutic alliance and engagement and so may in itself increase risk further.

Another challenge for the service is being able to undertake assessments of clients in a timely manner while also ensuring they are comprehensive and address both the evaluation and management of risk. The development of program guidelines and an intake and referral policy and procedure are central to managing this issue. Clear policies providing guidance for prioritizing referrals as well as time lines for the provision of verbal and written feedback to referrers are required. Even with these steps, and regardless of the reporting and legislative responsibilities of the referrer, Forensicare is often in the position of taking some responsibility for a potentially high-risk client without yet having assessed him or her. Forensicare must consider its responsibilities in relation to issues such as duty to warn and breach of confidentiality, particularly when an individual is awaiting assessment and has not yet formally become a registered client of the service. To manage these tensions, the PBP has increasingly taken on the role of providing tertiary advice, support, and guidance to services and individual practitioners while the individual is awaiting a PBP assessment. This is an effective way to encourage other services to make use of their skills and expertise in an informed way, minimizes any inclination to wholly defer to the "experts" in community risk management, and promotes the use of evidence-based practice in this area (see Russell & Darjee, 2012, for further discussion of this issue).

The other significant challenge for a PBP service model in a socialized health care environment is to find and maintain a funding source. The service model takes a public health approach to reducing the overall impact of violence and other problem behaviors in the community. This approach is analogous to a public health campaign to prevent deaths from heart attack. Encouraging healthy eating and exercise through population wide measures reduces the risk at a population level without having to undertake the virtually impossible task of identifying the specific individuals who are at extremely high risk of actually having a heart attack. In the problem behavior context, a public health approach means treating the risk factors for sexual or other forms of violence in as large a sample as possible, thereby reducing the overall risk in that group. This removes the need to attempt to accurately predict the small number of clients who may actually go on to commit serious violence because their risk is lowered along with that of all other group members. Based on this premise, the PBP employs specialist mental health clinicians who engage in treatments designed to reduce the risks associated with problem behaviors. These clinicians would typically receive funding via a health or mental health funding stream. However, the signature criterion of the PBP service model is that clients need not be diagnosed with a mental illness to access treatment. This creates a funding dilemma because, while the outcomes of treatment have a public and individual health function, clients are not "typical" consumers of health funding. Forensicare initially overcame this dilemma by funding the PBP from within their existing budget. Despite the potential for negative outcomes that is always present when working with a high risk population, the executive made the decision to provide and continue funding in the initial years of the program. What began as a research project in the early 2000s is now viewed as an integral part of the service, and Forensicare has navigated its way through the funding dilemma to secure finance from both the health and justice sectors. Identifying a secure funding source will be a key consideration for any service aiming to develop a similar program model.

Staff Profile

The staffing profile of the PBP has remained largely unchanged since 2004. Specifically, the staffing complement has remained at four psychology positions since its inception, with the later addition of a full-time PBP manager (a senior psychologist). The program also receives input from psychiatrists and psychiatric registrars and offers a small number of student placements and internships each year. Owing to the specialized nature of the work undertaken within the PBP, all staff providing psychological services in the program are clinical psychologists with specific additional expertise in forensic psychology,

forensic assessments (such as court-ordered reports and assessment of risk of violence), and interventions with those at risk of offending. In addition, expert forensic psychiatrists provide monitoring and supervision of high-risk sexual offenders on antilibidinal medication as well as general psychiatric assessment and input to other PBP clients as required. Although some staff members have developed expertise in particular problem behaviors or treatment approaches, all PBP staff provide both primary care and secondary consultations across the range of problem behaviors.

PBP OPERATIONS AND CASE STUDY

This section provides an overview of PBP intake, assessment, and treatment processes, with a case study demonstrating how each works in practice. The case study is an amalgamation of information from a number of clients that presents a "typical" PBP referral for stalking behavior. It provides an example of the types of information clinicians usually receive at intake and what they would try to collect during the assessment. A risk assessment and a threat assessment are outlined, along with basic information about the treatment program that the PBP would aim to deliver in this type of case.

Referral and Intake Process

Referrals to the PBP are managed through a centralized intake system in which an identified intake worker receives the referral and presents it, with supporting documentation, at a weekly intake meeting. It is at this meeting that referrals are discussed to determine whether they are appropriate for the program and their level of priority (low, medium and high). Referrals to the PBP that are considered of high priority are those where evidence-based risk factors are identified in referral documents that place the individual at an increased and imminent risk to the community. Such factors may include recent specific threats, a history of violence (including sexual violence), access to and history of weapon use, lack of social supports in the community, an identified victim/victims and access to these victim/s, unstable mental state, and current substance abuse. A further consideration is whether the individual has assessment, treatment, and support available via other nonspecialist forensic mental health services; or whether his or her problem behavior and the risk associated with that behavior warrants specialist forensic intervention that cannot be provided elsewhere.

Case Study: Intake

The intake worker was contacted by a psychiatrist at a local inpatient mental health unit. He described a current patient, Belinda, a 21-year-old woman who had been admitted three weeks previously after police transported her to hospital. On admission the police reported that Belinda was arrested after scratching "you will die" on the car of Matt, a man who had a restraining order against her. The police told the psychiatrist that Matt had taken out the restraining order because Belinda was stalking Matt's girlfriend, Julia, who had tutored Belinda in the past. The psychiatrist reported that although Belinda had been distressed on admission, she had quickly settled into the ward and was cooperative with all treatment. He described Belinda's open accounts of her "close and wonderful" friendship with Julia and told the intake worker that Belinda would dismiss any challenges to this perception of the relationship. When questioned about Matt, Belinda reportedly became guarded and evasive, saying that she did not wish to discuss him.

The psychiatrist reported that apart from some ritualistic behavior regarding the arrangement of her room and observable distress if anything was out of place, there were no indications of a mood disorder or anxiety during her admission. The rigidity with which she held the beliefs about Julia was considered to be of delusional intensity and a provisional diagnosis of delusional disorder was given. She had been commenced on antipsychotic medication 15 days prior to the referral, but there had been no noticeable attenuation of her beliefs. The psychiatrist requested a second opinion regarding diagnosis and what, if any, risk Belinda posed to Julia and Matt. He also asked if our service would be willing to treat her; or, at a minimum, assist them in putting together a treatment plan. At the intake meeting it was decided that the case should be given a high priority due to the presence of the threat and possible severe mental illness, and a joint assessment with a psychologist and a psychiatrist was scheduled.

Assessment

Once a referral is accepted at the intake meeting the client is allocated to either a psychologist or psychiatrist for assessment, with the former being more commonplace. In a small number of cases, a joint psychiatric and psychological assessment may be warranted; for example, when a client is presenting with both complex problem behaviors and significant and ongoing psychiatric symptoms that may be linked to the problem behaviors. A typical assessment is likely to take between two and six hours in the form of a semistructured interview, covering areas such as childhood, adolescence and adulthood, educational and employment history, relationship and sexual history, psychiatric and medical history, drug and alcohol use, and offense history. In assessing these domains, it is essential to obtain corroborative information, including criminal history reports, police charge sheets, and previous mental health assessments/reports. Often collateral information is sourced from the family or friends of the client, with their consent. In some cases police informants and/ or correctional officers are contacted if insufficient information about the offending behavior is available. This information is viewed in conjunction with results from psychological tests, which are administered in the majority of cases to guide formulation and treatment recommendations. Such testing is tailored to the individual and his or her presenting problem behaviors and will typically comprise some measure of socially desirable responding, personality testing, and other supplementary tests as required. In most cases a structured risk assessment using a set of professional judgment guidelines (e.g., the HCR-20 [Webster, Douglas, Eaves, & Hart, 2002] or RSVP [Hart et al., 2003]) is also completed and informs the results of the wider assessment. This comprehensive assessment process allows the assessor to develop an explanatory formulation of the problem behavior, including a functional analysis, which considers psychological, psychiatric, and social determinants of the behavior. A written report is provided to the referrer outlining the conclusions of the assessment and providing recommendations for management. In some cases, where risk level and lack of other support services warrants, this may include a recommendation to attend the PBP for ongoing treatment.

Case Study: Assessment

Belinda was brought to the clinic by a nurse a week after the intake was accepted. She presented as a slim, immaculately groomed young woman. She engaged well, and her emotional responses were appropriate to the topics of discussion. The tone, rate, and rhythm of her speech were unremarkable. There was no evidence of perceptual abnormalities and her thought form was normal with no evidence of thought disorder. Although she was somewhat preoccupied with Julia, she was easily enough redirected and could discuss other matters. Her attention and concentration were largely normal.

Background Information

In this case the assessment included information obtained from Belinda in addition to collateral information from her mother (interviewed on the telephone with Belinda's consent) and from the police informant who had taken Belinda to the local hospital.

Belinda was from a wealthy background and there was no evidence of maltreatment, neglect, or abuse within the family. She had no siblings and stated that she had always been shy and would rather play by herself as a child than join in with others; she added that generally this was still true for many of her current activities. She had excelled academically and on completing high school went straight to university to study history. Her only current social involvement was with her local church; she said that she didn't know many people there very well, but was praised for being a quiet achiever. She explained that she had never worried about making friends as she enjoyed spending time on her own and kept herself quite busy. She reported that she had never had a boyfriend but identified herself as heterosexual.

Belinda strenuously denied ever using or experimenting with any form of drug, expressing her disgust at those who did. She stated that she drank the occasional glass of wine when dining with her family but on special occasions only. She described a pedantic approach to her studies and general chores, and laughingly stated that she had always been "somewhat obsessive" about keeping her bedroom neat and tidy, spending a lot of time ensuring that her clothes and possessions were just as she wanted. She acknowledged being "something of a perfectionist" and "a neat freak." Beyond acknowledging that she "sometimes gets stressed and anxious," she denied experiencing any symptoms indicative of mental illness.

Stress and anxiety became a problem after Belinda commenced a master's degree approximately a year earlier. She found the work challenging and became upset if she did not obtain her usually excellent grades. When she began having difficulty with a compulsory unit, she became convinced she was going to fail despite all evidence to the contrary. She became increasingly anxious, had difficulty sleeping, and began to have panic attacks. Concerned over the level of distress their daughter was experiencing, her parents thought that a tutor might help to alleviate her unrealistic fears. They therefore approached the course coordinator, who recommended Julia, a confident, friendly student who was a year ahead of Belinda. They also suggested that Belinda attend the student counseling service. Although Belinda refused the counseling, the tutoring sessions were scheduled twice weekly in the university library. The impact was dramatic, and with Julia's assistance, Belinda's anxiety about her studies quickly reduced.

Belinda's Account of the Stalking

Although Belinda and Julia never met socially, if Julia had time they would occasionally go for coffee after the tutoring session. Belinda reported that a few weeks after the tutoring commenced she began to regularly text message or email Julia to ask if she would be able to have coffee after the next session. She reported that she would often text Julia just to see how she was doing or what she was up to. Belinda reported that she continued to send "a few" messages after their tutoring arrangement ended at the end of the semester and that Julia had replied, although not every time. Belinda stated that she began to make an effort to see Julia around campus more often because she missed seeing her friend every week with tutoring, but she found this difficult because Julia's other friends didn't like her and seemed eager to make her leave. She denied receiving any messages asking her to stop contacting Julia.

When asked why she had pursued the friendship with Julia, Belinda explained that from the outset she had known that Julia was "special." She spoke with great enthusiasm about how Julia had gone out of her way to help her through a time of crisis and of the strong bond that had formed between them. She was adamant that Julia had done this because they were friends and that they had become so close that they were like sisters. When the questioning turned to why restraining orders had been taken out against her, Belinda became angry, stating that she was convinced that it had been the work of "the others" trying to come between her and Julia because they were jealous of their friendship. When it was pointed out that Julia had contacted the police in regard to the breaches of the order, Belinda stated that she could not believe it was Julia as "a friend just wouldn't do that, it's not the way it works." Although she did not believe that Julia would be frightened by her behavior as "she knows I wouldn't hurt anyone," she acknowledged that the death threat that she had scratched into Matt's car was designed to scare him off. She denied that she would ever act on this threat.

Collateral Information

The police officer informed us that Belinda's intrusive behavior initially made Julia feel uncomfortable; therefore she tried to avoid Belinda and not reply to her communications so as to discourage her. In response, Belinda began to send up to 40 messages and emails a day. In these messages she stated that Julia was her best friend and that they needed to meet to talk things over. Julia sent Belinda an email asking her not to contact her again. Shortly after, Julia's friends began to experience hang-up phone calls and strange occurrences, such as repeatedly having a flat tire with no puncture, or taxis arriving at their homes in the middle of the night after receiving bookings for that address. After Julia arranged to have Belinda's telephone number and email address blocked, the messages stopped for three days, but then recommenced with the texts sent from public telephones and emails from various newly created accounts.

Approximately three months after the harassment began, Julia and Matt, her boyfriend, arrived home to find Belinda waiting on the footpath opposite their house. Matt lost his temper and began yelling at Belinda that she was a "loony" and needed to get a life rather than hassle Julia. Belinda just continued to stand there silently, watching. The next morning they went to the police and were advised to obtain a restraining order. An interim order was put in place with a court date set for three weeks' time.

Over the next week Belinda continued to send and deliver letters and cards to Julia in which she declared her eternal friendship. When Matt went to his car one morning to find the words "you will die" scratched into the paint work, the police were notified and Belinda was taken to the local police station for questioning. It was during this interview that Belinda began to rock back and forth, gouging her arms with her nails till she bled, prompting them to call the duty doctor and take her to the local hospital.

Psychometric Testing

Several psychometric instruments were administered, including measures of personality (Personality Assessment Inventory) (Morey, 1991), anger (Anger Disorder Scales) (DiGuiseppe & Tafrate, 2004), and impression management (Paulhus Deception Scales) (Paulhus, 1998). The results supported the clinical impression that Belinda was a perfectionistic young woman with high internalized standards regarding behavior and performance. The items she endorsed suggested the presence of rigid rules and inflexibility

in many areas of life, including unrealistically high moral beliefs and ideals in respect to interpersonal relationships. Her responses also indicated a personality style characterized by obsessive and dependent traits. Across the various instruments a pattern emerged suggesting a lack of insight, rigidity in dealing with personal problems, and overcontrolled or suppressed anger. There was no indication of attempts at impression management; however, Belinda showed above average levels of self-deceptive enhancement.

Diagnosis

Although there had been questions as to whether Belinda's thoughts about Julia were psychotically driven, her thoughts and beliefs, taking her history and presentation into account, were considered more consistent with overvalued ideas in the context of an obsessive-compulsive personality rather than evidence of erotomanic or other delusions. There was good evidence of a long and ego-syntonic history of preoccupation and rigidity with orderliness, perfectionism, and very rigid and inflexible views on moral issues. While similarities with the features of Asperger's syndrome were considered, this was discounted due to Belinda demonstrating a capacity for empathy, general social skills, and reciprocity when required; and the absence of other markers of repetitive and stereotyped patterns of behavior, interests, and activities. There was also no evidence of motor clumsiness or atypical use of language. On this basis, a provisional diagnosis was made of obsessive–compulsive personality disorder with a differential diagnosis of monodelusional disorder. Given the changed diagnosis, it was recommended that Belinda be taken off antipsychotic medication and her beliefs and preoccupation with Julia closely monitored for changes.

Structured Risk Assessment

The Stalking Risk Profile (SRP) (MacKenzie et al., 2009) is a structured professional judgment tool used to guide risk assessment in stalking situations. The SRP focuses on the assessment of a specific stalking situation, and assesses for a range of static (fixed) and dynamic (changeable) risk factors related to stalking. Risk judgments are made about the risk of persistence (the likelihood that the current stalking episode will continue over time), the risk of stalking-related violence, and the risk that the stalker will experience significant psychosocial harm as a result of his or her behavior. Typologies of different stalking behaviors are used to tailor the risk assessment to the particular circumstances of the case (see McEwan, Pathé, & Ogloff, 2011, for further information). Belinda's behavior was consistent with an Intimacy Seeking stalker and she was assessed against the risk factors for that profile.

Using the SRP, the risk of Belinda persisting with her stalking behavior towards Julia and the secondary victims in the short to medium term was assessed as high, indicating a strong need for immediate interventions to help reduce risk. Her risk of continued stalking was increased relative to others because of the nature of some of her behaviors, such as sending unsolicited materials and breaching legal directives, in addition to psychologically relevant risk factors such as the presence of personality disorder, cognitive distortions regarding the victim and her own behavior, and a strong sense of entitlement to the victim's time and attention. In addition, a number of contextual risk factors were present, namely Belinda's social isolation and the possibility of accidental or deliberate encounters due to a shared study environment and Belinda's knowledge of the location of Julia's home.

Even in the context of continued stalking behavior, Belinda was assessed as presenting a low risk of stalking-related violence to Julia and Matt. This indicated little need for specific interventions to reduce the risk of violence. Relatively few risk factors were present (only approach behaviors, property damage, and elevated anger [towards secondary victims], and some evidence of emotional overcontrol). There was no indication of any risk factors suggestive of increased risk of imminent violence (homicidal ideation, suicidal ideation, high-risk psychotic phenomena, or last-resort thinking). In the context of intimacy seeking stalking, threats are not routinely considered a risk factor as they occur relatively rarely and are not often related to violence in this group. A specific threat assessment revealed that Belinda was not engaging in any violent fantasies about harming Julia or Matt and had no plans or means to do so. She stated that the threat was an attempt to scare Matt into withdrawing from the relationship because Belinda felt that he was a negative influence on Julia. There appeared to be no reason to override the original risk judgment based on this information. Given that the stalking was considered likely to continue, regular reassessment of the risk of violence would be warranted to assess for change in this and other risk factors.

Belinda was judged to be at moderate to high risk of experiencing psychosocial harm as a consequence of her behavior, indicating that she was likely to require assistance to cope with the negative social and legal sequelae of her stalking. Most importantly, Belinda demonstrated poor resilience to stress, problems with the expression of anger, preoccupation with Julia and misinterpretation of Julia's actions, and ongoing social isolation. Particularly concerning was the potential for any significant deterioration in Julia's mental state to contribute to increased risk of stalking-related violence. Helping Belinda to improve her problem-solving and stress-management skills, and gradually reduce her reliance on the perceived relationship with Julia, would be central to improving her longer-term psychosocial outcomes and reducing other risks.

Formulation

A formulation is a theory-based explanatory narrative that is commonly used in mental health to hypothesize why a client is presenting in a particular way at a particular time. In this case, the formulation is an attempt to explain why Belinda may have engaged in stalking behavior. Formulation pulls the information from the assessment together and guides the targets and manner of subsequent treatment (See Hart, Sturmey, Logan, & McMurran, 2011, for further discussion of forensic case formulation).

Belinda engaged in intimacy seeking stalking of a former acquaintance and other related secondary victims. A number of factors may have predisposed Belinda to stalking in pursuit of a relationship and then when she perceived that she was being rejected. There is evidence of difficulties forming social relationships from a young age, and while this had not previously presented problems, Belinda has had few experiences of successful reciprocal social relationships on which to model her behavior. There is also long-standing evidence of a tendency toward perfectionism and associated rumination, with difficulties adapting and coping if her high internal standards cannot be met. In this context, there is some evidence that Belinda has difficulty managing strong negative emotions, with catastrophizing and heightened anxiety in response to perceived failure. There is no evidence of maltreatment or the modeling of aggression in Belinda's early life that might predispose her to react with threats or intimidation when experiencing interpersonal conflict, nor does this appear to be a pattern of behavior associated with the presence of antisocial beliefs and attitudes.

Belinda's stalking behavior in this case appears to have been precipitated by a strong belief that she shared a friendship with Julia, when in fact no such relationship existed. Her initial intrusive behaviors were inept attempts to maintain contact with someone whom she perceived to be a friend, and she failed to attend to normal social cues indicating that her overtures were unwanted. When her approaches were not accepted, Belinda found it increasingly difficult to moderate her emotional response (in accordance with the aforementioned long-standing difficulties in this area). There is some evidence that Belinda had idealized Julia to the extent that she could not accept that Julia would not want to be her friend, and so externalized blame and her anger about Julia's responses onto Julia's friends and boyfriend. At particular times she was unable to manage her negative emotional state and would engage in behaviors that would make her feel better, such as seeing Julia or warning her friends and boyfriend to stop interfering. Her emotional arousal and consequent stalking behavior seems to have been maintained by obsessive rumination about Julia and others' interference in their "friendship." She appears to have had little ability to moderate her angry responses or reframe her experiences so as to stop the behavior without feeling humiliated or let down. Central to Belinda's ongoing behavior is her continuing belief that Julia is actually interested in a friendship with her and her misinterpretation and distortion of events in a manner consistent with this belief. At present this is not considered to be a delusional belief; rather, it is a consequence of her cognitive rigidity and poor social skills, although ongoing monitoring of her beliefs about Julia in the absence of antipsychotic medication is necessary.

Although these predisposing, precipitating, and perpetuating factors mean that it is considered likely that Belinda's stalking behavior will continue in the short to medium term, Belinda also has a number of considerable strengths that can be built upon to help her cease her behavior. She has support from her immediate family and the church, and, outside of the context of this stalking episode, clearly has prosocial beliefs and values. She does not engage in substance misuse and at present is not suffering from a serious mental illness, both of which could act as disinhibiting factors if they were present. Moreover, Belinda is an intelligent woman who may be able to engage in psychological interventions designed to help her reframe her experiences in a manner that can help her to let go of her attachment to Julia. Given the high risk of persistent stalking behavior and a moderate risk of psychosocial harm, Belinda was judged to be suitable for treatment at the PBP.

Treatment

Treatment of any problem behavior in the PBP adheres to Andrews and Bonta's (2010) risk, needs, and responsivity principles, using structured risk assessment to identify clients who present at moderate or high risk and so are appropriate for behavior-specific treatment. Relevant risk factors that may be pertinent treatment targets are identified from the risk assessment tools, supplemented with functional analysis of the problem behavior. Treatment is oriented toward the cessation of the problem behavior and the formulation is used to prioritize treatment targets and responsivity factors. This allows treatment plans to focus on the client's criminogenic needs, but also to be individualized and tailored to the specific problem behavior context. Individual treatment may also be an entry point to other group programs that may be operating within Forensicare, such as anger management or social skills groups. Individual psychological treatment may be supplemented by clinical management of any contributory mental disorder; therefore pharmacological treatment may be warranted. Depending on the client and the nature of the medication, this can be managed by PBP psychiatrists or by an external medical provider.

Drawing on current research knowledge and best practice, treatment guidelines have been developed for the various problem behaviors; however, all incorporate a comprehensive functional analysis of the behavior and share similarities in their use of cognitive behavioral techniques. While clients present with a variety of different problem behaviors, the functional analysis often reveals similar targets for psychological treatment, such as offense-supportive cognitive distortions and underlying beliefs and attitudes, emotional dysregulation and impulsivity, and problem solving, social, and interpersonal skills deficits. As outlined previously, treatment is tailored to the individual; thus the length of time in treatment varies depending on the individual's needs and his or her progress in relation to treatment goals. To evaluate a client's progress and ensure that treatment remains beneficial and effective, all PBP clients are subject to a clinical review by the clinical team at the commencement of treatment and then at a minimum of six-month intervals. Clients are also subject to a clinical review prior to discharge from the service. This peer review system also ensures that client's risks are regularly monitored and reviewed and that risk management plans are appropriate. Examples of risk management strategies that may form part of a client's risk management plan include monitoring of the nature and frequency of deviant sexual thoughts or homicidal fantasies; restricting access to high-risk situations, including to a specific victim or victim group through employment or family/social relationships or access to the Internet; identification of a support network, including crisis services; increased support and monitoring during periods of increased environmental stressors or triggers; and use of pharmacological intervention such as antilibidinal medication for high-risk sex offenders.

Case Example: Treatment

The treatment program implemented with Belinda and described below highlights specific treatment targets that were relevant to her stalking behavior. Wider discussions of treating stalking behavior in a manner consistent with the problem behavior model can be found in MacKenzie and James (2011) and Mullen, Pathé, and Purcell (2009).

Drawing from the above formulation, the identified treatment targets in Belinda's case were prioritized, with the immediate focus on helping Belinda to refrain from stalking Julia on her release from the hospital. Central to this was the fact that Belinda initially did not perceive her behavior as a problem for Julia or herself. The first two-hour session, conducted while Belinda remained in hospital, therefore focused on identifying the pros and cons of her behavior. Belinda was encouraged to think about some of the costs so that she was more inclined to want to desist, at least in the short term. This involved a discussion about what she really wanted to achieve with her intrusions, what she actually had achieved, and education about stalking. The local stalking legislation was shown to Belinda and the risks that she was running by engaging in the intrusive behavior were outlined. This was quite motivating for Belinda and she was willing to work on short-term strategies that might help her not to contact Julia or Matt and so stay out of trouble with the police. These strategies were very practical and involved limiting her time on the university campus, giving her car keys to her parents so she could not drive to Julia's house if tempted, and developing distraction and avoidance techniques that she could use as alternatives if she was so emotionally aroused that she felt that she just "had" to see Julia. She also identified the pastor at her church as someone that she could call and talk to if she needed to vent. He was contacted to discuss the situation and agreed to act as a crisis contact.

Following the assessment, it was recommended to Belinda's treating team that she be taken off antipsychotic medications, as these were not warranted by the new diagnosis. While still in hospital, Belinda was engaged in conversation about other medications that could help her manage her rumination and distress more effectively. Belinda recognized that anxiety could cause her problems (referring to her trouble with her studies) and felt that medication might be helpful for this. She did not feel that medication would assist her with any of her emotional responses to the situation with Julia. An initial prescription for the anxiolytic medication sertraline was provided by the referring psychiatrist, with ongoing management of the medication being the responsibility of Belinda's general practitioner in the community. After the first month of treatment there was a noticeable reduction in Belinda's preoccupation with Julia, and her level of rumination decreased to a more manageable level, allowing for further psychological interventions.

With the stalking behavior under some level of control in the first two weeks, the focus of treatment moved to more medium- and long-term needs. A joint formulation was developed with Belinda to help her develop some sense of why she might have engaged in this behavior in the first place. This involved working with her to undertake a functional analysis of individual examples of stalking behavior (e.g., sending a letter or attending Julia's home), and then building a more comprehensive shared formulation focusing on predisposing and precipitating factors that might be relevant. This process was guided by the above preexisting formulation but also took into account additional factors that Belinda felt were important. Establishing a shared explanation for the behavior not only helped Belinda to understand it in an objective way, but also increased her willingness to work on changing the things that were seen as contributing to the behavior.

In Belinda's case the priority treatment targets were identified as the cognitive distortions she held about her relationship with Julia, her lack of thought as to the consequences of her actions, and her difficulties managing her experience and expression of emotion. Cognitive distortions were framed as "unhelpful thoughts and attitudes" in the sessions, with a shared position that they were unhelpful to Belinda because they made her feel bad and increased the chance that she might do things that could cause her legal trouble. Challenges to "unhelpful thoughts and attitudes" were developed that Belinda could use when she started to ruminate about the situation, which was an identified trigger for engaging in an intrusive behavior. Belinda's rigid cognitive style and her ongoing emotional investment in her "friendship" with Julia were significant responsivity factors affecting her ability to challenge misperceptions about her own behavior. Given this, less attention was paid to the impact on the victim in the initial stages and more to the impact of her behavior on Belinda herself. Over time, greater attention was given to Julia's perceptions and the likely effect of Belinda's behavior; however, Belinda never really let go of her belief that Julia had originally wanted "at some level" to be her friend, even if this was no longer the case. She was able to accept that Julia and Matt would have been scared by her approaches and the threat, and regretted causing them fear.

The other primary treatment target in the first two to three months was helping Belinda to develop some emotional regulation skills that she could use when faced with a triggering thought or experience (such as an accidental meeting with Julia at university). This first involved basic psychoeducation about emotions and feedback from the psychometric testing about how Belinda experiences and expresses emotions. Belinda worked on recognizing early signs of emotional arousal and ways of expressing this appropriately at an earlier stage. Some physical anxiety reduction strategies were taught and practiced over a number of weeks, and tied to the cognitive challenges and other behavioral responses as alternatives to engaging in stalking behavior when emotionally aroused.

This skill development work was specifically aimed at reducing the likelihood of continued stalking in the medium term. Clearly there were also underlying factors related to elevated risk of recurrent stalking in the long term, and these became the focus of subsequent sessions. By the fourth month of treatment, sessions were focusing on improving Belinda's communication and social skills, so that she felt more able to express herself to others (while still practicing the cognitive and emotional regulation skills previously outlined). Initially this work was undertaken in individual psychology sessions with role plays and homework tasks, with a subsequent move to identifying opportunities for social activities and developing friendships through church and university clubs. Throughout this "experimental" period, Belinda continued to bring examples of interactions into sessions that could be discussed and examined to gradually improve her ability to read others' meanings and communicate her own effectively.

One of the initial challenges in working with Belinda was her investment in the friendship with Julia. This was partly due to the lack of other social relationships, meaning that relinquishing Julia would lead to almost total isolation. Quite early in the treatment program, after discussion with Belinda's parents, it was agreed that Belinda could purchase a puppy that she would have responsibility for at home, which was hoped would provide her with an alternative emotionally satisfying relationship. The attention that a puppy requires was an effective diversion from thoughts of Julia in the short term and, over time, dog ownership also provided social opportunities through attendance at obedience training classes. Belinda very much enjoyed the routine and structure of dog training and her high-achieving nature led her to pursue this into the competitive arena, where she and her pet began to enter local obedience competitions. Gradually, this hobby not only took up more of Julia's spare time, but also introduced her to people with similar interests with whom she could form friendships.

Belinda saw a PBP psychologist for two hours a week for seven months and then attended three monthly "booster" sessions to help her consolidate her skills. She continued to be prescribed sertraline by her GP and reported being happy with the reduction in her anxiety and rumination. The GP reported her intention to review the need for the prescription at the end of 12 months. While Belinda initially found it very difficult to divert her attention from the stalking situation, she was able to understand that her behavior was problematic for her and carried significant costs. The primary initial motivation for Belinda to attend treatment was fear of the potential legal ramifications, although over time she also acknowledged that her behavior had been inappropriate and she did not want to frighten people in this way in the future. During the course of treatment Belinda pleaded guilty to breaching the intervention order, and the property damage charges were dropped when she paid for repairs to Matt's car. Because she had voluntarily attended treatment and had no previous convictions, she received a fine and a 12-month good behavior bond. At the completion of the treatment program, Belinda's risk of recurrent stalking toward Julia or another victim was assessed as low. The risk factors that remained present were a history of stalking, some social isolation (although significantly improved), personality disorder, and the possibility of future accidental contact with Julia at the university. Belinda had developed viable plans for dealing with this type of triggering event as well as some improved ability to manage interpersonal conflict and resultant stress. She was advised that if she felt she needed further help with a specific situation or behavior in the future, she was welcome to self-refer.

INTERNATIONAL IMPLEMENTATION OF THE PROBLEM BEHAVIOR FRAMEWORK

The PBP has attracted considerable attention within Australia and internationally since it was conceived. In some cases this has influenced the development of similar services in other areas. Perhaps the best publicized is the National Stalking Clinic in London. The clinic is a specialist service for the assessment and treatment of stalkers and stalking victims and is an initiative of the North London Forensic Service, part of the Barnet Enfield and Haringey Mental Health NHS Trust. The clinic was established following a visit by senior clinicians to the PBP in May 2011 and opened in November 2011. It is closely modeled on the PBP and offers psychological and psychiatric assessments of stalkers for courts and probation services, mental health agencies, and other social services (incorporating risk assessment as standard). Individual psychological treatment is available to those under legal orders, although it is not always recommended. Like the PBP, the NSC also offers tertiary consultations about handling ongoing stalking cases, although they have a closer relationship with local police services than has been established in Australia. In a departure from the current PBP model, the NSC also offers assessment and treatment services to some victims of stalking.

Another service influenced by the problem behavior framework is the Serious Offender Liaison Service (SOLS), which commenced operations at the end of 2012, superseding the former Sex Offender Liaison Service (Russell & Darjee, 2012). Based at the Orchard Clinic, Royal Edinburgh Hospital (part of the NHS Lothian forensic mental health service), the SOLS receives referrals for sexual offending, stalking, domestic violence, arson and other serious violence. Like the PBP, the SOLS does not require a conviction for referral. Clients who have a diagnosed mental illness or learning disability are excluded from the service, as they can access forensic mental health services elsewhere; however, if these individuals' management is complicated by

comorbid personality disorder or paraphilia, referrals are accepted. The SOLS has a slightly different service model than the PBP, developed from the preexisting service for high-risk sexual offenders. Staff at the clinic (specialist psychiatry, psychology, social work, and nursing staff) most often provide tertiary consultation and advice to referrers and less often undertake an assessment themselves. At present the service does not offer treatment, instead focusing on helping the referring agency to intervene and manage cases in a psychologically informed way. A particularly exciting element of the SOLS is their integration with the local policing units, who have a statutory duty to monitor sex offenders on the sex offenders' register. This is consistent with the SOLS' aim to provide clinical consultation, assessment, and advice to help criminal justice agencies with the management of personality-disordered and paraphilic sexual and violent offenders in the community.

At the other end of the United Kingdom, on the south coast of England, the Hampshire Stalking Consultancy Clinic started in May 2012 for a six-month pilot with the support of the local forensic mental health and police services. This clinic—consisting of a consultant clinical psychologist, a consultant forensic psychiatrist, a detective chief inspector from the Hampshire police, and a probation officer—was initiated by practitioners who identified a need for local multiagency work with regard to stalking identification and management. The clinic runs once a month on a case consultation, review, and formulation model. Cases are usually brought by the police or probation service personnel and can involve instances of suspected stalking or postconviction behavior problems. When appropriate, interview and structured risk assessment are used to help guide sentencing, treatment, and management planning. At the time of writing, the pilot program was continuing with an intended evaluation at completion to determine whether it will be continued.

In Australia, community forensic mental health services (CFMHS) outside Victoria have begun to develop their own problem behavior-oriented approaches, although within the bounds of existing mental health funding. In New South Wales, the Sydney CFMHS uses a problem behavior assessment approach, with all clients referred due to combined mental illness and offending behavior. At present they are not able to expand their service provision beyond those with a diagnosed mental illness, although this will hopefully occur in the future. In mid-2012 the CFMHS based in Brisbane, Queensland, began an innovative program delivering problem behavior-focused treatment to clients of general mental health services via a Community Forensic Outreach Service (CFOS). Clients engaging in stalking, sexual deviance, arson, querulous complaining and related behaviors are referred for risk or threat assessment. Where a recommendation is made for problem behavior-specific treatment, a CFOS clinician travels to the general mental health service to help the generalist clinician deliver interventions designed to reduce the problem behavior. The CFOS clinician provides written resources to the general mental health clinician, but a core aspect of the program is to build capacity to deal with problem behaviors outside of the forensic mental health service. The program is in a pilot phase and evaluation will be undertaken in the future.

We are less familiar with services in North America that use a problem behavior framework, although one service that we know of has independently developed this general approach. The Intrapsychic Clinic in San Diego, California, is a private psychology clinic that provides assessment and treatment to clients who have engaged in stalking, intimate partner violence, general violence, and problematic sexual behavior. Treatment at this clinic is offered in group format (grouped by type of problem behavior) and guided by repeated risk assessments using structured professional judgment tools. The primary difference between this and the other services using a problem behavior framework is a dual focus on psychodynamic therapy in addition to cognitive-behavioral approaches. Clients' attachment style and disordered attachment are considered key to their problem behaviors and therefore are incorporated into the psychological treatment provided.

CONCLUSION

The problem behavior framework offers a new type of service model that has great potential to bridge gaps in mainstream and forensic mental health services and the criminal justice system. For the individual client, the problem behavior framework can assist in understanding and communicating about complex and sometimes frightening behaviors in ways that can lead to change. At an organizational level, the presence of services such as the PBP means that there is somewhere to go when a threat or risk assessment reveals the need for treatment and management. In the absence of such a service, individuals with problem behaviors would likely not receive help to change their behavior, and instead be subjected to punitive measures that do little to decrease risk over time. While each of the services described above applies the problem behavior framework in a different way, they share the common goal of helping people whose behavior brings them into conflict with the law and other members of the community. Helping these people to access informed assessment and treatment services is consistent with mental health professionals' duty to act in the best interests of their clients and with their wider duty to prevent harm to the community. In this type of work, expertise in structured risk assessment and evidence-based threat assessment is an absolute necessity. Only by providing well-founded and appropriately qualified risk and threat assessments can forensic mental health clinicians identify where treatment and management is most required and where a perceived threat may not actually exist.

ACKNOWLEDGMENTS

The authors wish to thank Dr. Stephen Allnutt, Dr. Rajan Darjee, Detective Chief Inspector Linda Dawson, Dr. Frank Farnham, Dr. Michele Pathé, and Dr. James Reavis for providing information about the international services described in this chapter.

KEY POINTS

- Threat assessments of people who engage in problem behaviors such as violence, stalking, threatening, fire setting, or sexual offending often reveal a range of underlying psychological and social factors that increase risk but cannot be effectively managed by law enforcement alone.
- The skills of forensic mental health clinicians can and should be used to treat people who engage in these types of potentially high-risk behaviors, but current models of service provision (which focus on mental illness) exclude the majority of these individuals from assessment and treatment.
- The problem behavior model provides a recognizable referral pathway for clients of criminal justice and mainstream mental health agencies who are assessed as moderate or high risk to access specialist forensic mental health services based on the nature of their *behavior*, rather than the presence of a mental disorder or criminal conviction.

- The problem behavior model offers a framework for understanding why an individual might engage in a particular problem behavior so as to facilitate efforts to change the behavior and reduce risk over time.
- Applying the problem behavior model to practice requires an understanding of the research literature relevant to specific types of offending behavior, including threat and risk assessment, offender treatment and rehabilitation, and the role of psychopathology in different types of offending.

REFERENCES

Andrews, D. A., & Bonta, J. (2010). *The psychology of criminal conduct.* New Providence, NJ: Matthew Bender.

DiGuiseppe, R., & Tafrate, R. C. (2004). *Anger disorders scales (ADS).* Toronto: Multi-Health Systems.

Gannon, T. A., & Cortoni, F. (2010). *Female sexual offenders: Theory, assessment and treatment.* Chichester, UK: Wiley.

Hart, S. D., Kropp, R. P., Laws, D. R., Klaver, J., Logan, C., & Watt, K. A. (2003). *The risk for sexual violence protocol (RSVP): Structured professional guidelines for assessing risk of sexual violence.* Burnaby, BC: Mental Health, Law and Policy Institute, Simon Fraser University.

Hart, S., Sturmey, P., Logan, C., & McMurran, M. (2011). Forensic case formulation. *International Journal of Forensic Mental Health, 10,* 118–126.

Maden, A. (2007). *Treating violence. A guide to risk management in mental health.* Oxford, UK: Oxford University Press.

MacKenzie, R. D., & James, D. V. (2011). Management and treatment of stalkers: Problems, options and, solutions. *Behavioral Sciences & the Law, 29,* 220–239.

MacKenzie, R. D., McEwan, T. E., Pathé, M. T., James, D. V., Ogloff, J.R.P., & Mullen, P. E. (2009). *Stalking risk profile: Guidelines for assessing and managing stalkers.* Melbourne, Australia: StalkInc. and Centre for Forensic Behavioural Science, Monash University.

McEwan, T. E., Pathé, M., & Ogloff, J.R.P. (2011). Advances in stalking risk assessment. *Behavioral Sciences & the Law, 29,* 180–201.

Morey, L. C. (1991). *Personality assessment inventory.* Lutz, FL: Psychological Assessment Resources.

Mullen, P. E., Pathé, M., & Purcell, R. (2009). *Stalkers and their victims,* 2nd ed. New York: Cambridge University Press.

Paulhus, D. L. (1998). *Paulhus deception scales (PDS): The balanced inventory of desirable responding-7.* Toronto: Multi-Health Systems.

Russell, K., & Darjee, R. (2012) Managing the risk posed by personality disordered sex offenders in the community: A model for providing structured clinical guidance to support criminal justice services. In C. Logan & L. Johnson (Eds.), *Managing clinical risk: A guide to effective practice* (pp. 88–114). Abingdon, UK: Routledge.

Warren, L. J., MacKenzie, R., Mullen, P. E., & Ogloff, J.R.P. (2005). The problem behavior model: The development of a stalkers' clinic and a threateners' clinic. *Behavioral Sciences and the Law, 23,* 387–397.

Webster, C. D., Douglas, K. S., Eaves, D., & Hart, S. D. (2002). *HCR-20: Assessing risk for violence,* 2nd ed. Burnaby, BC: Simon Fraser University.

26

Threat Assessment in the US Navy and Marine Corps

DORIAN VAN HORN

Threat assessment in the US military presents multiple challenges. In particular, the relative ease of access to weapons within the military increases both the quantity and complexity of the threats that must be addressed. Accurately analyzing potential threats posed by military members can also be complicated by the stress of deployments, separation from family, inability to discuss work problems at home due to restrictions on sharing classified information, frequent duty station moves, and the typically young age of military members. Recently, the potential effects of posttraumatic stress disorder and traumatic brain injury on military personnel have received a significant amount of attention. These silent wounds do not always manifest themselves immediately but remain a concern for the military and its investigators. Threat assessments must also take into account that the military community is not limited to just uniformed personnel. Although they may have different challenges, the military's civilian and dependent populations face stressors that are similar to the ones faced by the military's uniformed members. All of these factors combine to create an extremely dynamic and challenging environment for accurately predicting when a potential threat will escalate into violence.

The Department of the Navy is a unique military department in the Department of Defense because it includes two uniformed services—the US Navy and the US Marine Corps. These services have uniformed personnel assigned on bases, submarines, and ships all over the world. In addition to the men and women in uniform, the US Navy and Marine Corps employ civilians such as doctors, nurses, engineers, teachers, bankers, gardeners, mechanics, security, administrative staff, social workers, and other government workers. Bases also include dependent spouses and children. Located on military installations are dry cleaners, fast-food establishments, veterinary services, gas stations, churches, hospitals, libraries, movie theaters, day care centers, grocery stores, department stores (called exchanges), barbers, and schools. Military installations are a microcosm of our larger society, with all its problems, relationships, and work-related stressors.

THE NAVAL CRIMINAL INVESTIGATIVE SERVICE

Within this microcosm, the Navy Criminal Investigative Service (NCIS) is responsible for conducting felony criminal investigations and counterintelligence activities for the Department of the Navy. Although the NCIS is staffed almost entirely by civilian personnel, its history and culture are closely connected to the Navy and Marine Corps, which it serves. NCIS employs approximately 1,200 civilian special agents who operate in over 140 locations around the world. After being trained at the Federal Law Enforcement Training Center in Glynco, Georgia, NCIS agents serve at all Navy and Marine Corps bases in the United States and overseas. A special agent is assigned to each aircraft carrier in the Navy and they voluntarily deploy to the war zones to conduct criminal and intelligence missions. Essentially, wherever the Navy and Marine Corps have a presence, NCIS agents are assigned to investigate and respond to criminal, counterterrorism, and counterintelligence concerns. Criminal investigations are a core NCIS mission, and agents can be tasked to investigate a wide variety of crimes. Types of crimes investigated by NCIS include but are not limited to rape, death, child abuse, child sexual assault, espionage, terrorism, sabotage, narcotics, piracy, assault, procurement fraud, robbery, and burglary.

As the Department of the Navy's felony investigative arm, NCIS has investigative responsibility for all crimes punishable under the Uniform Code of Military Justice with confinement of more than one year. The Uniform Code of Military Justice is the federal law that provides the foundation for the military's criminal justice system. As a practical matter, the Uniform Code of Military Justice generally applies only to uniformed personnel while they are serving on active duty. Under the Uniform Code of Military Justice, members accused of violating a punitive article are entitled to many of the same kinds of rights as defendants in civilian criminal justice systems. They have the right to be represented by a military attorney at no cost to them. They have the right to remain silent. They have the right to a trial (called a court-martial), which can be heard by either a military judge alone or by jurors (called members). Despite these similarities, the military criminal justice system differs from most other systems in that the authority to refer a case to court-martial does not rest with prosecutors. Instead, depending upon the severity of the offense, different levels of military commanders are authorized to determine whether a court-martial would be appropriate. For minor infractions that do not merit a court-martial, a commander could decide to administer nonjudicial punishment, which is an administrative procedure with limited types of punishment.

The criminal investigations mission of NCIS can be more complicated when a civilian member of the Department of the Navy's community is accused of a crime. Unlike uniformed personnel on active duty, civilians suspected of a crime are generally prosecuted in either a federal or state criminal justice system. Also, civilians who have committed a crime while overseas could potentially be prosecuted under the laws of the foreign country where the crime was committed. When the investigation of crimes committed by uniformed personnel is coupled with the investigations of crimes committed by the Department of the Navy's civilian population, it becomes clear that the criminal investigation mission of the NCIS requires its special agents to investigate a wide variety of criminal activities that could be prosecuted in diverse jurisdictions. In order to maximize its effectiveness with this broad mission, NCIS emphasizes crime prevention by utilizing proactive strategies that minimize the likelihood of criminal activity.

THE NCIS THREAT MANAGEMENT UNIT

As part of its proactive approach to stopping crime before it occurs and because of an increase in workplace violence, stalking, and threatening communications, the NCIS established the Threat Management Unit (TMU) in 1996. The TMU is a 24-hour capability used to provide immediate analysis and assessment of threatening behaviors. The TMU analyzes and assesses potential threats posed by any member of the Department of the Navy. Threat assessment and threat management aim to provide a behavioral risk assessment that places the verbal communication and/or threatening behavior on a continuum of potential violence (Turner & Gelles, 2003) and to offer recommendations regarding investigative strategies and security-related solutions. Threat assessment is about behavior, not profiles. There is no "type of person" who perpetrates targeted violence (Fine & Vossekuil, 1999). Since threat assessment is evidence-based, it examines behaviors and situations to determine risk. Violence is a dynamic process. Threat assessment is not about determining whether someone is a "violent person." Rather, it attempts to identify the circumstances or situations in which individuals might pose a threat to themselves or others (Deisinger et al., 2008). The TMU has investigated allegations of murder for hire, terrorism, stalking, workplace and school violence, insider threat, destruction of property, high-risk domestic violence, and serial crimes like arson and rape. The TMU also has the capability to assist with antiterrorism and counterintelligence investigations. If one examines these activities closely, individuals engaged in stalking or surveillance will be seen to exhibit similar behaviors. Whether a suspect is stalking a girlfriend or surveilling a building, the person is attempting to disrupt operations or cause fear without getting caught. In both instances, the person is looking for vulnerabilities in behaviors and security procedures of the target in an effort to manipulate the situation to advantage.

When it was originally established, the TMU consisted of one agent and one operational psychologist who were assigned to work threat investigations on a part-time basis. Over the next few years, the TMU grew to one full-time division chief with responsibility for the NCIS TMU program, two full-time special agents based in headquarters, and one operational psychologist. This small team was responsible for developing all TMU training, procedures, and protocols while they worked TMU investigations occurring throughout the world. After this modest growth, the TMU quickly proved that it could successfully prevent crimes. With the success of the TMU, more and more commands within the Department of the Navy requested TMU support. In response to this increased demand, the unit has grown to include 30 TMU trained investigators stationed around the world. In addition to the other duties as criminal, counterintelligence, or counterterrorism investigators, these investigators receive specialized training at least once a year in order to assist their field offices with threat assessment/threat management investigations.

Under its current organizational structure, the NCIS TMU operates very efficiently. A division chief oversees the entire program and two headquarters-based special agents each have responsibility for investigations that originate in an area covering half of the world. The operational psychologist consults on any case that is deemed to be significant. Every year the NCIS headquarters team provides specialized threat assessment/threat management training to the 30 TMU trained special agents and investigators. The training and utilization of these field personnel saves significant funding. By investing a negligible amount of training funds, the NCIS receives a significant gain by developing this important investigative capacity. The special agents and investigators trained by the headquarters TMU are already seasoned investigators. The training they receive does not teach them how to investigate. Rather, the training teaches how to look at a case differently. The training explains how to utilize resources, recognize behaviors of concern and warning/danger signs, and implement strategies to stop

or mitigate the behaviors of concern. The training teaches what questions to ask and how to develop a case. All the special agents and investigators in the NCIS TMU are volunteers. By requesting the additional training, they are volunteering to take on extra responsibilities. However, TMU trained special agents or investigators are not always the lead agents in TMU investigations in their areas of responsibility. Instead, they simply use their training to provide other agents with expert consultation when the need arises.

THE NCIS TMU PREVENTS CRIMES

Because of its proactive approach to crime prevention, the goal of the NCIS TMU is not necessarily to arrest a suspect. Rather, the TMU focuses on seizing the initiative and stopping improper behavior from escalating or moving forward. For many in law enforcement, this is a difficult concept to grasp. Nevertheless, experience has proven that the concept works exceptionally well in the military. The TMU does not wait to become engaged until after a crime has been committed. By addressing threatening behavior before it escalates into a crime, a commanding officer may be able to save a career instead of having to send someone to jail or having to attend a funeral. The TMU also allows commanders to spend more time focused on accomplishing their operational missions because the TMU reduces the number of crimes committed by service members and thereby decreases the administrative burdens associated with prosecuting crimes in the military. By helping to stop crimes before they occur, the TMU facilitates proactive leadership within the Department of the Navy.

The TMU provides commanders and NCIS investigators with ongoing consultation. The TMU reviews all of the information gathered and then provides a written assessment to the case agent with responsibility for the investigation. This information is used by the case agent to make investigative decisions and brief other stakeholders as necessary. Throughout the pendency of an investigation, there might be more than one assessment completed. As the subject's behavior changes, so does the assessment. The assessments are completed with only the case information available at the time. The more information the TMU has to work with, the more accurate the assessment.

The NCIS TMU's headquarters element reviews and oversees all investigations involving threats or behaviors of concern. The headquarters TMU desk officers and/or the division chief review the investigations for general oversight and provide guidance and supervision to the field agents when necessary. In all, the NCIS TMU works approximately 180 TMU investigations a year, most of which fall into the categories of domestic violence and workplace/school violence. Many of these investigations are quickly determined to be low-risk concerns. Even if they are classified as being of low risk for violence, a full and inclusive investigation is completed. For the investigations thought to be of high risk for violence, the TMU addresses all issues on a high-priority basis and provides constant monitoring and reassessment. Any investigation can quickly turn into a volatile situation. The TMU's headquarters personnel improve communications within the NCIS TMU community by using a group email address that includes all NCIS TMU personnel. Any NCIS employee can use this email address to raise an issue with the entire NCIS TMU community. This email address has proven useful when a trained NCIS TMU agent has been absent from the office and untrained personnel are faced with a threat management issue.

INVESTIGATIVE STRATEGIES UTILIZED BY THE NCIS TMU

From the start of an investigation, the TMU works side by side with the special agent assigned as the lead investigator. The TMU provides consultation on the investigation. It can also provide investigative leads to follow and questions to ask both witnesses and the suspect. The TMU generally recommends more questions into the background and surrounding events. In most cases, criminal investigators focus on the facts immediately surrounding the reported crime. In TMU investigations, agents investigate the reported concern, but prior events, other incidents, and reactions by the suspect are also explored. Researching the possibility of ideas leading to action (Turner & Gelles, 2003), behaviors can reveal significant information the assessor can use during the immediate investigation and also during interviews and interrogation. By giving the reported concern more context, agents are more likely to achieve their goal of stopping a crime before it happens or preventing an escalation in violence. Upon being notified of a potential threat, the agent's first job is to ascertain the following:

- Who made the threat (or who is causing the concerning behavior)?
- Is the threat aimed at an installation?
- Is the threat against a specific person?
- Is the threat against a specific command or the military in general?
- What was the exact verbiage used to make the threat?
- How was the threat made?
- How was the threat reported?
- Are there witnesses to the threat or to the concerning behavior?
- Have there been prior concerns related or unrelated to this incident?
- If there have been prior incidents, how were they addressed?

As in every investigation, requested details will include full biographical data on the suspect and the potential victim. If the suspected individual is military, the command will provide the service member's Service Record Book for review. The Service Record Book details biographical data and military history. Military history includes duty stations, trainings, disciplinary actions, and command evaluations. This information is vital because it indicates whether the service member has had special weapons training and has been in trouble in the past and identifies past duty assignments.

Open-source and official database checks should always be conducted to see what other pertinent information can be gleaned about the subject, the situation, and the victim/target. Open-source information can include Facebook, Google, news sources, and so on. Official database checks can include but are not limited to the following:

- National Crime Information Center (NCIC), which is the US central database for tracking crime related information
- Defense Central Index of Investigations (DCII), which records all military investigations
- Law Enforcement Information Exchange (LInX), which is a joint regional and state project run by the NCIS to share law enforcement data
- Family Advocacy Program (FAP), which provides clinical assessment, treatment and services for military members and families

There are several ways in which the NCIS learns of threats or concerning behaviors. Because commands can notify the NCIS at any time, special agents are on call 24 hours a day, 7 days a week. The NCIS also has a continuously manned battle watch called the Multi-Threat Alert Center (MTAC) to monitor world-wide concerns. The MTAC has the ability to contact any NCIS agent at any time regardless of where they are stationed. If the MTAC receives a report, the information is documented and passed along to the responsible NCIS special agent. The MTAC maintains several hotline numbers, which can be used by private citizens as well as military members.

The NCIS also learns about threats through its Text Tip reporting system. Anyone can text in an anonymous concern through this system from anywhere in the world. A reported concern will be immediately reviewed and addressed. Other options for reporting concerning behavior include in-person reports as well as reports made by mail, telephone, and email. In receiving reports, the TMU prefers to acquire *exact* verbiage of all communications made by suspects. For threat management purposes, there is a significant difference between "I'm going to kill you" and "I'm going to shoot you." Both have the potential for violence, but stating "I'm going to shoot you" implies access to a weapon and specificity. This could be an indicator that the suspect's behavior is escalating toward violence.

Once a concern is reported, a determination must be made as to whether the threat is predatory in nature. If a threat appears to be predatory, it is planned, purposeful, and goal-oriented (Meloy, 2000). Next a determination needs to be made as to whether the target is a high priority. If the target is a high-level or senior military official, immediate notification will be made to the NCIS special agents who protect that individual. If the target is a naval ship, the command will be notified. While NCIS is notifying the responsible command, the TMU will attempt to determine the veracity of the report and what steps need to be taken immediately to ensure the safety of all involved.

TMU special agents and investigators attempt to determine who made the threat and where the individual is currently located. Location is important because the TMU wants to know if the individual has the ability to carry out the threat. Time and distance can be an asset or a liability for law enforcement depending on where the suspect and the victim are located. If the threatening individual does not have immediate access to the victim or target, whether he or she can obtain access to the victim or target is one of the first issues to be investigated. The TMU will also initially want to know the following:

- What are the command concerns regarding this threat or behavior?
- Are dependents or other civilians involved?
- Is the subject experiencing marital problems?
- Are there any concerns arising from a military deployment by the subject?
- Is the subject struggling with financial concerns?
- Has the subject been in trouble before? For what?

The TMU will request as much information as possible about the nature of the relationship between the subject and the victim or target. The subject's history of violence needs to be fully investigated and fully documented. It is important to note any prior concerning behaviors or threatening comments. The investigating agent should review US Department of Defense, state, and local records to see if the subject has been involved in any prior investigations as either a victim or subject. If the subject has been listed in a previous investigation, a complete review of the prior investigation(s) should be conducted to determine if there is any relationship to the current concern. In recording prior incidents, it is important to note when they occurred, where they occurred, who was involved, all known circumstances surrounding the event, and the outcome of each.

Once an investigation has been opened, the TMU will attempt to gather as much information as possible about the victim/target and the subject. By collecting and providing the TMU with as much information as available, the TMU's ability to provide an accurate assessment is increased. Specifically, the TMU will ask the investigator to ascertain the type of relationship the victim has with the subject. Typical questions that should be asked include the following:

- Does the subject work with the potential victim?
- Is he or she in a leadership position?
- Is he or she currently or previously married or romantically involved?
- Does the subject suspect a romantic rival?
- Have there been any threats against a third party?

- Is the situation complicated by a either a current or past romantic relationship?
- Are family members or members of the household involved? How?
- Have there been threats to harm family pets?
- Is there no known relationship?

The TMU will interview all the potential victims and witnesses. Typical questions asked during these interviews will include these:

- Why does the victim think that he or she was targeted?
- What information can the victim provide about the subject or about the situation?
- What were the reactions of the potential victim?
- How did the witnesses respond?
- How did the subject respond?
- Is the victim afraid? Why or why not?
- Are the witnesses afraid? Why or why not?
- Is stalking involved?
- Have there been harassing telephone calls or text messages?
- Is the subject using social networking sites on the Internet to annoy or threaten the victim?
- Is the subject using social networking sites on the internet to gather information about the victim?
- Is the subject trying to find out information about the target/victim through third parties?
- Has vandalism been a problem?
- Have there been prior threats or other behaviors of concern?
- Does the victim think that he or she has control over the situation? (How and why is important to note)
- What is the frequency of the incidents?
- Was there a triggering event?

Questions about triggering events provide helpful information. Specifically, the TMU will request details from the victim's and witnesses' perspective and eventually, when the subject is interviewed, from his or her perspective. These details may include the following:

- What made the behavior start and stop?
- Did the behavior stop because a third party intervened?
- What do the parties think would have happened if the third party had not intervened?

- What has the subject said to the victim(s) and/or potential witnesses?
- Could potential aggravating factors exist?
- If so, what could be potential "aggravating" factors (alcohol abuse, mental health concerns, or access to weapons)?
- Has the subject ever talked about suicide? The NCIS TMU is always concerned if a subject is having suicidal thoughts. If a person has decided that death or any type of violence will solve his or her problems, that person should be treated as a dangerous person (Warren, 2006).

Collection of any 911 tapes provides a lot of information that can be useful in a threat investigation. Tape recordings of telephone conversations can provide exact verbiage, potential witnesses, and more accurately show the potential level of anger or frustration being expressed. Despite their value, 911 tapes are not always available. That is especially true in many overseas locations. When a 911 tape is not available, an investigator should interview any emergency operators or responders to document the details of the contact.

If the victim or the subject has injuries, they need to be well documented. Documentation of the injuries should be accomplished by obtaining medical records and photographic evidence of the injuries. Photographic documentation should occur over several days, as bruises change over time. Bruising might not show up on the first day of an attack but will more than likely be visible a day or two later. In order to obtain access to a victim's medical records, he or she should be asked to give a release that permits the investigator to access the records. Reviewing these files can reveal prior injuries or incidents that may have been considered minor at the time, but now show a pattern of escalation.

It can be very useful to put all of the facts learned during an investigation into a time line. The time line should include all significant events in the subject's history as well as outcomes and responses. Putting events in a sequential order can help to reveal patterns of violence. Creating a time line can facilitate the investigation in other ways. A time line can be used during the interrogation, to check facts, provide potential leads, and, if necessary, for court purposes.

Military protective orders should be a consideration in any investigation where there is a potential for future violence. Military protective orders are direct orders from the subject's command limiting what actions the subject can take. For instance, military protective orders can preclude the subject from having any contact with the victim. The command could also direct the service member to temporarily move out of his or her home and into a barracks room. Alternatively, the command could restrict leave and direct the service member to remain on base. If the service member violates a military protective order, he or she can be held accountable by the command.

Despite the benefits of military protection orders, they do have some limitations. For instance, only military authorities can enforce a military protective order. Civilian law enforcement authorities cannot react to a violation of a military protective order. As a result, a military protective order can be used in conjunction with a restraining order to maximize the protection provided to a victim. A restraining order is issued by a state court to limit a subject's contact with a potential victim by keeping the two separated. Because a restraining order may not be enforceable outside of the state court's jurisdiction, it would not be enforceable overseas. If a subject violates a military protective order or a restraining order, the TMU recommends imposing immediate consequences.

If the subject agrees to talk to law enforcement authorities, the TMU strongly recommends interrogating the subject of an investigation in every case. Determining when to interrogate the suspect depends on the circumstances of the investigation. Investigators will want to hear the subject's perspective on the incidents and what he or she thought as the incident occurred. During the interrogation, the investigator should ask the following questions:

- What made you pick this target?
- What outcome were you hoping for?
- What planning was involved?
- What did you accomplish toward your goal?
- What brought you to this point?

Listening and learning the subject's side of the story gives the subject a voice. It can explain why he or she engaged in the concerning behavior and possibly shed light on how to deter future violence. On occasion, the subject truly does not realize that his or her actions were causing concern. In these cases, simply learning that the behavior prompted a criminal investigation can be enough of a consequence to stop a subject from committing any future acts of violence.

NCIS agents always ask for a permissive search of the subject's belongings. The purpose is to look for possible weapons or journals and to review the computer to see if the subject was blogging, discussing, or researching anything that could be considered concerning. Photographs, videos, phone records, and social networking sites are reviewed. All electronic media are evaluated and documented by specially trained professionals.

In every instance the subject is released to his or her command after interrogation. In cases where there is a concern for safety, the TMU will recommend that the command refer the subject to medical to evaluate his or her health and potential for violence. The TMU can only make a recommendation to the subject's command because NCIS agents cannot refer a military member for medical evaluation. Only a service member's command can make such a referral. However, NCIS agents can provide the medical team with an investigative history so that a complete medical evaluation can be made.

Additionally, the NCIS normally recommends that the command assign someone to conduct a "welfare check." A welfare check can be conducted by anyone in command, but TMU generally recommends that a senior enlisted person be instructed to stay in contact with the subject to periodically check on his or her welfare. A welfare check does not cost anything, but the dividends can be tremendous. It shows the subject that the command cares about his or her safety and welfare. It also gives NCIS and the command the opportunity to learn about any further concerns.

Throughout the investigation, all information will be documented in the case file and the command will be briefed throughout the pendency of the investigation. At the conclusion of the investigation, the command will be provided with an overall report. The command will then review the entire report and make a determination of how to dispose of the case. After the command has resolved the case, the investigation will be reported out and the investigation will be closed. If new information becomes available or additional concerning behavior is reported, the investigation can be reopened or a new investigation can be initiated.

CASE STUDY

(The names and locations have been changed. Additionally, some investigative actions have been deliberately left out. This information does not change or in any way alter how the writer detailed the investigation or the TMU response.)

The NCIS received a report from a local police station about a military member who was asking strange questions about a local shopping mall. Apparently an enlisted service member, Ed, had contacted the shopping mall where his wife worked and asked unusual questions of mall security. These questions were concerning enough that the mall security contacted local law enforcement, who in turn contacted the NCIS.

As background, Ed, age 19, and Sheila, age 18, had dated for approximately two months prior to getting married. Several months into the marriage, Ed enlisted in the US Navy. When Ed enlisted, Sheila was pregnant with their first child. Ed was trained in security and sent to a remote duty location outside of the United States. Sheila gave birth while Ed was overseas. Shortly after the birth of their child, Sheila filed for divorce. Because of his remote location, Ed had never seen his child. During the divorce proceedings, Ed was still stationed outside of the United States. However, he found out or suspected that Sheila was romantically involved with another man. Sheila worked part-time at a fast-food restaurant in a local mall. The man she was dating worked at the same mall as a security officer.

In the military, Ed was assigned and trained in security. He had training in law enforcement and basic surveillance. Utilizing his law enforcement skills, Ed researched the mall where his wife worked. He took note of the entrances, the exits, and the building's overall design. Ed was able to find out the phone number of mall security, which he used to call them on at least four occasions. During at least two of these calls, Ed used a different name to identify himself. He told mall security that he was employed as a protection specialist and was hired by a wealthy sheik who wanted to shop at the mall. During the phone calls, Ed asked questions about the law enforcement response time should he need to contact them on the sheik's behalf. He asked about emergency exits and where their alarms would be received. He told them not to be concerned if he was seen wearing a weapon, as this was necessary for the sheik's protection. He inquired about whether or not the mall security personnel were armed and the number of security personnel who were on duty. He also asked about shift changes and who would be on duty when he was in the area.

Mall security became suspicious about the phone calls. They recorded the telephone number and

called it back the next day. Ed answered the phone and admitted to having called them. Subsequently, the security guard who had been dating Shelia asked her if she knew Ed. Sheila explained that she and Ed were divorcing and involved in a custody dispute. Mall security contacted local law enforcement and gave them all the information. In turn, the local law enforcement office contacted the NCIS for assistance. The NCIS TMU was immediately made aware of the situation and began providing guidance.

Initially, the command reported that Ed had recently been seen by medical and had only lately been cleared to return to full duty. Ed had become despondent shortly after Sheila gave birth to their child. He was initially offered the opportunity to travel back to the United States to see the baby, but he declined. Shortly afterwards, however, he became depressed. Several of his coworkers became concerned about his behavior and contacted base authorities, who went to his barracks room to check on him. When security arrived at his room, Ed became angry and threatened that he would either hurt himself or "kill everyone in his duty section."

After the command referred Ed to medical for an evaluation, the command learned that Ed was struggling with anger, depression, occupational stressors, and sleep disturbance. While at medical, Ed indicated that he suppressed his moods until he was alone, stating "I bottle it up until I explode." Ed also reported crying nightly to his wife via telephone. He also identified occupational stressors because he was in a job that he did not want to have. Instead of working for base security, Ed wanted to work in the medical field. He reported an inability to sleep, nightmares, and frequent hand washing. The medical evaluation reported he had a possible obsessive compulsive disorder and anxiety.

In response to being asked what he hoped to achieve and how medical could help him, Ed wrote, "Control my mood. Help me to not be so sad. Help to control my anger." He inconsistently described his relationship with his wife as "loving, close" and including "stormy arguments." He also reported being sexually abused by a babysitter but did not provide any details explaining the abuse. His questionnaire also revealed a drinking problem and that Ed was feeling, angry, sad, anxious, panicky, envious, hopeless, regretful, ashamed, numb, annoyed, depressed, energetic, confused, bored, lonely, tense, helpless, and jealous. Ed indicated that he felt like a nobody who was worthless, useless, ugly, and unattractive.

He revealed that he was confused and could not think clearly. He had difficulty making friends and felt that people did not like him. Ed explained that he constantly made mistakes and felt that he could not do anything correctly. Ed also stated, "I will soon be recognized by the world for who I am."

Ed was prescribed several antidepressants. Shortly after he started using these medications, he reported experiencing chronic sleep problems. He was subsequently taken off antidepressants and prescribed diazepam (Valium) for about two months. During this time, Ed's duty weapon was removed from his custody. Later, during the TMU investigation, Ed revealed that the loss of his weapon caused him additional stress. As Ed continued to take his medications and follow through with medical, he began to show improvement. Because the command was unaware of his phone calls to the mall, the command put Ed back on a full duty status and returned his weapon.

Because of the remote location of the duty station, the closest NCIS agent was located in another country about five hours away by plane. It was clear from the beginning that command cooperation would be necessary to prevent a potential tragedy. The command reported that Ed had recently requested leave to attend court hearings for custody of his child. Interviews revealed that he planned on staying with his grandparents, who lived in a town close to the mall. Because he was an avid hunter, Ed's grandfather had several weapons in the house.

Armed with this information, TMU suggested that Ed's leave be canceled until the investigation was complete. TMU developed a list of very detailed questions for use by the NCIS agents in the field in gathering behavioral and actionable details. In addition to normal investigative protocols, the TMU recommended asking Sheila the following questions:

- Why were she and Ed divorcing?
- Was she aware if Ed had any suicidal ideations?
- Had Ed ever threatened her?
- Is Sheila dating? If so, who? (A new boyfriend is a potential target)
- Is Ed aware Sheila is dating? Does he know who she is dating?
- Has Ed ever made a threat against anyone else?
- How did Ed react when he learned Sheila wanted a divorce?

- How did Ed react to stress? What are his triggers? How does he normally de-escalate?
- What are Ed's coping skills?
- How often does Sheila communicate with Ed? Who initiates the communication?
- How does the conversation end?
- Is she keeping information away from Ed? Why?
- Has Ed ever become violent with her? What were the circumstances?
- Are there visitation plans for the baby? Is she concerned about the baby's safety?

The TMU asked to have Ed's parents and grandparents interviewed for the following information:

- How does Ed cope with stress?
- What did Ed communicate to them about his problems with Sheila?
- Who does Ed trust?
- Do they communicate with Sheila? What information are they getting from her?
- Are they familiar with any incidents where Ed became violent? Can they provide details?
- Has Ed ever expressed suicidal ideations?
- Did Ed tell them about his phone calls to the mall?
- Has Ed ever expressed any homicidal thoughts?

During her interview, Ed's mom stated that Sheila began to talk about divorcing Ed almost immediately after giving birth to their child. Ed's mom cited their constant arguments as the reason for the separation. She also stated that Sheila would often threaten to keep the child away from Ed unless he provided her with more financial support. His mom stated she never saw Ed become physically violent. Ed's grandparents were interviewed and reported Ed was not a violent person. They denied knowing any reason why he would call the mall and ask about security.

Although the command had provided information about Ed previously, TMU requested answers to further questions, such as the following:

- How did he respond when his weapon was removed?
- What kind of sailor is Ed?
- Has there been a change in his work behavior? How?
- What kind of job stressors does Ed have?

- How does he cope with stress?
- How do they anticipate that Ed will react to having his leave denied?

Interviews of Ed's military coworkers generally portrayed Ed as an individual who was prone to lying and was considered a "loner." None of Ed's coworkers thought that he was violent, but at least one fellow sailor stated that she was afraid to work with Ed because of a rumor that he had threatened to kill himself or "shoot everyone in his duty section." She also overheard Ed make disparaging comments about Sheila and heard him say that he hated Sheila.

The TMU also recommended that Ed be interrogated. In order to prepare for his interrogation, the TMU recommended the following questions:

- What did Ed plan on doing when he got back to the United States?
- What did Ed plan on doing at the mall?
- Why did Ed solicit so much security information about the mall and local police response time?
- Does Ed have a parenting plan for his child?
- How does Ed feel about his wife dating other men?
- What are Ed's feelings for Sheila?
- Does Ed want to stay in the military?
- Who is Ed angry with? Why?
- Has Ed had any suicidal or homicidal thoughts?
- Has Ed been researching anything which could be viewed as concerning to command and or NCIS?
- What does Ed feel about his leave being canceled?
- What are Ed's future plans?

As the investigation was progressing, TMU recommended several investigative steps, including the following:

- A search of Ed's computer, social networking sites, and personal effects (journals, notebook) that could contain evidence of suicidal or homicidal ideation and/or attack planning.
- A review of the contents of his computer for documents, websites visited, or emails reflecting the same.
- A review of his Navy email account and cell phone records to identify with whom he had contact regarding any attack plans.

- A determination of Ed's access to firearms through individuals at home other than his grandparents.
- An assessment of Ed's training and skill sets in firearms, surveillance, and other operational skills that could be used to carry out a violent attack.
- A review of Ed's Service Record Book to see if the military provided him with countersurveillance training and if there were any issues during his training.
- An assessment of Ed's history of violence with Sheila and others. Sheila reported that Ed had been violent with her in the past but only mentioned one incident.
- Identification of situations where Ed acted out violently and the specific triggers to his violent behaviors.
- Identification of the outcomes and consequences of the behavior.
- A determination of whether Ed had a history of communicating threats and his behavior following the threats (e.g., threatening to kill someone and then damaging that person's property).
- Interviews with coworkers, family, and Ed himself to determine how he normally copes with stressful situations.
- An attempt to determine when and why he resorts to poor methods of coping. Is there a triggering event?
- Identification of those who were providing information from home to Ed. He knew that Sheila worked at a fast-food restaurant at the mall and that she was dating a mall security officer. How did he obtain this information?

These investigative steps yielded important information. For example, a forensic analysis of Ed's laptop computer showed that he had schematics of the mall and that he had been researching high-temperature accelerants. The analysis also showed that Ed had been researching child pornography, but no pornography was ever found. The investigators also found two documents created by Ed that appeared to be long rants expressing negative feelings toward his command and the Navy. In both documents, Ed threatened to harm himself and others aboard his base. In addition to the evidence found on Ed's computer, his telephone records revealed that Ed called Sheila's home and mobile phone numbers excessively, although most of the calls went unanswered. Ed called Shelia 377 times in a four-month period and made as many as 33 calls in one day.

As the information was reported to the TMU, a behavioral assessment was completed. The assessment concluded that based on the information presented there were several risk factors that significantly increased Ed's risk for violence. He was struggling with his divorce and custody issues. He was unhappy in his occupation and displayed several pre-attack behaviors that heightened the concern. Most significantly, his extensive research into the mall where Sheila worked suggested that he had thought through how to launch an attack. This behavioral assessment was verbally briefed to command and later to medical personnel.

As the information was gathered, the NCIS TMU recommended a multitiered management plan. Ed's responses to medical, especially the comment, "I will soon be recognized by the world for who I am," remained a significant concern. First, the NCIS TMU recommended that Ed's leave be canceled to prevent him from going home. Although attending a custody hearing was a legitimate reason for leave, keeping Ed at his remote duty station would prevent him from harming Sheila, her new boyfriend or anyone else back home. The TMU recommended monitoring Ed's reaction to the news that his leave had been canceled. This information needed to be passed along to the mental health professional. It could also be used as either a positive sign that Ed understood why his actions caused concern, or a negative sign if he appeared to become enraged or threatening.

The idea that Ed might try to commit suicide also remained a significant concern. As a result, the TMU recommended that Ed be evaluated by appropriate medical personnel. The TMU was willing to provide the mental health professional with all pertinent case information so that an accurate diagnosis could be obtained. Additionally, the TMU suggested that the command assign a more senior enlisted sailor to act as a "welfare check" person. In response, Ed's command assigned a Navy Chief to conduct checks on Ed's welfare. This person was able to act as Ed's sounding board in addition to keeping the command informed of Ed's ability to cope with his situation.

The TMU also recommended that the command work with the local military attorneys to ensure that Ed's personal legal issues were being addressed. Because the command was going to cancel his leave, Ed would be unable to attend any court proceeding.

He would remain overseas. The TMU recommended that command legal get in touch with the appropriate legal personnel in the United States to make sure that Ed's rights were protected during the custody hearing.

The command appreciated the NCIS TMU recommendations and immediately addressed all the concerns. Ed was seen by medical personnel, who were able to diagnose him. Shortly thereafter, Ed began treatment and working with a counselor. Ed slowly moved to a more positive state of mind. Because his command worked with Ed and his attorney back in the United States, Ed's divorce was finalized and he was awarded regular visitation once he returned to the United States. Ed reported that he was satisfied with the way in which his legal needs had been addressed. Ed was moved out of his position with base security and into a medical position. Ed reported that he was hoping to enter the medical field when he first enlisted and was very pleased with his new assignment. He began to accept the divorce and to figure out a parenting plan so that he could maintain a relationship with his daughter.

SUCCESSFUL OUTCOME

Because of the immediate participation of the TMU and the cooperation of the command, local law enforcement, and the local legal system, a possible tragedy was averted. Ed went through his mental health evaluation and was placed on medication. The command and mental health worked with him to make sure his work and personal life issues were being addressed. As a result, Ed successfully returned to a full duty status and has not expressed any further suicidal ideations. Throughout the investigative process, Ed was treated with dignity and respect. Everyone cooperated and all were willing to work together to do what was best. In the end, everyone remained safe and alive.

OVERVIEW OF THE TMU INVESTIGATION

This investigation crossed multiple boundaries and presented some unusual challenges. At least five NCIS offices were tasked with investigative steps. This, like every NCIS investigation, was worked by a team of special agents striving for a common goal—to get accurate information quickly. Communication is extremely important in working these types of investigations. Throughout the investigation, the lines of communications were kept open. Everyone stayed apprised of the investigation's current status. The obstacles of distance, multiple agents, and multiple locations (spanning three countries and several jurisdictions within the United States) were overcome by keeping all affected parties informed of the situation and events. NCIS TMU Headquarters was kept constantly aware via email and phone calls.

In this investigation, distance assisted in a positive outcome. Although the primary agent assigned to this investigation had to fly multiple times to Ed's duty station to conduct briefings and interviews, Ed's inability to have access to Sheila and her new boyfriend gave the NCIS TMU time to work out a successful outcome. It would have taken approximately four days and multiple plane flights for Ed to reach Sheila. The investigators had time to interview all the appropriate people and to work with medical. By leveraging the factors of time and distance, the NCIS TMU and command increased the likelihood that targeted violence would be avoided. However, there was always a concern that Ed would try to hurt himself or potentially his shipmates. In order to mitigate those risks, the command did everything it could to make sure that Ed was provided all available resources—legal, medical, and social.

Although the command canceled his leave, it helped Ed to address his legal and personal issues. The command's willingness to get Ed the help he needed made for a fast and proper medical diagnosis. The command made it possible for Ed to report to all counseling appointments for as long as deemed necessary by medical personnel. It provided a person to check up on his welfare so that Ed could have someone to use as a sounding board and could also vent his feelings. This person also kept the command advised of Ed's overall status. The command provided all information needed to complete a full and complete investigation. With TMU's support, the agents in the field were able to ask all the right questions and gather all the proper information so that a solid assessment could be completed. Ed's willingness to help himself contributed to the success of this investigation. Ed understood that the path he was headed on would not have ended well for him and possibly others.

The command knew enough to contact NCIS immediately when the concern became known. The special agent knew that the TMU could assist with this investigation and had the confidence to ask for assistance from fellow special agents. It was important to gain the trust of the command, medical, the victims and witnesses, and, most importantly, Ed. Without everyone's cooperation and the willingness to do the right thing, this investigation might have had a much different outcome.

The command was made aware that if another issue arose, the TMU and NCIS were prepared to re-engage. Teamwork and the ability to act quickly and decisively were the key elements for a successful outcome in this investigation. Utilizing all tools available, the TMU, medical, legal, and command authority all played a significant role in keeping all parties safe. In the end, Ed's cooperation and willingness to help himself was really what saved his career.

When the agents interrogated him, he was treated with respect and provided with information about the concerns. The NCIS afforded him the opportunity to help himself. He admitted to what he had done and fully cooperated with the mental health professionals. Because he was honest, they were able to accurately diagnose and treat him. Everyone (Ed, Sheila, Ed's family, mall security, local law enforcement, and command) had a hand in successfully averting a tragedy. Teamwork, a solid investigation, communication, and cooperation were essential to avoiding a potentially violent situation.

CONCLUSION

Working threat assessment/threat management investigations in a military environment is challenging. The stress of deployments, youth, separation of family, inability to discuss work due to classification, and frequent moves to new duty stations can significantly affect a person's ability to cope. When a person makes poor choices that could cause potential harm to another, a command, or an installation, the NCIS TMU has the obligation and the ability to investigate. The TMU provides an immediate analysis and assessment of threatening behaviors. The TMU also provides behavioral risk assessments, placing the communication and/or threatening behavior on a continuum of potential violence and offering recommendations for investigative strategies and security-related solutions. Threat assessment examines a person's behavior, situation, and stressors in an effort to identify the potential risk and impact of any interventions.

ACKNOWLEDGEMENT

The views expressed in this chapter are my own and do not necessarily represent the views of NCIS, the US Navy, or the Department of Defense.

KEY POINTS

- The TMU is cost-effective. Everyone assigned is already a trained investigator. Only three or four employees work for the TMU on a full-time basis. The special agents and investigators in the field are already trained investigators. Their work for the TMU is a collateral duty for them. The NCIS has to fund training only once a year.
- Special agents and investigators working for the TMU are volunteers. They enjoy the challenges and therefore are able to provide the commands with good, solid investigations.
- TMU investigations are challenging and dynamic. As the behavior changes, so does the assessment.
- In order to work a good TMU investigation, the most important element is good communication. Communication with the command, with medical, with other agents, and with the victims and witnesses is vital. Good communication builds trust.

REFERENCES

Fein, R., & Vossekuil, B. (1999). Assassination in the United States: An operational study of recent assassins, attackers, and near-lethal approachers. *Journal of Forensic Sciences, 44*, 321–333.

Meloy, J. R. (2000). *Violence risk and threat assessment: A practical guide for mental health and criminal justice professionals.* San Diego, CA: Specialized Training Services.

Deisinger, G., Randazzo, M., O'Neill, D. & Savage, J. (2008). *The handbook for campus threat assessment & management teams.* Boston: Applied Risk Management.

Turner, J. T., & Gelles, M. G. (2003). *Threat assessment: A risk management approach.* Binghamton, NY: Haworth Press.

Warren, L. J. (2006). Managing the client who threatens violence. *InPsych: Bulletin of the Australian Psychological Society, 28*, October, pp. 20–21.

27

Assessing Threats by Direct Interview of the Violent True Believer

J. REID MELOY AND KRIS MOHANDIE

Individuals who are "violent true believers" encompass a variety of personalities with very different social, cultural, and emotional backgrounds. They may be interviewed by law enforcement, intelligence, or military personnel in many different roles, such as detainee, arrestee, military combatant, defendant, suspect, or witness. The length of the interview may also vary from a few hours to multiple sessions over an indefinite period of time while such an individual is detained. Regardless of the differences across personality and situation, the definition of the "violent true believer" we are using remains the same: an individual who appears to be committed to an ideology or belief system, whether secular or religious, that advances the killing of the self and/or others as a legitimate means to further a particular goal (Meloy, 2011; Meloy et al., 2001).

Among violent true believers, moreover, there appear to be a number of different types; these include the (1) unwavering true believer, (2) the affiliative true believer, (3) the opportunistic true believer, (4) the criminal true believer, (5) the betrayer true believer, (6) the psychotic true believer, and (7) the fledgling true believer. These types, their needs/sensitivities, and the approach behaviors recommended to the interviewer are detailed in the *FBI Law Enforcement Bulletin* (Meloy, 2011).

We concern ourselves here with general comments and recommendations regarding the interviewing of such individuals. These guidelines are not binding and should be treated with the skepticism, until proven otherwise, and openness to modification that they deserve. They are based on the combined clinical and forensic interview experience of the authors, who are trained in forensic and police psychology, as well as multiple interviews with approximately a dozen personnel from the FBI, CIA, Army Intelligence, Department of Defense, and state law enforcement who are currently involved or extensively experienced in both foreign and domestic interviewing of individuals meeting our definition of the violent true believer.

PREPARATION

The greatest mistake made by interviewers of these individuals is the failure to prepare before the interview begins. Preparation falls into four categories: (1) selecting the interviewer, (2) gathering data before the interview, (3) defining the approach and direction of the interview, and (4) choosing the place for the interview.

1. *For most interviews there should be no more than two interviewers.* If a translator is needed, he or she should be the only other person in the room. Translators should be directed to translate the exact words the interviewee speaks. Care should be taken that an emotional relationship does not develop between the interviewee and the translator. One way to accomplish this is to have a different translator for each

interview. *The same interviewers, however, should be used across all interviews.* Observers should be watching the interview from another location and not be present in the room. We discourage group interviews of one individual for several reasons: (a) they dilute any chance of a bond forming between interviewer and interviewee; (b) multiple interviewers will raise anxiety and fear in most interviewees, which will usually limit data collection unless these emotions are being intentionally provoked for a specific reason; (c) multiple interviewers, in some cases, will provide a platform or an audience for a few interviewees to manipulate or provide disinformation; (d) multiple interviewers may set up a situation where there is competition among interviewers to ask the best question or score the most points, which usually leads nowhere and may provoke criticism among the interviewers toward each other or among agencies, thus reducing effectiveness.

There should be reasons for the selection of the interviewer. There may be a desire to bring in someone who reflects the culture, nationality, race, ethnicity, and religion of the interviewee. On the other hand, a person very different from the interviewee may evoke other feelings, which could lead to much useful information.

The age of the interviewer is a factor to be weighed. An interviewer who is younger than the interviewee may stimulate fatherly or authority feelings in the latter, which can be useful with certain types of violent true believers (Meloy, 2011). On the other hand, an older, more authoritative, and dominant interviewer may be selected to stimulate childlike or adolescent feelings in the interviewee. Emotions in the interviewee, both situationally evoked and historically based (transference), are always present and can be used as a source of control and manipulation for behavioral intelligence.

The gender of the interviewer is also very important. Violent true believers are typically men and see women in very constrained and domesticated roles. A female interviewer will evoke emotion in the interviewee, which can be purposefully used as long as it is thought about beforehand and identified when it occurs.

The skill level of the interviewer should be carefully assessed, and experience should be highly valued if it has been productive in past interviews.

2. *Interviewers need to do their homework.* They should have a working knowledge of the culture, society, politics, and religion from which the interviewee comes; they should also study any personal data or intelligence available on the interviewee beforehand. This is important for two reasons: it helps establish rapport with the interviewee if there is rudimentary knowledge of his or her background; and it helps the interviewer identify moments when he or she is being lied to or manipulated because the information known beforehand is inconsistent with what is said during the interview. An information grid that identifies facts known prior to the interview is useful for tracking deception, verifying truth, and identifying new information.

3. *The interviewer should define the approach and direction of the interview.* Each interview should be customized to the interviewee, the time frame, and the purpose of the interview. Will the approach most useful to this interviewee be authoritative and dominant? Or should the approach be done by a younger interviewer with a desire to learn from the interviewee? Is there time to build rapport with the interviewee before specific questions are asked, or is there an imminent threat? Should the interview be postponed until there is time for rapport building? Will there be time for multiple visits with the interviewee over the course of several days, weeks, or months? What is the goal to be achieved by the end of the first interview? If strategic and tactical information is revealed during the first interview, a healthy skepticism is useful given that it may be purposeful disinformation. On the other hand, all interviews are successful if one of the goals is to gather *behavioral* data on the interviewee for use in subsequent interviews.

4. *The location of the interview is very important.* Does the interviewer want to convey a sense of privacy and respect for the interviewee? Is this reflected in the choice of the room? Should the interviewee know the transportation route to the interview place? Is safety and security adequate to manage any violence during the interview? How close will the interviewer sit to the interviewee? Should there be a table between them? Should food or drink be served during the interview to establish a sense of hospitality? Are there certain artifacts or symbols that should be present in the room—perhaps to build an alliance or to intimidate—and what do they convey to the interviewee?

In most situations, the interview room should not allow for the psychological escape of the interviewee. In other words, there should be no distracting views, pictures, furniture, or other artifacts to make it easier for him to be inattentive. If there are objects, props, or views in the room, they should be there for a purpose—that is, to facilitate the goals of the interview.

The 17th lesson in the *Al Qaeda Training Manual* (UK/BM-162 translation) teaches the interviewee to expect "psychological warfare and intellectual combat." Harsh words and torture are also expected. "The room is ordinary, containing one or more desks, some chairs, and some torture devices, as needed." There is also a directive that "the brother should memorize the appearance of the interrogation building, its interior, and the appearance of the officers. The interrogation is a major opportunity for the group as long as the brother is tactful, bright, and observant.... one should concentrate heavily on the route and try to memorize any signs in order to benefit operations and plan development."

Behaving in ways that are consistent with the interviewee's training will build confidence for the interviewee. Behaving in ways quite different from what he expects may confuse and disorient him. This is "cognitive dissonance," and will create a state of mind that exerts pressure on the individual to change his expectations and perceptions of the interviewer. For example, if the interviewer is civil, patient, and polite over the course of many interviews, this will not be expected and will increase stress. On the other hand, knowledge that no physical torture will be used by American military, intelligence, or law enforcement personnel also builds confidence. Interviewee behaviors that are consistent with the *Al Qaeda Training Manual*—such as asking to see a medical examiner before the interview begins and asking that evidence of his "torture" be entered into any official report—indicate that the interviewee is familiar with the manual.

PLACEMENT BEFORE AND AFTER THE INTERVIEW

Isolation of the interviewee before and after the interview will, over time, increase his attachment to the interviewer. Human beings, with few exceptions, are biologically hard-wired to form bonds to other human beings, regardless of their race, culture, nationality, or religious belief. This will happen whether the interviewee wants it or not. Researchers for many years have known of the "Stockholm syndrome," wherein hostages form emotional attachments to their captors. Recent research refers to this as "traumatic bonding"

(Dutton & Painter, 1993), and it has been shown that this form of bonding is increased if there is (1) a large power differential between the two individuals, and (2) aversive consequences are intermittent and unpredictable. For example, a lengthy and harsh interrogation followed by the offer of food, drink, or comfort is *a negative reinforcement* (the withdrawal of a noxious or unwanted stimulus). This will tend to stimulate the bond to the person who is perceived to have eliminated the discomfort.

Attachment can be increased by using one's personal name and disclosing certain personal information. The limits of self-disclosure and whether the self-disclosure is a fabrication or the truth must be decided before the interview begins and consistently followed. If personal history is fabricated by the interviewer to establish rapport, the details must be simple and completely memorized, since the details of a "false self" are much more difficult to recall than an actual personal history.

Attachment is a powerful biological force in all humans, and it can also affect the interviewer. For example, feelings of gratitude or sympathy for the interviewee are emotional signs that the interviewer is also developing a bond. These feelings need to be carefully monitored so that they do not distort the direction or the outcome of the interviews. Awareness of these feelings, even if disliked, is far superior to attempts to deny them.

Whether or not isolation is used depends, of course, on the legal status of the interviewee and the nature of the detention, if any. If possible, the interview should be the interviewee's only "job" for the day and his only significant emotional contact.

If the interviewee has access to his associates before and/or after the interview, it should be assumed that he will communicate data from the interview to his associates. This can serve a useful purpose if done intentionally—for example, the interviewer may disclose certain information to the interviewee that the interviewer wants disseminated to others. Housing individuals in groups also provides an opportunity for *cross-talk monitoring*: assessing what is said from one individual to another and also assessing the various behaviors of individuals within the group. For example, Who is in charge? Who is dominant? Who is isolative? Who controls the conversations? Who is dependent on whom for certain favors or supplies? Assessing the *status* of the individual within his group is very important to ascertain his leadership qualities and the amount of information he likely possesses. Individuals from the lower echelon of the group typically do not know; those from the higher echelon typically do not talk. Separation or segregation of individuals in custody by level of cooperation and commitment to the cause should be seriously considered, since it prevents the recruitment of more ambivalent individuals.

ESTABLISHING RAPPORT

This is the most important part of the interview and provides the emotional vehicle for the conveyance of useful information or intelligence. Rapport may not guarantee credible information, but the lack of rapport will certainly impede it.

Rapport can often be established by doing five things:

1. *Smiling.* This is a universal gesture of goodwill regardless of culture, nationality, or religion. Research indicates that individuals who receive a smile from another feel accepted and not judged. Smiling will also be unexpected by the violent true believer. Although the Al Qaeda manual states that kindness may be used initially, in subsequent meetings it is predicted that the subject will be "blindfolded, beaten, and tortured."

2. *Listening carefully.* Most people do not listen to each other in an open and patient manner. If the interviewer is attentive, nonjudgmental, and shows interest in the other person, a very positive emotional dynamic will be put in place, even if the interviewee is very distrustful and hates what the interviewer represents (the FBI, Americans, infidels, etc.). His resistance to the interviewer will be emotionally challenged by his desire to be heard. In listening, tilt the head forward and slightly to the side (Dreeke, 2011).

3. *Finding something in common.* Identify a characteristic that is shared between the interviewer and interviewee and point it out. It could be marriage, a child, a common geographical area visited, a certain amount of education, or interest in a certain sport. Find it and say it. In times of war or combat, "the enemy" is always characterized as completely different from oneself. This is never true because all combatants are human beings and share certain desires, such as a home, family,

security, and the welfare of one's children. Soldiers in all wars are deeply disturbed when they find photos of family members in the pockets of the "enemy" soldier they have just killed (Grossman, 1995). In one instance, a strong bond was established between interviewer and interviewee in a cave in Afghanistan because they both were freezing for hours as the interview was conducted—and both survived the chilling temperature through the night. Their shared trait was their need for warmer clothing and their vulnerability as human beings to the cold (Soufan, 2011).

4. *Mirroring the interviewee.* This refers to mimicking the interviewee's body language and words, which takes attention and practice. If it is done too obviously, it will be noticed and rapport will not arise. It may mean sitting the same way, making similar gestures, using some of the same words, even using similar emotional tones of voice. For example, in the Islamic religion, whenever Mohammed, Jesus, or Moses—their three great prophets—are mentioned, the name is followed by the statement, "blessings and peace be upon his name."

5. *Avoiding blunders.* Allowing the soles of one's shoes to face another person is considered an insult in the Arabic culture. Displaying a cold and unfriendly demeanor is considered an insult. Conveying impatience, such as glancing at one's watch or tapping one's fingers on the table, is considered an insult. Certain gestures may be an insult. Study the culture and know what the blunders are (Nydall, 1996).

THE LINE OF QUESTIONING

All interviews require patience and flexibility. Depending on the time frame, interviews should be done in two- to three-hour increments over the course of days or weeks. Predictability should be avoided, however, since it builds confidence and reduces stress. Interviews should be done at any time, day or night. The length of time accomplishes three things: first, it conveys to the interviewee that the interviewer considers him important; second, it allows time for establishing rapport; and third, it creates fatigue in the interviewee, which may lead to inadvertent admissions. If the interviewee absolutely refuses to cooperate by sitting mute, the interview should not be terminated early, as this only reinforces the uncooperative behavior. If necessary, the interviewer and interviewee can sit and stare at each other for the original length of the interview. Establishing artificial time constraints also builds rapport because it signals that there is an end in sight (Dreeke, 2011) and will typically reduce stress in the interviewee if that is the goal.

The key to interviewing the violent true believer is to get him talking about anything. Open-ended and nonjudgmental questions, such as, "Why do you think America finds itself in the situation it's in right now?" gives control and permission to the interviewee to talk. Other questions, such as "Tell me about Islam," or "Tell me about your work," are more personal but still convey a sense of interest in the history and belief system of the interviewee. Above all, *do not challenge the religion or ideology of the violent true believer.* For example, to begin arguing with the interviewee as to whether or not the Koran justifies killing unbelievers will invite anger and a refusal to continue.

Approaching the subject with a wish to understand and allowing him to brag about his history, sacrifice, beliefs, or family will go a long way toward establishing rapport and accessing information. Later on, more personal questions—such as, "Did you join a mosque?" "How old are you?" "Whom did you admire in the mosque?" "How did your friends react to your decisions?" "What did you have to give up?"—can all lead to inadvertent admissions or to facts that will either fill in unknown gaps in intelligence or may confirm other facts that had not yet been verified.

Probably the most important technique in questioning is to freely use the phrase, "Tell me more," or "Please explain that more to me so I understand." Showing admiration is also very useful. Compliments are particularly important in the Arab cultures and can lead to unintended but critical admissions. Nonverbal expressions, however, must be congruent with the words chosen. For example, using the phrase "tell me more," and then glancing at one's watch will stimulate distrust in the interviewee.

The line of questioning should move from the least anxious and threatening content to the most. For instance, impersonal questions about the history of one's country or religion can be followed by questions about the interviewee's own religious upbringing or conversion. Remote history is usually much less threatening than recent history. Questions about female members of the family will be very threatening to any fundamentalist and should be avoided,[1] while questions about distant male relatives will be much less threatening. Getting an interviewee to talk about his life and development as a terrorist—although he may consider himself a soldier—helps us understand how he operates. Move slowly and carefully from "there and then" to "here and now."

Questions should also move from open-ended to more closed questions, such as "Where were you born?" "When were you born?" "Have you attended school?" "Who were your friends in school?" "What countries have you lived in?" "When?" "Where?" "Have you ever been to the United States?" All of these questions require a specific answer that can often be verified. They are also more personal and may raise the anxiety of the interviewee. Fact-specific questions may also be accompanied by physical evidence, which is either shown to the interviewee or left in the room where the interviewee can see it. These items may evoke emotion in the interviewee if they have personal importance or may provide evidence that contradicts what he has said before. Props should be used only if a specific purpose has been identified for them.

In one case, the interviewee was shown photos of some of the 9/11 terrorists—he did not know that they were identified on the planes and were dead—and told that they were talking about him. His emotional reaction led him to reveal that he knew some of them. He was subsequently confronted with the photos again and told that they were the 9/11 terrorists and were dead. His inability to deny personal knowledge of the men led to his extreme emotional distress and the revelation that Al Qaeda was responsible for the attacks (Soufan, 2011).

Persistent questioning in the same areas may be required to yield useful information. Re-asking questions an hour or two after the question was answered in detail the first time can betray lying or falsification because the answer may be slightly different.

One interviewer recommends a three-step approach to the line of questioning: (1) give the individual a doubt about his belief—for example, by behaving civilly and politely over time even though he hates Americans and believes they are evil; (2) give the individual a potential reward for cooperation, such as information about or contact with his family; and (3) ask God for guidance of the interview itself and the interviewer and interviewee as a team, which may induce a sense of guilt if the individual has just lied or deceived the interviewer.

EMOTION

Contrary to popular belief, emotion is always present in thought and influences thinking. In addition to the content of the interviewee's words, he is also communicating emotionally and behaviorally. Stress will typically increase emotion and cortisol levels, and emotions are accompanied by arousal of the autonomic nervous system. This involuntary portion of human physiology is behaviorally evident in muscle tension and tightness, more rapid and shallow breathing, increased heart rate, flushing, and perspiration. Stress reactions are very difficult to conceal and easy to identify.

Telling *which* emotion is aroused in the interviewee by attempting to read the feelings communicated by his facial expressions and his body language is notoriously difficult. Emotions can also be falsified to help conceal other emotions. On the other hand, most people cannot voluntarily move the particular facial muscles needed to realistically falsify distress or fear (Ekman, 2001).

Certain facial expressions of emotion —happiness, fear, anger, disgust, sadness, and surprise— are universal and appear in all people regardless of age, sex, race, or culture (Ekman, 1992). The *rules for display* of emotion, however, may differ from culture to culture. For instance, one researcher found that when Japanese subjects watched emotionally arousing films while alone, their expressions were no different than those of Americans. In a group, however, the Japanese subjects would mask any negative emotion with a polite smile (Ekman, 2001).

Emotions need to be monitored during interviewing, but their specificity or meaning will not be accurately identified without extensive exposure to the interviewee and knowing the display rules of his culture. For example, the *Al Qaeda Training Manual* teaches patience and steadfastness while being interrogated, yet also urges the brother to use emotional tirades against the interviewer. This is best responded to with calmness and then the question, "Are you finished?" Certain violent true believers are going to be much more comfortable ranting and raving against the interviewer than others, depending on their emotional experience and personality makeup.

In all cases, the interviewer should not react emotionally to any emotionality in the interviewee, whether genuine or feigned, unless there is a specific reason for doing so. He or she should maintain a calm, controlled presence unless there is a specific reason for abandoning this stance that has been decided in advance.

CALIBRATION

This is an interviewing technique through which the interviewer establishes the normative responses of the interviewee to various questions and answers. It is the interviewer's measurement of the interviewee's typical behavior (verbal and nonverbal) when he lies or tells the truth. Calibration can be done only if the interviewer spends a lot of time with the interviewee and is able to ask certain *control questions*, the answers to which will tell him whether the interviewee is lying or telling the truth. Calibration means looking for unusual behavior in the interviewee. For instance, knowing the birthplace of an interviewee can be used to determine his level of autonomic arousal—and other facial and body postures—if he gives a false answer to the question "Where were you born?" This calibrates his behavior when he lies and it can be expected when he lies again.

The importance of calibration is that it accounts for individual differences among interviewees and keeps the interviewer from making simple mistakes, such as assuming that when individuals lie they all behave the same way, when in fact they do not.

DECEPTION AND MANIPULATION

There is no absolute, infallible way to detect lying or deception. In fact, emotion should not be used to determine whether a person is lying. There are clues to deception that do not depend on calibration, such as slips of the tongue, tirades, emblematic slips, and micro expressions; the reader is referred elsewhere to study these phenomena (Ekman, 2001).

We would like to summarize, however, nine precautions suggested by Ekman (2001) in interpreting behavioral clues to deceit:

1. Become aware of how you interpret behavioral clues to deceit and the basis for your hunches, so you can recognize your mistakes.
2. There are two dangers in detecting deceit: disbelieving the truth and believing a lie.

3. The absence of a sign of deceit is not evidence of truth; the presence of a sign of deceit is not always evidence of lying.
4. Understand your own bias and preconceived notions about the interviewee and how these will distort your judgment of deceit.
5. Emotion may not be a clue to deceit, but a clue as to how a truthful person feels when suspected of lying.
6. Many so-called clues to deceit are signs of more than one emotion.
7. Analyze the gains or losses of the interviewee if he lies.
8. Never reach a final conclusion concerning lying based solely on your interpretation of behavioral clues. Like the polygraph, they never provide absolute evidence.
9. If one lies, it is much easier to conceal than to falsify information.

The most effective means for detecting lying or deceit is the comparison of facts across multiple sources of information (e.g., comparing statements to each other, or comparing statements made in interviews with physical evidence found on the interviewee). The truth dwells in the details. *The most common mistake made by interviewers in detecting deceit is being misled by the special skill they think they possess to detect deceit.*

COUNTERMEASURES

The interviewee may use countermeasures during the interview, and the degree to which he attempts to thwart the interview may be a measure of his involvement with a terrorist group.

A countermeasure is a behavioral tactic to defeat the purpose of the interview. For example, the *Al Qaeda Training Manual* specifies the following countermeasures:

1. Reveal some secrets.
2. Ask to be seen by a medical examiner when there is no medical problem.
3. Ask that evidence of torture be entered in the proceedings.
4. Ask that the interrogation be repeated because of torture.
5. Raise your voice; curse the interrogator back.
6. Be patient, resistant, silent, and prayerful.
7. Proudly take a firm and opposing position.
8. Pretend the pain is severe by bending over and crying loudly.

9. Pretend to be naïve and ignorant.
10. Take advantage of visits to communicate with brothers outside prison.
11. Shout slogans out loud from inside the prison cars to impress people.
12. Be steadfast.

The most common countermeasure appears to be the cover story that the individual's behaviors or travels are only to teach or study Islam.

SPECIFIC CULTURAL ISSUES

The Criminal Profiling Unit of the Florida Department of Law Enforcement has developed some specific insights into Islamist behavior (Porter & D'Ambrosia, 2002) that we find important to reiterate as a component of interviewing. These data points are limited to the investigation of terrorism originating in the Middle East (Nydell, 1996).

Personal and group dynamics. Physical behavior will often appear animated when stress or anxiety are applied. Lying is acceptable and common in daily interactions with others to maintain or restore personal image. Having trust betrayed is extremely significant. Shaming should be avoided at all costs. Hospitality is an important component of a person's personal image and status. Permission should always be asked to interview a female member of a family, and shaking hands with a female interviewee should be avoided unless initiated by her.

Primary interviewing. Be sensitive to cultural differences by learning them beforehand. Avoid shame and embarrassment by conducting the interview in a private setting. Know the country of origin of the interviewee and learn something about his customs and cultures. Get a clear verbal commitment from the interviewee to tell the truth. Do not refuse hospitable gestures, such as offers of food or drink. Maintain eye contact. Be prepared to state that you practice your religious faith regularly. Do not discuss illness. Be prepared to sit close to the interviewee. Do not directly ask about women in the family. Make an effort to pronounce personal names correctly. Aggressive interviews will likely result in early termination.

The Arabic cultures are more formal than ours. When in doubt, behave and dress in a conservative manner. Recognize the importance of hospitality, generosity, and piety in the culture.

CONTINUITY OF DATA COLLECTION

It is exceedingly important that a coherent record be kept of the cooperation, resistances, and sensitivities of the interviewee that is sufficiently detailed and fully accessible to subsequent interviewers. The absence of continuity of data collection defeats most of the reasons for interviewing the violent true believer.

TEAMWORK

The *Al Qaeda Training Manual*, lesson 18, stresses the importance of teamwork. "Team work is the only translation of God's command, as well as that of the prophet, to unite and not to disunite. Almighty God says, 'And hold fast, all together, by the Rope which Allah stretches out for you, and be not divided among yourselves.'"

Teamwork is critical in interviewing the violent true believer, whether it involves the careful selection of the interviewer, the compiling of data from previous interviews, or the debriefing of other analysts or agents following the interview. Competition among individuals and among agencies through obstructive behavior or the withholding of information while interviews and interrogations proceed is the surest way to destroy our own teamwork and contribute to our defeat in the war against terrorism.

KEY POINTS
• The most common mistake in interviewing is an absence of preparation.
• Placement before and after the interview can be used to foster attachment.
• The most important part of the interview is establishing rapport.
• Develop a line of questioning, but be patient and flexible.
• Emotion is always present in thought.
• Certain emotions are universal, such as anger and fear, but the rules for display of emotion vary from culture to culture.
• The technique of calibration can be used to establish the normative responses of the interviewee.
• There is no absolute, infallible way to detect deception.
• The interviewee may use countermeasures during the interview.
• Cultural issues can be critical to the success or failure of the interview.
• Continuity of data collection and teamwork are keys to success.

ACKNOWLEDGMENTS

We would like to thank the following individuals and groups for their contributions to this paper: the Behavioral Science Consultation Team of the CITF, DOD; Florida Department of Law Enforcement; SSA Vincent Sullivan; SA Joseph Navarro; James Beisterfeld; Dr. James Turner; SSA William Teater; and Dr. Margaret Nydell. Others have made very important contributions but wish to remain anonymous. Any errors, mistakes, or omissions, however, are solely the authors'. The views expressed in this chapter are those of the authors, and are not the official opinions, procedures, or policy of the Federal Bureau of Investigation. This chapter has been approved for publication by the FBI.

NOTES

1. Fundamentalist belief systems, whether secular or religious, tend to both idealize and control the women under the guise of protecting them from other male sexual interests; thus arises the threat to patriarchal dominance and possession if an interviewer shows any interest whatsoever in the females within the family.

REFERENCES

Dreeke, R. (2011). *It's not all about "me."* Amazon Publishing.

Dutton, D., & Painter, S. (1993). Emotional attachments in abusive relationships: A test of traumatic bonding theory. *Violence and Victims*, 8, 105–120.

Ekman, P. (1992). An argument for basic emotions. *Cognition & Emotion*, 6, 169–200.

Ekman, P. (2001). *Telling lies*. New York: Norton.

Grossman, D. (1995). *On killing*. Boston: Little, Brown.

Meloy, J. R. (2011). Violent true believers. *FBI Law Enforcement Bulletin*, 80, 24–32.

Meloy, J. R., Hempel, A., Mohandie, K., & Shiva, A. (2001). The violent true believer: homicidal and suicidal states of mind. *J Threat Assessment*, 1, 1–12.

Nydell, M. (1996). *Understanding Arabs: A guide for westerners*. Yarmouth, ME: Intercultural Press.

Porter, W., & D'Ambrosia, L. (2002). *Terrorism: the interview process*. Investigations and Forensics Program, Criminal Profiling Unit, Florida Department of Law Enforcement, Tallahassee, FL.

Soufan, A. (2011). *The black banners*. New York: Norton.

I think you know me well enough, Watson, to understand that I am by no means a nervous man. At the same time, it is stupidity rather than courage to refuse to recognize danger when it is close upon you.

SHERLOCK HOLMES
ARTHUR CONAN DOYLE,
The Final Problem
December 1893

INDEX

Page numbers followed by "t" indicate a table and "f" indicate a figure.